WAR AND DIPLOMACY

IN

THE FRENCH REPUBLIC

*An Inquiry into Political Motivations and the
Control of Foreign Policy*

FREDERICK L. SCHUMAN

WITH AN INTRODUCTION BY QUINCY WRIGHT

"*Les hommes ne supprimeront la guerre que le
jour où ils l' auront comprise*" —PROUDHON

HOWARD FERTIG

NEW YORK · 1969

First published in 1931

Howard Fertig, Inc. Edition 1969
Reprinted by special arrangement with The University of Chicago Press

Preface to the 1969 edition

Copyright © 1969 by Frederick L. Schuman

Library of Congress Catalog Card Number: 68-9635

PRINTED IN THE UNITED STATES OF AMERICA
BY NOBLE OFFSET PRINTERS, INC.

TO LILY

PREFACE TO THE 1969 EDITION

ALL authors feel honored when an early book is deemed worthy of republication as it was initially written. My thanks are due to Howard Fertig. My hopes are that new readers of this long (but, I believe, never dull) work will find something of value by way of insight into what now remains, more than ever, mankind's most dangerous and potentially fatal problem.

Aging writers are not always the best judges of the contemporary value of their research, thinking, and writing in the days of their youth. But if I were asked to evaluate the present case, my reply would run somewhat as follows. This volume is concerned with the ways by which foreign policy was formulated and executed in the Third French Republic (1871-1940). Those ways were not radically changed in the Fourth Republic (1946-1958) nor in the Fifth (1958). Each of these regimes, save the Fifth thus far, was ultimately discredited and cast down by virtue of major misconceptions and miscalculations on the part of policy-makers in the field of foreign affairs. In each instance the mistakes were passively supported or actively endorsed by most patriots, bewitched by the cult of the sovereign nation-state and by a quest for national power, profit, and prestige in a world of international anarchy.

These patterns of civic motivation and international conflict are more than ever with us as the twentieth century enters the final third of its allotted time on our calendar. Many earlier manifestations of the dilemma of modern mankind are set forth in documented detail in the pages that follow: colonial conquests; the dubious art of undeclared war; the diplomacy of the Dual Alliance and the Entente Cordiale, which divided Europe into hostile coalitions foredoomed to clash in arms; the tragedy of errors in 1914, for which, as far as I know, no better account of French policy has appeared in the intervening years despite further documentation of details; and above all—of special interest to Americans—the full story of how French powerholders sought, with results which were to prove both brutal and transitory, to impose their will by force on a remote community in Southeast Asia and thereby got themselves involved, through arrogance and stupidity, in a hopeless war with China. This conflict was as "absurd" (to quote de Gaulle), albeit not as tragic, as America's hopeless war in Vietnam.

From a broader prospective, these pages outline a frame of reference (particularly in the closing chapter) for thought and action toward the age-old goal of emancipation from violence in the relations among nations, and toward peace and order and cooperative activity in the service of the family of man. These hopes proved vain in the 1930's, thanks to human addictions to types of loyalties which, unless transcended, spell renewed violence under conditions ensuring disaster and, prospectively, irreparable catastrophe. The frame of reference here proposed bore little resemblance to the literature of international relations in the 1920's and 1930's. Unhappily, it also bears little resemblance to the "new" literature of international relations in the 1960's, with its dominant themes of a valueless "behaviorism" and "empiricism." Scientific quantification and computerizing, while often useful and necessary, can deal only with means towards ends. If *Homo sapiens* is to find the road toward survival and salvation, he must arrive at redefinitions of ends through greater moral and political wisdom than he has thus far displayed.

Last, but far from least, I must note that this work was inspired, as was a series of later works by other young scholars, by Quincy Wright —to whom all of us have all our lives been enormously indebted for his erudite and prolific contributions to the study and teaching of International Law, International Organization, and the Preconditions of World Order. The sequel of my own work of 1931 was *International Politics,* first published by the McGraw-Hill Book Company in 1933, with a seventh edition appearing in 1968-69. The sequel to Quincy Wright's brilliant studies of the 1930's was his detailed and definitive two-volume work, *A Study of War,* first published by the University of Chicago Press in 1943 and since revised and republished several times. This should remain required reading for all citizens and political leaders seriously concerned with the continuation of life on our planet.

As I look back over the years, I suspect that the best brief judgment of this book was set forth in the final paragraph of Quincy Wright's original Introduction. But let readers judge for themselves.

FREDERICK L. SCHUMAN

Portland State College,
Portland, Oregon
September, 1968.

PREFACE

ACCORDING to well-established traditions in academic circles, a preface to a work of this kind, should consist of three parts: a statement of the origins and purposes of the study, an apology for its weaknesses and limitations as testimony to the modesty of the author, and a word of acknowledgment to those whose assistance has contributed to whatever value the work may have. All prefaces, moreover, should be brief, unless written by Bernard Shaw or Walter Lippman. Bearing these precepts in mind, the writer offers the following preliminary observations for the perusal of the prospective reader.

The investigation which has culminated in the publication of this study of the conduct of French foreign relations was originally undertaken as a segment of a project of cooperative research into the causes of war which was begun in 1927 by various members of the social science departments at the University of Chicago. The present study was initiated in 1928 in consultation with the Causes of War Committee, presided over by Professor Quincy Wright. It was pursued in Chicago and in Paris during 1929 and 1930 and was brought to substantial completion in the early summer of the present year, just prior to the Hoover debt moratorium proposal of June 21, which initiated the protracted negotiations still in progress at the time of publication. These negotiations and their aftermath have perhaps revealed more clearly to the English-speaking world than any other single series of events since the occupation of the Ruhr the diplomatic interests and objectives of the French Republic in present-day Europe. These interests and objectives comprise the substance of that remarkably successful political and financial hegemony over the continent which France has established since the Armistice. If they are misinterpreted and made the targets of unreasoning attack by critics in other States, the reason is largely to be found in a lack of understanding of the stakes of diplomacy and of the sources from which foreign policy springs in the State System in which France has always played such an important rôle. It is the author's expectation that this volume will aid in revealing the controlling factors in international relations generally and in French foreign affairs particularly, and thereby contribute to a better understanding of diplomatic events, past, present, and to come.

From a broader point of view, the study is also intended to throw light upon the general problem of war and peace in the Western State System. That problem may be approached from various angles and the succeeding units of the series, of which this is the first volume to be published, will employ a variety of orientations and techniques in analyzing the situations

vii

out of which modern wars arise. The present approach seeks to analyze constitutional and administrative structures and the dynamic political forces which underlie the formulation of foreign policy. This analysis should prove to be of interest not merely to students of French politics and diplomacy, but to all who are concerned with the control of foreign policy everywhere. The analysis has inevitably involved a consideration of the patterns of international relations as a whole. Such conclusions and suggestions as are offered are pertinent to the whole problem created by the periodical use of armed violence in the contacts between sovereign States. If the writer's efforts to maintain an attitude of scientific detachment toward his subject matter has been successful, the result should prove useful not merely to academic social scientists and students, but to all who are interested in the currents of contemporary world politics.

No one is in a better position than the author to appreciate the limitations of a study of this kind. The foreigner who attempts to observe any phase of a national culture which is essentially alien to him is almost certain to fall into errors of fact and interpretation which no amount of careful scholarship can entirely remove. To employ a phrase which Clemenceau applied, unjustly no doubt, to Poincaré, his garnering of facts may leave him in a position where he knows everything, but understands nothing. On the other hand he brings to his task an objectivity and a perspective which few natives possess in studying their fellow-citizens. Lord Bryce's classic study of *The American Commonwealth* and Lowell's equally classic work on *The Government of England* testify to the ability of foreign observers to see more of the realities of foreign government and politics than those who are too close to them. The Anglo-Saxon observer of Latin European institutions is, of course, faced with peculiar difficulties of language and national psychology not present to the same degree in the ventures which have been mentioned. These difficulties have been apparent to me throughout the present study. I can only hope that my analysis has gained through the virtue of detachment whatever it has lost through lack of life-long familiarity with French life and customs.

As for content and method, it should perhaps be emphasized that the work is not intended in any sense as a complete diplomatic history of the Third French Republic. The diplomatic episodes and events which are described in the second part of the book are merely a few selected cases out of many which might have been chosen for the purpose of illustrating concretely the functioning of the constitutional and political machinery for the handling of French foreign affairs. Others might well have made a different selection from the vast mass of available material. It is my conviction, however, that the generalizations drawn from the assembled data are valid for all phases of French foreign policy and would be substantiated rather than vitiated by an extension of the same method to other possible cases.

The historical evidence itself is adduced, wherever possible, from original documentary sources. The fact that at the time of writing only a small beginning has been made toward the publication of the French pre-war diplomatic correspondence means, obviously, that an indeterminate amount of relevant evidence is still unavailable to the diplomatic historian. I feel, however, that the material at hand in the various *Livres Jaunes*, in the *Journal Officiel*, in the published diplomatic correspondence of other governments, and in secondary sources has been fairly adequate for the purposes of the present study. The vexed question of "war guilt" is not discussed in traditional terms in the following pages for reasons set forth in the text. But the two chapters on 1914 set forth as clearly and accurately as the available evidence permits the rôle of the French Government in the initiation of the Great War. Other chapters reveal the goals and methods of French diplomacy since the Peace Conference. The book is not an indictment and still less an apologia, but rather, in intention at least, a behavioristic account of those patterns of social action which underly French foreign policy and which have their exact counterparts in the foreign policies of all other Great Powers. Documentary sources at present unavailable will throw further light upon many aspects of the narrative. But in all probability they will not modify substantially the major conclusions reached either as to the content of French foreign policy or as to the methods through which it is carried out.

My first acknowledgments of indebtedness must go to the Social Science Research Council, which enabled me, through the grant of a fellowship, to spend the autumn and winter of 1929–1930 in Paris, and to the Social Science Research Committee of the University of Chicago, which extended financial assistance in the earlier phases of the study. As for my friends in France, my thanks are due to innumerable unnamed officials in libraries, government offices, and elsewhere whose courtesy, patience, and helpfulness were of invaluable assistance in enabling me to secure the materials needed for the study. I take pleasure in making personal acknowledgments to Professor Joseph Barthélemy, pioneer scholar and outstanding authority on the conduct of French foreign relations, for granting me the benefit of his aid and counsel; to M. Georges Cahen-Salvador, Secretary-General of the National Economic Council, for giving me a clearer conception of the work of the organization which he serves; to M. Pengeaud, *Directeur des Archives* at the Quai d'Orsay, for granting me access to the library of the Ministry and assisting me in locating relevant material; to M. Jacques Kayser, Secretary-General of the Radical Socialist Party, for advice and assistance; to Professor Maurice Caudel, MM. Henri and Florian Chardon, MM. Alexandre and Aubert Lefas, Professor Louis Lefur, and M. Jules Priou for their kindness, hospitality, and sundry services too numerous to mention; and last, but far from least, to my good friend, Madame Simon of 3 rue Berthollet, without whose cordial and unfailing solicitude for the comfort of her American *pensionnaires* my sojourn in Paris would have been less pleasant and less profitable.

Among my American friends who have assisted me in various ways, my warmest thanks are due to Professor Quincy Wright, who originally inspired the study and who later read the entire manuscript and offered many valuable suggestions in the course of its preparation. His kindness in writing the Introduction to the work is also greatly appreciated. Most of the chapters in the second section were read by Professor Bernadotte E. Schmitt, and the two concluding chapters by Professor Harold D. Lasswell and Dr. S. McKee Rosen, all of the University of Chicago. I am grateful to all of these gentlemen for their useful criticisms and suggestions. I am likewise indebted to Professor Walter R. Sharp, formerly Fellowship Secretary of the Social Science Research Council, for putting me into contact with various people in Paris, for reading and commenting upon the third chapter, and for permitting me to read in manuscript his own excellent study of *The French Civil Service* and to use from it his chart of the personnel of the foreign service. I am also grateful to Professor J. Gilbert Heinberg of the University of Missouri for his kindness in permitting me to use the material which he gathered on the personnel of French Cabinets. Among my own students who have rendered first aid at critical moments I am grateful to Miss Helene Kitzinger for doing some of the spade work for Chapter XI, and to Miss Dorothy Blumenstock for clerical aid in putting the manuscript in final form. Mr. Sol Spector and Miss Brita Berglund are particularly deserving of my thanks for assisting in the preparation of the index. Justice also requires a word of thanks to Mr. George Sorel, from whom I cheerfully acknowledge the theft of the title of the concluding chapter, and again last, but not least, to my wife for her encouragement and good humor in the face of my absorption in the labor of composition.

A time-honored formula obliges me to say that while all of these people have added to any merit the work may possess, none of them is answerable for any of its defects, for which I assume full responsibility. I close in the hope that this work may contribute slightly to international understanding and to a more adequate comprehension of the scourge of war and its cure.

FREDERICK L. SCHUMAN.

THE UNIVERSITY OF CHICAGO,
September, 1931.

CONTENTS

PART III

THE DYNAMICS OF FOREIGN POLICY

INTRODUCTION

THE present volume represents an effort to apply the methodology of the social sciences to the investigation of a problem which is universally recognized to be of decisive significance for the future of western civilization. Major wars have been followed by periods of general interest in the problem of war and peace. But in the period since the World War this interest has been more intense, more organized, and more effective upon the utterances and actions of the statesmen than hitherto. There has been a mass of writing on the subject, historical, analytical, polemical, philosophical, and literary, but the appearance of this volume indicates a conviction that there is room for more.

Dr. Schuman's study of war and diplomacy in the French Republic is designed neither to recapitulate historical data nor to offer a panacea, but to investigate as objectively as possible certain aspects of the situations from which recent wars have arisen. It is hoped that a gradual accumulation of studies which like this utilize the points of view and the methods of the contemporary social sciences may eventually prove useful both in theory and in practice.

It has been with this thought that the Social Science Research Committee at the University of Chicago has supported since 1927 a cooperative investigation of the Causes of War. Numerous studies have proceeded in connection with this investigation and, while it is anticipated that summaries of the results of the investigation will from time to time be published, it is thought desirable to publish special studies which have an independent interest as they are completed.

The project began with no theory of the causes of war but with a series of approaches suggested in several meetings of members of the departments of political science, economics, history, sociology, anthropology, geography, and psychology at the University of Chicago in the spring of 1926. Certain of these suggestions were selected for detailed study by research assistants working under the direction of members of the university staff or, as in the present instance, by members of the staff themselves. Thus, such unity as the project may eventually acquire will be a result of final synthesis rather than of initial analysis.

It is clear that governments of states are immediately responsible for the initiation of most modern wars. Governments differ from each other according to the type of men in positions of power and according to the constitutional structures which more or less determine the classes or sections of the population which shall exert influence and the degree of deliberation and breadth of participation which shall precede important decisions. One might expect to find that the frequency of war in the foreign relations of a given state is related to the type of governing personality and constitutional structure which prevail in the state, but before such an expectation can be tested detailed descriptive accounts on a somewhat common model of these personalities and constitutional structures operating in a number of states in the same international milieu must be available.

Dr. Schuman's study is an effort to present such a model. He has attempted to analyze the factors entering into the formulation of French foreign policy by combining the methods of the diplomatic historian with those of the political scientist. France was chosen because no comprehensive study of its personnel and structure for conducting foreign relations is available, because it is a country of importance in all major international transactions, and because its history abounds with wars of various kinds.

The study in successive parts describes the constitutional structure of France with enough of its history to indicate the spirit of its institutions; sets forth the operation of this structure in a selected list of international transactions with due attention to the personalities of the officers as well as the powers of the offices; and finally synthesizes this material according to types of activity involved which are classified as treaty making, war making, and the formulation of foreign policy.

While comparative studies are necessary before final conclusions can be reached, Dr. Schuman's investigation hardly encourages the idea that constitutional forms determine the character of foreign policy. Rather he suggests that foreign policy springs from independent roots, from the conception of the personality of the state and the interest of the entire population in the prestige of this personality in relations with other states. Thus, the policy of a particular state results from the manifestations of this general interest as well as many lesser interests of groups, parties and individuals in the peculiar international environment of the state, while the form of its constitutional structure and the personality of its leaders are, in the main, an adaptation to the necessities of this policy. Instead of structure determining policy, Dr. Schuman sees policy, in the main, determining structure. He recognizes, it is true, that "the constitution does impose certain restraints and limits upon the action that may be taken by a particular government," but these restraints generally bow before serious exigencies. It follows that Dr. Schuman would search for a solution of the problem of war and peace not within the state but in the relations of states, not in the constitution but in international organization and in modification of the basic popular interests which present world culture inculcates. So long as these remain constant, democratic control of foreign policy within the state or other reforms of constitutional structure can have but a limited effect.

QUINCY WRIGHT.

UNIVERSITY OF CHICAGO,
September, 1931.

ABBREVIATIONS

J.O.Ch. or *Sén.: Journal Officiel de la République Française—Annales de la Chambre des Députés* or *Annales du Sénat: Débats parlementaires*, Imprimerie du Journal Officiel, Paris. (Unless otherwise indicated, all references are to that portion of the *Journal Officiel* containing the parliamentary debates, always dated as of the day following the session reported.)

Rap. Budget, Ch. or *Sén: Rapports fait au nom de la commission des finances chargée d'examiner le projet de loi portant fixation du Budget Général de l'Éxercise, 18-* or *19-* (Ministère des Affaires Étrangères) *Chambre des Députés* or *Sénat;* Imprimerie de la Chambre des Députés *or* du Sénat, Paris.

L.J.T.: (Livre Jaune, Tunis) Ministère des Affaires Étrangères, *Documents diplomatiques, affaires de Tunisie, 1870–1881,* Imprimerie Nationale, Paris, 1881.

L.J.T.Supp.: (Livre Jaune, Tunis, supplement) Ministère des Affaires Étrangères, *Documents diplomatiques, affaires de Tunisie—supplément, avril-mai, 1881,* Imprimerie Nationale, Paris, 1881.

L.J.Tonkin: (Livre Jaune, Tonkin) Ministère des Affaires Étrangères, *Documents diplomatiques, affaires du Tonkin, convention de Tien-Tsin du 11 mai 1884, incident de Lang-Son,* Imprimerie Nationale, Paris, 1884.

L.J.C. et T.: (Livre Jaune, China and Tonkin) Ministère des Affaires Étrangères, *Documents diplomatiques, affaires de Chine et du Tonkin, 1884–1885,* Imprimerie Nationale, Paris, 1885.

L.J.Siam: (Livre Jaune, Siam) Ministère des Affaires Étrangères, *Documents diplomatiques, affaires de Siam, 1893–1902,* Imprimerie Nationale, Paris, 1902.

L.J.Haut-Mekong: (Livre Jaune, Upper Mekong) Ministère des Affaires Étrangères, *Documents diplomatiques, affaires du Haut-Mekong,* Imprimerie Nationale, Paris, 1893.

L.J.Siam et Haut-Mekong: (Livre Jaune, Siam and Upper Mekong) Ministère des Affaires Étrangères, *Documents diplomatiques, Affaires du Siam et du Haut-Mekong,* Imprimerie Nationale, Paris, 1896.

L.J.Mad.: (Livre Jaune, Madagascar, series of five, indicated by dates) Ministère des Affaires Étrangères, *Documents diplomatiques, affaires de Madagascar, 1881–1883; 1882–1883; 1884–1886; 1885–1895; 1896;* Imprimerie Nationale, Paris, respectively, 1883, 1884, 1886, 1895, and 1896.

L.J.L'A.F.R.: (Livre Jaune, Franco-Russian Alliance) Ministère des Affaires Étrangères, *Documents diplomatiques, L'Alliance Franco-Russe,* Imprimerie Nationale, Paris, 1918.

L.J.Maroc: (Livre Jaune, Morocco) Ministère des Affaires Étrangères, *Documents diplomatiques, affaires de Maroc, 1901–1905,* Imprimerie Nationale, Paris, 1905.

F.Y.B.: (French Yellow Book) Ministère des Affaires Étrangères, *La Guerre Européene, 1914,* Imprimerie Nationale, Paris, 1914.

L.N.: (Livre Noir, Black Book) *Un Livre Noir,* 2 vols., Librairie du Travail, Paris, 1922.

D.D.F.: (French diplomatic documents) Commission de publication des documents rélatifs aux origines de la guerre de 1914, *Documents diplomatiques française, 1871–1914,* Imprimerie Nationale, Paris, 1929–.

B.D.: (British Documents) British Documents on the Origins of the War, 1898–1914, Vol. XI: Foreign Office Documents, June 28–August 4, 1914, London, 1926.

G.P.: (Grosse Politik) *Die grosse Politik der europäischen Kabinette, 1871–1914,* Sammlung der Akten des Deutschen Auswärtigen Amts, 40 vols., Berlin, 1922–1927.

PART I

THE STRUCTURE OF THE MACHINE

CHAPTER I

THE THIRD FRENCH REPUBLIC

1. La Grande Nation

THE conduct of foreign relations may be approached from a variety of angles and for a variety of purposes. The increasing attention which has been paid to the subject since 1919 has been motivated largely by a desire on the part of students to further the democratization of foreign policy, apparently on the assumption that a democratically controlled foreign policy is likely to be a pacific one.[1] Studies have also been undertaken from the point of view of constitutional law,[2] of administrative organization, of personnel management,[3] and the like, with the relatively limited and specific objectives implied in the approach of public law and administration. The traditional approach of the diplomatic historian, whose objective is to present an accurate factual account of the chronological development of international contacts, has tended to center in recent years about the question of relative responsibility for the initiation of the Great War.

In view of this diversity of objectives and methods of approach, it seems appropriate at the outset to indicate briefly the general point of view from which the present study of the foreign affairs of France is undertaken. The present work aims at an analysis and interpretation of the machinery for the conduct of foreign relations in the Third French Republic in the light of the basic behavior patterns of States in the Western State System. These behavior patterns may be regarded, for the most part, as manifestations of that complex of attitudes, ideals, sentiments, and policies described by the somewhat vague term of "nationalism." It is submitted, not as an *a priori* assumption, but as a helpful hypothesis upon which to proceed, that the behavior of States toward one another is conditioned by their position in the State System of which they are an inseparable part, much as the behavior of individuals is conditioned by the social *milieu* in which they are born and have their being; that the "self" of a nation, like that of a single personality, is a product of the interaction of inherent characteristics and the social environment; that this process of conditioning as it has gone on between the

[1] J. Barthélemy, *Démocratie et politique étrangère*, Paris, 1917; F. R. Flournoy, *Parliament and War*, London, 1927.

[2] Quincy Wright, *The Control of American Foreign Relations*, New York, 1922.

[3] J. M. Mathews, *American Foreign Relations*, New York, 1928; H. K. Norton, "Foreign Office Organization" *Annals of the American Academy of Political and Social Science*, CXLIII, Philadelphia, May, 1929.

3

States comprising Western European civilization during the past five centuries has led to the growth, spread, and intensification, within each State, of the emotions and ideology of national patriotism; that the attitudes so generated have been the major factors controlling the behavior of these States toward one another; and that, more specifically, the functioning of the machine for the conduct of foreign affairs in France is intelligible only when viewed as an expression of French nationalism. The control of French foreign relations will be dealt with here primarily as an aspect of French nationalism, with such attention to constitutional and legal phases as is necessary to understand the machinery of its operation.

Social consciousness of common nationality, with its attendant mass emotions of national pride, ethnocentric patriotism, and antipathy toward the alien beyond the frontier, was a phenomenon which appeared relatively early in France. Local loyalties and feudal allegiances were merged into a broader nationalism here earlier than in any other modern State with the possible exception of England. The genesis of French nationalism may indeed be traced to the long series of conflicts between the Valois kings and "perfidious Albion" comprising the Hundred Years' War. Out of the humiliation of Crecy, Poitiers, and Agincourt, out of the suffering and bitterness of a protracted and apparently hopeless struggle against the invader, emerged the desperate politico-religious enthusiasm which made Jeanne d'Arc the first national political leader of modern France. Not only was final victory gained in the conflict, but loyalty to the monarch was gradually transformed into patriotism for the nation. Like the other nationalisms of Western Europe, French nationalism was born of war and was, at its conception, an extension of allegiance from king to country.

Throughout the whole formative period of French nationalism, the king was the symbol of the nation. His glory and prowess on the field of battle, as well as in the less exciting works of peace, were associated with the grandeur of France. This association helps to explain the royalist leanings of many extreme French patriots and the undoubted patriotism of all French royalists. If modern France was not created by her kings, she was at least created in the name of her kings, and to the popular mind the two things are not very different.

More significant perhaps, from the point of view of the traditional content of French nationalism, was the international position which France occupied from the beginning of so-called "modern times" to the middle of the nineteenth century. France was ever the first State of Europe—first in national unity, first in population and wealth, first in diplomatic prestige and military power. Her neighbors, with the exception of the House of Hapsburg and distant Russia, were small States, like the Netherlands; weak States, like Spain; or mere conglomerations of petty principalities. Germany, like Italy, was but a "geographical expression." England alone was the enemy to be feared, not because she approached France in power, but because of her insular immunity from invasion and her formidable sea forces. And, in the interest of security, prestige, and the balance of power, England, after 1689, was usually to be found aligned with the weak continental States which felt themselves menaced by the might of France. This coalition, in its various forms, was always sufficiently powerful to prevent any permanent establishment of French control over the continent. Not only did British diplomacy achieve this goal, but it succeeded in 1763 in wresting from France her colonial empire in America and India and, in 1813 to 1815, in checkmating the most nearly triumphant French attempt at the conquest of Europe.

Retrospection usually softens the sting of defeat and enhances the pride of victory. The Parisian of to-day has about him constant reminders of Rivoli, Austerlitz, and Jena, while Blenheim, Trafalgar, and Waterloo are forgotten—unless he goes to London, which is seldom. The French patriot boasts a purple past for his nation, such as no other State can claim. His heritage shines with the names of Francis I, Richelieu, Louis XIV, and Napoleon. He is accustomed to think of his country as the arbiter of the destinies of Europe and as the foremost military power of the world. The traditional ideology of French nationalism is thus almost inseparable from the legacy of glory in arms.[1] This is perhaps no more true of French nationalism than of others. But the Frenchman can point to a longer, brighter record of victory in diplomacy and war than any of his neighbors. This fact inevitably conditions all his basic attitudes toward foreign affairs. Nowhere else has national patriotism struck deeper roots and flowered so luxuriantly. Nowhere else can the diplomat whose policies seem to serve "national interests" count upon such unanimous and enthusiastic support from the mass of the citizenry.

2. L'Année Terrible

The tragic events of 1870 and 1871 furnish the point of departure for any consideration of the political institutions of contemporary France. They also shape the entire course of French diplomacy throughout the period of the present study, constituting, as they did, a diplomatic revolution which left *la Grande Nation* prostrate before a powerful and united Germany. More than the dignity and prestige of Louis Napoleon perished at Sedan. More than the Napoleonic tradition and the fabric of the Second Empire were dragged in the dust at the fall of Paris to the Prussians. The whole international position of France in the European State System was demolished under the blows of Bismarck. The hegemony over the continent which France had exercised for three centuries and which even the fall of the first Bonaparte had not destroyed now passed into other hands. Henceforth France, defeated and truncated, was to occupy a position of dimmed prestige and uneasy insecurity, in painful contrast to the glory of mastery and the pride of power of the past.

[1] *Cf.* Appendices of C. H. Hayes, *France—A Nation of Patriots*, New York, 1930.

The origins of the Franco-Prussian War are sufficiently well known to obviate the necessity of any extended treatment of them here.[1] From the halcyon days of the victory over Russia in the Crimea and the humbling of Austria in Italy in 1859, the Second Empire had sunk to a level from which the most desperate diplomatic expedients of Napoleon III were unable to raise it. While French troops lingered in Rome, Algeria, and Mexico, the "blood and iron" methods of the great Prussian Chancellor eliminated Austria from German affairs in the Seven Weeks' War of 1866 and at a single stroke achieved the creation of the North German Confederation. Napoleon's pitiable efforts to secure territorial "compensations" in the Rhenish Palatinate, Belgium, or Luxembourg were uniformly unsuccessful in the face of Bismarck's firmness. His attempts to secure diplomatic sympathy and support abroad fell on deaf ears. France was isolated as a result of Napoleon's blunders and his ambitions of territorial aggrandizement. Nevertheless, the Emperor felt that the arms of France might still achieve what diplomacy had failed to win. He counted upon war to prevent complete German unification and to restore for himself and his dynasty the waning loyalty of his subjects. Bismarck shrewdly analyzed the situation, decided that war was "inevitable," and determined to utilize the efficient military machine which he had at hand to overthrow France and incorporate the South German States into the Union.

The eagerness with which the Government of the Second Empire snatched at the bait which Bismarck held out was indicative of an optimistic but ill-founded confidence in the outcome of the impending struggle. Not content with Prince Leopold's relinquishment of the Hohenzollern candidacy to the Spanish throne, Napoleon III demanded that the renunciation be repeated and be made in perpetuity. William I's refusal to comply with this demand, as presented by Ambassador Benedetti, was reported curtly by Bismarck in the famous "Ems Dispatch," which he knew would be "a red flag to the Gallic bull." On July 14, 1871, the Chambers, at the Emperor's suggestion and with the apparent support of public opinion, declared war on Prussia in a great manifestation of belligerent, patriotic enthusiasm. Victory seemed certain. But France was diplomatically isolated because of the feeling abroad that she was playing the rôle of the aggressor. The South German States joined Prussia. Bismarck's war machine, with Von Moltke at the throttle, overwhelmed the Imperial armies. On September 3, the Emperor, with the last important French field army, was captured at Sedan and the road to Paris lay open to the invaders.

In the agony of defeat the Third French Republic had its birth. On September 4, a group of self-appointed Republicans under the leadership of Léon Gambetta proclaimed the deposition of the Bonaparte dynasty and the establishment of the Republic in the Hôtel de Ville of Paris. The Empress Eugénie fled to England and a provisional "Government of National De-

[1] For a brief account, see E. Bourgeois, *History of Modern France*, pp. 161–173, Cambridge, 1919.

fense" was formed to rule the country, pending the restoration of peace. Despite a *levée en masse* and frenzied efforts to organize resistance, the outcome of the war was never in doubt. Strasbourg capitulated in September, and Metz in October. The invaders laid siege to Paris, whose defenders were compelled to surrender on January 28, 1871, after a winter of starvation and suffering. An armistice was followed by the election of a National Assembly which ratified the preliminaries of peace on May 1. On May 10, the Treaty of Frankfort was concluded. France was forced to cede Alsace-Lorraine to the conqueror and to pay an indemnity of five billion francs. In the Hall of Mirrors at Versailles, Bismarck had proclaimed the German Empire on January 18. Germany emerged triumphant and a united nation. France had suffered a humiliation to her dignity and national pride more bitter, more rankling, than any she had experienced since the middle ages.

The electoral campaign of February, 1871, for the naming of the National Assembly, resulted in the victory at the polls of some 500 Monarchists as against only 200 republicans. This was perhaps a reflection less of the political views of the French nation than of the war-weariness of an electorate which supported the group committed to peace as against the Republicans who favored a continuation of the hopeless struggle. This Monarchist Assembly—chosen to take action on the treaty with Germany—was to constitute the Government of France for the next five years. It named Adolphe Thiers as "Chief of the Executive Power" and regarded the "Republic" as a temporary arrangement to be tolerated only until a new monarch could be chosen. But the issue of Monarchy vs. Republic was one which the members of the National Assembly postponed in the face of another problem of much more fundamental importance.

Whatever differences of opinion might exist at Versailles over forms of government, the members of the Assembly were one in support of the social and economic order of private property and industrial capitalism. This order was suddenly threatened by the insurrection of the Commune of Paris. At the end of the siege, a group of Radicals, Marxian Socialists, and Anarchists united in common opposition to the *bourgeois* Monarchist Assembly, and organized the Republican guardsmen and the disgruntled workers of the city into a kind of proletarian dictatorship, governed by a revolutionary joint committee. This body repudiated the authority of the National Assembly in March, 1871, took over the administration of the capital, and proposed that France be transformed into a loose federation of self-governing communes in which economic control and political power would pass into the hands of the wage earners. To this defiance, Thiers and the Assembly had but one response: suppression by force. The foreign war between States was transformed into a civil war between classes. The struggle was now to be waged not with lock-out, strike, and sabotage, but with rifle, bomb, and barricade. The second siege of Paris by the troops of the National Assembly began on April 1, with the tricolor of French *bourgeois* parliamentarianism pitted against the red flag of international social revolution.

The suppression of the Commune constituted the bitterest and bloodiest episode in the history of the European labor movement, prior to the Russian revolution. As always in class warfare, quarter was neither asked nor given. The besiegers in growing numbers advanced upon the beleaguered city in the face of stubborn and heroic resistance, made vain by the superior military resources of the National Assembly. A breach was soon made in the fortifications near the St. Cloud gate by the Versailles troops and the conflict became a series of ferocious combats within the metropolis. Barricades were demolished by artillery fire. Public buildings were burned and hostages were executed by the frenzied defenders. Prisoners were slaughtered by thousands. Paris became a shambles. Quarter by quarter, street by street, block by block, the desperate workers and soldiers of the capital were forced back, mowed down, and drowned in blood. By the end of May the invaders had broken all organized resistance and could proceed at leisure to the merciless extermination of the surviving bands of the defenders. Defiant to the end, the last of the Communards fell before the firing squad against the east wall of the cemetery of Père Lachaise—still red after the lapse of half a century with the flags and wreaths of Socialists and Communists throughout the world, left in tribute to the martyrs of '71. The new régime, whether Republican or Monarchist, had been made safe for capitalism. The French *bourgeoisie* had compensated itself for its national humiliation at the hands of Germany by a signal victory over its enemies within the gates.[1]

3. THE CONSTITUTION OF 1875

On August 31, 1871, the National Assembly enacted the Rivet law (proposed by Charles Rivet, Deputy from the Corrèze and a friend of Thiers) by which it conferred upon Thiers the title of "President of the French Republic." The President was made responsible to the Assembly and was intended to keep office only temporarily until the factions of the Monarchists could agree upon a candidate for the throne. The precise relationship between the President, the Ministers, and the Assembly remained obscure. It was enough for the moment that a workable governmental system had been devised until the Assembly, which regarded itself as a constituent as well as a legislative body, should prepare a constitution and choose a king. When Thiers, who had been a constitutional Monarchist, at length decided that a Republican Constitution was more likely to meet with popular approval, he was forced out of power in May, 1873, and his project rejected.

That the Monarchist Assembly was finally obliged, paradoxically, to draw up the Republican Constitution which has furnished the legal basis of the Government of France ever since was due only to the inability of

[1] Bourgeois, *History of Modern France*, pp. 207–215; Cf. P. O. Lissagary, *History of the Commune of 1871*; E. Lepelletier, *Histoire de la Commune de 1871*, etc.

the various royalist groups to reach an agreement among themselves. The Bonapartists were discredited. The Legitimists supported the claims of the Count of Chambord, grandson of Charles X, while the Orleanists championed those of the Count of Paris, grandson of Louis Philippe. With the fall of Thiers, the election to the Presidency by the Assembly of the staunch monarchist, Marshal MacMahon, and the formation of the "coalition" ministry of the Duc de Broglie, a compromise was reached whereby the Count of Chambord was to ascend the throne as Henry V, with the Count of Paris as the heir-apparent. But "Henry V," true to the Bourbon tradition of learning nothing and forgetting nothing, refused to renounce the white flag of absolutism and the principle of divine-right monarchy, as the Orleanists demanded. This new impasse led to a revulsion of popular feeling toward republicanism and obliged the Assembly to draw up provisional "Constitutional Laws" to operate until the aged Count of Chambord should be gathered unto his fathers and leave the way clear for the Count of Paris to accept the kingship. In November, 1873, MacMahon was made President of the "Republic" with a term of seven years. A Committee of Thirty, provided for by a law of September 20, was already preparing a project of a Constitution for the Assembly's consideration. The task was arduous and progress slow. Only when the despairing Orleanists threw sufficient support to the Republican program in January of 1875 did it become possible to carry a resolution through the Assembly (by the narrow vote of 353 to 352) providing definitely for the term, election, and reeligibility of the President.

Thereafter the work went forward more rapidly. On February 24, 1875, by a vote of 435 to 234, the Law on the Organization of the Senate was passed. On February 25 the Law on the Organization of the Public Powers was carried by 425 to 254. Finally, on July 16, the Law on the Relations of the Public Powers was approved, 520 to 84, and the Constitution of the Third French Republic was completed—if one may use such a term to describe the most fragmentary, incomplete, and unsystematic of modern constitutions. Its sketchy character is a result of the situation out of which it grew. It was a compromise between Monarchists and Republicans. It was intended to be capable of easy modification when the prospects for monarchy should brighten. That it remained as the permanent foundation of the Government of France was a consequence of circumstances which the National Assembly did not foresee. These circumstances frustrated the hopes of the royalists and insured the permanence of the Republic. As a result the three fundamental laws of 1875 remain the Constitution of France, brief, partial, and illogical as they are.[1]

Viewed broadly as an instrument of government, these laws are entirely lacking in many provisions ordinarily contained in such documents in other

---

[1] See Appendix A, p. 423 below for the text and the two amendments of July 22, 1879, and December 9, 1884; on the work of the National Assembly, *Annales de l'assemblée nationale*, especially Vol. XXXVI; and G. Hanotaux, *Histoire de la France contemporaine*, Vols. I, II, and III.

countries and also in the earlier revolutionary constitutions of France itself. There is no bill of rights. There is no provision for the method of appointing ministers or of electing members of the Chamber of Deputies. There is nothing dealing with the judiciary, the budget, or local government. There are no declarations of abstract principles or academic theories of the State. The Constitution is severely practical and limited in scope. It may be amended by a simple majority of the two houses of the legislature meeting as a unicameral National Assembly at Versailles. It possesses, therefore, none of the sacrosanct character of the American Constitution, but may be changed at the will of the Government, as in Great Britain, with only a difference of location and procedure to distinguish the constituent and legislative functions of the Parliament. In fact, the amending power has been sparingly used. On the other hand, the laws of 1875 have been supplemented by a whole series of statutes and decrees which, in their totality, comprise the actual working Constitution of the Third Republic.[1]

4. PARLIAMENTARY DEMOCRACY

The general principles of the organization and operation of government in France have been treated at length by numerous writers and need only be outlined briefly here.[2] As they have worked themselves out in practice, they have given the Third Republic a parliamentary system approximating that of Great Britain and roughly similar to the political machinery found elsewhere on the continent in countries accepting the theory and practice of *bourgeois* democracy. This parliamentary system differs markedly from the "Presidential" type of republican government prevalent in the United States and Latin America. Instead of a separation of powers between independent legislative, executive, and judicial departments, all authority is vested in the law-making body, to which the acting executive is responsible. Instead of an independent, powerful, and popularly elected chief executive, whose activities are checked and balanced by the other branches of the Government, the titular head of the State is an irresponsible figurehead, all of whose acts must be countersigned by ministers answerable to parliament. While the principles of the parliamentary system were not clearly discernible in all their ramifications to the framers of the Constitution of 1875, they have been unreservedly accepted in the practice of French public life.[3]

After considerable discussion the National Assembly decided to establish a parliament of two houses rather than one. The Senate, or upper house, as

---

[1] *Cf.* H. Leyret, *Le gouvernement et le parlement*, pp. 17–32, Paris, 1919, and J. Barthélemy, *Le gouvernement de la France*, pp. 11–20, Paris, 1919.

[2] L. Duguit, *Traité de droit constitutionnel*, Paris, 1924, 5 vols.; A. Esmein, *Droit constitutionnel français*, Paris, 1921, 7 vols.; J. Bryce, *Modern Democracies*, Vol. I, pp. 208–336, New York, 1927; Barthélemy, *op. cit.*; E. M. Sait, *Government and Policies of France*, New York, 1920; etc.

[3] *Cf.* Lindsay Rogers, *The French Parliamentary System*, Columbia University Press, 1931, announced, but not yet published at the time of writing.

provided for by the law of February 24, 1875, was designed to be somewhat removed from the direct control of the electorate and to constitute a moderating influence on the popular lower chamber. Of a total of 300 members, all to be over forty years of age and in the enjoyment of full civil and political rights, 75 were to be appointed for life by the National Assembly, to be replaced by the Senate itself as vacancies occurred, and 225 were apportioned among the departments on the basis of population. By the statute of December 9, 1884, all future vacancies were to be filled by elections in the departments, life membership being thus abolished in favor of a uniform term of nine years, with one-third of the Senators retiring triennially. Since this change, all members of the Senate are named by electoral colleges in the departments, consisting of the department's representatives in the Chamber of Deputies, the members of the departmental general council, the members of the *arrondissement* councils within the department, and one to twenty-four delegates from the communal councils, depending on their size. This system of indirect election of Senators has given rise to some criticism and several reform proposals, but in view of the generally satisfactory nature of the French Senate and the high esteem which its members enjoy, there would seem to be little prospect of France following the American example of direct popular choice. Since 1919 the Senate has consisted of 314 members, including those from Alsace-Lorraine.

The Chamber of Deputies consists of 612 members who must be voters and at least twenty-five years of age and who are simultaneously elected by universal manhood suffrage for a four-year term. The first electoral law of November 30, 1875, provided for the election of Deputies from single-member constituencies, the *arrondissement* being the normal electoral area. By the law of June 16, 1885, this *scrutin d'arrondissement*, as it was termed, was transformed into a *scrutin de liste* by which all the Deputies from a department were elected on a general ticket by all the voters of the department. On February 13, 1889, the single-member district system was restored. It was again replaced, forty years later, by the *scrutin de liste* by the law of July 12, 1919, which also introduced a modified form of proportional representation. The most recent change, back again to *scrutin d'arrondissement*, was carried through in July, 1927. These confusing shifts have been due in large part to the view taken by the parties in power of the advantages to themselves of the alternative systems.

The two Chambers are in theory equal in power and dignity. All legislation must be passed by a majority of both houses. Each draws up its own rules of procedure, elects its own president and its "bureau" and chooses its own commissions. The two bodies meet jointly as a National Assembly at Versailles only to amend the Constitution and elect the President of the Republic. For all other purposes, they meet separately in Paris—the Senate at the Palais Luxembourg in the Latin Quarter, and the Chamber in the Palais Bourbon, some two miles away, on the left bank of the Seine opposite the Place de la Concorde. In each house, members are free to introduce bills on their own initiative, as *propositions de loi*, though the bulk of important legislation originates with the Ministry, government bills being known as *projects de loi*. In the event of disagreement between the two chambers, measures may be referred to a special joint commission. The Chamber has the right to first consideration of finance bills, while the Senate has certain judicial functions not shared by the lower house. In fact, however, the latter is the dominant chamber. With rare exceptions the responsibility of the Ministry is to the Chamber rather than to the Senate or to both houses. The power of the President, with the consent of the Senate, to dissolve the Chamber before the expiration of its four-year term has been exercised only once, in 1877. As a result of these practices, and of the whole parliamentary system, the Senate tends to approach the position of the English House of Lords rather than that of the American Senate. If it plays a larger rôle in legislation than the former, it does not enjoy the special powers and influence of the latter.[1]

The President of the Republic is an honorary, titular executive like the British monarch rather than a powerful, responsible head of the administration. He is elected by a majority of the National Assembly for a term of seven years and is immediately and indefinitely reeligible. In the event of his death or resignation a new President is at once chosen for a full term—thereby eliminating any necessity for a Vice President. Curiously enough, there are no legal qualifications specified for the Presidency except in the amendment of 1884 which bars members of formerly reigning families. The President is vested with an imposing list of powers.[2] Gambetta declared that the Constitution created "the strongest executive power ever established in a democracy."[3] Ten years later, M. J. Weiss could assert with equal truth that "The fundamental principle of the Constitution is or ought to be that the President hunts rabbits and does not govern."[3] The explanation lies in the doctrine of Presidential irresponsibility, under which it might almost be said, as is said of the English King, that he reigns but does not rule.[4] He lives in the Palais d'Élysée and is surrounded with much of the pomp of royalty. He is the symbol of the State and the spokesman for the nation. But he is not head of the Government. The constitutional requirement of a ministerial counter-signature for all his acts deprives him almost completely of personal power in politics or administration.[5] He must, in the nature of things, conduct himself with absolute impartiality or run the risk of being forced

[1] Barthélemy, *op. cit.*, pp. 33–64; Duguit, *op. cit.*, IV, Chap. II.

[2] H. Leyret, *Le Président de la République*, pp. 11–12, Paris, 1913.

[3] *Ibid.*, p. 12.

[4] Barthélemy, *op. cit.*, pp. 86–100.

[5] Leyret, *op. cit.*, pp. 31–42, 109–122; G. de Lubersac, *Les pouvoirs constitutionnelles de la Président de la République*, pp. 20–25, Paris, 1913.

out of office by those he has offended politically, as was the case with President Millerand in 1924.[1]

Actual executive power resides in the ministry. The President, to be sure, names the ministers. But since each ministry can hold office only so long as it enjoys the confidence of the majority of the Chambers, the President's function here is largely limited to that of acting as a kind of moderator or impartial secretary for the party leaders in Parliament. He has little or no personal discretion.[2] He is obliged to pick a "President of the Council" or Premier, who can command the support of the Deputies. In each ministerial crisis, it falls to him to achieve a solution. His choice of a new Premier is countersigned by the retiring Premier. Because of the multiplicity of parties his task is often difficult and allows him somewhat more freedom of choice than the king enjoys in England. But fundamentally, as is always the case in the parliamentary system, the Premier, though chosen in name by the President, is chosen in fact by the party groups commanding a majority in Parliament.

Each new Premier must distribute the portfolios of the various departments or Ministries among his prospective colleagues with this in view. He usually keeps for himself that of the Ministry of the Interior. Each minister is the administrative head of an executive department, of which he takes charge with the assistance of his personal *cabinet* or staff which he brings into office with him. The ministers collectively, plus the under-secretaries, constitute the *conseil des ministres*, presided over by the President of the Republic, and the *conseil de cabinet*, presided over by the Premier or *président du conseil*. The two bodies, with the exception of the presiding officer, are identical in personnel. The former is recognized in law, meets usually twice a week, and makes decisions on all questions of the exercise of the executive power. The latter is extra-legal, meets ordinarily once a week, and discusses questions of general policy and relations with the Chambers. The size of the ministry (using the word now as referring to all the members of the *conseil*) varies from time to time and depends on the wishes of the Premier himself. In recent years the tendency has been toward larger ministries, with an increasing number of under-secretaries of state. Both the ministers and the under-secretaries are always members of the Senate or Chamber, more frequently of the latter body than the former.[3]

"The ministers shall be collectively responsible to the Chambers for the general policy of the government, and individually for their personal acts." In these words, the law of February 25, 1875, states the basic principle of parliamentary government everywhere. A ministry enjoys continued tenure of office so long as it has the support of the Chambers. When it is defeated in a vote of confidence, its resignation is obligatory. In practice, as already

---

[1] Duguit, *op. cit.*, IV, pp. 551–558.
[2] Leyret, *op. cit.*, pp. 45–74.
[3] Leyret, *op. cit.*, pp. 59–78.

noted, responsibility is to the Deputies rather than to the Senators, though the Constitution makes the ministry answerable to both houses. The collective nature of the responsibility requires the ministry to leave office as a body, though individual ministers may at times resign in the face of adverse criticism without affecting their colleagues. Parliament is thus the maker and breaker of ministries, the source of all executive authority, and the axis about which the whole governmental machinery of the Third Republic revolves.

5. THE PRACTICE OF POLITICS

The aspects of this constitutional framework which have a bearing on the control of foreign relations will be examined in detail in the following chapter. For the present it will be useful to turn from the form to the substance of Gallic politics and to attempt a sketch of the French party system. The colorfulness, the variety, and the tumult and the shouting of the French political scene make it difficult of comprehension and evaluation by English and American observers, accustomed as they are to the division of the electorate into two parties, usually distinguishable only by their names and by the fact that one is in power and the other is out. On the continent party fragmentation, fervid partisan enthusiasms, political intransigeance, and all the sound and fury of coalitions constantly dissolving and reforming, are inevitable concomitants of public life wherever parliamentary democracy continues to be practiced. These phenomena are typical of politics in France and are peculiarly representative of the French temperament. A literary discussion in a Montmartre café, a dispute over the merits of a new artist in the *Salon des Indépendents*, or an entr'acte argument regarding a new work at the *Opéra Comique* are more revealing of the workings of the French mind in the political realm than any amount of study of party platforms or parliamentary groups. Brilliant wit, penetrating criticism, ideological hairsplitting, a propensity to pursue every idea to its logical conclusion, a contempt for opportunism and suspension of judgment—these are characteristic of the French mentality in all its rich and variegated manifestations. Since the Frenchman does not cease to be a Frenchman when he becomes a political animal, these attributes are as marked in politics as elsewhere.

The French party system is accordingly marked by a bewildering multiplicity of programs and groups and a kaleidoscopic fluidity of movement. What one commentator calls an "undisciplined independence of political beliefs" places a premium upon political philosophizing and merciless logic-chopping, and discourages strong party organization and unity and coherence within the party groups.[1] Generally speaking, French political parties are little more than loosely knit committees of parliamentarians and journalists who draw up programs and give their blessing to candidates for office whom

[1] R. L. Buell, *Contemporary French Politics*, pp. 1–45, New York, 1920.

they approve. In Parliament and in the country, party lines are vague, confused, and overlapping. The names adopted by different groups change frequently and are misleading to the uninitiated observer. Within each group there is often the same minute gradation of opinion between the extremes which is to be found in the party system as a whole.[1] With few exceptions the control excercised by the parliamentary group over its members, and by the central party organization over its adherents in the provinces, is undisciplined, uncertain, and fluctuating.[2] These factors help to explain the instability of coalitions and the frequency of the recurrent dramatic overturns and prolonged ministerial crises which lift French political life above the level of self-complacent monotony and give it much of the zest, suspense, and hysteria of a gala performance at the *Grand Guignol*. While the great army of the permanent civil service carries on the work of routine administration with regularity and continuity behind the scenes, the actors before the public are free to indulge in duels of ideas, liaisons of convenience, and all manner of political acrobatics, to the immense edification and diversion of the forty million spectators.

These circumstances render impossible in a limited space any adequate treatment of French party history and organization. Suffice it to say that in the early decades of the Republic the numerous factions divided themselves broadly into Republicans and Monarchists, with the latter in the majority at the beginning. The former gained constantly in numbers and prestige as the Monarchists were discredited by internal dissensions and by the reverberations of the Boulangist movement, the Dreyfus affair, and similar episodes which threw the bulk of the electorate into the Republican camp. While the Republicans, freed from the urgent necessity of united action, divided and redivided into many groups over the issues of clericalism, social legislation, regulation of industry and the like, the Monarchists became a dwindling minority sitting on the extreme right of the Chamber. The extreme left, representing the dissatisfaction of the disgruntled industrial proletariat with the *bourgeois* social and economic order, was slow in reconstituting itself after the crushing of the Commune. The execution or exile of its leaders and the abhorrence with which its cause was regarded by the conservative peasantry and middle classes were serious obstacles to effective organization for political action. In 1905, however, the Unified Socialist party was created by the fusion of the Marxist faction, led by Jules Guesde, and the Reformist wing, led by Jean Jaurès.

By 1914 five distinct bands were discernible on the political spectrum, with numerous lines within each and shadings on the edges. On the extreme right was a handful of *Royalists*, still divided between Bourbonists and Bonapartists. Next came a well-organized Catholic party, accepting the

---

[1] J. Carrère, G. Bourgin et A. Guerin, *Manuel des partis politiques en France*, pp. 23–25, Paris, 1924.

[2] Buell, *op. cit.*, pp. 48–78.

Republic and championing the social program of Pope Leo XIII, but demanding the repeal of the anticlerical laws. This group was established in 1901, with the name of *l'Action Libérale*, and next to the Unified Socialists was the most compactly organized and best disciplined party in France. In the center were two loose groups of bourgeois Republicans of a less conservative temper, comprising the *Republican Opportunists* of various shades and names, and sundry aggregations of *Radicals*. These groups had cooperated from 1900 to 1910 in an anticlerical bloc, but had split by 1914 on newer issues. Such groups as the Progressist Republicans, the Democratic Alliance, the Republicans of the Left, the Unified Radicals, the Radical Socialists, etc., joined, parted, and rejoined in a dizzy waltz. On the extreme left sat the Unified Socialists, constituting the largest single party in the Chamber and committed, verbally at least, to revolutionary Marxism and uncompromising opposition to the *bourgeois* parties. With the war, however, the majority of the Socialists, in France as elsewhere, became good patriots and joined the *Union Sacrée* of all parties.

The end of the war found two great groupings in opposition, the *Bloc National* posing as a continuation of the *Union Sacrée* and standing firmly against socialism in all forms, and the *Cartel des Gauches* or Federation of the Left, comprising the more liberal or radical groups of the Republicans and having the support, if not the cooperation, of the Unified Socialists. The *Cartel*, with the Radical Socialist party as its backbone, was victorious in the 1924 elections and took over the reins of power in the Herriot Cabinet. Two years later, as a result of the fall of the franc and the financial crisis, the *Union Nationale* of all but the extreme right and left groups rallied to the support of Poincaré and maintained a party truce until the autumn of 1929 when the Radical Socialists and their allies revolted against the conservative character of the Poincaré coalition. Since that time liberty of action has been resumed by all groups and the parliamentary scene has taken on much of its pre-war aspect.[1] The extremes, however, have grown in numbers, discipline, and influence. On the ultra-right *l'Action Française* constitutes a noisy, intensely nationalistic, antiparliamentary group of Royalists, while on the ultra-left, as a result of the split in the Socialist ranks in 1920, there has appeared the Communist party as the French section of the Communist International—equally noisy and antiparliamentary, and committed to violent international social revolution and the dictatorship of the proletariat.[2]

At the beginning of 1930 the groups in the Chambers, as seated from right to left, comprised the following factions, with the voting strength obtained in the general election of 1928 and subsequent by-elections to fill vacancies:[3]

[1] Carrère, etc., *op. cit.*, pp. 9–22.

[2] *Ibid.*, *passim;* G. Gautherot, *Le monde communiste*, Paris, 1927.

[3] *Political Handbook of the World*, Yale University Press, p. 61, 1930; and Carrère, etc., *op. cit.*, pp. 25–28.

SENATE		CHAMBER OF DEPUTIES	
(To October 20, 1929)		(To December 31, 1929)	
President: M. Albert Lebrun		President: M. Fernand Buisson	
(elected June 11, 1931)			
Right	9	Belonging to no group	45
Republican Left	22	Popular Democratic	19
Republican Union	77	Republican-Democratic Union	97
Democratic and Radical Union	32	Left Republicans	64
Democratic Left	150	Unionist and Social Left	17
Socialist	15	Democratic and Social Action	30
Belonging to no group	8	Radical Left	52
Total	313	Independent Left	15
		Republican Socialist	35
		Radical and Radical Socialist	118
		Socialist	100
		Communist	10
		Not inscribed	7
		Total	609
		(Total authorized by law—612.)	

It will be seen that party names in the two houses by no means correspond. It should also be said that party lines in the center groups are confused and shifting and that such a mathematical tabulation as the table above attempts may give a false impression of the fixity of alignments. The prevalence of such names as "republican," "democratic," "radical," and even "socialist" is misleading if they are taken as an indication of doctrines or programs. More frequently they are of historical interest only or represent a use of catchwords to win popular support. The Radical Socialist party, for example, is neither radical nor socialist as a Marxian understands those terms, while the Republican Left in the Senate is a right group just next to the Royalists. Such paradoxes of terminology are characteristic of French party history throughout the whole period of the Third Republic. If the multiplicity of groups is in part due to a propensity to pursue each political idea to its logical conclusion, the final result, paradoxically again, is the antithesis of logic, with its chaos of misnamed factions and its perpetual ferment and confusion. To pick out the threads of effective control in such a maze is a task which taxes the wits of the student of French parliamentary life no less than those of the party leader who is called upon to form a ministry which will command a majority.

Chapter II

THE GOVERNANCE OF FOREIGN RELATIONS

1. The President

IN France, as in the other States of the Western State System, the control of foreign affairs was traditionally a prerogative of royalty during the formative period of modern international relations. From the earliest times to the great Revolution, the subject matter of diplomacy and international law dealt mainly with the dynastic relations and territorial ambitions of royal families and foreign policy was largely a personal affair of the king. The vague constitutional checks which limited his freedom of action to a degree in internal matters were almost entirely absent in his dealings with foreign Powers. War, peace, alliances, treaties, friendships, and enmities were the handiwork of the monarch and his immediate advisers. Here his absolutism within the nation was supreme, limited only by outside forces inherent in the nature of the State System of which he was a part.[1]

This tradition was a product not only of royal absolutism but of the very nature of foreign affairs as well. The determination of foreign policy and the handling of the problems of diplomacy do not lend themselves to treatment by a deliberative assembly or a judicial body. It is therefore not astonishing that the tradition of exclusive executive control of foreign relations has persisted into the period of *bourgeois* democracy, though the executive has been made responsible, in form at least, to the legislature or the electorate in most other respects. In France, as elsewhere, the executive continues to play the major rôle in foreign relations and such efforts at the democratization of foreign policy as have taken the form of legislative participation have been only partly successful in changing the situation which prevailed in the *ancien régime*. Only three articles of the Constitution of 1875 deal directly with foreign affairs and all reflect the survival of the tradition referred to above.[2] One gives the President control over treaty

---

[1] J. Barthélemy, *Démocratie et politique étrangère*, pp. 87–89.

[2] Loi Constitutionnelle du 16 juillet 1875 sur les rapports des pouvoirs publics . . . Article 8. Le président de la République négocie et ratifie les traités. Il en donne connaissance aux Chambres aussitôt que l'intérêt et la sûreté de l'État le permettent.—Les traités de paix, de commerce, les traités qui engagent les finances de l'État, ceux qui sont relatifs à l'état des personnes et au droit de propriété des Français à l'étranger, ne sont définitifs qu'après avoir été votés par les deux Chambres. Nulle cession, nul échange, nulle adjonction de territoire ne peut avoir lieu qu'en vertu d'une loi.

Article 9. Le président de la République ne peut declarer la guerre sans l'assentiment préalable des deux Chambres.

negotiation and ratification, subject only to the requirement of informing the Chambers as soon as the interest and security of the State permit and the further requirement of securing the consent of the Chambers for all treaties affecting peace, commerce, territory, finances, and the personal and property rights of French nationals abroad. Another requires the assent of the Chambers for declarations of war. The third, dealing generally with the powers of the President, confers upon him the right to dispose of the armed forces of the country and to receive diplomatic representatives.

These provisions would appear to place the President of the Republic in a position of great power and responsibility as the spokesman of the nation and the master of diplomatic negotiations and military operations.[1] Here, as in all other fields of executive action, however, the orders of the President must be countersigned by a minister who assumes political responsibility for any exercise of power. In accordance with the well-established principles of the parliamentary system, power is exercised in the name of the President, but not by the President as an individual.[2] Only the ministers individually, and the Cabinet collectively, are responsible for the Government's foreign policy. They may always escape responsibility for, and at the same time nullify, the personal acts of the President by refusing their countersignature. In practice, of course, the initiative comes almost always from the ministers rather than from the President. In foreign affairs, as in others, the President's rôle is mainly figurative and ceremonial and he is constrained by the constitutional system to accept a position of political inactivity which makes the office irksome to ambitious political leaders. Poincaré, for example, declares that for these reasons he had no desire for the Presidency in 1913, but was persuaded to accept it as a duty by Léon Bourgeois.[3] While such disclaimers must frequently be received with skepticism, it is undoubtedly true that the French Presidency does not afford the opportunities for policy determination and vigorous leadership which an active politician desires.

One would not be justified in concluding from such considerations, however, that the President has no voice whatever in foreign affairs. On the contrary, it is generally conceded that his opportunities for influencing policies and for playing an effective personal rôle are probably greater in the sphere of international relations than in any other. If he cannot act independently of the ministry, he shares with the British monarch the power to advise, to admonish, and to warn; and he can so conduct himself as to

---

Loi Constitutionnelle du 25 fevrier 1875 relative a l'organisation des pouvoirs public . . . Article 3. Le président de la République . . . dispose de la force armée. Il nomme à tous les emplois civil et militaires . . . les envoyés et les ambassadeurs des puissances étrangères sont accrédités auprès de lui . . . (For full text see Appendix A, p. 423 below.)

[1] Barthélemy, op. cit., pp. 102–103, 145–153; S. R. Chow, Le contrôle parlementaire de la politique étrangère en Angleterre, en France, et aux États Unis, pp. 115–117, Paris, 1920.

[2] H. Leyret, Le Président de la République, pp. 77–90, 1913.

[3] R. Poincaré, Au service de la France, III, pp. 33–63, Paris, 1928.

augment or weaken the effect of action taken by the Cabinet.[1] The precise influence which he may exercise in this way depends upon imponderable personal relationships and upon his capacity for the subtleties of leadership from behind the scenes. Sadi-Carnot played an important personal rôle in consumating the Franco-Russian Alliance and in establishing better relations with the Vatican. Loubet, through his public ceremonial activities and his personal contacts with Edward VII and Victor Emmanuel III, greatly furthered the work of Delcassé. Poincaré, at the time of his election to the Presidency, was Premier and Minister of Foreign Affairs and it has been alleged by his critics that as President he continued to exercise the functions of foreign minister and played an important secret rôle in strengthening the Franco-Russian Alliance and preparing the stage for 1914. President Millerand virtually forced Briand out of office in January, 1922, by his opposition to the Premier's policies, but so far overreached himself that he, in turn, was forced out of the Presidency by the victorious Left groups after the election of 1924.[2] It is clear from these and other instances that the French President can and does exert an influence of no negligible importance in foreign affairs despite the apparently innocuous position accorded to him by the parliamentary system.

2. The Ministry

In general, executive control in France means control by the Cabinet rather than by the titular executive. The Cabinet or ministry is the actual executive, chosen from and answerable to Parliament, and it is entrusted with the responsibility of policy formulation in domestic and foreign affairs. Within the Cabinet the Minister of Foreign Affairs is, of course, primarily responsible for the conduct of business with foreign Governments. The organization of his department and his position in it will be examined in the following chapter. For the moment it will suffice to note certain general aspects of the Cabinet's control of foreign policy.

In theory the ministry acts as a unit at all times. The Premier is presumably only *primus inter pares*. He confers with his colleagues in the weekly Cabinet meetings, where deliberations are secret and no minutes are kept.[3] In the discussion of questions of international relations the voice of the Minister of Foreign Affairs will naturally have greatest weight. The Ministers of War, of Marine, and of Colonies may also express themselves, as may any of their other colleagues on matters affecting their own sphere or the

---

[1] Chow, *op. cit.*, pp. 128–129.

[2] See below, Chaps. VII, VIII, and X; *cf.* L. Rogers, "The French President and Foreign Affairs," *Political Science Quarterly*, XL, pp. 540–560.

[3] This rule, observed since 1832, makes it difficult to ascertain exactly what occurs at Cabinet meetings. When General Weygand came before the Cabinet with a pencil and bloc-notes in 1919 he was told that at the council of ministers one does not take notes. J. Barthélemy, "La conduite de la politique extérieure dans les démocraties," lecture at the Dotation Carnegie, Paris, December 19, 1929.

policy of the Government in general.[1] Discussion is informal and decisions are reached not by counting noses but by threshing out questions until a consensus of opinion is arrived at. Once an agreement is reached, the Cabinet acts as a unit in presenting it and defending it before the Chambers. Every effort is made to preserve the appearance of unanimity,[2] though there are numerous instances of lack of unity in the Cabinet, which is natural in view of its composite character. Occasionally this results in the resignation of individual ministers or even of the whole Government. More frequently, however, the Minister of Foreign Affairs enjoys a relatively free hand and is subjected to supervision or criticism by his colleagues only when his policies demand the immediate expenditure of large sums of money or lead to a diplomatic "crisis."

The Premier's rôle as leader of the Cabinet is again not reducible to precise terms but depends on personal and political considerations. Ordinarily the Minister of Foreign Affairs has a greater freedom from control by the Premier than do his colleagues in the ministry. The tradition of continuity in foreign policy and the relative lack of interest in the intricacies of diplomacy place him in a favored position in this respect. Often the Premier will be indifferent to foreign affairs and entrust their conduct entirely to the minister at the Quai d'Orsay. This was the type of relationship which prevailed between Delcassé and the various Premiers under whom he served. More rarely the Premier may take the portfolio of the Ministry of Foreign Affairs himself or use his foreign minister as a rubber stamp to approve such foreign policies as he may himself decide upon. This seems to have been the relationship between Clemenceau and Pichon during the war and the Paris Peace Conference. Still more rarely, one may find Premier and Minister of Foreign Affairs of different schools of policy acting in collaboration. Briand and Poincaré are good examples of this peculiar situation. While differing markedly in their views, they worked together in the Poincaré Cabinet of November 11, 1928, which endured until the end of July, 1929, when Briand assumed the Premiership because of Poincaré's illness.[3] One may say, in general, that the constitutional rule of the solidarity of all the ministers in the conduct of foreign policy is qualified by the personal relations existing between the Premier, the Minister of Foreign Affairs, and their colleagues.

3. Parliament

The preponderant rôle in the conduct of foreign relations which the Constitution gives to the President, and which is exercised by the Cabinet,

[1] The Ministry of Colonies was created on March 20, 1894; its duties were formerly handled by the Quai d'Orsay. *Cf.* E. Simond, *Histoire de la Troisième République*, p. 65, Paris, 1921.

[2] Barthélemy, *loc. cit.*

[3] When he assumed the Premiership Briand declared that he had always been in complete accord with Poincaré: "Nous avons été, quoi qu' on ait pu dire ou penser, en plein et complet accord sur toutes les questions, délibérées toujours ensemble puis au sein du Gouvernement." (*J.O.Ch.*, July 31, 1929.) Cited by Barthélemy, *loc. cit.* There is, of course, no documentary record to confirm or refute such a statement.

is limited in various ways by the participation and supervision of the Chamber of Deputies and the Senate. Parliamentary control results both from specific provisions of the Constitution and from the whole nature of the governmental system. According to the former, Parliament must give its assent to declarations of war; it has the right to be informed of the terms of treaties as soon as the interest and security of the State permit; it must approve treaties of peace and commerce and those affecting the finances of the State and the personal and property rights of Frenchmen abroad before they are "definitive"; and it must approve by law all cessions, exchanges, and acquisitions of territory.[1] In these matters action is taken by majority vote in each Chamber. The French Senate, unlike the American, does not enjoy a constitutionally privileged position in the ratification of treaties and diplomatic appointments. The precise meaning of these constitutional provisions in practice can be determined only by an examination of cases and a detailed analysis of the treaty power and the war power.[2] The constitutional rule as to treaties is that the President, *i.e.*, the Cabinet, has the sole authority to negotiate and to ratify. The enumerated exceptions, calling for parliamentary action, are strictly interpreted and are not to be expanded into a general principle requiring legislative participation in treaty making.[3] The less definite forms of legislative control which flow out of the general nature of the parliamentary system are alike in that they are almost all exercised not during the course of action but after the event by way of approval or criticism "sur les faits accomplis."[4] The executive acts more or less freely on its own authority and responsibility. Action having been taken, Parliament examines it *ex post facto* and renders its judgment.

Pushed to its logical termination, this process of judging takes the form of a vote of confidence or of lack of confidence in the Government. In the latter case, the resignation of the ministry is imperative and a new ministry must be constituted which will command the support of a majority in the Chambers. But ministries are overturned very infrequently on clear-cut issues of foreign policy. The purpose of the opposition parties is not to clarify issues but to turn the Government out of office. The end justifies the means thereto. Questions of international relations are usually less convenient as pretexts than issues of domestic politics. When they are dragged into the arena of parliamentary combat, they are usually so mingled with, and obscured by, personal considerations, domestic problems, partisan prejudice, and all the exigencies of political acrobatics that the final vote is in no sense an accurate register of parliamentary opinion of the foreign policy of the ministry, nor even a logical outcome of the discussion of foreign affairs

[1] Articles 8 and 9 of the Constitutional Law of July 16, 1875.

[2] See below Chaps. XII and XIII, pp. 305*f.*, 334*f.*

[3] Barthélemy, *Le gouvernement de la France*, pp. 124–132; "C'est en somme le gouvernement seul qui fait la grande politique internationale," p. 126.

[4] Barthélemy, *Démocratie et politique étrangère*, p. 132.

which has perhaps preceded the vote. This is also true to a degree of domestic questions, but it is doubly true in foreign affairs, in which the Deputies and Senators seem noticeably less interested. As Professor Barthélemy has long since pointed out, the members of Parliament are much more concerned with the details of administration, in which they should not meddle, than with general policies, in the determination of which they are supposed to play a major rôle.[1] As a result, Parliament's power to turn out the Cabinet is scarcely an effective means of legislative control of the executive's handling of foreign relations. A butcher's cleaver cannot perform the work of a surgeon's scalpel.

More significant, though less spectacular, is Parliament's control over the purse. The annual budget furnishes a means of supervision, criticism, and direction which is one of the most important liaisons between the legislature and the executive.[2] In the Senate the Commission of Finances prepares annual reports on the budgets of the various ministries, including that of the Quai d'Orsay. The Commission of the Budget of the Chamber does the same for the lower house. The reports on the Ministry of Foreign Affairs usually run into several hundred pages and give a minute and detailed account of proposed expenditures by the department. They are prepared by the commissions in cooperation with the officials of the ministry and are ordinarily accompanied by elaborate reports on the budgets of the protectorates. The Senate reports are relatively brief and are confined to financial and administrative problems except for occasional treatments of general policy by an enterprising *rapporteur*. The longer Chamber reports usually include, in addition, a survey of the year in international relations, arranged by countries, primarily informative but sometimes critical of the Government's policies. The reports during the years of the Great War were only a few pages long and purely formal, consisting usually of recommendations for the transformation of provisional into definitive credits.[3] The post-war reports have often been somewhat brief, fragmentary, and uncritical.[4] But the preparation of the reports furnishes an opportunity for an annual investigation into the work of the Quai d'Orsay by the parliamentary commissions which is of great value in acquainting the Chambers with the administrative and technical problems of foreign affairs, if not always with the broader implications of general policies.

---

[1] "Les députés dominent et dirigent l'administration dont ils ne devraient pas s'occuper, alors qu'ils abandonment pour ainsi dire aux ministres la direction de la politique générale au dedans et surtout au dehors," Barthélemy, *op. cit.*, 137.

[2] *Ibid.*, p. 132.

[3] For an expression of regret over the fact that the disappearance of the regular budget had rendered fictitous all parliamentary control of expenses see p. 12 of 1916 *Senate Report*, 445.

[4] Chambre des Députés et Sénat, *Rapports—Budget générale de l'exercise* 19— (Ministère des Affaires Étrangères), published annually in two series. Hereinafter referred to as *Rap. Budget, Ch.*, or *Rap. Budget, Sén.*

The presentation of these reports to the Chambers is made the occasion for a general debate on the budget, frequently involving a more or less extensive discussion of foreign policy. Since 1914 the annual budget has been so enormous and has usually been presented so late in the legislative year that discussion has been cut short. In 1926, by voluntary agreement of the groups in the Chamber, the general discussion of the budget of the Ministry of Foreign Affairs was entirely suppressed. The congestion of parliamentary business, the number and complexity of the problems before the Chambers, and the nature of parliamentary procedure combine to render a well-organized and fruitful discussion of foreign affairs difficult. As in most national legislatures, long monologues are sometimes delivered for the edification of the speaker and his constituents with no intention of affecting votes, changing opinions, or influencing policies.[1] These circumstances diminish the utility which the budget debates might otherwise have as a means of parliamentary control.

The interpellation is another means to the same end of which much the same statement might be made. It is a familiar device whereby the members of Parliament may put questions to the ministers and inaugurate a general debate on the replies, followed by a vote of confidence.[2] The majority supporting the Government can determine what questions shall be discussed and can avoid embarrassing issues. In practice the number of interpellations on foreign policy is very small. From November, 1925, to July, 1926, the period of Locarno and the entrance of Germany into the League of Nations, only two debates on foreign affairs took place in the Chamber. Never has Parliament debated the foreign policy of France at the annual League assemblies.[3] Interest is lacking and issues are befuddled by domestic politics. A vote of confidence may mean no more than that the Chamber prefers not to overturn the ministry at that particular moment, even though it may disapprove of its policies. No one familiar with the use of the interpellation in the French chambers can avoid skepticism regarding its value as an instrument for the supervision and control of foreign policy.

Little more can be said for oral and written questions put to the ministers by members of Parliament. These devices, while similiar to the interpellation, can be more easily employed and do not require a vote of confidence. The number of oral questions on foreign policy is absurdly small. Two were put in 1907, four in 1908, three in 1909, and four in 1912.[4] According to the present rule two questions may be put to the ministry twice a week. They are almost always on domestic matters and better calculated to express the views of the questioner than to elucidate a reply from the ministers. The "system-

[1] *Cf.* comments on this in Barthélemy, "La conduite de la politique extérieure, etc.," Dotation Carnegie, Paris, January 16, 1930.

[2] P. de Saint-Mart, *Étude historique et critique sur les interpellations en France*, Paris, 1912, *passim.*

[3] Barthélemy, *loc. cit.*

[4] Barthélemy, *Démocratie et politique étrangère*, pp. 135f.

atic silence" and evasiveness of the latter reduce the usefulness of the procedure still further.[1] Written questions were introduced into the Chamber in
1909 and into the Senate in 1911. The Deputy, M. de Presseuse, designed
this device to facilitate parliamentary control of foreign policy. It was
accepted on the condition that the minister might at his discretion refuse to
respond "dans l'intérêt du pays."[2] There have been almost five thousand
questions a year put to the ministers under this rule. About half relate to the
interpretation of fiscal laws. Of the balance, many are essentially pointless
or naïve or calculated only to direct the attention of the public to the questioner. Very few relate to foreign policy. Professor Barthélemy, speaking
both from academic study and practical experience in parliamentary life,
declares laconically: "Mais quant à des questions de politique étrangère,
l'objet même pour laquel les questions écrites avaient été créés, il n'y en a
pas."[3]

There remains for consideration what are probably the most active and
effective instrumentalities of parliamentary control: the Senate and Chamber
Commissions on Foreign Affairs. Prior to 1914 the Chambers were organized
into "bureaux," chosen by lot, from which special, temporary committees
were picked to consider each treaty or each question of foreign relations as
it arose. This clumsy arrangement was gradually replaced by a committee
(commission) system similar to that found in most other legislative bodies.
In June, 1914 (owing chiefly to the initiative of M. Louis Marin), eighteen
permanent grand commissions were established in the Chamber, each to
consist of forty-four members chosen from among the Deputies by proportional representation at the beginning of each Parliament for a term of four
years. Number 10 was the *Commission des Affaires Extérieurs, des Protectorats
et des Colonies*, the first members of which were named June 30, 1914. In 1920
its name was changed to *Commission des Affaires Étrangères*.[4] In February of
1915 the Senate followed suit in creating a similar permanent commission.[5]
These commissions, of which that of the Chamber is the more active and

---

[1] Barthélemy, "La conduite, etc.," Dotation Carnegie, January 16, 1930.

[2] *Op. cit.*, p. 136.

[3] *Loc. cit.* During the legislative sessions of the Chamber of Deputies in 1926, 631 interpellations were presented, of which only 97 were discussed, as compared with 51 oral questions and
10,476 written questions. (Chambre des Députés, *Etat des Travaux Législatifs*, LXXXIX, pp.
10–11.) During 1927, 113 interpellations were asked and 99 oral and 13,264 written questions were
put. (*Ibid.*, LXXXIX, pp. 21–22.) During 1928, demands for 95 interpellations were presented, of
which 14 were discussed, with 11 oral questions and 3,013 written questions. (*Ibid.*, XC, p. 15,
and XCI, pp. 11–12.) During the first half of the ordinary session of 1929, 192 interpellations, 26
oral questions, and 2,381 written questions were addressed to the Government in the Chamber.
(*Ibid.*, XCI, pp. 20–21.) No compilation known to the writer gives the proportion of these interpellations and questions which dealt with foreign policy, but it is safe to say that it was extremely
small.

[4] Ch.d.D., *États des Travaux Législatifs*, LXXV, pp. 145f.; LXXXII, p. 136; Barthélemy,
Démocratie et politique étrangère, pp. 130–131.

[5] *Ibid.*, p. 131.

important, prepare reports on treaties and other matters of foreign relations submitted to them by the Chambers (with the exception of the budget), keep in constant touch with the Quai d'Orsay through their *rapporteurs d'informations*, submit questionnaires and receive replies, and call the foreign minister and his immediate subordinates before them for interrogation and discussion. They constitute the nearest approach yet devised to an effective organ of parliamentary control and direction of foreign policy and they exercise an appreciable, if somewhat imponderable, influence on the activities of the Ministry.[1]

Enough has already been said to indicate that the various forms of parliamentary supervision, with the possible exception of the last mentioned, leave much to be desired from the point of view of those who hold that the conduct of foreign affairs should be placed under the constant and effective scrutiny and supervision of parliament. Whether this ideal is possible of attainment is questionable. Its merits can be more conveniently discussed in other connections. Much more important is an analysis and evaluation of the past and present methods of control as they have operated in concrete situations. An effort will be made in the chapters which follow to assess the influence of the devices and organs listed here in shaping the conduct of policy, in the hope that this will make possible a more detailed and concrete evaluation of the whole system of control.

4. THE COURTS

No such survey of the formal controls of foreign affairs as is here being undertaken would be complete without some mention of the rôle of the judiciary, as well as of the executive and legislature. In dealing with France, however, very little can or need be said on this score. The American principle of the separation of powers is foreign to the parliamentary system; and the courts, not being policy-determining organs in any sense, have no direct voice in the handling of international problems, which is still a political rather than a judicial function. The questions which arise here revolve rather about possible conflicts between international engagements and national law, which the courts must somehow reconcile. Such questions are important and not infrequent in the United States, with its Federal form of government and its check-and-balance arrangements. Treaties are enforced as part of the "supreme law of the land" (Article VI of the Federal Constitution) and under the American system of judicial review are enforced as law in ordinary litigation, with the courts accepting the views of the political branch of the Government as to their interpretation. State statutes in conflict with treaties are not enforced. As between a treaty and a conflicting Federal law the most recent prevails.[2] In France such questions seldom arise. The courts enforce law as enacted by Parliament, and Parliament's interpretation of the Con-

---

[1] Barthélemy, "La conduite, etc.," Dotation Carnegie, January 16, 1930, *Cf. infra*, pp. 316*f*.

[2] Quincy Wright, *The Control of American Foreign Relations*, pp. 196–204.

stitution and of treaties is final, with no judicial veto to correct the legislature's mistakes. Treaties are in no sense part of any "supreme law" to be enforced as against an inferior law by the Court of Cassation as the United States Supreme Court enforces them against conflicting State, and anterior and conflicting Federal legislation.[1] Only on rare occasions have the courts been called upon to choose between a treaty and a conflicting statute. This perhaps suggests that a national legislature which is not placed under suspicion by judicial review tends to be more scrupulous in its observance of international obligations than one not considered so trustworthy. One French authority holds that a treaty may supersede a law, but only to the degree required to fulfill the strict letter of the international obligation.[2] Usually the latter is incorporated in statutory form and the problem is hypothetical rather than actual. If no well-established principle has emerged to deal with such cases, it is because of their extreme rarity in fact.[3]

The Council of State, as the highest administrative court, has similarly no functions of importance in connection with foreign affairs. It has a section on legislation and foreign affairs and the Minister of Foreign Affairs can secure an *avis* from this section or from the council as a whole on his projected decrees. These relate, of course, to the internal administration of the Ministry and of the diplomatic and consular services abroad and not to policy formulation. The council passes only upon the legality of decrees, although the line between legality and expediency is sometimes shadowy. The commissions of the Chambers secure advice from the Council of State only through the ministers and may occasionally request information on some point of law touching foreign affairs. Except for this, and certain limited functions connected with naturalization,[4] the Council of State has no voice in foreign relations. Neither it nor the regular courts have any formal control over policy.[5]

[1] Chow, *Le contrôle parlamentaire de la politique étrangère en Angleterre, en France et aux États Unis,* p. 185.

[2] For a discussion of this, with examples, see L. Michon, *Les traités internationaux devant les chambres,* pp. 222–227, Paris, 1901.

[3] French courts have not been entirely consistent in their views on the legal status of treaties. *Cf.* Quincy Wright, "The Legal Nature of Treaties," *American Journal of International Law,* 1916, X, pp. 706–736.

[4] *Cf.* Frantz Despagnet, "Du rôle du Conseil d'État dans la naturalisation," *Revue du droit public et de la science politique,* I, pp. 101–114, 1894.

[5] The writer is indebted for certain information upon which these statements are based to M. Aubert Lefas, member of the *section de contentieux* of the Council of State.

Chapter III

THE MECHANISMS OF DIPLOMACY

1. The Minister of Foreign Affairs

THE central figure in the machinery outlined in the preceding chapter is obviously the Minister of Foreign Affairs. In his hands rests the immediate responsibility for the determination of policy and the conduct of relations with foreign Powers. He works in greater or lesser degree in cooperation with, and under the supervision of, the other agencies of the Government who have a voice in foreign affairs: the President, the Premier, the other ministers in the Cabinet, the parliamentary commissions, etc. But ordinarily he works alone, through the tools at his command at the Quai d'Orsay, and the diplomatic and consular services abroad. He is called to account only rarely when his mistakes lead to crises or his policies lead to results which arouse general interest. The importance of his activities is frequently in inverse ratio to the amount of attention paid to them. And yet, his task is one of enormous complexity. As Professor Barthélemy observes: "He is like an organist before an instrument with innumerable keys, where the least false note may have the most serious repercussions."[1]

He differs from his colleagues in that he himself must play the organ at the Quai d'Orsay while the other ministers, knowing little of music, may content themselves with calling the tune in their respective departments and having their subordinates render the selections desired. Parliamentary government has been defined as government by a committee of amateurs who direct permanent experts. With rare exceptions this holds true of all the ministers in the French Cabinet. But the holder of the portfolio of foreign affairs cannot be a layman or amateur entirely unfamiliar with the technical details of the work of his staff, though in fact he is usually without personal diplomatic experience. He is constantly called upon to do work of a technical character himself: drafting communications, receiving representatives of foreign Powers, sending instructions to agents abroad, etc. Not only must he be an expert functionary, in distinction from his colleagues, who need only be intelligent politicians, but he must be a statesman as well if he is to be genuinely competent to handle the duties of his office.[2]

---

[1] Barthélemy, *Démocratie et politique étrangère*, p. 153, 154-160; and S. R. Chow, *Le contrôle parlementaire de la politique étrangère*, pp. 117-125.

[2] "Entre toutes les administrations centrales, c'est aux Affaires Étrangères que la personnalité du Ministre joue le rôle le plus effectif, car il n'y est pas uniquement, ni même principalment, chargé de centraliser dans ses bureaux le travail d'administration annexés; il doit être d abord le premier diplomat de son pays." (*Rap. Budget, Ch.*, 1921, No. 2020, p. 47.)

All of these factors, coupled with the usual absorption of the Premier, the other ministers, and Parliament in their own work give to the Minister of Foreign Affairs a peculiarly personal responsibility and a unique opportunity for uncontrolled policy determination. If the Minister of Foreign Affairs is also Premier, as is sometimes the case, this is all the more true. Even when the two posts are not combined, the foreign minister can usually pursue a personal policy within the limits imposed by the traditions of his office, the pressure of the permanent staff, the "national interests" of France, and the crossfire of criticism from without. He can commit the nation to engagements which cannot be conveniently disavowed and he can embark upon a course of action which may vitally affect the welfare, the security, and even the very existence of the State without being made answerable to any higher authority for his conduct until after decisions have been made and acted upon.[1]

In view of these considerations, it seems at first sight astonishing that France, during the sixty years between 1871 and 1931, should have had no less than fifty successive Ministers of Foreign Affairs.[2] The instability of Cabinets under the Third Republic is proverbial. During the period under consideration seventy distinct Cabinets were formed and overthrown—a situation which would seem to spell chaos in foreign as well as in domestic affairs. During the fifty-four-year personal rule of Louis XIV (1661 to 1715) only four persons held the office of foreign minister: Hughes de Lionne, Armand de Pomponne, Colbert de Croissy, and Colbert de Torcy. The comparison, however, is misleading. A new Cabinet in the Third Republic more frequently than not means merely a reshuffling of portfolios and a slight change of personnel. Only forty-three different individuals served as premiers in the seventy Cabinets mentioned. Only thirty-seven different individuals served as foreign ministers. There would thus seem to be a slightly greater continuity and stability at the Quai d'Orsay than in the office of the *président du conseil*. And while each Cabinet has an average tenure of less than a year,[3] this is not at all typical of the situation at the Ministry of Foreign Affairs. The shortest tenures on record are those of Leon Bourgeois (two days in 1914) and Herriot (one day in 1926). On the other hand, the longest tenures run into many years, as indicated by the tables on page 30.[4]

During thirty-one and a half years out of a total of sixty-one, the portfolio of the Ministry of Foreign Affairs has been held by the five men here listed, each with an average tenure of over six years. These tenures have not, of

[1] Barthélemy, "La conduite, etc.," Dotation Carnegie, December 19, 1929.

[2] See Appendix B, p. 427 below. While France had forty-three ministries from 1870 to 1920, Spain had twenty-eight, Italy sixteen, England fifteen, Germany ten, and Austria-Hungary nine. *Cf. Rap. Budget, Ch.*, 1921, No. 2020, pp. 47–48.

[3] From 1870 to 1920 France had forty-three Cabinets with an average tenure of fifteen months. If the calculation is made from 1870 to 1931, there were seventy Cabinets with an average tenure of ten months.

[4] *Cf.* Appendix B, *infra*, pp. 427–431.

LONGEST CONTINUOUS TENURES OF OFFICE BY MINISTERS OF FOREIGN AFFAIRS

Delcassé	84 months	(June 28, 1898 to June 17, 1905)
Briand	62 months	(July 23, 1926 to —*)
Pichon	52 months	(October 25, 1906 to March 2, 1911)
Décazes	48 months	(November 26, 1873 to November 23, 1877)
Ribot	34 months	(March 17, 1890 to January 11, 1893)
Poincaré	28 months	(January 15, 1922 to June 9, 1924)

LONGEST TOTAL TENURES OF OFFICE BY MINISTERS OF FOREIGN AFFAIRS

Briand	114 months*
Delcassé	98 months
Pichon	86 months
Hanotaux	44 months
Poincaré	40 months
Total	382 months, or an average tenure of 76 months.

* To September of 1931.

course, been continuous. Delcassé holds the record for the longest continuous tenure, while Briand has the longest total service to his credit. It is obvious that such a situation signifies a continuity of policy and leadership which is strikingly exceptional in France and keeps the Quai d'Orsay relatively free from the acrobatics of politics. A foreign minister with a short term is constrained by his inexperience and the pressure of facts to follow the lead of his predecessor. Only the few statesmen who have held the office for a number of years have been able to give a decisive turn to the course of policy. This is broadly true of all the ministries and of the Cabinet as a whole. At the Quai d'Orsay it insures an even greater stability and continuity than elsewhere because of the relatively long intervals of continuous tenure of office by a few individuals such as are found in no other department.

Certain other statistical aspects of the office are not without interest. Only one minister, Bonneville, was without parliamentary experience at the time of his appointment. Of the remainder, twenty-four were Deputies and twelve were Senators when they assumed office for the first time. Ten became Senators subsequently. Seventeen of the thirty-seven were Premiers at one time or another. The Presidency of the Republic was attained by five: Fallières, Casimir-Périer, Poincaré, Millerand, Doumergue. Poincaré served as foreign minister both before and after his Presidency. Of the twelve Presidents of France since 1870, five served at the Quai d'Orsay. Only eight of the thirty-seven foreign ministers had previous diplomatic experience at the time of their appointment. It is clear from what has already been said that an amateur at the Quai d'Orsay is in a peculiarly difficult position and is probably influenced to a greater degree than his colleagues by the permanent staff of his Ministry. This may easily mean that the initiative in policy formulation may actually come from the permanent bureaucrats rather than from the responsible minister. In terms of vocational background and interest, twenty of the thirty-seven were lawyers or jurists, eight were primarily journalists, six were professors, one was an engineer (Freycinet), one a chemist (Berthelot), and one a business man (Décazes). A little less than half of the total number attained distinction as journalists or writers. All of them might be described by an Extreme Left critic as having the economic interests and political attitudes of the *bourgeoisie* who constitute the backbone of the Third French Republic. In terms of age groups, the office has usually been filled by men well advanced in years. Only five came to the office under the age of forty-five: Gambetta (43), Fallières (42), Ferry (45), Hanotaux (41), and Bourgeois (45). Ten were sixty or over at the time of their appointment. In general, then, the French Minister of Foreign Affairs is usually a middle-aged lawyer with journalistic experience who has been a member of the Chamber of Deputies, but has had little first-hand contact with diplomatic problems.[1]

2. The Quai d'Orsay: Organization

The plain, gray stone building which houses the staff of the Ministry of Foreign Affairs is located on the left bank of the Seine on the Quai d'Orsay, from which it takes its traditional name. It lies just to the left of the group of structures comprising the old Palais Bourbon, where the Chamber of Deputies now meets, and near the foot of the ornate bridge named after the Tsar Alexander III, reminiscent of the most fateful achievement of the diplomacy of the Third Republic—the Franco-Russian Alliance. To the rear stretches the *Esplanade des Invalides*, beyond which is *l'École Militaire*, France's war college, and the tomb of the Man of Destiny—Napoleon I— France's mightiest warrior and hallowed symbol of the glory of conquest and prowess in arms. These associations are not without their significance, for at the Quai d'Orsay it is never forgotten that "war, like diplomacy, is but another instrument of policy. In times of peace, foreign policy has diplomacy for its tool; in times of war, foreign policy is one with the conduct of hostilities."[2]

The historical origins and development of the French foreign office need not detain us here. Prior to 1880 the Ministry was organized much as it had been under the Second Empire, the Second Republic, and the July Monarchy of Louis Philippe. The basic decrees of May 1, 1832, and December 26, 1869, had created three great "services": the Minister's *cabinet* and Secretariat, the Dispatch and Receipt of Correspondence, and the Protocol Service. In addition to these groupings, there existed the two great "directions" of political affairs and of commercial affairs, subdivided into geographical sections, a Division of Archives, with a bureau of chancelleries attached to it, and a Division of Funds and Accounts. Except for the creation in 1875 of

---

[1] For the biographical data upon which these generalizations rest, the writer is indebted to Professor J. Gilbert Heinberg of the University of Missouri. *Cf.* his Tables on the Personnel of French Cabinets, February 19, 1871–October 22, 1929, in "The Personnel of French Cabinets," *American Political Science Review*, XXV, pp. 389–396, May, 1931.

[2] M. Raiberti in *Rap. Budget, Ch.*, 1917, No. 4108, p. 1.

a bureau of translators, attached to the *cabinet* of the minister, no changes were made in the framework of the central administration with the establishment of the Third Republic. Modifications of the old machinery were required, however, by the new problems raised by the changing international situation. A report presented to the National Assembly in March, 1874, by Emmanuel Arago indicated the nature of the reforms needed, but for the moment no action was taken. In 1877 Décazes submitted an elaborate report to the President of the Republic "On the Organization of the Services of the Ministry of Foreign Affairs," which attacked the artificial separation between the political and commercial divisions and which led to the creation, by executive decree, of a Committee of Foreign Services to insure community of views and unity of action between them.[1]

With the coming into office of Freycinet in 1880 more sweeping reforms were introduced. The organization of the political and commercial divisions was made symmetrical and three new divisions were established: a Personnel Service, the functions of which had previously been performed for the consular service by the commercial division and for the diplomatic service by the political division; a *service du contentieux*, detached from the political division and subdivided into sections of public and private law; and a new division combining the divisions of archives and of funds and accounts. The *cabinet* of the minister was improved by the addition of a Press Service and a Code Service. This rearrangement was at once attacked as too theoretical and during the course of the next few years many new changes were introduced, some of them restoring the old scheme and others making minor modifications in the arrangement of bureaus and offices within the divisions. These changes were so numerous and frequent that they were without lasting results save an illogical confusion in the organization of the Ministry. A project for general reorganization was submitted to the Chambers in 1899, but rejected by the Commission of the Budget because of the expense involved.[2]

Following the appointment of Stephen Pichon as minister, a Commission of Administrative Reforms was established in 1906, the recommendations of which were embodied in a decree of April 29, 1907. The political and commercial divisions were at last united in a single division, to which the Archives were attached, while a new Division of Technical and Administrative Affairs was established. A Bureau of Communications was also created in the political and commercial division for the purpose of aiding in the coordination of the various services by distributing summaries of information sent in by French agents abroad and pertinent news items and comment in French and foreign papers. A commercial and financial counselor was likewise established in this division to study economic questions. The latter office was abolished in 1910, by a decree of August 13, which also brought into existence the Bureau of French Schools and Culture Abroad.[3]

[1] *Rap. Budget, Sén.*, 1913, No. 148, pp. 34–35.
[2] *Ibid.*, pp. 35–38, for a detailed account of these changes.
[3] *Ibid.*, pp. 38–41.

The story of the structure of the Ministry since the Great War is much the same: a bureau added here or abolished there; offices within divisions shuffled now this way, now that; subdivisions established, suppressed, restored. It is noteworthy that in practically every case administrative changes are achieved through decrees of the Executive rather than by the passage of statutes.[1] This might be expected to insure consideration of such problems only by mature experts and experienced officials whose advice could be readily secured and promptly acted upon. In practice this has usually been the case. And yet it is difficult to discern any logical line of development in the changes which have taken place, except for a tendency since the Great War toward expansion. If there has been any coherence or unity or planned direction behind the successive rearrangements and reorganizations, they elude the outside observer. It would appear rather that each new decree has been motivated by a pressing emergency, an immediate problem, a novel idea of a minister or high functionary, or some other factor having no relation to any broad view of the work of the Quai d'Orsay or the desirability of a structural scheme based upon the nature of that work. If the present organization approximates such a scheme, it is a result of accident or of sporadic, piecemeal reforms. These considerations raise questions of the greatest interest to students of administration. They are not sufficiently relevant to our main purpose here, however, to warrant stopping to discuss them. In any case, it is being increasingly recognized that structural arrangements are less important than personnel management in determining the effectiveness of a given bit of administrative machinery.[2]

At the time of writing, the Quai d'Orsay is organized into six major divisions and four independent offices as shown in the accompanying diagram. In this scheme of things, the Secretary-General is second in importance to the minister himself. The office is a post-war creation, designed to relieve the minister of the burden of dealing personally with the innumerable questions of personnel and the details of administration which are constantly arising. This is particularly important when the minister is also Premier. The Secretary-General must be prepared at any time to take over the duties of the minister. He acts at all times under the latter's direction as the administrative head of the staff at the Quai d'Orsay and in the diplomatic and consular posts abroad.[3] He is not a liaison agent between the Ministry on the one hand and the Cabinet and Parliament on the other, as a true parliamentary under-secretary would be. Some have urged that he be given this function.[4] In practice, however, he is the minister's right-hand man and the highest

[1] For references on the decrees from 1907 to 1915 see Barthélemy, *op. cit.*, p. 160.

[2] *Rap. Budget, Sén.*, 1913, No. 148, pp. 41–43. *Cf.* L. D. White, *Public Administration*, pp. 206f., New York, 1926.

[3] The functions of the Secretary-General are defined in the following concise language in the decree of January 20, 1920: "Le S. G. exerce, sous l' autorité et au nom du Ministre, la haute direction de tous les services," *Rap. Budget, Ch.*, 1921, No. 2020, pp. 48–50.

[4] *Ibid.*

of the permanent officials, having the rank of ambassador and playing the rôle formerly played by the chief of the division of political and commercial affairs. His office was created by simple executive decree, with the tacit approval but not the specific authorization of Parliament.[1] This again

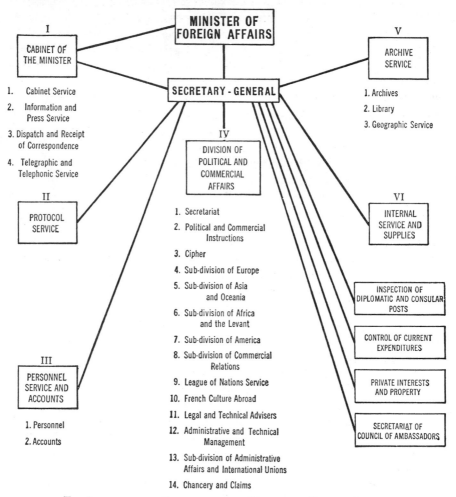

I
CABINET OF THE MINISTER

1. Cabinet Service
2. Information and Press Service
3. Dispatch and Receipt of Correspondence
4. Telegraphic and Telephonic Service

II
PROTOCOL SERVICE

III
PERSONNEL SERVICE AND ACCOUNTS

1. Personnel
2. Accounts

MINISTER OF FOREIGN AFFAIRS
SECRETARY - GENERAL

IV
DIVISION OF POLITICAL AND COMMERCIAL AFFAIRS

1. Secretariat
2. Political and Commercial Instructions
3. Cipher
4. Sub-division of Europe
5. Sub-division of Asia and Oceania
6. Sub-division of Africa and the Levant
7. Sub-division of America
8. Sub-division of Commercial Relations
9. League of Nations Service
10. French Culture Abroad
11. Legal and Technical Advisers
12. Administrative and Technical Management
13. Sub-division of Administrative Affairs and International Unions
14. Chancery and Claims

V
ARCHIVE SERVICE

1. Archives
2. Library
3. Geographic Service

VI
INTERNAL SERVICE AND SUPPLIES

INSPECTION OF DIPLOMATIC AND CONSULAR POSTS

CONTROL OF CURRENT EXPENDITURES

PRIVATE INTERESTS AND PROPERTY

SECRETARIAT OF COUNCIL OF AMBASSADORS

THE ADMINISTRATIVE STRUCTURE OF THE MINISTRY OF FOREIGN AFFAIRS

demonstrates the fluidity of administrative organization in France and the possibility of inaugurating extensive modifications of the existing machinery without the intervention of the legislature. The post of Secretary-General has been held much of the time since its creation by M. Philippe Berthelot.

The *cabinet* of the minister is an institution found in all the great executive departments. The name has no reference to the *conseil du cabinet*, i.e., to

[1] *Ibid.*, p. 49.

the whole group of the ministers, but is applied here to the small staff of personal assistants which each minister picks himself and brings into office with him. This group is not a consultative body, but a personal office staff, designed in part as a check on the influence of the permanent bureaucracy on the minister.[1] The organization of the *cabinet* has also been fixed by executive decrees, of which those of February 13, 1912, and July 23, 1918, are the most important.[2] Its principal task at the Quai d'Orsay is to handle correspondence and audiences for the minister and to act as a liaison between the minister and the permanent officials.[3] The information and Press Service of the *cabinet*, which handles the exceedingly important and delicate work of relations with the public and the newspapers, is under the immediate supervision of the Secretary-General. One section supplies information to journalists, another makes a digest of the foreign press for a daily bulletin which is widely circulated among the officials at the Quai d'Orsay and the diplomatic and consular officers abroad, the other ministers and the parliamentary commissions, and a third section makes detailed studies of special questions on request and sends out periodical bulletins to French representatives abroad to keep them in touch with home developments.[4] The routine work is, of course, done by permanent clerks, but the heads of the *cabinet* are the minister's own appointees. They are frequently chosen from the professional foreign service.

The Protocol Service, the second of the major divisions of the Ministry, is, in a sense, the "adviser on etiquette" of the Quai d'Orsay. It is the custodian of the traditions of ceremonial which seem amusing or unnecessary to the layman but which constitute an indispensable lubricant on the wheels and gears of the machinery of diplomacy. The procedure of official receptions of members of the diplomatic corps and of distinguished foreigners, the rights, privileges, and immunities of diplomats, the forms of diplomatic communications and international agreements all fall within the scope of its activity. It is also entrusted with the task of making nominations to the Legion of Honor of foreigners and of Frenchmen residing abroad and of giving advice on the reception of foreign decorations conferred on French agents. In all these matters the influence of democratic doctrines has in no sense diminished the importance of this service nor lessened the reverence for court usages and the forms and ceremonies of royalty.[5]

The functions of the Division of Personnel Service and Accounts are indicated by its title. It has charge of personnel administration in the

---

[1] H. K. Norton, "Foreign Office Organization," *Annals of the American Academy of Political and Social Science*, Supp. to Vol. CXLIII, pp. 12–13.

[2] For contents see *Rap. Budget, Ch.*, 1921, No. 2020, pp. 50–52.

[3] *Ibid.* This report emphasizes the necessity of administrative experience and tact on the part of the members of the *cabinet*.

[4] Norton, *loc. cit.*, pp. 65–66; *Rap. Budget, Ch.*, 1908, No. 2015, pp. 22–24.

[5] *Rap. Budget, Ch.*, 1921, No. 2020, pp. 52–53.

foreign services and at the Quai d'Orsay. In collaboration with the heads of
the services immediately concerned, it makes nominations to office, handles
questions of advancement and promotion, recommends officials who have
distinguished themselves for membership in the Legion of Honor, and
examines all budgetary questions affecting the status of agents in the Ministry or abroad. These functions were originally scattered about among other
offices and bureaus, then concentrated in a section of the Minister's *cabinet*,
and more recently constituted into an autonomous service.[1] The Accounts
section of the service prepares the budget of the Ministry in collaboration
with the other services and the budget commission of the Chamber, super-
vises the expenditures authorized by the budget, and constitutes a central
accounting house for the Ministry. The maintenance of an independent section for the control of current expenditures would seem to involve an unnecessary duplication of functions.[2]

The Division of Political and Commercial Affairs is by far the largest
and most important in the Ministry, and its chief stands next to the Secretary-
General in prestige and influence at the Quai d'Orsay.[3] It was created in 1907
by the fusion of the separate divisions dealing with commercial and political
matters, a necessary step to the proposed administrative amalgamation of
the diplomatic and consular services. A detailed examination of each of its
fourteen subdivisions would involve an analysis of the minutiae of administration which would throw little light on the broader problems under consideration. It will be noted that four of the fourteen subdivisions are
organized geographically, on bases familiar in every foreign office, for the
receipt of information coming in from French agents abroad in their
respective regions. Of the remaining subdivisions, only a few call for special
attention.[4] The League of Nations Service is a recent creation, established for
the purpose of centralizing French contacts with the League and indicative
of the importance attached to the Geneva organization at the Quai d'Orsay.
The subdivision of French Culture Abroad is particularly interesting. Its
general task is to encourage the expansion of French influence through
literary, artistic, and academic channels.[5] The University and School section
attempts to encourage the teaching of French language and literature abroad
and in recent years has concentrated its efforts in the East European satellites
of France, the Baltic States, Poland, Czechoslovakia and Jugoslavia, seeking

[1] *Ibid.*, pp. 53–54.

[2] *Ibid.*, p. 62.

[3] *Ibid.*, pp. 57–61, and Barthélemy, *op. cit.*, pp. 160–163.

[4] For details, see *Rap. Budget, Ch.*, 1921, No. 2020, *passim.*

[5] "Le présent résumé nous permettra d'apprecier l'intérêt captivant, l'importance de premier
ordre, qui s'attache à cette question, encore beaucoup négligée chez nous, de l'expansion. Il ne
faut pas oublier, en effet, qu'une nation isolée ne peut rien aujourd'hui par elle-même; sa sécurité
et sa prospérité, si elle est unie, lui viènnent de la sécurité qui lui conquiert sur les champs de
bataille de l'univers sa puissance politique, économique et intellectuelle," *Rap. Budget, Ch.*,
1921, No. 3131, p. 16.

fellowships and aids for students of these and other countries in France and endeavoring to establish French chairs in foreign universities. "Culture" thus becomes the tool of high policy. The literary and artistic Section and the section on "Tourism," Sports, and the Cinema engage in cultural propaganda on many fronts designed to enhance French prestige abroad and to counteract the corresponding efforts of supposedly hostile States.[1] The legal and technical adviser, who works with a small staff and in occasional consultation with professors of law at the Sorbonne, is an official of no small importance, since his word tends to be final with the minister on the legal aspects of international controversies. Questions of conflicts of laws, of nationality, extradition, rights of French citizens abroad and of foreigners in France, passports, international litigations, private claims, and technical cooperation in the enforcement of what has been called "international social legislation" through the great public international unions are handled by subdivisions 12, 13, and 14, as shown in the diagram.[2]

The fifth major division, that of the Archives, maintains a library of some 80,000 volumes at the Ministry in addition to a geographical service with atlases, maps, and charts for the use of the staff. The Archives proper consist of the vast mass of historical records, documents, and diplomatic correspondence accumulated over the centuries, classified in such fashion as to be accessible to the staff of the Quai d'Orsay and to such outside scholars as may receive authorization to do research at the Ministry. The sixth division, that of Internal Service and Supplies, is concerned with the maintenance of the buildings and grounds of the Ministry and the purchase of necessary materials.

3. THE QUAI D'ORSAY: PERSONNEL

The administrative machine which has been sketched above is manned by over 400 permanent officials and employees at the Quai d'Orsay, exclusive of the diplomatic and consular services abroad which contain about 600 officials in addition.[3] The recruitment and management of this small army of public servants involves problems of major interest to students of personnel administration. While an exhaustive treatment of these problems here would again carry us away from our main task, it is important to secure a general picture of the situation. What manner of people work in the offices at the Quai d'Orsay? How do they secure their positions? What rules govern their advancement and promotion? What is their attitude toward their work?

[1] *Ibid.*, pp. 16–45.

[2] *Cf. Rap. Budget, Ch.*, 1921, No. 2020, pp. 61–62; 1910, No. 361, pp. 118–136; 1911, No. 1237, pp. 88–96.

[3] The decrees of June 14 and July 21, 1918, provided for 217 officials, exclusive of the personnel of the *cabinet* and non-commissioned agents and auxiliaries (*Rap. Budget, Ch.*, 1921, No. 2020, pp. 10–12). The personnel list of the Ministry, as of March, 1930, contained 392 names, not including guards, concierges, etc.

These and similar questions do not in every case admit of definitive answers on the basis of the information available, but must wait upon detailed studies of personnel management in the French public service. Nevertheless the broad outlines of the system of personnel administration are clear and can be briefly indicated.

In general, the higher posts at the Quai d'Orsay are filled from the ranks of the diplomatic and consular services while the lower posts are filled by promotion from the permanent staff or by direct recruitment. Article 1 of the decree of June 15, 1918, provided that the posts of director of divisions, assistant director, chief of services, head and assistant head of bureaus, *rédacteur, secretaire archivist, attaché classeur,* and *premier chiffreur* should be reserved to agents taken from the foreign service. While the salaries of these officials are fixed by the central administration, they are under the rules of advancement and promotion prevailing in the diplomatic and consular staffs.[1] The *directeurs,* the *chefs de service,* and the *sous-directeurs* are named by a decree of the President of the Republic and the others by an *arrêté* of the minister. Numerous decrees set forth in considerable detail the qualifications for each office. They vary so greatly because of the different kinds of work to be done that generalization is difficult.[2]

The decree of September 22, 1913, instituted a regular system of formal examinations for admission to the foreign services and gave a greater guarantee of competence and permanent tenure than had existed under the loosely organized and informal system of recruitment prevailing hitherto. Since the staff of the Quai d'Orsay was recruited largely from the ranks of the foreign service, the benefits of the new system extended automatically to the central administration. Recruits came largely from the nobility and wealthy families in the pre-Republican period. The *haute bourgeoisie* and the *nouveau riches,* with increasing numbers from the middle and even lower *bourgeoisie,* now supply a large proportion of the entrants, since only people of considerable financial means are able to send their sons to the *École Libre des Sciences Politiques,* which is the semiofficial training school for the public service. The entrance examinations for admission to both the Quai d'Orsay and the foreign services are prepared by, and given under the supervision of, a board of examiners, and, while possibly somewhat less severe than in England, require the equivalent of more than a bachelor's degree if the candidate is to hope for success. About forty applicants take the examinations annually, of whom less than half are passed.[3] All assignments and promotions are made on the recommendation of the Director of Personnel. Promotions are based on efficiency rather than seniority, though an official must ordinarily serve a minimum number of years (usually three) in one rank before he can

[1] *Rap. Budget, Ch.,* 1921, No. 2020, pp. 10–12.

[2] For a survey see *ibid.,* pp. 83–93.

[3] Norton, *loc. cit.,* pp. 32–33 and 42–43. Owing to the virtual suspension of recruitment during the war, 226 applicants entered the service from May, 1918, to August 1, 1920. *Rap. Budget, Ch.,* 1921, No. 2020, p. 90.

THE MECHANISMS OF DIPLOMACY

be promoted to the next. Advances from inferior to superior positions are purely discretionary if they involve no change of rank or class. If they do involve such a change, discretion is limited by seniority rules.[1] M. Philippe Berthelot, Secretary-General at the time of writing, has the rank of ambassador. M. Leger, *chef du cabinet*, is a minister plenipotentiary of the second class. M. Becq de Fouquières, *chef du service du protocole*, is a minister plenipotentiary of the first class, as is M. Harismendy, *chef du service du personnel*. Lower officials have lower ranks in the diplomatic or consular ‘scale, while subordinates have no diplomatic ranking.

Salaries have long been notoriously inadequate in the central administration. The officials of the foreign services have been paid on a gold-franc basis since the war and have accordingly not suffered severely from the fluctuations in the value of the franc prior to its stabilization in 1928. Even here, however, salaries have been comparatively low: ambassadors, 40,000 fr. yearly (about $8,000); ministers of the first class, 28,000 fr.; ministers of the second class, 22,000 fr. running down to 11,000 fr. for secretaries of the third class; consuls general, 18,000 fr.; consuls of the first class, 16,000 fr.; consuls of the second class, 14,000 fr., down to interpreters, 6,000 fr. (decree of July 1, 1919). These figures are supplemented by variable allowances adjusted to the cost of living at the various posts.[2] By the decree of February 22, 1920, *directeurs* at the Quai d'Orsay received 25,000 fr. to 30,000 fr. (paper); *chefs du service* and *sous-directeurs*, 18,000 fr. to 22,000 fr.; *chefs de bureau*, 11,000 fr. to 14,000 fr.; and *rédacteurs*, 6,000 fr. to 11,000 fr.[3] Despite certain subsequent increases, the depreciation of the franc from over nineteen cents to four cents has rendered the present salary scale entirely insufficient by any standard. Doubtless the efficiency and morale of the personnel has suffered accordingly, though to the outside observer it appears that the existing system of personnel administration at the Quai d'Orsay has resulted in a generally high standard of competence among the members of the staff.

A word as to the total cost of maintaining the Ministry may not be out of place at this point. The budget of the department before the Great War exhibited a remarkable stability and uniformity, as shown by the following table of representative years:[4]

1800	fr. 5,923,732
1850	9,928,564
1871	12,847,895
1880	15,785,674
1890	17,640,819
1900	19,546,035
1910	22,638,225
1913	21,758,246

[1] *Ibid.*, pp. 94–127.
[2] For an elaborate treatment of this see *ibid.*, *passim.*
[3] *Ibid.*, p. 122.
[4] *Rap. Budget, Ch.*, 1913, No. 3318, pp. 200–201.

In 1871 the total State budget was 1,693,793,000 fr. By 1913 it had grown to 4,738,603,000 fr. In other words the budget of the State almost tripled in size while that of the Ministry of Foreign Affairs did not even double. If allowance is made for the gradual decline in the purchasing power of the franc, the increase is even less. Despite the alarm to which this situation gave rise in certain quarters, it is perhaps not surprising in view of the fact that the constantly expanding functions of the modern State have affected diplomacy least and last. The war, of course, completely upset the normal trend of budgetary developments, here, as elsewhere, both because of the extraordinary expenses imposed by war needs and because of the depreciation of the currency. By 1920 the annual budget of the Ministry had reached the figure of 310,893,621 fr., an increase of 1,487 per cent over 1913. By 1924 it had fallen to 139,858,118 fr., 613 per cent of the 1913 figure, and in 1925 to 129,486,347 fr., 561 per cent of 1913.[1] The 1929 budget was 244,232,150 fr. in a total State budget of 51,624,957,183 fr.[2] In terms of gold francs this would be about 48,846,000 fr. out of a total of 10,324,991,000 fr., as compared with 21,758,246 fr. out of 4,738,603,000 fr. in 1913. Both figures thus approximately doubled in the intervening sixteen years.

In the Senate report on the 1930 budget of the Ministry (over 280,000,000 fr.) M. Henri Bérenger pointed out that while the total had almost tripled since 1914, the administrative expenses had only doubled. The expenses for the dissemination of French culture abroad had increased sixfold and those for international administration and organization had been multiplied by 140. This he attributed to the needs arising out of the enormous expansion of international contacts and the politics of "intercontinentalism" which has followed the Great War.

> The human generation which is growing up is intercontinental by its birth-right. Intercontinentalism will remain the formula of the twentieth century. All the literature and all the art of all the nations are impregnated with it, as well as their politics and economics. A new order is in process of arising which imposes on the France of to-day a foreign policy of peace and security, the technique of which demands novel methods and enlarged means.[3]

4. THE DIPLOMATIC AND CONSULAR SERVICES

The relation between the central administration at the Quai d'Orsay, which has just been described, and the representatives of France in foreign countries might be compared to the relationship between the brain and spinal column of the nervous system and the network of nerve endings spread over an organism, transmitting sensory impressions to the centers and receiving from them impulses to glandular or muscular action. The analogy is a familiar one and the general relationships between the field services and the central headquarters in any foreign office is too well known to require labored

[1] *Rap. Budget, Ch.*, 1924, No. 509, pp. 86–93.
[2] *J.O.Ch.*, December 30, 1928; *J.O.Sén.*, December 30, 1928; Annex 748.
[3] *Le Temps*, March 19, 1930.

description. The field services of the Quai d'Orsay consist of some 600 officials and employees, not counting the subordinate agents at the diplomatic and consular posts who are recruited locally and are not subject to the established regulations.[1] This total includes fifteen ambassadors; twenty-one ministers plenipotentiaries of the first class, and forty-one of the second; thirty-seven consuls general; fifty-two consuls of the first class, and seventy-two of the second; ninty-three of the third class; and a whole host of lesser agents in embassies, legations, and consulates.

By decrees of September 22, 1913, and November 15, 1920, a rough equivalence of grades was established in the two services, as follows:[2]

DIPLOMATIC SERVICE	CONSULAR SERVICE
Ambassador.	
Minister plenipotentiary of the first class.	
Minister plenipotentiary of the second class.	
Counselor of embassy.	Consul General.
Secretary of embassy, first class.	Consul of the first class.
Secretary of embassy, second class.	Consul of the second class.
Secretary of embassy, third class.	Consul of the third class.
Attaché of embassy.	Vice consul.
Chancellor.	
Chancery attaché.	
Chancery clerk.	
First dragoman or first interpreter.	
Dragoman or interpreter.	
Student dragoman or interpreter.	

The introduction of examinations for entrance into the service took place relatively early. By the decree of August 18, 1856, an examination was given for admission to the post of student consul. For all other posts, appointments were made on the basis of certain minimum educational qualifications and a specified number of years of service in the lower ranks. The decree of February 1, 1877, required entrance examinations for attachés in the central administration and for secretaries of the third class. These examinations were made competitive by the decree of July 10, 1880. The lower posts in both the diplomatic and consular services were filled from the same competition. In 1882 the grade of counselor of the embassy was created and assimilated to that of consul general, while the three grades of consuls and of embassy secretaries were likewise assimilated. These early efforts at establishing an equivalence of rankings were abandoned in the decrees of November 12, 1891, and October 22, 1892, but restored by those of May 29, 1902, and March 15, 1904.[3]

At the time of writing a single examination is given for entrance into either the diplomatic and consular divisions, as shown in the accompanying

[1] Decree of November 15, 1920, *Rap. Budget, Ch.,* 1921, No. 2020, pp. 18–19.
[2] *Ibid.,* pp. 82–83.
[3] *Rap. Budget, Sén.,* 1913, No. 148, pp. 53–58.

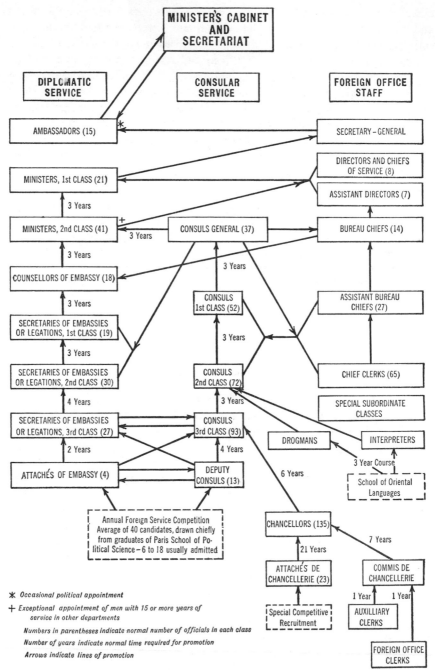

PERSONNEL OF THE FRENCH FOREIGN SERVICE

(Adaped from Walter R. Sharp, *The French Civil Service*, Chap. XI, The Macmillan Company, 1931).

chart of recruitment and promotion. Under the terms of the decree of January 17, 1907, the examination is held annually. Candidates must be French citizens over twenty-three and under twenty-seven years of age who have fulfilled the requirements for military service and who have either the degree of *licencié* in law, letters, or science; or have diplomas from a specified list of schools. Accepted candidates receive three months' probation at the Quai d'Orsay, where they are questioned, instructed, and given a ranking of professional aptitude, and then admitted to the grades of *attaché d'ambassade* or *consul suppléant*. A separate examination is given for admission to the chancelleries (decree of May 24, 1908), but assistant clerks (*commis auxilliaires*) are chosen without examination by the diplomatic and consular agents, subject to the ratification of the department, and these are frequently promoted to the grade of *commis de chancellerie*, thus entering the service without taking any examination whatever. They must have fulfilled their military obligations, have served for one year, and have been recommended by their immediate superiors before promotion (decree of November 15, 1920). Student dragomans and interpreters are recruited exclusively from graduates of *l'école des langues orientales vivantes* who are of French nationality, twenty eight years of age, and discharged of their military obligations (decree of November 15, 1920). It is possible for officials to pass from the ranks of the chancery, dragoman or interpreter services into the consular service and thence into the diplomatic service and up to the grade of minister plenipotentiary of the second class, after fifteen years of service—all without examination (Article 5, decree of November 15, 1920). Such distinguished diplomats, as Bompard, Barrère, and Paul and Jules Cambon, entered the service and attained to the highest posts without any examinations. This is exceptional, however, and the remaining loopholes for promotion to the highest posts without examination are few. In general, entrance into the service is now by competitive tests which give an assurance of competence.[1]

The issue of the fusion of the diplomatic and consular services is an old one in France. As early as 1876, Emmanuel Arago strongly urged in the Senate the desirability of amalgamation, emphasizing the artificiality of the distinction between political and commercial affairs in modern international relations and the economy and convenience of fusion. His proposal was attacked in its details by Décazes, then Minister of Foreign Affairs, and failed of adoption by a vote of 112 to 143.[2] Décazes, however, had himself urged this reform five years previously as *rapporteur* of the Chamber's Budget Commission. Active discussion of the problem went on for many years thereafter, stimulated by allegations of scandalous favoritism in the era before competitive examinations.[3] Reforms were gradually introduced, but up to the time of writing the fusion of the political and commercial divisions of the

---

[1] *Rap. Budget, Ch.*, 1921, No. 2020, pp. 83–88.

[2] *J.O.Sén.*, December 7, 1876.

[3] E. Hippeau, *Histoire diplomatique de la troisième République*, pp. 295–328, Paris, 1889.

Quai d'Orsay has not been followed by a corresponding amalgamation of the diplomatic and consular services abroad. An equivalence of grades has been established and those seeking a career can transfer their activities from one service to the other without undue difficulty. To this degree the two services are assimilated and the present situation is not unlike that prevailing in the American foreign service under the Rogers Bill of 1924.[1] It seems unlikely that any further steps toward complete amalgamation will be taken in the near future.[2]

Other problems which are of current interest revolve about the relationship between the foreign service and the foreign agents of the Ministry of Commerce and the question of geographical zones. As to the former, a statute of August 25, 1919, created a number of commercial attachés and commercial agents serving in the Ministry of Commerce but under the control of the heads of diplomatic missions abroad and intended to give practical information and advice on commercial problems and to assist in the extension of French business interests in their districts. The utility of their services is generally conceded and it has been urged that a body of financial attachés, and perhaps of press attachés as well, should be created. It is argued in some quarters, however, that the divided allegiance and responsibility which have resulted are undesirable and that all such officials should be incorporated into the ranks of the regular foreign service under the exclusive control of the Quai d'Orsay.[3] Another reform which has been repeatedly urged in the reports of the Chamber Budget Commission is the division of the entire foreign service into great geographical zones, between which there should be no transfers or promotions. This step, it is argued, would insure greater competence on the part of the agents within each area and prevent transfers from one end of the earth to the other, which confront representatives with new problems and situations unrelated to their past experience.[4]

That the foreign service of the Third French Republic compares favorably with that of any other Great Power, in terms of training, competence, astuteness, and general efficiency, few will dispute. Its organization has been briefly sketched. Its rôle in the control of foreign relations will be examined in connection with the incidents and episodes of diplomatic history which are analyzed in the chapters which follow. If it has almost always attained to high achievements in the chess game of world politics, it is because all patriotic Frenchmen echo the fervent hope expressed at the end of one of the admirable reports of the Chamber Budget Commission:

[1] J. M. Mathews, *American Foreign Relations*, pp. 304f., New York, 1928.

[2] *Rap. Budget, Ch.*, 1921, No. 2020, pp. 72–75. Promotions are made by recommendation of a *conseil d' avancement*, made up of the heads of the several divisions on the basis of service ratings and seniority. The slowness of the promotion rate is shown by the accompanying chart. Salary advances in all of the lower posts require two years service at each level. *Cf.* Walter R. Sharp, *The French Civil Service*, The MacMillan Company, Chap. IX, New York, 1931.

[3] *Rap. Budget, Ch.*, 1921, No. 2020, pp. 76–80.

[4] *Rap. Budget, Ch.*, 1921, No. 3131, pp. 5–6; 1920, No. 802, pp. 11–12.

May our diplomats, better recruited, better selected, with a preparation longer and more adequate, better administered, better housed, better paid, better supervised and stimulated, better known and better loved—may our diplomats of to-morrow be worthy of our soldiers—our soldiers of yesterday, our soldiers of the future![1]

[1] *Rap. Budget, Ch.*, 1921, No. 2020, p. 160. Professor Walter R. Sharp has suggested to the writer, on the basis of his own observations, that in the French bureaucracy only the foreign service has retained undiminished its pre-war prestige value, while the other branches have suffered a considerable loss in terms of attracting able young men to careers in them.

PART II

THE MACHINE AT WORK

PART II

INTRODUCTION: NOTES ON METHOD

IN undertaking to examine the practical operations of the constitutional and administrative machinery which has been sketched in the preceding chapters various alternative methods of procedure are available. The entire diplomatic history of the Third French Republic might be reviewed from a perspective largely neglected by diplomatic historians, *i.e.*, that of the internal procedures by which foreign policy has been formulated, administered, and controlled. This method will not be adopted in the present study, partly because of considerations of space and proportion, and partly because of certainty that the outlines of the forest would be obscured by the trees. Since the objective of the study is not to retell the ofttold tale of the historical evolution of French foreign relations, nor even to treat those phases of the story which are regarded as of salient importance by historians, but rather to throw light upon the functioning of the internal agencies and forces which initiated and controlled the diplomatic and military action of the French Government, no useful purpose would be served by re-examining in its entirety the whole narrative of diplomatic events. Certain of these events must therefore be selected for detailed analysis. Those selected must be genuinely representative of the various patterns of political behavior which have appeared throughout the entire story of French foreign relations. The scientific soundness of the conclusions is obviously dependent upon the basis of this selection and the validity of its assumptions.

Various bases of selection at once suggest themselves. In the natural sciences random samples, picked out of a large mass of relatively homogeneous data, may be utilized legitimately for purposes of observing uniformities and formulating generalizations. In dealing with the phenomena of human society, however, and especially in dealing with past social events which can be observed only from written records, the assumptions behind the method of random sampling are frequently vitiated by the heterogeneity of the data and by the constant presence of immeasurable variables. Where the phenomena under investigation are present in a very large number of cases and can be reduced to statistical terms, this method may be profitably employed. Examples can readily be found in the subject matter of anthropometry, cultural anthropology, demography, human geography, statistical sociology, certain phases of economic research, and, in the field of political science, in inquiries into political attitudes, public personnel administration, non-voting, election practices and the like. But the phenomena of international relations are not, on the whole, reducible to terms which justify handling in this fashion. Some other basis of selection must therefore be found.

An arbitrary classification of data on the basis of distribution in time or space is sometimes used to avoid bias arising from lack of homogeneity in the data as a whole. Time segments, picked at regular intervals, might be chosen. A detailed analysis of French diplomatic action during every fifth year, for example, or during a given month of every year, or during a small segment of each decade might supply evidence relevant to the purposes of the present study. Or, correspondingly, an analysis might be made of French diplomatic action, during a fixed interval of time, in certain chosen areas: a portion of Africa, a region of Asia, a country of Latin America, and a nation of Europe, for example. But the objections to this method of selection are obvious. Life in all its aspects is a continuous process, with each "present" conditioned by the past and conditioning the future. The content of diplomacy during a given time interval is meaningless except in terms of what has gone before and of what comes after. Forms and procedures, moreover, while relatively constant under a given constitutional system, are subject to change from time to time. A selection of data based on equal time intervals would therefore not be necessarily representative of the processes of the present day. Similarly the world-wide integration and international interdependence which characterize the Western State System during the whole period of the present study make a selection of data on a geographical basis equally misleading. It is impossible to localize all diplomatic incidents and difficult to classify the areas of the world into categories which are equally significant and worthy of equal weight.

A selection on the basis of the ends or objectives of diplomatic action next suggests itself. The ends or objectives are in themselves subjective values in the minds of diplomats, but to the outside observer they may be treated as phenomena capable of furnishing a basis of classification of the whole mass of data. One may, for example, select instances of diplomatic action looking toward the acquisition of territory. Every diplomatic episode in the creation of the French colonial empire would fall within this category. One may pick out instances of diplomatic action designed to secure economic advantages for French nationals: the negotiation of commercial treaties, the acquisition of economic concessions and privileges in "backward areas," governmental encouragement of loans and investments and the like. Other actions are designed to protect citizens abroad, to enhance diplomatic prestige, to increase military strength, to provoke or prevent war, to preserve or reestablish peace, or to attain "security" through alliances or disarmament or arbitration treaties or the promotion of international organization. The entire mass of diplomatic data can readily be classified under such headings. But if such objectives are used exclusively as a basis of classification, they may involve the observer in a serious logical fallacy which undermines the validity of the method. Within the classification are assumed the conclusions which should emerge from the data. If these various motivations are taken for granted—either as Aristotelian major premises or as scientific hypotheses—the data will almost inevitably be so shaped and handled as to demonstrate the presence of the assumed motivation in each instance studied. Further, if only incidents are chosen which appear to have been governed by a given objective, the data will inevitably prove the dominance of that objective. A little reflection, moreover, upon the actual behavior of diplomats, ministers, parliamentarians, and journalists in concrete instances will show that motives are almost always mixed, frequently difficult to ascertain, often confused and fluctuating and never capable of furnishing a guide for a selection of evidence which will lead to scientific conclusions.

Similar objections apply to any classification based exclusively upon the consequences of diplomatic action. One action leads to acquisition of territory, another to a loss; this to a diplomatic rebuff, that to a signal success; one to an alliance, another to a war, still another to a peace conference; and so on. But success and failure are relative terms and results are always evaluated in accordance with subjective values, even by the pragmatist. They furnish no valid basis for classification and selection unless they can be reduced to objective terms. As regards the techniques of diplomacy, means to ends vary infinitely with situations and with the skill and subtlety of diplomats themselves. Unplanned blundering which leads to results generally accepted as desirable often assumes in retrospect the dignity of great statesmanship. Carefully reasoned calculation, if unsuccessful, takes on the appearance of ineptitude, stupidity, chaotic groping devoid of plan or meaning. A classification of data based upon the tools or methodologies of diplomacy can only be confusing and unrealistic. On the other hand, specific means or techniques in concrete situations are distinguishable from constitutional and political procedures, which, with possible variations, are adhered to in all situations and exhibit observable uniformities which can usefully be described in any analysis of the conduct of foreign affairs.

It would seem to follow from these considerations that the raw materials of such an investigation as the present one cannot easily be fitted into any comprehensive scheme of *a priori* categories without destroying their context, distorting their meanings, and reading into them causal relationships which may be purely hypothetical. The investigator must resort to a somewhat different approach in making his selection. The approach employed here resembles somewhat the case method of legal research. Certain "cases" in the diplomatic history of the Third Republic have been chosen for analysis—the word "case" being used here to describe a particular series of related diplomatic events, each exhibiting a more or less clearly definable sequence of developments from a specific origin to a specific conclusion. The subject matter of diplomatic history may be thought of in terms of such sequences or episodes without doing violence to the material itself nor to any established canons of logic or scientific procedure.

The question may properly be raised as to what constitutes a case or episode, since a diplomatic case, unlike a legal case, is not defined and limited by an obvious, objective criterion. Here the judgment of the traditional diplomatic historian may be accepted with few qualifications. To him, as to the student of the control of foreign policy, the whole sequence of diplomatic events is clearly divisible into episodes or topics. Each of these consists of a succession of developments, culminating in a well-defined result or conclusion, to which the antecedent events bear an obvious relationship in a chain of causation. In some cases the result or conclusion constitutes the attainment of a definitely formulated objective, with the preceding events the steps by which the end was achieved. The acquisition of Syria, the control of Morocco, the conclusion of the Franco-Russian Alliance are examples. Here the unifying element in the various phases of the episode is the conscious pursuit of a definite goal. In other cases a result is arrived at, which is not the realization of an aspiration or policy—which, indeed, may be quite contrary to what was desired—but which, in retrospect, can be seen to have been brought about by certain anterior acts or events. The causal relationship here is not one growing out of an objective for the accomplishment of which various means are devised and put into execution, but one which flows out of the interaction of uncontrolled forces leading to a diplomatically significant consequence. The outbreak of the Great War, the rift in the *Entente Cordiale* between 1922 and 1925, the occupation of the Ruhr, the interallied intervention in Russia in 1918 and 1919 are all examples of this type of episode. In the former instances, the conscious execution of a particular policy defines the nature and limits of the case. In the latter, the case is defined by the objective consequences of a series of contributory events. In other words, the present classification of the data into cases or episodes is based not upon goals nor upon consequences exclusively, but upon a combination of the two growing out of the basic relationships of time and causation between anterior and posterior events.

In the present study, as in most diplomatic histories, attention will be concentrated upon cases which are politically significant, *i.e.*, which eventuate in a result or conclusion altering the power, position, or status of France with regard to other States. Possible cases of a routine nature will at once come to mind which are of little or no political importance. The test of political importance is the degree to which the sequence of developments produces, or is designed to produce, a modification of the diplomatic position of the State in the State System. Such a modification may take the form of a change in title or control of territory, in international alignments, in relative military strength, in diplomatic prestige and the like. A war, an occupation of land, an alliance, a conquest of territory are obviously in this category. On the other hand, such instances as the conclusion of an extradition treaty or consular convention, accession to a public international union, participation in an international exposition, or extension of relief to victims of a natural catastrophe in a foreign State would generally be recognized as cases of a non-political character, in which the result or conclusion has no immediate and observable effect upon the power and prestige relationships of Great Power politics. Some cases, such as the recognition of new governments and the protection of citizens abroad, might fall into either category, depending upon circumstances. The line between the two types of cases is admittedly difficult to draw, but it is not essential for present purposes to make a hard-and-fast line of demarcation. The distinction is merely pointed out to emphasize the orientation of the present inquiry toward those cases which have obviously changed the international position of France and affected its national destinies in relation to other Powers.

Cases of this kind can be conveniently divided into three broad classes: (1) acquisitions or losses of territory; (2) alliances, political understandings, and treaties of peace; and (3) wars, interventions, and other coercive measures. The following table suggests itself for the diplomatic history of the Third French Republic:

I. Acquisitions or Losses of Territory

A. Europe:
> Alsace-Lorraine (lost, 1871; recovered, 1919)
> The Saar Valley (under occupation, 1919–1935)
> The Rhineland (under occupation, 1919–1930)

B. Africa:
> Tunis (acquired, 1881)
> Equatorial Africa (1884)
> Senegal (1637–1889)
> Mauritania (1893)
> Dahomey (1893)
> French Sudan (1893)
> Madagascar (1896)
> Algeria (1830–1902)
> Niger (1912)
> Morocco (1898–1912)
> Cameroon (lost, 1912; regained as a mandate, 1919)
> Togoland (mandate, 1919)

C. Asia and Oceania:
> Tahiti (1841–1881)
> Annam (1884)
> Tonkin (1884)
> New Caledonia and dependencies (1854–1887)
> Laos (1892)
> Syria and the Lebanon (mandate, 1922)

II. Alliances, Political Understandings, and Treaties of Peace

A. Military Alliances with:
> Russia (1891–1917)
> Allied and Associated Powers (23) at war with the Central Powers (1914–1919)

    Poland (Treaty of February 19, 1921)
    Belgium (exchange of letters, September 15, 1920)
    Czechoslovakia (Treaty of August 31, 1922)
    Jugoslavia (Treaty of November 11, 1927)
    Roumania (Treaty of June 10, 1926)

B. Political Understandings with:
    Great Britain (1904–1919)
    Members of the League of Nations (56) (1920–)
    Great Britain, United States, and Japan (Four-Power Pacific Pact, 1922–)
    Germany, Great Britain, Italy, and Belgium (Locarno treaties, 1925)
    United States and other signatories of Kellogg-Briand Pact (1928)

C. Treaties of Peace with:
    Germany, signed at Frankfort, May 10, 1871
    Germany, signed at Versailles, June 28, 1919
    Austria, signed at St. Germain, September 10, 1919
    Hungary, signed at Trianon, June 4, 1919
    Bulgaria, signed at Neuilly, November 27, 1919
    Turkey, signed at Sèvres, August 10, 1920
    Turkey, signed at Lausanne, July 24, 1923

III. OUTBREAKS OF WAR AND RESORT TO COERCIVE MEASURES SHORT OF WAR

A. Declarations of War with:
    Germany, August 3, 1914
    Austria-Hungary, August 12, 1914
    Bulgaria, October 16, 1915
    Turkey, November 5, 1914

B. Resort to Coercive Measures Short of War against:
    China (1884–1885; 1899–1900)
    Siam (1892–1893)
    Russia (1918–1921)
    Germany (1922–1924)
    Etc.

In this enumeration of cases, Lists I, II, *A* and *C*, and III, *A*, are complete, including all instances in the diplomatic history of the Third French Republic of acquisitions or losses of territory, declarations of war, and treaties of peace. List II, *B*, might well be extended to cover international agreements of lesser political importance, such as disarmament and neutralization treaties, debts pacts, etc. List III, *B*, might be extended almost indefinitely if an enumeration were undertaken of every instance in which the French Government, in its diplomatic controversies, resorted to displays of force, military expeditions, armed interventions, pacific blockades, or other acts of retorsion or reprisal. The number of such instances in Asia and Africa is legion. Almost every territorial acquisition, listed under I, involved some military or naval action, but it appears logical to place such instances under the first heading, since the result or conclusion of the case was not the utilization of coercive measures but the assumption of title to, or control over, new territory. Similarly, under List II, many "unequal" alliances and political understandings might be listed which led to the ultimate extinction of the independence of the weaker party and a territorial gain by France. Tunis,

Madagascar, Morocco, and Annam offer examples. Here again the conclusion of the episode was not the signature of the preliminary agreement but the territorial acquisition.

In making a selection of a small number of typical cases for detailed analysis, out of all of those enumerated, the criterion of choice has been determined by the purposes of the investigation: to examine the control of French foreign affairs with particular reference to the situations out of which wars arise. In applying this criterion to the cases listed, it has seemed best to omit entirely those enumerated under Treaties of Peace, since attention is to be centered not on the termination of war but on its initiation. The treaty-making process, however, will be reviewed in Part Three of the study, among the internal procedures for the handling of foreign affairs. In surveying the other cases it is obvious that all declarations of war and all resort to coercive measures short of war are relevant to the present inquiry. The crisis of 1914, the occupation of the Ruhr in 1923, and the hostilities with China in 1884 have been selected as representative episodes of this type. The Chinese episode, for reasons which will be obvious from the narrative, has been considered as a sequel to the acquisition of Tonkin. In making a selection from the other cases terminating in an acquisition of territory, the geographical distribution of the episodes and the utilization of warlike measures have been considered. Tunis, Madagascar, and the series of events leading to the acquisition of Tonkin, Annam, and Laos have been chosen for detailed treatment. All involved the use of military force. The first is one of several such cases in North Africa and the Sahara. The second is the focal point of French diplomacy in the Indian Ocean. The third constitutes an important series of cases in French colonial expansion in Southeastern Asia. Among the military alliances and political understandings, the Dual Alliance and the *Entente Cordiale* have been selected. Both contemplated the use of military force against other States in certain specified contingencies. Both were of fundamental importance in the crystallization of the hostile coalitions which clashed in the Great War. The post-Versailles alliances and ententes are too recent to admit of detailed study and too current to be viewed in their proper perspective.

The cases chosen are obviously not all of the same intrinsic importance, nor do they include all of the instances which the diplomatic historian would discuss in a well-proportioned treatment of French diplomacy under the Third Republic. Even within the limits imposed by the purposes of the present investigation, a very different selection would be quite possible and permissible. It is the writer's conviction, however, that most of the other possible cases are less illuminating than those chosen and would add relatively little to the evidence adduced. The eight chapters which follow will take up these cases in a roughly chronological order. Three colonial "wars," ending in territorial gains, two liaisons with European States, altering the balance of power, one outbreak of a war of the first magnitude, and one military occupation of the territory of a neighboring State complete the list. It is hoped that these episodes will reveal clearly the practical operations of the machinery for handling foreign affairs in the Third French Republic and that they will justify certain conclusions on the topic under investigation. It is believed, moreover, that these conclusions would be supported by an extension of the same method to other possible cases.

CHAPTER IV

THE TAKING OF TUNIS

1. THE PRELUDE

MESSIEURS, the change of ministries which has been effected during our separation is not one which will modify the general direction of public affairs. The policy which we submit is not new to you. It is you yourselves who have inspired it. We remain faithful to the line of conduct which is clearly demanded from the debates of the last session of the two chambers.[1]

With these words M. Jules Ferry, Premier and Minister of Public Instruction and Fine Arts, presented his Cabinet to the Chambers on November 9, 1880.[2] The Freycinet Cabinet had resigned during the interval between the sessions of Parliament because of internal dissension over the application of the decrees against religious associations. Its successor was pledged to the enforcement of the anticlerical laws. The major portion of Ferry's ministerial declaration dealt with the necessity of purging education of clerical influences and of enforcing the letter of the law. As for foreign relations, he asserted:

The Government will communicate to parliament the diplomatic documents relative to the negotiations which have followed the signature of the Treaty of Berlin, and particularly those which refer to the most recent incidents in eastern affairs. You will find there the proofs of our good relations with all the Powers, of the pacific spirit which animates them all, and of the constant efforts of the European entente to prevent new collisions . . . The maintenance of common deliberations is the surest guarantee of the peace of Europe; the Government of the Republic has not ceased to carry to them that spirit of disinterestedness and of peace of which no one is dubious and which merits for republican France the esteem and the confidence of the world.[3]

From these words no one could anticipate that the ministry which had just assumed office was to be one of the most momentous in the diplomatic history of the Republic and was to launch France upon an unprecedented program of colonial expansion. Nor could anyone unfamiliar with the secret discussions of the preceding Cabinet and the obscure bargainings at the Congress of Berlin have anticipated the events of the following spring in North Africa. Behind the scenes and away from the troublesome light of publicity, the stage had already been prepared for a daring diplomatic and military adventure. If Bismarck, the "honest broker" of Berlin, had not

---

[1] *J.O.Ch.*, November 10, 1880.

[2] *Ibid.*, *Jules Ferry, président du conseil, instruction publique et beaux-arts; J. Cazut, justice; Barthélemy-Saint-Hilaire, affaires étrangères; Constans, intérieur et cultes; J. Magnin, finances; Général Farre, guerre; Vice-Amiral Cloué, marine et colonies; Sadi-Carnot, travaux publics; Tirard, agriculture et commerce; Cochery, postes et télégraphes.*

[3] *Ibid.*

definitely encouraged French expansion, in the hope of diverting attention from the *revanche*, he had at least adopted an attitude of benevolent indifference.[1] M. Waddington, then French Minister of Foreign Affairs, reported to the Marquis d'Harcourt, French ambassador at London, his conversations with Lord Salisbury at Berlin, in which the latter, with Disraeli's confirmation, gave him assurances that England would raise no obstacle to the natural development of French policy in Tunis. "England has no special interests in this region which could possibly lead her to view with apprehension or distrust the legitimate and expanding influence of France."[2] Two years later this assurance was repeated.[3] Ferry's predecessor, Freycinet, in accord with Gambetta, had already cast longing eyes on Tunis. M. Théodore Roustan, French Consul General and chargé d'affaires, had been instructed to open negotiations with the Bey for a treaty of protectorate. Difficulties had developed, however. "Authorize me to disembark a company of marines," Roustan had written, "and the Bey will sign." Freycinet was obliged to leave office before he could act on this suggestion. But he left the situation in good hands. " 'The fruit is ripe', I said to him (Ferry). 'You may pick it at the propitious moment.' "[4]

It is clear that Ferry's African policy was not written on a clean slate, but was a logical outcome of preceding developments. Tunis had been a center of interest ever since the alliance between Francis I and the Sultan had given France a privileged position in North Africa. Henry III had sent a French consul to Algiers in 1564 and another to Tunis in 1577.[5] Early commercial contacts, interspersed with wars waged by the Marseillais upon the Algerian and Tunisian pirates in the early seventeenth century,[6] had developed into a political interest which had culminated in the conquest of Algeria in the 1830's. Fifty years later Algeria's eastern neighbor was to fall victim to a like fate. The steps by which this was achieved constitute one of the most illuminating chapters in the history of French diplomacy. What were the motives of the conquest? Who made the important decisions? What methods of procedure were employed? What was the attitude of Parliament, the public, and the press?

Inquiry into human motivations always involves peculiar difficulties of analysis and evaluation which are the perpetual despair of historians.

---

[1] For a refutation of the Italian allegation that Bismarck had offered Tunis to Italy, and upon the latter's refusal to France, see *Discours et opinions de Jules Ferry* (P. Robiquet, ed.). IV, pp. 532–541. Bülow, however, had made such a suggestion. On Bismarck's policy, *cf.* W. L. Langer, "The European Powers and the French Occupation of Tunis," *American Historical Review*, XXXI, pp. 55f.

[2] Lord Salisbury to Lord Lyons, August 7, 1878, *L.J.T.* Supplement, pp. 69–70.

[3] *Ibid.*, pp. 71–72.

[4] C. de Freycinet, *Souvenirs*, pp. 168–169, Paris, 1913.

[5] P. Grandchamp, *La France en Tunisie au début XVIIe siècle*, I, pp. ix–xxi, Tunis, 1921; L. Foucher, *De l'évolution du protectorat de la France sur la Tunisie*, pp. 34–49, Paris, 1897.

[6] Grandchamp, *op. cit.*, III, pp. v–x.

A priori adherence to any fixed theory of interpretation is almost certain to be misleading, while deductions from accumulated data may frequently lead to reading into a situation a logic and simplicity entirely foreign to the minds of those dealing with it. In the sphere of political behavior these difficulties are multiplied by the necessity under which those in power constantly find themselves of erecting a façade to give their activities the most pleasing appearance possible in the public view. M. Barthélemy-Saint-Hilaire, Ferry's Minister of Foreign Affairs, declared in a circular addressed to French diplomatic agents abroad, under date of May 9, 1881, that the Government's frankness had rendered unnecessary any further explanations of the Tunis expedition.

The policy of France in the question of Tunis has always been inspired by but a single principle; and this principle which suffices to explain all our conduct toward the Regency for the past half century, is the absolute obligation which we are under to assure the security of our great Algerian colony.[1]

The importance of this obligation was set forth at length, along with the necessity of redressing wrongs inflicted on French nationals by the Regency, and made the basis of a Yellow Book of some 300 pages of documents issued by the Ministry of Foreign Affairs. The security of existing possessions is a familiar argument for the acquisition of contiguous territory and it was used extensively and effectively in the present instance.[2] The foreign minister also emphasized the purity of the Government's motives and its anxiety to do the natives of Tunis good in the interest of all the world. "It is a sacred duty which a superior civilization owes to less advanced peoples."[3]

In contrast with this official interpretation, one may note the equally familiar explanation of the economic determinist:

The security of the interests of French holders of Tunisian bonds and also the desire to conserve concessions and industrial privileges for French nationals were important motives which were not formulated in a precise fashion but which preoccupied the Government as shown even in its official communications, despite the care it took to hide them.[4]

From this point of view the acquisition of Tunis was merely another chapter in the history of economic imperialism, undertaken in the interest of concessionnaires and bondholders, and entirely innocent of the political considerations and lofty disinterestedness which loom so large in the official apologia.

The difficulties of locating responsibility and assessing motives are in proportion to the obstacles in the way of unraveling the tangled skein of Tunisian diplomacy. Veiled barterings between foreign offices, clashing

[1] *L.J.T.*, pp. xvii–xxiv.

[2] In 1905 it was similarly argued that Italian acquisition of Tripoli would endanger French security in Tunis and should be prevented. *Cf.* R. Millet, *Notre politique extérieure de* 1898 *à* 1905, pp. 92–98, Paris, 1905.

[3] *L.J.T.*, p. xxiv.

[4] Foucher, *op.cit.*, p. 60.

colonial ambitions, and curiously involved financial transactions mingle with the grievances of alien property owners, the fears and hesitancies of the Bey, the obscure machinations of consuls, and the raids of border tribes in complex and fascinating orchestration. The basic *motif* is simple and familiar: a weak State, remnant of the long declining culture of Islam, is brought into contact with the powerful States of the West, is made the victim of their clashing ambitions, and finally succumbs before *force majeure*. It is the complex counterpoint and the innumerable variations which are difficult to follow and which are most significant for present purposes.[1]

The piece begins, as such pieces frequently do, with the measures by which the weaker party becomes financially obligated to the stronger. The Government of the Bey, practically independent though still acknowledging the suzerainty of the Sublime Porte, found itself embarassed in the 1850's by its inability to make payments on the local bonds which it had issued. By 1862 these had reached the sum of 28,000,000 fr. and three years later the Bey, in all innocence, leaped from the frying pan into the fire by contracting a foreign loan of 35,000,000 fr. He received only 5,000,000 fr., along with several worthless ships and cannon and a lot of valueless copper, the balance disappearing into the pockets of the local officials and foreign financiers who had arranged the transaction. The best revenues of the Regency were turned over to the money-lenders. Taxes were increased to meet current expenditures and new loans were contracted to pay interest on the old. Threats of revolt within, and the clamor of creditors without, led to a crisis. Since most of the foreign bondholders were French, the Government asked the French Consul-General in November, 1867, to name a French official to manage the Bey's finances. An Anglo-Italian-French commission was established for this purpose in 1869, in which the French had a preponderant voice. This *commission financière* acted as the agent of the creditors whose Governments gave it their support. The Tunisian debt had now reached 160,000,000 fr. But the commission's anxiety to protect the bondholders resulted in increasing disorder in the finances of the country, which, in turn, led the creditors to seek alternative methods of protecting their interests. In France the cry arose for a guarantee of the Tunisian loans by the French Government. In the columns of *l'Économiste Français*, Leroy Beaulieu began urging political annexation for financial and economic reasons.[2]

Meanwhile the Bey's embarrassments were increased by his relations with foreign investors and concessionnaires. In 1870 he had granted two important concessions of arable land, one to an Italian agricultural colony at Jedeida, and one to the French Count de Sancy at Sidi Tabet on the banks of the Medjerdah. The Italian company at once demanded jurisdiction over the inhabitants, quarreled with the Arabs, withdrew its agents, made

[1] S. H. Roberts, *History of French Colonial Policy*, I, pp. 259–266, London, 1929.

[2] Foucher, *op. cit.*, pp. 59–90, and P.H.X. (d'Estournelles de Constant), *La politique francaise en Tunisie*, pp. 32–71.

demands for heavy damages which led to a clamor for a military expedition in the Italian press, and finally agreed to arbitrate the dispute. Sancy, on the other hand, secured capital by forming a partnership with Mrs. Mary Frances Ronalds of the United States and operated a stud and dairy farm with some success. Presently, however, he sold out his rights to a M. Wyse, who proceeded to quarrel violently with Mrs. Ronalds and to bring suit against Sancy for selling rights he did not possess. The French Consul General, Baron de Billing, who arrived in May of 1874, was friendly to Sancy and Mrs. Ronalds and the unfortunate Wyse was soon arrested and jailed on the order of the French consular agent, Cassas. Early in 1875, however, M. Roustan became Consul General and chargé d'affaires. Wyse was released and Mrs. Ronalds departed in disgust. In July, 1877, Roustan induced the Bey to grant Sancy another concession as compensation for losses incurred in the first. When the second grant was revoked on the ground that Sancy had not fulfilled its terms, Roustan protested vigorously and on January 7, 1879, dispatched a severe ultimatum which led to the confirmation of Sancy's grant. The following year he transferred all his rights to the *Société Marseillaise*.[1]

In December of 1878 Signor Licurgo Maccio had arrived on the scene as Italian Consul General with great pomp and military display. The Italian Premier, Cairoli, was alarmed at the prospect of a French descent on Tunis and was determined to secure Tunis for Italy or at least frustrate possible French designs.[2] Not to be outdone by his French rival, Maccio bestirred himself on behalf of Italian concessionnaires. His request for permission to lay a telegraph cable from Cape Bon to Sicily was declined by the Bey as a prospective violation of the alleged telegraph monopoly which France had secured by three concessions granted in 1859 and 1861. These grants did not legally constitute a monopoly, but the Bey could ill afford to antagonize Roustan. Both the French and Italian consuls next turned their attention to the railway connecting the city of Tunis with the sea at La Goulette. This line was in the hands of an English company which had secured the concession in 1871. While the Italian Rubattino Company was negotiating for its purchase in London, M. Gery, for the French Company of Bône-Guelma, effected its purchase in Paris for 2,605,000 fr., on condition of the approval of the contract by the chancery division of the British High Court of Justice. When the Rubattino interests, in high dudgeon, attacked the sale as void, the British vice-chancellor annulled the contract and ordered the line sold at auction. Though the French and Italian Governments agreed not to intervene, Maccio and Roustan were at sword's points. The latter went so far as to forbid the Bey to transfer the line to the Italians regardless of the results of the auction. But in July, 1880, the Italian Government enacted a law granting an annual guarantee of 609,000 fr. to the Rubattino Company,

---

[1] F. Despagnet, *La diplomatie de la troisième République et le droit de gens*, pp. 221–223, Paris, 1904; A. M. Broadley, *Tunis, Past and Present, The Last Punic War*, I, pp. 149–180, London, 1882.

[2] Langer, *loc. cit.*, pp. 74f.

which then outbid Gery and secured the line for 4,125,000 fr. Roustan was obliged to see the line transferred to the Italian Company, but at once demanded compensatory privileges for French interests.[1] Diplomatic threats, rumors of troop movements, and the presence of a French fleet had the desired effect and Roustan secured the concessions of the port of Tunis and the railway line from Tunis to Bizerta and Sousse for the Bône-Guelma Company.[2]

In this contest it would be too easy to assume that M. Roustan and Signor Maccio, and the members of the French and Italian Cabinets who encouraged them in their activities, were acting as catspaws for concessionnaires and investors and that the only issue was whose nationals should secure the profits of the economic exploitation of Tunis. Even the most insistent of economic determinists would doubtless concede the influence upon the situation of certain political interests and motives having little to do with the struggle for concessions. There is, to be sure, very little point in attempting to differentiate sharply between political and economic motivations in modern world politics. But from the point of view of the control of policy, it is of some importance to ascertain whether the initiative to decisive action came from interested financial and commercial groups, bringing pressure to bear upon indifferent or reluctant government officials, or from the officials themselves who adopted a line of conduct having no direct relation to private economic interests but in the pursuit of which such interests could be used as convenient tools. While generalization on such a delicate point is dangerous, it appears reasonably clear from an examination of the available evidence that in the present instance the latter hypothesis is more tenable than the former.

As already noted, the fate of Tunis had become a subject of diplomatic conversations before disputes regarding concessions had reached an acute stage. The Regency had long been looked upon with hungry eyes by the nationalistic statesmen of the newly created Kingdom of Italy. As the portion of Africa nearest to Sicily and the site of ancient Carthage, it had a certain sentimental value for the diplomats at Rome. From the viewpoint of the Italian Government, it was ear-marked as an Italian possession. Many thousands of Italians had settled there, a number vastly in excess of the nationals of France or of any other Power, and the Italian Government was not above encouraging their economic activities and stimulating investment in order to claim that a vigorous policy was justified by these tangible interests.[3] France, with the contiguous colony of Algeria, was the obstacle to be feared. And in French official circles there were many who had long envisaged the extension of French control over the Regency as a desirable

[1] *L.J.T.*, Nos. 158, 163, 165, and 171.

[2] Despagnet, *op. cit.*, p. 223; Broadley, *op. cit.*, I, pp. 180–190. Langer regards the Rubattino affair as decisive at Paris. Action was delayed because of uncertainty regarding the attitude of the new Gladstone Cabinet, *loc. cit.*, pp. 255f.

[3] In 1881 there were 700 French in Tunis and 11,200 Italians. In 1921 the French numbered 71,000 and the Italians 89,000. Roberts, *op. cit.*, I, p. 286.

possibility. Freycinet, Ferry, Barthélemy-Saint-Hilaire, and Roustan were of this group. Bismarck, moreover, had shrewdly calculated that French acquisition of Tunis would embroil Paris and Rome, contribute to the continued isolation of France, and perhaps throw Italy into the arms of the Central Powers. By virtue of this very fact the French annexationists were obliged to play their hand with caution. There is no reason for supposing that German encouragement was a factor of appreciable influence in determining their policies. While German consent was a practical necessity, the appearance of German instigation had to be avoided. France emerged from the Congress of Berlin with the assurance that neither Germany nor Great Britain would object to the extension of French influence in Tunis.[1]

On October 14, 1878, Waddington, Minister of Foreign Affairs in the third Dufaure Cabinet (December 13, 1877, to February 4, 1879), had informed Rome that while France had no desire to annex the territory of the Bey, it must insist on the maintenance of tranquillity, the orderly management of Tunisian finances, and the security of Algeria.[2] Waddington was Premier from February 4 to December 28, 1879, but the time was not ripe to act. The position of his successor, Freycinet (December 28, 1879, to September 23, 1880), has already been indicated. Roustan, on the scene, continued his efforts to increase French influence over the Bey by a vigorous championship of the economic interests of French nationals and by resisting Italian encroachments at every opportunity. Maccio countered his efforts by encouraging the circulation throughout Tunis and Algeria of the inflammatory, anti-French journal, *Mostakel*, printed in Arabic and published in Sicily.[3] Roustan, in turn, apparently induced various commercial groups interested in Tunisian trade to subsidize a large section of the French press in favor of a more vigorous policy. *Le Temps* declared "He who touches Tunis touches France" and the Havas Agency began to broadcast dispatches hinting at a French protectorate.[4] In December, 1880, the Deputy Léon Renaud arrived in Tunis with a project for a *Crédit Foncier* and a demand for exclusive permission to issue bank notes to the amount of all sums advanced as loans, coupled with a governmental guarantee of repayment. In presenting him to the Tunisian Prime Minister, Roustan reassured the latter as to rumored troop movements in Algeria and declared that the projected financial arrangements would consolidate the relations of mutual friendship between the two countries.[5] The Bey unearthed a French protest of 1873 against a similar projected arrangement with Messrs. Ranking of London and declined the offer in the face of Renaud's irritation and Roustan's veiled threats.[6] The

[1] *Supra*, p. 57; A. Debidour, *Histoire diplomatique de l'Europe*, pp. 41–45, Paris, 1917.

[2] R. Valet, *L'Afrique du Nord dévant le parlement au XIXme siècle*, pp. 168f., Paris, 1924.

[3] Roustan to Freycinet, August 2, 1880, *L.J.T.*, No. 91; E. Hippeau, *Histoire diplomatique de la troisième République*, pp. 379–407, Paris, 1889.

[4] Broadley, *op. cit.*, I, pp. 194f.

[5] *L.J.T.*, No. 171, December 21, 1880.

[6] Broadley, *op. cit*, p. 193; P. Gaffarel, *Notre expansion coloniale*, pp. 29–42, Paris, 1918.

hatrassed Bey, in resisting Roustan's advances, could only say: "We are all in the hands of God, and if force is to overcome right and justice, all I can do is to leave my fate and that of Tunis to Him."[1]

The early months of 1881 were marked by increasingly bitter disputes over concessions. On January 3, 1881, Barthélemy-Saint-Hilaire instructed the Marquis de Noailles, French Ambassador in Rome, to inform the Italian Government that France could not permit the establishment of any other Power in Tunis.[2] The *Société Marseillaise*, meanwhile, was involved in a dispute with a British subject, Mr. Levy, regarding the latter's right of preemption under Moslem law over the lands of General Khereddine, adjoining his own, which the general had sold to the *société*. When Roustan's agents ejected Levy's from possession,[3] the British Consul General strongly objected. Roustan thereupon announced that the land was French property and summoned two additional French warships to Tunisian waters. His agents withdrew, however, when two British warships appeared and Levy was left in control.[4] Roustan alleged that the Bey's Government had opposed the transfer to the *société*.[5] Further wrangles followed between Roustan and Maccio over conflicting railway and telegraph concessions.[6] Roustan always urged that the French Government should support its nationals vigorously in these disputes[7] and Barthélemy-Saint-Hilaire, ever anxious to block Italian ambitions, accorded all the diplomatic support which was asked, though sometimes recommending caution and courtesy on the part of the French Consul General.[8] Every effort was made to obstruct the activities of the Italian concessionnaires and to facilitate those of the French, while

[1] Broadley, *op. cit.*, I, p. 196.

[2] Valet, *op. cit.*, pp. 173f.

[3] *L.J.T.*, No. 183, January 17, 1881.

[4] *Ibid.*, No. 193, February 12, 1881.

[5] *Ibid.*, Nos. 169 and 170, October 22, 1880, and December 7, 1880; Broadley, *op. cit.*, I, pp. 198f.

[6] *Ibid.*, I, pp. 201–210.

[7] "La Société Marseillaise, une fois entrée en possession, n'aura pas de peine, je crois, à se défendre contre toutes les attaques, qu'elles viennent du Gouvernement Tunisien ou des tiers, si elle est assurée de l'appui du Gouvernement de la République." (*L.J.T.*, No. 171, R. to B.St.H., December 21, 1880.)

In connection with a demand for damages advanced by the Bône-Guelma Company against the Tunisian Government for suspension of work on a telegraph line at Hamman-Life, due to an anterior concession granted to one Signor Mancardi: "Avant de donner suite à cette requête, je ferai un nouvel effort auprès du Bey, et si j'échoue, comme c'est probable, je transmettrai la protestation en l'appuyant au nom du Gouvernement de la République." (*L.J.T.*, No. 187, R. to B.St.H., February 3, 1881.)

[8] *L.J.T.*, No. 172, B.St.H. to R., January 6, 1881; No. 176, B.St.H. to R., January 12, 1881; No. 195, B.St.H. to R., February 17, 1881: " . . . En vous invitant à appuyer, dans la mesure du possible, les justes réclamations des concessionnaires français, je vous faisais observer que l'introduction d'une demande d'indemnité pécuniaire risquerait d'être prématurée tant que nous ne serions pas décidés à la soutenir par une action énergique . . . "

Roustan charged the Bey with discrimination and confiscation and insisted that the Italian actions were aimed directly at France.

This friction over economic interests was a mere surface manifestation of an irreconcilable conflict of national policies. In such a situation, the ordinary methods of diplomacy could lead only to deadlock. An appeal to force was expected on both sides. In view of the repeated warnings from Paris, the Italian Government knew that military action on its own part would lead at once to the gravest international complications. It therefore hesitated. At the French capital, the internal situation did not admit of any action which might savor of aggression. A plausible pretext must be found which would give to a military expedition the appearance of a defensive measure.[1]

2. THE CONQUEST

In the desert lands to the east of the ill-defined Algerian frontier there had lived from time immemorial wild nomadic tribes which acknowledged allegiance to no one and which constantly raided one another's lands in quest of cattle or booty. These raids frequently carried them across the imaginary line which was supposed to separate the territory of France from that of the Bey of Tunis. The Bey paid no great heed to "Algerian" raiders into his own domains, but he had often been obliged by French protests to punish raiders who crossed into Algeria from Tunis and to pay indemnities for their depredations. For a decade prior to 1880 such protests had been made periodically and had for the most part been answered to the satisfaction of Algerian officials.[2] The Governor-General of Algeria, M. Albert Grévy, was entirely convinced of the sincerity and good intentions of the Bey and had no sympathy with the suggestions which Roustan began making in September of 1880 that French troops should be used against raiders on the Bey's territory. He pointed out to Barthélemy-Saint-Hilaire that diplomatic methods had always resulted in satisfaction to injured French nationals and he emphasized his disagreement with Roustan's point of view. In September the foreign minister had agreed with the Governor-General. By January of 1881 he had swung around to Roustan's position,[3] much to Grévy's uncomprehending dismay:

For, I repeat, even if it is a matter of dealing with tribes entirely independent of the Bey, they are in reality on the territory of the Regency, and one can only resort to this mode of repression after having exhausted all diplomatic means. To-day, the moment has not come to act, since the Bey offers a kind of Conference to regulate these questions and conversations have begun . . . In résumé, although I agree with you that we have every interest in not leaving unpunished the

[1] On the story (unsubstantiated) that the French decision was due to the infidelity of Maccio's mistress, who revealed plans of an imminent Italian expedition to a French agent, see Valet, *op. cit.*, p. 176: "Si le nez de Cléopâtre avait été plus court . . . "

[2] *L.J.T.*, Nos. 59, 79, 85, 97.

[3] On Roustan's attitude see generally *L.J.T.*, Nos. 171–210.

Tunisian bands which make incursions or commit crimes on our territory, I believe that it is necessary to exhaust all the means of conciliation compatible with our dignity while at the same time not permitting any grievance to pass without informing our diplomatic agent at once regarding it.[1]

This conciliatory attitude did not long survive the combination of continued frontier raids and the determination of Roustan and Barthélemy-Saint-Hilaire to make the most of them. The Minister of Foreign Affairs was always favorably disposed to forcible action if only a convenient and plausible pretext could be found. Roustan strengthened his resolution and sought to create the pretext. Grévy was won over as soon as he perceived that the objective was not the suppression of the frontier raids but the conquest of Tunis. M. Géry, president of the Bône-Guelma Railway, listed some sixty-nine acts of violence along the line from September 1, 1878, to April 20, 1881—most of which, however, consisted of throwing stones at trains or placing obstacles on the tracks.[2] The Governor-General himself subsequently enumerated 2,379 crimes or misdemeanors committed in Algeria by Tunisians between 1870 and 1881, of which 1,540 were thefts.[3]

On February 17, 1881, Grévy reported to the Ministers of Foreign Affairs, War, and Interior that the Kroumir tribesmen had violated the frontier.[4] It is possible that these raids were deliberately engineered by Roustan for his own purposes.[5] In any case, the affair was of no great moment. The Kroumirs retired and offered hostages and an indemnity, which Grévy refused, preferring to deal directly with the Bey.[6] When Barthélemy-Saint-Hilaire transmitted Roustan's dispatches for comment to General Farre, the Minister of War, the latter expressed his conviction that measures should be taken to prevent such raids in the future by demanding from the Bey the right to punish the Kroumirs directly and also "to increase our legitimate influence in the Regency."[7] Desultory negotiations with the Bey terminated in a conference, during the course of which Grévy, on the advice of General Forgemol, authorized the occupation of Soukahrras, on the Algerian side of the line but a Kroumir stronghold.[8] On March 30, some 500 Kroumirs crossed the line near La Calle—whether in retaliation or without provocation is not clear—and engaged in a combat with the French forces, which suffered a loss of four killed and six wounded.[9] Roustan, while reporting the measures of the Bey to restore order, continued to urge military action. On

---

[1] *L.J.T.*, No. 97, G. to B.St.H., January 21, 1881.

[2] *L.J.T.*, Annex to No. 153, Géry to B.St.H., April 24, 1881.

[3] *L.J.T.*, Supplement 286, Grévy to B.St.H., May 20, 1881.

[4] *L.J.T.*, Nos. 101 and 106.

[5] Broadley alleges that Roustan communicated with two professional dealers in border disturbances with this end in view. See Vol. I, pp. 204*f*.

[6] *L.J.T.*, No. 110, March 7, 1881.

[7] *L.J.T.*, No. 112, March 13, 1881.

[8] *L.J.T.*, No. 117, April 1, 1881.

[9] *L.J.T.*, No. 119, April 1, 1881, "Report of General Osmont."

April 6, Barthélemy-Saint-Hilaire instructed him to inform the Bey of the French intention to punish the tribes. In Roustan's opinion,

it is desirable always that our military operations be conducted with a force and rapidity sufficient to discourage all desire for disorder as well as all attempts at resistance. One can make known to the Bey that once the principal aim of the expedition is attained, our troops will regulate their movements according to his attitude.[1]

While the Bey protested at the proposed violation of his territory, he agreed not to resist the French invasion. The French foreign minister disclaimed all responsibility for the consequences of resistance, instructed Roustan to remain at his post as long as possible, and assured the Powers of the sincerity and good intentions of the French Government in resorting reluctantly to force.[2]

The fate of Tunis was thereby sealed. A pretext has been found and the Regency could now be seized under cover of "the absolute obligation which we are under to assure the security of our great Algerian colony."[3] What had been happening meanwhile at Paris, where the final decision to act had been taken? Ferry, himself, it is clear, had been favorable from the outset to a policy which would eventuate in the extension of French influence in North Africa. He had always been a conservative, patriotic, *bourgeois* Republican, waging incessant war on communards, socialists, pacifists, internationalists, and liberals of all shades.[4] His background and mentality were those of the imperialistic expansionist. The inner springs of action of the imperialist mind are everywhere much the same, though policies and rationalizations change incessantly with periods and circumstances. Allegations of personal profit are unconvincing. As for the interests of concessionnaires, what *bourgeois* statesman would not favor their protection? But, at bottom, territory is desired for the glory of the State, its pride of possession, its prestige in expansion. The will to power is its own justification. All else is the façade of apologetics. Ferry was seldom consistent in his own statement of his motives. Now the purpose is to lift the lowly to salvation. The superior race "does not conquer for its own pleasure, for the purpose of exploiting the feeble one, but to civilize it and raise it up to itself."[5] Again the end is to seek an outlet for French industry and capital. "Colonies are for rich countries a most advantageous place for capital investment . . . Eh! oui, pour les capitalistes!"[6] Political control is followed by economic preponderance. Trade follows the flag. Self-determination is "pure political metaphysics." Justifications are adjusted to conditions and the probabilities of their being accepted. They are means to ends and not statements of ends.

---

[1] *L.J.T.*, No. 135, April 8, 1881.
[2] *L.J.T.*, Nos. 138–146.
[3] *Supra*, p. 59.
[4] A. Rambaud, *Jules Ferry*, pp. 517–522, Paris, 1903.
[5] *J.O.Ch.*, March 27, 1884, cited in Rambaud, pp. 316–317.
[6] *J.O.Ch.*, July 28, 1885, cited in Rambaud, pp. 388–394.

But the means were not simple. Many obstacles had to be overcome. From the President of the Republic, Jules Grévy (January 30, 1879, to December 2, 1887), Ferry had little to fear, despite his early opposition to the project. But in the Cabinet, in the Chambers, in the press and the public were many skeptics, critics, and enemies. The Royalist Right and the extreme Left could be counted upon to fight every Cabinet and all its deeds at every opportunity. The disasters of the Second Empire, moreover, had left a heritage of anticolonial and antiwar sentiment. Even ardent patriots, in a day when patriotism was synonymous with hatred of Germany, were suspicious of a man who had an Alsacian wife and who had received his secondary schooling at Strasbourg. According to Clemenceau, Ferry was Bismark's tool and acted under "the humiliating protection of Germany."[1] The foreign minister, Barthélemy-Saint-Hilaire, was an old secretary of Thiers, as conservative as the executioner of the communards, and a political adversary of Gambetta who had been strongly opposed to "dangerous adventures" but whose views were modified by Freycinet. Saint-Hilaire was much criticized for a policy of "pusillanimité et de crainte." General Farre was unpopular, suspected of irresoluteness and lack of energy, and at best little inclined to daring projects. To add to the difficulties, 1881 was an election year. Ferry was dubious. But throughout the winter of 1880–1881 Baron de Courcel, director of political affairs at the Quai d'Orsay, constantly urged a military expedition upon the doubting ministers. Barthélemy-Saint-Hilaire was won over and even Gambetta himself,[2] much to the delight of Roustan who had consistently worked in the same direction. Long before the Kroumir raids the Cabinet had secretly decided to seize the first favorable opportunity to act. But action required money and money required the consent of the Chambers. Ferry rightly judged that a public avowal of the intention would be fatal. Recalling the motto of Louis XI: "to rule is to dissimulate," he perceived the necessity of the utmost caution in dealing with Parliament.

On April 4, 1881, General Farre appeared before the Deputies, to whom he declared:

In the presence of these events, which surpass all that has happened hitherto in the way of incursions of Tunisian tribes over our frontier, the Government has taken measures to enable it to repress the present raids and to prevent others in the future. As soon as we have gathered the necessary forces to act against the pillagers, we will act with all the energy which such a situation demands.[3]

Three days later he deposited in the bureau of the Chambers a project for an extraordinary credit of four million francs for the Ministry of War and 1,695,276 fr. for the Ministry of Marine to meet the expenses "of the

---

[1] Rambaud, *op. cit.*, pp. 395f.

[2] Valet, *op. cit.*, p. 169, and pp. 177f.

[3] *J.O.Ch.*, April 5, 1881.

operations against the Kroumirs on the frontiers of Tunis."[1] Favorable action was at once taken by the Budget Commission, whose *rapporteur*, M. Amedée le Faure, recommended approval by the Deputies. In the Chamber, M. Jules Delafosse challenged the ulterior motives of the Government in invading Tunis without a declaration of war and urged that the credits be voted only for the chastisement of the Kroumirs. If the Government had other purposes they should be made known.[2] This ineffective and unanswered interrogation gave rise to no discussion and the credits were voted unanimously, with fifty members of the Right abstaining.[3] The small credits asked, however, were obviously out of all proportion to the extensive military and naval preparations under way. The Cabinet's exact intentions were kept veiled. The issue was befogged by vague talk of "guarantees" to be demanded of the Bey. In order to reassure the parliamentarians, Ferry spoke before the Chamber on April 11. Following the President's reading of several demands for interpellations on the question, Ferry asked either an adjournment of the entire discussion for one month (by which time he hoped his goal would be gained) or an immediate discussion (in which he could still conceal the goal behind soothing words). The Chamber voted for the latter. Later in the day, M. Janvier de la Motte accused the Cabinet of asking for wholly inadequate credits in order to escape explanations and of carrying on a belligerent enterprise without the consent of Parliament.

In response, Ferry declared that the military operations were designed only to punish the Kroumirs and to obtain guarantees and satisfaction for the future. "The Government of the Republic does not seek conquests; it has no need of them." (Loud applause on the Left and Center.) But the security of Algeria must be protected. In a month, the Chambers would reconvene and all necessary explanations would be given at that time. To appear thus evasive and on the defensive was a tactical error. M. Lenglé asserted that the Premier's statement was wholly inadequate. In his view, Parliament had been given less information than the press or foreign governments, and private financial interests were drawing the country into costly adventures. Ferry's denial of the accusation was followed by a declaration from M. Cuneo d'Ornano, on behalf of his colleagues of the Right, that the Chamber had voted the credits asked exclusively for the repression of the Kroumirs. He proposed an *ordre du jour*, terminating the debate, couched in these terms. Several alternative proposals were made, one condemning the silence of the Government, one recalling that wars cannot be waged without the authorization of Parliament, and one lauding the conduct of the Cabinet. Ferry insisted that only the latter was acceptable. It was passed by a vote of 322 to 124. "The Chamber, approving the conduct of the Government and,

[1] Valet, *op. cit.*, p. 179.

[2] *J.O.Ch.*, April 8, 1881; *cf.* Despagnet, *op. cit.*, pp. 224–225.

[3] *J.O.Ch.*, April 8, 1881; the Senate followed suit without discussion the following day. *J.O.Sén.*, April 9, 1881.

full of confidence in its prudence and its energy, passes to the order of the day."[1]

With the Chambers adjourned for four weeks, Ferry breathed a sigh of relief. While France celebrated Easter, the decisive blow could be struck in Tunis. When Parliament reassembled, Ferry could present it with a *fait accompli*. Meanwhile he had concealed his hand, kept the Deputies in ignorance of his real plans, and secured the support or acquiescence of all but a handful of oppositionists. To be sure, Henri Rochefort, editor of *L'Intransigeant*, boldly ridiculed the expedition and even doubted whether the Kroumirs existed at all.[2] Other journals of the opposition press followed his lead. This campaign might ultimately prove embarrassing. But for the moment the Cabinet had its hands free.

On April 5, 1881, the Bey of Tunis received the report of his investigators who declared that the alleged invasion of Algeria by the Kroumirs was entirely problematical and that, in any event, the tribes were ready to submit to the Bey's decision.[3] On the same day Roustan informed him of the impending French incursion. His protests were met by requests for cooperation and other devices designed to gain time, while an army of 30,000 troops was secretly assembled. At the end of April, General Fergemol scattered the little bands of vagrant tribesmen without difficulty and dispatched a large force by sea to descend upon the Tunisian capital.[4] The city was soon surrounded by General Breart's soldiers and resistance was hopeless. The French commander submitted an ultimatum, demanding that the Bey at once sign the draft treaty which had been sent by Barthélemy-Saint-Hilaire to Roustan on May 10.[5] In its outlines, this agreement had been drawn up shortly after the Congress of Berlin.[6] In its final form it commenced with the customary innocuous prelude: "The Government of the French Republic and that of His Highness, the Bey of Tunis, wishing to prevent for all time the renewal of the disorders which have recently occurred on the frontiers of the two States and on the coast of Tunis, and desirous of binding more closely their former relations of friendship and good neighborliness, have resolved to conclude a convention for this purpose, in the interest of the two high contracting parties."[7] The ten articles which followed made no mention of the word "protectorate," but effectively destroyed the existence of Tunis as an independent State, by giving France control of all Tunisian foreign relations, guaranteeing the person and territories of the Bey, imposing a

[1] *J.O.Ch.*, April 12, 1881.

[2] *L'Intransigeant*, April 25, 1881, and following.

[3] Text in Broadley, *op. cit.*, II, pp. 368–370.

[4] *L.J.T.*, Nos. 216*ff.*

[5] Text in *L.J.T.*, Supplement 267. *Cf.* P.H.X., *op. cit.*, pp. 463–465 and Broadley, *op. cit.*, I. pp. 313–315. On military operations, Broadley, I, pp. 247–308, and P.H.X. pp. 123–178 and 213–258.

[6] Foucher, *op. cit.*, pp. 124–135.

[7] *L.J.T.*, Supplement, 267, B.St.H. to Roustan, May 10, 1881.

French military occupation on the country, and providing for the reorganization of the public finances with French assistance. The French Minister of Foreign Affairs referred to it as a "treaty of alliance and guarantee."[1] The "friendship and good neighborliness" was that of the lion for the lamb—with the lamb inside undergoing the process of digestion. The Bey and his advisers were terrified by the French bayonets and vague threats against their persons. On May 12, 1881, the Bey attached his signature to the document, known henceforth as the Treaty of Bardo, and complained pathetically to the Grand Vizier that he had submitted only under pressure and compulsion.[2]

On the same day, Ferry spoke to the reassembled Senators and Deputies: "Durable guarantees are necessary to our security. It is from the Bey of Tunis that we demand them. We desire neither his territory nor his throne. The French Republic has solemnly repudiated all notions of annexation, all ideas of conquest, in launching this expedition; it renews the same declarations at this hour when the end is near."[3] On the next day, May 13, he announced the signature of the treaty to Parliament, expressing his satisfaction with it and his hope of ratification, while Barthélemy-Saint-Hilaire transmitted to the bureaus of the Chambers the Yellow Book of justification which had been carefully prepared in advance at the Quai d'Orsay. He reassured foreign governments by announcing that the Bey had become the "ally" of France. Public opinion seemed divided. Many rejoiced, "fond of fine deeds in arms and of military expeditions, in love with the army, especially at this period when all minds were turned toward the revanche."[4] The opposition press continued its campaign of ridicule. On May 23, Parliament discussed the treaty. Technically, it might have been regarded as outside those categories of international agreements requiring legislative approval under the Constitution. But Ferry knew that such an interpretation would weaken rather than strengthen his position. M. Delafosse assailed this embarkation on the perilous seas of colonial imperialism, and Clemenceau, the "tiger," who revelled in the slaughter of Cabinets, accused the Government of keeping the Chambers in ignorance of its intentions, of acting without authority, and of prejudicing the diplomatic position of France in Europe. M. Cuneo d'Ornano asserted that the use of the man-power and wealth of the nation for the protection of purely private interests was inadmissible and suggested that five articles of the treaty be suppressed, leaving only those strictly necessary for the security of the Algerian frontier. In the Senate, M. Paul Rémusat, *rapporteur* for the commission which had examined the project for ratification, sought to justify the Cabinet in advance by pointing out that the agreement was not a treaty of peace, since diplomatic relations had never

[1] *L.J.T.*, Supplement, 274, May 13.
[2] Broadley, *op. cit.*, I, p. 318.
[3] *J.O.Ch.*, May 13, 1881.
[4] Valet, *op. cit.*, p. 190.

been severed and the Chambers had never been asked to declare war. M. de
Goutant-Biron declared the treaty objectionable, but said that Parliament
must uphold the Government in the face of an accomplished fact. Ferry
made no response. In the Senate the treaty was approved unanimously and in
the Chamber by a vote of 430 to 1, with the three opposition speakers
abstaining.[1]

3. THE AFTERMATH

But the population of Tunis was less disposed to acquiescence in the
conquest than were the members of the French Parliament. A national insurrection against the invaders broke out in the south, aided by the withdrawal
of a portion of the French forces and the desertion to the rebels of large
contingents of the Bey's troops.[2] New military expeditions were required.
To finance them more money was needed. And money required appropriations
by Parliament. The small credits already granted were wholly insufficient
to pay the costs of the original invasion, to say nothing of further operations.
Ferry could wage undeclared war on Tunis and destroy the independence of
the Regency by a sudden blow, while he calmed the Deputies with deceptive
phrases, but he had no legal means of financing the conquest without the
consent of Parliament. Explanations he found embarrassing and he always
made them with the utmost reluctance. He had already supplemented the
funds granted by taking sums out of other chapters of the budget during the
parliamentary recess—a procedure of doubtful legality, since he did not even
consult the Council of State.[3] But it was clear that the Chambers must be
asked for more appropriations. Ferry could only hope that a nicely calculated
appeal for patriotic support and for the execution of the treaty which he had
so shrewdly secured would suffice to carry the day.

On June 9, 1881, General Farre asked another credit of 14,226,000 fr.
Despite new protests at the hypocrisy of the Cabinet, the credit was approved
unanimously in both houses,[4] in part from a conviction that expenditures
already made must be paid for. Notwithstanding the vote, the Cabinet felt
its strength declining. A general election was scheduled for September 18.
Constans, Minister of the Interior, conceived the idea of advancing the date
to August 21 to enhance the Government's chances of success. Unrest in
Algeria led to an interpellation in which the Cabinet was charged with
weakening the garrisons for the Tunis expedition. A vote of confidence was
obtained by the narrow margin of thirty votes.[5] The necessity for a new
punitive expedition was used by the opposition as the basis for a series of

[1] *J.O.Ch.*, May 24, 1881; *J.O.Sén.*, May 28, 1881.
[2] A detailed account of the uprising and its suppression will be found in Broadley, *op. cit.*, II,
passim.
[3] P.H.X., *op. cit.*, p. 262.
[4] *J.O.Ch.*, June 10 and 15, 1881, and *J.O.Sén.*, July 3, 1881.
[5] 249 to 219, *J.O.Ch.*, July 1, 1881.

violent attacks upon the Government's policies. Rochefort in *L'Intransigeant* openly accused the Cabinet of taking Tunis in order to raise the price of Tunisian bonds and named Roustan as the agent of the operation. At the suggestion of the Minister of Foreign Affairs, Roustan brought suit for defamation against the fiery editor, and the trial which dragged through the summer and fall added fuel to the flames of controversy.[1] On July 26, Clemenceau sought to overturn the Cabinet in an interpellation on Tunis and on the proposed change in the election date. The Government survived by the close vote of 214 to 201.[2] On the following day, Ferry, by two decrees, declared the legislative session closed and ordered the elections for August 21.

While the opposition made the most of the issue in the campaign, the election cannot be said to have turned on the Tunis question. Very infrequently does a problem of foreign policy clearly determine the outcome of a national election. In the result of the polling, Ferry was somewhat strengthened by the success of the Republican groups against the Monarchists. In the old Chamber the former had controlled 394 Deputies out of 535. In the new, the Republicans numbered 457 as against 90 Royalist reactionaries. Within the Republican ranks, however, Ferry could not reckon with anything like united support. He preferred postponing explanations as long as possible and in defiance of the demands of the extreme Left for an immediate convocation and a full investigation into the situation in North Africa, he deferred the opening of the new Parliament until October 28. This evoked a manifesto from the Parisian Deputies, strongly condemning the whole Tunisian policy of the Government for embroiling France with the rest of Europe. With 50,000 troops needed to cope with the rebellion, eighty four battalions were withdrawn from the garrisons in France and the class of 1876 was kept under the colors. The latter order led to such widespread public resentment that it was withdrawn on September 17.[3]

When the new Chamber met, the insurrection in Tunis had been all but wiped out. There was, nevertheless, a general demand among the Deputies for a "Grande Ministère" of all the Republican groups, headed by Gambetta. This sentiment was not entirely motivated by the results of Ferry's policy in Tunis, but was undoubtedly augmented by such considerations. Assured of the ultimate success of his plans, Ferry was perhaps content to retire for a time, leaving to others the none too pleasant task of dealing with the remaining difficulties. But first he must be "vindicated," before he could withdraw with good grace and undiminished prestige. On October 28, the opening day, Ferry read a telegram to the Chambers from General Saussier, announcing his entry into Kairouan, the rebel stronghold. He was greeted with mocking laughter and cries of "C'est une comédie!" Three demands for interpellations on Tunis were made at once and Ferry declared that he welcomed dis-

---

[1] Broadley, *op. cit.*, II, pp. 247–281.

[2] *J.O.Ch.*, July 27, 1881.

[3] Robiquet, *Discours et opinions*, V, pp. 1–4.

cussion as soon as possible. In the stormy debates which followed, the Premier abandoned the tactics of passive resistance and took the initiative in assailing his opponents.

> Messieurs, it is not without profound surprise and—I dare to say it—a little humiliation, that I see myself under the necessity, at a date so close to the events, to recall on this platform that the expedition to Tunis has been a national cause, and that it was a response to patriotic needs . . . To send reinforcements to an expedition in order to execute a treaty subscribed to by the nation, for the purpose of putting into effect the clauses of a treaty to which the nation had given its signature, was, on the part of the Government, to fulfil a duty, and there can be no question here of dictatorship nor of infringement on the legislative power.[1]

The former Chamber, in voting credits, argued Ferry, had authorized the Government to execute the Treaty of Bardo. For the present Chamber to repudiate its execution would be a repudiation of the decision of its own majority. Credits had not been exceeded and expenditures had not been made without authorization. The execution of the treaty was a most elementary duty of patriotism. France had rendered Christian civilization a great service by crushing the Holy War in Tunis and striking a mortal blow at Moslem fanaticism. France's political and military interests in Tunis should be inviolable. "Do not touch, with however light a hand, these two great interests: do not touch France; do not touch the Army!"[2]

The opposition, aware now of the duplicity of the preceding spring, assailed Ferry furiously—for incurring unauthorized expenses, for misrepresenting the meaning of the credits voted, for withdrawing troops to deceive public opinion and thereby encouraging rebellion, for sending to death 782 sons of France. On November 8, Clemenceau, with the support of the Left, successively demolished Ferry's arguments and demanded a parliamentary inquiry. The entire expedition, he insisted, was undertaken in the interests of the Bône-Guelma Railway Company, the *Société Marseillaise*, and the *Crédit Foncier*. The ministry had deceived the Chambers and the country, had exceeded the credits voted, and had waged war without the authorization of Parliament.[3] Ferry replied in a four-hour discourse, interrupted by frequent denials and objections. The Government, he said, had never, despite repeated solicitation, supported in any manner the private interests referred to. It had been forced to act by the effect on public opinion of the pleas of the French colony in Tunis.[4] All charges of deception were false. Patriotism required the enforcement of the Treaty of Bardo. By this time the Chamber was in a tumult of disorder. Clemenceau's demand for an inquiry was rejected, 312 to 161. The pure and simple order of the day (a vote of confidence in the Cabinet) was likewise rejected 312 to 176. In the utmost confusion, the Chamber successively rejected some sixty *ordres du jour*, three demands for investigations, and two for criminal prosecutions. Gambetta finally

---

[1] *J.O.Ch.*, November 6, 1881.

[2] *Ibid.*

[3] *J.O.Ch.*, November 11, 1881.

[4] This was another product of Roustan's skillful strategy; *cf.* Broadley, *op. cit.*, I, pp. 210*f.*

intervened with an appeal to patriotism. On his proposal, the exhausted Deputies mustered a majority of 355 against 68 in favor of the resolution: "The Chamber, resolved on the integral execution of the treaty subscribed to by the French nation, May 12, 1881, passes to the order of the day."[1] Ferry was vindicated. On the following day he tendered his resignation to the President of the Republic and was succeeded by a new ministry headed by Gambetta (November 14, 1881, to January 30, 1882).

The battle was won, even with the sacrifice of the Premiership. Military force, appeals to patriotism, executive initiative and duplicity had triumphed over constitutional principles and parliamentary control. Eight hundred French soldiers had lost their lives. Forty-five million francs had been spent.[2] Attacks on the treaty continued in the Chambers and in the press and, in December, Rochefort was absolved by a Paris jury from any criminal responsibility for his attacks upon Roustan.[3] Ferry was out of office and his enemies rejoiced. But he had taken Tunis, in the face of the indifference and opposition of the nation, and had launched France upon an imperial career which was to make her the second colonial Power of the world. In the face of this achievement, all else seemed insignificant. Even Gambetta was won over. On December 2, the Chamber voted the supplementary credits which he asked, in response to his plea for the execution of a treaty which permitted "neither the annexation nor the abandonment" of Tunis. "We must assure the development of our colonies, both economically and politically, and we must protect them, when that is necessary, against the ambitions of certain Powers, and that is what we have done in occupying Tunis."[4]

From the point of view of world politics, the French *coup de force* had far-reaching reverberations. The Turkish Government, claiming suzerainty over Tunis in the face of the French contention that it had been independent,[5] protested bitterly but in vain against the conquest and the treaty of protectorate.[6] The British Government, appealed to by the Porte and the Bey, assumed an attitude of friendly disinterestedness, contenting itself with references to the unfavorable effect on English opinion of the French action and tart comments on the discrepancies between the declarations and the behavior and the French Government.[7] But at Rome indignation approached

---

[1] *J.O.Ch.*, November 11, 1881; see also Robiquet, *Discours et opinions*, V, pp. 5–98; and Valet, *op. cit.*, pp. 210–228.

[2] 44,449,981 fr. up to December 31, 1881, P.H.X., *op. cit.*, p. 262.

[3] Broadley, *op. cit.*, II, p. 281.

[4] *J.O..Ch*, December 2, 1881.

[5] For the substance of the French argument, see Foucher, *op. cit.*, pp. 98–121.

[6] *L.J.T.*, Supplement, 234, 238–242, 249–254, 267, 271, 277, and 283.

[7] *L.J.T.*, Supplement, 285, Lord Granville to M. Challemel-Lacour, May 20, 1881, in response to No. 282, B.St.H. to Lord Lyons, May 16, 1881: "Votre excellence rappelle qu'en plusiers occasions dans mes entretiens avec Elle, j'ai repoussé l'idée d'une conquête ou d'une annexation à la France d'une partie quelconque du territoire tunisien. Je ne fais aucune difficulté de vous répéter ici ce que je vous ai dit déjà, et je puis vous affirmer que nos arrangements avec le Bey ne comprennent aucune stipulation que ne soit conforme aux assurances que je vous ai données."

a state of frenzy. Freycinet had promised the Italian Ambassador, General Cialdini, in 1880, to do nothing in Tunis without informing him. Ferry felt himself not bound by his predecessor's promise and took the Italian Government by surprise.[1] Vigorous protests against the invasion were followed by vain appeals to the other Powers to act. When the news of the Treaty of Bardo was received, the Cairoli Cabinet was overturned (May 14, 1881). Cairoli had been a friend of France, but his blunderings and indiscretions had been factors of no small importance in influencing Ferry's decision.[2] Cairoli proceeded to Berlin and commenced the negotiations which culminated a year later in the Triple Alliance. Deep as was Italian resentment at Austria's continued possession of "Italia Irredenta," it was overcome by a deeper resentment at Rome's defeat in the "Last Punic War." The new Carthage had been snatched away under Rome's very eyes. Italy threw her lot with the Central Powers, past and potential enemies of France.[3] From 1881 dates the bitter enmity between France and Italy which was only temporarily submerged in the Great War and which has reappeared in acute form in recent years as one of the most serious dangers to world peace.

From the point of view of the domestic control of French foreign policy, the significance of the story is too obvious to require elaboration. An imperialist-patriot Premier had shrewdly seized an opportunity for national expansion at the expense of a weak and helpless State, unable to defend itself and coveted by a rival Power. There is no evidence to show that he profited personally from the venture or acted at the behest of investors and concessionnaires. It would be more correct to say that he used French economic interests in Tunis as a lever in diplomacy and in dealing with Parliament and public opinion. Encouraged by the permanent officials at the Quai d'Orsay and aided by a foreign minister and a diplomatic agent on the scene who were neither hesitant nor scrupulous in advancing their conception of the interests of France, he guided and anticipated the sequence of events and struck when the iron was hot. His circumlocutions and inconsistent explanations are not indicative of any lack of foresight or planning, but only of the necessity which he was constantly under to act with the utmost circumspection in order to avoid arousing the opposition of Parliament and public opinion to a project which would have been repudiated had it been openly avowed. He accomplished his task with skill and subtlety. His greatest allies were gullibility and inertia on the part of the legislature in the face of executive initiative, and indifference and ignorance of the facts on the part of the "public," which he took no pains to correct. Neither the power of the purse, nor the right of interpellation, nor all the strategy of parliamentary manoeuvering enabled the Chambers to prevent the achievement of the goal. Neither the attacks of the opposition press nor the exigencies of a national

---

[1] Freycinet, *Souvenirs*, pp. 169–170.

[2] Langer, *loc. cit.*, p. 264.

[3] Debidour, *Histoire Diplomatique*, I, pp. 47–52.

election sufficed to stir public sentiment from an attitude of acquiescence, which was at first fearful and reluctant and then complacent and content in the face of success and appeals to patriotic pride. A small group of men, fearful of public disapproval and therefore determined to act surreptitiously, behind a façade of misrepresentation, had pushed the nation into a policy, the consequences of which the entire country was obliged to assume, but which was essentially their own creation.

Chapter V

THE WHITE MAN'S BURDEN IN THE FAR EAST

1. Tonkin

DESPITE the almost complete destruction of the early French colonial empire in the Orient by Great Britain in the Seven Years' War (1756 to 1763), Southeastern Asia remained a center of French economic and political interests throughout the eighteenth and nineteenth centuries. At the delta of the Mekong, which empties into the South China Sea, directly opposite Borneo, lies the ancient land of Cochin-China, at the end of the great land mass between the Malay peninsula and the Philippine Islands. It had become an object of the colonial ambitions of the Second Empire and had been conquered with some difficulty between 1859 and 1867.[1] The region was looked upon as the outlet for the profitable trade of Southern China and, during the early sixties, French agents secured an ascendant influence in the Kingdom of Cambodia, to the north of Cochin-China, long a victim of the rivalry between Annam to the east and Siam to the west. The Treaty of Oudong of August 11, 1863, went far toward making the kingdom a French protectorate.[2]

The Third French Republic inherited Cambodia and Cambodia's quarrels and frontier disputes with her larger neighbors. French relations with Tu-Duc, the Emperor of Annam, were especially strained over the area of Tonkin (or Tong-Kin) at the mouth of the Red River, which had been conquered by the Annamites in 1802. The latter had never acquiesced in French commercial and military penetration of the river basin and attacked the French posts in 1872. Reinforcements were dispatched to their assistance under Francis Garnier and on November 20, 1873, the French marines drove the Annamites out of the citadel of Hanoï. While the conquest proceeded piecemeal, Admiral Dupré dispatched his agent, Lieutenant Philastre, to negotiate with the Annamite authorities. The Emperor, however, summoned to his aid against the French the bands of Chinese bandits and mercenaries known as the *Pavillons Noirs* (Black Flags), backwash of the great Taiping Rebellion, and, on December 21, Garnier was slain at their hands and his small force compelled to withdraw. The Cabinet at Paris, headed by the anti-

---

[1] Debidour, *Histoire diplomatique*, I, pp. 67*f.*; Despagnet, *La diplomatie de la troisième République*, pp. 121*f.*

[2] A. Bouinas et A. Paulus, *L'Indo-Chine française contemporaine*, I, pp. 1–24, 455–460; II, pp. 775–778, Paris, 1885. *Cf.* texts of other early treaties in Appendixes.

colonial Duc de Broglie, was frightened at the prospect of a costly and dangerous adventure in the Far East at a time when Germany seemed still threatening and ordered the retirement of the expedition. Philastre negotiated a treaty to which Admiral Dupré and Tu-Duc attached their signatures on March 15, 1874.[1]

The Annam treaty of 1874, which was supplemented by a commercial convention signed the following August, furnishes the most convenient point of departure for a consideration of French policy in Indo-China. The treaty was ratified, after a brief discussion, in the Chamber, where its real significance was entirely overlooked.[2] It constituted a partial abandonment of French efforts to acquire Tonkin and the establishment of a veiled and ambiguously defined protectorate over Annam. Paradoxically, it recognized the complete independence of Annam and failed to terminate the vague suzerainty which the Chinese Empire exercised over its ruler.

His Excellency, the President of the French Republic, recognizes the sovereignty of the King of Annam and his entire independence *vis-à-vis* every foreign Power, whatever it may be, promises him aid and assistance, and engages to give him, on his demand and freely, the support necessary to maintain order and tranquillity in his States, to defend him against every attack, and to destroy the piracy which desolates a portion of the coasts of the Realm. (Article 2.) In gratitude for this protection, His Majesty, the King of Annam, engages to conform his foreign policy to that of France and to change nothing in his present diplomatic relations. (Article 3.)

Provision was also made for the gift by France to Annam of five steamships, 100 cannon, 1,000 rifles, specified quantities of ammunition, and the services of military and marine instructors and engineers. In return Tu-Duc opened to commerce the three ports of Hanoï, Haïphong, and Quinh-On, in each of which 100 French troops were to be stationed and French consuls were granted exclusive jurisdiction over foreign residents. France abandoned territorial claims to Tonkin and received a guarantee of unimpeded navigation for unarmed ships up the Red River to the Chinese frontier.[3]

During the next six years the treaty gave rise to numerous difficulties. Navigation on the Red River was frequently impeded by pirates with whom the Annamite authorities were unwilling or unable to deal. Foreigners expected a protection from French officials which they could not give under the terms of the agreement. Allegations of the mistreatment of French agents and private citizens were made and led to reparations which were regarded as inadequate. Tu-Duc continued to consider himself a vassal of the Celestial Empire, to send tribute to Pekin, and to call upon China for assistance in

[1] On these early developments see Despagnet, *op. cit.*, pp. 122–123; Bouinas et Paulus, *op. cit.*, I, pp. 25–35; J. Dupuis, *Les origins de la question du Tong-Kin*, Paris, 1896, *passim;* H. Gautier, *Les Français au Tonkin*, pp. 151–273, Paris, 1885.

[2] *J.O.Ch.*, August 6, 1875.

[3] Text in Gautier, *op. cit.*, pp. 315–318; on the difficulties of its interpretation, Bouinas et Paulus, *op. cit.*, II, pp. 80–89, and Debidour, *op. cit.*, I, pp. 67–73.

various ways, asserting that his procedure was entirely in harmony with Article 3 of the treaty. The French cited Article 2 in refutation of this claim, but obviously had under it no right of uninvited intervention. With the local French authorities determined to interpret their rights as broadly as possible and the Annamites determined to confine them to the narrowest possible limits, satisfactory relations were difficult to maintain and the "protectorate" remained a dead letter.[1] Successive Cabinets in Paris contented themselves with "watchful waiting."

Only when M. de Freycinet became Premier and Minister of Foreign Affairs on December 28, 1879, was an active and energetic defense of French interests contemplated. The Minister of Marine and Colonies, Vice Admiral Jauréguiberry, was asked by Freycinet to prepare plans for an expeditionary force to occupy the upper reaches of the Red River and a credit of 2,700,000 fr. was obtained from the Chamber for the enforcement of the treaties of 1874.[2] Before action could be taken, however, Freycinet was succeeded as Premier by Jules Ferry, September 23, 1880, and as Minister of Foreign Affairs by the more cautious Barthélemy-Saint-Hilaire, who was disposed to acquiesce in the claims of Marquis Tseng, Chinese Minister in Paris, that China retained sovereignty over Annam and could never accept the Franco-Annamite treaty of 1874. Ferry, here as in Tunis, was inclined to a vigorous assertion and expansion of French influence, less because of legal rights or tangible interests, than out of a general desire to enhance French prestige by an energetic colonial policy. And here, as in Tunis, he could count upon German friendliness or even support, while he was less obliged to reckon with other Powers than in North Africa. He decided to augment the small French garrisons permitted by the treaty. Aside from dangers of diplomatic complications, there was the rising tide of domestic opposition to colonial ventures to be reckoned with, augmented by the controversy over the Tunis expedition. While determined to prepare an expeditionary force "sans bruit," he sought to avoid the appearance of one and in July, 1881, asked the Chamber for credits under the pretext of preserving order. Naval forces must be sent up the Red River to chastise the Pavillons Noirs. "We are charged with maintaining order in the country. For this, we do not have sufficient forces. It is these forces which we ask of you. We do not wish to make conquests; we wish to have a situation which is honorable, and at this moment it is not honorable."[3] The Deputies granted the credits with little discussion and forgot them with as little regret. Ferry's design was to create a situation which would make possible the imposition of an effective protectorate over Annam. But he moved with caution and apparently with a less clear perception of the relation of means to ends than he had shown in dealing with

---

[1] *Ibid.*, I, p. 69; Despagnet, *op. cit.*, pp. 365–370; E. Hippeau, *Histoire diplomatique de la troisième République*, pp. 445f., Paris, 1889.

[2] Hippeau, *op. cit.*, p. 452.

[3] *J.O.Ch.*, July 18, 1881.

Tunis. Nothing of importance had been done when his ministry fell in November.

The short-lived Gambetta ministry which followed (November 14, 1881, to January 30, 1882) did nothing beyond assuring Tseng that France intended to execute the 1874 treaty and that Chinese sovereignty over Annam was only of historical interest.[1] When the Governor of Cochin-China, LeMyre de Vilers, ubiquitous imperialist, urged action, Gougeard, Minister of Marine and Colonies, forbade all movements of ships and troops.[2] Vilers resigned in disgust, but the Cabinet refused to accept either his resignation or his advice. The second Freycinet ministry (January 30 to August 7, 1882) was of a different mind and continued work on the original plan of an expedition. It decided to send a small force from Saigon, in Cochin-China, up to the coast to the Red River delta in Tonkin. Henri Rivière, who had distinguished himself by the repression of the native rebellion in New Caledonia in 1878, was chosen as commander and sailed from Saigon on March 26 with two vessels and 400 men. Following his ill-fated predecessor, Garnier, he ascended the Red River and stormed the citadel of Hanoï on April 25, 1882.[3]

This employment of violence evoked an immediate protest from the Chinese Government as suzerain of Tonkin and Annam. Marquis Tseng in Paris demanded an explanation. Freycinet, in reply, professed ignorance of the event, which was scarcely plausible, even though Rivière was acting under orders from the Governor of Cochin-China, and the spring and summer passed with the French expeditionary force remaining inactive at Hanoï and the French and Chinese Governments exchanging views on the subject which seemed irreconcilable. Tu-Duc, having made no such request for aid in the maintenance of order as the treaty contemplated, regarded the expedition as an unprovoked invasion of his territory and called upon China for military aid. From a legal point of view the French case was extremely weak. From an economic point of view, the expedition was designed to clear the Red River of pirates and other obstructions to French commerce with South China, in which the source of the stream was located. While potentially of considerable value, since freight on a ton of goods to Yunnan cost 450 fr. up the Red River as compared with 880 fr. up the Yangtse,[4] this trade was as yet undeveloped. Freycinet, Ferry, and their supporters at Paris who favored such action would seem to have been motivated by the usual considerations of prestige and expansionist diplomacy, though the immediate objective was to prepare the way for the growth of commerce. This, in turn, would further their political designs. Economics and politics were, in fact, inextricably intertwined. The drive to action, however, came from politicians

[1] January 1, 1882; Debidour, *op. cit.*, I, p. 70.

[2] Gautier, *op. cit.*, p. 340.

[3] *Ibid.*, pp. 342f.; Bouinas et Paulus, *op. cit.*, II, pp. 89–121, and Bouinas et Paulus, *La France en Indo-Chine*, pp. 44–50, Paris, 1886.

[4] S. H. Roberts, *History of French Colonial Policy*, II, p. 425, London, 1929.

rather than merchants. But whether war with China should be risked for the sake of Tonkin was dubious. M. Bourée, French Minister at Pekin, reported Chinese military preparations and asserted that hostilities were inevitable if the French policy of force was continued. The members of Parliament, moreover, were displaying increasing restlessness over the colonial and foreign adventures sponsored by the Freycinet Cabinet. Relations with England were strained over Egypt, torn by the rebellion of Arabi Pasha and the Holy War of the Mahdi in the Sudan. When the Government demanded a credit of 9,410,000 fr. for the occupation of a portion of the Suez Canal, the Chamber overturned the ministry by decisively rejecting the policy which it had pursued.[1]

On August 7, 1882, Eugène Duclerc became Premier and Minister of Foreign Affairs in a new Cabinet, pledged to conduct itself with that "reserve and prudence" which Parliament had demanded.[2] Bourée at Pekin resumed negotiations and on November 27, 1882, signed an agreement with the Chinese Government providing for the evacuation of Tonkin by the Chinese forces which had filtered in, the establishment of a neutral zone on the frontier, and a qualified recognition of the French protectorate. In December Vice Admiral Jauréguiberry, still Minister of Marine and Colonies, was obliged by Duclerc to abandon a project for a credit of eleven million francs for the purpose of reinforcing Rivière and organizing the definite occupation of Tonkin. The Premier expressed his satisfaction with the terms Bourée had secured and Rivière was ordered not to attack the Chinese forces surrounding Hanoï.[3] Had Duclerc remained in power it appears entirely likely that the objects sought could have been gained by peaceful means. But the Cabinet was divided on internal policies and resigned on January 8, 1883. Portfolios were reshuffled and Fallières took the helm, only to retire within three weeks because of ill health and to be succeeded on February 21 by the second ministry headed by Jules Ferry, who was destined to remain in office for over two years. The death of Gambetta in 1881 had resulted in his followers forming themselves into a Radical group which controlled the balance of power between the Republicans and the Royalists. Only a skillful leader could maintain a stable coalition in the face of this new alignment. Ferry returned to office, pledged to put an end to parliamentary chaos and to protect the Republic from its enemies. He bespoke vigor, energy, efficiency. Foreign policy would be one of peace, but not of inaction.[4]

[1] *J.O.Ch.*, July 30, 1882. The vote was 416 to 75.

[2] Ministerial Declaration read in Chamber and Senate, *J.O.*, August 10, 1882.

[3] Gautier, *op. cit.*, pp. 350*f.*; and Hippeau, *op. cit.*, pp. 452*f.*

[4] "Messieurs, la politique extérieure de ce cabinet, comme celle de tous ses prédécesseurs, depuis douze ans, ne peut être qu'une politique de paix. La paix est le premier besoin et l'intérêt profond de toute grande démocratie. Mais une politique pacifique n'est pas nécessairement une politique inactive. Partout, dans toutes les questions, où nos intérêts, où notre honneur sont engagés, nous voulons, nous devons maintenir à la France le rang que lui appartient." Ferry's Ministerial Declaration, *J.O.Ch.*, February 23, 1883.

As was to be expected, Ferry repudiated Duclerc's Chinese policy. The agreement of the preceding November was rejected and Bourée was recalled from Pekin by the new foreign minister, Challemel-Lacour, on March 5. Rivière was reinforced and a course embarked upon, under Ferry's leadership, which could result only in war—a war unwanted even by Ferry but an inevitable consequence of his underestimation of Chinese determination and fighting capacity, his naïve belief that China could be disposed of as readily as Tunis, and his disposition to close his ears to all, like Bourée, who were well informed and counseled peace. Marquis Tseng reasserted the Chinese claim to suzerainty over Annam and offered China's good offices in dealing with Tu-Duc. Challemel-Lacour rejected the suggestion. When Tseng pointed out the bad effect on Franco-Chinese relations of the continued presence of French troops in Tonkin, the French Minister was again cold. On March 23, Rivière left Hanoï, which the Pavillons Noirs at once invested, in order to attack Nam-Dinh, where the French advance was blocked by Annamite and Chinese forces. The latter were defeated, but Rivière was obliged to return to Hanoï by the gravity of the situation in his rear. In a sortie against the besiegers on May 19, 1883, the company which he was leading fell into an ambush and he, like Garnier, was slain with his followers by the pirates of the Black Flags.[1]

The news of this incident created a great sensation in France and strengthened Ferry's appeal for credits. On May 15, the Chamber had voted 5,300,000 fr. for reinforcements. On the twenty-sixth, following several amendments by the Senate, the credits were revoted unanimously and the Cabinet dispatched a fleet under Admiral Courbet and a military expedition of 4,000 men. In Tonkin, war was undertaken in earnest to insure effective control of the country by French forces. In Paris and Pekin, recriminations were exchanged. The Chinese Government insisted on its rights and demanded the withdrawal of the French troops as a condition of further discussion. Challemel-Lacour rejected all the Chinese claims and in November negotiations were broken off. Ferry took the post of Minister of Foreign Affairs at the same time and declined all responsibility in case of conflict between the French troops and the Chinese forces in Tonkin.[2] In Annam the French display of force and the death of Tu-Duc combined to produce a capitulation. On August 25, 1883, the French commissioner, Harmand, with the support of Admiral Courbet, imposed the Treaty of Hué on the new ruler, Disiep-Hoa. The latter accepted unreservedly the French military, diplomatic, and financial protectorate, an unqualified right of French intervention, complete French control of Tonkin, and the annexation to Tonkin of the provinces Ha-Tinh, Ngue-Ann, and Thanh-Hoa; and of the province of Binh-Thuan to Cochin-China. The annexation provisions were in excess of Harmand's instructions and were made in contemplation of the eventual absorption of

[1] Gautier, *op. cit.*, pp. 375f.
[2] Hippeau, *op. cit.*, pp. 453–458.

all of Annam into the French possessions. In view of repeated declarations to Parliament and to the Chinese Government that France had no annexationaist designs and in view of the vigorous attacks on Ferry's dissimulation by Clemenceau and the opposition,[1] these clauses were dropped from the final Treaty of Hué of June 6, 1884, by agreement between Ferry and M. Tenot, *rapporteur* to the Chamber.[2]

On May 11, 1884, China had acquiesced in the Annamite surrender by signing the Convention of Tien-Tsin with the French naval commander, Captain Fournier, by which France agreed to respect and protect against any aggression the Tonkin frontier of China, and Pekin agreed to grant freedom of trade between Annam and China, to be regulated by a treaty of commerce under conditions as advantageous as possible for French merchants.

The Celestial Empire, reassured by the formal guarantees of good neighborliness which are given it by France as to the integrity and security of the southern frontiers of China, engages: first, to withdraw immediately, behind its frontiers, the Chinese garrisons in Tonkin; second, to respect in the present and the future the treaties concluded or to be concluded between France and the Court of Hué." (Article 2.)[3]

Apparently peace was now assured. Ferry had gained Tonkin and the Annam Protectorate and had secured Chinese acknowledgment of both. Except for his peculiar method of dealing with certain unforeseen developments, the issue would have been closed by the Convention of Tien-Tsin. In fact, however, the agreement marked the beginning of a period of hostility in Franco-Chinese relations of unprecedented bitterness.

2. WAR WITH CHINA

In his communications to Fournier, immediately following the signature of the convention, Ferry had insisted on the evacuation of Tonkin by the Chinese with the utmost possible dispatch.[4] Fournier informed General Millot, the French commander at Hanoï, that the evacuation must be complete by June 6, under threat of the forcible expulsion of the Chinese garrisons.[5] Messages traveled slowly in China, however, and time was required for the movement of the troops behind the frontier. The Chinese, moreover, regarded the evacuation as contingent upon the signature of a definitive treaty.[6] The impetuosity of the French military commanders would brook no such delay. On June 23, a French column, advancing north of Bac-Lé was fired upon by bands of guerillas and irregulars. The Chinese army near by reported that it wished to avoid any friction, was familiar with the terms of the convention, and asked six days to reach the frontier. Colonel Dugenne

[1] *Cf. J.O.Ch.*, October 31 and December 10, 1883.

[2] Despagnet, *op. cit.*, pp. 379f.

[3] *L. J. Tonkin*, pp. 5–7; on the details of the negotiations, Nos. 1–20, May 2, to May 16, 1884.

[4] *L.J.Tonkin*, Nos. 10, 13, 14.

[5] *Ibid.*, Nos. 16–18.

[6] *Ibid.*, No. 27.

refused to grant the requested delay or to halt his own advance. He ordered his force forward to Langson and came into conflict with the Chinese, who greatly outnumbered his own men. The French force lost seven killed and forty-two wounded and was compelled on the following day to beat a hasty retreat, with a further loss of eleven killed and thirty-six wounded.[1] The first French reports of this incident made it appear that the Chinese had attacked the French without provocation in flagrant violation of the convention.[2]

Ferry ordered Patenôtre, who had just signed that Treaty of Hué with Annam and who was proceeding to Pekin, to demand reparation and instructed M. Semallé, chargé d'affaires at the Chinese capital, to protest energetically and insist upon an indemnity.[3] The Tsong-Li-Yamen, or Chinese foreign office, transmitted its views early in July through Li-Fong-Pao, its minister in Paris. It declared that the French forces had opened the attack, contrary to the convention, protested against the naval demonstration already under way, and suggested that the troops of both countries keep their respective positions and avoid further hostilities, pending an arrangement for mutual evacuation.[4] Ferry at once rejected this proposal, insisted that the French column had been a victim of a premeditated ambush, and demanded immediate evacuation by the Chinese forces.[5] On the same day (July 4, 1884), General Millot dispatched a full account of the Langson affair to Vice Admiral Peyron, Minister of Marine and Colonies, with the facts substantially as given above. Patenôtre, at Shanghai, played into the hands of the naval officers who were apparently itching for an opportunity to ply their trade of war. On July 6, he expressed his agreement with the view of Admirals Courbet and Lespés that further negotiations would be useless and recommended an ultimatum.[6] Three days later Ferry presented his "final" demands to Li-Fong-Pao at Paris: immediate Chinese evacuation of Tonkin through an imperial decree to be published in the *Pekin Gazette*, and reparation of "at least" 250,000,000 fr. These demands, he hoped, would be considered

as a new proof of our amicable disposition toward China . . . We are expecting that a satisfactory reply on these two points will be made within the week which follows their presentation by our representatives. Otherwise, we shall be under the necessity of assuring ourselves by direct action the guarantees and the reparation which are due us.[7]

[1] Millot to Peyron, July 4, 1884; *ibid.*, No. 36. *Cf.* No. 21, which reached Paris on June 26·

[2] *Ibid.*, No. 21. "Le *guet-apens* de Bac-Lé (c'est le nom qu'on donna bientôt en France à cet incident) eut dans notre pays un immense retentissement et fut le point de départ d'une série d'opérations qui allait donner à la guerre du Tonkin une importance et une gravité tout autres que celles qu'elle avait jusqu'alors paru avoir aux yeux du monde politique," Debidour, *op. cit.*, I, p. 74.

[3] *L.J.Tonkin*, Nos. 23–24.

[4] *Ibid.*, No. 33.

[5] *Ibid.*, No. 34.

[6] *Ibid.*, Patenôtre to Ferry, July 6, 1884.

[7] *Ibid.*, No. 39, Ferry to Li-Fong-Pao, July 9, 1884.

Ferry's motives in presenting these exorbitant demands furnish an interesting subject of speculation. Even were he acting on the assumption that the facts of the Langson incident were as originally reported, his ultimatum was calculated to achieve not a just settlement of the controversy but a humiliating surrender on the part of China as an alternative to war. In fact, however, he was undoubtedly familiar with the actual events as reported by Millot to Peyron on July 4. Any supposition of ignorance on his part presupposes either an almost criminal neglect to secure the facts from his Minister of Marine or a deliberate withholding of Millot's dispatch on the part of Peyron. The latter assumption, though improbable, is more plausible than the former, which is entirely out of keeping with Ferry's character. In such a crisis, the influence of the militarists and navalists is likely to be thrown on the side of war. In the present instance, the French Marine, or at least the French naval commanders in Far Eastern waters, were in favor of the use of force. At least one member of the diplomatic staff, Patenôtre, was in agreement with them. On the whole, however, it seems likely that neither the influence of Patenôtre nor the pressure of the Marine was decisive. The impetus to action leading to war came from Ferry himself. His own original position, as well as the attitude of the patriotic public, based as they were on the initial "ambush" story, made the issue one of "national honor." There could be no turning back, even if Ferry were so disposed. But he was not so disposed. This is not to say that he wanted war. No statesman in such a position "wants war." But he may want certain other things which he thinks may be worth war—particularly if he calculates that the war will probably be of short duration and that victory will be easy. Ferry was not the man to neglect an opportunity to enhance French diplomatic prestige at the expense of a weaker State from whom nothing was to be feared. He had always gained by the use of force in such instances, in Tunis, in Annam, in Tonkin. He saw no reason to suppose that he would not gain again. His Cabinet supported him. Parliament and public opinion would object only in the improbable event of a dangerous and costly struggle—and even then opposition could be minimized by appeals to the pride of patriotism. A diplomatic triumph in the Orient would afford compensation for the loss of Egypt to Great Britain and the union of Italy with Germany and Austria-Hungary. An unacceptable ultimatum, a judicious use of military and naval pressure, and China would capitulate. Triumph would be cheap.

The ultimatum was delivered at Pekin by Semallé on July 13. The Chinese reply accepted the demand for evacuation, but denied responsibility for the Langson affair and threatened an appeal to the Powers on the basis of International Law.[1] On the day of the delivery of the ultimatum Peyron instructed Admiral Courbet to send all his ships to Foochow, on the South China coast, and to Kelung, on the island of Formosa, which were to be occupied as "gages" if the demands were rejected. In accordance with the logic of the

[1] *L.J.Tonkin*, Nos. 40, 46, 47, 48.

military mind, Courbet was authorized to seize Chinese ships carrying "contraband of war" or seeking to force the "blockade" of the River Min, and to prevent by force all Chinese war preparations, which were to be regarded as "equivalent to an attack."[1] From a legal point of view, these instructions were of course preposterous, since no war existed. Ferry expressed his satisfaction with the publication of the Imperial Decree for evacuation of Tonkin on July 16, but insisted on the pecuniary indemnity and agreed to halt naval operations until August 1, only on condition that nothing but the amount of the indemnity be discussed in the pending negotiations.[2] Following a Chinese appeal to the Powers, he authorized Patenôtre to discuss the indemnity with Chinese agents at Shanghai and to open negotiations for a definitive treaty on the basis of the convention of May 11.[3] Patenôtre offered to accept 200,000,000 fr. payable in three years if a prompt solution were reached. Ferry repeated that the principle of an indemnity was undebatable.

If they object that the indemnity thus calculated (on the basis of grants to the families of the killed and wounded at Langson and the additional expense of maintaining land and naval forces) does not reach the sums which we claim, you can reply that the affair of Langson had prevented the repatriation, already ordered, of a portion of our troops, that it has inspired an extreme distrust among our compatriots, and that, in order to meet the just demands of public opinion, we shall be obliged to maintain our military and naval forces on the footing of to-day for at least a year.[4]

The Chinese plenipotentiaries at Shanghai were unmoved by such arguments. They pointed out that Chinese acceptance of the indemnity principle would be an admission, in advance of discussion, of Chinese violation of the convention of May 11. Finally, under protest, they offered Patenôtre 3,500,-000 fr. which he refused,[5] announcing, on August 1, that France resumed complete liberty of action.[6]

On August 5, Admiral Lespés attacked and destroyed the defenses of Kelung.[7] This action marked the beginning of hostilities, though war was never formally declared on either side. Ferry subsequently asserted: "We remain in a state, not of declared war, but of reprisals, always ready to reopen negotiations."[8] Diplomatic relations were at no time completely severed. But the nine months of fighting which followed were marked by all the incidents of open warfare. It has become commonplace to say that wars are usually blundered into by statesmen rather than deliberately desired and plotted. This, however, is the defense of diplomats whose policies have resulted in a war in which their State was defeated or which has unleashed

[1] *Ibid.*, No. 44, Peyron to Courbet, July 13.
[2] *Ibid.*, Nos. 50, 53, 56, 59.
[3] *Ibid.*, No. 63, Ferry to Patenôtre, July 23, 1884.
[4] *Ibid.*, No. 66, Ferry to Patenôtre, July 27, 1884.
[5] *Ibid.*, Nos. 75, 76.
[6] *L.J.C. et T.*, No. 6, Patenôtre to Ferry, August 2, 1884.
[7] *Ibid.*, No. 22.
[8] *Ibid.*, No. 42, Ferry to Patenôtre, August 18, 1884.

a catastrophe of such magnitude for all concerned that its authors seek scapegoats instead of laurels. In the Western State System, the statesman is ever concerned with such intangible but none the less controlling considerations as "national honor," "vital interests," diplomatic prestige, the balance of power and the like. These are the standards by which he judges policy. These are the values for which he juggles with territory, economic opportunities, and the other stakes of diplomacy. He serves the State, in its dealings with other States, by the alternative, or frequently complementary, methods of diplomacy and war, discussion and force, compromise and coercion. Having determined his goal in a concrete situation, he must ascertain what method, or what combination of methods, is most likely to lead to its achievement. This will depend upon his foresight and his ability to predict the consequences of a given policy on other interested parties and on the course of events. War results when those in control of policy decide that more is to be achieved by violence than by procedures of peace. Such a decision may be an almost instinctive defense reaction or a rationalization of aggressive purposes.

The Sino-French War of 1884 and 1885 was a result of Ferry's refusal to abandon the position he had originally taken and of his conviction that the goals implied in this position could be more readily obtained by force than by discussion. As a question of law, more can be said for the Chinese side than for the French. But, given on the one hand a disposition to use force, and on the other a disposition to resist force by force, the question was one of power, not of law. The Tsong-Li-Yamen believed (correctly, as subsequent events showed) that it could better resist the French demands by fighting than by unsupported negotiation. Ferry believed (erroneously) that he could better obtain his goal by coercive violence than by talking alone. Had he not gained Tonkin and Annam by an astute combination of diplomacy and force? But just as he misjudged the strength of Chinese diplomatic resistance to his demands, so he misjudged the capacity of China to resist effectively the use of violence to obtain their fulfilment.

With the military and naval events of the war, we need not concern ourselves in detail. When it became apparent that China would not yield to threats and a display of force, Ferry and his advisers were confronted with the baffling problem of inflicting sufficient injury, from distant bases of operations, on the huge hulk of the Chinese Empire to compel it to sue for peace. This had to be done, moreover, in such fashion as not to expose French interests or territory to undue danger from Chinese resistance. Foreign Powers must not be antagonized to the point of imperiling the success of the venture. Great Britain, fortunately, was heavily occupied with the revolt in the Sudan. In France, Parliament and public opinion, being clearly opposed to the war, must be soothed by the appropriate phrases and catchwords to divert attention from the main issue. Time was of the essence of the problem, since protracted hostilities would involve dangerous complications abroad and an embarrassing necessity for credits and explanations at home. If China could be struck down with the secrecy and dispatch with which Tunis had been conquered, these difficulties could be obviated. Unfortunately, China was not a weak State across the Mediterranean but a vast empire on the other side of the globe. In war, political difficulties and diplomatic problems resolve themselves into questions of strategy. Ferry was an astute politician, but certainly not a military tactician, and his diplomacy in the Orient had more of the rude violence of bowling than of the skill and subtlety of chess.

From the outset, the situation was too complicated by factors beyond Ferry's control to justify optimism. As early as July 31, the unfavorable military prospects led Ferry to reduce his indemnity demands to 50,000,000 fr.[1] On August 16, in the face of Chinese recalcitrance, 80,000,000 fr. were insisted upon.[2] Another "ultimatum" was presented to Pekin on August 19, with a forty-eight-hour time limit and a threat of rupturing diplomatic relations and seizing further "gages."[3] While Patenôtre complains of the fatal consequences of indecision and inaction and urges the occupation of Foochow, the Chinese Minister at Paris requests his passports.[4] When Admiral Courbet bombards the forts at Foochow, destroying the arsenal and fleet, with no diplomatic result, Patenôtre agrees with Courbet and Lespés on the necessity of striking a blow in the north near Pekin.[5] The Minister of Marine, Peyron, is disturbed over the transport of Chinese troops in "neutral" ships and urges a declaration of war to prevent this,[6] but Ferry does not dare to endanger the ministry by making such a demand on Parliament. Action in the north is delayed because of fear of diplomatic complications, until the strengthening of the fortifications of Port Arthur and Wei-Hei-Wei and the advance of winter make action impossible. By mid-October even Courbet thinks a decisive blow in the north no longer feasible and demands reinforcements for further operations in the south.[7] In the southern theater of hostilities victories alternate with reverses and the Chinese Government remains adamant. Counsels are divided. Lemaire, the French Minister at Hué, tells Ferry on November 24 that, after all, effective pressure can be exerted only in the north against Pekin. The government should at least send Courbet thirty ships and 7,000 men to enable him to destroy Port Arthur and blockade the Gulf of Petchili.[8] Courbet complains dismally that his fleet is immobilized by the absence of a legal state of war while British vessels carry Chinese troops, money, and munitions to Formosa, which he is

[1] *L. J.C. et T.*, No. 5, Ferry to Patenôtre, July 31, 1884.

[2] *Ibid.*, No. 39, Ferry to Patenôtre. Ferry was encouraged to make his demand by the attitude of the Chambers.

[3] *Ibid.*, No. 47.

[4] *Ibid.*, Nos. 52–54, 55, 60.

[5] *Ibid.*, Nos. 59–71.

[6] *Ibid.*, No. 73, Peyron to Ferry, August 30.

[7] *Ibid.*, No. 114, Patenôtre to Ferry, October 15, 1885.

[8] *Ibid.*, No. 142, Lemaire to Ferry, November 24, 1884.

trying to occupy.[1] From St. Petersburg, Ambassador Appert assures Ferry that only an attack on Pekin will have results, since the Formosa operations are no more than "the sting of a wasp on the back of an elephant."[2] In February, Langson in Tonkin is at length recaptured. Indecisive fighting proceeds in Formosa and Ferry at last decides on the evacuation of Kelung, much to Patenôtre's disgust.[3] Some crumbs must be salvaged when the whole loaf is unobtainable and he is encouraged by news that the Cabinet has decided on the permanent occupation of the Pescadores. "The acquisition of the Pescadores will be, perhaps, the sole enduring advantage, outside of Tonkin, which we will gain from our struggle with China; it is essential not to let them escape."[4] But on March 23 and 24, the forces under Négrier are decisively defeated at Langson and compelled to withdraw. Thus ingloriously ends the military history of the struggle.[5]

Ferry's difficulties were greatly increased by the attitude of other Powers toward the "war." When Pekin appealed to the United States to exercise its good offices under the Sino-American treaty of 1858, Secretary of State Frelinghuysen offered his mediation to Paris.[6] He suggested that the Chinese offer to submit the indemnity question to the arbitration of the President of the United States be accepted by France as a method of avoiding war.[7] Ferry declined these proposals with thanks, and regrets that they had been made.[8] China next sought the mediation of Germany, after the Hamburg boerse had petitioned the Chancellor to oppose any French blockade of the treaty ports.[9] Ferry instructed the French Ambassador at Berlin to decline all German offers of mediation.[10] In September, 1884, however, the German, British, and American chambers of commerce in Shanghai, all demanded the intervention of their Governments to end an intolerable situation.[11] A month later, the American Minister at Pekin offered American arbitration to Patenôtre, a proposal which was repeated two weeks later with a suggestion of a 5,000,000 fr. indemnity.[12] At the same time Great Britain proferred her mediation and early in November both the British and American Governments renewed their pleas.[13]

---

[1] *Ibid.*, No. 162, Patenôtre to Ferry, January 9, 1885.

[2] *Ibid.*, No. 163, Appert to Ferry, January 9, 1885.

[3] *Ibid.*, Nos. 182, 185, Patenôtre to Ferry, March 12 and 16, 1885.

[4] *Ibid.*, No. 189, Patenôtre to Ferry, March 20, 1885.

[5] *Ibid.*, Nos. 195, 198, 210. For a detailed history of the campaigns see Bouinas et Paulus, *L'Indo-Chine français contemporaire*, II, pp. 286–408.

[6] July 23, 1884, *L.J.C. et T.*, No. 1, Frelinghuysen to Morton.

[7] *Ibid.*, No. 6.

[8] *Ibid.*, No 66, August 29, 1884.

[9] *Ibid.*, Nos. 67, 92.

[10] *Ibid.*, No. 94.

[11] *Ibid.*, No. 97.

[12] *Ibid.*, Nos. 102, 117.

[13] *Ibid.*, Nos. 119, 128.

All these offers were rejected by Ferry. Yet he realized that he could ill afford to antagonize the Governments which made them by continuing the conflict indefinitely, and on October 11 he instructed Patenôtre to resume negotiations with no mention of an indemnity, but with equivalent territorial and economic compensations.[1] The military as well as the diplomatic situation enabled China to refuse all such demands and the negotiations again broke down, while Frelinghuysen made known the willingness of the United States to mediate or arbitrate alone or in conjunction with Great Britain or Germany or both.[2] In January the British Government, by way of observance of its neutral obligations, forbade French war vessels to refuel at British ports in the Orient.[3] The detrimental effect of the war on Chinese foreign trade naturally disposed the Governments of the other commercial Powers to seek peace and to look with disfavor upon the French attitude. While none seemed ready to intervene, it was apparent that a prolongation of the indecisive struggle would lead to undesirable international complications.

Even more embarrassing to Ferry was the position of Parliament. Despite the obvious existence of war,[4] the Premier could not risk the overthrow of the Cabinet by asking the Chambers for a formal declaration, as the Constitution required, and felt obliged to pretend that all the military and naval operations were merely reprisals. He was at all times dependent upon Parliament for credits to finance the struggle. To avoid arousing strong opposition, he was obliged to ask for money in small amounts. From May of 1883 to March of 1885, nine separate demands for credits were addressed by the Government to the Chamber: 5,300,000 fr.; 9,000,000; 20,000,000; 38,363,000; 10,811,000; 3,460,000; 1,875,000; 43,422,000; and finally (and fatally) 200,000,000 fr.—the sums demanded rising or falling with the exigencies of the military situation in China and the parliamentary situation at home.[5] The amounts asked were always insufficient and such was the power of the Opposition that Ferry was compelled to make military plans dependent upon parliamentary action. The bombardment of Foochow in August was delayed until Parliament had expressed its confidence in the Government by voting credits.[6] Members of the Opposition demanded economy, peace, and the arbitration of the dispute—all to no avail. During the autumn, Parliament was not in session, and Ferry could act more freely. The extreme Left Deputies, however, addressed a protest to President Grévy on September 1 against the waging of war by the Government without the consent of Parliament and in violation of the Constitution.[7]

[1] *Ibid.*, No. 110.
[2] *Ibid.*, No. 134, November 8, 1884.
[3] Debidour, *op. cit.*, pp. 77*f.*
[4] *Cf.* Despagnet, *op. cit.*, pp. 389–395.
[5] *Cf.* Freycinet, *Souvenirs*, pp. 266–269.
[6] *L.J.C. et T.*, Nos. 30, 39, 41; *J.O.Ch.*, August 15, 1884.
[7] Despagnet, *op. cit.*, p. 383.

When the Chambers reconvened, Ferry was bitterly assailed in a four-day debate on China and Tonkin.[1] But he wrung from the Deputies a credit of 16,147,368 fr. for 1884 and secured an additional appropriation for 1885 of 43,422,000 fr., by a vote of 342 to 170. After heated debate, the Chamber expressed its determination, 295 to 176, "to enforce the full and entire execution of the Treaty of Tien-Tsin" and its confidence in the energy of the Government "to compel respect for the rights of France."[2] The Senate approved the credits by a vote of 189 to 1, allowing itself to be persuaded of their necessity even more easily than the Chamber, by the usual arguments for the sanctity of treaties and appeals to patriotic emotionalism. Ferry sought to gain all the diplomatic and military advantage possible from this endorsement,[3] but with no great success. Dissension in his own household was an additional source of anxiety. In the midst of the debates on the constitutional revision of the composition of the Senate, Waldeck-Rousseau, Minister of the Interior, threatened to resign, in the face of the pleas of Ferry and Grévy that he remain. When Ferry declared that the entire Cabinet would go out with him, he agreed to remain, despite his pessimism over the future of the ministry.[4] General Thibaudin, Minister of War, had resigned in October and been replaced by General Campernon. The latter wished to confine the land operations of the war to the delta of the Red River in Tonkin. Opposed in this by Ferry and the other members of the Cabinet, he resigned on January 3, 1885, and was replaced by General Lewal.[5] When, on January 14, Ferry told the Chamber that the vote of November obliged the Government to use all the means at its disposal to enforce the Treaty of Tien-Tsin, he secured a vote of confidence by the much reduced majority of 280 to 225.[6] While the military operations failed to bring peace, the Government's majority was dwindling to dangerously small proportions. Ferry was assailed by both the extreme Right and the extreme Left as "Tonkinois," "Tunisien," and "Malgache," and the opposition, headed by Clemenceau in Parliament and by Henri Rochefort in the press, constantly painted the Chinese situation as one leading to a national catastrophe.

Under the circumstances discretion appeared the better part of valor and Ferry decided to beat a secret retreat from the position he had originally taken. With great circumspection and a determination to conceal his moves from even his own diplomatic agents, he availed himself of the services of Mr. James Duncan Campbell, commissioner and non-resident secretary of the Inspector-General of the Imperial Chinese Maritime Customs. Campbell, at Paris, was the agent of Sir Robert Hart, the Inspector-General at Pekin,

[1] *J.O.Ch.*, November 24, 1884f.
[2] *J.O.Ch.*, November 29, 1884.
[3] *L.J.C. et T.*, Nos. 143 and 152.
[4] H. Leyret, *Waldeck-Rousseau et la troisième République*, pp. 392f, Paris, 1908.
[5] Despagnet, *op. cit.*, p. 384.
[6] *J.O.Ch.*, January 15, 1885.

and was authorized by the Tsong-Li-Yamen to act as China's secret representative at the French capital. In mid-January, Hart urged Campbell,
on China's behalf, to seek a pacific solution of the controversy.[1] Ferry
welcomed this opportunity and, on February 28, the Emperor transmitted
the draft of a protocol through these secret channels which Campbell was
authorized to sign.[2] Ferry communicated with Campbell with the greatest
caution, taking into his confidence only M. Billot, director of political
affairs at the Quai d'Orsay.

In the devious and involved conversations which ensued, Ferry insisted
upon the utmost secrecy. He abandoned all claims for an indemnity and
sought compensation in commercial advantages and railway concessions,[3]
without, however, obtaining any definite assurances on these points. He
asked some direct word from the Tsong-Li-Yamen, "in order to cover my
responsibility toward the Government and the Chambers."[4] This word, he
said, could be transmitted in the utmost secrecy to the French Consul in
Tien-Tsin. This was done in due time, and the way was thus prepared for the
signature of the protocol at Paris on the basis of the Chinese terms. This
extraordinary procedure was resorted to by Ferry because of his realization
that Patenôtre, who had contributed to the initiation of the conflict, was
unacceptable to the Chinese as an emissary of peace and would doubtless
be an obstacle rather than a help in the negotiations. To remove him and
replace him by another emissary would be equivalent to a reproof to an agent
who had faithfully followed instructions and might be publicly interpreted
as a sign of a change of policy on the Premier's part. Change could only mean
recession from the original position which Ferry had so stoutly adhered to.
Since "saving face" is no less important to a French minister than to a
Chinese official, Ferry chose to ignore Patenôtre and to conduct secret negotiations himself with Hart through Campbell, with Billot as his aid.

The much neglected Patenôtre, who had received only the vaguest information from Ferry regarding these discussions, learned of the transmission
to Paris of the communication of the Tsong-Li-Yamen from the consul himself, M. Ristelhueber, and expressed himself pessimistically regarding these
obscure goings-on in which he played no part. But with great magnanimity
he announced his willingness to efface himself, if such was Ferry's desire.[5]
The conclusion of final arrangements in Paris rendered this sacrifice unneces-

---

[1] *L.J.C. et T.*, No. 165, Hart to Campbell, January 17, 1885.

[2] *Ibid.*, No. 176, Hart to Campbell, February 28, 1885.

[3] *Ibid.*, Nos. 178–180.

[4] *Ibid.*, No. 186, Ferry to Campbell, March 17, 1885.

[5] "M. Ristelheuber a recu de M. Hart avis que Li-Hong-Tchang lui ferait une communication
qui, d'áprès vos ordres, devait être tranmise directement à Paris. Je suis prêt à m'effacer si telles
sont réellement vos instructions; mais les défiances de M. Hart à l'égard de la légation ne vous
semblent-elles pas suspectes? Tout le monde sait ici par ses propres indiscrétions qu'il est en
pourparlers avec vous. Que signifie alors ce prétendu mystère? En outre pourquoi M. Hart recourt-
il maintenant à l'intermédiare de Li-Hong-Tchang?" *L.J.C. et T.*, No. 191, Patenôtre to Ferry,
March 21, 1885.

sary. By March 30, the protocol was ready to sign. It consisted of only three articles and constituted a complete abandonment of Ferry's initial demands of the preceding July.[1]

1. On the one hand, China consents to ratify the convention of of Tien-Tsin of May 11, 1884, and, on the other hand, France declares that she pursues no end other than the full and entire execution of this treaty.

2. The two Powers agree to cease hostilities everywhere, as quickly as the orders may be given and received, and France agrees to raise immediately the blockade of Formosa.

3. France agrees to send a minister to the north, that is to say, to Tien-Tsin or to Pekin, to arrange a detailed treaty, and the two Powers will then fix the date for the withdrawal of troops.[2]

Before this document could be signed, however, disaster had overtaken the Cabinet. On March 25, unfavorable reports were received of General Négrier's expedition operating in Tonkin, north of Langson. Ferry was violently attacked in the Chamber and obtained the *ordre du jour* of confidence by only 259 votes against 209.[3] Four days later came the news of the abandonment of Langson, the wounding of Négrier, and the rout of his forces. This was coupled with a needlessly alarming dispatch from General Brière de l'Isle: " . . . Whatever happens, I hope to be able to defend all the delta . . . "[4] All Paris was thrown into a furor. It appeared that the great catastrophe long predicted by the opposition had at last befallen. The ministers, the Deputies, and the public were in a frenzy. "I do not believe," wrote Waldeck-Rousseau to his mother, "that Waterloo produced such a panic."[5] Everyone suspected the worst in Tonkin while the French occupation of the Pescadores on March 29 escaped notice.[6] Ferry was deserted by almost the entire press, with the exception of *Le Temps* and *La République Française*. The Premier, caught in the entanglements of his secret discussions with Campbell, was in no position to reveal the imminence of peace, on terms which now would have the appearance of a weak surrender in the face of the Chinese victory. Two special sessions of the Cabinet were held and the advice of Waldeck-Rousseau in favor of immediate resignation prevailed. The leaders of the two chief groups supporting the Government, the *Union républicaine* and the *Union démocratique*, sought to induce Ferry to quit without appearing before the chambers. He refused and determined to face his enemies, if only to go down to defeat.[7]

On March 30, Ferry went before the Deputies. Pandemonium greeted his arrival. His demand for a credit of 200,000,000 fr. was met with jeers.

[1] *Ibid.*, Nos. 192, 193, 199.

[2] *Ibid.*, No. 207.

[3] *J.O.Ch.*, March 26, 1885.

[4] Rambaud, *Jules Ferry*, p. 365.

[5] Leyret, *op. cit.*, p. 416.

[6] Debidour, *op. cit.*, I, pp. 94–97; "En réalité, la France avait été vaincue, non sur quelque champ de bataille indo-chinois, mais dans les couloirs et la salle des séances du Palais-Bourbon," Rambaud, *op. cit.*, p. 383.

[7] Leyret, pp. 410*f.*; Rambaud, pp. 359–371.

Clemenceau's rapier became a bludgeon. No discussion was possible, he asserted. "It is no longer a minister, they are no longer ministers, whom I have before me. They are the accused. They are accused of high treason, they, whom the hand of the law would not hesitate to crush if there existed in France any principle of responsibility and justice!" Alexandre Ribot followed in the same vein. Fiery denunciation poured in upon the Cabinet from all sides. The credits were rejected, 306 to 149. "The Chamber, resolved to make all sacrifices to maintain the integrity of the national honor and confident of the bravery of the army, blames the faults committed, regrets not having known the truth until now, and passes to the order of the day." While an angry mob attempted to storm the Palais Bourbon and the Quai d'Orsay, shouting "Down with Ferry!" "Death to Ferry!" the beaten Premier took a hidden door out of the Chamber.[1]

Despite these dramatic events, the secret conversations with Campbell drew to a close. The Chinese Court was content to make peace upon the terms already agreed to, without taking advantage of the fall of Langson to its troops.[2] Ferry hesitated to bind his still unchosen successor by signing the protocol. M. Billot of the Ministry of Foreign Affairs was unable to sign without a grant of full powers from President Grévy, which the latter was reluctant to grant. On April 3 Hart reported the impatience of the Tsong-Li-Yamen to Campbell and warned that a week's delay might ruin the work of the past three months.[3] On the following day the protocol was signed, by Campbell for China and by M. Billot for France. The entire procedure reveals the ease with which the foreign minister can personally inaugurate and complete negotiations which remain secret even from the diplomatic service. A permanent official at the Quai d'Orsay, at the behest of a repudiated Premier, brought to a close by the stroke of a pen an international conflict of almost a year's duration. An "explanatory note" provided for an armistice, contained a schedule for the cessation of hostilities, and contemplated the early conclusion of a definite treaty of peace, amity, and commerce.

On the same day on which the Chinese Government ratified the Convention of Tien-Tsin (April 6), Henri Brisson became Premier in a "Cabinet of union and conciliation" in which Freycinet was again Minister of Foreign Affairs. In the declaration which he read to the Chambers on April 7, Freycinet confined his references to China to an expression of the Government's determination to compel the observance of the original convention of May 11, 1884.[4] Not until April 17 did he make known to the diplomatic

[1] *J.O.Ch.*, March 31, 1885; Freycinet, *Souvenirs*, pp. 279–283.

[2] *L.J.C. et T.*, No. 200, Hart to Campbell.

[3] *Ibid.*, Nos. 201–205.

[4] "Nous demanderons à la Chine le respect de nos droits tels qu'ils résultent des traités, tels qu'elle les a reconnus elle-même dans la Convention du 11 mai 1884: heureux si des négociations suffisent pour atteindre ce but, mais résolus à le poursuivre par les armes, décidés aussi à ne pas

service the terms of the agreement which had been signed on April 4.[1] At his order, M. Cogordon, a *sous-directeur* at the Quai d'Orsay, had a two-hour interview with Campbell on April 19, in which it was agreed that a short and simple treaty of peace on the basis of the Campbell-Billot protocol should be concluded.[2] French evacuation of Formosa and the Pescadores was accepted and Freycinet sought special tariff privileges and railway concessions. The commercial treaty, however, was to be left to later negotiations. On May 11, Freycinet sent to Patenôtre the draft treaty of peace which he had agreed upon with Campbell at Paris.[3] On June 9 the treaty of ten articles was signed at Tien-Tsin by Patenôtre and Li-Hong-Chang. The festivities which ensued were marred only by the death of Admiral Courbet in the Pescadores on June 11 and the unexpressed regret which Patenôtre must have felt at the futility of a war from which he had expected so much.

The new treaty of Tien-Tsin differed little from the original one. France again agreed to respect and guarantee the Chinese frontier of Tonkin, (Article 1). Each party was to deal with pirates and pillagers on its own side. The frontier was to be charted by a special commission and China agreed to quit Tonkin and to respect all past and future treaties between France and Annam (Article 2). In the special convention regulating land commerce over the Tonkin frontier, French trade would be granted lower tariff duties than those prevailing in the treaty ports (Article 6), and China agreed to address herself, though not exclusively, to French industry and the French Government for railway construction (Article 7). France was to evacuate within one month all Chinese territory which had been occupied (Article 9). The question of the indemnity for the Langson affair, for the sake of which the war had been ostensibly fought, was conveniently disposed by discreet silence on both sides.[4] China had successfully resisted the French demands and had emerged from the combat with such laurels of victory as remained.

3. SIAM

Eight years after the Chinese war, France became involved in another conflict in the Far East—this time with the ancient Kingdom of Siam, bordering on Cambodia and divided from Annam by the River Mekong. As early as the seventeenth century, projects of a French protectorate over Siam had been discussed. French missionaries, arriving in 1662, on the heels of the

---

modifier la caractère de l'expédition sans le consentiment du Parlement. Le sentiment de ce que nous devons à nos héroïques troupes de terre et de mer et à leurs chefs nous trouvera d'ailleurs facilement unanimes," *J.O.Ch.*, April 8, 1885.

[1] *L.J.C. et T.*, No. 238.

[2] *Ibid.*, No. 241.

[3] *Ibid.*, No. 252.

[4] Text in *L.J.C. et T.*, No. 281, Patenôtre to Freycinet, June 13, 1885.

Portuguese, the Spaniards, the Dutch, and the English, had been well received, and had created a friendly feeling toward France at the Siamese Court. When the Dutch appeared to be threatening the integrity and the independence of the kingdom, Constance Phalkon, First Minister of the King Pra-Narai (1656–1688), turned to France for aid. In 1680 he sent an embassy to Europe, carrying rich presents, letters for the Pope and Louis XIV, and an offer of the cities of Bangkok and Mergui to France. Unfortunately, the expedition was lost in a storm off the cost of Madagascar. A new mission arrived in 1684, however, and expressed the desire to their monarch to receive a French diplomatic mission in Siam. The "Sun King" sent one the following year, chiefly for the purpose of converting Pra-Narai to Catholicism. While the Siamese King and his ministers sought an offensive and defensive alliance against the Dutch, the French representatives insisted on the monarch's baptism, a ceremony to which he remained singularly indifferent. The only result was a treaty of December 5, 1685, providing for religious freedom and the protection of missionaries. The determined ruler sent a new mission to France in 1686, again asking for a protectorate. A French mission, accompanied by 630 troops, left for Siam in 1687, with the triple task of conversion, conquest, and commerce promotion, but its leaders were divided as to the relative importance of the three duties, and the entire project failed of achievement. An antiforeign revolution in 1688 led to the death of Phalkon, the deposition of the King, the destruction of French influence, and the ascendency of new leaders friendly to the Dutch.[1]

Not until the middle of the nineteenth century did the Quai d'Orsay interest itself again in Siam—and then not for the conversion of the King, nor the assumption of a protectorate over the country, but for the acquisition of commercial privileges. In 1826 the Siamese had concluded a commercial treaty with Great Britain, which had long since replaced the Netherlands as the great trading and imperial Power in the South China Sea and the Bay of Bengal. Seven years later the United States secured the same privileges granted to the British by a most-favored-nation treaty. The British treaty of 1855 granted most-favored-nation treatment and the rights of extraterritoriality; again the United States followed suit in the following year. After much hesitation and delay, Montigny, French Consul at Shanghai, was dispatched to Siam to secure the same privileges for France. The treaty of August 15, 1856 not only placed French nationals in a position of equality with Americans and Britishers, but allowed French warships to ascend the Menam River up to Pak-Nam and thence, on condition of warning the Siamese authorities, to Bangkok.[2] Despite francophil inclinations on the part of the Siamese, French indifference and the diplomacy of Downing Street gave Great Britain a predominant influence in the kingdom. The establish-

[1] C. Seauve, Les rélations de la France et du Siam, pp. 1–23, Paris, 1908.

[2] Ibid., pp. 25–52; text of treaty in Bouinas et Paulus, L'Indo-Chine française contemporaine, II, pp. 788–790.

ment of French control at Saigon, however, near the mouth of the Mekong, cut off an important outlet to the sea for both Siam and Annam and wrecked the designs of these States upon Cambodia, which became a French Protectorate in 1863. By the treaty of July 15, 1867, Siam recognized the protectorate, renouncing all its own claims to suzerainty over Cambodia, and France, in return, ceded to Siam the Cambodian provinces of Battanbang and Angkor. A boundary commission was established to define the frontier but it never accomplished its task. The problems of conflicting territorial claims were left in abeyance, while French activities were concentrated in Annam and Tonkin.[1]

Apparently with British encouragement, the Government of Siam, in the late eighties, adopted an unfriendly attitude toward the expansion of French territory and influence in the region of its frontiers. Cochin-China, Cambodia, Annam, and Tonkin had each in turn fallen prey to French imperialism. Perhaps frightened by the movement of the juggernaut in its direction, and possibly encouraged by the successful resistance of China to French demands in 1884 to 1885, Siam began fishing in the troubled waters of the Upper Mekong in the confused and anarchic hinterland of the Laos. Here Chinese bandits, French agents, British officials, and venturesome traders jostled one another before an unorganized and defenseless native population. Boundaries were vague and territorial claims everywhere conflicted. France asserted title to the entire east or left bank of the Mekong, and a portion of the right bank on the basis of the implications of the treaty of 1867, while Siam sought to extend its control over all of the right bank on the not unreasonable assumption that the river itself was the logical frontier between its own lands and French Annam.

Late in 1885, Pavie was appointed French vice consul at Luang-Prabang in the realm of the Laotians. When he arrived at his post in February of 1887 he found the Siamese installed on the right bank of the Mekong. In October he became president of a Franco-Siamese Commission to study the frontier. With great foresight, he persuaded the principal chief of the Pavillons Noirs, who were operating in the vicinity, to accept French control, and induced the local Siamese commander to respect the *status quo*. In March, 1889, the Siamese administrators agreed to do likewise. The formal negotiations would thus be opened with all the advantages on the French side. But the Siamese Government protested, disclaimed the agreements of its agents, and countered the French moves by occupying the entire right bank and a portion of the left.[2] Pavie thereupon refused to negotiate. Leaving Bangkok, he continued his geographical explorations in the disputed area and at last decided to return to Paris to confer with the appropriate authorities on a future policy. In the French capital he urged upon the Ministers of Foreign Affairs and Colonies a vigorous defense of the French protensions and met with a favor-

[1] Despagnet, *La diplomatie de la troisième République*, pp, 546–548.
[2] Seauve, *op. cit.*, pp. 55–67.

able reception.[1] In June, 1892, he returned to Bangkok as minister pleni-potentiary with instructions to press the French claim energetically.

In the preceding September the Siamese agents on the Upper Mekong kidnapped the Annamite official at Tran-Ninh, the Bambien of Tong-Xieng-Kham, who had asked French support against the Siamese "invasion." In September, 1892, two French nationals, MM. Champernois and Esquilot, were expelled from Outhène and a month later M. Massie, the French agent at Luang-Prabang, committed suicide, supposedly because of despair at his isolation and the insults of the Siamese.[2] These incidents produced something of a sensation at Paris and led the Chambers to approve of the Government's position. On February 4, 1893, M. Théophile Delcassé, the Colonial under-secretary of state in the second Ribot Cabinet (January 11 to April 4, 1893), announced to the Deputies that France would insist upon the entire left bank of the Mekong.[3] In March, Pavie demanded of the Siamese Government the immediate evacuation of the left bank, the release of the Bambien, a disa-vowal of the conduct of the Siamese agents in the affairs of Outhène and Tran-Ninh, and the payment of reparations.[4] A warship was dispatched to Bangkok to support the French demands. The Siamese suggestions of an investigation and arbitration of the dispute were rejected and when "satis-faction" was not forthcoming, French troops were ordered to oust the Siamese from the posts they had occupied.

This decision to resort to force was again a result of the initiative of the ministry, confident of parliamentary support and the acquiescence of public opinion, so long as success was assured and dangerous complications with powerful States were avoided. Pavie, who might be called the Patenôtre of the war with Siam, was the agent on the scene who recommended violence as a more effective diplomatic weapon than discussion. The Premier, Charles Dupuy (April 4 to December 3, 1893), was absorbed in domestic matters. In his Cabinet (notable for including among its names for the first time that of Raymond Poincaré as Minister of Public Instruction), Jules Develle re-mained Minister of Foreign Affairs, holding the post he had occupied in the brief Ribot ministry. He had been Minister of Agriculture in the three preceding Cabinets and felt reasonably secure in his position. He was left a relatively free hand by the Premier. In collaboration with General Loizillon (War), Vice Admiral Rieunier (Marine), and Delcassé, who continued as under-secretary of state for Colonies, he formulated a policy of coercion which was designed to enhance French territory and prestige at Siam's expense. The Siamese had hoped for British support and had engaged the Belgian jurist, Rolyn Jacquemins, to refute the French arguments. But arguments and protests were futile when French columns occupied Stung-

[1] Auguste Pavie, *Mission Pavie—Indo-Chine*, I, pp. 214f., Paris, 1911.

[2] Seauve, *op. cit.*, pp. 69–78.

[3] *J.O.Ch.*, February 5, 1893.

[4] Seauve, *op. cit.*, pp. 70-76; Despagnet, *op. cit.*, p. 549.

Treng, the island of Khône, Ai-Lao, and portions of the left bank of the Mekong. These operations, which went on during May, 1893, encountered no effective resistance from the Siamese forces, who, for the most part, retired peaceably before the French troops. "Incidents" were almost inevitable, however. A Captain Thoreux and his convoy were captured at one point by the Siamese, and at Keng-Kiek Inspector Grosgurin and his escort were slain. The French Government demanded explanations, ordered Admiral Humann to proceed at once to Saigon, put the garrisons of Indo-China on a war footing, and sent a battalion of the Foreign Legion as reinforcements.[1] The Siamese returned the Captain to French custody, with a disavowal and offer of reparations, but took the view that the death of Grosgurin was an inevitable incident of warfare.

Suspicions of British support of Siam were rife. In March, Lord Roseberry assured Waddington that Great Britain had no interest in the Franco-Siamese conflict, while Lord Dufferin at Paris told Develle that France would never find the British in her way in this controversy. In June the French press began speaking of the advisability of a naval attack on Bangkok. Though Develle denied the intention, Sir Edward Grey, speaking in the House of Commons on July 29, said that the British Government was unfamiliar with French designs and had sent three war vessels to Siamese waters. Develle's complaints were met with assurances that the sole purpose of the expedition was to protect British subjects.[2] Le Myre de Vilers was sent as Minister Extraordinary to Siam shortly afterwards. In his instructions of July 8, Develle told him to demand reparations, indemnities, and recognition of French rights on the left bank, while disclaiming any designs on Siamese independence and refusing to deal with any foreign advisers of the Government at Bangkok. If the demands were refused, he was to withdraw to the French warships which would institute a blockade. At the same time the Siamese Government was informed that since "certain foreign governments" had resolved to increase their naval forces at Bangkok, France was sending two additional war vessels to join the one already there.[3]

The battleship Lupin was already anchored at Bangkok, which is well up the River Menam, emptying into the sea below Pak-Nam. In July, Captain Bory arrived at the river mouth with L'Inconstant and La Comète. Pavie had insisted that the vessels should anchor at Pak-Nam, the port of Bangkok, as authorized by the treaty of 1856. The Siamese Government refused his demand. In the face of threatened resistance, Pavie, at Bangkok, ordered Bory to halt his vessels before Pak-Nam, in accordance with instructions just received from the Quai d'Orsay.[4] Admiral Humann, however, ordered him to proceed to Bangkok as originally planned, being apparently in ignorance

[1] Seauve, op. cit., pp. 80–81.
[2] Despagnet, op. cit., p. 550.
[3] Seauve, op. cit., p. 82.
[4] Despagnet, p. 552. According to Seauve (p. 83), these instructions did not arrive until July 14.

of the latest diplomatic decisions. Bory, either out of ignorance of Pavie's orders or out of a feeling that his first duty was to his superior officer in the Marine, obeyed the latter's command. A passage was forced through on July 13, in the face of the fire of the forts, which sank the pilot boat and slightly damaged the warships, with a loss of three killed and three wounded. Develle then decided that the ships should remain at Bangkok with the *Lupin*, ready to bombard the royal palace but not firing unless attacked or threatened.[1]

On July 18 Develle presented in the Chamber an exposé of Franco-Siamese relations which he repeated in the Senate two days later. He declared that despite the recent incidents the Government wished to avoid war with Siam because of the cost and the danger of complications with Great Britain. It would accordingly limit its activites to the demonstration at Bangkok, while insisting on reparation for all wrongs done and a full recognition of all French claims.[2] The cries of "respect for French rights" and "indispensable guaranties" carried the order of the day unanimously in both houses in favor of the Cabinet's policies. So long as the parliamentarians were not pinched too sharply by demands for large credits affecting their constituents' pocketbooks, and so long as the Government seemed to be steering clear of extended and dangerous adventures, the Chambers were prepared to sanction the undeclared war which Develle and his colleagues in the ministry were waging. Thus reinforced, Develle felt free to press the issue. Pavie presented the French demands in full on July 20: first, formal recognition by Siam of the rights of Cambodia and Annam to the left bank of the Mekong and the islands in the stream; second, complete evacuation, within one month, of all the Siamese posts on the left bank; third, reparation for the attacks on French agents and war vessels; fourth, punishment of the guilty and indemnities to the families of the victims; fifth, two million francs for French nationals who had suffered from Siamese exactions; sixth, a deposit of three million francs to guarantee the execution of these engagements. These demands were presented in a forty-eight-hour ultimatum, under threat of a diplomatic rupture and the immediate imposition of a blockade. Two hours before the time limit expired, the Siamese Government declared itself ready to give satisfaction on all points, but unwilling to give up the islands or the territory left of the Mekong and north of 18 degrees without a guarantee of common use by the adjoining States. On July 26, 1893, Pavie withdrew to the ships and the blockade began on Humann's orders.[3]

The blockading squadron did not limit itself to intercepting only Siamese vessels, in accordance with the established rules of pacific blockade, but barred all commerce with Bangkok—a step permissible only as a war measure

---

[1] Seauve, p. 82, and Despagnet, pp. 552–553. A full military and diplomatic account of the war is contained in Pavie, *op. cit.*, I, pp. 214–252; VI, pp. 311*f.*

[2] *J.O.Ch.*, July 19, 1893.

[3] Despagnet, pp 553–556; A. de Pouvourville, *L'affaire de Siam*, pp. 205–268, Paris, 1897.

and especially injurious to the British who enjoyed 90 per cent of the trade. War had not been declared by the Chambers, however, and Develle disclaimed any intention of inaugurating a state of war in the official sense. On July 25, Grey, in the Commons, asserted that the blockade was obviously belligerent. Much uncertainty prevailed and the situation promised to become increasingly embarrassing. Develle had officially fixed July 31 as the date of the beginning of the blockade. On July 30, Lord Roseberry learned from the British Minister at Bangkok that the French commander had ordered the British gunboats to leave the river. Such a demand was wholly unacceptable, and in London war was expected to ensue. So grave was the danger that an appeal for support was made to the Kaiser who was visiting at Cowes. On July 31, however, news was received that the earlier dispatch was a result of a misunderstanding. No such order had been given by the French commander, though his subordinates had acted discourteously. Thus there disappeared, as quickly as it had arisen, what has been called the gravest crisis in Anglo-French relations before Fashoda.[1]

Siamese expectations of British support were disappointed. The British Government took the view that a speedy settlement was preferable to a prolongation of the conflict, so long as France was not cherishing designs on Siam's independence nor contemplating serious encroachments on her territory. Siam had, in fact, submitted before the Franco-British war scare arose. On July 29, the Siamese representative in Paris, possibly on British advice, informed Develle that Siam would accept all the conditions of the ultimatum. On the thirtieth, the foreign minister made two new demands: French occupation of the river and port at Chantaboum until Siamese evacuation of the left bank of the Mekong was completed, and Siamese acceptance of a neutralized zone adjacent to the river and the frontier, within which Siam would keep no armed forces save police. Siam had no alternative but to submit. Her capital was at the mercy of the French naval forces and no aid was forthcoming from foreign quarters. The capitulation was followed by the lifting of the blockade on August 4.[2]

The subsequent negotiations culminated in the treaty of October 3, 1893, signed by Le Myre de Vilers for France and Prince Devawongse-Varoprakar for Siam. By its terms Siam renounced all claims to the territory on the left bank of the Mekong and the islands in the river (Article 1), agreed to forbid all armed vessels on the waters of the Grand Lake, of the Mekong, and of their tributaries (Article 2), and undertook to construct no fortifications and keep no armed forces save police in the provinces of Battanbang and Angkor and within a zone of twenty-five kilometers on the right bank of the Mekong (Articles 3 and 4). Within these territories no customs duties were to be established until a special agreement had been reached for the revision of the

[1] For a full account of this incident, see W. L. Langer, *The Franco-Russian Alliance*, pp. 325-333, Harvard University Press, 1929.
[2] Despagnet, pp. 556-558.

Treaty of 1856 (Article 5). The French Government was authorized to establish coal and wood stations on the right bank of the Mekong and consular offices wherever convenient, and French citizens were granted a right of free circulation in the specified zones. An annexed convention provided for the delivery of the Bambien and the trial of various persons involved in the offenses against French and Annamite agents by the Siamese authorities, with a French judge assisting who had a right to demand a retrial. France was to occupy Chantaboum pending the complete execution of the convention, apparently in lieu of the suggested deposit of money. No indemnity was demanded and no territorial annexations were provided for.[1]

The leniency of these terms is explicable only by the tentative Anglo-French agreement which had already been reached regarding Siam. On July 31, Develle and Dufferin had agreed to create a commission to assign limits to the proposed intermediate zone between the French possessions in Tonkin, Annam, and Laos, and the British territory to the west in Burma. Develle had named M. Jusserand, then an official in one of the geographical subdivisions of the Quai d'Orsay, and M. Paul Revoil, chief of his *cabinet*, as the French members. Messrs. Phipps and Austin Lee represented the British Government. The four met for the first time on October 16 at the Quai d'Orsay, but failed to agree because of a lack of precise topographical information. But it was agreed that navigation, transit, and communication should remain free in the intermediate zone and that neither party should seek advantages not accorded to the other. The "open door" was thus to be maintained and a joint investigation was to be made on the scene.[2] It is not clear from the record that these discussions were linked up with the terms of the Siamese peace treaty. The two problems were inseparable, however, and it appears reasonably well established that the treaty of October 3, 1893, reflected a decision on Develle's part to seek his ends not by taking full advantage of his opportunities to coerce Siam but by reaching an *entente* with Great Britain.

Prolonged negotiations followed the conclusion of the treaty, because of its alleged non-execution on the part of Siam. The French continued to hold Chantaboum and to object to the degree to which Siamese authority was exercised in the neutral zone. Endless discussion went on year by year, until a new convention was signed at Paris on October 7, 1902, by Delcassé and the Siamese Minister, fixing the frontier, allowing Siam to keep troops in the Mekong basin, giving France a right of protection over persons born within the French protectorates and their children, and providing for French participation in the construction of public works along the Mekong.[3] By

[1] *L.J.Siam*, pp. 1–4.

[2] *L.J.Haut-Mekong*, Casimir-Périer to Maurice Lebon, with attached documents of the Develle-Dufferin agreements; *cf.* Seauve, *op. cit.*, pp. 89–97.

[3] *L.J.Siam*, No. 79; *cf.* No. 80, Delcassé to Dutasta, October 25, 1902: " . . . La préparation d un vaste champ d'expansion pour notre industrie a été une de mes principales préoccupations . . . "

the new frontier, France gained a substantial triangle of territory west of the Mekong, on the right bank. Chantaboum was not finally evacuated until January of 1904. On February 13, 1904, a new convention modified the frontier once more to the advantage of France and the Treaty of March 23, 1907, ceded to France a large block of territory northeast of Chantaboum in return for the suppression of the right of protection referred to above and the relinquishment to Siam of a small area around Kratt seized three years previously.[1]

In all these negotiations, in which France gained all and more than had originally been demanded, Siam was little more than a silent third party. France and Great Britain were the real bargainers. As early as 1896 the two Powers had agreed to "uphold the independence of the Kingdom of Siam," to neutralize the basin of the Mekong, to divide it into spheres of influence, and to exclude any third Power.[2] Siam was thus spared the fate of Annam and Cambodia by the stalemate between the two great imperial Powers in the Indo-Chinese peninsula. Her "independence" was preserved, though not without large losses of territory to both her powerful neighbors, because neither Great Britain nor France would permit the other to destroy it and was unwilling to risk the dangers of unilateral action. If Siam emerged from the "war" of 1893 with small losses, the explanation is to be found here and not in Franco-Siamese relations themselves. Larger stakes of diplomacy dictated an Anglo-French *rapprochement*. If Develle and Delcassé could wage war on Siam on their own initiative and without reference to constitutional formalities, they could no less easily choose compromise in preference to conflict with the British Empire and mend their sails accordingly. Siam was the victim and the beneficiary of this decision.

[1] Seauve, *op. cit.*, pp. 97–120; R. Millet, *Notre politique extérieure de 1898 à 1905*, pp. 36–75, Paris, 1905.

[2] *L.J.Siam et H.M.*, Declaration of January 15, 1896.

CHAPTER VI

MADAGASCAR

1. WAR

I N the southern Indian Ocean, off the southeast coast of Africa, lies the
huge island of Madagascar, larger in area than France itself, and in-
habited by a congerie of tribes and peoples who came originally from the
African mainland or from the South Sea islands, some thousands of miles
to the east. On the central plateau dwell the so-called Hovas, a Polynesian
people, who dominate the more primitive races scattered along the northern
and eastern coasts and who established, in the seventeenth century, the
Kingdom of Emyrna or Merina, to which most of the other tribes were
compelled to acknowledge allegiance. Since the island lies directly athwart
the south African trade route to the Indies, it early became an object of
European interest. In 1642 Richelieu participated in the establishment of the
Société de Madagascar for the purpose of colonization and Louis XIII ordered
French agents to take possession of it in the name of the King. Efforts at
European settlement proved impractical, however, and had entirely ceased
by the end of the century. Several French posts were again established on the
coast in 1810, taken by the British in 1811, partially reoccupied in 1819, and
finally abandoned.

During the early nineteenth century the island was frequently a bone of
contention between the missionaries, traders, and military agents of Great
Britain and France. Several minor French expeditions were dispatched to
the coasts—the most important in 1829 and 1845—but met with such vigor-
ous resistance from the Hovas that they were without permanent results.[1]
Only along the northwest coast, where the power of the Hovas was feeble,
were the French able to establish a foothold. In 1840 Tsimiharo, chief of the
Sakalaves, often at war with the Hovas, ceded to France all his rights in
Ankara, the northern region of the island, and on the near-by islets, Nossy-
Mitsou and Nossy-Faly, receiving in return an annual pension from France.[2]
This "protectorate" was never recognized by the Hova Government, which
defeated the Sakalaves and established small garrisons in the region. On
September 12, 1862, the French Government signed its first formal treaty
with Madagascar, then ruled by Radama II, who granted commercial,

[1] *Cf.* P. Gaffarel, *Notre expansion coloniale en Afrique*, pp. 257–269, Paris, 1918; and L. Brunet,
La France à Madagascar, pp. 1–194, Paris, 1895.

[2] *L.J.Mad.*, 1881–1883, No. 1, Baudais to Gambetta, November 16, 1881.

property, and religious rights to French nationals, subject to the regulations of local law. The monarch was assassinated the following year, but a second treaty of August 8, 1869, with Queen Ranavalo-Manjaka II confirmed the rights granted by the first. She was recognized as the ruler of the whole of the island and no effort was made to enforce the "protectorate" on the northwest coast, though it was never formally renounced by Paris.[1]

After 1870, French nationals in Madagascar encountered less friendly treatment at the hands of the Hova authorities, because of the alleged influence of English Methodist missionaries and other British subjects. In 1881, the Queen prepared to take effective possession of the northwest coast. Ferry, determined as always to protect French "rights" everywhere, decided to resist these "encroachments." The legal bases of the French "protectorate" were shaky, but the Premier was determined to make the most of the agreements of the 1840's with the Sakalave chieftains. Baudais, French Consul and Commissioner at the Hova capital, Tananarive (or Antananarivo), was instructed to protest vigorously against the action of the Queen's Government.[2] His efforts were vain and he concluded that "all protests made without the support of a certain force in the waters of Madagascar will always have the same result."[3] Another source of difficulty was the recently enacted Law No. 85, based on an old Madagascar custom, by which all land was declared to be the property of the Queen and its alienation to foreigners was forbidden. When the heirs of M. Laborde, former French Consul, who had died in 1878, claimed his estate, valued at over one million francs, obstacles were interposed by the Hovas on the ground that title to land could not be transmitted under the new legislation. Offers of compensation were made, but the French Government took the view that the law amounted to confiscation and was in violation of Article 4 of the Treaty of 1868.[4] Baudais suggested a naval demonstration to compel the withdrawal of the Statute, which, he declared, menaced the rights of all French property owners on the island. The Hovas took the view that since the law did not prevent French nationals from buying land but only forbade its sale by the Queen's subjects, it was no violation of the treaty.[5]

Freycinet, Minister of Foreign Affairs and Premier from January to August of 1882, was moved to caution by the internal situation and the realization that the sentiment which had opposed the Tunis adventure would scarcely welcome a policy of force in Madagascar in defense of French property holders. He was especially anxious to avoid any appearance of designs against Hova independence, lest foreign complications and domestic opposition should undermine the position of the ministry. He advised

---

[1] Despagnet, *La diplomatie de la troisième République*, pp. 345f.

[2] *L.J.Mad.*, 1881–1883, No. 1.

[3] *Ibid.*, No. 2., Baudais to Gambetta, December 1, 1881.

[4] *Ibid.*, No. 2.

[5] *Ibid.*, No. 3.

Baudais to defend French rights and interests by diplomatic representations at their violation, but to avoid impatience or precipitate action. Baudais adopted an imperious attitude, expressed increasing alarm over Hova designs on the northwest coast, and finally left the capital in June, 1882, after anti-French demonstrations and several acts of violence against French nationals.[1] Shortly afterwards he ordered the chancellor of the consulate, who was maintaining a slender thread of diplomatic contact, to withdraw to the coast at Tamatave, to which he himself had retired, and told Freycinet that France must demand complete satisfaction or "abandon" Madagascar.[2]

Under these circumstances, the Hova Government dispatched a special diplomatic mission to Paris. It arrived in October and opened negotiations with Decrais, director of political affairs at the Quai d'Orsay, Billot, director of political and commercial claims, and Admiral Peyron, chief of the general staff at the Ministry of Marine and Colonies. These gentlemen had been named for the purpose by Duclerc, the new Premier and Minister of Foreign Affairs, and seemed to share the views Baudais had expressed rather than those of Freycinet. They were unyielding in the face of arguments that the French "protectorate" in the north had no sound legal foundation and insisted on an interpretation of the Treaty of 1868 which would make Law No. 85 a violation of French rights. In the preceding discussion the problem of the "protectorate" had loomed largest. The Hova delegates now offered to recognize French claims, withdraw their posts, and remove their customs offices in the disputed region, on condition that the French withdraw their protests against the Hova legislation and accept, in lieu of an unqualified right of French nationals to hold property in Madagascar, an arrangement based upon renewable twenty-five-year leaseholds. This solution was rejected by the Quai d'Orsay and the negotiations were broken off.[3]

In November the Hova delegates went to London, where they received some sympathy in the press but no offer of diplomatic support. Lord Lyons, the British Ambassador in Paris, informed Duclerc, however, that hostile action on the part of France would endanger the entire white population of the island and asked him to exercise caution.[4] Duclerc, in reply, contented himself with restating the French grievances. A British tender of good offices was coldly received, as was the copy of the article of the renewed treaty between Great Britain and Madagascar relating to property rights. The British Government pointed out that British subjects were granted leaseholds with all the advantages of ownership for any term specified in the contract and hoped that a similar arrangement might be made with France.[5] When no response was forthcoming, it asked whether it should

---

[1] *Ibid.*, Nos. 6–14.
[2] *Ibid.*, No. 15.
[3] *Ibid.*, Nos. 23–28, 40.
[4] *Ibid.*, No. 35.
[5] *Ibid.*, No. 37.

transmit any further views of the French Government to the Hova representatives. On January 24, 1883, Duclerc told Lyons that in his opinion no useful purpose would be served by so doing.[1]

This obvious determination to obstruct a peaceful settlement with the Hovas is in striking contrast to the conciliatory attitude usually assumed in similar disputes between Great Powers. The Government at Tananarive was prepared to grant the French territorial claims in the north and the substance of the property rights demanded. Duclerc's refusal to accept the offer cannot be explained by his solicitude for the interests of French property owners nor by his self-righteous defense of French legal rights. It is clear that he, like Bauvais and certain officials at the Quai d'Orsay, were entertaining more ambitious political designs on Madagascar and were seeking to use the occasion as an opportunity for putting them into execution.

This group was undeterred by the fall of the ministry on a domestic issue and the coming into office of the brief ministry of Fallières (January 29 to February 21, 1883). The new *ad interim* Minister of Marine and Colonies, De Mahy, was an advocate of forcible measures. He brushed aside opposition and ordered a squadron under Admiral Pierre to sail from Toulon for Madagascar.[2] On February 15, 1883, the fleet took to the high seas. Its instructions, as supplemented by the orders of Charles Brun, new Minister of Marine in the second Ferry Cabinet (February 21, 1883, to April 6, 1885), contemplated the destruction of the Hova posts in the north, the occupation of Majunga on the northwest coast, the seizure of the customs there, and the dispatch of an ultimatum to the Queen. The ultimatum was to demand Hova recognition of French rights of "sovereignty or (*sic*) protectorate" on the northwest coast, full enforcement of the 1868 Treaty, and an indemnity of one million francs.[3] The same terms were outlined in the dispatch sent to Baudais by Challemel-Lacour, the new foreign minister.[4] This was the diplomacy of war. Yet Parliament, which constitutionally possesses the power to declare war, had not even been consulted on the policy which was adopted. Ferry's attitude toward the Chambers was doubtless dictated in part by the eternal irritation of the executive at legislative control and in part by the realization, already confirmed by painful experience, that his imperialistic foreign policies, if openly avowed, would not command the support of the Deputies. He felt obliged to move behind a façade of verbiage, with a minimum of publicity as to what his purposes actually were.

Admiral Pierre reached Madagascar in April. Majunga was seized and the Hovas driven from the north coast. The ultimatum was delivered on June 1, 1883, and rejected.[5] The important port of Tamatave on the east

---

[1] *Ibid.*, Nos. 39, 40. The date is erroneously given in the Livre Jaune as 1884.

[2] L. Brunet, *L'oeuvre de la France à Madagascar*, p. 17, Paris, 1903.

[3] *L.J.Mad.*, 1882–1883, No. 5, Brun to Pierr, March 17, 1883.

[4] *Ibid.*, No. 8, Challemel-Lacour to Baudais, March 25, 1883.

[5] *Ibid.*, No. 25.

coast was then bombarded and occupied. Repeated Hova assaults were repulsed with heavy losses and the city placed under a state of siege. The French Vice Consul was made mayor and the foreign consuls, not being accredited to the French authorities, were deprived of their functions.[1] Foreign protests obliged Challemel-Lacour to rescind the last two measures and declare that the occupation was only temporary.[2] The British Government was particularly irritated at Pierre's conduct in ordering the British Consul to leave within twenty-four hours, in severing communications between British vessels and the shore, and in arresting the consul's secretary and a former missionary, Mr. Shaw, on a charge of trying to poison the French soldiers.[3] Shaw was finally released and was paid an indemnity of 25,000 fr. out of the secret funds of the Ministry of Foreign Affairs in order to avoid a parliamentary debate which might increase the friction between the two Governments.[4] Admiral Pierre having fallen ill and died on his way back to Marseilles, Admiral Galiber continued his work by occupying several more points on the coast. The summer and autumn of 1883 passed in desultory operations which were without the desired effects. With no prospect of a Hova capitulation and with Ferry heavily involved in the Far East, the Premier now took the portfolio of foreign affairs himself and resumed negotiations in November, but with no immediate result.[5]

Ferry now made a serious effort to secure peace, apparently influenced not only by the lack of success in coercive measures and their increasing cost, but by the restiveness of Parliament and the suspicions of the British Government. In January of 1884 he told Baudais that every effort should be made to reach an understanding. In the projected treaty, Baudais might suppress all references to French rights over the island. It would be sufficient for the Hova Government to engage itself "not to occupy any territory nor exercise any authority in the region which was the object of the arrangements concluded by France with the Sakalaves in 1841 and 1842." He might even consent to the relinquishment of Majunga, asking only the north coast of the island from Vohemar to Mourounsang. Majunga and Tamatave would be occupied, however, until the indemnity was paid.[6] These terms, which Ferry seemed to regard as liberal and as a recession from his original demands, were a result of his discussion of the situation with his new Minister of Marine, Vice Admiral Peyron. "It is not, as you know, any thought of conquest which has led us to Madagascar, but only the necessity under which

[1] *Ibid.*, No. 15.

[2] *Ibid.*, No. 26, Challemel-Lacour to Baudais, July 31, 1883.

[3] *Ibid.*, Nos. 19–22.

[4] *Ibid.*, Nos. 28, 30, 33–40; *cf.* Despagnet, *op. cit.*, pp. 350–354; and Brunet, *op. cit.*, p. 18.

[5] *L.J.Mad.*, 1882–1883, Nos. 43 and 48.

[6] *L.J.Mad.*, 1884–1886, No. 1, Ferry to Baudais, January 11, 1884. The new formula of the "protectorate" in the north was at first suggested in June of 1883. *Cf. L.J.Mad.*, 1882–1883, No. 16, Ferry to Baudais, June 19, 1883.

we find ourselves to assure respect for our conventional rights and the reparations due to our nationals by an energetic demonstration."[1] A month later Baudais acknowledged receipt of these communications, but asserted that any concessions would be interpreted as a sign of weakness. He would therefore demand new pourparlers and be conciliatory then, but not in advance.[2] If Ferry expected a permanent diplomatic official who had been encouraged in making extreme demands to execute an abrupt about-face on new instructions dictated by the exigencies of domestic politics and the difficulties in Indo-China, he expected too much. Baudais had no enthusiasm for the rôle of peacemaker, despite Ferry's anxiety for an agreement. Admiral Galiber was similarly instructed by Peyron to renew negotiations on the new basis and reported his intention of collaborating with Baudais in a task which must necessarily have been distasteful to a naval commander.[3] He said he would demand an indemnity of 10,000,000 fr. Ferry reduced it to 3,000,000 fr.[4] Both Galiber and Baudais perhaps calculated that Ferry's instructions need not be taken at their face value and that no harm would result from delay.

At Tamatave they resumed discussions with M. Rainandrianamanpandry who sued for peace on behalf of the Queen. Baudais presented Ferry's formula. When asked what territory it included, he evaded an answer. The Hova Prime Minister's offer to cede the islets of Nossy-Mitsou and Nossy-Faly was rejected. Rainandrianamanpandry was too shrewd to sign away the birthright of his sovereign in an ambiguous clause. He pleaded for honorable treatment. "Would it not be a great glory for France to permit a feeble Power to maintain its independence and grant to it her friendship, to the end that this Power may march along the road of progress and civilization and exchange with her the fruits which accrue from them?"[5] Galiber replied that France had no designs on the independence of Madagascar. France merely sought to protect the territory of the Sakalaves. All of Rainandrianamanpandry's efforts to secure a delimitation of this territory were fruitless. Madagascar must accept the formula. Finally, after laborious debate, Baudais consented to read the treaties of 1841 and 1842, and pointed out that the territory affected was less than a third of the island. The Hova delegate replied that the treaties were worthless, since Tsimiharo ceded what he did not possess. When Galiber was asked the town where Tsimiharo lived, he admitted his ignorance, but insisted that Tsimiharo was a real person who had ceded real rights, whether he possessed them or not. But the Hovas had occupied the region since 1824 and these rights were never enforced by France. No matter. They must be enforced now. Over what territory do

---

[1] *L.J.Mad.*, 1884–1886, No. 2, Ferry to Baudais, January 14, 1884.

[2] *Ibid.*, No. 3, Baudais to Ferry, February 13, 1884.

[3] *Ibid.*, No. 4, Galiber to Peyron, February 16, 1884.

[4] *Ibid.*, Nos. 5, 6, March 1 and 2, 1884.

[5] *Ibid.*, No. 7, Baudais to Ferry, March 13, 1884, Annex II, Address of February 21.

they apply? Over the territory affected by the treaties of 1841 and 1842. But the treaties are invalid. So the discussion goes around and around. All of the Hova offers of specifically defined territory are rejected. Baudais, in a burst of irritated frankness, at length admits that he desires a protectorate over all the inhabitants north of 16 degrees south latitude. French honor forbids the abandonment of these peoples. "What peoples?" asks Rainandrianamanpandry. "We will not discuss that!" rejoins Baudais. "Indicate a parallel to us!" Long silence. The Prime Minister suggests a secret treaty indicating when the Hovas may recover possession of their territory. Baudais champions open diplomacy. If France demands a third of the island, Rainandrianamanpandry must have time to reflect. Baudais and Galiber wax sarcastic. War goes on unless the terms are met. The conference ends in deadlock and the final response of the Prime Minister on March 5 declares that the Queen cannot abandon all the northern region of the realm to the anarchy and pillage which will result if the Hova authority is withdrawn. She will cede various islands, give a money payment, and guarantee that if any part of Madagascar is ever ceded to a foreign Power, France will receive an equal share. This is refused and discussion ceases.[1]

On March 27, 1884, Ferry received what was probably an unexpected support from parliament. In the Chamber, M. de Lanessan inaugurated a long discussion of colonialism by his interpellation of the Government's Madagascar policy. While blaming the Cabinet for undertaking a military expedition without the authorization of the Chambers, he insisted on a vigorous defense of French interests. Ferry admitted that the "bad faith" of the Hovas had forced the Government to war. This confession, which was grave from a constitutional point of view, met with little criticism. Only M. Georges Perin pressed the attack, pointing out the omissions in the *Livre Jaune* issued by the Quai d'Orsay, especially on the Shaw affair, and demanding an examination by a special commission. But the Deputies were indifferent. Peace with victory seemed to be impending in Indo-China and Ferry was enjoying great popularity. The Chamber resolved to maintain all the rights of France in Madagascar by a vote of 437 to 26.[2] The Senate followed suit. Ferry, in elation, at once cabled Baudais: "This vote, characterized by an accord without precedent among all the parties, ought to be brought by all possible means to the knowledge of the Government of Tananarive and ought to serve as a guide to the French negotiators."[3] Galiber was replaced by Admiral Miot, who sailed on April 9. Ferry sent orders not to renew negotiations until his arrival with new instructions.[4] On Ferry's advice, Peyron instructed Miot to negotiate only for reparations, an indemnity of 3,000,000 fr. and recognition of the treaty rights of French

[1] *Ibid.*, No. 7, Annexes I–VII.
[2] *J.O.Ch.*, March 28, 1884.
[3] *L.J.Mad.*, 1884–1886, No. 8, Ferry to Baudais, March 28, 1884.
[4] *Ibid.*, No. 9, April 3, 1884.

nationals. The northwest coast was to be effectively occupied and not made a subject of further discussion.[1] Negotiations were, in fact, renewed on April 3 and again broken off five days later, with the same deadlock as before. Baudais assured Ferry that the vote of the Chambers would have no effect unless supported by troops. In his opinion an effective military expedition against the Hova capital was the *sine qua non* of success.[2] Ten thousand men would suffice to capture Tananarive. Negotiations would then eventuate as desired.[3] He continued to express his impatience at Hova efforts to renew discussion and at lack of military action from France, pointing out the dangers of delay in view of the discovery of gold near Tananarive and the acquisition of numerous advantageous ninty-nine-year leaseholds by British subjects.[4]

Military operations were resumed, but not on the large scale which Baudais thought necessary. The coast town of Vohemar was completely destroyed in July and a blockade was enforced. Such actions Baudais thought useless. The Hovas must be attacked in the heart of the island.[5] For such a campaign, however, large sums of money would be required and Ferry was reluctant to demand extensive credits in view of the unsatisfactory results of his policy of coercion in China. In May, Peyron asked 5,000,000 fr. "for the expenses occasioned by the events in Madagascar."[6] In the ensuing discussion in July, the credits were presented as essential to secure respect for French rights. Perin assailed the report of the commission which recommended approval of the demand, on the ground that the policy which it contemplated would involve a long and costly adventure and possible complications with England. In response to the denials of the *rapporteur*, M. de Lanessan, he accused the commission of abandoning its original plan of occupying only the northern portion of the island and of substituting for it a program for the conquest of all Madagascar. The Cabinet, he asserted, had adopted the new program of the commission. Ferry denied this, probably truthfully, since the initiative in planning more extensive military operations had come from Baudais and was then taken up by Ferry and Peyron with the approval of the Chamber Commission, before which Ferry appeared twice. There was, as yet, no avowal of any intention of securing control of the entire island. However desirable this may have seemed to Ferry, it appeared beyond the range of practical possibility. Perin, to the applause of the Left, assailed the whole philosophy of colonialism, pointed to the joy with which French colonial entanglements were greeted in the German press, and proposed voting against the credits. A lengthy debate followed, at the end

[1] *Ibid.*, Nos. 11, 12.

[2] *Ibid.*, Nos. 13, 14, Baudais to Ferry, April 8, 1884.

[3] *Ibid.*, No. 18, Baudais to Ferry, May 9, 1884.

[4] *Ibid.*, Nos. 20 (June 4) and 22 (September 27, 1884).

[5] *Ibid.*, No. 21, August 2.

[6] *J.O.Ch.*, May 20, 1884.

of which the Deputies approved the credits, 360 to 81. Ferry closed by declaring that the Chamber had committed itself to the Government's policy by the vote of March 27 and asserting that the only object of the ministry was the protection of established French rights in Madagascar.[1]

2. PROTECTORATE

On October 25, 1884, Baudais, in a long dispatch to Ferry, recommended a complete reversal of policy—or, perhaps one could better say, an extension of policy beyond anything which had hitherto been seriously considered. The blockade and the naval operations which had dragged through the summer had had no result. After all, declared Baudais, Hova predominance over the entire island was indisputable. Safely ensconced on the great table land of Imerina, the Hovas would always remain masters of the country. This fact should be utilized and not combated by the French. The logical solution of the problem would be a French protectorate over all of Madagascar, exercised through the Hovas. "It is not necessary to suppose that the Hovas will come themselves to offer us the Protectorate . . . We need to go to them, even to Imerina, to overturn the present Government, if it is necessary, and impose the Protectorate."[2]

No reply to this by Ferry is published. From October of 1884 to February of 1885 is a blank in the *Livre Jaune*, which, with the diplomatic archives still closed, can be filled only from secondary sources of information. Certainly Ferry, by personal predilection, would not view unfavorably the objective which Baudais suggested. But ends require means. The war with China was going badly. Troops could not be spared for the conquest of Madagascar without greatly increasing the already menacing unrest in Parliament and public opinion over the Government's foreign and colonial policies. One can picture Ferry, in the midst of his embarrassments in the Orient, toying with the idea and reluctantly rejecting it as impossible of achievement. Yet it was destined to bear fruit—even though in the bearing it was to bring about the ruin of him who sowed the seed.

As has already been noticed, the Ferry ministry was overturned at the end of the following March because of the situation in China and Tonkin. The diplomatic and strategic stalemate in Madagascar continued. The blockade was relaxed to the point where it existed in name only. Several posts in the north had been abandoned. The French occupation of the ruins of Vohemar was without effect. Baudais foresaw an indefinite continuation of the deadlock, barring a French invasion and attack upon the Hova capital.[3] Admiral Miot took the same view, except that he believed that a march on Tananarive would be costly, difficult, and impractical. If the French had supposed in the beginning that the affair could be settled by a

---

[1] *J.O.Ch.*, July 21, 1884.

[2] *L.J.Mad.*, 1884–1886, No. 23, Baudais to Ferry, October 25, 1884.

[3] *Ibid.*, Nos. 24, 25.

few cannon shots, they now knew better. In his opinion, the wisest course of action would be to resume negotiations for a protectorate over all of Madagascar. Such a protectorate would require only a small garrison in the country, while a conquest would demand the maintenance of at least 6,000 troops in the island for twenty years. A protectorate would probably be accepted, thought Admiral Miot, after a few military successes, such as the recapture of Majunga; after which negotiations could be reopened by new agents who were without animosity and *persona grata* to the Hovas. He would await reinforcements for this purpose. "These reinforcements . . . will draw the country into enterprises very costly, very prolonged, and very painful, if they have any purpose other than the imposition of a protectorate. And this protectorate can be discussed only by men who were in no way involved at the beginning of hostilities." Admiral Galiber, Minister of Marine in the Brisson Cabinet, transmitted this report to Freycinet, again Minister of Foreign Affairs, with a recommendation that it be acted upon.[1] Freycinet at once agreed and made preparations for sending a new emissary, who would have the innocuous title of Special French Agent in the Indian Ocean, to resume negotiations.[2] In this fashion an important decision of national policy was taken by the Ministers of Marine and Foreign Affairs on the advice of the naval commander on the scene.

The second act of the drama thus gets well under way. Baudais has sketched the plot and wishes to execute what he has designed. But the naval officer has no confidence in the diplomatic agent whose ideas he accepts. In Miot's view, Baudais' belligerency and unpopularity among the Hovas will prevent the success of the project. Miot's superior, Galiber, who had worked side by side with Baudais eighteen months previously in seeking to bully and hoodwink the Hovas into accepting the original French terms, has no hesitation in casting his former colleague aside. He and Freycinet work out the details of the new program which the Cabinet approves. The two ministers are in complete accord. Freycinet agrees to be guided only by Miot and concedes that Baudais may be an obstacle. The special agent will go to Madagascar. If he finds no chance of negotiations he will proceed to Zanzibar and no one will be the wiser. If he thinks negotiations can be resumed, he will send Baudais to Paris "to enlighten me (Freycinet) on the situation," reveal his full powers, and enter into discussions with the Hovas in accord with Miot. All will thus be effected with secrecy, neatness, and dispatch. Here, as in the Chinese war, circumventing his own agents becomes an important part of the foreign minister's task.[3]

Freycinet was obliged to observe great caution, however, in carrying out this scheme of action. The Hova Government seemed indisposed to consider serious negotiations and parliament had to be reckoned with in Paris.

[1] *Ibid.*, No. 26, Galiber to Freycinet, June 17, 1885.
[2] *Ibid.*, Nos. 27, 28, June 21 and 24.
[3] *Ibid.*, No. 30, Freycinet to Galiber, June 26, 1885.

Receipt of another dispatch from Baudais led Galiber and Freycinet to agree to bid their time for a bit.[1] On July 11, 1885, Camille Pelletin in the Chamber strongly criticized the Government's policies, "which make us attack Tunis because we have Algeria, Tonkin because we have Cochin-China, and Madagascar because we have Réunion."[2] The anticolonial sentiment which had overthrown Ferry in March was more powerful than ever. The Cabinet was pledged to a foreign policy of care and circumspection.[3] Toward the end of July a four-day debate took place in the Chamber on the whole subject of colonial imperialism, occasioned by the Government's demand for credits to finance the Madagascar operations. On the twenty-fifth, Perin argued for the rejection of the credits and the abandonment of the island. Conquest had been disclaimed and would be costly and unprofitable. A limited occupation would be a compromising enterprise. "We ought to save ourselves for other battlefields." Freycinet, adroitly concealing the recent decision of the Cabinet, declared that there was no question of occupation, but merely of protecting acquired rights. Brisson declared this to be the view of the entire Government. On the twenty-eighth, Ferry spoke at length in justification of his entire foreign policy. The economic advantages of imperialism and the white man's civilizing mission were emphasized. Colonies were not compensations for lack of power and prestige in continental diplomacy. They were a means of augmenting power and prestige. "Nations are great only through activity which develops them; it is not by pacific expansion that they are great at the present hour." Clemenceau and the extreme Left objected to this thesis, but on July 30 the Deputies approved the Madagascar credits, 291 to 142, and on August 4 the Senate did likewise, 189 to 22—all for the alleged purpose of maintaining the *status quo* and defending the established rights of France on the island, with Parliament in ignorance of the secret decision of the Cabinet to impose a protectorate. The Chambers presently adjourned, with new elections scheduled for October.[4]

The Minister of Foreign Affairs could now proceed with his program, without fear of embarrassing publicity and parliamentary demands for explanations. On August 19, 1885, Freycinet asked Patrimonio, French Consul General at Beyrout, to undertake a special mission of four or five months in the Indian Ocean. Upon his acceptance, he was asked to come to Paris for instructions, meanwhile keeping his appointment a secret.[5] A month later Patrimonio received his orders at the Quai d'Orsay. He was to proceed to Madagascar and use his full powers as Minister if Miot so recommended. If not, he was to make no mention of his authority until his return to France. A draft treaty of nineteen articles was given him by Freycinet, by which

---

[1] *Ibid.*, No. 30, Note 1.
[2] *J.O.Ch.*, July 12, 1885.
[3] *Cf.* Ministerial Declaration, *J.O.Ch.*, April 8, 1885.
[4] *J.O.Ch.*, July 28, 29, 30, 31, 1885; *J.O.Sén.*, August 5, 1885; *cf.* Despagnet, *op. cit.*, pp. 354–355.
[5] *L.J.Mad.*, 1884–1886, Nos. 31–34.

"Her Majesty the Queen accepts the protectorate of France as it is defined in the following articles."[1] Three days later, Freycinet received a dispatch from Baudais, dated August 27, which was, to say the least, astonishing. Baudais, perhaps suspecting that he was in danger of being superseded, had evidently sought to push matters to a swift conclusion and confront Freycinet with a *fait accompli* which would reflect credit on himself. Without keeping the Government adequately informed of his movements,[2] he availed himself, apparently with Miot's consent, of the services of Désiré Maigrot, the Italian Consul, to reopen negotiations with the Hova Prime Minister. Discussions went on through the summer, the Prime Minister objecting to the use of the word "protectorate" and Baudais insisting upon its retention in the French text of the proposed treaty, which would be authentic. Maigrot returned to Tamatave from Tananarive on August 25, bringing a formal refusal on the part of the Hovas to accept the conditions so long as they involved a surrender of sovereignty.[3] Several days before receiving this information, Freycinet had learned from the Italian Chargé in Paris of Maigrot's work, which had led to suggestions of Anglo-Italian mediation. He politely declined the offer and thanked the Italian Government for the services of its agent.[4]

Baudais had all but ruined Freycinet's carefully formulated scheme. He was recalled at once to Paris, where he was questioned on October 10 by Brisson, Galiber, and Freycinet, who concluded that he had begun negotiations on June 25 and continued them until August 27 without informing the Government. On October 15 he was removed from office. While technically at fault, he was in one sense a victim of the duplicity of his superiors. He had merely sought to execute the plan he himself had suggested and they had accepted. He had overreached himself and failed. Freycinet's irritation at the interposition of Italy and his anxiety lest the whole plan should now fall through were doubtless mitigated by his pleasure at the favorable opportunity which Baudais had thus provided for his own elimination.

Though the election of October 4 resulted in a repudiation of Ferry's colonial policies and a strengthening of the opposition parties, Freycinet pushed on. Patrimonio was instructed to confer with Miot and to act discreetly.[5] The two agreed to strike out the word "protectorate" from the proposed treaty, but Patrimonio was pessimistic and kept his mission a secret.[6] He repaired to Zanzibar, where he learned of new Hova overtures.[7]

[1] *Ibid.*, No. 35, Freycinet to Patrimonio, September 22, 1885.

[2] The implication of the *Livre Jaune* is that he acted in secret and entirely without authority. It is possible, however, that several dispatches were left unpublished in order to strengthen the Government's case.

[3] *Ibid.*, No. 36, Baudais to Freycinet, August 27, 1885 (received September 25), Annexes I–IV.

[4] *Ibid.*, Nos. 37, 38, September 28, 29, 1885.

[5] *Ibid.*, No. 40, Freycinet to French Vice Consul at Aden, October 3, 1885.

[6] *Ibid.*, No. 43, Patrimonio to Freycinet, Tamatave, October 25, 1885.

[7] *Ibid.*, No. 44.

He was thereupon granted full power to act, sent to Tamatave, and authorized to make several minor modifications in the draft treaty.[1] At Tamatave he dealt with General Digby Willoughby, commander of the Hova army, and M. Rainizanamanga, son of the Prime Minister, as the Hova representatives. On December 17, 1885, on board the *Naiade* in the harbor of Tamatave, Patrimonio, Miot, and Willoughby signed the treaty which ended the war and was intended to regulate future Franco-Madagascar relations.[2] On receiving word of it on the twenty-second, Freycinet promptly notified foreign Governments and thanked Patrimonio and Miot in complimentary terms.[3] The text of nineteen articles[4] provided that France would represent Madagascar "in all its external relations. The Malgaches abroad will be placed under the protection of France." (Article 1.) "A Resident Agent, representing the Government of the Republic, will preside over the foreign relations of Madagascar, without meddling in the internal administration of Her Majesty the Queen." (Article 2.) He will reside at Tananarive and have a right of private and personal audience with the Queen (Article 3). French citizens were granted extraterritorial rights and Madagascar agreed to pay 10,000,000 fr. on account of claims and reparations (Article 8). Pending payment, Tamatave was to remain under French occupation (Article 9). The Bay of Diego-Suarez was subject to permanent French occupation (Article 15), and France agreed to aid the Queen in protecting her States (Article 11). No mention was made of the "protectorate" on the northwest coast nor of Law No. 85, save a guarantee of the rights of French citizens under previous agreements.[5]

In Parliament, meanwhile, the Government continued to ask for credits "to maintain the established rights of France in Madagascar." On November 22, it requested 79,000,000 fr. for Tonkin and Madagascar. *Rapporteur* Hubbard, on behalf of the majority of the commission which examined the project, recommended a large reduction of this figure, on the ground that the ministry ought to content itself with the preservation of French treaty rights and renounce all territorial claims. When Freycinet, on December 23, announced the signature of the treaty at Tamatave, he was greeted with ironical laughter, his declaration being regarded as a ruse to win over doubters. The next day the Government demanded 30,000,000 fr. for the expeditionary corps in Tonkin. The commission reduced the credit to 7,500,000 fr. The Government's figures were at length adopted, but by such a feeble majority (274 to 270) that the Brisson Cabinet resigned.[6] The ministries of this period were almost all obliged to retire in the face of the anticolonial opposition, but only after they had gained their ends.

[1] *Ibid.*, No. 45, November 13.

[2] *Ibid.*, No. 50.

[3] *Ibid.*, Nos. 52, 53, December 23, 24.

[4] *Ibid.*, No. 57.

[5] G. Hanotaux, *L'affaire de Madagascar*, pp. 299–304, Paris, 1896.

[6] *J.O.Ch.*, December 30, 1885; Despagnet, *op. cit.*, pp. 355–358.

Freycinet headed the next Cabinet (January 7 to December 11, 1886) and submitted the new treaty to the Chambers for approval. He expressed his optimism over the happy combination of internal sovereignty and French control of foreign affairs and asserted that French moral influence would civilize and improve internal administration. Some contended that the treaty constituted an abandonment of former French rights in Madagascar. Others viewed it as a dangerous entanglement. "But," as one commentator puts it, "as almost always in parliamentary assemblies, the critics were dominated by the preoccupation of national interests or even by after-thoughts of internal politics; the juridical character of the treaty, and its legal consequences, of which the future was soon to show the importance, remained almost unperceived."[1] The Deputies recommended ratification, 436 to 28, on February 27 and the Senators by a great majority, without balloting, on March 6.[2] As a result of Freycinet's astute diplomacy in handling Parliament and the Hova Government, France had gained a protectorate over Madagascar. What its fruits would be, remained to be seen.

3. ANNEXATION

No sooner was the ink dry on the manuscript than controversy began over the meaning of the agreement which had been signed on December 17, 1885. The word "protectorate" had not been employed, because to the Hovas it signified loss of sovereignty and virtual annexation, to which they had not consented. In response to Willoughby's inquiries, Miot and Patrimonio sent him an interpretative letter on January 9, 1886, in which it was stated that "external relations" as used in Article 1 referred only to political relations in the narrow sense, that the "protection" to the States of the Queen was to be granted only when solicited, that the military escort of the French agent would be limited to fifty men and would not enter the royal palace, etc. In a postscript, the French delegates observed: "You have asked us if the Government of the Queen may, as in the past, continue to negotiate treaties of commerce with Foreign Powers. Without doubt, so long as these treaties of commerce are not contrary to the stipulations of the treaty of December 17, 1885."[3] This letter, being signed and accepted prior to the ratification of the agreement, was properly regarded by the Hovas as an authoritative and binding interpretation of its terms. They conducted themselves accordingly and in the following summer borrowed 20,000,000 fr. from British capitalists at 7 per cent and opened up negotiations for a commercial treaty with Great Britain without consulting the French Government. Freycinet protested, repudiated the Hova interpretation of Article 1 in a statement to the English press and a declaration in the Chamber of July 15, 1886, and seemed determined to construe French rights under the treaty

[1] Despagnet, op. cit., p. 359.
[2] J.O.Ch., February 26 and 28, 1886, and J.O.Sén., March 7, 1886.
[3] Hanotaux, op. cit., pp. 305–308.

as broadly as possible.[1] He was embarassed by the obvious soundness of the Hova contention that the interpretative letter of January 9 was binding on both parties. Miot and Patrimonio, by their eagerness for an agreement, had bungled matters as badly as had Baudais by his obstinacy, and with results far more serious. The attitude of the Hovas led to protests in the press and demands in the Chamber for vigorous action by the Government. Freycinet declared that the Cabinet was in favor of a pacific policy but would demand absolute observation of the text of the treaty. He was sustained, 285 to 102.[2]

Under such unfavorable circumstances the unhappy history of the protectorate began, destined to culminate a decade later in a more costly war and the complete extinction of the independence of Madagascar. The details of the prolonged diplomatic controversies of the late eighties and early nineties are without interest and are scarcely germane to present purposes. Successive French Cabinets sought to utilize the treaty of 1885 to establish a maximum of French control over the island and to reduce Hova sovereignty and foreign influence to negligible proportions. The Government at Tananarive, on the other hand, interpreted the limitations on its sovereignty as narrowly as possible, on the basis of the letter of January 9 and of general principles of treaty interpretation. These divergent positions led to conflict on many points. Could the Hova Government negotiate commercial treaties with third States without consulting France? Could it grant exequaturs to foreign consuls or must they be granted by the French agent? Could it grant economic concessions to nationals of foreign Powers without French consent? All these questions were answered very differently at Paris and at Tananarive. Irritation became chronic. Sporadic outbreaks of violence and acts of discrimination or injustice against French citizens increased. In its difficulties the Hova Government found sympathy and support among the British missionaries and in the British press. British entrepreneurs secured large concessions of mines, forests, and farms, which the French foreign minister conceded to be within the right of the Hovas to grant, but which he looked upon with anxiety because of their possible political implications. The Quai d'Orsay sought to safeguard the economic resources of the island for French exploitation. Those who stood to profit from effective French control of Madagascar were not blind to their opportunities. The primary motivations of the Ministry, however, seem to have been of a political and diplomatic character. Prestige, honor, influence, glory—the elevation or abasement of *la Grande Nation* in the European State System—these were the imponderable but controlling stakes of the game which the French Government was playing with the Hovas.[3] The purchase and importation of arms by the Hovas led to fresh warnings and threats.[4] Mutual protests and

---

[1] *J.O.Ch.*, July 16, 1886.

[2] *J.O.Ch.*, November 30, 1886; Despagnet, *op.,cit.*, pp. 360–364.

[3] *Cf.* Address of Ribot, *J.O.Ch.*, October 30, 1892; and of Develle, *J.O.Ch.*, May 17, 1893.

[4] *L.J.Mad.*, 1885–1895, Nos. 22f.

recriminations dragged on for months and years, until it was apparent to all that neither party to the dispute could impose its will on the other without a radical readjustment of their relationship.

On January 22, 1894, Casimir-Périer, Premier and Minister of Foreign Affairs, declared in the Chamber, in the time-honored formula, that it was the Government's intention to protect all the rights of France in Madagascar. Louis Brunet delivered himself of a long, patriotic address, warmly seconding the Premier's statement and insisting upon the necessity of vigorous action to compel observance of the treaty of 1885. At the close, he proposed a vote of confidence which received the unanimous support of the Deputies: "The Chamber, resolved to sustain the Government in whatever it undertakes to maintain our situation and our rights in Madagascar, to restore order, to protect our nationals, to make our flag respected, passes to the order of the day."[1] Thus supported, the Ministry reinforced the French garrisons on the island and prepared for energetic action, while the Hovas continued to insist on their right to confer exequaturs on foreign consuls and augmented their own military preparations in anticipation of efforts at coercion. The Cabinet of Casimir-Périer fell in May and he was succeeded in the Premiership by Charles Dupuy (May 30, 1894 to January 26, 1895), who named as his foreign minister the erudite and prolific historian, Gabriel Hanotaux, to whom he granted a relatively free hand in the conduct of foreign affairs. Hanotaux' colleagues were no less disposed to a vigorous policy than himself: Raymond Poincaré, Minister of Finance, General Mercier, Minister of War, Félix Faure, Minister of Marine, and Delcassé, Minister of Colonies. But in spite of the blank check which Parliament had given the Cabinet in the preceding January, the Dupuy ministry was none too certain of its parliamentary majority and felt obliged to avoid any precipitate action in Madagascar which could not be plausibly rationalized.

In Madagascar itself matters were rapidly approaching a crisis. On August 28, 1894, the French Resident-General telegraphed to Hanotaux that he could no longer be responsible for the safety of French citizens and asked that measures be taken for their evacuation.[2] Such measures could be taken only in contemplation of an effective military expedition to coerce the Hovas—or, what was unthinkable, of an abandonment of French pretensions to control. While the Chamber would probably not sanction the latter, it was not yet ready, in Hanotaux' opinion, to authorize the former. Time must be gained before the moment would be ripe to act. He so informed the French agents in Madagascar[3] and resorted to the expedient of dispatching a special diplomatic mission to Tananarive in what would have the appearance of a last effort at peaceable settlement. The purpose, however, was not to preserve peace but to afford time for evacuating the French

---

[1] *J.O.Ch.*, January 23, 1894; *cf.* L. Brunet, *La France à Madagascar*, pp. 265–289.

[2] *L.J.Mad.*, 1885–1895, No. 44.

[3] *Ibid.*, No. 46.

nationals and for preparing parliament for military action. Le Myre de Vilers was chosen for the task. He had been First Civil Governor of Cochin-China and French Resident-General in Madagascar after 1886.[1] He reached Tananarive on October 12 with instructions to evacuate the French inhabitants in the interior to the coast and to negotiate a supplementary convention protecting French rights under the treaty of 1885.[2] He carried out the former task and then submitted to the Queen a draft agreement giving the French Resident-General an unqualified control over foreign affairs and concessions and granting to the French Government the authority to undertake the construction of public works and to maintain such military forces on the island as it deemed necessary.[3] As was expected, this proposal was rejected and a counterproject presented, by which France would renounce all of her treaty rights and restore complete independence to the Hova Government.[4] Vilers left Tananarive October 27 and departed from Madagascar a month later.[5]

On November 13, Hanotaux went before the Chamber with a plea for the use of force. He reviewed the terms of the protectorate treaty, the refusal of successive French Cabinets to concede the validity of the interpretative letter, the policy of the Hovas, the dispute over exequaturs, and the record of crimes and acts of violence directed against French residents. He recalled that the Chamber had always favored a vigorous enforcement of French rights. Vilers had been sent to withdraw the 250 French citizens in Tananarive to the coast and to report on the situation. The foreign minister stirred the Deputies to mirth by ridiculing the Hova counterproject, and assured them that the Government would leave Parliament complete liberty of action. No expenses had been incurred, no troops had been sent, except by the preceding ministry in the previous May. Decisive action or complete evacuation were the only alternatives. The Government could not contemplate the latter because of the economic value of Madagascar and the damage to French diplomatic prestige which its abandonment would entail. Effective military action was a patriotic duty. There would be no foreign complications, since the other Powers, including Great Britain, had recognized the French protectorate. A force of 15,000 men and a credit of 65,000,000 fr. would be necessary to occupy the capital and make the French masters of the whole island. In the face of such a disarming appeal to patriotism the "liberty of action" of the Deputies could be exercised in only one way. Mercier suggested a special commission to consider the credit, and the Premier urged immediate action. A motion of the Left for an extraordinary commission of thirty-three members was rejected, 348 to 153, and a regular commission of eleven members was chosen for the purpose.[6]

---

[1] A. Pavie, Le Myre de Vilers, Paris, 1918, passim.

[2] L.J.Mad., 1885–1895, No. 47.

[3] Despagnet, op. cit., pp. 518–536; Brunet, L'Oeuvre, etc., pp. 25–38.

[4] L.J.cit., No. 53; G. Grandidier, Le Myre de Vilers, pp. 64–67, Paris, 1923.

[5] L.J.cit., Nos. 50–55.

[6] J.O.Ch., November 14, 1894; Hanotaux, L'affaire de Madagascar, pp. 76–137.

On November 23, Hanotaux delivered another long discourse, dwelling on the economic value of the island and the 100,000 fr. which the Chamber had voted annually since 1891 for its development. But there were motives for action nobler than these materialistic considerations. French citizens must be protected. French colonists who had gone to Madagascar in good faith under the promise of protection must be rescued. The prestige and moral force of the entire foreign policy of the Republic required decisive measures.[1] On November 26, after a prolonged discussion, the Deputies voted, 372 to 135, to grant the credits asked.[2] The Senators followed suit, 267 to 3.[3] On December 7, 1894, the project became law. 43,500,000 fr. were available for the Ministry of War, and 21,500,000 fr. for the Ministry of Marine. Hanotaux' skillful tactics had won the Chambers over to a military expedition of such magnitude that its outcome could scarcely be doubtful.

An expeditionary force under the command of General Duchesne was fitted out and the campaign began with the taking of Tamatave on December 12.[4] This was war. It was not preceded by any ultimatum, except for Vilers' threats and warnings and an announcement of French intentions which he sent to the Hovas after the occupation of the coast city. Nor was it preceded by any declaration of war by the Chambers. As usual in such cases, the ministry waged war without this constitutional formality, with the Chambers acquiescing. The operations were presented in certain quarters as a mere suppression of a rebellion, but they had all the earmarks and results of war in the international sense. The Government did not regard them as war, but conducted the operations in accordance with the laws of war, at least in their earlier phases.[5] The Hova resistance, though determined, was never serious, but the unhealthful climate and the occasional breakdown of transportation led to heavy losses on the part of the expeditionary corps.[6] Desultory fighting throughout the winter was without effect and was accompanied by minor disputes with other Powers and considerable indecision at Paris as to what future action should be taken. The sale of arms to the Hovas by British firms and the enlistment of numerous British subjects in the Hova army led to much unofficial friction. The United States ignored the French operations, on the ground that war had never been declared and that it had never recognized the French protectorate. The conviction by the French authorities of an American negro landowner and former American consul, Mr. Waller, on a charge of furnishing military information to the enemy, and the imposition of a sentence of twenty years' imprisonment led to a great outcry in the United States and to a somewhat acrimonious exchange of views between

[1] *J.O.Ch.*, November 24, 1894; *Ibid.*, pp. 38–166.
[2] *J.O.Ch.*, November 27, 1894.
[3] *J.O.Sén.*, December 7, 1894.
[4] *L.J.Mad.*, 1885–1895, No. 59.
[5] *Cf.*, Despagnet, *op. cit.*, pp. 708, 709.
[6] Grandidier, *op. cit.*, pp. 71–106; Brunet, *L'Oeuvre*, pp. 25–155.

Hanotaux and the American State Department, terminating in American acquiescence in Waller's condemnation. Except for such incidents, other governments remained officially indifferent to the French policy.[1]

At Paris the Dupuy Cabinet gave way to the third Ribot ministry (January 26, 1895, to November 1, 1895), but Hanotaux remained at the Quai d'Orsay. His original intention was to secure a renewal of the protectorate arrangements of 1885, on a basis which would admit of no such misunderstandings as had developed during the past ten years. Such were Duchesne's original instructions. At the end of March, Hanotaux ordered him to take Tananarive.[2] This difficult operation required reinforcements and was accomplished, in the face of disease and Hova resistance, at the expense of several thousand casualties. Tananarive fell to the invaders on September 30, 1895. Meanwhile, the prolongation of the conflict, the heavy losses in men and money, and the experience of the past had raised doubts in the Cabinet, the Chambers, and the Press as to whether the old formula of a "protectorate" was the most suitable as a basis of a new settlement. After extended discussion, Hanotaux sent new instructions to Duchesne on September 18, advising him that he might suppress the treaty project and simply demand Hova submission by unilateral declaration.[3] His cable was sent by way of Majunga and did not reach Tananarive until after October first. On that day, Duchesne had signed a new treaty with the Government of the Queen,[4] which consisted of a restatement in unequivocal terms of the arrangements of 1885, with such modifications as would assure effective·French control. Duchesne did not feel it expedient to insist, after a few days' interval, on the new formula of his latest instructions. The treaty was therefore adhered to as the basis of the new relationship.[5]

But in the French capital the treaty had few friends and many critics. The Ribot government fell on October 28 on a domestic issue and was replaced by the ministry of Léon Bourgeois (November 1, 1895, to April 29, 1896), in which Maurice Berthelot, a chemist of some distinction, became Minister of Foreign Affairs. The new Cabinet proceeded to take measures apparently contemplating the complete annexation of Madagascar, rather than the continuation of the protectorate. By decree of November 11 the administration of the island was transferred from the Quai d'Orsay to the Ministry of Colonies.[6] Other steps were taken toward placing internal administration in the hands of French agents.[7] On November 27, 1895, Berthelot presented a

[1] Despagnet, pp. 709f.

[2] *L.J.Mad.*, 1885–1895, No. 60, March 29, 1895.

[3] *Ibid.*, No. 63.

[4] *Ibid.*, No. 60, Annex I for text of seven articles.

[5] *Ibid.*, No. 67; cf. A. Lebon, *La politique de la France en Afrique*, 1896 to 1898, pp. 109–113. This work was republished in 1928, with some additional documents under the title: *La pacification de Madagascar*. The following references are to the earlier work.

[6] *L.J.Mad.*, 1885–1895, No. 70.

[7] *Ibid.*, No. 71.

declaration of the Government's views to the Chambers which in all probability constitutes the most chaotic jumble of legalistic inconsistencies
ever read in the Palais Bourbon. He asserted that the *rebellion* of the Hovas
against the French *protectorate* had been subdued, and that their submission
had been incorporated in a *treaty*. The island was now a French *possession*.
The Government was preparing the text of a new *treaty*, more precise than
that of October, which would be submitted to the Chambers. *Sovereignty*
had passed to France.[1] Madagascar thus became an unparalleled juristic
monstrosity—not so much because of a chemist's ignorance of the fundamental legal concepts which he handled so cavalierly, as because of his
desire to placate all shades of opinion in the Chamber by a purposely ambiguous statement of the situation. When Laroche was appointed Resident-
General of France at Tananarive, he was informed that Madagascar was
henceforth a French possession under French sovereignty. His instructions
from Berthelot referred to Hanotaux' dispatch of September 18 and suggested
a number of modifications in the treaty of October 1, to be secured in the
form of a unilateral declaration on the part of the Queen. The authority of
the Hova Government was not to be unnecessarily weakened, however,
since France would be dependent upon its cooperation in controlling the
island.[2] In accordance with these suggestions, Laroche secured from the Queen
on January 18, 1896, a declaration of five articles by which she acknowledged
French possession of the island, accepted French control of foreign affairs,
the right of France to maintain such military forces as should be necessary
to the exercise of its authority, the control of internal administration by the
Resident-General, the obligation to introduce such reforms as the French
Government might desire, and the authorization of the French Government
for all loans.[3] This declaration was intended to be a one-sided capitulation
rather than a contractual engagement. Instead of clarifying the legal situation it led to confusion worse confounded.

A series of decrees of the Minister of Colonies organized the administration of the new "possession."[4] The Hovas were meanwhile disarmed and
a portion of the French troops withdrawn. The former Prime Minister,
Rainilaiarivony, was imprisoned and later deported to Algeria and a new
one, M. Rainitsimbasafy, who was more friendly to the French, installed in
his place. The Queen objected to him, supposedly because of his obesity
and senility, in view of the old Madagascar custom of making the Prime
Minister the spouse of the ruler.[5] He was finally accepted, on condition
of the temporary lapse of this quaint folkway. The Queen remained ruler

---

[1] *J.O.Ch.*, November 28, 1896; *L.J.Mad.*, 1885–1895, No. 69.

[2] Text in Lebon, *op. cit.*, Annex A, December 11, 1895, pp. 257–265. *Cf.* Memorandum from
M. Guieysse, Minister of Colonies, to M. Bourde, pp. 265–279.

[3] *L.J.Mad.*, 1896, p. 1; Lebon, p. 114, Note 1.

[4] December 11, 28, 29, 1895, January 7, 28, 1896. Lebon, *op. cit.*, pp. 116–118.

[5] *Ibid.*, pp. 121–123.

"by the grace of God and the will of the French Republic."[1] On the surface all seemed quiet on the island. Beneath the calm exterior, however, smoldered the deep resentment of a proud people deprived of independence by superior force.

What followed throughout the spring and summer of 1896 is a familiar story in the history of western imperialism. With its details we are not here concerned. It follows the general pattern of similar events elsewhere, both before and since. It has almost exact counterparts in the Philippines, Haiti, Nicaragua, the Sudan, South Africa, India, Morocco, Syria, Tunis—everywhere, in fact, where the "backward peoples" of the dawn or twilight regions of the earth have dared to resist the domination of the nation-states of the West. A brief military campaign crushes local resistance and established foreign authority in the centers of population. A deceptive period of "peace" ensues. In the hills and forests of the hinterland, however, the fires of rebellion glow more fiercely, away from the foci of control. "Bandit" raids and sporadic acts of violence occur. The puppet government maintained by foreign bayonets finds its power ebbing away and it has neither the authority nor the desire to "restore order." Bands of "brigands" gather in the highlands and descend on isolated outposts. Ambuscades and massacres are followed by the dispatch of additional troops by the conquerors. By April Madagascar appeared to be on the verge of anarchy. Extensive insurrections, recurrent revolts, and guerilla warfare continued in spite of the efforts of the French military authorities to perform their "civilizing" mission through wholesale slaughter and terrorism, mass executions of unarmed prisoners, and the savage destruction of villages and towns by fire and sword.[2] Nothing sufficed to stem the tide of rebellion save force to the utmost. New troops were poured in. A state of siege was proclaimed over large parts of the island, which was divided into military districts. Province by province, town by town, almost foot by foot, the invaders were obliged to pursue their work, burning, slaying, destroying all in their path in the face of the frenzied resistance of the infuriated natives.

At Paris, the demands of the Government for new credits to deal with the situation enabled the opposition to bring about the downfall of the Cabinet. On April 21, 1896, the Senate, by 171 to 90 votes, expressed its lack of confidence in the ministry, which resigned without waiting for similar action by the Deputies.[3] The new Cabinet, headed by Jules Meline, was destined to remain in office over two years (April 29, 1896, to June 28, 1898). Hanotaux again became Minister of Foreign Affairs. His past record was assurance that the Ministry would continue the Madagascar policy of its predecessor and stop at nothing to crush the rebellion. The legal con-

[1] Memo. of Guieysse to Bourde, *ibid.*, pp. 265–279. On February 11, 1896, Berthelot notified the Powers that France had taken "possession" of Madagascar. *L.J.Mad.*, 1896, No. 3.

[2] See official dispatches on the methods of repression employed in Lebon, *op. cit.*, pp. 121–133.

[3] *J.O.Sén.*, April 22, 1896.

fusion was still in need of being resolved. On May 30, the Government submitted to the Chambers a *project de loi* of one article, declaring Madagascar, and its dependent islands, a French colony. André Lebon, the new Minister of Colonies, informed Laroche of this step, presenting it as necessary to deal with the diplomatic difficulties with Great Britain and the United States. Both Powers protested against French efforts to exercise jurisdiction over their nationals and against French proposals for a preferential tariff in the island, contrary to their own treaties with the Hovas, and both demanded information as to the meaning of "taking possession" in the absence of formal annexation.[1] M. Le Myre de Vilers presented a detailed report in favor of the Government's project on behalf of the Chamber commission which had examined it. He emphasized the distinction between annexation and assimilation and declared that the measure would give France complete control of the situation without involving a substitution of French administrative machinery for local authority.[2]

The presentation of this report was followed by long and jumbled debate, marked by charges and countercharges, complete confusion as to the juristic aspects of the problem, and much heat with little light on the subject of the abolition of slavery.[3] The Government had taken the view that an institution so deeply rooted in native ways of life could not be suddenly destroyed without producing serious difficulties. The Chamber Commission of Colonies and the commission charged with examining the annexation proposal had both examined the facts in their secret sessions and come to the same conclusions. When the matter was discussed on the floor of the Chamber, however, the carefully prepared transitional steps of the ministry were swept aside in a storm of opposition sentiment and uninformed humanitarianism.[4] Unanimously, the Deputies declared: "Slavery being abolished by the fact that the island is declared a French colony, the Government will take measures to assure immediate emancipation." Thus instructed, the Government acted accordingly, with results not always calculated to contribute to the restoration of peace and order.[5] The Chamber also approved the project for the formal annexation of Madagascar, 329 to 82.[6] The Senate gave its approval on July 11 and the annexation was proclaimed by law on August 6. Foreign governments were so notified and accepted the new status without protest, though diplomatic controversy over tariff questions continued for a time with Great Britain.[7] The last vestiges of Hova independence were thus extinguished and the confusion which had existed for over a decade was at least partially resolved.

[1] Lebon, *op. cit.*, pp. 133–135.
[2] *Ibid.*, pp. 137–141.
[3] Brunet, *L'Oeuvre*, etc., pp. 247–332.
[4] *J.O.Ch.*, June 21, 1896.
[5] *Cf.* Lebon, pp. 159–173.
[6] *J.O.Ch.*, June 30, 1896.
[7] Lebon, pp. 141–147.

The last act of the drama is a chapter in military tactics and colonial administration rather than in diplomatic history. Laroche, with his well-intentioned efforts to keep down expenses and preserve amicable relations with the Hova Government, was scarcely the official to deal with a widespread insurrection against French rule. He was made scapegoat for the entire situation by the public and the press. His relations with the military authorities gave little promise of a speedy subjugation of the rebels. Blood and iron demanded new leaders. General Gallieni, experienced in colonial warfare, was sent in August with four companies of the Foreign Legion and reached Tananarive in September. At the same time that Laroche received the order to abolish slavery, September 14, he was invited to return to France, leaving to the military commander all his civil and military powers throughout the island. Gallieni, while instructed to exercise tact and to avoid atrocious acts of repressions as far as possible, was authorized to pacify the country by all the means at his disposal.[1] The chambers gave their approval.[2] Prince Ratsimamanga, father of the Queen, and Rainandrianamanpandry, now Minister of the Interior, were courtmartialed for complicity in the rebellion and shot on October 12. The Prime Minister installed by Duchesne resigned and was not replaced. On February 27, Gallieni, on his own initiative and against the advice of the ministers at Paris, deposed the Queen. The Cabinet and the Chambers approved and Gallieni was made governor.[3] The rebel bands were driven from their burning villages and scattered to the forests. Crushed by superior armaments and strategy, the survivors gradually submitted to the inevitable. Recalcitrant groups carried on incessant guerilla warfare in the hills until they were hunted down and done to death. Not until the spring of 1902 were the Sakalaves of the north and west subdued. The wilderness of the south did not yield to the conquerors for several years thereafter. At length the last embers of revolt were stamped out and bloodshed and repression gave way to "peace." At the cost of millions of francs and thousands of lives, French honor and diplomatic prestige were preserved. French merchants and investors were given a new privileged field of operations and a new gem was added to the crown of the French colonial empire.[4]

Here, as in the conquest of Tunis, of Annam, of Tonkin, the machinery for the control of foreign affairs in the French Republic had run true to form. The same policies are pursued by different men and different Cabinets, dictated by a common nationalism and a common conception of the French position in the European State System. In the executive offices, always

[1] Lebon, *op. cit.*, Annexes C, D, and F.

[2] *J.O.Ch.*, July 17, 1896; *J.O.Sén.*, November 4, 1896.

[3] Lebon, pp. 209–226.

[4] A detailed account of these operations will be found in F. Hellot, *La pacification de Madagascar*, Paris, 1900; *cf.* Grandidier, *op. cit.*, pp. 129–151. One thousand and ninety-two French soldiers lost their lives and a very much larger and indeterminate number of natives. See map in F. H. Roberts, *History of French Colonial Policy*, II, p. 284.

sensitive to the nuances of diplomacy and the economic interests of French citizens abroad, the decisions are taken which drive the nation along the path of war and empire. In the legislative halls, there is opposition—of the eternal opposition, which, like poverty, is ever present, of the nationalism of the Right, of the nationalism of the Left. Ministerial schemes must be kept secret until they are beyond changing, or must be cleverly presented as manifest obligations of patriotic duty. While diplomats and soldiers carry out the Cabinet's plans in the field, with such cooperation and effectiveness as they can muster, the ministers at home must wheedle, cajole, plead, and implore the Chambers for money, for legislation, for support. But the public is hostile to dangerous adventures. It remembers too well the Second Empire. More often than not it supports the opposition against the government. Ferry is punished for acquiring Tunis and overthrown for securing Indo-China. Gambetta, determined not to renounce French rights in Egypt, is cast down. Freycinet is balked. Bourgeois and Berthelot suffer for taking Madagascar. No expansionist ministry, during this early period of a national inferiority complex, can take Parliament into its confidence. If secret diplomacy must be supplemented by war, the Chambers cannot be asked to declare it. Small credits are asked. Ultimate aims are concealed.[1] Money is spent and territory is taken and the Deputies and Senators are asked, not to make decisions, but to approve what has already been done. With astute maneuvering and adroitly phrased rationalizations of patriotic pride, love of military glory, and the demands of diplomatic prestige, parliament and the public can be won over, so long as reasonable success is met with in the field and the cost in men and money is not too great. The astute politician plays the right keys and obtains the tune he desires. If he produces too many discords, he gives way to a new player. But the piece goes on. The French empire is created through daring, deceit, and a convenient lapse of memory regarding constitutional technicalities. The nation is led by its nose, it knows not whither. Philosophically, it accepts what it finds on its arrival and lives to praise the leaders who led it to goals of glory in the face of its own doubtings.

[1] "Mais, il faut le dire à l'excuse du Gouvernement, elle était indispensable. La dissimulation est la base de toute bonne politique et on ne fait pas d'un plan de campagne l'objet d'un débat public." R. Valet, *L'Afrique du Nord devant le Parlement*, p. 234, Paris, 1924. *Cf.* J. Caillaux, *Agadir*, pp. 7–8, Paris, 1919.

CHAPTER VII

THE DUAL ALLIANCE

TO the historian who surveys the past half-century of European diplomacy from the vantage point of 1914 and its aftermath, there is apparent a clear line of causality running through the narrative from the Treaty of Frankfort of May, 1871, to the outbreak of the Great War forty-three years later. So obvious does the logical sequence of events appear in retrospect that it takes on the majestic aspect of Destiny—of a fatal and uncontrollable flood-tide which carries peoples and governments along in its flow and admits of no freedom of course nor choice of destination. While commentators are perhaps too prone to fall into the ancient error of *post hoc ergo propter hoc*, it is undeniable that the story lends itself to such treatment and that this type of presentation more readily renders intelligible the chronology of events than any alternative method of handling the data. The scholar who would pause to consider the rôle of accident, the play of chance, the limits of liberty, or the deeper motivations of behavior becomes at once involved in philosophical and psychological problems with which the historian cannot seriously concern himself in an age of specialization, fragmentation of knowledge, and an absence of any effectively coordinating synthesis of the various social disciplines.

Yet, it is precisely here that one must stop to search for facts and to strive for their interpretation if light is to be thrown upon the processes by which policies are formulated and executed by the statesmen of the nation-states. In the tangled interrelationships of their ensemble, these policies proceed inexorably, like the movements of a great symphony, driven on by the harmonies and dissonances generated by their juxtaposition. But it is in the counterpoint and variation of each melody and motif that the forces of creation are to be found. Lacking a "chef d'orchestre" to conduct the Concert of Europe, each section, each group of musicians composes and plays its own tune—not in oblivion, however, of those of the others. The diplomatic historian can listen to the total effect and prepare his program notes on the basis of the entire score. The student of behavioristic politics must look to each part, and study at first hand the creative efforts which produced it. Without postulating any freedom from the influence of external stimuli on the part of the players, he must seek to analyze the mechanisms by which effective stimuli are selected out of the mass and produce a given response, which, in conjunction with many other responses, results in the social situations with which the diplomatic historian is directly concerned. Putting the problem differently, one who is concerned with the control of foreign policy must use the data of the past not as the raw stuff of generalizations flowing from assumptions of causality or destiny, but as a means of minute analysis of men and motives which will illumine the fundamental patterns of politics as well as the nature of the whole State System into which they are woven.

The Franco-Russian Alliance need not be dealt with here as a topic of diplomatic history. As such it has already been treated at length by able historians.[1] The French, and to a lesser degree, the British diplomatic documents, still in process of publication at the time of writing, will throw further light on the story. It is already sufficiently clear, however, to permit the acceptance of the later histories as definitive. From the point of view of the present study, interest in it centers in the situation at Paris and the activities of the officials, publicists, and private citizens which resulted in its consummation and development. What happened is known. Why it happened and at whose behest is by no means so simple a problem.

1. FORGING THE BLADE

Thought and action at the Quai d'Orsay during the period between the Franco-Prussian War and the Franco-Russian entente of 1891 were conditioned by the new diplomatic position in which France was placed as a result of the unification of victorious Germany and the international system erected by Bismarck for the isolation of the defeated enemy and the maintenance of the *status quo*. The Iron Chancellor's distinction between "satiated" States, asking nothing better than the preservation of what is, and hungry States, seeking territorial and political readjustments, has become a familiar one. Sedan, Frankfort, and the loss of Alsace-Lorraine left France in the latter category and Germany, after 1871, in the former. The "lost provinces" were a source of bitter humiliation and resentment to every patriotic Frenchman.[2] Very few there were who shared the objectivity and dispassionate calm of the poet Verlaine, who is reputed to have thanked heaven that good music would at last be available when told that the Germans were at the gates of Paris. Bismarck reckoned with the general bitterness in France to the extent of perceiving the necessity of keeping Germany strong and supported by strong allies, while France remained weak and isolated. His encouragement of French colonial ventures has already

---

[1] See the exhaustive bibliography in W. L. Langer, *The Franco-Russian Alliance*, 1890–1894, Cambridge (Mass.), 1929, pp. 421 ff. In the following pages reference is made to the works of Cyon, Daudet, Debidour, Freycinet, Hansen, Michon, Welschinger, etc.

[2] "France, including the annexed districts of Alsace and Lorraine, had become one body, powerfully conscious of its unity and nationality; if one of its members suffered, all suffered together. Bismarck had mutilated a living body and the wound would not heal; it was to remain an awful open sore, threatening the peace of Europe for fifty years." S. B. Fay, *The Origins of the World War*, I, p. 52, New York, 1929.

been noticed. He perhaps did not foresee that the sense of injury would rankle indefinitely and lead to a desire for a *revanche* which would become the keystone of French foreign policy.

The *revanchards* in France were first to be found among the Monarchists, who claimed a monopoly of ultra-patriotism. The poet-soldier, Paul Déroulède, created the League of Patriots for agitation in Alsace-Lorraine and sought aid for the cause abroad.[1] His place was later taken by Maurice Barrès. Since the movement was associated with hostility toward the Republic, it suffered somewhat from the decline of royalism and the growing strength and stability of the Republican groups. It ceased to express itself so generally in irresponsible appeals to arms and demands for war or for a belligerently anti-German foreign policy. It persisted, however, as a popular feeling, only awaiting the leader who could translate it into terms of political possibilities.[2] Despite official disclaimers of any connection between colonial expansion and the lowered diplomatic prestige of France in Europe, parliamentary and public approval of successful imperialism was unquestionably due in large part to the renewed feeling of pride and power which overseas possessions always afford the patriot. If Germany was impregnable behind the Bismarckian system, buttressed as she was by the Austro-Hungarian Alliance of 1879,[3] France might secure compensation for her defeat elsewhere, even though Bismarck was mistaken if he supposed that these adventures would weaken France or reconcile her to her lot on the continent. If Italy was alienated and led to join the Central Powers in the Triple Alliance of 1882, Tunis at least was gained. Asia and Africa offered compensatory satisfactions. But colonies were not enough. Though an imperial domain second in size only to Great Britain's was created, the good patriot regarded it as a means to the *revanche* on the continent rather than as a substitute therefore.

This attitude was not confined to official circles or to the ruling classes, but permeated all groups and classes. At no point could it be said to have reached definite formulation into a program which was consciously accepted by large numbers of people. In the later period, when a program was envisaged by a small group of statesmen and diplomats, it was kept a carefully guarded secret and never spoken of openly. In the earlier period there existed only an unformulated aspiration toward a restoration of the traditional position of *la Grande Nation* in the councils of Europe, a recovery of the territory taken by Germany, and a general enhancement of French power and prestige. Any step on the part of the Government which seemed to tend in this direction without obviously endangering the security of the country was certain of public approval. Yet nothing must be done which raised anew

[1] Jules Claretie, *Paul Déroulède*, Paris, 1883.

[2] H. E. Barnes, *The Genesis of the World War*, pp. 383–388 New York, 1926; *cf.* E. Hippeau, *Histoire diplomatique de la troisième république*, p. 64, Paris, 1889.

[3] See Langer, *op. cit.*, Chap. I; Hippeau, pp. 239–264.

the specter of a German invasion of an isolated France. The problem of the Quai d'Orsay was to evolve a policy of paradoxes which would be pacifically belligerent and assure peace and security without precluding the final attainment of the *revanche*.

This was a diplomatic problem which defied solution so long as Bismarck remained arbiter of the destinies of Europe. He perceived the possibility of a combination between Germany's eastern and western neighbors even before he had accomplished his mission of German unification.[1] His work done, he realized that the continued enjoyment of its fruits depended upon preventing the consummation of such a union. Despite occasional friction, the Tsar and his advisers were usually friendly toward Germany, indisposed to pourparlers with the radical French Republic, and much less irritated by German hegemony on the continent than by British and Austrian resistance to Russian expansionist ambitions in the East. Bismarck spared no efforts to retain this friendship. It was cemented by the Reinsurance Treaty of 1887, successor to the "Dreikaiserbound" and the pact of 1881.[2] Those in France who counted upon an anti-German orientation of Russian policy could only wait with fasting and prayer for the hoped-for diplomatic revolution. As early as 1881, Gambetta observed to Jules Hansen, a naturalized Frenchman of Danish origin, close to Russian Embassy circles:

> France is condemned to play a humble rôle in Europe and ought to observe great reserve until she possesses a very strong army. The creation of that army is our present task. I occupy myself with it every day and it is the object of my principal preoccupation. When we possess a powerful army we will find allies, I have no fear on that subject. I have often envisaged this possibility with General Skobelev, whom I love and esteem very much.[3]

During his brief premiership, Gambetta sent Count Chaudordy to Russia with instructions to work for an entente. "The time has not yet come for us to sleep with Russia, but it is time to commence the courtship."[4] He felt that Bismarck's attitude required caution, but that German efforts to estrange France from Russia and Great Britain must be resisted.[5] Gambetta's successors returned to the pro-English orientation of Waddington, which spelled Russian hostility because of Anglo-Russian friction. Ferry, while perhaps not indisposed in principle to collaboration with Russia,[6] was too occupied with

[1] According to Delcassé, Bismarck foresaw this possibility in April of 1856. J. Hansen, *Ambassade à Paris du Baron de Mohrenheim*, p. 77, Paris, 1907.

[2] A. Debidour, *Histoire diplomatique de l'Europe*, pp. 82–84, Paris, 1917.

[3] J. Hansen, *L'Alliance Franco-Russe*, p. 6, Paris, 1897. As Premier, Gambetta took immediate steps to fill the vacant embassy post at St. Petersburg and proposed to do everything desired to suppress the nihilists in Paris, *ibid.*, p. 9.

[4] E. de Cyon, *Histoire de L'Entente Franco-Russe*, p. 32, Paris, 1895.

[5] "L'Allemagne voudrait nous attirer dans son orbite et nous éloigner de l'Angleterre et de la Russie. Tenons-nous bien; gardons l'alliance avec ces deux puissances en réserve pour l'avenir." This statement was made by Gambetta, at a dinner on July 28, 1881, to Freycinet, who regarded it as an indication that Gambetta's attitude was more cautious than in 1880. *Souvenirs*, p. 175.

[6] Rambaud, *Jules Ferry*, p. 399; and Hansen, *L'Alliance*, p. 14.

other problems to formulate any policy in this direction. There were individuals in both countries, official and unofficial, who were working for a *rapprochement* for a variety of reasons—diplomatic, economic, sentimental, or personal. Alexander III had, at first, little confidence in the French Republic. But the ambassador whom he sent to Paris in 1884, Baron Arthur Pavlovitch de Mohrenheim, was a partisan of an entente, as was also, in lesser degree, General Appert, the French Ambassador at St. Petersburg. When Freycinet recalled Appert in 1886, and spoke of replacing him by General Billot, whom the Tsar refused to accept because of an apparent disregard of the formalities by the French Government, Mohrenheim was recalled and the embassies remained vacant for several months. During his absence from Paris, Mohrenheim prepared a *mémoire* on the expediency of a Franco-Russian understanding which was transmitted to the Tsar by his foreign minister, de Giers. Toward the end of the year Laboulaye was appointed ambassador and courteously received on the Neva, and Mohrenheim returned to the Rue de Grenelle.[1]

The resurgence of militant nationalism in France, associated with the name of General Boulanger, led to increasing attention in the press to the possibility of closer relations with Russia. According to Hansen, President Grévy was in favor of a pacific *rapprochement* for protection against Germany.[2] Déroulède and the League of Patriots redoubled their agitation for the *revanche* and General Boulanger, Minister of War in the Goblet Cabinet (December 11, 1886, to May 30, 1887), went so far as to write a letter to Alexander III proposing an alliance. This move seems to have been an outcome of the work of Mohrenheim and Flourens, the Minister of Foreign Affairs. Goblet was opposed to such direct solicitation, and when Mohrenheim received discouraging news from Giers, M. de Vogüe, the private agent who was to have gone to St. Petersburg with the proposal, was detained in Paris.[3] When Flourens, in a Cabinet meeting, accused Boulanger of irregularity in this connection, the Minister of War disclaimed all responsibility and even denied the existence of the letter.[4] Boulangism, in fact, increased the Tsar's apprehensions and lack of confidence in France, since it stood for a policy toward Germany of foolhardy belligerency of which the Tsar strongly disapproved. As the tide of the movement ebbed, he became more favorably disposed. When the Tirard ministry fell at the end of March, 1888, and it seemed likely that Charles Floquet, president of the Chamber, would become foreign minister in the next Cabinet, Mohrenheim is alleged to have informed President Carnot (December 3, 1887, to June 25, 1894)

[1] Debidour, *op. cit.*, I, pp. 110–112; Hansen, *Ambassade*, pp. 14–22; *L'Alliance*, pp. 15–22.

[2] "Elle (Allemagne) menace la Russie aussi bien que la France; ces deux pays doivent donc, par des moyens pacifiques, se soutenir mutuellement," May 6, 1887, Grévy to Hansen, *Ambassade*, pp. 41–42.

[3] Debidour, *op. cit.*, I, pp. 126–128; Hansen, *Ambassade*, pp. 34–36.

[4] Lord Lytton to Lord Salisbury, March 30, 1888, in B. Willson, *The Paris Embassy*, pp. 291–292, New York, 1927.

that the Tsar would be displeased. Floquet had cried "Vive la Pologne!" in the Palais de Justice in 1867 during the visit of Alexander II. He now became Premier and Minister of Interior, while Goblet took the portfolio of foreign affairs and Freycinet that of War. The latter's reorganization of the army had a favorable effect on Russian official opinion, as did Floquet's break with Boulanger. With the dissolution of the League of Patriots in February of 1889, the flight of Boulanger to Belgium, and the crushing of his movement in the fall elections, the Tsar felt reassured as to the stability of the French Republic.[1]

In preparing Russian and French opinion for an entente, the influential Russian journalist, Michel N. Katkof, and his friend and Paris correspondent, Elie de Cyon, played an important rôle. Katkof was a loyal monarchist, an orthodox churchman, and an extreme Pan-Slavist nationalist who secured the ear of the Tsar by his impassioned advocacy of the vigorous suppression of the Polish rebellion in 1863. He founded the Russian political press by securing permission to treat of political questions in his *Russian Messenger* and *Moscow Gazette*. His anti-German sentiments led him to turn his attention in 1886 to a possible reorientation of Russian foreign policy. Cyon had been instrumental in bringing the Grand Duke Nicholas, brother of the Tsar, in contact with French military and political circles in 1879, and at Katkof's suggestion began sounding out French opinion on an entente. At first he found support only in the Orleanist paper *Soleil*, and in *La Patrie* of the Bonapartists. He was obliged to make haste slowly. In August of 1886 he secured from Madame Juliette Adam, chauvinist *revancharde* and Russophile, the directorship of the *Nouvelle Revue*, through which he carried on his propaganda, despite his unfriendly relations with Mohrenheim and the criticism of the radical press.[2] Katkof sought to wean the Tsar away from what he regarded as the pro-German influence of Giers.[3] In the spring of 1887 he definitely opened his campaign against the Triple Alliance and in favor of a French entente, not because of love for France or hatred of Germany but because of what he presented as the necessity of Russia's resuming her independence of action in continental politics.[4] Katkof and Cyon worked in close collaboration, assailing Bismarck, Giers, and Mohrenheim, exploiting the war scare of 1887, and urging Franco-Russian financial and political collaboration. Apparently at the suggestion of the Russian Minister of Finance, Cyon took steps to form a French financial syndicate in order to transfer the market for Russian Government bonds from Berlin to Paris. Katkof gained many enemies and died in 1887 in the midst of bitter con-

---

[1] Hansen, pp. 44–50 and 80–81; Debidour, I, pp. 133–136.

[2] Winifred Stephens, *Madame Adam*, Chaps. XVI and XVII, New York, 1917.

[3] Cyon, *Entente franco-russe*, pp. 152–206.

[4] To Katkof French republicanism was an abomination, but the alliance was "une fatale et désagréable nécessité." *La République française*, August 26, 1887, quoted in Q. Michon, *L'Alliance franco-russe*, pp. 4–5, Paris, 1927.

troversy over his aims and motives.[1] The importance of these journalistic activities has doubtless been exaggerated, but they were of considerable effect in both France and Russia in strengthening the opinion of groups favoring a Franco-Russian entente.

In 1888 began the long series of financial transactions which were to precede and accompany the consummation of the entente. The Tsar's Government had for a long period of time floated loans in the Western European money markets for railway construction and public works and for the purpose of meeting the persistent deficits in the Russian State budget.[2] Anglo-Russian friction had made London less suitable than Berlin for such purposes. Between 1875 and 1884 several Russian State loans were floated in Berlin with Bismarck's approval and the cooperation of the Russian State Bank. But in 1887, in retaliation for Russian tariff policy and the ukase forbidding alien land ownership near the western frontier, Bismarck ordered Russian Government bonds struck from the list of securities eligible for collateral loans at the Reichsbank. This measure was accompanied by a German press campaign against Russian credit and was interpreted as a veto on further Russian flotations in Berlin. St. Petersburg turned to the only other available source of loans—the Paris Bourse. Cyon had already negotiated a minor conversion loan for Russia with the Rothschilds. His motives in doing so were definitely political, though the Russian Ministry of Finance was concerned chiefly with its pecuniary needs. Giers feared that Russian borrowing in Paris might arouse German hostility, but at length consented. Toward the end of 1887 a group of financiers, headed by the Danish banker Hoskier, asked the French Cabinet to authorize the listing of Russian Government bonds on the Bourse. The Floquet Cabinet gave its consent, with the political possibilities of the situation clearly visible at least to Goblet and Freycinet, Ministers of Foreign Affairs and War. In December of 1888 a Russian loan of 500 million francs at 4 per cent was issued at 86 fr. 45 c. It was at once so heavily oversubscribed that two more were issued in the following year, for 700 and 1,200 millions respectively, and during 1890 three more issues appeared, for 260, 360, and 41 millions.[3] At the same time, military contacts between the two countries became closer. When the Grand Duke Vladimir, brother of Alexander III, visited Paris and studied the army reforms which Freycinet had introduced, he was greatly impressed with the new Lebel rifle. In 1888 General Fredericks, on behalf of the Russian Government, proposed that 500,000 be manufactured in the French national factories and sold to Russia. Freycinet asked a guaranty that the guns would never be used against France and even

[1] Cyon, pp. 24–38, 207–354.

[2] *Cf.* M. Margaine, *Rapport . . . sur le Livre Jaune rélatif à L'Alliance Franco-Russe*, Chambre des Deputies, 1919, No. 6036, p. 7.

[3] J. Viner, "International Finance and Balance of Power Diplomacy, 1880–1914," *Southwestern Political and Social Science Quarterly*, IX, pp. 2–5, March, 1929. Fay, *op. cit.*, I, pp. 107–108; Debidour, *op. cit.*, I, pp. 136–138.

suggested a military convention. Assurances were given by Mohrenheim and the rifles were in due time manufactured and shipped to Russia.[1]

These transactions, as well as Russian official gratitude for French willingness to arrest nihilist plotters in Paris, were straws in the wind.[2] No great political significance was as yet attached to them at St. Petersburg. At Paris there were hopes. The reactionaries and conservative nationalists continued to urge an entente. Delcassé, in June of 1887, declared that France and Russia were the counterpoises to the Germanic colossus in the east and the west of Europe, "just as, at the north and south of Asia, they are obstacles to the encroachment of China and England. Everywhere the same enemies, everywhere the same interests, everywhere the same aspirations. It is astonishing that an entente so natural has been so long in being established."[3] In July, 1887, the *République Française* emphasized the common interest of both countries in combating German domination.[4] Leroy-Beaulieu, on the other hand, argued that an understanding would give Russia all the advantages and France all the obligations and might draw the Republic into a disastrous war.[5] Grévy seemed indifferent and Jaurès and the Left were opposed to any union with the Tsarist autocracy. With parliamentary and public opinion divided, the outcome would depend upon executive initiative. The trend of policy at the Quai d'Orsay, in turn, depended upon the attitude of St. Petersburg, which hinged largely on German policy and developments in the Mediterranean and the Near East.

The kaleidoscopic complexities of the general diplomatic situation and of domestic politics at Berlin cannot be discussed here.[6] Russian foreign policy was dominated by the exigencies of the drive toward Constantinople and the Straits and by the resistance which this ambition encountered from Great Britain and later from Austria-Hungary. Bismarck had cleverly constructed his international system so as to keep both Russia and Austria within its orbit, despite their diverging policies, and to placate England and Italy, who were agreed upon the maintenance of the Mediterranean *status quo*. But a choice between St. Petersburg and Vienna would some day become imperative. Only a political genius of Bismarck's caliber could expect to ride both horses indefinitely. The Mediterranean agreements of 1887 seemed detrimental to both French and Russian aspirations and created common grievances. Bismarck's dismissal in March of 1890 was due in large part to the anti-Russian bent of William II who was convinced by Baron Holstein and other advisers that the renewal of the Reinsurance Treaty of 1887 would be contrary to the spirit of the Triple Alliance and would

[1] Hansen, *L'Alliance*, pp. 84–86.

[2] *Ibid.*, pp. 55–58.

[3] Cited in Michon, *op. cit.*, p. 9.

[4] *République Française*, July 26, 1887.

[5] *Revue des deux mondes*, February 15, 1888.

[6] A full account of these developments will be found in Langer, *The Franco-Russian Alliance*, Chaps. I–VI.

antagonize England. Despite the willingness of Giers to renew the arrangment it was allowed automatically to lapse in June. The Anglo-German Heligoland Treaty of the same date, moreover, created the impression at St. Petersburg that Berlin was lending aid to the Mediterranean policy of Russia's traditional enemy in the East. These developments led the Russian diplomats to conclude that that continued collaboration with Germany was incompatible with the pursuit of their aims in the Balkans and the Bosphorus, and to consider seriously the reorientation of their policy which Katkof had urged.[1] The change in the diplomatic situation which was symbolized by the fall of Bismarck led the Russian statesmen to lend an ear to French overtures.

These overtures did not come from a single source, nor can any individual be given credit for the formulation of the policy of the entente with Russia. The idea had long since permeated official and unofficial circles in Paris to such a degree that the personal responsibility for taking final action was almost a matter of chance. The Russians themselves had made unofficial soundings in 1879 and 1886.[2] In what fashion and under what circumstances aspirations could be translated into action depended upon the opportunities presented by the ever changing diplomatic situation and upon the exigencies of French and Russian domestic politics. One name stands out above others in the final accomplishment of the task. It is that of Charles de Freycinet—scientist, mathematician, engineer, collaborator with Gambetta in the organization of the National Defense in 1870 and 1871, and thrice Premier and Minister of Foreign Affairs in the French Republic.[3] In the Floquet Cabinet of April 3, 1888, he became Minister of War, a post which he held in five successive Cabinets until January 11, 1893. During this period he headed his fourth ministry (March 17, 1890 to February 27, 1892). It is not without significance that the Dual Alliance was consummated, on the part of France, by one who was not only an astute and calculating politician, but a military administrator as well, holding the portfolio of war.[4] He had toyed with the idea of a Franco-Russian entente for years. To him, as to so many of his compatriots, it seemed the logical way out of French diplomatic isolation. It was the corollary of the reorganization of the French army. He was not an irresponsible *revanchard*. But a strong France, in alliance with Russia, could again deal with Germany on a basis of equality. And then . . . ? But nothing was possible until the diplomatic changes accompanying the removal of Bismarck from the European scene cleared the way for the transformation of the existing financial and military collaboration between France and Russia into a political understanding.

[1] Fay, *op. cit.*, I, pp. 90–96.

[2] Langer, *op. cit.*, p. 92, Note 28.

[3] December 28, 1879, to September 23, 1880; January 30, 1882, to August 7, 1882; January 7, 1886, to December 11, 1886. See the sketch of his early life in H. Depasse, *De Freycinet*, Paris, 1883.

[4] Hansen, *Ambassade*, p. 80: "M. Freycinet a certainement été le ministre français qui a le plus contribué à l'Alliance Franco-Russe."

Freycinet apparently acted in full accord with the President of the Republic, Carnot, with Ribot, the Minister of Foreign Affairs, and with Barbey, the Minister of Marine. He kept in his own hands, however, the many threads of the diplomatic skein and dictated the design to be woven. The initiative came from the Minister of War on the Rue de Solferino rather than from the Quai d'Orsay. His military reforms had already impressed Russia favorably and afforded an opportunity for contacts with Russian military leaders and members of the royal family. When the Grand Duke Nicholas, Commander-in-Chief of the Russian Armies, visited Paris in May of 1890, Mohrenheim invited Freycinet to meet him. The two discussed army administration and military cooperation, and the Romanov was agreed that the two armies ought to act as one in time of war.[1] Russian friendship was strengthened by new arrests of nihilist conspirators in Paris at the end of the month. Laboulaye was well thought of at St. Petersburg, but Freycinet employed Hansen as a supplementary channel of communication to the Tsar, through Ratchkovsky, a friend of Prince Obolensky, who was a confidant of Alexander III.[2] The beginning of the more or less regular exchange of military missions marked the progress of Freycinet's plans. In the summer of 1890 General Boisdeffre visited the Russian capital and spent two weeks observing the encampments at Krasnoë-Selo and the manoeuvers at Narva. Contacts were thus established between the general staffs and plans were even discussed for common action in the event of an attack. Laboulaye asserted that military cooperation would naturally follow French aid in equipping the Russian infantry and that the *rapprochement* had become a reality, despite the deplorable defect of the French Constitution which deprived French diplomacy of the advantage of secrecy.[3] About the same time, Freycinet and Barbey began sounding out the attitude of St. Petersburg toward receiving a French naval squadron at Cronstadt. The Tsar replied evasively and the matter was postponed.[4] Toward the end of the year, however, Barbey received reassuring information from the French Naval Attaché at St. Petersburg and Freycinet began secret preparations for a naval mission, which the two ministers revealed to the Cabinet only when they were well advanced.[5]

Curiously enough, these hidden pourparlers on the part of the Premier were accompanied for a time by public manifestations of a Franco-German *rapprochement*. The fall of Crispi at Rome in January of 1891 and German anxiety regarding the stability of the Triple Alliance led the Kaiser to adopt a conciliatory attitude toward France. During the preceding year, scientific and artistic contacts had been increased and there was much discussion in the French press of the advantages of some kind of definite understanding with

[1] Freycinet, *Souvenirs*, p. 442.
[2] Michon, *op. cit.*, pp. 12–14.
[3] *L.J.*, *L'Alliance Franco-Russe*, No. 1, L. to Ribot, August 24, 1890.
[4] Michon, pp. 15f.
[5] Freycinet, pp. 443–444, 464–471.

Berlin.[1] Probably in the hope of capitalizing on this sentiment, the Kaiser approved the plans of his mother, the Empress Victoria, to visit Paris, ostensibly *incognito* and for non-political purposes. She arrived on February 18, 1891, and expressed her friendship and her desire for an abandonment of the *revanche*, which irritated the ultra-nationalist press. Her sojourn at the German Embassy and her visits to Versailles and St. Cloud aroused a storm of patriotic indignation in Paris, which was stirred to frenzy by Déroulède and his followers. The Empress departed on the twenty-seventh, amidst the bitter recriminations of the press of both countries. The Kaiser was furious and spoke of mobilization. He accused Freycinet of responsibility, though the latter had taken every precaution to avoid a disturbance, and the attitude of the French Government was correct at all points.[2] All hopes of Franco-German reconciliation were shattered. Mohrenheim declared that the Russian accord with Paris was now "solid as granite," while Giers took advantage of the opportunity to say that "the *entente cordiale* which has been so happily established between France and Russia is the best guarantee of peace. While the Triple Alliance ruins itself in armaments, the intimate accord of the two countries is necessary to maintain a just balance of power (*pondération des forces*)."[3]

The spring and early summer of 1891 witnessed the final preparations for the consummation of the union. Discussion of the French naval visit had been resumed in January and Freycinet renewed suggestions of a more definite understanding. Early in April, Laboulaye, following his instructions from Ribot, sounded out the Russian Government on its attitude in the event of Franco-German hostilities. The reply was apparently still evasive.[4] Giers could say, with satisfaction: "France is at our feet. We should show bad grace to complain of it. She has done everything to secure a treaty, but despite the most urgent insistence, she has not obtained it."[5] The Russians remained wary of possibly dangerous commitments. They attributed to the French dissatisfaction with their attitude the last-minute refusal of the Rothschilds to handle another loan, though the bankers gave as their reason the refusal of the Tsar's Government to cease its persecution of the Jews and there is no evidence of official pressure upon them.[6] Hoskier offered his services, but Mohrenheim urged the participation of the *Crédit Foncier*, under Government control. The Minister of Finance, M. Rouvier, granted the necessary authorization somewhat reluctantly and with the understanding that the procedure was exceptional. The loan was finally issued in October, under somewhat unfavorable conditions and with results which

[1] Langer, *op. cit.*, pp. 139–141.

[2] Freycinet, *Souvenirs*, pp. 458–459; Debidour, *op. cit.*, I, pp. 165–169.

[3] L.J.L'A.F.R., No. 2, Ribot to Laboulaye, March 9, 1891.

[4] Langer, *op. cit.*, pp. 147–148.

[5] Giers to Ghika, Roumanian Minister, in "Bülow to Caprivi," May 2, 1891, *Die grosse Politik der europäischen Kabinette*, VII, No. 1498; cited in Langer, p. 148; Michon, p. 14.

[6] Margaine, *rapport*, pp. 13–17.

were not entirely satisfactory.[1] It is impossible to say that Freycinet and Ribot brought financial as well as diplomatic pressure to bear upon Russia in this way, as they did on Italy at the same time in the hope of detaching her from the Triple Alliance.[2] The pressure at Rome failed and the Triplice was renewed in June. The secrecy of its terms, as well as ignorance of the details of Anglo-Italian commitments aroused new apprehensions on the Seine and the Neva which were influential in furthering Freycinet's scheme. The cordiality of the Kaiser's reception in London in July was grist for the mill.[3]

But Franco-Russian relations had been somewhat cool since April. The Tsar, as a friendly gesture, visited the French exposition in Moscow in May, but Freycinet demanded more than small favors. *Le Matin* and *Figaro* waxed bitter over the Russian attitude. Ribot instructed the French Ambassador at Constantinople to take a strong stand in opposition to Russia in the dispute over the use of the door of the Church of the Nativity in Bethlehem by the Franciscans and the Greek Orthodox monks. Giers and his colleagues were made to see that they need expect nothing without a *quid pro quo*.[4] Germany, moreover, was regarded as threatening in the spring of 1891 and the direction of German policy was very influential in driving Giers and the Tsar to a decision. Great Britain was well disposed toward Berlin and was committed, in collaboration with Italy, to the maintenance of the Mediterranean *status quo*—which meant opposition to Russian designs on the Straits as well as to French expansionist schemes in North Africa. The Tsar's Government saw itself faced with isolation and estrangement from the only friendly Power in Europe if the French demands were longer evaded. An invitation was extended to the French squadron to visit Cronstadt. The rest was understood. Freycinet, Ribot, and Barbey had played their cards skillfully and could now feel certain that the Tsar would at last agree to what he had thus far resisted.

On July 23, 1891, the French squadron under Admiral Gervais anchored before Cronstadt and was received by Russian officialdom and the populace with unbridled enthusiasm. For a fortnight the French officers and sailors were wined, dined, and fêted wherever they went—St. Petersburg, Peterhof, and Moscow. The Tsar listened bareheaded to the forbidden revolutionary anthem of the *Marseillaise* and no pains were spared to impress the world with the intimacy of the new *liaison*.[5] The demonstration was clearly intended by the Russian Government as a challenge to the Triple Alliance and England. Giers had already made the expected advances to Laboulaye. Ribot informed Carnot and Freycinet and told the ambassador that any proposition which Russia might make would be welcome. Relations should

[1] Viner, *loc. cit.*, pp. 5–7.
[2] Langer, pp. 156*f.*
[3] *Ibid.*, pp. 170–178.
[4] *Cf.*, Langer's comments on the astuteness of this move, *op. cit.*, p. 180.
[5] Debidour, *op. cit.*, I, pp. 169–171.

be strengthened in order to maintain peace and "a certain equilibrium of forces in Europe." The two countries must act together in the face of any threat to peace in view of the renewal of the Triple Alliance and the indirect adherence of Great Britain to it.[1] "It is, moreover, understood that if one of the Powers of the Triple Alliance comes to mobilize its forces, France and Russia, without having need of prior consultation, will mobilize theirs immediately and simultaneously."[2] Giers wished the agreement extended to any threat to peace, whether involving the Triplice or not.[3] Ribot agreed, recognizing that St. Petersburg was bargaining for French support against England and still seeking to avoid definite commitments as far as possible. On the Neva there was no disposition to accept an obligation to go to war to assist France in the recovery of Alsace-Lorraine, and on the Seine there was no desire to further Russia's eastern ambitions.[4] The negotiations were marked by much caution and some suspicion, with the Tsar and Giers reluctant to accept all the French demands. It was at last decided to summon Mohrenheim home for consultation.[5] He arrived on August 16, fresh from extended conversations with Freycinet and Ribot, and he apparently persuaded the Tsar to accept the substance of the French demands.[6] He returned to Paris and communicated to Ribot the draft of letter from Giers dated August 19 and embodying the French proposals.

On August 27, 1891, Mohrenheim and Ribot exchanged the letters at Paris which constituted the first formal documentary embodiment of the Dual Alliance. They contained two general principles which were a compromise between the extreme French and Russian positions. The two Powers would consult one another on all questions jeopardizing the general peace. In the event of a threat of peace, and especially in case of aggression, they would agree upon measures to be adopted immediately and simultaneously.[7] Delegates should be appointed as soon as possible for practical study of the measures contemplated.[8] Ribot and Freycinet urged that this be done at once. The Russians, having conceded all they desired to at the moment,

[1] *L.J.L'A.F.R.*, Nos. 3, 4, 5.

[2] *Ibid.*, Annex to No. 5, R. to L., July 24, 1891.

[3] *Ibid.*, No. 7, L. to R., August 7, 1891.

[4] Langer, *op. cit.*, pp. 188f.

[5] *L.J.L'A.F.R.*, Nos. 8-16.

[6] Hansen, *Ambassade*, pp. 118-120.

[7] "1. In order to define and consecrate the cordial understanding which unites them, and desirous of contributing in common agreement to the maintenance of the peace which forms the object of their sincerest aspirations the two Governments declare that they will take counsel together upon every question of a nature to endanger the general peace.

2. In case that peace should be actually endangered, and particularly if one of the two parties should be menaced with an aggression, the two parties undertake to reach an understanding on the measures whose immediate and simultaneous adoption would be imposed on the two Governments by the realization of this eventuality." *L.J.L' A.F.R.*, No. 17, Mohrenheim to Ribot, August 27, 1891.

[8] *Ibid.*, No. 18, Ribot to Mohrenheim, August 27, 1891. *Cf.* Hansen, *L'Alliance*, pp. 58-78.

hung back once more. Giers insisted on absolute secrecy and declared in September that he believed that the agreement already formulated corresponded to the needs of the present situation.[1] Freycinet, Ribot, and Mohrenheim met Giers in Paris in November. The Russian Minister, doubtless with tongue in cheek, sought to reassure the French that Russia had no designs on Constantinople or the Straits. Russia desired only peace. The Tsar wished time to reflect before accepting any definite military obligations in the event of German or Austro-Hungarian mobilization. War might be delayed, but would some day be inevitable.[2] For the present, concerted action in the eastern Mediterranean for the preservation of the *status quo* was sufficient. At Constantinople Paul Cambon and Nelidoff were instructed by their respective Governments to collaborate to this end. The first fruit of the entente was thus the adoption of a common policy in the Near East—one which represented neither all that France desired nor the attainment of Russian hopes, but one which constituted a workable basis of united action.[3]

2. TEMPERING THE STEEL

Freycinet had not obtained all he desired. There was no assurance of united action in the agreement. From the point of view of the Quai d'Orsay it was but a point of departure for more definite obligations. But at all events the Bismarckian system was no more and Russia was withdrawn from the orbit of the Triple Alliance. French isolation was ended. *La Grande Nation*, no longer able to act alone and set Europe by the ears with impunity, had at last gained a powerful ally with whose assistance great things might eventually be accomplished, even though the nature and purposes of such assistance were not as yet clearly defined. The *revanche* and the recovery of the lost provinces were still in the distant future. But the diplomatic hegemony of the continent which Germany had enjoyed since 1871 was undermined and the coalition which she had created for the maintenance of the *status quo* was now faced by another coalition designed to change the existing territorial and political equilibrium. So much France and Russia had in common. Without this the alliance would have been impossible. But since Russian ambitions centered in the Near East and French aspirations were limited to the west, and neither Government was as yet prepared to be drawn into unknown dangers for the sake of the aspirations of the other, the Dual Alliance too was obliged to bide its time and profess its devotion to peace and to the balance of power as a means of preserving it.

It is obvious that the initiative had come from Paris. France, with a definite grievance, was naturally much more interested in the entente than Russia, whose ambitions were much less clearly formulated and involved not a certainty but only a possibility of conflict with other Powers. Within

[1] *L.J.L'A.F.R.*, No. 19, Mohrenheim to Ribot, September 21, 1891.
[2] *Ibid.*, No. 21, Ribot's résumé of the views of Giers, November 21, 1891.
[3] *Ibid.*, Nos. 22–27.

France the initiative had come from a relatively small group of ministers. They were not dealing with remote territories nor with obscure problems in which the nation had little interest, but with a national cause. Patriotic public opinion and parliamentary sentiment could be counted upon to approve any measures not too obviously dangerous which would end French isolation and open the possibility of realizing, in some form, the deepest aspirations of French national consciousness. The precise character of these measures must, in the nature of things, be left to the executive officials handling the nation's foreign affairs, to Freycinet, Ribot, Barbey, Carnot, and their colleagues and successors. Secrecy and dissimulation were necessitated not by the fear of public or parliamentary opposition but by the exigencies of the diplomatic situation. With rare exceptions, this was fully appreciated by the Deputies, the Senators, and the journalists. The new departure did not require, in any direct or immediate fashion, the voting of credits or the dispatch of military expeditions, as was the case in empire building. There were no frenzied debates nor indignant demands for explanations. Freycinet, Ribot, and Mohrenheim could refer vaguely to "unity," "sympathy," and "friendship" between the two countries in their public statements and evoke the enthusiasm or acquiescence of all politically significant groups save a handful of extreme Left leaders.[1] The nation understood and approved —what, how, or why was of little moment.[2] Political mysticism furnished a release from the unhappy realities of France's international situation. All the conversations, which have been reviewed, were conducted in deepest secrecy and the terms of the agreement, and of the supplementary accords which followed it, were never, until 1918, revealed to anyone outside of a small group of ministers, permanent officials at the Quai d'Orsay, and a few diplomatic representatives abroad. None of the agreements fell within the categories of treaties requiring parliamentary approval for ratification. The Cabinet could withold the terms in the interest of the security of the State without violating the Constitution in any way. It did so for the entire period of the alliance.

A detailed account of the subsequent evolution of the Franco-Russian Alliance would involve a full treatment of European and Asiatic diplomatic history from 1890 to 1917. Here it will be sufficient to deal with the political situation at Paris as it influenced, and was influenced by, the commitments with Russia. Freycinet at once sought to perfect what were, from his point of view, the incomplete and unsatisfactory arrangements of August, 1891. At the end of the month he dispatched Hansen to Denmark, at Mohrenheim's suggestion, to present to Alexander III, then visiting the country, an *aide mémoire* urging the necessity of a military convention. In the event of an attack by the Central Powers, he argued, France and Russia would be at a

---

[1] *Cf.* extracts from addresses of August and September, 1891, in Hansen, *Ambassade*, pp. 120–125.

[2] Debidour, *op. cit.*, I, pp. 174–179.

serious disadvantage with no prior agreement on mobilization or military cooperation:

> To remedy this state of affairs, which may become very dangerous and lead to France and Russia being defeated separately, it is highly necessary to conclude with all speed a military convention between the two countries of which the essential stipulation will be that at the first news of the mobilization of the Triple Alliance, Russia and France will mobilize immediately all their forces . . . And if, as is very essential, this convention is held absolutely secret, it will give us in our turn a great advantage over our adversaries . . . Our victory is probably dependent on it.[1]

Hansen left Paris September 1 and at Fredensburg asked Ratchkovsky to transmit this memorandum to Prince Obolensky who would bring it to the attention of the Tsar. This channel of secret communication was employed by the French Government and by Mohrenheim for almost ten years.[2] Hansen was an old friend of Mohrenheim's and a warm partisan of the alliance. He reported that the Tsar would give serious consideration to the proposal on his return to Russia.[3] At the conference with Giers in Paris on November 21, the reluctance of the Russian Government to accept further obligations was obvious. The Tsar's insistence on caution and secrecy was increased by the troubled diplomatic situation in the winter of 1891 and 1892 and the disastrous famine in Russia.[4] Montebello, the new French Ambassador at St. Petersburg, declared that Giers favored a military convention, but that the Tsar's attitude precluded any immediate discussion of it.[5] Freycinet, in collaboration with General Mirabel of the French General Staff, worked out a detailed plan for military cooperation against Germany, but getting Russia to accept it was quite another matter.[6] The Russian press campaign against the French suggestions was strengthened by the fall of the Freycinet Cabinet in February of 1892.[7]

Loubet became the next Premier (February 27 to December 6, 1892), but Ribot and Freycinet retained their posts and continued to work for a military agreement.[8] Montebello sent the Mirabel memorandum to the Tsar on March 8, with certain modification to make it more acceptable, but Alexander III persisted in evading the issue.[9] So long as the French Government was unwilling to support the Russians against England, the Russians would refuse to support France against Germany.[10] Alexander, in fact, sought, not

---

[1] Text in Hansen, *Ambassade*, pp. 133–135.

[2] *Ibid.*, pp. 126–129.

[3] Freycinet, *Souvenirs*, pp. 487f.

[4] Langer, *op. cit.*, Chap. VIII.

[5] *L.J.L'A.F.R.*, No. 23, Montebello to Ribot, December 11, 1891, *cf.* Michon, *op. cit.*, pp. 22–25.

[6] *L.J.L'A.F.R.*, No. 28, Annex.

[7] *J.O.Ch.*, February 18, 1893.

[8] Freycinet, *Souvenirs*, pp. 499–510; Debidour, *op. cit.*, I. pp. 179f.

[9] *L.J.L'A.F.R.*, Nos. 28, 29, and Annexes.

[10] Langer, pp. 241f.

without some success, to improve Russo-German relations by meeting the Kaiser at Kiel in June. The prospects of gaining Russian consent for the military convention appeared increasingly dismal.[1] The French ministers became depressed and irritable. Ribot told Montebello to speak directly to the Emperor, since Giers was a "timorous spirit who fears too definite engagements and who loves circumlocutions."[2] The agreement must be signed early in July, or early in August at the latest. If no agreement was reached he would have to take the question before the Cabinet to relieve himself of responsibility.[3] This was an obvious effort to play upon the Tsar's fear of publicity. Gloom reigned in Paris. On July 14, an inspired article appeared in *Figaro*, entitled "Alliance or Flirtation?" which suggested that perpetual dallying was imprudent and that the year's courtship must be followed by a marriage contract.[4] Still the Russians hung back from commitments which would antagonize Berlin and make Russia a catspaw to pull the French chestnuts out of the German fire.

General Boisdeffre, Chief Adjoint of the General Staff, was invited to attend the Russian manoeuvers in August, and Ribot hoped to utilize his mission to press the issue. He was sent as military attaché of the embassy and reached St. Petersburg on August 1 with a new draft of a convention for military cooperation against Germany, which was to be signed not only by the Russian Minister of War, but also by the Minister of Foreign Affairs, and, if possible, by the Tsar.[5] He at once got in touch with General Vannovski, Minister of War, and General Obruchev, Chief of the Russian General Staff, who made numerous objections to the French terms and even to the whole project of a convention. The Russians were determined not to be embroiled in a Franco-German quarrel not involving Austria-Hungary. The French were determined not to be involved in a Russo-Austrian quarrel not involving Germany. The result was a neat compromise. Both would mobilize in the event of mobilization by either Germany or Austria-Hungary or Italy. Both would attack Germany in the event of a German or German-supported Italian attack upon France or in case of a German or German-supported Austrian attack upon Russia.[6] The precise meaning of the agreement

[1] Michon, *op. cit.*, pp. 26–33; *L.J.L'A.F.R.*, Nos. 32, 34.

[2] *Ibid.*, No. 35.

[3] *Ibid.*, Nos. 38, 39.

[4] Langer, *op. cit.*, pp. 255–256.

[5] *L.J.L'A.F.R.*, Nos. 45, 47, R. to Mont., July 22, 28, 1892.

[6] "1. If France is attacked by Germany or by Italy supported by Germany, Russia will employ all her available forces to attack Germany. If Russia is attacked by Germany or by Austria supported by Germany, France will employ all her available forces to fight Germany.

"2. In case the forces of the Triple Alliance, or of one of the Powers composing it, should mobilize, France and Russia, at the first news of the event and without the necessity of any previous concert, shall mobilize all their forces immediately and simultaneously and transport them as near to the frontiers as possible.

"3. The available forces to be employed against Germany shall be, on the part of France 1,300,000 men, on the part of Russia 700,000 or 800,000. These forces shall fight with all their

had been the subject of much controversy,[1] but this seems a concise and accurate statement of the obligations assumed.

That the Russians should have been willing to accept these terms, despite their earlier resistance, was doubtless due to the Anglo-Russian crisis in Central Asia and the Russian desire to secure a French guaranty against German support of England.[2] Ribot apparently would have preferred to keep France free from any quarrel which did not directly involve Germany, but he consented to the compromise draft.[3] Before submitting it to the Tsar, Obruchev desired Boisdeffre's signature. Ribot urged Freycinet to accept it on August 12, observing that "we have already encountered so many difficulties of all kinds that I can appreciate his (Boisdeffre's) impatience to end the matter."[4] Freycinet agreed. The Tsar approved the draft "on the whole," but insisted on a consultation with Giers, who was ill in Finland. Giers made no objection, but asked that he be allowed to consider the draft "à tête reposée."[5] Alexander approved "in principle" on August 17.[6] With this the matter ended for a time, until Giers should see fit to sign the agreement and secure its ratification by the Tsar. It had been signed only by Boisdeffre and Obruchev, and Ribot did not regard it as binding.[7] He reported Carnot's approval on August 27 and urged all haste in making it definitive.[8] In the discussions which followed, both sides suggested further modifications, the Russians insisting on absolute secrecy and showing anxiety lest they be drawn into a French war of revenge against Germany, and the French being disturbed by the constitutional scruples of President Carnot and the danger of being drawn into Austro-Russian quarrels in the Balkans.[9] In the course of these conversations Boisdeffre observed to the Tsar that mobilization was equivalent to a declaration of war, and it was so understood on both sides.[10] Freycinet and Ribot saw Giers at Aix on September

---

might with all speed, so that Germany will have to fight on the East and the West at the same time." Text in *L.J.L'A.F.R.*, No. 71, Boisdeffre, to Freycinet, August 18, 1892. See also No. 56, Boisdeffre to Freycinet, August 10, and No. 57, Montebello to Ribot, August 10.

[1] *Cf.* Langer, pp. 261*f*.

[2] *Ibid.*, pp. 265–269.

[3] *L.J.L'A.F.R.*, No. 62.

[4] *Ibid.*, No. 62, R. to F., August 12, 1892; also Nos. 47, 52, 65.

[5] *Ibid.*, No. 69, Montebello to Ribot, August 17, 1892.

[6] *Ibid.*, No. 70, M. to R., August 19, 1892 " . . . Nous sommes arrivés à un résultat avec une rapidité surprenant. Je n'osais pas l'espérer."

[7] *Ibid.*, Nos. 71, 75.

[8] *Ibid.*, No. 74.

[9] *Ibid.*, Nos. 73–80; *cf.* Michon, *op. cit.*, pp. 26–40.

[10] No. 70, Boisdeffre to Freycinet, August 18, 1892: " . . . L'Empereur m'a parle ensuite de la mobilisation au sujet de l'article 2. Je lui ai fait rémarquer que la mobilisation c'était la déclaration de guerre; que mobiliser c'était obliger son voisin a en faire autant; que la mobilisation entraînait l'exécution des transports stratégiques et de la concentration . . . 'C'est bien comme cela que je le comprends,' m'a répondu l'Empereur." This language renders dubious Renouvin's statement that the phrase had reference only to mobilization by the enemy. (*Les*

5, but secured no assurance of ratification.[1] At the end of October they again urged upon him the desirability of signing the convention in view of the German menace and the possibility of publicity with a change of ministry.[2] This was a dangerous move, since the Tsar had wanted to make the agreement voidable if it became known, but the French ministers perhaps calculated on the needs of the Russian treasury as a guaranty against hasty unfavorable action at St. Petersburg. Giers continued to be evasive and by winter it was clear that early Russian ratification of the agreement was out of the question.

As Professor Langer has pointed out in his masterly analysis of the whole situation, the Russian Government had no desire to ratify an agreement which seemed to be directed primarily against Germany.[3] Despite tariff difficulties, a *rapprochement* ensued between Berlin and St. Petersburg. At the same time the stench of the Panama scandal in Paris offended the nostrils of the Tsar and alarmed him by its political implications. It caused the fall of the Loubet Cabinet on November 28.[4] Ribot became Premier (December 6, 1892, to January 11, 1893), but Freycinet resigned on January 11 because of the attacks directed against him, and Ribot was obliged to constitute a new Cabinet (January 11 to April 4, 1893) with Jules Develle as foreign minister, General Loizillon as Minister of War, and Delcassé as Minister of Colonies. Mohrenheim was implicated in the general corruption, but was cleared of blame by the Chamber commission of inquiry. A letter from Carnot to Alexander III early in April partially assuaged the Tsar's anger.[5] The new Ribot Cabinet was overthrown in turn at the end of March and Dupuy became Premier (April 4 to December 3, 1893) with Develle and Loizillon retaining their respective portfolios. Such goings-on were not calculated to increase the Tsar's confidence in a "republic of atheists and rascals." Montebello informed Develle of the situation, blamed the changes proposed by Freycinet and Ribot for the delay in the ratification of the convention, and urged that the original compromise text be adhered to.[6] French anxiety was increased by the new German military law,[7] but the Tsar would do nothing despite

---

Origines immédiates de la guerre, pp. 309–310, Paris, 1927.) This point was of great importance in the crisis of 1914. Renouvin concedes the insincerity of Sazonov's pretense of continuing negotiations after mobilization had been ordered. The military authorities, in 1914, as in 1892, knew that "mobilization means war" and that the Russian general mobilization on July 30, 1914, closed the door to peace. For a discussion of the significance of the original phrase in 1914 see B. E. Schmitt, *The Coming of the War*, 1914, II, pp. 249–256, Charles Scribner's Sons, New York, 1930; and S. B. Fay, *The Origins of the World War*, II, pp. 479–481, New York, 1928.

[1] *L.J.L'A.F.R.*, No. 79.

[2] *Ibid.*, No. 80.

[3] Langer, *op. cit.*, Chaps. IX, X, XI.

[4] *J.O.Ch.*, November 29, 1892.

[5] Hansen, *Ambassade*, pp. 143–154.

[6] *L.J.L'A.F.R.*, No. 82, M. to D., May 20, 1893.

[7] Debidour, *op. cit.*, I, pp. 182f.

continued pressure. Through Hansen, Develle sought a return visit of the Russian squadron to a French port, doubtless hoping for another Cronstadt. The Russians were favorably disposed, if the matter could be handled without offending Germany, but no date was set. For St. Petersburg, the enemy was not Germany, but England. Russia was interested in the convention with France only in so far as it bore upon this conflict. Fortunately, from the point of view of the ratification of the agreement, Anglo-French, as well as Franco-Italian, relations were becoming increasingly strained. In Egypt and the Far East, Downing Street and the Quai d'Orsay were at odds. These clashes, coupled with naval rivalry in the Mediterranean, led to British efforts at closer relations with the Triple Alliance, which in turn led the Russian diplomats to give renewed attention to the French agreement. The Siamese crisis and the "war scare" of the summer were followed by an announcement that a Russian squadron would visit Toulon in September or October. Russia was still dependent upon the Paris Bourse for loans. A British fleet, moreover, was to visit Taranto in Italy and there seemed a growing danger that the Triplice might become a Quadruple Alliance by the accession of England. Since France seemed disposed to stand shoulder to shoulder with Russia against Great Britain and to abandon, or at least postpone, the *revanche* against Germany, the Russians were less and less averse to ratifying the convention of the preceding August.[1]

On October 13, 1893, Admiral Avellon, with a squadron of five vessels, anchored at Toulon, and the Tsar, then in Denmark, boarded a visiting French war vessel, and again listened to the *Marseillaise*. The Russian sailors in France were lionized. Parades, banquets, toasts, and effusive demonstrations were again the order of the day. Care was taken, however, to emphasize the pacific character of the alliance, and Berlin remained calm and on good terms with both Paris and St. Petersburg.[2] Great Britain was the enemy and the hostility of French opinion toward perfidious Albion was at a high point.[3] Develle renewed pressure for the ratification of the convention, but the diplomatic exchanges of the autumn were not reproduced in the *Livre Jaune* and still remain secret. The Tsar seemed reassured as to the pacific intentions of the French statesmen.[4] Casimir-Périer became Premier and Minister of Foreign Affairs in December (December 3, 1893 to May 30, 1894) and expressed his impatience at further delays.[5] On December 27 Giers at last attached his signature to the Boisdeffre-Obruchev agreement in its original form, and on January 4, 1894, Montebello responded in an identical note which

---

[1] Michon, *op. cit.*, pp. 44–47, and Langer, *op. cit.*, pp. 334ff.

[2] Langer, pp. 348–353.

[3] Sir Thomas Barclay, *Thirty Years, Anglo-French Reminiscences*, pp. 111–113, London, 1914.

[4] *L.J.L'A.F.R.*, No. 90.

[5] "Si le Tsar ne veut plus de notre alliance, qu'il le dise! Nous nous orienterons autrement." Quoted in Michon, p. 45. *Cf.* Margaine, *Rapport*, pp. 26–44.

made the convention a definitely binding obligation on both sides.[1] St. Petersburg had finally accepted the alliance in full, but only as a purely defensive arrangement with a France pacifically disposed toward Germany and not likely to employ it rashly for the recovery of the lost provinces. Germany, in fact, viewed the situation with complacency, ignorant, of course, of the exact terms of the alliance, but well aware of the Franco-Russian intimacy.[2] It was the English who felt themselves menaced by the marriage of France to the "bear that walks like a man."[3]

The military convention, like the original agreement, was signed and ratified in secret. "Ratification" on the part of France consisted merely of the exchange of notes referred to. The agreement was not signed by the President of the Republic. Its constitutionality, and its binding effect as an international obligation, might therefore be questioned, though, so far as the present writer has been able to determine, this problem has never been dealt with seriously by any of the numerous commentators.[4] It was not submitted for approval, nor even revealed to the Chambers. This was not in violation of the Constitution, since neither of the agreements fell within any category specified in Article 8 of the Constitutional Law of July 16, 1875. The constitutional question centers about the power of the signatories to bind the State. According to Article 8, treaties are negotiated and ratified by the President, whose acts are validated by the countersignatures of his ministers. But can the ministers bind the State by an instrument which is not signed by the President? President Carnot thoroughly approved of both agreements, but he signed neither of them. The political agreement was signed by Ribot as Minister of Foreign Affairs, and the second only by Boisdeffre, Chief Adjoint of the General Staff, on Ribot's instructions, and later confirmed by the exchange of notes between the French Ambassador and the Russian foreign minister. Technically, it would seem doubtful whether a minister's signature alone can bind the State and even more dubious whether the mere signature of a military officer, even though approved by the Cabinet, constitutes a valid international obligation. Both instruments would appear to have the character of "executive agreements," binding upon the ministers and upon their successors at their option, rather than of treaties binding on the State. The problem of their legal effect was never raised except by the Russians prior to their signature. St. Petersburg was apparently convinced that the final arrangements obligated not only the Government of the day in Paris but the French nation for all time to their secret commitments. Finely drawn

[1] *L.J.L'A.F.R.*, No. 91, Annex, G. to M., December 27, 1893; and No. 92, M. to G., January 4, 1894.

[2] Langer, *op. cit.*, p. 355, Note 15 and p. 392*ff*.

[3] Debidour (*op. cit.*, I, p. 194) speaks of the alliance as concluded in March of 1894 and Hansen (*Ambassade*, p. 164), in the spring of 1894. The *Livre Jaune* of 1918 (Nos. 91, 92) corrects this error in the earlier accounts.

[4] *Cf.* Fay's erroneous statement that the President has no power to conclude secret agreements, *op. cit.*, I, p. 116.

distinctions are not, of course, very useful in dealing with a Constitution as loose, fragmentary, and flexible as that of the Third French Republic. In point of fact, all the succeeding Cabinets, and, with few exceptions, the Deputies and Senators as well, regarded the alliance as a binding obligation upon the State and raised no question of the constitutionality of its origin. This was sufficient for all the practical purposes of high politics. The constitutional point is worth raising only for the light which it throws on the scope of executive freedom in handling foreign affairs.

Public opinion, as measured by press comments and declarations of leaders, was almost unanimously behind the alliance. Lucien Millevoye and Henri Rochefort were the first publicists to hail it with enthusiasm. They were presently followed by *Le Gaulois*, *L'Autorité*, *Le Journal des Débats*, *Figaro*, *Le Petit Journal*, *Éclair*, *Radical*, *Liberté*, and *Le Temps*. By the spring of 1894 the press was a unit in singing the praises of the new dispensation, though ignorant of its terms and commitments.[1] The Toulon manifestations led to outbursts of almost delirious joy. The *revanchards* were naturally elated at what they regarded as the means to their end. The radicals developed the fanciful notion that the alliance was a frank and open agreement, possessing none of the sinister secrecy of the Triple Alliance.[2] The conservatives, supported by the military and clerical groups, welcomed it as a tool of reaction in domestic politics. The Autocrat of All the Russias must not be alienated by radical agitation and revolutionary reforms. "Little by little the Alliance was exploited for the ends of internal politics and social reaction. There, in embryo, existed the profound vice which was to prevent us from counseling the Tsar to a progressive policy which would have saved Russia."[3] The radicals and socialists deplored falling into the arms of the Romanovs, but accepted it as a national necessity. The patriotic population at large gloried in the pomp and pageantry of Cronstadt and Toulon and hailed joyously the prospects which the alliance was supposed to hold out for the rehabilitation of French diplomatic prestige and the eventual restoration of *la Grande Nation* to its traditional place in world affairs.[4] Voices of dissent

[1] Hansen, *Ambassade*, pp. 165–166; Michon, *op. cit.*, pp. 51–61.

[2] Clemenceau asserted in *Justice*, October 15, 1893: "C'est de la diplomatie au grand jour, un peu bruyante, peut être, mais par sa simplicité, par sa candeur même, exempte des vices et des périls de l'autre." Flourens, in *Le Journal* of October 30: "C'est l'alliance entre deux grands peuples maîtres de leur destinée et qui n'ont rien à cacher. C'est la politique franche, loyale, à la lumière du grand jour, sans dissimulation et sans réticence." Quoted in Michon, p. 57. Such statements were echoes of the fanfare of Cronstadt and Toulon.

[3] Michon, *op. cit.*, p. 59.

[4] Gabriel Menod, in the *Contemporary Review* of November, 1893, characterized the French national temper as follows: "Another difficulty in the way of every ministry is that France, now that the difference between the Monarchists and the Republicans has been composed, feels the need of some stimulating excitement. She is in love with stir and pageantry, with glitter and bustle. With no liking for distant adventures, she suffers from being compelled to inaction in Europe . . . Nothing is produced, either in literature or in art, which excites enthusiasm. Yet we feel the need for action, for something to admire, something to believe in. There is a

were few. Few perceived the implications of the new departure, as embodied
in the secret texts, and still fewer the essentially divergent interests of the
parties whose union was being celebrated. Only Tolstoi could say ironically
that because naval officers had eaten and drunk to excess, listened to and pronounced stupid and mendacious words, all the millions of French and
Russians who had neither eaten nor drunk nor indulged in stupid mendacities
pretended to love one another with peculiar affection.[1]

3. THE SWORD OF DAMOCLES

On November 1, 1894, Alexander III was gathered unto his imperial
fathers at Livadia. All France went into mourning and the Republic was
appropriately represented at the obsequies by Generals Boisdeffre and
Berruyer and by Admiral Gervais. The new Tsar, Nicholas II, pledged the
continuation of his father's policies and eternal friendship for France, his
marriage to Princess Alice of Hesse, with the Kaiser's benignant approval,
to the contrary notwithstanding.[2] Germany stood behind Russia in her Far
Eastern ambitions and France dragged along as a poor third in protesting
against the Treaty of Shimonoseki of April 17, 1895, which victorious Japan
sought to impose on a prostrate China. On June 10, 1895, Millerand, then a
socialist, interpellated the third Ribot ministry on its policies and expressed
surprise that it had run the risk of drawing the nation into a conflict in the
Orient without the assent of the Chambers and under the terms of an accord
which had not been divulged to Parliament. Hanotaux, as Minister of
Foreign Affairs, declared that he believed the Government had reflected the
sentiments of the country in informing St. Petersburg that "France placed in
the first rank of her preoccupations consideration for her alliances. We are
disposed then to support with all the effectiveness possible the views of the
Imperial Government concerning the conditions of peace between Japan and
China." This quotation from a diplomatic dispatch was the first official
mention of the word "alliance" and evoked prolonged applause from the
Deputies. Goblet said that if a treaty existed, it should be published. Ribot
declared that he had nothing to add to Hanotaux' statement. France had
allied its interests with those of another nation for the sake of peace and the

---

longing for something nobler and greater in the life of the country. The very eccentricities of the
decadent and 'symbolic' writers and of the impressionists in painting are the sign of the longing
for what is new and better . . . There is in France . . . a certain fermenting dissatisfaction,
a yearning for an unknown ideal. The great danger . . . is the existence of a state of inaction, of
languid *ennui*, side by side with the longing for activity, . . . an intellectual and moral chaos
from which may spring some sudden outburst. It may be war, it may be social revolution, it may
be a pacific moral and intellectual revival." Quoted in Barclay (*op. cit.*, pp. 105–106), who
suggests that popular enthusiasm for the *revanche* and, therefore, for the alliance, was due to this
feeling.

[1] Quoted in H. Welschinger, *L'Alliance Franco-Russe*, p. 10, from *L'Ésprit chrétien et le patriotisme*,
Paris, 1919.

[2] H. Simond, *Histoire de la troisième République*, pp. 34–37, Paris, 1921.

"balance of power." The alliance had been ratified by the entire country, if not by Parliament. The Deputies approved this cryptic declaration, 362 to 105.[1] In the general enthusiasm at the official admission that a definitive alliance had actually been concluded, it was forgotten that France was hitched to the Russian chariot through a secret bargain the terms of which were unknown to all but a favored few in the ministry.

In October of the following year the Tsar and Tsarina visited Paris after a tour of the continental capitals. Amid speeches, banquets, toasts, parades, and reviews, Nicholas laid the cornerstone of the most ornate bridge over the Seine, named after Alexander III and connecting the Place de la Concorde, where Louis XVI lost his head, with the Quai d'Orsay, where reposed the texts of the agreement which was to make possible the war which was to provoke the revolution which was to cost the last of the tsars his throne and his life. He visited the frontier with Gervais and Boisdeffre. He wined and dined with statesmen, diplomats, journalists, and parliamentarians. He left 100,000 fr. for the poor of Paris, who were like the rich, as Anatole France once observed, in enjoying that majestic equality of the law which forbade both to steal bread or to sleep at night under the bridges. Everywhere once more was indescribable enthusiasm. Barthou, Minister of the Interior, pointed out that a moderate internal policy was essential for a lasting accord with Russia. The people of Bordeaux learned from M. Raynal that the alliance imposed upon France the necessity of combatting socialism.[2] The extreme Left was attacked in the name of patriotism. Jaurès assailed the reaction and demanded to know why the citizens of the Republic must grovel before the Tsar.[3] "If Parliament abandons to a kind of diplomatic mandarinate the conduct of the affairs of France, the Republic itself is only a word . . . The hour is come to tell Parliament and the nation the truth. Parliament will betray its mandate if it does not demand it in its entirety."[4] Millerand spoke in similar vein, though the Government and the great majority of the parliamentarians and the journalists resisted all inquisitiveness.[5] On November 21, 1896, Millerand declared in the Chamber that republicanism demanded publicity and only Parliament could determine peace or war. The destinies of France could not be disposed of without her consent. The Government must reveal the nature of the Franco-Russian engagements. Hanotaux replied that all that could be said in public had been said by the Tsar and President Faure. A superior interest made it impossible for him to add anything. Jaurès observed that silence had become the duty of patriotism and national honor.[6]

[1] *J.O.Ch.*, June 11, 1895; *cf.* Simond, *op. cit.*, pp. 119–121.
[2] *Le Temps*, October 17, 1896.
[3] *Petite République*, August 14, September 1, 1896.
[4] *Le Matin*, October 12, 1896.
[5] Michon, *op. cit.*, pp. 66–75.
[6] *J.O.Ch.*, November 22, 1896.

Meanwhile money flowed out of France into Russia as freely as the wine at the great festivals of friendship. Four days after the "ratification" of the military convention by Giers, the French Government came to the rescue of Russian credit by warning against speculative attacks on Russian securities in the French press and by sending police to watch the operations on the curb market.[1] The occasional qualms of Montebello and the Minister of Foreign Affairs over the state of Russian public finances were calmed by the French Minister of Finance. Late in 1894 the Rothschilds underwrote a new loan of 100,000,000 fr. Montebello declared it not a convenience, but a necessity and expressed his skepticism regarding the Russian budget for 1895. Vauvinaux, Chargé at St. Petersburg, pointed out the fictitious and dangerous character of Russian financial operations. At length, in 1897, even the Minister of Finance, then M. Cochery, expressed his alarm to the Minister of Foreign Affairs over the large and continuous flotations and suggested that some control be exercised.[2] But nothing was done. Each ministry sought to place responsibility upon the other. Finance was made the handmaiden of high politics and the Russian Government was granted a free market for loans in which official supervision became a mere administrative ritual. Caillaux, as Minister of Finance, protested to Delcassé against the introduction of Russian internal bonds on the bourse in 1899 and vetoed their listing. He again expressed his fears when Montebello reported a grave financial crisis in Russia: "I recognize that since Russia is our ally, it is very difficult for us to close our market to her . . . But . . . "[3] Delcassé was reassuring and insisted upon a liberal attitude. In 1906, following the last Russian loan to be admitted to the Berlin Boerse and the conclusion of the Algeciras Conference, French objections were withdrawn to the flotation of a huge loan of 2,225,000,000 fr. Despite the approval of Finance Minister Poincaré, the bankers were dubious. Only when Premier Rouvier appealed to their patriotism and pleaded with them to help the Russian Government "restore order" did they agree to float the loan.[4] In these and subsequent issues, the Minister of Finance frequently asked the advice of the Minister of Foreign Affairs who regularly declared that he had no objection to the listing of Russian securities. They were regularly listed and subscribed to by investors on the assumption that Government approval was a guaranty of their soundness. But the Government approved for political reasons only—to strengthen the alliance, to win Russian diplomatic support, to speed Russian military preparations, and the investors were none the wiser until all was lost in the holocaust of war and revolution.[5]

[1] Viner, *loc. cit.*, p. 7.

[2] Margaine, *rapport*, text of letter of July 6, 1897, pp. 109–112.

[3] *Ibid.*, p. 122, letter of November 13, 1900.

[4] Michon, *op. cit.*, pp. 132–139.

[5] Margaine, *rapport*, pp. 106–126.

These financial transactions have been interpreted, not without reason, as the means by which the Romanov autocracy maintained its control of Russia in the face of its own corruption and incompetence and the rising tide of revolt. Unfavorable reports on the state of Russian finances were regularly disregarded by the French Ministers of Finance and Foreign Affairs, and objections and protests were brushed aside. To those who wished to see, it was apparent that the Russian budget had a constant deficit and that Russian officials constantly resorted to all kinds of shabby devices to conceal the rottenness of the whole financial fabric of the Tsarist State. Without the French loans it seems reasonably certain that the reactionary ministers of the weak-willed Nicholas II could never have staved off for so long the popular clamor for reforms and a constitution.[1] The Revolution of 1905 stirred doubts in France as to the wisdom of such a policy. In Russia the Constitutional Democrats, the Social Democrats, the Peasants' Union, the revolutionary soviet of St. Petersburg, and other bodies announced that the nation would some day repudiate loans contracted in support of the autocracy. Anatole France warned his investing compatriots that they were subscribing to oppression, to crime, and to madness. Even the conservative Leroy-Beaulieu suggested that no new loans should be floated without the approval of a Russian national assembly.[2] The Russian loan of 1906 was nevertheless approved unconditionally by Poincaré and Rouvier. The Russian Union of Unions condemned it as a crime against the nation, and Jaurès and the Socialists in France assured the French investors that they were earning the hatred of the entire Russian people. The Chamber of Deputies was one of the few European parliamentary bodies which sent no greetings to the newly formed Russian Duma. The Socialists repeatedly protested against the Government's loan policy but in vain.[3] By 1914 over 17,000,000,000 fr. had gone to Russia: about 12,000,000,000 in State bonds, 4,500,000,000 in industrial securities, and the balance in provincial and municipal bonds.[4] During the Great War and after, 7,400,000,000 fr. in addition were loaned to the support of Tsarism, some 391,000,000 fr. of this total being expended during the Russian civil war on behalf of the counter-revolutionary White

---

[1] "C'est alors que le sort, non seulement de la Révolution mais des réformes, l'avenir du constitutionalisme, la transformation du déspotisme en un régime libérale et parlementaire fut réellement entre les mains de la France. La tsarisme était à sa merci, ruiné et discrédité, il suffisait de lui réfuser tout emprunt tant qu'un régime moderne ne serait pas définitivement établi en Russie, ce que, en apportant aux emprunts la guarantie des réprensentants de la nation, eut constitué pour les porteurs français la meilleuse des sécurités." Michon, op. cit., pp. 129–130.

[2] Ibid., p. 132, from Courrier Européen, July 28, 1905.

[3] J.O.Ch., February 7, 1907; January 21, 1909; June 29, 1908, etc. Pichon regularly condemned intervention in Russian internal affairs and defended the loans as serving French "national interests."

[4] Michon, op. cit., p. 127; also pp. 142–150 on the loan policy. Cf. infra., pp. 395–396. Feis' estimate of pre-war French investments in Russia is only 11.3 billion francs. This figure is perhaps nearer the truth than Michon's larger figure. In any case Russia was the market for about one-quarter of the total French capital invested abroad in 1914.

Armies pledged to overthrow the Soviet régime and repay the imperial debt.[1] This staggering total of over 24 billions of francs (about five billion dollars) has been repudiated by the Soviet Government and will in all probability never be repaid, even in part. Few living Frenchmen will contend that the tune was worth the piper's price.

The policy which approved the constant loaning of money to Russia expressed itself also in efforts to strengthen the political and military bonds between the two Governments. In the autumn of 1896 the Tsar visited Paris once more and in the following year President Faure returned the courtesy. Expressions of friendship and eternal fraternity were profuse and enthusiastic.[2] There began thus a whole series of pilgrimages of French Presidents to St. Petersburg. Clemenceau and the Radicals at first complained of the uselessness of an Alliance which was dedicated to the preservation of the "German peace" when France desired the recovery of the lost provinces. The Socialists continued to object to secret commitments. But successive foreign ministers revealed nothing save their ability to formulate reassuring platitudes. On August 1, 1898, an anonymous article appeared in the *Revue de Paris*, presenting the thesis that the alliance would fulfil its function only when it had definitely checked the continental hegemony of Germany. In this process, the Balkan States, especially Serbia, would play an important rôle. France must summon Russia to the aid of the oppressed and to a realization of her mission toward European civilization. A year later, the new foreign minister, Delcassé, went to St. Petersburg for the purpose of modifying the military convention to give it the same duration as the accord of 1891, instead of leaving it dependent upon the duration of the Triple Alliance. The Tsar consented and on August 9, 1899, Delcassé exchanged notes with the Russian foreign minister, Muraviev, confirming the arrangements of 1891, now with the object of "the maintenance of the 'balance of power'" as well as of the general peace and envisaging common action in the event of a disturbance of the equilibrium in the Balkans or through the break-up of Austria-Hungary.[3] The new accord, like its predecessors, was kept rigidly secret and Delcassé spoke of his visit as a mere formality.[4] It marked the beginning, however, of French support of Russian ambitions in the Balkans and the East. In September, 1901, the Tsar again visited France and the usual festivities were renewed.[5] In March, 1902, following the conclusion of the Anglo-Japanese Alliance, Delcassé signed new accords requiring France and Russia to consult on means of safeguarding their interests in the event of aggression in the Far East by a third party. In response to inquiries in the

---

[1] For an itemized analysis see *Rap. Budget, Ch.*, 1927, No. 4875, pp. 104–107.

[2] Debidour, *op. cit.*, I, pp. 239–240.

[3] *L.J.L'A.F.R.*, Nos. 93, 94, 95. Michon interprets this as giving the alliance an entirely new significance. *Op. cit.*, pp. 84–89.

[4] Margaine, *rapport*, pp. 65–66.

[5] Barclay, *Thirty Years*, pp. 206–208.

Chamber regarding the possible consequences of Russian penetration of Manchuria, Delcassé asserted that France and Russia were as one in their desire to protect the integrity of China.[1]

The Russo-Japanese War of 1904 and 1905 was a severe strain on the alliance. Immediately before its outbreak, Delcassé assured the Senate of its improbability and of the certainty of Russian victory if it came.[2] Great Britain's alliance with the enemy of France's ally in the Far East placed the Quai d'Orsay in a delicate and perilous position. But Delcassé escaped unscathed.[3] The foreshadowings of the *Entente Cordiale* sufficed to ward off the danger. Jaurès and his Socialist colleagues once more warned of the risks of secret commitments and insisted, in vain, upon publicity.[4] The defeat of Russia and the outbreak of revolution were greeted in the French press with pained surprise. The Russian liberal movement was condemned as treason and almost the entire Right press condoned Bloody Sunday and the brutal repressions of the Black Hundreds. Jaurès, Anatole France, and other Left leaders demanded an end of the alliance as useless, shameful, and criminal;[5] but Delcassé took refuge in patriotic duty and advocacy of indifference to Russian internal problems. Before the Treaty of Portsmouth was signed, Nicholas II met the Kaiser at Bjerkoe on the Gulf of Finland and allowed himself to be persuaded to sign an anti-British defensive alliance with Germany. This astonishing document was concluded by the two sovereigns in secret, but rumors of its nature soon leaked out. Warnings and regrets reached Delcassé from French representatives all over Europe, but the foreign minister made light of the treasonable behavior of the Tsar. The agreement was indefinitely suspended and never became operative, but it revealed the unreliable character of France's ally, as the defeat in the war with Japan revealed the impotence of the whole Tsarist structure.[6]

Following the frustration of its ambitions in the Orient, the Russian Government sought compensation in Persia and the Near East. The age-old dream of the conquest of Constantinople and the Dardanelles, which had been discouraged by the French at the close of the century,[7] was revived. Izvolsky became Minister of Foreign Affairs and entered upon a series of secret bargainings, often concealed from Paris, with the object of preparing the way for the execution of this scheme. Accords were concluded with Japan and Great Britain. The Triple Alliance must be placated, since it

[1] *J.O.Ch.*, March 25, 1902.

[2] *J.O.Sén.*, December 26, 1903.

[3] "La résponsibilité de Delcassé était écrasante. Mais le contrôle parlementaire sur la politique extérieure est tellement une dérision en France que la position de ce ministre ne fut même pas ébranlée," Michon, p. 103.

[4] Michon, pp. 103–112.

[5] *L'Humanité*, January 28, February 5, 1905; *L'Aurore*, January 31, 1905; Michon, pp. 115–123.

[6] *Ibid.*, pp. 123–126; Margaine, *rapport*, pp. 92–93; 126–127; Welschinger, *op. cit.*, pp. 62–87; Fay, *op. cit.*, I, pp. 172–177.

[7] Michon, pp. 75–77.

could not yet be defied. Bosnia and Herzegovina were offered to Austria-Hungary and duly annexed in 1908. But Izvolsky failed to secure his *quid pro quo* and felt that he had been tricked. His bitterness against Aerenthal played its part in the events to come. The Russian agreement with Italy of October of 1909, to maintain the *status quo* in the Balkans, was not revealed to the Quai d'Orsay until three years later. The ministers of the Tsar felt too certain now of French support to be overscrupulous as to their methods.[1] If negotiations failed, perhaps a Balkan league against Turkey—usable later against Austria-Hungary—would be more successful. At the end of 1910 Izvolsky became Russian ambassador in Paris and bestirred himself to secure French support of the Russian Near Eastern policy by continuing the wholsale bribery of the French press and by direct representations to the foreign minister. He apparently desired a blank check which would give St. Petersburg complete liberty of action, with no question of French objections, supervision, or even consultation. The old assurances were given anew by De Selves, Minister of Foreign Affairs in the Caillaux Cabinet (June 27, 1911, to January 10, 1912), but they were not enough.[2] The curiosity and precision of George Louis, French Ambassador on the Neva, were embarrassing. But the fall of Caillaux and the coming into power of Poincaré as Premier and Minister of Foreign Affairs (January 14, 1912, to January 18, 1913) were reassuring.

The details of Izvolsky's activites and the policies of Poincaré can be more conveniently discussed in connection with the immediate background of 1914. The final formal agreement cementing the Dual Alliance prior to Sarajevo was the naval convention of July 16, 1912, proposed and negotiated on Russian initiative. This supplement to the military convention of 1892 was strongly favored by the new French Premier. The original convention had no application to naval cooperation. In fact, the French Naval Staff, corresponding to the military general staff, was not established until 1902 and the Russian counterpart a decade later. The naval convention was signed in secret by Admirals Aubert and Lieven, and by Delcassé and Grigorovitch, the naval ministers. A month later it was "ratified" by an exchange of notes between Poincaré and Sazonov. It was designed to further Russian plans against the Straits and was based on the strategy of British control of the North Sea, French of the Mediterranean, and Russian of the Black and Baltic Seas.[3] Soon afterward the third squadron of the French fleet was transferred from Brest to Toulon. In August, 1912, Poincaré made the first of his two visits to Russia to discuss further plans of naval cooperation and to urge an Anglo-Russian naval convention. These conversations became known and contributed to the general insecurity and suspicion which hung over Europe

---

[1] Michon, *op. cit.*, pp. 154–168; Fay, *op. cit.*, I, Chap. V. It should perhaps be noted that the Franco-Italian agreement of 1902 was likewise not revealed to Russia.

[2] See *J.O.Sén.*, April 6, 1911, for Ribot's defense of the alliance.

[3] *L.J.L'A.F.R.*, Nos. 96–107; Michon, pp. 174–185.

in the spring of 1914.[1] Poincaré had become the black magician of German "encirclement." The Russian war chariot was driving furiously toward the Balkans and the Straits, with the French following hard behind.

* * * * * *

The agreements which have been reviewed unquestionably constituted the most important series of international engagements entered into by the French Republic. They formed the pivot around which the alignments shaped themselves to make possible 1914. They staked on the fortune-wheel of war not only Alsace-Lorraine and the *revanche*, but the lives and property of millions of Frenchmen, and even the very existence of France as a national State. Yet during the entire period of their existence they were never made public; their commitments were never an object of informed discussion in Parliament or the press; they were never passed upon at a national election; they were never submitted to the Chamber and the Senate for approbation, criticism, or disapproval; their constitutionality and expediency were never debated before a legislative body or a judicial tribunal in France. They were exclusively the secret creation of a little handful of men occupying ministerial posts—theoretically answerable to Parliament and the electorate, but in such matters answerable to no one save themselves, their predecessors, and successors. Even within the Cabinet, there is no evidence to show that these fateful obligations were ever made the object of searching analysis and criticism, involving a general discussion among the ministers of their implications and alternatives. They were the products of the Ministers of War, Marine, and Foreign Affairs, of a few individuals at the Quai d'Orsay, and in the army, navy, and diplomatic service. The actions of these individuals were, in practice, not reviewable. It was enough to wrap themselves in the cloak of patriotism and to present the obligations to which they had committed the nation as necessities of national honor and national interests. Parliament, the public, and the press acquiesced. The Constitution, the parliamentary system, and the democratic tradition availed nothing in the face of the will of the uncontrolled and uncontrollable oligarchs of diplomacy and war.

These individuals were not free agents working in a vacuum, however. French statesmen, heirs of a great tradition, have seldom taken any but a realistic view of the problems of diplomacy, *i.e.*, a view based upon a thorough knowledge of the system in which they were working and a keen appreciation of the relationship of means to ends. The ends themselves are not subject to any appreciable degree of control or freedom of choice. They are dictated by the nature and rules of the game of *Realpolitik*. The political goals of balance-of-power and prestige diplomacy may be shaped and colored by economic, humanitarian, or religious considerations, but only within the limits imposed by the political State System itself. The Dual Alliance,

[1] Fay, *op. cit.*, I, pp. 325–330.

like the Triple Alliance, was a natural outgrowth of that system, successor of many such combinations in the past and predecessor of many others in the future. It was "inevitable" in the sense that its genesis and development were determined by the basic features of the State System which has given birth to so many similar liaisons and by the particular positions occupied by France and Russia in that system during the period under consideration. These factors thus impose fairly rigid limits on the choice of means as well as condition the ends themselves.

The creators of the Franco-Russian Alliance in Paris acted as one would expect statesmen everywhere in the Western State System to act under similar circumstances. The later diplomats who utilized and developed it were under a like compulsion. Whatever freedom they exercised was a freedom not to choose between ultimate ends, which were determined by the international position of France after the Treaty of Frankfort, nor between alternative combinations as means, which were precluded by factors beyond their control in foreign capitals, but a freedom to participate in the shaping of the alliance and, to a lesser degree, of the general diplomatic situation in such a way as to make it serve their predetermined purposes. And this, in turn, amounted only to an ability to make use of such opportunities as presented themselves "accidentally" (*i.e.*, in a fashion undetermined and uncontrollable from the Quai d'Orsay), to postpone or hasten the ultimate day of reckoning with Germany. Their decisions here depended upon an anticipation of consequences. Like all European statesmen, they failed to foresee the catastrophic character of a resort to arms by the Great Powers under modern economic and technological conditions. Here is a point at which their "realism" was unrealistic. But in general they acted with a clear consciousness of their objectives and of the agencies for their achievement. Their motivations were conditioned by the State System in which they lived and their policies were controlled by their own judgments of the stresses and strains and the shiftings of power and prestige in the relationships of the great coalitions which faced one another across the armed frontiers.

CHAPTER VIII

THE ENTENTE CORDIALE

1. DELCASSÉ AND THE SUDAN

WHEN in June, 1898, the Méline ministry fell and Henry Brisson, for the second time, succeeded in forming a Cabinet of the Left, he called to the Quai d'Orsay a statesman who was destined to enjoy a longer continuous tenure of office than any of his predecessors and who worked with impressive effectiveness for a period of almost seven years to reorient the foreign policies of France in accordance with his own ideas.[1] Théophile Delcassé was born in 1852 at the foot of the Pyrenees, in the pleasant country of the Midi, whose sunshine no doubt contributed to what would have been an amiable disposition if the indefatigable energy, crisp precision, and strength of will of this stocky little man had allowed him leisure for cultivating friendships. Like so many French politicians he began his Paris career as a journalist. He was an ardent follower of Gambetta and presented himself for election to the Chamber in his home Department in 1885. He retired in favor of another candidate, however, and did not reach the Palais Bourbon till four years later, when he was elected from Foix, which consistently reelected him for many years thereafter. On January 17, 1893, he was named under-secretary of state for Colonies in the Ribot ministry. When this position was elevated to ministerial rank in the following year, Delcassé became the first Minister of Colonies, a post which he filled with distinction. He was an expansionist of the school of Ferry and Freycinet, and always insisted that French power and prestige on the continent depended upon a vigorous colonial policy. He was equally interested in foreign affairs and in the development of the navy and often spoke his mind regarding them in the Chamber.[2]

His first achievement as Minister of Foreign Affairs was preparing the way, at the invitation of Madrid, for the peace conference at Paris which closed the Spanish-American War. He has been described as one of those rare mortals who shape their lives according to a predetermined plan and who attain to the goals they have set for themselves through continuous

[1] Despite the importance of the man and his work, there is no adequate biography of Delcassé available in French or English. The nearest approach to one is the pamphlet sketch by Reynald cited below. The present chapter is not intended to fill this gap, but merely to outline the diplomatic achievements of Delcassé from the point of view of the control of policy.

[2] G. Reynald, *La diplomatie française: l'oeuvre de M. Delcassé*, pp. 5–16, Paris, 1914; G. H. Stuart, *French Foreign Policy from Fashoda to Sarajevo*, pp. 3–8, New York, 1921.

and well-planned efforts.[1] While this may be a rationalization in retrospect which minimizes the rôle of chance and the opportunism which must, in greater or lesser degree, mark the work of every statesman, it seems reasonably clear that Delcassé, at the very beginning of his long term, had certain fairly definite and carefully formulated ideas as to the policy he should pursue. His general objectives were those of all Franch foreign ministers of the period: the enhancement of French prestige, the weakening of the diplomatic hegemony of Germany, the utilization of opportunities to recover for France what had been lost at Sedan and after. He differed from his predecessors, and especially from the anglophobe Hanotaux, only in his conception of the specific policies through which these ends were to be gained. The Russian Alliance was already a reality. Delcassé's success in strengthening it by the accords of 1899 has already been noted.[2] But in view of Russia's preoccupation in the Far East, Delcassé did not expect too much from the alliance. France must seek to increase her own power and prestige by a further development of her colonial policy, involving the acquisition of additional territory. His eyes rested longingly on Morocco, which must not be allowed to fall to any other Power and which, as a French possession, would neatly round out the French North African empire and greatly strengthen the French position in the Mediterranean. The Sudan also offered possibilities. But rival imperial Powers must be reckoned with—Italy, Spain, and, above all, Great Britain. To antagonize them would be to imperil the diplomatic advantages of colonial expansion.[3] They must be placated, and, if possible, pulled away from the orbit of the Triple Alliance and oriented toward Paris. These two goals, which seemed at the outset almost paradoxical, were equally important in Delcassé's scheme of action. The steps by which he successfully put these policies into execution will be sketched in the pages which follow.[4]

Throughout his career at the Quai d'Orsay, Delcassé discreetly refrained from any fanfare of trumpets or excess of publicity regarding his purposes and methods. While avoiding Parliament as much as possible, he gained the confidence of all parties, whose leaders were absorbed for the most part in the heated polemics of the Dreyfus case and the great controversy over the separation of Church and State. His position remained firm in successive Radical Cabinets, of whose general outlook and policies he disapproved. During the first year, from June of 1898 to June of 1899, Brisson succeeded Méline, Dupuy succeeded Brisson, and Waldeck-Rousseau succeeded Dupuy

[1] Reynald, *op. cit.*, p. 5.

[2] *Supra*, p. 155.

[3] In Delcassé's own language: "Le problème était celui-ci: établir la prépondérance de la France au Maroc, par conséquent augmenter sa puissance dans la Méditerranée, sans s'aliéner, en se conciliant au contraire, les puissances dont la position dans la Méditerranée se signalait d'elle-même à nos préoccupations." *J.O.Ch.*, November 10, 1904.

[4] For a brief survey of the development of his policies, see R. Millet, *Notre politique extérieure de 1898 à 1905*, Paris, 1905, *passim*.

in the Premiership. With Waldeck-Rousseau, Delcassé was fairly intimate. When he resigned in June of 1902, a new Cabinet was constituted by Émile Combes (June 7, 1902, to January 23, 1905). Toward both Combes and his successor, Maurice Rouvier (January 23, 1905, to March 14, 1906), Delcassé was cool and aloof. Both Parliament and his colleagues in the Cabinet granted him a free hand to handle foreign affairs as he saw fit. Profiting from their preoccupation with other matters, he conducted his office with almost complete independence, vouchsafing only brief and occasional explanations to an aquiescent Chamber and public. With the representatives of foreign Powers he was uncommunicative, secretive, cautious, and unpopular.[1] In a different setting he might not have enjoyed such freedom of action. But the anxieties and apprehensions of the eighties, with which Ferry had to cope, had passed away before the prospect of a Europe at peace and a France strong by its own power and by its alliance in the east. Delcassé waged no undeclared wars and asked for no expensive military expeditions. He could better accomplish his ends through silent and secret paths about which Parliament and the press knew little and cared less.[2] But he was none the less the consistent apostle of *Realpolitik*. He joined Germany in sabotaging the Tsar's well-intentioned efforts to secure armament limitation at the First Hague Peace Conference of 1899—a step which he described as "senseless."[3] He was ever ready to protect the claims and interest of French nationals abroad when it seemed diplomatically advantageous to do so.[4] Such was the outlook and position of the man who has been aptly called the "the nemesis of Bismarck."

The diplomatic structure of the Iron Chancellor was already crumbling when Delcassé took office. Italy's adherence to the Triple Alliance had been due to resentment at the taking of Tunis by France. She sought to use it to further her colonial ambitions in North Africa, but in view of German reluctance to support adventures which might antagonize Great Britain, France, and Turkey, Crispi's hopes of acquiring Tripoli were frustrated.[5] When the military expedition in Abyssinia met with disaster, he was overthrown and succeeded by the Marquis di Rudini, who initiated a policy of

[1] E. N. Anderson, *The First Moroccan Crisis*, 1904–1906, pp. 8–10, Chicago, 1930.

[2] "Pendant sept ans, M. Delcassé a poursuivre une conception personnelle de la politique extérieure de la France; il s'agissait de rétablir l'équilibre européen contre l'hégémonie allemande et d'étendre notre empire colonial, notamment dans le Nord de l'Afrique, on lui reproche très vivement de certain côtés, d'avoir exercé une sorte de dictature, d'avoir poursuivre cette politique, bonne en elle-même, sans en informer le Parlement, le Président de la République, ni même son président du conseil de 1902 a 1905, M. Combes. Mais ces diverses autorités constitutionelle, n'auraient-elles pas dû montrer, en temps opportun, une plus vive curiosité?" J. Barthélemy, *Le Gouvernement de la France*, p. 128, Paris, 1919.

[3] *G.P.*, XV, No. 186.

[4] See for example the Socialist criticism of his action in dispatching a squadron to Mitylene in 1901 to coerce Turkey into meeting the financial claims of French citizens. *J.O.Ch.*, November 4, 1901 and January 20, 1902.

[5] S. B. Fay, *The Origins of the World War*, I, pp. 141–144, New York, 1928.

rapprochement with France. Delcassé was quick to take advantage of the opportunity thus presented. In the spring of 1898, before he took charge at the Quai d'Orsay, he visited Barrère, the French Ambassador at Rome, and held conversations with Marquis Visconti-Venosta, the Italian foreign minister.[1] Two years previously, a Franco-Italian convention had been signed by which Italy at last recognized the French protectorate in Tunis in return for commercial privileges. Delcassé assured the Marquis that there was room in the Mediterranean for both Powers and devoted himself to winning Italian good will. In 1899 a commercial treaty put an end to the long tariff war between the two countries. The Anglo-Franch convention of March, 1899, irritated the Italian statesmen by its implication of eventual French control of Tripoli, but Barrère extended assurances that France would not stand in the way of Italian ambitions. "Under conditions" Delcassé was prepared to support the Italian aspirations. He drove a hard bargain, and on December 14, 1900, Visconti-Venosta and Barrère reached a somewhat ambiguous secret agreement by which Italy secured a pledge that France harbored no designs on Tripoli and Paris secured what was interpreted as a free hand in dealing with Morocco. Delcassé announced the *rapprochement* in the Senate[2] and in the following April a French fleet visited Italian ports.[3] President Loubet bestowed on Victor Emmanuel the Grand Cross of the Legion of Honor and an Italian squadron was warmly greeted at Toulon.

So much done, the rest was made easy by Signor Prinetti, the Francophile Italian foreign minister from 1901 to 1903. Through Barrère, Delcassé made more explicit the reciprocal recognition of rights in Tripoli and Morocco and sought an agreement to render harmless to France the pending renewal of the Triple Alliance. In June, 1902, he obtained Prinetti's secret assurances that the alliance contained nothing directly or indirectly aggressive toward France. Delcassé informed the Chamber that "in no event and in no manner will Italy become either the tool or the auxiliary of an aggression against our country."[4] On November 1, Barrère and Prinetti exchanged notes providing for the maintenance of Italian neutrality in case of a direct or indirect attack against France, even if France were obliged to take the initiative in a declaration of war as a result of a direct provocation.[5] These secret commitments, quite out of harmony with the spirit, if not the letter, of Italy's obligations to Germany and Austria-Hungary, gave Italy a foot in both camps. In 1903 Victor Emmanuel and his queen visited Paris, and in 1904 President Loubet and Delcassé visited Rome. The French foreign minister had taken a long step toward detaching Italy from the Triplice and had secured Italian assent to French penetration of Morocco. At the same time Spain, ever

---

[1] Reynald, *op. cit.*, pp. 30–31.

[2] *J.O.Sén.*, February 11, 1901.

[3] Anderson, *op. cit.*, pp. 21–24.

[4] *J.O.Ch.*, July 3, 1902.

[5] Texts in Fay, *op. cit.*, I, p. 147, and Anderson, pp. 31–32.

anxious over Morocco's future, was conciliated by a secret partition agreement in October of 1902. This document, however, was not signed by the Spanish Government which, in the final outcome, secured a smaller share of the spoils than had been allotted to it in the agreement, but it was proof that Delcassé had established good relations with both of France's Latin neighbors in the Mediterranean.[1]

Far more important, from the point of view of the broader purposes of Delcassé's diplomacy, were the problems of Anglo-French relations. On July 10, 1898, twelve days after he had taken the portfolio of foreign affairs, an event took place in the remote wilds of Africa which was destined to bring the two countries to the verge of war. Several French officers, under the command of Captain Marchand, accompanied by 120 Senegalese, landed upon a small and desolate bit of ground on the left bank of the White Nile, some sixty miles downstream from the mouth of the Sombat, which carried the waters of the Abyssinian high-lands into the valley and marshes south of Egypt. They had started out from the Atlantic coast two years previously and with infinite labor and courage had traversed the jungles, deserts, and swamps of north central Africa and reached their destination at Fashoda, where the French flag was planted and an encampment established. Six weeks later a steamboat, once belonging to the fleet of Gordon, who had perished at Khartoum, and now manned by the Arab rebels of the Mahdi who had overthrown Anglo-Egyptian rule in the Sudan, appeared, attacked the post, and finally withdrew to the north before the French rifle fire. Early in September the vessel was captured by the gunboats of General Kitchener, whose forces had crushed the Mahdist revolt at the Battle of Omdurman and who now learned of the presence of the mysterious intruders some hundreds of miles to the south. With five steamers and a strong force, Kitchener started up the river and on September 19 reached Fashoda. Courtesies were exchanged and Marchand was informed that Great Britain could not tolerate French occupation of any part of the Nile Valley. His orders were precise, however, and he refused to retire. But he consented to the hoisting of an Egyptian flag and the tension gradually eased. The two forces settled down to a joint occupation of the point of land, pending further orders from their respective Governments.[2]

This incident was the dramatic culmination of many decades of Anglo-French colonial rivalry in the Dark Continent. The details of its antecedents are less important, from the viewpoint of the rôle of Delcassé, than its immediate results and ultimate consequences. As far back as 1890, the Ubangi country and the Upper Nile had been looked upon as a field of French expansion northward and eastward from the French Congo. Marchand's instructions of February and June, 1896, had ordered him to establish French title to the White Nile region and to cultivate friendly relations with the

[1] Anderson, *op. cit.*, Chap. III.
[2] M. B. Giffen, *Fashoda, The Incident and Its Diplomatic Setting*, Chap. I, Chicago, 1930.

Mahdists, sworn enemies of Great Britain. He was expected to reach his destination in the fall of 1897, but a recession in the waters of the Bahr-el-Ghazelle caused delay. Attempts were also made, without success, to reach the Nile through Abyssinia. These efforts were secret, but on March 28, 1895, Sir Edward Grey, Under-secretary of State for Foreign Affairs, had declared that any French advance into the Nile Valley would be regarded as an "unfriendly act"—a statement which drew a sharp retort from Hanotaux anent the impropriety of making vast paper claims to unoccupied territories.[1] In subsequent discussions, during 1897 and 1898, the British Government adhered to its position and Hanotaux made the same reservations. The British had been seriously contemplating the subjugation of the Sudan for several years, in part out of a desire to anticipate the French designs.[2] Kitchener and Marchand were thus the spear-points of rival imperialisms, meeting under circumstances likely to lead to serious friction.

Here was an adventure after Delcassé's own heart—veteran expansionist that he was. But enthusiasm for the path of empire must not be allowed to obscure the realities of the situation. Marchand's little band was impotent. No reinforcements could be got to it for eight months, while the British in control of the Nile Valley could reach Fashoda in force in as many days. On September 8 the foreign minister informed Sir Edmund Monson, the British Ambassador, that this French expedition might be encountered somewhere up the river, that Marchand was only an "emissary of civilization" with no power to take possession of territory, and that all questions of principle should be reserved for direct discussion at home.[3] He professed ignorance of Marchand's whereabouts even after the English papers had reported them.[4] Once the news was known, the press on both sides of the Channel burst forth into claims, counterclaims, and recriminations which became more heated as the controversy progressed and the deadlock tightened. Prophecies of war became rife. Business was suspended. The French Mediterranean fleet passed Gibraltar in the night and proceeded to Cherbourg while preparations for hostilities were begun in the English Channel ports.[5] In the diplomatic conversations, the British Government demanded Marchand's immediate withdrawal and rested its case upon Egyptian sovereignty over the Bahr-el-Ghazelle and (inconsistently) on the right of conquest by Kitchener. Delcassé replied with arguments that the territory was unoccupied, that it had been taken possession of first by the French, and that (again inconsistently) it was not British but Egyptian territory.[6] Both sides were unyielding. The tension tightened and an open break seemed imminent.

---

[1] *J.O.Sén.*, April 5, 1895.

[2] Giffen, Chap. II.

[3] *Ibid.*, pp. 34–35.

[4] B. Willson, *The Paris Embassy*, 1814–1920, pp. 323–324, New York, 1927.

[5] T. Barclay, *Thirty Years*, pp. 144–150.

[6] Giffen, pp. 37–64.

Delcassé had thus inherited from Hanotaux a quarrel with the Power he hoped to conciliate. The European balance of power was no less important in his calculations than colonial expansion. Great Britain was unentangled as yet, but he could ill afford to risk a war over Fashoda with the greatest naval Power. Germany stood always on the flank—officially neutral but waiting. Delcassé had abandoned Hanotaux' efforts at a *rapprochement* with Berlin. If there had even been an opportunity for a Franco-German accord, it had passed.[1] As for Russia, Delcassé might have reasonably hoped for a common front against the colonial rival of both Paris and St. Petersburg. But the hope was vain; the Tsar had no interest in Africa and had just summoned a peace conference. Witte, Muraviev, and Koropatkin, all ministers, visited Paris in October on various missions, and made it plain that no Russian support would be forthcoming.[2] The British attitude was one of belligerent insistence. France was torn by the Dreyfus affair and by the fall of the Brisson Cabinet in the midst of the dispute.[3] Delcassé might have escaped the odium of capitulation by refusing to participate in the Dupuy ministry, but he remained at his post to carry through the distasteful task of surrendering as gracefully as possible.[4]

When endless discussion had gotten nowhere and Monson threatened to present an ultimatum, Delcassé cried, "No! No! Not that! That would be irreparable!"[5] The Cabinet met and decided. On November 4, 1898, it was announced that the Marchand mission would not be maintained at Fashoda. On December 11 the redoubtable captain and his little force quit the left bank of the White Nile and the war danger was passed.[6] But Salisbury remained truculent. No concession of a trade outlet on the Nile was obtained by Paul Cambon in London and the problem soon became one of delimiting frontiers. Toward the end of the year, Sir Edmund Monson, speaking at the banquet of the British Chamber of Commerce in Paris, sought to reassure French opinion regarding the motives of British policy. But the French Government must avoid provocations:

I would earnestly ask them to discountenance and to abstain from the continuance of that policy of pinpricks which, while it can only procure an ephemeral gratification to a short-lived ministry, must inevitably perpetuate across the Channel an irritation which a high-spirited nation must eventually find intolerable.[7]

This led to a new explosion in the French press, causing the British Embassy, at Salisbury's suggestion, to issue a *communiqué*, declaring that the ambassador had been misunderstood.[8] Such incidents revealed the difficulties

[1] *Ibid.*, Chap. VIII.
[2] *Ibid.*, Chap. IX.
[3] *J.O.Ch.*, October 26, 1898.
[4] Giffen, Chap. VII.
[5] Reynald, *op. cit.*, p. 21.
[6] Giffen, pp. 76–77.
[7] Quoted in Willson, *op. cit.*, p. 328.
[8] *Ibid.*, pp. 329–330.

in the way of an accommodation. On March 21, 1899, however, an agreement was signed, fixing the Nile-Congo watershed as the line east of which Great Britain, and west of which France, promised to acquire neither territory nor political influences.[1] Delcassé was relieved. The most serious crisis of Anglo-French diplomacy under the Third Republic had been weathered without war.

2. Great Britain and France, 1904

Fashoda is frequently presented as the turning point of Anglo-French relations which prepared the ground for the diplomatic revolution effected by Delcassé five years later. It is no longer possible, however, to read into the situation a causal connection between the convention of March, 1899, and the later agreements. While Delcassé unquestionably favored a *rapprochement* with Great Britain from the beginning,[2] the effects of the conflict over the Sudan left him discouraged and embittered. Hostile threats and warnings still filled the press and the occasion seemed as inauspicious as possible for the realization of Delcassé's early hopes. In fact, French resentment against Great Britain ran so high that an entente with Germany seemed almost possible in the spring of 1899. The specter of isolation again loomed and dampened the ardor of the *revanchards*. Russia seemed a weak reed to lean upon and Delcassé's strengthening of the Dual Alliance on his visit to Russia later in the year was an unrevealed secret.[3] Berlin was not averse to profiting from Anglo-French friction and overtures came both from Wilhelmstrasse and the Quai d'Orsay. Bülow was dubious, however. Delcassé was not disposed to press the issue. This eddy of cordiality across the Rhine was but a backwash of the Bahr-el-Ghazelle. Genuine friendship seemed out of the question between the enemies of '71, whatever their relations with other Powers might be.[4]

But British policy had reached the crossroads and might be directed toward either of the two continental coalitions, depending upon circumstances. Delcassé would have been unable to secure its reorientation in the direction he desired but for the exigencies of Anglo-German relations. Chamberlain, Colonial Secretary in the Salisbury Cabinet, was a vigorous champion of cooperation with the United States and Germany. He had the support of Balfour, Lord Lansdowne, and the Prince of Wales (the future Edward VII) and his popularity and business connections made him an influential figure. The Kaiser's previous efforts to gain a British alliance now seemed to promise success. In view of the friction with France and

[1] Giffen, Chap. VI; and Stuart, *op. cit.*, pp. 38–40.

[2] When he took office he declared: "I do not wish to leave here, I do not wish to leave this armchair, until I have reestablished a friendly understanding with England." Quoted by Stuart, *op. cit.*, p. 12, from Bérard, "La politique française" in *Revue de Paris*, July 1, 1905.

[3] *Supra*, p. 155.

[4] Anderson, *op. cit.*, pp. 41–51; Giffen, *op. cit.*, Chap. X.

Russia, Chamberlain had made an unofficial offer of a defensive alliance to Berlin in March, 1898. But Bülow, Holstein, and even the Emperor were suspicious and indifferent. The Kaiser and Bülow visited England in November, 1899, and Chamberlain renewed his overtures.[1] The Chancellor continued to be evasive and to suggest special bargains. Lansdowne, the new Foreign Secretary, was favorable and discussions continued, but Salisbury was skeptical and Bülow distrustful. Lansdowne finally decided that the obstacles were insuperable and the negotiations ended in a fiasco—primarily because of Berlin's vague desire to retain a "free hand," which in practice meant rejecting in turn the opportunities for closer relations with Russia, France, and Great Britain and throwing the latter into the arms of the former.[2]

This breakdown of the Anglo-German alliance negotiations, coupled with the increasing realization in London of continental unfriendliness as shown by the Boer War and the dangerous situation developing in the Far East, disposed Downing Street to give renewed attention to French relations and to the possibility of an entente with the Quai d'Orsay. The Anglo-Japanese Alliance of 1902 gave added security to British interests in the Orient. But it obligated the parties to come to the assistance of one another in the event of an attack by two or more Powers. The clashing imperial ambitions of Russia and Japan were already threatening war in Manchuria. Should France support Russia the *casus foederis* might become operative—and no British statesman could view with equanimity the prospect of a conflict with both members of the Dual Alliance. Here was an additional incentive to efforts to reach an understanding with Paris and perhaps to give form to the dreams of Delcassé.[3]

The problem was by no means simple, however. A diplomatic understanding would be barren, if not impossible, without the support of the intangible but powerful forces of public opinion. The psychological gulf separating the peoples on either side of the Channel was as wide in the early years of the new century as it had ever been. Fashoda had left deep scars— naturally more painful to the loser. French distrust of "perfidious Albion" was unabated and Delcassé's political position in the Government was not such as to enable him to overcome this obstacle unaided. His efforts in this direction are probably not fully revealed by the evidence available. But fortunately for his purposes, others were preparing the ground for the seeds which he wished to sow. While the diplomatic initiative for the entente came from Delcassé, the necessary molding of public opinion was largely effected by the English. Major Roper Parkington and a group of his colleagues who were interested in closer economic relations between the countries, and who had arranged the visit of the Lord Mayor of London to

[1] *Cf.* H. Nicolson, *Portrait of a Diplomatist*, p. 94, New York, 1930.

[2] Anderson, *op. cit.*, pp. 52–80, and Fay, *op. cit.*, I, pp. 129–141.

[3] Anderson, pp. 81–87.

the International Exposition at Bordeaux in 1895, were bestirring themselves to bring about a solution of the political problems dividing the two Governments. With the encouragement of the Prince of Wales they established a society which took the name of "*Entente Cordiale* Association for the development of more cordial relations between the United Kingdom and France." Its activities met with a certain response in France and various articles in periodicals on both sides on the narrow seas began to urge a *rapprochement*.[1] Thomas Barclay, vice president of the British Chamber of Commerce in Paris, also played a rôle of no mean importance. His efforts to create a more friendly atmosphere met with appreciable success and in the autumn of 1900 he arranged a meeting of the Association of British Chambers of Commerce in Paris. Some six hundred representatives of eighty-five chambers of commerce came over and the affair was a great success. The enthusiastic welcome accorded to President Kruger of the Boer Republics militated against Barclay's designs, but the tone of the French press was restrained and anti-British demonstrations were subdued. Barclay worked ceaselessly through his business and press connections to create a more friendly attitude.[2]

These activities were largely motivated by a general humanitarian interest in the cause of peace and international understanding and by considerations of the gain to trade which would presumably accompany improved relations in politics and public opinion. Barclay, in looking back over his contribution, declared:

> The distinguishing feature of the present entente is that it found its most congenial soil among the business and popular elements of the two nations, and that, instead of being officially fostered, it was treated with indifference if not with discouragement, by the governing classes, until it overwhelmed them.[3]

This is something of an exaggeration, but it is probably true that the individuals and agencies which thus ploughed the ground for the diplomatic planting were not primarily interested in—or even aware of—the broader political implications of their cause. It was left for the Quai d'Orsay and Downing Street to reap the fruits in the harvest of *Weltpolitik*.

When Balfour succeeded Salisbury in 1902 the air was filled with suggestions of a general arbitration treaty between the two countries—a proposal sponsored by many prominent Britishers and by chambers of commerce on both sides. A group of Deputies under the leadership of Estournelles de Constant met in March, 1903, to discuss the possibility. Informal diplomatic conversations were commenced in April.[4] Early in May, the new monarch, King Edward VII, took the bold step of making an official visit to Paris. French coldness and indifference melted before the sovereign's affability and tactful emphasis upon more friendly relations. Paul Cambon, French

[1] J. L. de Lanessan, *Histoire de l'Entente Cordiale*, pp. 209–240, Paris, 1916.
[2] *Thirty Years*, pp. 157f.
[3] *Ibid.*, pp. 289–290.
[4] Anderson, *op. cit.*, p. 86.

Ambassador in London, later declared that the entente could not have been achieved except for the King's work in its behalf.[1] Tardieu also gives Edward VII credit for initiating the negotiations[2] and the general impression prevailed that the British Government had taken the lead. All these developments, however, were an outcome of Delcassé's long maturing aspirations. The projected arbitration treaty was definitely taken up late in May on Cambon's initiative. In July, 1903, President Loubet, Delcassé, and M. Étienne, Minister of Colonies, visited London, where felicitations were again exchanged. These visits were the Cronstadt and Toulon of the entente. The Commission on International Arbitration of the Chamber of Deputies had already been invited by the Commercial Committee of the House of Commons to visit the British Parliament. At the great banquet in Westminster Palace on July 22, Balfour and the leader of the Opposition, Campbell-Bannermann, expressed their enthusiasm for an arbitration agreement and Chamberlain urged a general entente.[3] During his sojourn in the British capital, Delcassé discussed outstanding difficulties with the Foreign Secretary. Étienne expressed to Lansdowne his fear of Germany, his belief in the efficacy of an Anglo-French combination to hold Berlin in check, and his confidence that such arrangement would lead to improved Anglo-Russian relations.[4] Delcassé, Étienne, Cambon, and Loubet were all in accord as to the desirability of an understanding and extended discussions were commenced with that end in view.

During these secret negotiations, which stretched out over the autumn and winter of 1903, Delcassé sought assurances that Great Britain would not obstruct French policy in Morocco, where the intimate relations of the Sultan's Government with Sir Arthur Nicolson and other British agents had given rise to anxiety at the Quai d'Orsay,[5] Lansdowne agreed on condition of the protection of British interests in Tangier and along the coast, the recognition of Spain's interest, and the maintenance of the "open door." An arbitration convention was signed on October 14, 1903. In reply to Cambon's further proposals, Lansdowne suggested that Egypt be included in the general political accord, but Cambon consented only to drive a closer bargain in Morocco in return for French recognition of the British occupation of the Nile. It was agreed that a subsequent settlement should be reached between France and Spain which should leave Madrid in possession of the Moroccan coast opposite Gibraltar. Lord Cromer, British Consul General and agent at Cairo, urged further concessions in order to strengthen British control of Egypt. Cambon asked more in Morocco than Lansdowne seemed

---

[1] London *Times*, December 22, 1920.

[2] *La France et les alliances*, pp. 60f., Paris, 1909.

[3] Lanessan, *op. cit.*, pp. 246–256.

[4] Conversation of July 2, cited by Anderson, *op. cit.*, p. 88, Note 20, citing *B.D.*, II, 293, No. 356. *Cf.* Fay, I, pp. 153–167.

[5] Nicolson, *op. cit.*, pp. 106–108.

willing to concede, alleging fear of German designs, proposing an agreement
to maintain the *status quo* within a radius of 500 miles of the straits as a
means of blocking them, and insisting upon a time limit to equality of
economic opportunity. Lansdowne would not be drawn into any anti-
German scheme, but by November an agreement on Egypt and Morocco was
practically reached and Delcassé felt justified in assuring the Chamber that
France would have the decisive word in the solution of the "Moroccan
problem."[1] At Delcassé's instigation, the Russian Ambassador discussed
Anglo-Russian friction in Manchuria and Asia generally with Lansdowne.
St. Petersburg was unwilling to limit its ambitions or to make any arrangements satisfactory to Japan and Great Britain, but British apprehensions were
relieved by assurances from Delcassé that France would take no part in any
Russo-Japanese conflict. This being settled, the British adopted a stiffer
tone in the Anglo-French discussions and by mid-January, 1904, a deadlock
was reached because of the British refusal to grant a territorial indemnity
for the relinquishment of French fishing rights off Newfoundland. Both
Lansdowne and Delcassé were indisposed to concessions through fear of
public opinion and the French foreign minister kept his colleagues in the
Cabinet uninformed of the details of the situation.[2]

On February 10, 1904, war began between Japan and Russia. Delcassé was
surprised and furious at the British refusal to cooperate in preventing or
stopping the conflict. His whole scheme was imperiled by this new development. But an accord with Great Britain was more essential than ever.
Lansdowne threatened to break off negotiations when Delcassé sought to
reopen the Newfoundland question at the end of March. The foreign minister
then ordered Cambon to sign the draft agreements. The ambassador did so
on April 8, 1904, and the *Entente Cordiale* became a diplomatic reality. It
consisted of three documents, only one of which, the convention relative to
Newfoundland and West Africa, affected the status of territory and required
parliamentary approval in France. In return for a limitation of French fishing
rights, Great Britain renounced her monopoly of navigation in Gambia,
ceded to France the island of Los, commanding the port of Konakry, and
redefined the Niger frontier in the interest of French navigation. A "declaration" confirmed the arrangements of January 15, 1896, regarding the basin
of the Menam in Siam, recognizing a British sphere of influence west of the
river and a French sphere to the east; embodied a reciprocal acceptance of the
French tariff in Madagascar and the British in Zanzibar; and agreed on new
arrangements to end the difficulties between French and British traders in
the New Hebrides. Another Declaration, by far the most important politically, concerned Egypt and Morocco. The French Government agreed to
recognize British rights in Egypt and to withdraw its demand for a time
limitation on the British occupation, while Great Britain, although accept-

---

[1] *J.O.Ch.*, November 23, 1903.
[2] Anderson, *op. cit.*, pp. 94–100.

ing the French disclaimer of any intention of altering the political status of Morocco, recognized the right of France to "preserve order" and to "provide assistance" and agreed to acquiesce in French action taken for these purposes if not detrimental to British rights (Articles I, II). The "open door" was to be maintained in Morocco for thirty years (Article IV). Spanish interests would be respected and the British and French Governments agreed "to afford one another their diplomatic support" in executing the declaration.[1]

This public agreement was supplemented by five secret articles, which left no reasonable doubt regarding Morocco's future. In the event of a modification of policy by the respective Governments toward Egypt or Morocco, the declaration would remain intact (Article I). British judicial "reforms" in Egypt and French suggestions for similar reforms in Morocco would be accepted (Article II). Articles III and IV frankly contemplated the division of Morocco into French and Spanish spheres of influence.[2] Stripped of casuistry, the accord meant that Delcassé had gained his end. With British support, he could proceed to the acquisition of Morocco, with no fear, he thought, of effective opposition from any other Power. Berlin was, of course, unacquainted with the secret articles of the bargain, which were not revealed until 1911, but it could suspect the worst. In the House of Commons, Mr. Gibson Bowles called the agreements a "compact of plunder" for the "partition of three new Polands" (Egypt, Morocco, and Siam) and the London *Times*, differing from Balfour's view, presented the entente as designed to check and weaken the Triple Alliance.[3] Barclay and his colleagues had never intended to give it this character and even in Germany few voices of alarm were raised. English opinion accepted the agreements unreservedly.[4]

Here was an immense triumph for the personal diplomacy of Delcassé. Great Britain was once more drawn into the continental balance of power on the side of France; the hegemony of Germany was by so much weakened; and French possession of Morocco was assured. But these implications of the secret articles were less clear to French opinion in general than to the Quai d'Orsay. The reaction to the entente in Paris was a divided one. The published provisions regarding Morocco were acceptable, but there were many objections to the French concessions in Egypt, Siam, and Newfoundland. Delcassé was obliged to promise the Chamber that he would reopen the Newfoundland question. Except for this, he gained much applause by the impressive and mouth-filling generalities with which he presented the accords to Parliament. The Deputies approved the Convention, 443 to 105 and the Senators, 215 to 37[5] The Chambers thus gave their approbation

[1] *L.J.Maroc*, 1904; *B.D.*, II, pp. 373f., No. 417.
[2] Anderson, pp. 103–104.
[3] *Ibid.*, pp. 105–106.
[4] Barclay, *op. cit.*, pp. 256–273; Debidour, I, pp. 290–295.
[5] *Cf.* debates in *J.O.Ch.*, November 3 to 10, and *J.O.Sén.*, December 5–7, 1904.

specifically to the convention on Newfoundland and West Africa, and by implication to the two declarations. The secret articles were jealously guarded at the Quai d'Orsay. But had they been known they would have facilitated rather than hindered ratification. The "nemesis of Bismarck" had scored a victory which obliterated the memories of Fashoda and foreshadowed new conquests. The resulting enhancement of French diplomatic power and prestige was sufficient to gain national approval for the new course. Only a few unheeded voices were dubious as to where it would lead.[1]

3. Paris, Berlin, and Tangiers

The processes and motivations of French imperialism in Morocco differ in no essential respect from its counterparts elsewhere at an earlier period. The story of Tunis or of Madagascar or of Indo-China might have been repeated, except for the changed attitude of Germany and the diplomatic revolution which made Morocco not merely a sphere of French colonial ambition and a theater of conflicting imperialisms, but an issue between the two great European coalitions. Delcassé's determination to acquire Morocco sprang from the usual impulses of prestige and balance-of-power diplomacy. The "security" of Algeria "demanded" the acquisition of a preponderant influence in the neighboring State.[2] Morocco would neatly round out the French empire in North Africa, carrying it across the continent from the borders of Egypt to the Atlantic. It would "strengthen" France politically and strategically in the Mediterranean. It would furnish a field of activity for French investors and traders. Delcassé's designs against equality of economic opportunity in the secret bargainings which were going on indicate his determination to utilize the occasion for the exclusive benefit of French commerce and finance—apparently not because French merchants and financiers insisted upon such advantages, but because economic penetration would further political designs. The influential *Comité d'Afrique*, organized in 1889, was agitating for annexation, but it represented politics, patriotism, and the Press rather than groups inspired by desire for pecuniary gain. Its program was substantially that which Delcassé adopted.[3] The details of earlier efforts at penetration, growing out of border raids and disputes over treaty interpretation, need not concern us here. By 1903 the Moroccan Sultan was in dire straits and Delcassé persuaded the banking house of Gautsch to loan him 7,500,000 fr.[4] Here, as elsewhere, finance was the handmaiden of diplomacy and borrowing by a small, backward State from the bankers of a great, imperial Power sounded the death-knell of its inde-

[1] Millet, *op. cit.*, pp. 168f.

[2] "La France, maîtresse de l'Algérie, et par l'Algérie, limitrophe du Maroc sur une immense étendue, est tenue de suivre ce qui s'y passe avec un intérêt singulier, dont nul ne saurait équitablement méconnaître la légitimité." Delcassé, *J.O.Sén.*, July 5, 1901.

[3] Anderson, *op. cit.*, pp. 5–8.

[4] *Ibid.*, p. 18.

pendence. The stage was already set for action. Delcassé had only to brandish the threat of the acquisition of Morocco by another Power to win the almost unanimous support of French opinion to his program.[1]

He had thus far met with marked success in preparing the diplomatic scene for the sequel. Italy had been placated. Great Britain had been won over to acquiescence in the French designs.[2] With Rome and London favorably disposed, Fez and the Porte could be disregarded. St. Petersburg would be of little aid in view of Russia's defeat in the conflict with Japan, but had given its approval. During most of 1904, Delcassé anticipated Russian victory. Anglo-Russian friction was still serious, but the Quai d'Orsay's new position enabled it to assume the rôle of mediator, as in the Dogger Bank affair.[3] Spain must be considered. But, after somewhat difficult negotiations, a convention was signed on October 3, 1904, by which Madrid adhered to the Anglo-French declaration. Sixteen secret articles divided Morocco into French and Spanish spheres of influence, drew the boundaries of the projected partition, and rendered public solicitude for the "open door" and the independence of Morocco a mere façade to conceal the real structure of annexationist diplomacy.[4] Delcassé took none of his colleagues in the Cabinet and Parliament into his confidence and gave only perfunctory and deceptive notice of the accords to the German Government.[5] With the ground thus prepared, he felt that he could proceed to a brilliant *finale* with no fear of dangerous complications.

It is customary to say, in retrospect, that the fatal error of Delcassé's diplomacy was his failure to take Germany into account in laying his plans for the acquisition of Morocco. He reckoned without Berlin—or supposed that the German Government would not oppose what the other Powers had accepted. The otherwise pleasant game of partitioning the territory of an independent State was transformed into a grave international crisis by the veto of Wilhelmstrasse. Whether this could have been avoided by prior bargaining with Berlin must ever remain a subject of fruitless speculation. Conceivably, Delcassé might have offered Bülow "compensations" in Central Africa, of a character comparable to those offered to Italy, Spain, and Great Britain, in return for German consent to the French program. But there is very little likelihood that French public and parliamentary opinion

[1] "Pour saiser l'intérêt, non point seulement considérable, mais capitale que nous avons à posséder près du sultan l'influence prépondérante, figurez-vous, pour une minute, une puissance étrangère installée dans les conseils du Maghzen.

"Quel est l'avenir réservé à la France?

"Au lieu de sa prospérité, n'est-ce pas de sa sécurité qu'il va falloir désormais avoir souci? Et le temps, et les soins, et l'argent que réclame l'exploitation méthodique des ressources de l'Algérie, n'est-ce pas, assurer son existence à la mettre à l'abri d'une agression qu'il les foudra avant tout et surtout dépenser?" Delcassé, *J.O.Sén.*, December 7, 1904.

[2] Debidour, I, pp. 281–285.

[3] *Cf.* Anderson, Chap. VII.

[4] *Ibid.*, pp. 118–125 and Reynald, *op. cit.*, pp. 32–37.

[5] Anderson, pp. 125–127.

would have approved such concessions to the victor of '71. At all events Delcassé contented himself with giving vague information on the Anglo-French negotiations to Prince von Radolin[1] and chose to proceed on the assumption that Germany was uninterested or, in case of opposition, could be checkmated by the diplomatic support which had been gained for France as a result of the recent understandings.

A series of accords with the Government of the Sultan during 1901 and 1902 had paved the way for French "pacific penetration" of Morocco.[2] A special mission under Count de Saint-Aulaire carried the text of the Anglo-French convention to Fez and offered the Sultan the friendly cooperation of the Republic in introducing reforms. The anxieties of the local authorities were soothed and Delcassé lent his support in the negotiations for a loan from the *Banque de Paris et des Pays-Bas*. On June 12, 1904, the transaction was completed, 62,500,000 fr. being advanced by a consortium of eleven French banks. The loan—at 5 per cent for thirty-six years—was guaranteed by 60 per cent of the customs duties of all the ports of Morocco, which were to be supervised and, if need be, collected, by French officials.[3] The French banks were given the preference in future loans. French good offices secured the release in June of the American citizen, Ion Perdicaris and his British son-in-law, Mr. Varley, who had been captured and held for ransom by the bandit, Raisouli, and French instructors were intrusted with the organization of a police battalion at Tangiers. French commerce, which held first place in Morocco's foreign trade, increased appreciably and French bankers, railway magnates, merchants, journalists, and fortune hunters licked their chops at the banquet of the *Comité du Maroc*, held on June 15 in anticipation of Delcassé's *pièce de résistance*.[4] The chef stirred the stew with a deft spoon. In October a conference was held in Paris, attended by the foreign minister, the Governor-General of Algeria, Jonnart, the commander of the French troops in southern Oran, General Lyautey and the French Minister in Morocco, Saint-René Taillandier. It was decided to dispatch a larger mission to Fez to institute police reforms, establish a State Bank, construct railways and harbor improvements, and extend French influence generally.[5] But the tide of anti-French sentiment was rising rapidly in Morocco and obstructed the task of Saint-René Taillandier's mission.

The winter of 1904 and 1905 was marked by increasing difficulties in the way of the consummation of Delcassé's design. The Russian armies were beaten back in Manchuria and the red flag of revolution was raised in St. Petersburg and Moscow. The German press began to exhibit alarm over the impending "Tunisification" of Morocco. Since the Sultan announced that henceforth

[1] *G.P.*, XX, No. 4.

[2] E. Dupuy, *Comment nous avons conquis le Maroc*, pp. 39–53, Paris, 1913.

[3] Anderson, *op. cit.*, pp. 128–131.

[4] Dupuy, pp. 68–72, Anderson, p. 132.

[5] D. to St.R.T., December 15, 1904, *L.J.Maroc*, 1901–1905, p. 179f., cited in Anderson, p. 133.

he intended to dispense with the services of foreign officials, the French Minister did not depart for Fez until January 11—and then only after threats and bluster had apparently wilted the Sultan's resistance. In Berlin suspicion of the French designs was growing and the German Government could not afford to be indifferent to the fate of Morocco. Germany enjoyed an important place in Moroccan commerce[1] and held second place in the carrying trade, being exceeded by Great Britain and followed by France and Spain.[2] The Mannesmann Brothers had important interests at Agadir and German trade was particularly important at Mazagan and Mogador. As early as September, 1903, the German Government, suspecting the purposes of Delcassé, instructed its ambassador at Madrid to consider ways and means of participating in any partition of Morocco which might take place.[3] In March, 1904, Bülow advised a naval demonstration at Tangier, but William II vetoed the suggestion. In April, Bülow sought to calm public opinion by speaking reassuringly of the Anglo-French agreements, which, in his opinion, were "not directed at any other Power" and would not injure German economic interests in. Morocco.[4] But German chagrin at the diplomatic revolution which Delcassé had effected was increased by the almost open disloyalty of Italy to the Triple Alliance. Bülow toyed with the idea of a German entente with Great Britain, but nothing was achieved beyond the conclusion of an agreement regarding Egypt and an arbitration treaty of July 12, 1904. The notion of an alliance with Russia and a revival of the *Dreikaiserbund* was also played with, but met with no success.[5] Under these circumstances the bogey of "encirclement" began to take form and resentment at Delcassé's studied indifference to Berlin waxed strong. German acquiescence in the partition of Morocco would have the appearance of a diplomatic defeat of the first magnitude, while German interposition could be plausibly defended and might serve as an entering wedge with which to undo Delcassé's work.

Officially, "thunderous silence" prevailed in Wilhelmstrasse.[6] Late in 1904 Herr von Kühlmann, the German chargé at Tangiers, visited Sir Arthur

---

[1] According to Dupuy, *op. cit.*, p. 77, the percentages of Moroccan foreign commerce enjoyed by Germany and France were as follows:

Year	Germany, per cent	France, per cent
1902	9.1	31.1
1903	9.6	31.7
1904	11.1	30.0
1905	9.9	46.3

[2] In 1901, 434,000 tons of British shiping called at Moroccan ports as compared with 260,000 German, 239,000 French, and 198,000 Spanish. Barclay, *op. cit.*, p. 276.

[3] Anderson, p. 137.

[4] *Ibid.*, p. 142.

[5] *Cf.* Anderson, Chap. X.

[6] Nicolson, *op. cit.*, p. 118.

Nicolson, who declared that the former, in the course of conversation, mentioned that

his Government did not consider that the Anglo-French Agreement had any official existence: it had not been officially communicated to the German Government, and had not consequently been officially accepted by them. France and Great Britain were, of course, at liberty to settle their own differences, but these were matters between these two countries alone, and in no wise affected the rights and interests of third parties. I cannot recollect . . . whether I reminded him that Prince Bülow had in the Reichstag publicly given his blessing to the Agreement; but in any case I considered Herr von Kühlmann's warning of sufficient importance to cause me to lose no time in acquainting my French colleague with what had been said. It was evident that Germany would not remain quiescent while France took Morocco in hand and that she expected that France would enter into negotiations for the purpose of obtaining her concurrence. On my informing my French colleague of what had passed and expressing my opinion that it foreshadowed German interference with French projects, he remarked, after a moment's hesitation—"Nous sommes parfaitement tranquils du côté de Berlin." Future developments showed that this confidence had no sound foundation. It was clearly an oversight on the part of France to have taken the consent of Germany for granted and not to have conversed with Berlin.[1]

In April, 1905, German agents in Morocco assured the Sultan of Germany's interest. The Sultan refused to discuss Taillandier's proposals for reforms except in the presence of a commission of Moroccan notables. The German Government interested President Roosevelt in the situation and assured the Sultan that Germany and the United States favored the maintenance of existing conditions. The efforts of the French Ambassador at Berlin to secure an explanation of von Kühlmann's guarded statements were without result.[2] On March 15, Bülow intimated that the Government would defend German economic interests in Morocco and five days later the press announced that the Kaiser would visit Tangiers. Bülow wrote to the Emperor: "Your Majesty's visit to Tangiers will embarrass M. Delcassé, thwart his plans, and be of benefit to our economic interests in Morocco."[3] William II was dubious, but the Chancellor prevailed upon him to go through with the show. The French and German newspapers were already at war and the Kaiser could not recede with dignity. Bülow instructed him to champion Moroccan independence, suggest German opposition to French designs, and commit Germany to nothing.[4]

On March 31, 1905, the Kaiser, after more last-minute hesitations,[5] landed at Tangiers on his way to Corfu and rode through the town on a Berber horse, amid the enthusiastic applause of the populace. Perhaps carried away by the excitement of the occasion, the monarch went somewhat beyond Bülow's advice in his extemporaneous address. He greeted the Sultan as an "independent sovereign" and expressed the hope that a free Morocco would remain open to the pacific commerce of all nations, "without monop-

[1] *Ibid.*, pp. 117–118.
[2] Dupuy, pp. 73*f.*, and Anderson, pp. 196–197.
[3] *G.P.* XX, No. 262.
[4] Anderson, pp. 190–191.
[5] *G.P.* XX, No. 285.

oly nor exclusion of any sort." He decorated the Sultan's representatives and recommended much caution in instituting reforms.[1] Germany had accepted Delcassé's challenge. The press of the entire continent was aghast. Paris and Berlin were at once at swords' points. The first of the great international "crises" which culminated in the tragedy of 1914 was thus inaugurated by Germany's resentment at the bargaining which Delcassé had indulged in and by her refusal to be excluded from negotiations over Morocco's future.

On the very day of the Kaiser's speech at Tangiers, Delcassé assured the Senators in the Palais du Luxembourg that nothing in French Moroccan policy could explain the hostility of the German press and that France would succeed in her efforts without ignoring any rights or injuring any interests.[2] The semiofficial *Temps* threatened a new Dual Alliance with England if Germany sought special privileges in Morocco.[3] The foreign minister instructed Saint-René Taillaindier to refuse all proposals for an international conference, as suggested in the German press, and likewise informed the Italian Government that France could not entertain such a. proposal.[4] But a blank refusal to discuss such an issue between two Great Powers raised the specter of war—and war could not be contemplated with Russia defeated in the Far East and in the throes of revolution. As early as March 22, Bilhourd, French Ambassador at Berlin, had advised Delcassé to seek an understanding with Germany or contemplate unpleasant surprises.[5] On the twenty-eighth, Tardieu, already an influential journalist, declared that Delcassé would give Germany satisfaction if it were solely a question of economic interests, and on April 4, M. Billy of the press department of the Quai d'Orsay asked Theodore Wolff, Paris correspondent of the *Berliner Tageblatt* how the German Government would receive a French overture.[6] On April 7, Delcassé declared his readiness to "dissipate any misunderstanding which . . . may still exist." He repeated the statement to Prince von Radolin on April 13 while dining at the German Embassy, denied that Saint-René Taillandier had claimed before the Sultan to have a mandate from Europe, and sought to explain away his past attitude toward Berlin.[7]

Delcassé's position before Parliament and the public was undermined by a variety of factors: general fear of dangerous complications with Germany; his own secretiveness; his friction with his Premier, Rouvier; general dislike induced by his long tenure of office; his flouting of the Left parties in his defense of the barbarities of the Tsarist repression in Russia—in short, by a combination of circumstances which singled him out as the object of concerted attack by many groups. On April 19 he was assailed in the Chamber

[1] Dupuy, p. 76; Anderson, pp. 193–195.
[2] *J.O.Sén.*, March 31, 1905.
[3] *Le Temps*, April 3, 1905.
[4] *L.J.Maroc*, 1901–1905, No. 239. See, in general, Nos. 228–240 and 266.
[5] *Ibid.*, No. 232.
[6] Anderson, p. 199.
[7] *L.J.*, Nos. 244f.

from all sides for compromising the nation and blundering in his calculation
of the German attitude. He refused further explanations, but was defended
by Rouvier on the ground that Germany had changed her Moroccan policy
in consequence of Russia's defeat. The Government was ready to entertain
any proposals which would safeguard the honor of the country and maintain
peace. He would himself supervise foreign policy henceforth, but Delcassé's
retention in the Cabinet was a question of confidence.[1] Delcassé threatened to
resign the same day, but was prevailed upon to remain by President Loubet
and by Ambassadors Paul Cambon and Barrère, both in Paris at the time.
On the twenty-sixth, Rouvier dined with Prince Radolin at the German
Embassy. He declared that Germany and France must under no circumstances quarrel over Morocco, where the *status quo* would be maintained and
foreign commerce would remain open to all. They must cooperate in preserving peace. Radolin had been assured by a friend of Rouvier that the Premier
did not identify himself with Delcassé, since the British navy "did not run
on wheels" and was unable to protect Paris. Bülow had already anticipated
Delcassé's removal as a consequence of the crisis.[2] It now seemed clear that
Rouvier, with the support of public opinion, was willing to sacrifice his
foreign minister in the interest of peace. On April 30, following rumors of
war and a panic on the Bourse, Rouvier informed Radolin that he had clipped
Delcassé's wings by taking charge of foreign affairs himself and suggested
a Franco-German accord on the basis of the Kaiser's declaration at Tangiers.[3]
It is not clear that Berlin took the initiative in "demanding Delcassé's head"
as the price of a settlement, but it is apparent that the Premier, the Parliament, and the public were willing, if not anxious, to dispense with the
services of one whose policies had produced such a critical situation.[4]

Bülow adhered to the formula of an international conference, which was
urged upon the Sultan and the Assembly of Notables by the provocative
Count Tattenbach at Fez.[5] The German Government, enjoying a certain
amount of moral support from President Roosevelt, who later congratulated
Bülow on the removal of that "unbelievable scamp," Delcassé,[6] sounded
out the Powers on a conference and on April 18 responded to the French
foreign minister's offer of the thirteenth by suggesting an exchange of ideas
between all the signatory Powers of the convention of Madrid of 1880. In
Great Britain sympathy was all on the side of France and on April 25 Sir
Francis Bertie, going somewhat beyond Lansdowne's own views, offered
Delcassé British support in resisting possible German demands for a port on
the Atlantic coast of Morocco.[7] With this welcome support, Delcassé con-

---

[1] *J.O.Ch.*, April 19, 1905.
[2] Anderson, p. 190.
[3] *Ibid.*, pp. 217–218.
[4] Fay, *op. cit.*, I, pp. 186–187.
[5] Dupuy, *op. cit.*, pp. 82–83.
[6] *G.P.*, XXI, A, Nos. 6896–6897.
[7] Anderson, pp. 210–211.

tinued to oppose a conference and to insist on a direct settlement with Berlin. In the face of some opposition from Radolin and Tattenbach, Bülow rejected all schemes of territorial compensation and insisted upon a conference as a means of keeping Germany's hands free for the future. Edward VII arrived in Paris on May 1, to give Delcassé further support, but Rouvier, fearful of war, was negotiating behind the back of his foreign minister. He sent his friend, M. Betzold, to Berlin to interview Holstein and persuaded Baron Eckhardstein, then in England, to communicate with Bülow and the Kaiser at Karlsruhe. These secret and unofficial agents were to promise Germany a coaling station and a strip of Moroccan coast, to suggest that the French Cabinet, while certain of British backing in the event of war, preferred not to seek it, and to intimate that Delcassé might disappear from the scene within a few weeks. These advances met with no success. Holstein clearly distrusted Delcassé, and Bülow was prepared "to await further developments with composure."[1] In view of this opposition, Rouvier became anxious and Bülow decided to press him to the wall. On May 16, Prince von Radolin announced that a *rapprochement* would be possible only when trust was restored."[2] Rouvier replied: "I understand you fully. Leave it to me." Through Betzold, he urged the German Government to be patient until an internal crisis offered a favorable opportunity for action.[3]

Delcassé was thus to be sacrificed to Rouvier's war fears and to the exigencies of a situation in which a pacific solution was imperative for France. Not only had Rouvier had no hand in the formulation of the policy which had led to the crisis (he became Premier on January 23, 1905, following the fall of Combes), but Delcassé had had a free hand in its formulation from the beginning. It had led to the extraordinary situation of the Premier taking control of foreign affairs out of the hands of his minister and finally causing his resignation in the interest of peace. Delcassé and his supporters took the view that the ignoring of Germany in the earlier negotiations was justified since she was not a Mediterranean Power, and that France should stand firm against all demands for the internationalization of the Moroccan question, which were regarded as bluff, designed to detach France from Great Britain and to pave the way for more extensive demands in the future. Rouvier felt that such a position would lead to dangerous international complications at a time when Russia was powerless and when, in France, neither the army nor the navy nor public opinion were prepared for war.[4] Delcassé was willing to run the risk in the confidence that Berlin would not, after all, resort to force. Rouvier was unwilling to take any risks at a time when war was unthinkable, and his view was supported by the great majority of the Cabinet, the Parliament, and the journals.

[1] Anderson, pp. 219–220.

[2] *Cf.* Memo. by Baron von Holstein, *G.P.* XX, No. 358, May 2, 1905.

[3] Anderson, p. 221, quoting Eckhardstein, *Lebenserinnerungen und politische Denkwürdigkeiten*, III, p. 204 and *G.P.*, XIX, Nos. 6659–6661.

[4] J. Caillaux, *Agadir*, pp. 20–23, Paris, 1919.

The German Government hinted darkly in Rome and Madrid of the danger of hostilities and persuaded Roosevelt to intercede with Great Britain, whom it represented as blocking a conference. The British Government rejected his advice, but Berlin was pleased at gaining the support of the American President, who later urged a conference on the French Ambassador at Washington.[1] When Count Tattenbach at Fez reported that Delcassé, through the French Minister, was threatening violence if the Sultan consented to a conference, Bülow made it clear to Rouvier that Delcassé must go. Herr von Miquel, counsellor at the German Embassy, transmitted this message on May 30. Rouvier was in despair. "I cannot cause M. Delcassé to fall because Germany frowns. I would be reproached always . . . always."[2] On May 28, Tattenbach telegraphed the Sultan's rejection of the French proposals and his approval of an international conference. While making veiled threats at Rome of a German invasion of France in the event of French military action in Morocco, Bülow, through Betzold, warned Rouvier on June 1 that Germany "would follow up the consequences if France continued the policy of intimidation and violence hitherto pursued by M. Delcassé."[3] The French foreign minister remained adamant and dickered for further British support. Though Lansdowne sought to tone down Bertie's enthusiasm, the fleet was ordered to be in readiness to descend on the German coast and discussions were begun between the military and naval officers of the two countries for cooperation in case of war. At Delcassé's suggestion, the British representative in Fez advised the Sultan against a conference and refused an invitation. Thus buttressed in his position, he was not at all disposed to make concessions, while Rouvier, as the recipient of German threats, felt obliged to dig his minister's political grave.

On June 5, the Chamber was thrown into a panic by the rumor of a report from Barrère at Rome that Germany was contemplating military action in the Vosges. On the same day Rouvier took Delcassé with him to President Loubet, assured the President that he was utterly opposed to his foreign minister's policies, and threatened to resign if a majority of the Cabinet did not support him. Almost simultaneously Delcassé received encouragement from Edward VII to remain at his post and from Lansdowne, through Cambon, a communication which he interpreted as a definite offer of a full military alliance with England.[4] On the sixth, the Cabinet met. Delcassé defended his position ably and urged acceptance of the British offer, the dispatch of identical notes to the Sultan from London, Paris, and Madrid declining the conference, and defiance of Germany, which, he asserted, would not fight in the face of a united front. Rouvier asserted that Berlin had threatened war if the British offer were accepted. The Ministers of War and

---

[1] *G.P.*, XX, No. 442.
[2] *G.P.*, XX, Nos. 6669 and 6674f.
[3] *G.P.*, XX, No. 6678. *Cf.* Anderson, pp. 224–225.
[4] *Cf.*, Anderson, p. 231, Note 121.

Marine emphatically declared France unprepared for hostilities. "Germany reproaches you with having debauched Italy," Rouvier flung at Delcassé. "Pardon me!" retorted the minister, "I was charged with the foreign affairs of France; I have not supervised the external relations of Germany."[1] Not a single minister supported Delcassé. With a final warning to his colleagues that Berlin would become more insolent than ever in the face of this capitulation, he tendered his resignation and Rouvier took his portfolio. Bülow had triumphed and was made a Prince on the same day by William II.[2]

Thus ended Delcassé's long term at the Quai d'Orsay. Rouvier justified his dismissal by arguing that his retention would have meant war. He fell amid a clamor of universal condemnation in France. Balfour was disgusted at French "weakness" and the *Entente Cordiale*, which the crisis had all but transformed into an alliance, was severely damaged. The German Government had gained its immediate objective and was satisfied. The fallen minister retired to the Chamber and interested himself again in naval affairs, breaking his silence on foreign policy only once, three years later.[3] His prestige was enhanced once more when friction with Germany continued and it was realized that he had been sacrificed at the behest of Berlin. On the eve of the Great War, he was appointed ambassador to Russia by Poincaré, who shared his views of foreign policy. While the German armies swept toward Paris in 1914 he again, by a kind of poetic justice, became Minister of Foreign Affairs and held the post during a critical and terrible year (August 26, 1914, to October 29, 1915). He died on February 22, 1924, vindicated in a sense by the appalling fruition of the seeds he had helped to sow.

The settlement of the Moroccan crisis which followed his downfall may be briefly sketched. Bülow at once dispatched a circular note to the Powers informing them of Germany's acceptance of the Sultan's invitation to a conference and asking them to do likewise. On July 8, as a result in part of Roosevelt's representations, Rouvier reluctantly accepted the conference formula in principle, but many months of difficult negotiations and of Anglo-German recriminations followed before the bases of the conference were worked out. When the conference met in Algeciras in January, 1906, the French and British Governments did all in their power to carry out the intention of the accords of 1904. In the outcome, Germany won in principle and France in practice. Bülow's victory was a Pyrrhic triumph.[4] The *Entente Cordiale* was strengthened and, despite all formulas to the contrary, the partition of Morocco was made a certainty. New "crises" followed. Agadir came in 1911 and Berlin was finally obliged to see Morocco divided between

[1] Reynald, *op. cit.*, p. 45.

[2] Anderson, pp. 211–233; Fay, I, pp. 187–189; Stuart, pp. 170–192; Reynald, pp. 38–47; *G.P.*, XX, Nos. 406, 418, 625.

[3] *J.O.Ch.*, January 24, 1908.

[4] "France has had her *revanche* in Morocco. Nobody who thinks dispassionately over the events of the last six years can fail to see that Germany was defeated in one of the keenest diplomatic contests in current history." Barclay, *op. cit.*, p. 282

France and Spain while Russia recovered and the "encirclement" of Germany by the Triple Entente became a reality. Berlin secured territorial "compensations" in Central Africa, thanks to the diplomacy of Caillaux. But in Europe the Quai d'Orsay had terminated the diplomatic hegemony of Germany and had created a coalition which could defy the Triple Alliance. Delcassé, in obscurity, saw victory snatched from his own defeat and the objectives he had set for himself achieved and surpassed.

Because of an usual combination of circumstances, Delcassé had perhaps enjoyed greater freedom from domestic constitutional and political control than any of his predecessors or successors. Successive Premiers granted him a free hand in handling the foreign affairs of the Republic. His colleagues in the Cabinet were relatively indifferent to his activities and, until the end, too impressed with the prestige of his long tenure of office and of his remarkable achievements to venture the criticism which might have been directed against a lesser figure. The world of the parliamentarians and the journalists was content enough to leave diplomacy in the hands of a veteran statesman while the nation worked itself into a frenzy over the Dreyfus affair and anticlericalism. Delcassé pursued his Grand Design in secrecy and security, far removed from the storm and turmoil of internal politics. He was accepted on faith. Only when his policies led to a grave international crisis, which raised the specter of war, did the Cabinet, the Parliament, and the nation at large rise to smite what it had hitherto praised and repudiate what it had sanctioned in silence for seven years.[1] Nothing could reveal more strikingly the *ex post facto* character of the usual controls exercised over the Minister of Foreign Affairs. In times of calm they are non-existent or ineffective in modifying trends of policy. In times of crisis they function with the blind indirection and senseless impetuosity of lightning.

The peculiarly personal character of the methods of French diplomacy under Delcassé should not overshadow the nature of his purposes and their relation to the international position of France in the European State System. Delcassé was a worthy heir to the national diplomatic traditions of *La Grande Nation*. He combined with a single-hearted devotion to France and to French power and prestige a clear insight into the unstable equilibrium of forces which constitutes the State System of the West and a keen vision of the means needed to enhance the value of French diplomatic stock and to

[1] "Nous avons vu récemment un ministre des affaires étrangères poursuivre, pendant sept ans, avec une volonté calme et persistante, un plan d'alliances politiques, qui ne manquait pas de grandeur. Pendant sept ans, il s'adonna à la mission qu'il s'était imposée, sans que le Parlement, trop absorbé par des matières qu'il jugeait plus intéressantes, lui suscitât le moindre obstacle: à piene lui posa-t-il quelque questions, sur une politique où étaient engagés les intérêts vitaux du pays. C'est avec un véritable sursaut de stupeur qu'il apprit un jour que cette politique pouvait amener pour la France une crise des plus graves. Il se débarrassa, en un tournemain, de l'auteur responsable de la politique que, par son silence, il avait approuvée pendant sept ans, et revint ensuite à ses occupations d'administration intérieure." J. Barthélemy, *Le gouvernement de la France*, pp. 127–128.

tip the delicate balance in favor of the Quai d'Orsay. Even in defeat he was doubtless more correct in his analysis of the situation than his enemies. He could not foresee that an international conference could, after all, be so handled as to preserve for France all the fruits of victory while giving the empty platter to Berlin. He saw in the proposal only the tool whereby Wilhelmstrasse hoped to cheat France of Morocco and wreck the *Entente Cordiale*. In retrospect, it is reasonably clear that Germany would not have resorted to war over Morocco even if Paris had remained adamant. Rouvier was frightened into surrender by Bülow's bluff and bluster. To say that Delcassé was playing with fire and laying the faggots for an international conflagration is only to say that he was a good patriot who served his State first and whose motivations and methods were those of realistic statesmen everywhere. It was precisely because of this that he attained such marked success in realigning the Powers to suit his ends and that he was looked upon by his successors as the major contributor to that diplomatic revolution which won Great Britain to the side of the Dual Alliance and detached Italy from the Triplice.

Chapter IX

1914: THE IRREPRESSIBLE CONFLICT

1. Poincaré and Izvolsky

THE circumstances under which Raymond Poincaré first attained to the Premiership of the French Republic are indicative of the dilemma of French foreign policy after the conference of Algeciras. In 1906 Berlin had won a tactical triumph in the "internationalization" of the Moroccan question. But the pressure of French imperialism was irresistible and the Act of Algeciras was step by step reduced to a nullity. Germany was prepared to accept French control of Morocco, but only at a price. On July 1, 1911, following the French occupation of Fez, the German gunboat *Panther* anchored at Agadir. This *coup* led to another "crisis" of a most serious character.[1] Bülow's successor, Bethmann-Hollweg, and the Foreign Secretary, Kiderlen-Waechter, finally indicated their willingness to grant France a free hand in Morocco—in return for the cession of the French Congo to Germany. This was a demand which even the conciliatory ministry of Joseph Caillaux (June 27, 1911, to January 10, 1912) could not accept. Through the services of a number of international financiers Caillaux carried on secret, unofficial negotiations, unknown to his foreign minister, De Selves, to Jules Cambon, the French Ambassador in Berlin, or to the British Government, which feared war over the issue.[2] Finally, two agreements were signed on November 4, 1911. In return for German recognition of the French right to establish a protectorate over Morocco, France was obliged to cede 100,000 square miles of the French Congo to Berlin, receiving a sham compensation in the form of a valueless strip of the Cameroons.[3] This accord was regarded by nationalists on both sides as a "defeat" and greatly embittered Franco-German as well as Anglo-German relations.

Only the African agreement, involving an exchange of territory, required parliamentary confirmation, but the two instruments were considered together by the Chambers. On December 22, 1911, a Senate commission of twenty-six members, headed by Léon Bourgeois and including many former ministers and diplomats, was appointed to consider the accords. The commission named as its *rapporteur* Raymond Poincaré, Senator from the Meuse,

---

[1] Cf. S. B. Fay, *The Origins of the World War*, I, pp. 246–250; G. H. Stuart, *French Foreign Policy*, pp. 275f.

[2] A. Fabre-Luce, *La victoire*, pp. 133–137; Harold Nicolson, *Portrait of a Diplomatist*, pp. 251–254, referred to hereafter as "Nicolson."

[3] Fay, I, pp. 277–293.

who had committed himself to vote for the treaties, despite the fact that they were distasteful to him. The Deputies from the eastern departments had declared their opposition to ratification, since they did not wish "to appear to subscribe to a *rapprochement* which, in the present state of things, would have a sad echo in our mutilated Lorraine."[1] Caillaux defended the agreements ably before the commission, but made the mistake of denying expressly the press rumors that he had conducted negotiations outside of the Quai d'Orsay. When Clemenceau asked De Selves to confirm the denial, which the members of the commission knew to be false, the foreign minister begged to be allowed not to reply. After the session, he transmitted his resignation to the Premier, who proferred his post to Delcassé, Minister of Marine, and invited Poincaré to assume the post Delcassé was to vacate. These manoeuvres failed in their object and on January 11, 1912, the Cabinet left office. President Fallières called upon Poincaré to form a new ministry. After some hesitation, he accepted, though distrusting the support promised by "that devil of a man," Clemenceau.[2]

From Caillaux to Poincaré was a step from conciliation and cooperation with Germany to a policy of vigorous self-reliance and determined assertion of national interests. Morocco had been gained, but at a price which French patriots resented as a national humiliation. Poincaré formed a strong "concentration" Cabinet, taking the portfolio of foreign affairs himself, and making Briand, Minister of Justice; Klotz, Minister of Finance; Millerand, Minister of War; Delcassé, Minister of Marine; and Steeg, Minister of the Interior. On January 16, 1912, the Chamber approved ratification of the accords with Germany almost unanimously. The Senate followed suit on February 11 by a vote of 212 to 42. In his ministerial declaration Poincaré defended the accords as permitting France to assume a protectorate over Morocco in cooperation with Spain:

It will permit us also to maintain between France and a great neighbor nation, in a sincerely pacific spirit, relations of courtesy and frankness, inspired by mutual respect for their interests and their dignity. More than ever, we intend to remain faithful to our alliances and our friendships. We will strive to cultivate them with that perseverance and continuity which are, in diplomatic action, the best guarantee of honesty and integrity. In order for a nation to be strong and respected, it is indispensable that it have a Government resolved to assume the responsibilities which fall to it and to exercise without default all the authority which your confidence may confer upon it . . . (In closing) . . . The army and navy will be the objects of our attentive solicitude. Like you, messieurs, we see in them the sacred supports of the Republic and the Fatherland.[3]

Beneath the surface the spirit of the *revanche* was again arising, under the pressure of successive humiliations inflicted by Berlin, and Poincaré was its fitting symbol and embodiment. He had been born in 1860 into a

---

[1] Poincaré, *Au service de la France*, I, p. 3; cited hereafter as "Poincaré."

[2] *Ibid.*, I, p. 17.

[3] *J.O.Ch.*, January 17, 1912.

middle-class family in Bar-le-Duc, Lorraine, and was ten years of age at the time of the Prussian invasion which prostrated his country and placed his home province under foreign domination. As a young man he became a lawyer and a journalist and made a large fortune at the bar. It was as a financier that he first attracted attention in the Chamber, which he entered at the age of twenty-seven. His first Cabinet post was that of Minister of Public Instruction in the first Dupuy ministry (April 4, to December 3, 1893). He held the same post in the third Ribot Cabinet (January 26, to November 1, 1895), having meanwhile served as Minister of Finance in the second Dupuy Cabinet (May 30, 1894, to January 26, 1895). Since he was a member of the Right, he went into eclipse with the ascendency of the anticlerical radicals, to emerge again as Minister of Finance in March, 1906, in the Sarrien Cabinet. In October, the Left, under Clemenceau, again took power, retaining it under Briand, Monis, and Caillaux, who was replaced in the Premiership, under the circumstances indicated, by the astute Lorrainer in January of 1912. He scathingly condemned the policies and methods of his predecessor, though recommending approval of the settlement of 1911 as a matter of honor and expediency. His very name was regarded a *défi* by the German Government.[1]

Within this short, fat, bearded little *bourgeois*, there burned an over-powering ambition, a tremendous energy for work, and a remarkable memory, which have led more than one commentator to agree that "No one since Bismarck's day has equaled him in sheer ability."[2] Behind a plain, unromantic exterior and a rigidly routinized, almost puritanical, life, surged an ardent patriotism, a love for glory, and a thirst for power which concealed and compensated for a natural timidity.[3] Combining the arts of the journalist and the politician, he still remained the lawyer, skilled in logic-chopping and in the type of simple, single-tracked reasoning which carried him with unswerving determination toward the goals he set for himself. He lacked the capacity for compromise and adjustment, and the intuitively accurate perception of the relationship of means to ends, which characterize the great statesman. But he excelled in administration, in executive leadership, in oratory of a kind—in all that required firmness, concentration, emotional intensity, and the single-hearted, almost fanatical devotion of the extreme Nationalist. He had many of the qualities of Delcassé, coupled with a certain shrewdness, lacking in subtlety, and a liking for displays of power which frequently mark introverted minds, unconsciously distressed by a false sense of their own deficiencies. In Poincaré the emotions of what might be termed the "inferiority complex" of the French national temper toward Germany became personalized and constituted the driving forces behind the action of the Quai d'Orsay in the period between Agadir and the Marne.

[1] S. Huddleston, *Poincaré, A Biographical Portrait*, pp. 34–55; *cf.* Fay, I, pp. 312–355.

[2] Fay, I, p. 314.

[3] Huddleston, pp. 13–25.

In September, 1910, fifteen months before Poincaré became Premier of France, Alexander Izvolsky, Russian foreign minister, got himself appointed ambassador at Paris and was succeeded at St. Petersburg by his under-secretary, Sergei Sazonov. This circumstance brought into conjunction the two men who, above all others in the coalition facing the Central Powers, were. determined to resist all further *démarches* by Berlin, to strengthen what had already become the Triple Entente, and to face unflinchingly the possibility that the next diplomatic crisis might lead to hostilities. Izvolsky, like Poincaré, was led by the bitterness of his past experiences to an attitude of suspicion and resentment toward the Triple Alliance. Austria-Hungary, rather than Germany, was his *bête noir*. He had become Russian foreign minister in May of 1906, after diplomatic service at Copenhagen, in the reactionary Cabinet of Goremykin. It was the period of the first Duma, of the twilight of the revolution, of the violent repressions of Stolypin and the Black Hundreds. He has been aptly described by Sir Arthur Nicolson, the British Ambassador at the Tsarist Court:

His intelligence was alert, quick, and subtle; but I must add that like all human beings he had his defects. I do not think that he ever quite understood the minds and feelings of his own countrymen, and on one or two occasions this misapprehension led him into serious difficulties. Again he was nervous and timorous, and was exceedingly sensitive to public criticism. This necessarily led to some want of continuity in his foreign policy and somewhat weakened the confidence with which one could depend on him. He was much impressed with the power and might of Germany, and was always anxious lest by any mischance he should give offense to her. He was also a little too eager to play a part in society, and he was exceedingly open to the influences of the fashionable world.[1]

During 1906 and 1907, Izvolsky was much occupied with Nicolson in discussing Anglo-Russian differences in Asia. In the course of the complex negotiations, which culminated in the signature of the convention of August 31, 1907, and the Anglo-Russian entente, he had seemed anxious not to offend Berlin and apparently had no thought of using the new understanding as a weapon against Germany.[2] But the events of 1908 left him transformed. Seeking new laurels, he turned to the Near East and the Balkans, striving for "freedom of the Straits" for Russia, *i.e.*, for a modification of Article 63 of the Treaty of Berlin of July 13, 1878, which, like earlier treaties, barred war vessels from the Dardanelles and the Bosphorus. Without clearly defining his objective, he entered into conversations with the Austrian foreign minister, Freiherr von Aerenthal, suggesting, as a *quid pro quo*, Austrian annexation of Bosnia and Herzegovina, under the occupation of the Dual Monarchy since 1878. In mid-September, 1908, he met Aerenthal at Buchlau in Moravia, and consented to Austrian annexation of the two provinces, expecting an opening of the Straits to Russian battleships in return. Turkey was paralyzed by revolution. On October 5, Bulgaria pro-

[1] Nicolson, p. 159.
[2] *Ibid.*, pp. 170–188.

claimed her independence and on the following day Aerenthal announced the Austrian annexation of Bosnia and Herzegovina. Great Britain and Italy at once protested. The Serbs were furious, regarding the two provinces as their own territory. Izvolsky, proceeding at the moment from Paris to London, suddenly realized that he would be unable to secure British and French consent for his half of the bargain. On instructions from St. Petersburg, he was now obliged to protest against the Austrian action which he had himself suggested. He had been duped, he felt. The fault was not in Aerenthal, but in himself. In the Russian capital, he was almost disgraced by his blunder. He sought to save his face, but Berlin supported Vienna and since Russia was unprepared for war over the issue, he was obliged, in March, 1909, to capitulate.[1] The Russian Pan-Slavists were furious and he was only too happy to retire to Paris to nurse his grievances. He had incurred a great diplomatic defeat. His personal resentment against Aerenthal, whom he never forgave, made him the bitterest and most determined spokesman for everything in Russian foreign policy which bespoke hostility to Vienna in the Balkans. Revenge became his consuming motive and his energies were henceforth bent toward preparing his own *revanche*.[2]

That France's ally should have been represented at Paris by a diplomat whose personal animosities strengthened his political intransigeance and aggressiveness precisely at a time when successive rebuffs by Berlin disposed the Quai d'Orsay to a similar attitude was a factor of no mean importance in the shaping of the future diplomatic situation. Yet it is easy to exaggerate Izvolsky's influence. Sazonov did not share his prejudices and in August, 1911, reached an agreement with Bethmann regarding Persia and the Bagdad Railway. Since Sazonov failed to confer with the British and French Governments regarding these conversations, irritation resulted in Paris and London. Pichon, foreign minister under Clemenceau and Briand, was severely criticized and found the Russian foreign minister "insupportable."[3] Such behavior on the part of the man who had been his assistant and who was now his superior perhaps increased Izvolsky's determination to turn Franco-Russian policy definitely against the Triplice, but with Briand and Caillaux he could do little. In the Agadir crisis he even encouraged the Quai d'Orsay to yield to Berlin, while Nicholas II advised Georges Louis, the French Ambassador, to "keep in view the avoidance of a conflict. You know our preparations are not complete."[4]

The advent of Poincaré altered the complexion of things. Izvolsky and the new Premier were never friends. Far from crediting the Russian Ambassador with bellicose intentions, Poincaré was irritated by his anxiety in

---

[1] Fay, I, pp. 251–258; B. E. Schmitt, *The Coming of the War*, 1914, I, pp. 126–128; cited hereafter as "Schmitt."

[2] Fay, I, pp. 264–270.

[3] Comment to Sir Francis Bertie, February 8, 1911, in Nicolson, p. 245; *cf.* Fay, I, pp. 275*f*.

[4] E. Judet, *Georges Louis*, pp. 156*f*; J. Caillaux, *Agadir*, pp. 142*f*; Fay, I, pp. 292–293.

1911 lest Russia be drawn into a war over Morocco. He regarded him as an intelligent, but vain, self-important, and somewhat untrustworthy individual.[1] According to his own account, he even asked for his recall in August, 1912, though he failed to press the matter.[2] His contacts with Baron von Schoen, the German Ambassador, were apparently more pleasant and more cordial.[3] Izvolsky, on his part, was full of praise of the Premier's energy and directness, though Poincaré suspected him of exaggerating his sentiments in his dispatches to St. Petersburg in order to enhance his own importance and secure more adequate information regarding Sazonov's designs, which were not always revealed to him.[4] The personal relations of the two men were thus characterized more by suspicion and friction than by cooperation and affability.

But politics were more important than personalities. Both men, for different reasons, favored closer Franco-Russian relations and common resistence to the Central Powers in any future crisis which might arise. Izvolsky, smarting from the Buchlau "betrayal" was intent upon gaining satisfaction from Aerenthal. If he shrank from war over Bosnia or Morocco, it was not because of pacific intentions, as Poincaré implies,[5] but out of a realization of Russia's unpreparedness for a conflict.[6] He continued his efforts and concluded a secret agreement with Tittoni, at Racconigi, on October 24, 1909, by which Italy pledged herself "to regard with benevolence . . . Russia's interest in the question of the Straits," while Russia gave a like pledge with regard to Italian ambitions in Tripoli and Cyrenaica. Izvolsky kept this bargain a close secret and did not reveal it to Poincaré until the outbreak of the Balkan wars.[7] When Italy prepared to seize Tripoli in 1911, Izvolsky, at Paris, at once saw Tittoni, now Italian Ambassador to France, and recalled the terms of the compact. Sazonov's assistant, Neratov, instructed Charykov to open the question of the Straits at Constantinople. Charykov informed his French colleague, Bompard, who suggested the necessity of British consent and informed De Selves. On October 1, 1911, Izvolsky, on Neratov's suggestion, took the matter up with the French foreign minister, who was much alarmed. The ambassador complained of De Selves' "ignorance" and emphasized the necessity of gaining a "good press." Great Britain reiterated her opposition to any one-sided "opening of the Straits" to warships for Russia's exclusive benefit. De Selves and Georges Louis, then at the Quai d'Orsay, framed a dilatory and non-committal reply, which was transmitted to Izvolsky in January, 1912. Meanwhile the Turks were furious and looked to Germany for support. The whole

[1] Poincaré, I, pp. 294–302.
[2] *Foreign Affairs*, October, 1925. p, 10.
[3] Poincaré , I, pp. 86–87.
[4] *L.N.* (*Un livre noir*), I, pp. 203, 216, 266, 281; II, pp. 14, 360, 570.
[5] Poincaré, I, pp. 317–318.
[6] Gouttenoire de Toury, *Poincaré, a-t-il voulu la guerre?*, pp. 16–18.
[7] Fay, I, pp. 407–408.

business ended in failure. Sazonov disavowed the negotiations. Charykov was made the scape-goat. Izvolsky had failed again.[1]

Poincaré was no more disposed than his predecessor to support Russian designs on the Straits and in the Balkans for their own sake. But Turkey and Austria-Hungary were the prospective victims of the realization of these designs. And behind Vienna stood Germany, "like a knight in shining armor" in the Kaiser's theatrical phrase. And to Poincaré the Lorrainer, Germany was always the enemy.[2] His determination to take a firm stand against Berlin in future controversies was perhaps an expression of a deeper and unconfessed resolution to do all in his power to regain the "lost provinces" for the Republic and to crush the German "menace" once and for all. This could be achieved not by diplomacy but only by war. Izvolsky was moved by corresponding resentments and ambitions. He, too, could gain his objective only by war—since diplomacy had failed. His war might take the form of a sudden Russian descent on the Straits, a Balkan league against Turkey, or a general war of the Entente against what remained of the Triplice. The first idea was toyed with and abandoned as impractical. The second was to be tried, but without the results hoped for. The third remained. "C'est ma guerre!" cried the Russian Ambassador in Paris in 1914.[3] Both Poincaré and Izvolsky were secretly or openly pursuing diplomatic objectives which could be realized only by a general conflict between the armed coalitions. Poincaré could not, in the nature of things, take the initiative. Russia would not fight for Alsace-Lorraine any more than she would fight for Morocco or the Congo. But, if war came, Russian and British support was essential for success. And Russia might fight for other goals in the Near East. The degree of support which Poincaré gave to St. Petersburg in pursuing these objectives is the measure of his willingness to face the prospect of a general conflagration. Conversely, from Izvolsky's point of view, France would not fight for the Straits or for Russian domination in the Balkans. But she might fight for other ends which would be served by a conflict arising out of these problems. French support of Russian Balkan policy must therefore be secured. Here was a community of interests which brought the two men together and enabled the Dual Alliance to be utilized against Germany to the advantage of both parties.

The very contemplation of this possibility made it essential to translate the *Entente Cordiale* into a binding engagement to cooperate against the Central Powers. Diplomatic cooperation had already been assured by the convention of 1904 and had been liberally extended in the controversies over Morocco. Russian support had not been forthcoming, since Russia was

---

[1] *Ibid.*, I, pp. 413–426, 361–364; A Pevet, *Les résponsables de la guerre*, pp. 16–20.

[2] Poincaré, I, Chap. V for his view of Germany; *cf.* V, pp. 1–2: "Mon pays natal n'a pas seulement connu, en 1870, les affres de l'invasion; il subi, après la paix de Francfort, l'épreuve d'une occupation prolongée et mes premiers souvenirs de collège sont assombris par des défilés de casques à pointe."

[3] Fay, I, p. 29, citing the *Diary of Lord Bertie of Thame*, I, pp. 2, 3, 66.

uninterested in the issue. The British Government had stood side by side with France against Berlin because of increasing commercial, colonial, and naval rivalry between Great Britain and Germany. But from the point of view of the Quai d'Orsay diplomatic support, unaccompanied by an assurance of military cooperation in case of war, was almost more dangerous than it was profitable. The Lansdowne-Cambon conversations of 1905 might have culminated in something closely approaching an alliance but for the fall of Delcassé. In December of that year Sir Edward Grey came to the British Foreign Office. He pursued the dubious policy of endeavoring to grant to the Quai d'Orsay the substance of an alliance without the form. Military and naval discussions were facilitated. Cambon seemed assured that France could count on British aid, though he was told that Great Britain reserved liberty of action. The Foreign Secretary sought to give the French as much encouragement as possible, without going to the point at which the Cabinet and Parliament would have to be informed of the commitments. In January, 1906, Lord Haldane began preparations for a British expeditionary force of 160,000 troops to operate against Germany in Flanders and Belgium. This involved a complete reorganization of the British Army and the drawing up of elaborate plans for transportation and cooperation with the French General Staff. By 1910 these plans were approaching completion, though their very existence was sweepingly denied by Haldane in response to German inquiries. In Paris and St. Petersburg, however, diplomatic action was based upon the assumption of British assistance in the event of war. These preparations were not revealed to the British Cabinet until 1912, and not to Parlia ment and the public until August 3, 1914, by which time they had reached such a degree of perfection that the issuance of mobilization orders took but a few minutes, the landing of troops in France but a few hours after the declaration of war, and the organization of the whole expeditionary force but two days.[1]

The year 1912 was a decisive one in this transformation of the entente. For a time there seemed a possibility of a British understanding with Germany. But the Haldane mission to Berlin in the winter of 1912 ended in failure and naval rivalry and political antagonism developed unchecked. For a moment the Quai d'Orsay had been uneasy. On a hint from Sir Francis Bertie, Poincaré sent an energetic dispatch to Paul Cambon on March 29, 1912, pointing out the danger to France of any Anglo-German neutrality agreement. On the same day the British Cabinet declined Bethmann's offer and the "danger" was ended. Poincaré recalled Cambon to Paris for consultation. On his return to London in April he informed the Foreign Office of the Premier's conviction as to the inevitability of war with Germany and his anxiety for more definite assurances of British aid in that eventuality. He was met by doubts which seemed evasions.[2] But when it was realized that

---

[1] Fay, I, pp. 192–214; F. R. Flournoy, *Parliament and War*, pp. 196–198.

[2] See Sir Arthur Nicolson's memo. to Grey on his conversation with Cambon of April 15, 1912, in Nicolson, pp. 267–269. For an older, but still useful account of Anglo-German rivalry, see B. E. Schmitt, *England and Germany 1740–1914*, pp. 139–218.

Von Tirpitz's naval plans were more "menacing" than had at first been supposed, it was decided to concentrate British naval strength in the North Sea. This involved a withdrawal of ships from the Mediterranean, where the protection of British interests might be left to France. But if French naval forces were concentrated here for such a purpose, Great Britain must assume the protection of the French northern coasts. The situation was thus ripe for putting the Anglo-French commitments into writing, as Poincaré desired in order to assure skeptics that Anglo-French relations afforded "security" to the Republic.[1] British naval plans continued to develop along the expected lines. On July 16, 1912, the Franco-Russian Naval Convention was signed. Poincaré instructed Cambon to press Grey for an agreement. The Foreign Secretary at last consented, but felt that he must inform the Cabinet of the past military and naval conversations going on during the preceding eight years. This was done, and, with the Cabinet's approval, Grey and Cambon exchanged the letters of November 22 and 23, 1912.[2]

These letters were the first formal written recognition of the implications of the military and naval conversations. Poincaré and Cambon believed that they had gained their end. Grey believed that he was safeguarding the liberty of action of the British Government by a specific agreement. The letters took the form of a consultative pact and a disclaimer of any obligations to cooperate in war.

> We have agreed that consultation between experts is not, and ought not to be regarded as, an engagement that commits either Government to action in a contingency that has not arisen and may never arise. The disposition, for instance, of the French and British fleets respectively at the present moment is not based upon an engagement to cooperate in war . . . However . . . I agree that, if either Government had grave reason to expect an unprovoked attack by a third Power, or something that threatened the general peace, it should immediately discuss with the other whether both Governments should act together to prevent aggression and to preserve peace, and, if so, what measures they would be prepared to take in common. If these measures involved action, the plans of the general staffs would at once be taken into consideration, and the Governments would then decide what effect should be given to them.[3]

To Poincaré this meant that British assistance was practically assured, though he denies Sazonov's statement that he so informed the Russian foreign minister in the summer of 1912.[4] If, in the event of war, hostilities were initiated under circumstances giving the appearance of German aggression, the moral obligation which Grey has assumed would leave the British no honorable alternative but to join forces with the French. The French General Staff, in fact, based its Plan XVII, which was used in the 1914 campaign, on the assumption that British naval aid was a certainty and British military aid a probability. Yet Grey continued to profess that his hands were free. In Berlin, where news of the Grey-Cambon letters somehow

[1] Poincaré, I, pp. 176f. and, generally, pp. 146–236.

[2] Fay, I, pp. 293–324.

[3] Grey to Cambon, November 22, 1912, in Fay, I, pp. 322–323, citing Grey, *Twenty-five Years* 1892–1916, I, pp. 94f.

[4] Poincaré, I, pp. 86f.

leaked out in the spring of 1914, it was clear to alarmists that the Triple Entente was gradually drawing its net of encirclement tighter about the Central Powers.[1]

2. THE AFFAIR OF GEORGES LOUIS

Among the various spheres of friction between the hostile coalitions, the Balkans and the Near East loomed largest after 1908, the year of the "Young Turk" revolution, the independence of Bulgaria, the Austrian annexation of Bosnia and Herzegovina, and the Aerenthal "betrayal" of Izvolsky. Pan-Slavism and the drive toward the Straits were the two wings of Tsarist imperialism, impelling Russia to intervene in Near Eastern affairs and to seek a predominant influence in the Balkan peninsula. Racial and religious mysticism, economic motivations, the power-and-prestige ideals of nationalists and militarists, all impelled the Romanov colossus to a course which was bound to run counter to the interests of other Powers. The friends and allies of St. Petersburg in London and Paris had no enthusiasm for these designs. But they were constrained to support them, with qualifications, in the interest of the balance of power. For Austria-Hungary, with her large and unruly Jugoslav population, the liberation and expansion of the Balkan Slavs under Russian auspices was a direct threat to her security and integrity. Germany stood behind Austria as her only reliable ally, and had fish of her own to fry in Turkey. The complex Balkan intrigues which made this region the focus of conflict between Vienna and St. Petersburg, and therefore between the Triple Entente and the Triple Alliance, had no direct interest for France. For Sazonov and Izvolsky it was enough to make certain of French support in any crisis which might arise as a result of the situation. This support Poincaré was prepared to extend—not because he favored Russian Balkan policies nor the methods by which they were pursued, not primarily because he was willing to help Russia secure the Straits in return for Russian aid in recovering Alsace-Lorraine, not because he wished to provoke war or was unaware that the Russian policies would probably lead to war,[2] but because any crisis which might arise would at once be an issue between the coalitions and he was committed to the solidarity of the Triple Entente as the only means of checkmating Germany. If war came, he would not shrink from it. Alsace-Lorraine and the *revanche* would be among the fruits of victory.

From 1909 to 1913 France was represented at St. Petersburg by Georges Louis, who was something of a thorn in the flesh of both Poincaré and Izvolsky because of his unsympathetic attitude toward their conception of Franco-Russian relations.[3] Elevated to the *direction politique* of the Quai d'Orsay by Delcassé, Louis was a partisan of a solid Franco-Russian front against Germany and an opponent of all suggestions of an anti-English

---

[1] *Cf.* T. Barclay, *Thirty Years*, p. 283; Poincaré, II, pp. 114*f.*

[2] *Cf.* Schmitt, I, pp. 64–66.

[3] E. Judet, *Georges Louis*, pp. 50–65.

continental bloc of which he found some support in Russia, especially on the part of Witte. He preferred Sazonov to his predecessor. But he had few illusions regarding Russian military strength and wished to keep the alliance in a state of stable equilibrium for the maintenance of peace. The Pan-Slavist Balkan policy of the Empire he regarded as a menace to peace which might well drag France into a disastrous adventure. He followed closely Russian-Italian relations and the contacts of Izvolsky and Tittoni, warning Poincaré of the perils of Russian duplicity and adopting an attitude of great caution and circumspection in dealing with Sazonov.[1] The Russian foreign minister naturally resented his efforts to check the development of Russian policy in the Balkans and to confine the alliance to its originally defensive character. He felt that the French Ambassador did not accurately transmit his views to the Quai d'Orsay, a result perhaps due more to Sazonov's evasiveness and changeability than to any remissness in Louis' part. Sazonov's agents, moreover, had discovered how to decipher the French diplomatic code and were spying upon the telegrams exchanged between Louis and Poincaré. In April, 1912, through a mistranslation of "ministry" as "minister," Sazonov read into one of Louis' dispatches a personal criticism of himself and instructed Izvolsky to secure his recall.[2]

The sequel throws much light upon the relationship between the foreign minister, the Quai d'Orsay, and the diplomatic service. Izvolsky, who was doubtless pleased by this opportunity, informed the Premier of Sazonov's desires. Poincaré apparently desired to avoid offending Louis and sought to handle the situation as discreetly as possible. At his suggestion, Maurice Paléologue, Louis' successor as director of the political section of the Quai d'Orsay, dispatched a communication to the ambassador on May 8, 1912,[3] informing him that the Russian Government had expressed a desire to have France represented at St. Petersburg by an agent who would show more activity in his political functions and social relations. The Premier, declared Paléologue, fully realizes that your inactivity is due only to ill health, but in view of Sazonov's statement that he no longer feels in contact with you, and in view of the importance of pending diplomatic problems, he begs you to place the embassy at his disposition. Louis, who enjoyed good health, who was an indefatigable worker, and who thought himself on good terms with Sazonov, was astounded by his summons and at once suspected Izvolsky of some secret machination to accomplish his removal. He contemplated sending a vigorous telegram to Poincaré, expressing his indignation and suspicion. When the Premier informed the Cabinet on May 10 of his decision to recall the ambassador, the ministers acquiesced, feeling that the matter was an internal affair of the Quai d'Orsay. Léon Bourgeois, Minister of Labor, and a friend of the ambassador, informed Madame Louis, then in

[1] Judet, *op. cit.*, pp. 131–203.
[2] Fay, I, pp. 332*f.*
[3] Text in Judet, pp. 28–29.

Paris, of the situation and suggested that she telegraph her husband to come at once to the French capital. She did so and Louis accordingly abandoned his original plan of protesting and asked Poincaré for permission to come to Paris for a hearing before a final decision should be taken.[1] This was an unusual request and perhaps savored of insubordination, but Poincaré granted it, repeating that Izvolsky had acted on Sazonov's instructions.[2]

The first public hint of Louis' recall appeared in Le Temps on May 13. On the sixteenth, Louis arrived in Paris. On the seventeenth, Marcel Hutin in L'Écho de Paris, ascribed the decision to Louis' lack of harmony with Sazonov and mentioned Deschanel as his possible successor. On the same evening Gandolphe (Maurice Herbette) declared in Liberté that Izvolsky and Paléologue had won the support of Poincaré as their accomplice against Georges Louis and condemned his recall as an indication of the unwholesome influence of the Russian Ambassador over the French Government. The question thus threatened to become a subject of political controversy in the press. During the night of May 17 the Havas Agency, apparently on the instigation of Poincaré or of someone else at the Quai d'Orsay, issued a note to the press, denying that the Russian Government had requested Louis' recall, saying that Poincaré had no intention of removing him, and declaring that he would remain, despite his own desire to be relieved of his post because of the state of his health. This falsified report of the situation added fuel to the flames. Jaurès in L'Humanité now asserted that Izvolsky and the Russian Government desired Louis' removal because of his opposition to the aggressive designs of St. Petersburg against Turkey.[3] Meanwhile, Izvolsky informed Sazonov that though he approved of Louis' removal, the matter was difficult and delicate and had best be dropped. Sazonov seemingly insisted on action, though Kokovtsov, the Russian Prime Minister, had reassured Louis and disclaimed responsibility. Poincaré at first bowed to Sazonov's demand, but after conferring with Louis in Paris, decided to send him back to the Neva, pending an investigation. By his own account, Poincaré had no quarrel with Louis and suspected Izvolsky's honesty in the whole matter.[4] Sazonov acquiesced, doubtless deploring Izvolsky's inability to control the French press more effectively, and Louis returned to his post.

It is reasonably clear that the initiative for Louis' recall had come from Sazonov. Izvolsky and Poincaré had agreed and Paléologue had been instructed to transmit the order. Louis' resistance, along with the debate in the press and the Premier's reluctance to precipitate a general discussion

[1] "10 mai 1912, Pour le Président du Conseil: La démarche que vous me signalez est en complete contradiction avec la language de M. Kokovtzoff et de M. Sazonoff. Je prie Votre Excellence de m'autoriser à partir pour Paris et de m'entendre avant décision. Georges Louis." Judet, p. 41.

[2] "11 mai, M. Izvolsky m'a confirmé pour la troisième fois qu'il m'avait parlé de vous sur instructions expresses de M. Sazonoff. Je vous autorise néanmoins à venir à Paris ou je recevrai volontiers vos explications. Poincaré." Judet, pp. 43–44.

[3] Gouttenoire de Toury, op. cit., pp. 18–68; Judet, pp. 66–82.

[4] Poincaré, I, pp. 358–388.

over the incident at a time when delicate negotiations were pending, led Poincaré to reconsider the matter. Izvolsky became the scapegoat. The thesis of a Poincaré-Izvolsky "conspiracy" to oust Louis is not supported by the evidence available. When Louis resumed his duties, he bestirred himself to secure a "vindication" and sent elaborate dispatches on his findings back to Poincaré. Kokovtzov and the Tsar seemed sympathetic and Sazonov himself declared that Izvolsky had placed him in a false light. Poincaré insisted that Izvolsky had acted on Sazonov's orders and apparently became increasingly irritated at Louis' reluctance to drop the matter. The ambassador finally established to his own satisfaction that the Grand Duchess Maria Pavlovna was at the bottom of the "intrigue" against him.[1]

These incidents contributed to Poincaré's decision to visit Russia in the summer of 1912. It was clear that the existing channels of communication between himself and Sazonov left much to be desired. Izvolsky he distrusted. Louis obviously did not have the confidence of the Russian foreign minister. And the Near Eastern situation was disquieting. When in March, 1912, Poincaré had inquired of Izvolsky regarding rumors of Russian military moves in the Caucasus, the Russian professed ignorance. The Premier insisted emphatically on the necessity of Franco-Russian consultation and collaboration in connection with any political enterprise not envisaged in the original alliance.[2] Izvolsky, in embarrassment, asserted that this was also Sazonov's view as shown by his desire to have Poincaré study secretly his questionnaire on Russian Near Eastern and Balkan policy. Poincaré replied that the problem was too serious to conceal from the Cabinet, but that in any case the French Government stood for the maintenance of Ottoman integrity and the *status quo* in the Balkans. Izvolsky seems to have neglected to quote Poincaré on these points to Sazonov, but the Premier instructed Georges Louis to bring the matter to the foreign minister's attention on his return to St. Petersburg. Sazonov seemed evasive and Poincaré began to suspect his frankness. On April 1st, Izvolsky had come to the Quai d'Orsay to tell of two secret agreements between Serbia and Bulgaria to maintain the *status quo* and act only in consultation with Russia. When Poincaré sought more information, the ambassador again professed ignorance. The Premier was uneasy and refused permission to list the Bulgarian loan on the bourse.[3] Briand and Bourgeois in the Cabinet urged the usefulness of direct contact with Sazonov. The press as a whole approved the project, though Jaurès

[1] Judet, pp. 83–130.

[2] "De toutes façons, répliquai-je, vous savez que le gouvernement de la République a toujours interprété notre alliance en ce sens que toute initiative non prévue par le pacte primitif, c'est-à-dire, toute entreprise de politique générale qui ne constitue pas une riposte à une attaque effective ou imminente de l'Allemagne, impose auz deux allies l'obligation préalable de se concerter. M. Sazonoff a declaré récemment à M. Georges Louis que le gouvernement impériale n'entreprendrait rien en Orient sans nous prévenir. Il ne suffit pas que vous nous préveniez; il est nécessaire que nous vous concertions." Poincaré, II, p. 27; also *L.J.* 1914, Nos. 16, 17.

[3] *Ibid.*, II, pp. 29–46.

and the Left had misgivings.[1] Briand was named Premier and Minister of Foreign Affairs *ad interim* and Poincaré left Paris on August 5, reaching the Russian capital on the ninth aboard the cruiser *Condé*.

The purpose of this visit was not to incite Russia to a more active Balkan policy, but to discover what Russia's Balkan policy was and to avert possible dangers to peace growing out of it.[2] Izvolsky, who was temporarily back in Russia, greeted the Premier and his party and accompanied them from St. Petersburg to Moscow. Poincaré discussed a variety of matters with Sazonov, including the Italo-Turkish War. He found the Foreign Minister "visibly as Italophile as M. Izvolsky."[3] He further learned, to his amazement, that a secret agreement had been signed under Russian auspices, on the thirteenth of the preceding March, constituting a Balkan league for military action against Turkey or Austria-Hungary. "C'est un instrument de guerre!" he exclaimed. No intimation of its contents had previously been vouchsafed the French Government. Poincaré hastened to assure Sazonov that French public opinion would not sanction any military action in purely Balkan matters if Germany did not, on her own initiative, provoke the application of the *casus foederis*. Russia could rely on French aid in case of war only if she were attacked by Germany or by Austria-Hungary backed by Germany.[4] Sazonov took cognizance of this position, but expressed to the Tsar his confidence in Poincaré and in the certainty of French aid in the event of war. Subsequent events were to prove the correctness of his interpretation.

. . . I am very glad to have had the occasion for making the acquaintance of M. Poincaré and of entering into personal relations with him, all the more so, because the exchange of views which I have had with him has left me with the impression that in his person Russia possesses a sure and faithful friend endowed with exceptional political ability, and with an inflexible determination. In case of a crisis in international relations it would be very desirable that our ally should have as her head, if not M. Poincaré himself, at least a personality possessing the same decision and as free from the fear of responsibility as the present French Prime Minister.[5]

Among other things, Sazonov expressed his distrust of Georges Louis, but agreed to consider the incident closed.[6] The removal of both Izvolsky and Louis was considered, but it was agreed that both men should remain at their posts for the time being. Poincaré urged haste in the construction of strategic railways through Poland and informed Sazonov of the Anglo-French plans for naval and military collaboration and the scheme of a British

[1] Gouttenoire de Toury, pp. 71–90.

[2] Fay, I, pp. 334–336.

[3] Poincaré, II, p. 109.

[4] "Après avoir reproché à M. Sazonov, au nom du gouvernement de la République, de ne nous avoir ni consultés ni prévenus, je n'avais qu'a courir maintenant au plus pressé et à tâcher de m'assurer par un contrôle vigilant que la Russie tiendrait sa promesse et se joindrait à nous pour empêcher une guerre d'éclater dans les Balkans." Poincaré, II, p. 117.

[5] *L.N.*, II, p. 345.

[6] Poincaré, II, p. 123.

expeditionary force to fight Germany on the continent, begging him to keep this confidence a secret even from the English. On his return from Moscow to the capital, he took up with Sazonov the proposal of the Austrian foreign minister, Berchtold, for international action by the Powers to restrain the Balkan States while urging upon the Porte a policy of progressive decentralization. Briand had given Berchtold a favorable reply. Sazonov was skeptical, but Poincaré, according to his own account, urged him to consider the plan as a means of averting war. With this last word of advice, he returned to France—certainly not reassured regarding the pacific character of Sazonov's purposes nor the honesty of his methods. Sazonov, on his part, was left secure in the confidence that French acquiescence could be gained for whatever warlike schemes he might devise and that French support could be counted upon in any eventuality. The Premier's warnings and admonition could be taken *cum grano salis*.[1]

Here, as always, Poincaré's conception of French national interests made Entente solidarity seem more important than the preservation of peace. After his return to Paris, he allowed a month to elapse before taking action, while Sazonov dallied with Berchtold's proposal, and war in the Balkans became imminent. On September 22 he suggested to the British Government that the Entente Powers agree on a formula for restraining the Balkan States and present it to Berlin and Vienna for acceptance. This was done with half-hearted support from Sazonov. The Balkans States were to be warned that no territorial gains as a result of war would be permitted. Berlin was favorable and by October 7 the consent of all the Powers had been secured. On the eighth, the Austrian and Russian Governments transmitted the warning to the Balkan capitals. On the same day, Montenegro declared war on Turkey and the First Balkan War began.[2] The broth which Sazonov had brewed boiled over the caldron. The dream of Izvolsky was brought a step nearer to realization, not, perhaps, with the connivance of Poincaré, but in the face of his doubtings and his reluctance to put pressure on Russia to keep the peace.

The rapid victories of the Balkan allies, culminating in Kirk-Kilisse and Lule-Burgas, gave pause to Sazonov's enthusiasm while it reassured French public opinion and lent support to Poincaré's declaration of loyalty to Russia. The Russian foreign minister feared a Bulgarian occupation of Constantinople and on November 2, without consulting the French Premier, who had already taken steps in the same direction, he presented to the Powers a complete program of intervention, embodying continued Turkish control of Adrianople and the capital, an autonomous Albania, and Serbian access to the Adriatic. Before Poincaré could recover his breath, Sazonov further informed him of his hopes of seizing the Bosphorus.[3] The Premier was

[1] *Cf*. Poincaré, II, pp. 158–170 with Sazonov's report in *L.N.*, II, pp. 338–345.
[2] Fay, I, pp. 434–438.
[3] Fay, I, pp. 338–339.

unenthusiastic, and fearful lest the Balkan Slavs be alienated from the Entente and lest Austria use the occasion to secure additional territory at their expense. Izvolsky welcomed this new interest in Balkan affairs and informed Sazonov that "Poincaré is perfectly aware of the fact that France may thus become involved in a warlike action. For the present, of course, he submits this question merely for our consideration, but in a conversation with me Paléologue freely granted that the proposed agreement might lead to some kind of active step."[1] When Serbia's occupation of northern Albania led to threats of force from Vienna, Izvolsky inquired as to what the French attitude would be in the event of a general war. He reported to Sazonov on November 17 that Poincaré desired Russia to take the initiative and rest assured of French support.[2] "And it (the French Government) admits very candidly and with all the necessary *sang-froid* that the final result of the present complications may impose upon it the necessity of the participation of France in a general war."[3]

Poincaré has hotly denied that this was the meaning of his statements to the Russian Ambassador[4] and he warned Georges Louis of Izvolsky's misrepresentations. But where the wish was father to the thought, it was easy for Sazonov to accept the interpretation which his ambassador put upon the Premier's words. The Russian Ambassador in Belgrade, Hartwig, incited the Serbs to extreme demands at Austria's expense. With Austrian and Italian encouragement, Albania declared its independence and neutrality on November 28. By early December, Austria and Russia were at swords' points over the issue of a Serbian outlet to the sea. Poincaré took no steps to restrain Russia, but contented himself with emphasizing again that France would support Russia only if Germany were involved. In Berlin and London steps were taken to preserve peace, and since Russia was not yet prepared to resort to arms, an agreement was finally reached by which Albanian independence was recognized and Serbian hopes of access to the Adriatic were frustrated. The later Serbian effort to secure compensation at Bulgaria's expense led to the outbreak of the Second Balkan War in June, 1913. That the Balkan crisis did not result in a general conflagration in the winter of 1912 and 1913, arising out of Russian support of Serbia against Austria-Hungary, was apparently due only to Sazonov's realization of the military unpreparedness of the Tsardom. He felt throughout that French support was assured in any eventuality. The Dual Alliance had become "balkanized." Here were the seeds of incalculable tragedy.

Meanwhile Poincaré had been elevated to the Presidency of the Republic. The term of President Fallières being on the point of expiration, it was the constitutional duty of the National Assembly to pick his successor. Poincaré

---

[1] *L.N.*, I, p. 342.
[2] *L.N.*, I, p. 346.
[3] *L.N.*, II, p. 20, January 30, 1913.
[4] Poincaré, II, pp. 336*f.*

declares that he was persuaded by Léon Bourgeois to put his name forward
as a candidate, though he had no desire to fill so inactive a post. He was
supported by the Nationalist and Catholic Right against Pams, Radical-
Socialist candidate of the Left. On the first ballot at Versailles he received 180
votes to Pams's 174, with the balance scattered. On the second ballot he
received 272 votes to Pams's 283; and on the third, 309 to his rival's 323.
Great pressure was brought to bear upon Poincaré to withdraw his candidacy, but, much to Clemenceau's disgust, he refused. On the fourth ballot,
he secured 429 votes (eight short of a majority) to Pams's 327, and on the
fifth, 483 to Pams's 298. He was thus elected President of France on January
17, 1913.[1] The Senators and Deputies seem not to have been influenced to any
appreciable degree in their choice by considerations of foreign policy. Only
Jaurès and the Socialists felt alarm on this score. Poincarè himself doubtless
calculated that he could continue to control foreign affairs to a large degree
from the Palais d'Élysée. Izvolsky, Sazonov, and the Russian nationalist
press rejoiced, though the charge that he was "elected by Russian gold"
would seem to be true only to the extent that Russian bribery of the French
press can be said to have influenced the result.[2] Poincaré at once resigned as
président du conseil and Briand formed his third Cabinet (January 18 to March
22, 1913) with Jonnart as Minister of Foreign Affairs. In his ministerial
address, Briand limited his references to foreign affairs to a declaration of
"fidelity to our alliances and our friendships as the immutable principle of
our foreign policy," a statement of satisfaction at the enhanced diplomatic
prestige of the Republic in its efforts to prevent war in close contact and
constant harmony with its friends and allies, and an expression of determination to serve the cause of peace by strengthening the means of national
defense.[3]

Jonnart, following Poincaré's cue, instructed Georges Louis to protest at
the various diplomatic *démarches* which Sazonov, without consulting France,
was undertaking at Berlin and Bucharest and informed Sir Edward Grey of
these incidents.[4] Izvolsky saw Jonnart for the first time on January 28 and
found him irritated and reproachful. Sazonov, on the other hand, reproached
the ambassador for not having made the Russian action seem acceptable to
the Quai d'Orsay.[5] On January 29 Izvolsky saw Poincaré once more—though
the latter minimizes the importance of this and later contacts and accuses the
ambassador of exaggerating the cordiality of his relations with the new
President as a means of meeting Sazonov's criticisms. He also charges Izvolsky with representing Poincaré's anxiety to be consulted on Russian decisions
as due to a desire to prepare French public opinion for a possible war growing

[1] Poincaré, III, pp. 33–63.
[2] *Cf. ibid.*, III, pp. 112–114.
[3] *J.O.*, January 25, 1913.
[4] Poincaré, III, pp. 77–82.
[5] *Ibid.*, III, pp. 90–93.

out of the Balkan imbroglio—a motive which Poincaré denies having had.[1] His continued distrust of Izvolsky made it all the more important that the Republic be represented at St. Petersburg by some one in Sazonov's confidence. The Russian foreign minister had complained, during the visit of the preceding summer, that Louis had accused him of belligerent designs against Turkey (subsequent events are sufficient proof of Louis' perspicacity in this particular) and had frequently misinterpreted his observations in his reports to Paris, a fault which Poincaré had again attributed to ill-health.[2] On January 29, 1913, Louis transmitted information of a secret agreement of 1902 between the Russian and Bulgarian General Staffs which had never been made known to Paris. Jonnart, probably at Poincaré's suggestion, expressed regret that Louis had not at once protested and emphasized to Sazonov that any independent Russian action in the Balkans would be contrary to the spirit of the alliance. On January 31, Louis responded to this implied criticism by asking leave to come to Paris to discuss the whole situation. Jonnart replied on February 5 that the Cabinet thought it best that he should remain at his post for the present.[3]

Early in February, Jonnart called upon Delcassé and asked him to assume the post of ambassador to Russia.[4] The veteran diplomat's hesitations, inspired by his political prospects in the Chamber, were overcome by the insistence of Briand and Poincaré. On February 17, 1913, Jonnart informed Louis that the gravity of the circumstances required that France be represented in Russia "by a political personage possessing particular authority, and who will be able to pursue his duties with an activity which the state of your health unfortunately forbids."[5] Georges Louis this time succumbed to his "diplomatic illness" without complaint. The details were arranged with the utmost formality. L'Écho de Paris announced the change with fulsome laudations of Delcassé and no mention of Louis' name. The deposed ambassador returned to Paris on March 24, convinced that Poincaré, acting as Izvolsky's tool, was responsible for his removal.[6] When the President asked him to keep silent, he replied that he did not need to be taught his duty. He was placed in the cadres de la disposition, where he had no duties. He was awarded the Grand Cordon of the Legion of Honor and retired at the end of the year, to write his Carnets and die in obscurity on April 7, 1917.[7]

Much has been made of the Georges Louis affair by Poincaré's critics by way of showing the influence exercised over the Premier-President by the

[1] Ibid., III, pp. 94–96.

[2] L.N., II, pp. 338–345.

[3] Judet, op. cit., pp. 209–214.

[4] This story appeared in the Russian journal, Vetscherneie Vremia, of February 22, and is cited by Judet, pp. 205f. It is not denied by Poincaré and would seem to be an accurate statement of the situation.

[5] Judet, p. 215.

[6] Ibid., p. 246.

[7] Ibid., pp. 235–253; Gouttenoire de Toury, op. cit., pp. 90-160.

Russian Ambassador. Enough has been said of the relations between the two men to show the falsity of this view. The incident is chiefly revealing for the light it throws on the relationships between the various officials in the French Government handling foreign affairs. As soon as Poincaré, Premier, was convinced that Sazonov was not fully revealing his hand in the Balkans to Paris and that Georges Louis did not possess his confidence, he considered his replacement a necessity, though inclined to accept Izvolsky's reports of Sazonov's views with a certain skepticism. But to provoke a bitter controversy in the press over the matter seemed too high a price to pay. The move of May, 1912, was therefore abandoned. Poincaré, President, denies that he exercised any influence whatever in the final recall of February, 1913.[1] But the new Premier and foreign minister were familiar with the President's views and disposed to defer to them in dealing with Russia. Among his first official acts as President was Poincaré's signature of Jonnart's recall of Georges Louis. The peculiar position of Poincaré enabled him to exert an influence on foreign affairs much greater than would normally be exercised by a French President. In February, 1913, there was no indication of Russian pressure, no hint of unfavorable press comment except for Jaurès perpetual misgivings, no danger of provoking an embarrassing political controversy. The knife accordingly fell, with Poincaré's approval, if not at his suggestion. The French and Russian press rejoiced. Stocks fell on the Berlin Boerse at the news of Delcassé's appointment, which German and Austrian journals attributed to Izvolsky's influence. Delcassé was a symbol of belligerent French nationalism. His appointment, like the conferring upon Poincaré by the Tsar of the Russian Imperial Order of St. Andrew,[2] epitomized the tightening of Franco-Russian bonds. He would be a poor instrument to restrain Sazonov's Balkan designs, but an excellent and sympathetic vehicle of communication, representative of all in French foreign policy which was most acceptable to Russian official circles. Here again Poincaré had imposed upon the Quai d'Orsay the view, from which he never wavered, that Franco-Russian solidarity was more important than peace.

One of the most extraordinary aspects of Franco-Russian relations at this time was the wholesale and systematic bribery of French newspapers by St. Petersburg in order to create a favorable public opinion of Russian policies and to safeguard the market for Russian bonds. This practice apparently began in 1897[3] and was developed extensively on the eve of the Russo-Japanese War and during the revolution of 1904 to 1906. The first transaction, amounting to 50,000 to 100,000 fr. monthly, were handled by Arthur Raffalovitch, secret agent of the Russian Ministry of Finance in Paris, through the *Banque de Paris et des Pays-Bas* and the *Crédit Algerien*.[4] The

---

[1] Poincaré, III, pp. 115–119.

[2] *L.N.*, II, pp. 30–33.

[3] Boris Souvarine, "L'Abominable vénalité de la presse française," *L'Humanité*, January 1, 1924.

[4] Letter to Kokovstov, August 30, 1940; *ibid.*, December 5, 1923.

editors of the politically Right papers, such as *Figaro* and *Liberté*, were the first recipients of Russian money. During 1905, 1,782,000 fr. were expended for this purpose. The *Société des Agents de Change de Paris* informed Raffalovitch that they could not admit new Russian loans to the Bourse unless 200,000 fr. a month were placed at the disposition of the French press for the duration of the war.[1] *Le Matin, Le Petit Parisien, Le Petit Journal,* and *Radical* were all bribed to minimize the importance of Russian defeats and revolutionary disturbances. The record for the following years is incomplete. But on October 23, 1912, Izvolsky, apparently learning for the first time of the subsidy system, wrote to Sazonov that, in his opinion, Poincaré favored the Russian Government resorting to this expedient. Kokovstov, now Russian Minister of Finance, placed 300,000 fr. at Izvolsky's disposal for this purpose. Poincaré has admitted his knowledge of the system, but alleges that the Austrian and Italian Governments resorted to the same practice and denies that he encouraged Izvolsky in it. He wrote to Kokovstov on November 18, 1912, denying that he had taken the initiative in the matter, but leaving Russia full liberty of action. "It is essential to distribute it (the 300,000 francs) as much as possible by successive installments, with much prudence and discretion."[2] Poincaré, hotly denying the various accusations against him, declares that he washed his hands of the whole affair soon afterwards and ceased to be interested in the consequences.[3] Franco-Russian solidarity was essential, even if it involved connivance in dishonesty and corruption.

The wholesale bribery, blackmailing, and racketeering which ensued is suggestive of American municipal politics rather than of the refinements of continental diplomacy. *L'Agence Havas, Le Temps, La Patrie, L'Echo de Paris, Gil Blas, Le Journal,* and a host of other metropolitan and provincial journals were on the Russian pay roll. The ultra-patriotic *Le Matin* was among the most venal. Twenty-six Paris papers were at one time on the list. André Tardieu was among the beneficiaries. In 1913 Poincaré and Briand encouraged the practice in order to combat the campaign against the three-year military service law. The details of these transactions, with documentary proof, the authenticity of which has never been successfully challenged, were published in the Communist (formerly Socialist) paper *L'Humanité* during December and January, 1923 and 1924,[4] and led to a demand by the Communist Deputy, Marcel Cachin, for an interpellation in the Chamber, which was voted down, 400 to 111.[5] No explanations were offered at the time by Poincaré, Klotz, Briand, or other participants.[6] The facts of the situation have been established beyond reasonable doubt.

[1] G. Michon, *l, Alliance Franco-Russe,* pp. 296–297.

[2] Poincaré, III, pp. 106–107.

[3] *Ibid.,* III, pp. 108–113.

[4] See especially issues of December 14 and 25 and January 1 to 16.

[5] *J.O.Ch.,* January 12, 1924.

[6] *Cf.* G. Lowes Dickinson, *The International Anarchy,* 1904-1914, pp. 43–46.

The venality of the French press is generally conceded and these incidents are probably not to be regarded as abnormal or extraordinary. The significant thing is that responsible ministers in the French Cabinet, including the man who, while the bribery was at its height, became Minister of Foreign Affairs, Premier, and President of the Republic, not only sanctioned this procedure, but gave it at least their tacit encouragement. The Quai d'Orsay regularly resorts to the same practice itself in dealing with the foreign press. The "secret funds" of the Ministry are apparently largely devoted to this purpose—and it seems probable that they are occasionally used to influence the French press as well. That Poincaré and his colleagues should have welcomed the opportunity to utilize Russian funds to influence French opinion in favor of Franco-Russian solidarity was a natural result of their diplomatic objectives and of their situation *vis-à-vis* Parliament and the press. The precise effect of Russian bribery in shaping French opinion is difficult to measure. That it had an important influence in the desired direction is undebatable. Since public opinion is obviously shaped primarily by the daily press, one may well doubt whether any opportunity existed under these circumstances for an objective presentation of the facts of French and Russian foreign policy to the French citizenry or for an intelligent comprehension of the issues and alternatives involved.

3. SARAJEVO

At 10:00 A.M., Sunday, June 28, 1914, the Austrian Archduke Francis Ferdinand, heir to the Hapsburg throne, reached the town of Sarajevo with his wife and party in the course of a journey through the southwestern privinces of the Dual Monarchy. A procession had been arranged through the gaily bedecked city, which was the capital of the disaffected Jugoslav province of Bosnia. As the royal car reached the Cumurja Bridge over the Miljacka River, a man stepped forward out of the crowd and hurled a bomb at the Archduke's party. The missile exploded in the roadway, wrecking the following car and wounding several bystanders. The would-be assassin was one N. Chabrinovitch, agent of the *Narodna Odbrana* and its adjunct, the Black Hand Society, formed in 1908 to oppose Hapsburg rule and work for the incorporation of Bosnia and Herzegovina into a Greater Serbia. He was arrested and the procession proceeded to the Town Hall, where the mayor made a speech of welcome. On the way back, along Appel Quai, the mayor's car turned left up Franz Joseph Street. The procession had been rerouted to proceed directly along the Quai, in view of the earlier attack. As the royal car stopped, owing to this mistake, Gabriel Princep, one of Chabrinovitch's fellow conspirators, stepped forward and fired two revolver shots point blank at the Archduke and his wife. Both died within a few minutes. Ten million men were to follow them into the grave before the final curtain fell on the tragedy which here began on a summer morning in this little Balkan municipality.[1]

The prelude and the sequel to the assassination cannot be discussed here. It was the work of Pan-Serbian terrorists, whose activities were acquiesced in if not encouraged by the Serbian General Staff at Belgrade and by responsible officials of the Serbian Government. It was the culmination of the efforts of Serbian nationalists since 1908 to undermine and dismember the Dual Monarchy. In Vienna it was clear to Count Berchtold and his colleagues that the security of the Empire depended upon the suppression of these subversive activities organized in the Serbian capital. In St. Petersburg it was equally clear that any Austrian "aggression" against Serbia must be resisted at all costs, or the whole Pan-Slavist program of expansion in the southeast would be frustrated. Vienna had triumphed in 1908. It had triumphed again in 1913, in blocking Serbian access to the Adriatic. The Second Balkan War in the summer of 1913—Serbia, Montenegro, Roumania, Greece, and Turkey against Bulgaria—had enabled the Turks to recover Adrianople and part of Thrace and had deprived Sofia of most of the spoils of victory in the earlier conflict. It left Bulgaria disgruntled and unresponsive to Russian overtures. The future of Russian influence in the Balkans lay in Belgrade. Another Austrian triumph over Serbia was intolerable to Sazonov and his colleagues. Any conflict between Vienna and Belgrade was at once an issue between Vienna and St. Petersburg. Since the practical defection of Italy from the Triple Alliance, Austria-Hungary, whose very existence as a State was menaced by the Pan-Serb agitation, was the only Power upon whom "encircled" Germany could rely for support in any international crisis. Behind Vienna stood Berlin. Behind St. Petersburg stood Paris. The issue was therefore one between the armed coalitions. The intricacies of these involvements are beyond the scope of the present investigation. The development of the crisis will be traced from the point of view of the Quai d'Orsay for the purpose of throwing further light upon the control of French foreign relations in the gravest diplomatic crisis in the history of the Third Republic.

It will be appropriate first to review briefly the course of French politics during the year from June, 1913, to June, 1914. The unusual influence of President Poincaré on foreign affairs and his relations with Sazonov and Izvolsky have already been indicated. Delcassé's sojourn at St. Petersburg had been terminated by ill-health (physical, not diplomatic) and he had been replaced by Maurice Paléologue, who well represented Poincaré's views.[2] At home the Briand Cabinet was overturned in March, 1913, and succeeded by the Barthou ministry (March 22 to December 10, 1913) with Pichon as Minister of Foreign Affairs. The Government supported the three-year military service law introduced by Briand as the only means of protecting the

---

[1] For full accounts of the incident and further references regarding it see Schmitt, I, pp. 175–257, and Fay, II, pp. 1–166.

[2] Poincaré, IV, pp. 29–30.

interests, dignity, and security of the Republic.[1] This proposal, though bitterly fought by Jaurès and the Socialists, was enacted into law and went into effect in the summer. The Doumergue Cabinet of December, 1913, was predominantly Left and included Joseph Caillaux as Minister of Finance. But for his alleged diplomatic improprieties in 1911 he might have become Premier. As it was, he might have been expected to influence Doumergue, who was also foreign minister, in the direction of an independent policy, designed to restrain Russian ambitions and maintain friendly relations with the Triplice. But the scandal resulting from his wife's murder of Gaston Calmette, editor of *Figaro*, in May, 1914, forced him out of the Cabinet. The general elections of May, 1914, resulted in Socialist gains and a general strengthening of the Left, despite some Radical losses, and of the opposition to the three-year law. Doumergue and his Cabinet resigned before the new Parliament met on June 1.

The ministerial crisis which followed was prolonged and difficult to resolve. The Left groups were bent upon the repeal of the three-year service law and the enactment of an extensive program of social legislation, both of which demands were bitterly resisted by the Right politicians, who, of course, had the full sympathy of Poincaré. The latter was, nevertheless, obliged by the party situation in the Chamber to pick Réné Viviani, leader of the Republican Socialists, to form a new Cabinet. On June 5, 1914, Paléologue returned from St. Petersburg and asked Briand to inform Viviani of his intention of resigning if the new Cabinet did not maintain the three-year service law. This threat was apparently made on his own initiative, though it expressed the views of Sazonov, Izvolsky, and Poincaré, all of whom seemed to be comtemplating the possibility of war acquiescently, if not with equanimity, and all of whom regarded the larger number of military effectives which the three-year law kept under arms as essential to the security of France and the alliance in view of German war preparations. Here was a question of public policy which was, by its nature, a matter for the prospective Cabinet to determine on its own merits. The election could validly be interpreted as a popular repudiation of the law under discussion. Paléologue's threat meant, in substance, that the St. Petersburg diplomats and militarists, with the support of the French President, the Quai d'Orsay, and the French Ambassador, were exerting pressure on decisions at Paris, while no group in the French capital was in a position to exert a corresponding pressure on Russian policy, with the possible exception of the bankers, who were treated as the passive instruments of Franco-Russian solidarity. Briand agreed that the Radicals and Socialists were "en train de perdre la France." On June 5, *Le Matin* published a St. Petersburg dispatch declaring that the majority of Russian statesmen regarded the three-year law as indispensable to the European balance of power and the solidarity of the Alliance. *Le Temps* and other papers followed suit in attacking the repeal proposal.

[1] *Cf. J.O.Ch.*, March 26, 1913.

One may venture the guess that Russian bribery of the editors played some part in shaping their attitude.[1]

Since the decision in the matter was virtually dictated by St. Petersburg, acting through Paléologue and Poincaré, the interest of Russia in the three-year law deserves a word of explanation. Kokovstov had conferred with Poincaré in Paris in the preceding November. According to the President, the three-year law was not suggested by Russia, but was a natural reply to the German "menace." Indeed, the initiative to war preparations came from Poincaré himself, who encouraged loans to assist Russia in building strategic railways and urged measures to accelerate Russian mobilization.[2] Izvolsky and Raffalovitch persuaded Doumergue and Caillaux in December, 1913, to authorize the flotation of 500,000,000 fr. worth of Russian railway bonds in France. Poincaré declares that neither he nor Barthou thought it necessary to give Russian bonds precedence over the needs of the French Government itself, but that the strategic importance of Russian railways made it imperative that they be built without delay and that it was to the political advantage of France to please her ally.[3] The Russian protest to Berlin in December, 1913, over the appointment of General Liman von Sanders as military adviser to the Turkish Army was supported by Bompard, French Ambassador at Constantinople, and by Paléologue, then still political director at the Quai d'Orsay. Izvolsky was enthusiastic: "M. Doumergue marche jusqu'à présent derrière nous sans hésitation."[4] But Doumergue, along with the British Government, urged restraint upon Sazonov and the problem was amicably settled.[5] Sazonov's anxiety to hasten war preparations was motivated by the feeling that the *status quo* in Turkey and the Balkans could not be long maintained and that any favorable opportunity ought to be utilized by Russia to secure control of the Straits. On January 13, 1914, he informed his fellow ministers that Delcassé had extended assurances that "France will go as far as Russia may wish." Kokovstov pointed out that war with Germany might result. Soukhomlinov, the Minister of War, declared that Russia was now prepared for any eventuality.[6] Obviously, France must likewise be prepared. Hence, Russian enthusiasm for the French three-year law and anxiety over the policies of the Left groups. Sazonov and Izvolsky were anticipating war. The latter's influence at St. Petersburg was

[1] *Cf.* G. Michon, *L'Alliance Franco-Russe*, pp. 248–254.

[2] Poincaré, III, pp. 315–325.

[3] *Ibid.*, III, pp. 350*f.*

[4] *Ibid.*, III, p. 353. *Cf. L.N.*, II, pp. 228*f.* Izvolsky's dispatches for this period reveal the care with which he watched, and sought to influence, French domestic politics.

[5] Fay, I, pp. 498–524. "The whole affair shows how even a serious Russian-German diplomatic crisis could be sensibly and peacefully settled, provided that Germany was willing to make some concessions, and that Russia was restrained by France and England from taking too extreme and hasty steps; and provided also that neither side paid too much attention to the hounding criticisms of its own jingo newspapers and military alarmists" (p. 523).

[6] Fay, I, pp. 525–541.

waning by the spring of 1914 and he even feared his recall,[1] but his conception of Russian foreign policy and of Franco-Russian relations was predominant at the Tsarist capital.

In view of Poincaré's advice[2] and Paléologue's threat to resign, Viviani assured the President that he would maintain the three-year law, at least temporarily, but he was unable to convince his followers in the Chamber and gave up the task of forming a ministry. Poincaré then summoned Alexandre Ribot, father of the Franco-Russian Alliance, to try his hand at Cabinet making. Ribot formed a Center-and-Right Cabinet on June 9, with Bourgeois as Minister of Foreign Affairs and Delcassé as Minister of War, and declared his loyalty to the three-year law before the Chamber of the twelfth. An *order du jour*, declaring that the Chamber "respectful of the will recently expressed by universal suffrage, resolves to give its support only to a Government capable of realizing a union of the forces of the Left," was passed, 374 to 187, and Ribot was obliged to resign.[3] Poincaré's chagrin was so great that he was tempted to quit his office.[4] On the following day an article: "La Russie est prête, la France doit l'être aussi," appeared in the *Gazette de la Bourse*, evidently inspired by Sazonov and Soukhomlinov. It demanded that France maintain the three-year law. "The greater the number of her soldiers in time of peace, the sooner she will be ready."[5] In desperation, Poincaré turned again to Viviani, whose followers now agreed to a compromise under which the three classes of soldiers then serving would not be discharged, though the existing law might be modified in the future. Viviani took the portfolio of foreign affairs and succeeded in forming a Left Cabinet with Bienvenu-Martin as Minister of Justice, Messimy as Minister of War, Malvy as Minister of the Interior, etc. On June 16, by a vote of 370 to 137, the Chamber expressed its confidence in the new Cabinet.[6]

Two days later, on June 18, ten days before the Sarajevo assassination, Paléologue told the new Premier that war was impending. Viviani asked when it would occur.

"It is impossible for me to fix any date," the ambassador replied. "However, I shall be surprised if the state of electric tension in which Europe lives does not end soon in a catastrophe."

"Well," returned the Premier, "if it must be so, we will do our duty, all our duty. France will find herself, as she has always been, capable of every heroism and every sacrifice. One will see again the great days of 1792."

"You are resolved then," queried Paléologue, "to maintain the military law in its entirety? I may affirm it to the Emperor Nicholas?"

[1] *Ibid.*, I, p. 537.
[2] See Izvolsky's comments on Poincaré's constitutional and political position in his dispatches in *L.N.*, II, pp. 14–22.
[3] *J.O.Ch.*, June 13, 1914.
[4] Poincaré, IV, p. 163.
[5] Pevet, *op. cit.*, p. 20.
[6] *J.O.Ch.*, June 17, 1914.

"Yes, you may assure him that the three years' service will be maintained without restriction and that I will let nothing happen which may enfeeble or loosen our alliance with Russia."[1]

The eve of Sarajevo thus found a Left Cabinet in power in France, committed, however, to a military program and a foreign policy dictated by St. Petersburg, Poincaré, the Quai d'Orsay, and the nationalist Right. French public opinion had been consistently poisoned for many years by the Russia-subsidized press and acquiesced in the situation. The May election had produced no change. The bribed papers exuded the most extravagant optimism regarding Russian financial solvency, political and social stability, and fighting capacity.[2] The loan policy of the Government confirmed this confidence. In the preceding dozen years, French investments in Russia had increased from 6,900,000,000 fr. to 11,300,000,000 fr. French capital had flowed into the Balkan countries even more rapidly—920,000,000 fr. in 1902, and 3,130,000,000 in 1914.[3] The "Balkanization" of the Dual Alliance was viewed with complacency by all save a small group of radicals and Socialists. Jean Jaurès, with prophetic insight, had written in the German Socialist organ *Vorwärts* in 1905:

> From a European war the Revolution might spring; and the governing classes would do well to ponder on that—but there might result also, for a long period, crises of counter-revolution, or furious reaction, of exasperated nationalism, of stifling dictatorships, of monstrous militarism, a long chain of retrograde violence, of base hatreds, of reprisals, of slavery. And as for us, we have no wish to play at this game of barbarous chance.[4]

The great French Socialist leader was always suspicious of the Franco-Russian Alliance, because of its influence in strengthening reactionary groups in France and because of his feeling that the Republic was being led toward catastrophe by the Tsardom. He urged Anglo-German conciliation as the mission of France. Though constantly denounced as a Germanophile traitor, he ceaselessly condemned French imperialism in its betrayal of the Act of Algeciras and sponsored a *rapprochement* with Berlin.[5] But his was a voice of the future, crying in the wilderness. Except for his followers, all significant opinion groups in France were either acquiescent or inspired by fervent patriotism to enthusiastic support of the Government's Russian policy.

The first reaction of the French press to the news of the crime at Sarajevo was not without its grim humor. The nationalistic Right papers were somewhat sympathetic toward Austria-Hungary and especially toward the old Emperor in his bereavement, as shown by the comments in *Le Temps* and *Le Petit Journal* on the evening of June 28. *Le Matin*, to be sure, con-

[1] Michon, *op. cit.*, pp. 250–252.
[2] *Ibid.*, pp. 238–247.
[3] Fay, I, pp. 402–403, Note 80.
[4] Cited in Margaret Pease, *Jean Jaurès*, p. 126.
[5] *Ibid.*, pp. 123–152.

demned the Archduke for favoring war on Serbia in 1909. The Left papers tended to condone the assassination. On July 1, Clemenceau in *L'Homme Libre* declared that the conspirators were inspired by Pan-Serb ideals and got their inspiration from Belgrade. In Jaurès own paper, *L'Humanité*, Marcel Sembat declared that Austria was herself responsible by the annexation of Bosnia and Herzegovina and described the criminals as exasperated patriots (July 1). *Le Guerre Sociale* asserted that the only crime committed was that of Austria-Hungary against the Serbs of Bosnia. *Le Temps*, on July 2, denied that the Serbian Government or people were in any way responsible.[1] There was no general feeling that the incident would lead to war or that it would involve Franco-German relations. *Le Temps*, to be sure, strongly opposed Jaurès' plea for friendship across the Rhine, on the ground that it would destroy the diplomatic achievements of forty years which had given France "liberty" and "security" (July 8) and a week later it glorified the Russian military colossus—a lead followed by *Le Matin* (July 18 and 20). Paléologue and Poincaré dissuaded Briand from accompanying the Prince of Monaco to the Kiel regatta at the end of June.[2] These were little flashes of the future. But the calm of early summer prevailed and few were alarmed by lightning without thunder.

When a Havas telegram first brought news of the murder, Poincaré was at the races at Longchamps. He showed it to the Austrian Ambassador, Count Szécsen, who at once returned to his embassy in the metropolis. On his return to the Palais d'Élysée, after the races, the President, in accordance with diplomatic usage, sent a telegram of condolence to Franz Joseph. Viviani visited the Count to express his regrets and instructed Dumaine, French Ambassador in Vienna, to extend condolences to Count Berchtold. On July 29, he expressed in the Senate the reprobation of the nation for the crime and its sympathy for the bereaved.[3] He did the same in the Chamber on the following day.[4] Both houses were absorbed in legislative work and in the budget and no discussion took place regarding the assassination.[5] On July 5, Szécsen called to thank Poincaré for his action. The President observed that political murders were usually the acts of isolated fanatics. Szécsen replied that the Serbs had sought for years to incite the South Slavs against the Dual Monarchy. Neither man was aware of the secret links between the conspirators and Belgrade. Poincaré remarked that the Serbian Government would be accommodating in facilitating a judicial investigation.[6] The Serbian Minister in Paris, Vesnitch, communicated to his Government the view of the French Government (probably transmitted by Viviani)

[1] J. F. Scott, *Five Weeks. The Surge of Public Opinion on the Eve of the Great War*, pp. 183–186.

[2] Poincaré, IV, pp. 168–169.

[3] *J.O.Sén.*, June 30, 1914.

[4] *J.O.Ch.*, July 1, 1914.

[5] J. D. Carter, *The Attitude of France in the Austro-Serbian Conflict*, 1914, pp. 59–62, Toulouse, 1927.

[6] *Cf.* Poincaré, IV, pp. 173–190.

that Serbia should remain calm and dignified and avoid giving cause for fresh accusations from Vienna.[1] No other steps seem to have been taken at the moment to influence the Serbian attitude toward the anticipated Austrian note.

During the early days of July the capitals waited for Vienna to act. But the Austrian Government bided its time. In Paris preparations proceeded for the projected visit of the President to St. Petersburg, which had been planned for July 20 to 23 in the preceding January.[2] The Cabinet doubted the wisdom of the trip in view of the diplomatic situation, but finally decided that a change of plans would needlessly alarm public opinion. Jaurès refused to vote credits for the voyage, on the ground that further Near Eastern entanglements were dangerous, but Viviani defended the alliance and the Chamber approved, 428 to 106.[3] On July 15, Poincaré and Viviani sailed from Dunkirk aboard the cruiser *France*. The President of the Republic and the Premier and Minister of Foreign Affairs were thus both absent from Paris during the critical days which ensued. M. Bienvenu-Martin was left as *ad interim* Premier and foreign minister. He had been Minister of Public Instruction in the second Rouvier Cabinet (January 23, 1905, to March 14, 1906) and Minister of Justice in the Doumergue and Viviani Cabinets. He was without diplomatic experience and yet was obliged by circumstances to play a major rôle in the gravest of all diplomatic crises. Poincaré and Viviani, as they traversed the North and Baltic Seas, were concerned with Russian-Swedish relations and especially with Anglo-Russian relations in Persia, which were threatening the solidarity of the Triple Entente. The uncertainty regarding Austrian plans toward Serbia was also a cause for anxiety, but war was not anticipated immediately. They reached Cronstadt on July 20. On the same day the Austrian ultimatum, which had been prepared in secret on July 14, was sent from Vienna to Belgrade, to be held there for delivery until the twenty-third, when Poincaré and Viviani would depart from Russia.[4]

The three days in Russia were filled with the receptions and ceremonies which had always accompanied such visits.[5] As the guests left the *France* in a launch, Poincaré and the Tsar sat chatting in the stern, the President taking the initiative and impressing the weak-willed Romanov with his own strength of conviction and powerful personality. At the banquet at Peterhof in the evening, toasts were drunk and perpetual loyalty pledged to the alliance which had now lasted almost a quarter of a century. The next morning Poincaré discussed the Persian situation with the Tsar, who did not accompany the party back to the capital because of the strikes and revolutionary labor disturbances taking place. Paléologue and Izvolsky were both present at most of these gatherings. The former presented the President

[1] Schmitt, I, p. 439.

[2] Poincaré, IV, pp. 3–6.

[3] *J.O.Ch.*, July 8, 1914; *cf. Le Temps*, July 9 and 21, 1914.

[4] Fay, II, pp. 277–278; Carter, *op. cit.*, pp. 74–95; Michon, *op. cit.*, pp. 255–258; R. Viviani, *As We See It* (transl. of *Réponse au Kaiser*), pp. 89–93.

[5] For details, see Poincaré, IV, pp. 221–280.

to his diplomatic colleagues at the reception at the Winter Palace on July 21. The British Ambassador, Sir George Buchanan, took the opportunity to present to Poincaré the suggestion of Sir Edward Grey that the Austrian and Russian Governments should discuss the situation together if the Serbian crisis became threatening. Poincaré discouraged him. Great Britain and France should advise Vienna to act moderately, he thought, but an Austro-Russian discussion "would be very dangerous at the present moment." Entente solidarity must be preserved. The President next met Szápáry, the Austrian Ambassador, and sought some indication of Berchtold's intentions. The ambassador merely observed that the judicial investigation was proceeding and that "we cannot tolerate, Mr. President, that a foreign Government shall allow murderous attacks to be prepared on its soil against our sovereignty." Poincaré tried to be conciliatory, but could not forebear observing that "Serbia has very warm friends in the Russian people. And Russia has an ally, France. What complications are to be feared here!"[1]

This interview produced an unfavorable impression on both sides. Poincaré expressed his anxiety to Paléologue. "Sazonov must be firm and we must support him," he declared. He feared that the Russian foreign minister might acquiesce in Austrian demands upon Serbia or might accept some compromise which could be interpreted as a diplomatic defeat for the Triple Entente. Szápáry found Poincaré "tactless" and "threatening" as compared with Sazonov, who was thus far "reserved and cautious," and calculated correctly that the French visitors would strengthen the Russians in resisting Vienna's plans for the chastisement of Serbia.[2] Poincaré and Viviani apparently discussed the situation with Sazonov in the evening. Early the next morning[3] the latter sent a long telegram to the Russian Embassy in Vienna, instructing the ambassador to confer with his French and British colleagues and to warn the Austrian Government against "irrevocable measures" which would not be tolerated at St. Petersburg, Paris, or London.[4] This communication arrived too late (3:00 P.M., July 23) to have any influence on the Austrian ultimatum to Belgrade. Later, after the pressure of festivities was over, Viviani, with the approval of Poincaré, telegraphed from Reval, at 1:00 A.M., July 24, to Dumaine, through Bienvenu-Martin, instructing him to confer with his British and Russian colleagues and to warn Berchtold against any intervention in the internal affairs of Serbia.[5] The Austrian note had been dispatched before this communication was even sent. In the British Foreign Office, Sir Eyre Crowe thought that the move recommended would produce "intense irritation" at Vienna, and Sir

[1] M. Paléologue *La Russie des Tsars*, I, pp. 9–10; Poincaré, IV, pp. 253–255.

[2] Szápáry to Berchtold, July 21, Austrian Red Book, I, 45, cited in Fay, II, pp. 281–282.

[3] This telegram is dated 4:00 A.M., July 22. Fay considers this an error and concludes from other sources that it was sent at 4:00 A.M., July 23, after Poincaré and Viviani had departed. Fay, I, p. 284, Note 24. *Cf.* Schmitt, I, p. 452.

[4] Text in Schmitt, I, pp. 452–453, citing Schilling's *Diary*, pp. 85–86.

[5] Schmitt, I, p. 454.

Arthur Nicolson feared it would be injudicious. Grey decided to postpone action.[1] Unlike Poincaré, he regarded the preservation of peace as more important than Entente solidarity—a difference in objectives occasioned by the difference in the geographical situation and the international commitments of Great Britain and France.

Meanwhile, the St. Petersburg festival had come to an end in a "champagne mood." On the evening of July 22 the Grand Duke Nicolas gave a banquet in Poincaré's honor, after a military review at Krasnoe-Selo. His wife, the Montenegrin Princess Anastasia, who was close to Russian military circles, showed to Paléologue a box filled with the soil of Lorraine, the French President's home province. She had the tables decorated with Lorraine thistle. During the meal she reflected the excitement and enthusiasm of the Russian Army commanders. "War is going to break out," she observed to the French Ambassador. "Nothing will be left of Austria. Our armies will meet in Berlin. Germany will be annihilated!" Paléologue apparently acquiesced in this pleasant prospect.[2] On the next day another review and a farewell banquet on board the *France* took place. At its close, the Premier asked Paléologue to prepare a *communiqué* for the press. He did so, concluding it with the statement that the "two Governments have reaffirmed the perfect concordance of their views and of their intention of maintaining the European equilibrium, especially in the Balkan peninsula." Poincaré concluded the toasts: "The two countries have the same ideal of peace in strength, honor, and dignity." Viviani objected to Paléologue's last phrase as seeming to implicate France too deeply in Russia's Balkan policy, but the ambassador declared that its suppression would lead to the suspicion that the Premier did not dare to speak of Franco-Russian agreement in the impending crisis. Viviani agreed and the wording was changed to "the perfect community of their views on the various problems which the preservation of the general peace and of the European equilibrium place before the Powers, especially in the East." "Très bien!" said Viviani. Poincaré, the Tsar, Sazonov, Izvolsky all approved the text which was at once dispatched to the Havas Agency.[3] At 11:00 o'clock the *France* steamed out of the harbor. The next morning, while still in the Gulf of Finland, it picked up a wireless message from Paléologue, summarizing the terms of the Austrian ultimatum to Belgrade, which had been delivered at 6:00 P.M. the preceding evening. Viviani at once telegraphed to London and St. Petersburg, suggesting that Serbia should offer every satisfaction compatible with her honor and independence and request an extension of the forty-eight-hour time limit while the Entente Powers should support this request at Vienna and try to arrange an international investigation in place of the proposed Austro-Serbian judicial inquiry.[4] On July 25 the party reached Stockholm, from which

[1] Fay, I, p. 284.
[2] Paléologue, *op. cit.*, I, pp. 14–15, 21.
[3] *Ibid.*, I, pp. 16–17.
[4] Poincaré, IV, p. 288.

Viviani renewed his suggestions, which were viewed unfavorably at St. Petersburg and London and forgotten. Poincaré and Viviani spoke to Nekludov, the Russian Minister to Sweden. The President expressed alarm at the crisis. Nekludov said "It means war." Viviani replied, "It is terrible, terrible, for if it means war for you, it most certainly also means war for us."[1] The party proceeded on its way, lost in the mists of the Baltic, while the shadow of disaster lowered over the continent. On the same evening, Izvolsky left St. Petersburg for Paris. At the Warsaw station, Paléologue bade him farewell. They were agreed as to the future: "Cette fois, c'est la guerre!"[2]

The most significant effect of this last visit of the heads of the French State to Tsarist Russia was to impress Nicolas and Sazonov with French willingness to follow them in any course they might choose and to strengthen their determination to resist the Austrian demands on Serbia. This was not an incitement to war, nor even, in so many words, a "blank check" to St. Petersburg. In fact, the results of the visit were minimized and viewed with complacency in German and Austrian circles.[3] But it was the inevitable result of Poincaré's insistence on Entente solidarity, which he regarded as essential to French security. Solidarity meant resistance to the Triplice and support of Russia in whatever policy it might adopt to make that resistance effective. Poincaré was only President of the Republic with no constitutional power of policy determination. But Viviani, who was in all respects a smaller, weaker, and less experienced diplomat, easily fell under the other's influence. In so far as French policy in the 1914 crisis was subject to conscious control (and, as will be shown, friction, disharmony, and misunderstanding developed at several points), that control was exercised by the powerful personality of Poincaré. After his departure from Russia Count Witte suggested that a meeting between the Tsar and the Kaiser be arranged at once to counteract the French President's influence on the impressionable Nicolas and calm public opinion, but nothing came of the proposal.[4] Sazonov and Paléologue informed Buchanan that three points had been established by the visit: (1) perfect community of views on peace and the balance of power, especially in the East; (2) a decision to act at Vienna to prevent any demands on Serbia equivalent to intervention in internal affairs and contrary to Serbian sovereignty and independence; (3) solemn affirmation of the obligations imposed by the alliance on the two countries.[5] Paléologue interpreted this understanding, coupled with Poincaré's own words, in such a way as to require repeated encouragement and assurances of French support to Sazonov as the latter took action in the days which followed looking toward mobilization and a general war.

[1] Schmitt, I, p. 455, citing (footnote) Nekludov, *Diplomatic Reminiscences*, p. 291.

[2] Paléologue, *op. cit.*, I, pp. 27–28.

[3] Schmitt, I, pp. 455–456.

[4] Schmitt, I, pp. 456–457, citing Huldermann, *Albert Ballin*, pp. 302–306.

[5] Fay, II, p. 286, citing *B.D.*, 101; *cf.* Poincaré, IV, pp. 279, 293–294, and Paléologue, I, p. 17.

Chapter X

1914: THE CRISIS OF THE ALLIANCES

1. Peace or War?

AT Paris, Szécsen presented a copy of the Austrian note to Bienvenu-Martin at the Quai d'Orsay at 10:30 P.M., July 24. With Poincaré and Viviani away, and in touch with the situation only through fragmentary wireless dispatches, a heavy responsibility fell upon the Minister of Justice and his adviser, M. Philippe Berthelot, assistant political director at the Ministry of Foreign Affairs. The political director, M. de Margerie, had accompanied the Premier to Russia. Bienvenu-Martin sent a résumé of the Austrian note to Viviani and to all the French ambassadors abroad, but refused to discuss its text. Dumaine, at Vienna, seemed dubious of Russian support of Serbia and somewhat sympathetic toward the Austrian point of view.[1] The note made ten demands on Belgrade, involving dissolution of the *Narodna Odbrana*, arrest of those implicated in the conspiracy, suppression of anti-Austrian propaganda, etc. Demands 5 and 6, requiring Serbian acceptance of Austrian collaboration in the investigation of the plot and in the suppression of subversive activities, went furthest in the direction of infringing upon Serbian sovereignty and were least likely of acceptance. The demands had in fact been formulated in the expectation of their rejection in order that Vienna might plausibly resort to war.[2] Vesnitch, the Serbian Minister in Paris, was without instructions from his Government. Berthelot told him on July 24 that Serbia must try to gain time by offering such satisfaction as was not incompatible with her dignity and sovereignty and by declaring her readiness to submit the dispute to international arbitration. This was in accordance with wireless instructions from the *France* and was not out of harmony with the suggestions Viviani had made to London and St. Petersburg.[3]

Both Bienvenu-Martin and Berthelot seem to have been interested primarily in preserving peace, though not at the cost of Entente solidarity, while Poincaré and Viviani were primarily interested in maintaining Entente solidarity, even at the cost of peace. Szécsen reported to Berchtold that Bienvenu-Martin had "avoided every attempt to palliate or defend in any way the attitude of Serbia," and had expressed the hope that the dispute

[1] Schmitt, I, p. 472, especially footnotes.
[2] *Cf.* Fay, II, Chap. V; and Schmitt, I, Chaps. VI and IX.
[3] Schmitt, I, p. 512, citing Bienvenu-Martin's circular of July 24.

would be peaceably settled in accordance with Vienna's wishes.[1] Even allowing for the ambassador's excessive optimism as to the French view, the discrepancy between the position of Bienvenu-Martin and that taken by Poincaré in talking with Szápáry at St. Petersburg is obvious. The German circular note, emphasizing the "incalculable consequences" which might follow in the event that other Powers intervened in the Austro-Serb conflict and insisting on "localization," was presented to Bienvenu-Martin, in the presence of Berthelot, by Von Schoen. The acting Premier was sympathetic with this proposal and hoped that Vienna would not make it impossible for other Powers to accept this solution. Berthelot likewise agreed that Serbia should accept the Austrian demands in principle and ask for explanations and details. In response to a query, Schoen was unable to say whether the Austrian note was intended as an ultimatum or as a basis of discussion. Schoen reported to his Government that France would cooperate with Germany in localizing the controversy.[2] There seems to be no doubt that this correctly represented the views of Berthelot and Bienvenu-Martin, who were, of course, unaware of the Austrian determination, encouraged by Berlin, to resort to war against Serbia. This was certainly not the view of Poincaré, who later condemned this German proposal as a "menace scarcely disguised and an anticipated repudiation of any attempt for a European concert."[3]

Under the circumstances, it was inevitable that the views of the President, which were shared by the Premier, should prevail over any disposition which the Quai d'Orsay or Bienvenu-Martin might have to accept the German formula of "localization." But the President and the Premier were still on the high seas. The Chambers were not in session, having adjourned for the summer[4] on July 15. There was therefore no opportunity for parliamentary discussion of the crisis. In the press, however, the Austrian note immediately became the subject of extended commentary. With remarkable unanimity, the more important papers (which, it is perhaps not irrelevant to recall, were in the pay of the Russian Government) strongly condemned the Austrian ultimatum and treated the German "localization" proposal as a ruse to enable Vienna to crush Belgrade. L'Écho de Paris declared on July 25 that Schoen's démarche meant: "Let Austria crush Serbia, otherwise you will have to reckon with Germany." It charged that a new coup d'Agadir was in preparation, while Great Britain was occupied with Ulster, and Russia with labor troubles, and the heads of the French Government were absent. Schoen at once protested against these accusations to the Quai d'Orsay, which disclaimed responsibility and agreed that the German Embassy should inform the Havas Agency that the Austrian note was not an ultimatum and that the

---

[1] Szécsen to Berchtold, July 24; Schmitt, I, p. 488, citing *Austrian Documents*, II, 9.
[2] Von Schoen, *Memoirs of an Ambassador*, pp. 178–180; cf. Schmitt, I, pp. 488–489.
[3] *Les origines de la guerre*, p. 214.
[4] *J.O.*, July 16, 1914.

only object of the German action was the localization of the conflict. The British Ambassador reported, significantly, that *L'Écho de Paris* "is known to be in close relations with the Russian Embassy."[1] Other papers followed suit. *Le Matin* asserted that Austria-Hungary was not treating Serbia as a civilized State and described Schoen's visit of the twenty-fifth as a threat from Germany to the Triple Entente. The Left papers, which were not on the Russian pay roll, were scarcely more receptive to the German overture. Clemenceau in *L'Homme Libre* emphasized Austro-German solidarity. *La Lanterne* accused Vienna of seeking to provoke war. Even *L'Humanité* followed the same vein. The press thus shared the view of Poincaré, rather than those of Bienvenu-Martin and Berthelot.[2]

In any case, the decisions controlling the next step had to be taken not at Paris or Berlin, but at St. Petersburg and Vienna. When Sazonov learned of the terms of the ultimatum on July 24—the morning after the departure of Poincaré and Viviani, he exclaimed, "C'est la guerre européenne!"[3] He told Szápáry nothing of his intentions, but accused Austria of wanting to make war on Serbia. Later in the day he protested against portions of the ultimatum and adopted a hostile and uncompromising attitude. Here, and later, Szápáry and Pourtalès, the German Ambassador, minimized Sazonov's determination in their dispatches to their Governments and created the impression in Vienna and Berlin that Russia would not come at once to the armed defense of Serbia. Sazonov saw Buchanan and Paléologue at luncheon on the twenty-fourth. He spoke of mobilization and sought from them a declaration of Entente solidarity. Buchanan was favorable, but could not commit his Government. Paléologue had no hesitation in declaring that France would give Russia strong diplomatic support and would, if necessary, fulfill all the obligations imposed by the alliance.[4] This and later assurances were given in the knowledge that Sazonov was as determined upon a final reckoning with Austria in the Balkans as Berchtold was determined upon a final reckoning with Serbia. Sazonov discussed the possibility of a partial mobilization of the Russian Army with General Yanushkevitch, Chief of the General Staff. At the conference of ministers at 3:00 P.M., July 24, it was decided to ask the Tsar's approval for mobilization of the four military districts of Kiev, Odessa, Moscow, and Kazan, and of the Black Sea Fleet, for the collection of war materials, and for the withdrawal of funds of the Ministry of Finance in Germany and Austria-Hungary.[5] According to Paléologue, Sazonov informed him that evening only of the last of these three ominous decisions. "Can I certify to my Government that you have not ordered any military measures?" "None, I assure you," replied the foreign

---

[1] Bertie to Grey, July 25, *B.D.*, 123, cited in Schmitt, I, p. 490, footnote.
[2] Scott, *op. cit.*, pp. 186–191.
[3] Schilling's *Diary*, p. 43, cited in Schmitt, I, p. 494.
[4] Buchanan to Grey, July 24, *B.D.*, 101, cited in Schmitt, I, p. 500.
[5] R. C. Binkley, "New Light on Russia's War Guilt," *Current History*, XXIII, pp. 533f.

minister.[1] The conference of ministers also authorized the dispatch of a telegram to Vienna, asking for an extension of time to Belgrade, while Prince Alexander of Serbia appealed to the Tsar for aid in case of an Austrian attack. Sazonov gave no advice to Serbia as to its reply.

On the twenty-fifth, Sazonov again appealed to Buchanan for Entente solidarity as the only means of preventing war[2] and also pleaded directly with London for the maintenance of the balance of power by British pressure on Vienna. Sazonov's view of the way in which the situation should be handled was thus identical with Poincaré's. A ministerial council met at Krasnoe-Selo on the twenty-fifth, with the Tsar, the Grand Duke Nicolas, and General Yanushkevitch in attendance. Here the foreign minister argued for a military gesture and it was decided to recall troops in training camps to barracks, to promote cadets to the officer ranks, to declare martial law in fortresses and on the frontier, to proclaim the "period preparatory to war," and to authorize Sazonov to order the mobilization of thirteen army corps and the Black Sea and Baltic Fleets whenever he should consider this step diplomatically advisable. These decisions were notified to the French and British Ambassadors the same afternoon and put into force the same evening. As noted above, Paléologue and Izvolsky were agreed, as the former bade farewell to the latter at the Warsaw station that night, that a general war was now unavoidable.[3]

The rôle of Paléologue is of prime importance from the point of view of French policy and its influence on Russian decisions. The steps summarized above were all taken before the expiration of the forty-eight-hour time limit of the Austrian note to Serbia and before any rupture of diplomatic relations between Vienna and Belgrade. They reflect Sazonov's determination to resort to war in the event of an Austrian attack upon Serbia. This decision, if carried out, would make "localization" impossible and a general war inevitable. From Poincaré and Paléologue the Russian foreign minister had received unqualified assurances of French support. On the evening of the twenty-fifth he saw Buchanan and Paléologue once more and informed them of the plan for partial mobilization. According to the British Ambassador, Paléologue declared that

he had received a number of telegrams from the minister in charge of the Ministry of Foreign Affairs, that no one of them displayed the slightest sign of hesitation, and that he was in a position to give his Excellency (Sazonov) formal assurance that France placed herself unreservedly on Russia's side.[4]

Sazonov thanked him and asked Buchanan what the views of his Government were. The British Ambassador replied that Grey did not despair of peace and thought it essential to gain time. Paléologue inquired as to whether

---

[1] Paléologue, I, pp. 24–25.
[2] B. to G., July 25, 8:00 P.M., B.D., 125, cited in Schmitt, I, p. 502.
[3] Schmitt, I, pp. 504–511.
[4] B. to G., July 25, 8:00 P.M., cf. Fay, II, pp. 326–328.

the British fleet would play the part assigned to it in the Anglo-French Naval Convention. Buchanan urged prudence and warned Sazonov that mobilization would mean war with Germany. But Sazonov replied that "Russia cannot allow Austria to crush Serbia and become the predominant Power in the Balkans, and, secure of the support of France, she will face all the risks of war."[1] The same evening Paléologue assured the Italian Ambassador that "France was ready to fulfil the obligations of her alliance in their entire scope." While the Entente Powers would do everything to ward off a European catastrophe, they were "convinced of the futility of their endeavors."[2] Paléologue, then, acquiesced in Sazonov's decision to precipitate a general war over the Austro-Serb quarrel and was prepared, like Poincaré, to support St. Petersburg to the end. Bienvenu-Martin certainly had misgivings and hopes of peace, but he hesitated to act on his own initiative and apparently did not feel called upon to instruct Paléologue to hold Sazonov in check. Had he been fully informed (as he was not) of the extent of Russian war preparations and the determination of St. Petersburg to force the issue, he might have sought to exercise a restraining influence. This is but one of the innumerable "might-have-beens" of the 1914 crisis. In point of fact, he seems to have been unaware of the imminence of disaster. He confessed to the British Ambassador in Paris later in the same day that he had no suggestions to make "except that moderating advice might be given at Vienna as well as at Belgrade."[3] The German solution of "localization" appealed to him, as it did to Grey, who did nothing with Paul Cambon's suggestion that he invite Berlin to approach Vienna with a mediation proposal by the other Powers until he should see the results of the German formula. Russian decisions were rapidly making "localization" out of the question. Paul Cambon saw "no way of averting the course of events."[4]

The Serbian reply to Vienna and Grey's various *démarches* need be considered here only in so far as they affected, or were affected by, action taken at Paris or by French agents abroad. The Serbian Government apparently received no specific advice from any of the Entente capitals regarding the terms of its reply. Hartwig, the Russian Minister, had dropped dead a few days previously and had not been replaced. Neither Great Britain nor France had regular ministers in Belgrade at the moment. Berthelot had advised the Serb Minister in Paris to seek to gain time and to offer to submit to arbitration. Whether he actually drew up a draft of a reply[5] is not clear. The reply was in accordance with Berthelot's advice, but its terms were the work of the Serbian Cabinet. At 3:00 p.m., July 25, Serbian mobilization was ordered.

[1] B. to G., July 25, 8:00 p.m. *Cf.* Schmitt, I, pp. 511–512.
[2] Schmitt, I, p. 512, footnote.
[3] Bertie to Grey, July 25, *B.D.*, 127, cited in Schmitt, I, p. 512.
[4] Cambon to B.–M., July 24, Schmitt, I, p. 513. *Cf.* Fay, II, pp. 327–328; Carter, *op. cit.*, 141–142.
[5] M. Morhardt, *Les preuves*, p. 71.

At 6:00 p.m. Pashich handed a copy of the reply to Baron Giesl at the Austrian Legation. Since the note was not an unconditional acceptance of the Austrian demands and Giesl's instructions left him no discretion, he left the Serb capital at 6:30 and diplomatic relations were severed.[1] The reply, while rejecting, outright, No. 6 of the Austrian terms, evading Nos. 4, 5, and 9, and accepting Nos. 1, 2, 3, 8, and 10, was conciliatory in tone and, naturally, made a favorable impression in the Entente capitals and even at Berlin. In Austria war preparations were ordered at once and July 28 fixed as the first day of partial mobilization. Berchtold was resolved on war with Serbia. The decisions already taken at St. Petersburg made the "localization" of such a war impossible. It remained to be seen what steps could be taken by other Powers to prevent a universal catastrophe.

The Paris press unanimously condemned the Austrian rejection of the Serb reply and with few exceptions stood for Franco-Russian solidarity, but was divided in its view of the rôle of Germany. *La Petite République* of July 27 said that it was clear that Berlin had not premeditated the Austrian blow and expressed confidence that the skies would soon clear. The *Radical* (July 26, 28, 29) pictured Germany as embarrassed rather than threatening. Izvolsky was delighted at the faith which most of the papers expressed in Russia. *Le Journal* of July 24, *Radical*, *Le Temps*, and *La Libre Parole* on the twenty-fifth, and *L'Écho de Paris* on the twenty-fifth and twenty-sixth all supported the position which St. Petersburg had assumed. Clemenceau in *L'Homme Libre* of the twenty-seventh declared that Russia could not consent to be annihilated (*sic*) while *L'Action Française* of the twenty-ninth asserted that France awaited action by her ally and expected the imminent appearance of the *casus foederis*. On the other hand, the Socialist Party manifesto of the twenty-eighth demanded that the French Government restrain Russian aggression and *L'Humanité* declared that Russia would be guilty of a grave fault if she enlarged the scope of the conflict. Even the chauvinistic *Le Matin* on the twenty-ninth hoped that Russia would not treat an Austrian occupation of Belgrade as a *casus belli*. But these were feeble and isolated voices, not likely to influence Bienvenu-Martin and Berthelot in their uncertainty so long as the bulk of the press supported Russia, was contemptuous of Grey's proposals and the "localization" formula, looked to Berlin to keep the peace, and was content-with a do-nothing policy on the part of France. On the evening of the twenty-seventh, peace demonstrations on the boulevards were broken up by the police, with some five hundred arrests. Smaller patriotic demonstrations also led to minor disorders. Among the populace of the metropolis there was neither a will to war nor a will to peace but only apprehension, which was transformed in the last few days of the month into belligerently anti-German patriotism as war seemed more and more imminent. By August 1, the public and the press were in the mood to support a French declaration of war on Germany. At no time was sentiment

[1] Fay, II, pp. 330f.; Schmitt, I, pp. 519–533.

for restraining Russia widespread or influential, a situation due in part, at least, to ignorance of Russian decisions.[1]

The Serb reply reached Paris on the twenty-sixth, and Bienvenu-Martin at once sent a notice of it to all French agents abroad, declaring that, although Serbia had accepted most of the Austrian demands, diplomatic relations had been severed, which indicated the intention of Vienna to adopt harsh measures toward Belgrade. The *France*, on the North Sea, picked up a wireless to this effect on the same day. When Szécsen spoke to Berthelot, the latter expressed astonishment at the Austrian rejection of the reply, but hoped for further negotiations on the basis of the Serb concessions.[2] Bienvenu-Martin's sympathetic reception of Schoen's plea for localization on the twenty-fourth had created the impression at Berlin that the French Government would cooperate with it with this end in view.[3] This impression was strengthened rather than weakened by Bienvenu-Martin's moves on the twenty-fifth and twenty-sixth, though it was completely at variance with the views of the Premier and the President, still on their way back from St. Petersburg and Stockholm. The British Ambassador in Paris also believed that Bienvenu-Martin favored localization and wrote that "the French Government will probably advise the Russian Government to moderate any excessive zeal that they may be inclined to display to protect their Serbian client."[4] Bienvenu-Martin admitted privately to Bertie that it would be difficult to bring French opinion to the point of fighting on behalf of Serbia.[5] As for Schoen, as soon as he received Bethmann's telegram on July 26, requesting the British and French Governments to exert a moderating influence on St. Petersburg for the localization of the conflict, he went to see Bienvenu-Martin and emphasized Austria's intention to take only police measures. He pointed out the necessity of Franco-German solidarity to preserve the general peace. The acting Premier declared that personally he "would be quite willing to have St. Petersburg calmed down," but that Germany should exert pressure on Vienna. Russia was moderate and had not committed any act which allowed doubt as to her moderation, asserted the Minister, obviously in ignorance of the progress of Russian plans for partial mobilization which had not yet been fully revealed to Paléologue. Schoen pointed out that German pressure on Austria was incompatible with the formula of localization. Bienvenu-Martin then suggested action at St. Petersburg and Vienna simultaneously by the four less interested Powers, but Schoen had no instructions on such a proposal. Bienvenu-Martin felt unable to commit himself

---

[1] Scott, *op. cit.*, pp. 191–205.
[2] Carter, *op. cit.*, p. 155.
[3] Bethmann-Hollweg to William II, July 25, cited in Schmitt, II, p. 9.
[4] Bertie to Grey, July 25, *B.D.*, 134, cited in Schmitt, II, pp. 10–11.
[5] B. to G., July 25, *B.D.*, 129, cited in Schmitt, II, p. 11.

to any action at St. Petersburg without consulting Viviani and therefore rejected Schoen's original suggestion.[1]

Berthelot, who was more suspicious of German motives, was not present at this important interview. Schoen saw him the same evening, however, and proposed a *communiqué* to the press which would state that the German Ambassador and the foreign minister, acting in an identical spirit of pacific solidarity, had examined means of preserving general peace. Berthelot refused, regarding the German moves as designed to gain a diplomatic victory for Vienna and Berlin, and insisted that peace could be maintained only by German pressure on Vienna to prevent an attack upon Serbia. Bertie advised Grey to urge the Quai d'Orsay to issue the notice Schoen had suggested. Grey refused, in turn, on the ground that he could not ask the French Government to risk the appearance of being detached from Russia.[2] Not only did Bienvenu-Martin hesitate to restrain St. Petersburg, since this would endanger "Entente solidarity," but the Quai d'Orsay refused even to authorize a statement to the press implying that France and Germany were cooperating to keep the peace. Nevertheless, a statement was issued by the Quai d'Orsay on the morning of the twenty-seventh, declaring, colorlessly, that Schoen and Bienvenu-Martin had had a fresh conversation and had "considered what measures might be taken by the Powers for the maintenance of peace."[3]

In these and later moves the issue was always between effective steps to preserve peace and the solidarity of the alliances. Berlin would consent to anything, except what was essential: pressure on Vienna to prevent war on Serbia. Paris would consent to anything, except what was essential: pressure on St. Petersburg to prevent war on Austria. Bienvenu-Martin was not immovable, but failed to appreciate the imminence of war moves in Russia and feared to take action on his own initiative. Berthelot, steeped in the atmosphere and traditions of the Quai d'Orsay, was more inclined to interpret every move made at Berlin as a device to hoodwink the Entente. The intransigeant views of Poincaré and Viviani have already been indicated and had already had their effect at St. Petersburg in leading Sazonov to believe that he would have French support in any eventuality. The Premier and the President, far off at sea, were unable to control the daily and hourly decisions at Paris, but their views were well represented by Berthelot, upon whom Bienvenu-Martin, as a diplomatic novice, was necessarily obliged to lean heavily. These views were also those of Izvolsky, who returned to Paris on July 27. "He is not an element of peace," wrote Bertie to Grey.[4] At dinner

[1] Schoen to Foreign Office, July 26; circular of Bienvenu-Martin, July 26; *F.Y.B.* (1914), No. 56; *L.N.*, II, No. 187, p. 278; for accounts of this, and subsequent conversations, with further documentary references, see Schmitt, II, pp. 11–17; Fay, II, pp. 387–393; Renouvin's *Les origines de la guerre*, pp. 94–97; Carter, *op. cit.*, pp. 162f.

[2] B. to G., July 27, and G. to B., July 28, *B.D.*, 193, 204, cited in Schmitt, II, p. 14.

[3] Schmitt, II, p. 14.

[4] July 27, *B.D.*, 192.

that evening, the Russian Ambassador told the counsellor of the British Embassy that war was inevitable because Great Britain had failed to declare her solidarity with Russia and France.[1] He had already seen Bienvenu-Martin, Berthelot, and Abel Ferry, the Under-secretary for Foreign Affairs, probably in the afternoon. He reported that Bienvenu-Martin was convinced that the German *démarches* were undertaken to separate France and Russia. "Altogether, I am surprised how correctly the Minister of Justice and his colleagues understand the situation, and how firm and calm is their determination to give us the most complete support, and to avoid the slightest appearance of disunity between us."[2] Bienvenu-Martin's "determination" had been hitherto mixed with doubts which were now resolved by the combined pressure of Izvolsky and Berthelot. Schoen's program was now doomed. He had written privately to Berthelot, reaffirming Germany's desire for solidarity with France, and visited Ferry in the afternoon to urge again French counsels of moderation at St. Petersburg. He personally agreed on the desirability of joint and simultaneous pressure at Vienna and St. Petersburg, but he knew that Berlin was still unwilling to hear of it. On the morning of the twenty-eighth, he again saw Bienvenu-Martin. Again the two positions were stated. The French minister declined to put pressure on Russia. The ambassador declared that Germany could not put pressure on Austria. Again deadlock. Izvolsky was delighted. He telegraphed the French refusal of the German suggestions the next day: "The Minister of Justice (Bienvenu-Martin) has not for a moment admitted the possibility of a moderating action at St. Petersburg."[3]

Throughout these days of suspicion and hysteria, those responsible for French policy treated the various proposals for the preservation of peace much as other Governments treated them, *i.e.*, from the point of view of their effect upon the diplomatic and strategic position of the hostile coalitions rather than from that of their effectiveness in preventing war. As Berlin could not risk alienating her only loyal ally, Vienna, so Paris could not risk alienating her only loyal ally, St. Petersburg. Both eyed London with fear and hope, uncertain of what the British decision would be in the event of war. Grey's first suggestion of July 20 for "direct conversations" between Vienna and St. Petersburg had been condemned by Poincaré as "very dangerous"—not to peace, obviously, but to Entente solidarity, which Poincaré always placed before peace.[4] Grey next suggested, on July 24, mediation by the other Powers between Austria and Russia. The French Ambassador, Paul Cambon, was dubious, since this might mean French pressure on St. Petersburg, and he favored mediation between Vienna and Belgrade, which would only mean restraining Vienna. He agreed with Count Benckendorff, the Russian Ambassador in London, on the necessity of Germany checking

[1] B. to G., July 28, *B.D.*, 216, cited in Schmitt, II, p. 16, note.
[2] Izvolsky to Sazonov, July 27, *L.N.*, II, pp. 281–282.
[3] *Ibid.*, July 28, pp. 283–284; *cf.* Viviani, *op. cit.*, pp. 136–140; and Schoen, *op. cit.*, pp. 180–187.
[4] *Cf.* Fay, II, pp. 362–369.

Austria-Hungary and failed to transmit Grey's proposal in its original form to the Quai d'Orsay. Late on the same day (Friday, July 24), Cambon went to Paris and did not return to London until the following Monday night. What he did in Paris is not recorded in the documents available. It is safe to guess that he did not weaken the stand of Bienvenu-Martin and Berthelot against localization and restraint of Russia. On the twenty-fifth, Grey proposed to St. Petersburg mediation between Austria and Russia by the four other Powers. Berlin was sympathetic, though clinging to the forlorn hope of localization, on the assumption that Russia would be satisfied with Berchtold's declaration that Vienna contemplated no acquisition of Serbian territory. But Benckendorff was opposed and no answer came from Paris.[1] During the night, news reached London of the Austro-Serb rupture. Grey now took the view that it was too late to hope for French pressure on Russia and cast about for means of restraining Vienna. On the twenty-sixth, he proposed a conference of ambassadors to discuss the issue and seek to mediate, whether between Austria and Serbia or between Austria and Russia was not clear. Berlin favored the latter, Paris the former. The German Government rejected this proposal, knowing that it would be distasteful to Vienna. Sazonov declared himself ready to consider the proposal if direct conversations with Vienna failed. But if it were a question of exercising any kind of moderating influence at St. Petersburg, he rejected it in advance.[2] Izvolsky's reassurances as to the attitude of Bienvenu-Martin on this point were sent the next day. On the twenty-seventh, Bienvenu-Martin, without waiting for word from Viviani, accepted Grey's suggestion, on condition that Berlin act first at Vienna.[3] But the plan was dropped in favor of "direct conversations" between Austria and Russia.[4]

Whatever prospects such conversations for preserving peace may have offered were greatly diminished by the dispatch of an Austrian declaration of war on Serbia to Nish (to which the Serb capital had already been moved) shortly before noon on Tuesday, July 28, exactly a month after the Sarajevo assassination. Vienna had originally planned to declare war about August 12, by which time Austrian partial mobilization would be completed, but news of Russian war preparations and anxiety over the diplomatic situation led Berchtold to act at once,[5] despite the dispatch from Szécsen on the previous day that Bienvenu-Martin and Berthelot seemed convinced that war by Austria on Serbia would make a general war inevitable and that "we shall have to listen to sharper words" when Poincaré and Izvolsky return.[6] In Paris suspicions of Berlin were aggravated by the news of the

[1] *Ibid.*, II, pp. 369–377.
[2] Sazonov to Benckendorff and Izvolsky, July 27, 1914, *L.N.*, II, p. 280.
[3] *Cf.* Fay, II, p. 390; Schmitt, II, p. 48.
[4] *Cf.* Fay, II, pp. 393–400; Renouvin, pp. 97–98.
[5] Schmitt, II, pp. 49–84; Fay, II, pp. 416–418.
[6] Szécsen to Berchtold, July 27, Schmitt, II, p. 17; *cf.* Izvolsky to Sazonov, July 27, *L.N.*, II, p. 82.

declaration.[1] Schoen's assurances were unconvincing.[2] In view of the impending return of Poincaré and Viviani, a memorandum for their information was prepared at the Quai d'Orsay, reflecting the views of Berthelot and the acting Premier. It rejected the "sophism" of the German suggestion of moderating counsels at St. Petersburg from Paris and London and insisted that action ought to be taken at Vienna by Berlin. Russia, up to the present, had "given proof of the greatest moderation," but "it is very desirable that Russia should lend all her support to the mediation project which Sir Edward Grey will present."[3]

2. Descent into the Maelstrom

Whether the Austro-Serb war would lead to a general conflagration depended upon the decisions taken by Russia and upon the German attitude toward the policy Vienna had adopted. Bienvenu-Martin still refused to take any moderating action at St. Petersburg further than to urge acceptance of Grey's mediation proposal. Paléologue's conviction as to the inevitability of a general war was naturally strengthened by the action of Vienna. Sazonov had already warned the Quai d'Orsay not to interfere, and Paléologue was not in the least disposed to try to halt what he regarded as the predestined course of events. The Russian foreign minister, in turn, had no doubt of the outcome. He ignored the Tsar's suggestion of the twenty-seventh that he take steps to arbitrate the Austro-Serb dispute before the Hague Tribunal.[4] He saw the French Ambassador shortly after the news of the Austrian declaration of war was received. Paléologue was already in receipt of direct instructions from Viviani, sent from the *France* on the preceding day:

Please say to M. Sazonov that France, appreciating as fully as Russia how highly important it is for the two countries to affirm their complete agreement with regard to the other Powers and to neglect no effort to bring about a solution of the conflict, is ready to give full support to the action of the Imperial Government for the purpose of maintaining the general peace.[5]

According to Paléologue's account he executed these instructions by beseeching the foreign minister to take no military measures on the German frontier and to be very circumspect on the Austrian frontier, lest the support of England be lost. He also asked Sazonov to agree to any measures Great Britain and France might take to preserve peace, emphasizing his own enormous responsibility because of the difficulty of communicating with Poincaré and Viviani. Sazonov objected that he was having great difficulty in restraining the general staff, but finally assented.[6] According to another account, Paléologue extended at the same time the assurance, on behalf of

---

[1] Fay, II, p. 408.
[2] *L.N.*, II, pp. 284–285; Schmitt, II, p. 224.
[3] Izvolsky to Sazonov, July 29, *L.N.*, II, pp. 286–287.
[4] Schmitt, II, p. 30.
[5] Viviani to Paléologue, July 27, Poincaré, IV, p. 335.
[6] Paléologue, I, pp. 33–34.

the French Government, "of the complete readiness of France to fulfil her obligations as an ally in case of necessity."[1] This was a repetition of earlier assurances, but coming on July 28 was bound to strengthen Russian enthusiasm for war. That Paléologue took such action is indicated by Sazonov's dispatch to Izvolsky of the twenty-ninth, telling him of his decision to hasten military preparations and to envisage the eventuality of war as inevitable:

. . . Please forewarn the French Government and at the same time express to it our sincere gratitude for the declaration which the French Ambassador has made to me in its name, to the effect that we may count completely on the support of France. Under the present circumstances, this declaration is especially valuable to us. It would be extremely desirable that England, also, without loss of time, should join France, seeing that this is the only means by which she will succeed in preventing a dangerous rupture of the balance of power.[2]

On the afternoon of the twenty-eighth, Sazonov, convinced that a general war was unavoidable and encouraged by Paléologue's assurances, instructed General Yanushkevitch, Chief of the General Staff, to proceed with the partial mobilization authorized on the twenty-fifth. The general, supported by Dobrorolsky, chief of the mobilization section, objected that partial mobilization would be technically very difficult to achieve and would seriously interfere with general mobilization later. While the decision hung fire, Yanushkevitch and his colleagues on the general staff acted on the assumption that general mobilization would be ordered and would begin on the thirtieth. On the twenty-ninth, the Tsar reluctantly consented to sign the order for general mobilization. During the afternoon, Dobrorolsky occupied himself with getting the necessary ministerial signatures, while Sazonov engaged in frenzied negotiations with Szápáry and Pourtalès, which ended in the usual deadlock. At 9:30 P.M., July 29, Dobrorolsky was ready to send out the necessary orders for general mobilization from the central telegraph office. At the last moment, a message came from Nicolas countermanding general mobilization and ordering the partial mobilization originally planned. This change of heart was apparently the result of the Tsar's correspondence with the Kaiser. At 11:00 P.M. Sazonov, still unaware of the Tsar's action, sent one of his assistants, N. A. Basily, to the French Embassy to inform Paléologue that thirteen army corps were being mobilized the same night to operate against Austria-Hungary and that general mobilization was being commenced secretly. Paléologue "jumped" at this and asked whether partial mobilization would not suffice for the moment. He was told that the general staff regarded it as technically impossible. The ambassador hoped that no measures would be taken without consulting the French General Staff.[3] Paléologue then composed a telegram to Paris and sent it by a secretary, who accompanied Basily, to the Russian foreign office, where it was to be put in the Russian cipher. While this was being done, word arrived of the

[1] Schilling's *Diary*, cited in Fay, II, p. 444 and Schmitt, II, p. 89.

[2] Sazonov to Izvolsky, July 29, *L.N.*, II, p. 289.

[3] Paléologue, I, pp. 35–36.

Tsar's decision against general mobilization. The secretary therefore omitted the last part of the telegram. The Quai d'Orsay was informed only of the order for partial mobilization. Paléologue approved his secretary's action and never informed Paris of the imminence of general mobilization on the night of the twenty-ninth, nor of the details of the somewhat confused and dangerous situation at St. Petersburg.[1]

Meanwhile Viviani and Poincaré had returned to France. During their four-day voyage from Stockholm to Dunkirk, they had received only the most meager and fragmentary news of the course of events—due in part to the efforts of the German wireless stations to interfere with communications between their cruiser and Paris and St. Petersburg.[2] According to Viviani, they received no news whatever on the twenty-sixth and twenty-seventh, except: "Satisfactory reply from Serbia; admirable in its moderation." On the twenty-seventh, Viviani dispatched his message to Sazonov, pledging French support of Russian efforts to maintain peace, which Paléologue transformed into a pledge to support Russia in war. On the morning of the twenty-ninth, they reached the French coast, entered Paris at noon, and drove from the Gare du Nord to the Palais d'Élysée to the applause of excited crowds, in which was heard an occasional voice shouting "À Berlin!" While news of the impending Russian mobilization had not been received, reports of German war preparations were arriving almost hourly. Viviani now relieved Bienvenu-Martin of his duties and Berthelot gave way to his superior, M. de Margerie, political director at the Quai d'Orsay, who had also returned on the *France*. They soon learned, with approval, of the pre-cautionary measures already taken by the Minister of War. Messimy, like Soukhomlinov and the militarists in Russia, was convinced of the inevita-bility of a general war and by his own admission was already urging a Russian invasion of East Prussia.[3] During the morning of the twenty-ninth French officers abroad were ordered to rejoin their corps. At noon the frontier wireless stations were put on a war footing. Fortifications were placed in order and defensive works begun. The French war preparations preliminary to mobilization had already progressed further than the German intelligence service had been able to discover and were further advanced than correspond-ing measures in Germany.[4] Viviani and Poincaré approved. The President found the French ministers "firmly united in a determination to do the impossible to avoid war and also to neglect no preparation for defense."[5] But the latter seemed more important than the former and whatever the possibilities were of checking the war fever at St. Petersburg, Poincaré and

---

[1] *Cf.* Schmitt, II, p. 113; Fay, II, p. 467.

[2] Viviani, *op. cit.*, pp. 95–97.

[3] *Cf.* G. Demartial, *La guerre de* 1914. *L'Évangile du Quai d'Orsay*, p. 24, citing Messimy, *Les heures tragiques d'avant guerre.*

[4] *Cf.* Schmitt, II, p. 226.

[5] Poincaré, IV, p. 371.

Viviani were even less inclined than Bienvenu-Martin to do anything which might endanger Entente solidarity.

One of Viviani's first acts was to ask Paul Cambon to request Sir Edward Grey to renew as soon as possible in Berlin his suggestion for four-Power mediation.[1] Again, nothing came of the proposal. Berlin was already putting pressure on Vienna to halt in Belgrade and seek a settlement by diplomacy or conference, but this suggestion would have no chance of success if Russia were to mobilize for war. The key to peace lay in St. Petersburg rather than in Berlin. If the French Cabinet and the Quai d'Orsay wished peace, they must act at St. Petersburg. If they preferred to follow Russia's lead into war rather than to run the risk of friction with Russia by acting effectively to prevent Russian mobilization and the outbreak of hostilities which would almost certainly follow, they could sit back passively and allow events to overtake them. In retrospect, they seem to have chosen the latter course, though at the moment the situation was confused and the inadequacy of Paléologue's dispatches failed to convey a true impression of the gravity of the decisions pending in the Russian capital. Late in the afternoon of the twenty-ninth, the Council of Ministers met under Poincaré. During its deliberations Schoen appeared to discuss the mediation proposal inconclusively and to announce that the French war preparations would oblige Germany to resort to like measures. Viviani replied that he would not feel uneasy if Germany took similar steps, but insisted that hope for peace remained.[2] The problem before the Cabinet, as Poincaré saw it, was to do nothing which would weaken the Russian Alliance and yet to induce St. Petersburg to show moderation. The first objective defeated the second. At the end of the meeting, Viviani told Izvolsky that all groups and classes in France were resolved to act in agreement with Russia.[3] Poincaré, Margerie, and Izvolsky were all agreed as to the unanimity of French public opinion in supporting this decision. Szécsen reported to Berchtold that the general impression in Paris was that Serbia had granted all that was possible and that Vienna's intransigeance was making a general war inevitable.[4]

At 2:00 A.M. on the night of July 29 and 30, Viviani was aroused at his home by Margerie, who communicated to him the dispatch of Sazonov to Izvolsky referred to above, in which the Russian foreign minister transmitted the warning of the German Ambassador of German mobilization if Russia did not cease her war preparations. Sazonov expressed his conviction that war was unavoidable, and indicated his gratitude for Paléologue's pledge of support.[5] The Premier and the Minister of War aroused Poincaré from his

[1] Viviani to Cambon, July 29, cited in Schmitt, II, p. 227.

[2] Schoen, *op. cit.*, pp. 190–191.

[3] Izvolsky to Sazonov, July 29, *L.N.*, II, pp. 288–289.

[4] Szécsen to Berchtold, July 30, cited in Schmitt, II, p. 230.

[5] *L.N.*, II, p. 289. Viviani, pp. 163–164. The Premier's account of this, as of other incidents is jumbled, inaccurate, and biased.

bed at the Palais d'Élysée and the three agreed on the draft of a telegram which was sent at 7:00 A.M., July 30, to the French Ambassadors in St. Petersburg and London:

As I have stated in my telegram of July 27, the Government of the Republic is determined to neglect no effort toward a solution of the conflict and to support the action of the Imperial Government in the interest of the general peace. On the other hand, France is resolved to fulfil all the obligations of the alliance. But, in the same interest of general peace and in view of the fact that conversations have begun between the Powers not directly interested, I think it would be well that in taking any precautionary measures of defense to which she thinks she must proceed, Russia should not immediately take any step which may offer Germany a pretext for a total or partial mobilization of her forces.[1]

This telegram is significant as representing the furthest point to which the French Cabinet was prepared to go in warning Russia against action which would precipitate a general war. That Poincaré should have been consulted before it was drawn up indicates the extent to which Viviani relied upon the President for counsel. That counsel always placed the obligations of the alliance before the maintenance of peace. The Russian Government was not clearly and unequivocably warned against general mobilization, the imminence of which was still probably unsuspected in Paris, though such a warning was implied in the telegram. It expressly stated France's resolution to fulfil the obligations of the alliance, i.e., to resort to war, if St. Petersburg thought this necessary. Far from checking the Russian militarists, it again granted them assurance of support, proferred platonic advice, and left the fateful decision to St. Petersburg. The telegram was shown to Izvolsky, who transmitted it to Sazonov. Along with it, the ambassador dispatched another communication, telling how Margerie had assured him (presumably early in the morning of the thirtieth) that the French Government had no desire to interfere with Russian military preparations, but thought it extremely desirable that they should be as little public and challenging as possible, in view of the continued pourparlers to safeguard peace. Messimy, reported Izvolsky, had said the same thing to the Russian military attaché in Paris, Count Ignatieff. "We could declare that in the superior interest of peace we would consent to slacken temporarily the measures of mobilization, since this would not prevent us from continuing and even intensifying our military preparations while we refrained, as far as possible, from the transport of troops en masse."[2] If Izvolsky's words correctly represented the views of the Quai d'Orsay and the Ministry of War, Messimy and Margerie at least would seem to have been aware that Russian general

---

[1] L.N., II, p. 290; Schmitt, II, pp. 231–232; cf. Poincare, IV, pp. 385–386; Viviani, p. 164. The various texts of this telegram differ slightly, but the translation given here conveys its sense.

[2] "Le Minister de la Guerre, développant la même idée, a dit au Comte Ignatieff, que nous pourrions declarer que dans l'intérêt de la paix nous consentons a ralentir temporairement les mesures de mobilisation, ce qui ne nous empêcherait pas de continuer et même de renforcer nos préparatifs militaires en nous abstenant, autant que possible, du transport en masse de troupes." Izvolsky to Sazonov, July 30, L.N., II, pp. 290–291.

mobilization was impending, though Paléologue's dispatch of the twenty-ninth, telling of partial Russian mobilization had probably not been received as yet and in any case threw little light upon the real danger at St. Petersburg. Poincaré has denied that Messimy and Margerie expressed themselves as Izvolsky reported,[1] though the two men themselves have remained discreetly silent on the point. The Cabinet met early the next morning and approved the text of the telegram, already sent by Viviani, who had consulted only Poincaré, Messimy, and Margerie in drafting it.[2] The diluted nature of its admonitions, coupled with Izvolsky's comments, was enough to convince Sazonov that he had a free hand and could count on French support in whatever course he followed. It is not unreasonable to conclude that Poincaré and Viviani were less interested in preserving peace by preventing Russian war moves than they were in delaying or concealing Russian military preparations for the purpose of throwing responsibility for war on Berlin.[3]

Sometime before noon of July 30, Paléologue received Viviani's telegram and transmitted it to Sazonov.[4] It may be assumed that the ambassador attached more importance to the renewed assurance of French support to Russia than to the advice against military measures which might give Germany an excuse for mobilization. Sazonov replied vaguely that certain secret precautionary measures had been suspended and concealed from Paléologue his real plans. Under pressure from military circles, Sazonov and Yanushkevitch were determined to convince the Tsar that general mobilization was a necessity. In the morning Pourtalès had asked whether Russia could not be content with the Austrian pledge of territorial disinterestedness vis-à-vis Serbia. Sazonov declared this insufficient and offered to cease military preparations only if Austria recognized that the conflict was a European question and declared herself ready to eliminate from her ultimatum the points which were contrary to the sovereign rights of Serbia.[5] This formula was communicated to the Powers, but Sazonov assured Izvolsky, very confidentially, that he would continue preparations for war unless he received a completely satisfactory reply from Vienna through Berlin.[6] He had no hope of peace and no intention of suspending general mobilization if he could persuade the Tsar to consent. Accompanied by General Tatishchev, he saw the monarch at 3:00 P.M. and pleaded eloquently for general mobiliza-

---

[1] Poincaré, IV, pp. 386–387, 408.

[2] L.N., II, p. 291.

[3] Cf. Schmitt, II, pp. 230–233; Fay, II, pp. 482–486.

[4] Paléologue gives the hour as 6:00 P.M., two hours *after* general mobilization had been ordered and too late to have any influence on the Russian decision. It seems clear from other sources, however, that the interview took place in the forenoon and served to confirm Sazonov's certainty of French support. Cf. Fay, II, p. 271, note 58; Paléologue, I, pp. 39–40; Poincaré, IV, p. 399.

[5] L.N., II, pp. 291–292.

[6] Ibid., p. 292.

tion. Nicolas was troubled and hesitant. But at 4:00 P.M. he capitulated. Sazonov at once phoned Yanushkevitch to do his duty, smash his telephone, and disappear for the day. By 5:00 he had secured the necessary ministerial signatures and the ukase was signed. For a moment Sazonov proposed to keep it secret, but found this to be out of the question, for technical reasons.[1] "Mobilization means war," Boisdeffre and Alexander III had agreed in August of 1892.[2] Such was the understanding at Paris and St. Petersburg in 1914, though in neither capital did it seem expedient to admit this. Sazonov had closed the door to peace, undeterred by Paléologue or the Cabinet in Paris. On July 31, the armed millions of the last of the Romanovs marched forth to battle.

The reception and treatment of the news by Paléologue and the Quai d'Orsay are significant. Early in the evening of July 30, Sazonov saw the British, German, and French Ambassadors. Buchanan telegraphed the Foreign Office at 6:40 P.M.: "It had been decided to issue orders for general mobilization." Pourtalès came to plead for time, while Berlin interceded with Vienna, and was told nothing about the mobilization order. Paléologue reported to Viviani:

> In a conversation which he had this afternoon with Count Pourtalès M. Sazonov was forced to the conclusion that Germany does not wish to pronounce at Vienna the decisive word which would safeguard peace. The Emperor Nicolas has received the same impression from an exchange of telegrams which he has just had personally with the Emperor William.
> Moreover, the Russian General Staff and Admiralty have received disquieting news concerning the preparations of the German army and navy. In consequence the Russian Government has decided to proceed secretly to the first measures of general mobilization.
> In informing me of this decision, M. Sazonov added that the Russian Government will none the less continue its efforts at conciliation. He repeated to me: "I shall negotiate until the last moment."[3]

This ambiguous and incorrect statement of the Russian decision was dispatched from St. Petersburg at 9:15 P.M. and received at the Quai d'Orsay at 11:25 P.M., July 30. Whether it was brought to the attention of Margerie and Viviani the same night is not clear. No record of any action taken by either of them on receipt of it is available. In any case, it conveyed the false impression, by the words "secretly" and "first measures" that Sazonov was following Viviani's suggestions. Poincaré declares that the French Government remained in ignorance of Russian general mobilization until the evening of July 31.[4] Neither Izvolsky nor the other Russian Ambassadors abroad were informed of it by Sazonov. Paléologue was the only source of information open to the Quai d'Orsay. Did Sazonov deceive Paléologue or did Paléologue deceive the Quai d'Orsay? The evidence available at the time of writing

[1] Fay, II, pp. 472f.; Schmitt, II, pp. 240–245; Renouvin, pp. 129–152, 178–191.
[2] *Supra*, p. 146, and Schmitt, II, pp. 249–256.
[3] Poincaré, IV, p. 403.
[4] *Ibid.*, IV, pp. 403, 408, 452f.; cf. Renouvin, p. 190, Note 3.

does not admit of an unequivocal answer. If Paléologue was a victim of Sazonov's duplicity, he was in a position to learn the facts from Buchanan, who reported them correctly and whom Sazonov might be supposed to have been more interested in deceiving in view of the uncertainty as to the British attitude. Paléologue either did not inform himself or preferred to suppress the facts. Even had he reported the general mobilization promptly and accurately, the die was cast and Viviani could have done nothing. Nor is it reasonable to credit the French Premier with any strong desire to halt the Russian war machine. The important point is that Paléologue was no more trustworthy as an interpreter of Russian views to Paris than Izvolsky was as an interpreter of French views to St. Petersburg.

The rôle of the permanent staff at the Quai d'Orsay in shaping the action of those responsible for decisions is also of interest. At 10:45 A.M., July 31, almost sixteen hours after the event, Paléologue telegraphed via Bergen: "The mobilization of the Russian Army has been ordered." This telegram, according to the Quai d'Orsay, was not received until 8:30 P.M. The cause of the delay, if there was one, is unknown. A possible hypothesis is that it was falsified at the Quai d'Orsay before being transmitted to Viviani. In the French Yellow Book, which appeared some weeks later, a falsified version was printed, which expanded Paléologue's ten words into ninety-seven, justifying the Russian mobilization by the prior general mobilization of Austria-Hungary (which, in fact, was ordered eighteen hours *after* the Russian ukase) and by the secret mobilization of Germany (which, in fact, had not taken place).[1] It is within the realm of possibility that this falsification was perpetrated at the Quai d'Orsay on the afternoon or evening of the thirty-first by Margerie or his subordinates, who may have been motivated by a desire to conceal Paléologue's negligence or duplicity or by a more general inclination to depict the fatal action of France's ally in presentable terms. It seems likely that the falsified version was submitted to Poincaré and Viviani and accepted by them at face value—though the chance that they subsequently authorized the falsification themselves is not precluded by the evidence. On the next day, Poincaré told Bertie that the Russian general mobilization was not ordered "until after a decree of general mobilization had been issued in Austria."[2] Poincaré later declared that he had confidence in the "fundamental accuracy" of the documents in the French

[1] "As a result of the general mobilization of Austria and of the measures for mobilization taken secretly, but continuously, by Germany for the last six days, the order for the general mobilization of the Russian Army has been given, Russia not being able, without serious danger, to allow herself to be further outdistanced; really she is only taking military measures corresponding to those taken by Germany.

"For imperative reasons of strategy the Russian Government, knowing that Germany was arming, could no longer delay the conversion of her partial mobilization into a general mobilization." F.Y.B., 1914, No. 118. On this and other falsifications, see Morhardt, *Les preuves*, pp. 162–210.

[2] Bertie to Grey, August 1, *B.D.*, 403, cited in Schmitt, II, pp. 299–300, note.

Yellow Book and quoted them in his speeches down to 1921.[1] Unless Poincaré was a party to deliberate misrepresentation, the suspicion would seem justified that the falsification of Paléologue's dispatch was the work of unknown persons at the Quai d'Orsay and that the erroneous time sequence it contained, as justification for the Russian mobilization, was accepted as a true statement of fact by Poincaré, Viviani, and the Cabinet on July 31 and August 1, 1914.

In Berlin the Russian action admitted of but one response. At 3:30 P.M., July 31, instructions were sent to Pourtalès and Von Schoen. The German Ambassador at St. Petersburg delivered an ultimatum to Sazonov at midnight: German mobilization would follow the already proclaimed *drohende Kriegsgefahr* unless Russia, within twelve hours, suspended every war measure against Germany and Austria-Hungary.[2] The instructions to Schoen cited the note to Russia, declared "mobilization inevitably means war," and asked an answer within eighteen hours as to whether France would remain neutral in a Russo-German war. A negative answer was of course expected, since the existence, if not the exact terms, of the Dual Alliance was known to Berlin. But if the response was affirmative, Schoen was to demand the surrender to German forces of the fortresses of Toul and Verdun as a pledge of neutrality, the two strongholds to be returned at the close of hostilities. This suggestion, which Schoen himself regarded as stupid, would have destroyed any disposition toward neutrality in Paris, had any existed, and was perhaps intended to have this result.[3] Schoen went to the Quai d'Orsay at 7:00 P.M., July 31, to deliver his message.

During the preceding twenty-four hours, French military preparations had been accelerated. General Joffre, Chief of the General Staff, had requested permission at a Cabinet meeting on the morning of the thirtieth to move covering troops up to the frontier. This was a wise measure from a military point of view, but to Viviani and Poincaré it was obvious that it would have the appearance of a belligerent gesture. The clash of strategists and diplomats led to a compromise according to which no reservists would be called up, the troops would march to their positions, they would purchase supplies rather than requisition them, and they would remain ten kilometers from the frontier "in order to prevent any contact between French and German patrols." The purpose of the last condition was to prevent frontier incidents, which might be given the appearance of French aggression, and to convince Great Britain of the pacific intentions of the French Cabinet.[4] Joffre consented

---

[1] *Cf. Current History*, September, 1930, pp. 1100–1102, "An Important Admission by Poincaré," by Von Wegerer.

[2] Schmitt, II, pp. 267–268.

[3] Schoen, *op. cit.*, pp. 192–193; Fay, II, pp. 528f.; Schmitt, II, pp. 269f.

[4] At Viviani's funeral, in September of 1925, Théodore Steeg, then Minister of Justice, gave him great credit for the ten-kilometer withdrawal, described it as "this gesture of sublime sincerity," and echoed the press in presenting it as a symbol of the innocence of France. *Cf.* Demartial, *op. cit.*, pp. 84–85. Viviani himself presents in the same light, *op. cit.*, pp. 192–198.

on condition that the order should not be literally applied.[1] The *Paris-Midi* of July 30 announced, erroneously, that the mobilization of four classes of reservists had been decided upon. The issue was at once seized by the police and the Minister of the Interior issued a denial.[2] The afternoon was filled with rumors of German troop movements and impending German mobilization. At 4:55 P.M. the order was sent out from the Ministry of War for the covering troops to take up their positions. In the evening, at 7:10, General Lyautey, in Morocco, was instructed to send seven battalions of troops to France without waiting for mobilization.[3] Viviani instructed Paul Cambon to inform Grey of German preparations in such a manner as to convince him of the imminence of German mobilization as a justification of the French measures and to emphasize the ten-kilometer withdrawal.[4]

Viviani was still toying half-heartedly with Grey's proposals for preserving peace. The British Foreign Secretary suggested on the thirty-first that Russia should agree to suspend her military preparations if Austria-Hungary should consent to negotiate after occupying Belgrade. At 5:00 P.M., July 31, twenty-four hours after the Russian general mobilization was ordered (or twenty-six hours, allowing for the difference in times), but three and one-half hours before the receipt of definite information from Paléologue regarding it, the Premier instructed the ambassador to urge Sazonov to adhere without delay to Grey's proposal. Despite Sazonov's duplicity and the negligence or connivance of Paléologue, Viviani was probably well aware of the imminence of war, having learned of the Russian mobilization at 3:30 from Jules Cambon in Berlin, and he dispatched this communication with an eye to public opinion and the British attitude rather than with any serious hope that it would prove acceptable or effective in preserving peace.[5] At 3:30 Joffre informed the Cabinet that the Germans were proceeding to the complete mobilization of the forces (which was certainly not the case, though the general may have been honestly mistaken) and refused to accept responsibility for further delay in calling up reservists. The news of the proclamation of *drohende Kriegsgefahr* in Germany helped the strategists to convince the diplomats and the Cabinet agreed to Joffre's proposal. At 5:40 P.M., July 31, the order was issued for the mobilization of the five army corps on the frontier, *i.e.*, *couverture* without restrictions, except for the ten-kilometer line, and Izvolsky was assured by Margerie that France would respond immediately to the mobilization of the German Army by the mobilization of her own forces.[6] Schoen was more optimistic over the situation and thought that even the Russian Ambassador was becoming more cautious, but Bertie reported that Izvolsky "goes about declaring that Russia is ready

[1] Fay, II, 489–492.
[2] Schmitt, II, p. 234, note.
[3] Schmitt, II, pp. 233–236.
[4] Viviani to Cambon, July 30, F.Y.B., 1914, No. 106. Quoted in Viviani, *op. cit.*, p. 192.
[5] *Cf.* Schmitt, II, pp. 296–297.

and war inevitable. What a fool, even if it be the truth!"[1] Izvolsky was apparently still in ignorance of the Russian mobilization and regarded the Berlin report of it as a German trick to provoke French mobilization.[2] The Cabinet refused the plea of the general staff to prevent the exodus of German and Austrian subjects in France, but authorized a decree prohibiting the exportation of war materials, in view of "the hostilities between Austria-Hungary and Serbia."[3] The correspondent of the London *Times* was given a list of German war preparations by the Quai d'Orsay and invited to present French mobilization, which might be ordered any moment, as a measure forced upon France by the German danger.[4] A more detailed statement of the German seizure of French locomotives and the cutting of railway lines across the frontier was prepared for Grey's perusal, and the British military attaché was informed that the Ministry of War anticipated German mobilization the same afternoon.[5]

When Schoen appeared at 7:00 P.M., July 31, with the German ultimatum, of which Cambon had already given warning from Berlin, he was thus confronted by a Premier who was still without authoritative information of the Russian general mobilization, but who, (under pressure from the general staff), had approved extensive military preparations on the part of France, who suspected, because of Joffre's allegations, that Germany was on the point of mobilizing, and who had been convinced by the military authorities that French mobilization was an imperative necessity which must be resorted to with the least possible delay. Control of policy was already in process of passing from the hands of the diplomats into the hands of the strategists, from the civil authorities to the militarists, from the Ministry of Foreign Affairs to the Ministry of War and the general staff. Schoen sketched the terms of the ultimatum to Russia and said that Germany would mobilize if the Russian Government did not give a satisfactory reply within twelve hours. "What would be the attitude of France in case of war between Germany and Russia?" Schoen, always conciliatory and pacific, says that he meant to suggest that the adoption of a neutral attitude on the part of France might also enable Germany to avoid war.[6] He made no mention of Toul and Verdun, since their occupation was to be proposed only in the event that France agreed to remain at peace. To Schoen's astonishment, Viviani replied that he "had no information about an alleged total mobilization of the Russian Army and Navy," and knew only of partial mobilization against Austria-Hungary and general precautionary measures. He hoped that the worst might be avoided. Margerie sat by, silent. Viviani promised an answer the next afternoon, following a Cabinet meeting. The ambassador reached

---

[1] Bertie to Grey, July 31, cited in Schmitt, II, p. 296, note.

[2] *L.N.*, II, p. 293. *Cf.* Schmitt, II, p. 298, note.

[3] *J.O.*, August 1, 1914, p. 7025.

[4] Bertie to Grey, July 31, Schmitt, II, p. 297; London *Times*, August 1, 1914.

[5] *Cf.* Schmitt, II, p. 298.

[6] Schoen, *op. cit.*, p. 194.

for his hat and asked the Premier to present his regards to the President of the Republic, an indication that he planned to leave his post. Viviani refused and begged Schoen to remain. Margerie joined the plea, but the ambassador now had no doubt of the outcome. He bowed and said that he would return the next day for an answer.[1]

Viviani at once informed the British and Russian Ambassadors and dispatched telegrams to Paléologue, saying that the reply would be to the effect that "France will be guided by her interests"—indicating his certainty of the result of the projected Cabinet meeting. He also asked for information about the alleged (sic) Russian general mobilization and hoped "that the Imperial Government, in the highest interests of peace, will on its part avoid everything which may precipitate the crisis"[2]—this, more than thirty hours after the Russian general mobilization had been ordered! At 9:00 P.M., July 31, there began at the Palais d'Élysée, under Poincaré, the momentous Cabinet meeting which was to decide the issue of peace or war for the French Republic. Margerie reported the progress of its deliberations to Izvolsky, who telegraphed to Sazonov that the German demand was regarded as a trap to provoke France into a declaration of war and that Paléologue's telegram of the morning, confirming Russian general mobilization, had just been received.[3] This telegram, which merely established definitely what Viviani already knew from a variety of other sources—Jules Cambon, Schoen, Havas dispatches from St. Petersburg, etc.—was supposed to have been received at the Quai d'Orsay at 8:30. The fact which it reported was the crucial fact of the entire crisis, upon which the peace of Europe hung by a hair. Yet, both Viviani and Poincaré have publicly admitted that they have no recollection of the hour at which it was deciphered (and possibly falsified) and no knowledge of whether it was even communicated to the Cabinet meeting.[4] This circumstance, coupled with their failure to exercise any effective restraining influence at St. Petersburg, strengthens the suspicion that they had already decided upon war and had no concern with the Russian mobilization except to present it to the public in as justifiable a light as possible.

The deliberations of the ministers were suddenly interrupted by the startling news of the assassination of Jean Jaurès. The great Socialist leader had always condemned the Dual Alliance and had been exerting himself to the utmost to bring French pressure on Russia to avert war. He had declared in his last speech in Brussels on July 28: "If appeal is made to secret treaties with Russia, we shall appeal to public treaties with humanity!" In the afternoon of his last day, he had seen Abel Ferry (having failed to find Viviani) and threatened the Government with dire consequences if it led the Republic into war for the sake of Serbia and Russia. "We will rise up, we will cry out the truth to the populace . . . even if they have to shoot us at the

[1] Schoen, pp. 193–195; Viviani, pp. 208–209; cf. Schmitt, II, 298–299; Fay, II, pp. 528–531.
[2] Viviani to Paléologue, July 31, 9:00 and 9:30 P.M., Poincaré, IV, pp. 452–453.
[3] Izvolsky to Sazonov, July 31, L.N., II, pp. 293–294.
[4] Cf. Poincaré's letter of January 9, 1923, in Morhardt, Les preuves, pp. 180f.

first street corner." In the evening, as he sat in a café with his Socialist colleagues, contemplating writing a long article for L'Humanité accusing Izvolsky of instigating the conflict, he was shot to death from behind by Raoul Villain, an ardent patriot who regarded him as a traitor because of his opposition to the three-year law and who was possibly incited to his deed by the Russian secret police in Paris.[1] The leader of the only political group in France which was determined that the nation should not be dragged to the slaughter behind the Tsarist war chariot was thus murdered at the very moment when the Cabinet was about to make the irrevocable decision. The ministers were apprehensive lest the Paris proletariat rise to avenge the crime and block mobilization. Viviani left the Cabinet meeting and went to Jaurès' bedside. Two regiments of cavalry were placed at the disposal of the prefect of police. But French nationalism was stronger than French social-ism. As the troops rode down the Boulevard Montparnasse, the crowds greeted them with enthusiastic cries of "Vive la France! Vive l'armée!"[2]

The Cabinet resumed its session and Viviani presently returned. At 10:30 the Premier was called out to receive an inquiry from the British Ambassador regarding the French attitude toward the neutrality of Belgium. He replied that France would respect Belgian neutrality unless it were violated by some other Power.[3] Viviani returned to the council and read to the ministers, with satisfaction, three telegrams from the French Ambassador in Rome, which made it clear that Italy regarded the agreement of 1902 as binding and would take no action, even if France declared war on Germany. It was known that Belgium would resist a German invasion and it was reasonably certain that Great Britain would support France, especially in the event of a German violation of Belgian neutrality. French military preparations were well advanced and the prospects of war could be viewed by the strategists with reasonable equanimity. There was apparently no question raised as to the technical application of the Dual Alliance to the situation. Russia had not been "attacked by Germany or by Austria supported by Germany,"[4] nor had any of the members of the Triple Alliance ordered mobilization prior to the Russian general mobilization. The Austro-Hungarian general mobiliza-tion had been ordered shortly after noon of the thirty-first. It was a response to the Russian action, though the Cabinet members in Paris were apparently unaware of this, or possibly believed, on the basis of Paléologue's falsified dispatch, that it had preceded Russian mobilization. In short, the casus

[1] Margaret Pease, Jean Jaurès, pp. 150–152; Michon, L'Alliance Franco-Russe, pp. 259–260; Scott, Five Weeks, pp. 181–183; Schmitt, II, p. 300, note. The murderer was not brought to trial but kept in prison for five years, safely away from the trenches, and on March 24, 1919, was adjudged "not guilty" and released, ten days after Émile Cottin, who had wounded Clemenceau on February 19, was sentenced to death by a military court. Cf. R. L. Buell, Contemporary French Politics, pp. 107–111.

[2] Cf. Schmitt, II, p. 300.

[3] Bertise to Grey, July 31, B.D., 382, cited in Schmitt, II, p. 301.

[4] Supra, pp. 145–146.

foederis, strictly interpreted, had not arisen. Russia had disregarded French advice and had taken the initiative in marshaling her forces for war. But since Poincaré, Viviani, and their less well-informed colleagues in the Cabinet had long since decided to support Russia in any eventuality, these considerations were irrelevant. It was only necessary to devise means to make Germany appear the aggressor.

While the discussions proceeded, the Austrian Ambassador, Szécsen, came to the Quai d'Orsay and was received by Berthelot. He reported that Vienna was prepared to renounce all territorial ambitions at the expense of Serbia and was ready, at last, to discuss the whole question with the Powers.[1] Berchtold had at length yielded to pressure from Berlin and from Szécsen himself. Berthelot replied, "It seems to be too late, for we have been overtaken by events."[2] He did not think it necessary to inform the Cabinet of this overture. Later in the night, after the Cabinet had decided on war, Szécsen sent a personal note to Margerie, expressing Austrian willingness to continue conversations with Russia in a friendly manner.[3] This was confirmed by a telegram from Sazonov, who suggested that negotiations might be opened in London with all the Great Powers participating.[4] But Sazonov, like Berchtold, Bethmann, and Viviani, was manoeuvering for position, in order to gain time and throw the odium for initiating the conflict on the prospective enemy while war preparations proceeded unabated.[5] The Quai d'Orsay followed suit. Early the next morning, Berthelot was authorized to send a telegram to Paléologue, Dumaine, and Barrère, at St. Petersburg, Vienna, and Rome, respectively, citing the overtures of Szécsen and Szápáry and declaring that peace might yet be preserved "if the desire of Berlin for peace is sincere."[6] The sole purpose of this communication was to present the German Government as the primary obstacle to peace. Had it been designed to facilitate negotiations, it would have suggested definite action on the basis of Szécsen's suggestions. The French Cabinet, in fact, had already decided on war and all else was hollow pretense.

Since Cabinet proceedings are always secret and unrecorded, little can be known of the details of the decision. It was apparently reached about midnight. If there were doubters in the Cabinet, they were silenced by Poincaré and Viviani, who felt certain that a German declaration of war on Russia was imminent. They were determined that the Republic should support Russia and accept the long-deferred opportunity for the *revanche.* How many of the ministers were familiar with the terms of the Dual Alliance is unknown. It is doubtful whether they were even discussed. Franco-Russian solidarity against Berlin and Vienna meant war and this was enough. At

[1] Izvolsky to Sazonov, August 1, *L.N.,* II, pp. 295–296.
[2] Memo. of Berthelot, July 31, Poincaré, IV, p. 465.
[3] *Ibid.,* IV, pp. 467–468.
[4] Sazonov to the Ambassadors, July 31, Schmitt, II, p. 312.
[5] *Cf.* Schmitt, II, pp. 313–315.
[6] 6:00 A.M., August 1, Poincaré, IV, pp. 465–466.

1:00 in the morning, Messimy emerged to inform the Russian military attaché "in a tone of enthusiastic sincerity" of the "firm decision of the Government for war." "He asked me," reported the attaché, "to confirm the hope of the French General Staff that all our efforts would be directed against Germany and that Austria would be considered as a negligible quantity."[1] At the same hour the corps commanders of the French Army were informed that the order for mobilization would probably be issued the following afternoon.[2] War was now, indeed, "inevitable"—and the ministers went home to their troubled sleep certain that the morrow would bring the call to arms.

3. ARMAGGEDON

In the developments at Paris which followed the decision, as in those which preceded it, one of the primary considerations of Viviani and Poincaré was to shape the situation in such fashion that Great Britain would be won to the side of the Dual Alliance in the impending conflict. The *Entente Cordiale* and the military and naval understandings which followed its consummation were not interpreted by the British Government as imposing upon it any binding legal obligation to come to the aid of France in the event of war. It was of the utmost importance to the Quai d'Orsay, therefore, to do nothing which would antagonize Sir Edward Grey and everything which would conciliate British opinion and increase the chances of British participation. On July 26, Jules Cambon had expressed to the German Foreign Secretary, Von Jagow, his confidence that Great Britain would stand with France and Russia in the event of war. The German minister was equally certain of British neutrality.[3] Grey endeavored to preserve peace by bringing pressure to bear on both of the continental coalitions—at Berlin, by veiled threats that Great Britain was to be reckoned with; and at Paris and St. Petersburg by vague warnings that Great Britain was not to be counted upon for support. He succeeded only in convincing the German Government of the certainty of British neutrality, and the French statesman of the untrustworthiness of the Government they had regarded as an ally.

On July 29, Grey was still saying that Great Britain would consult her own interests, had not made up her mind, and was free from engagements.[4] On the morning of the thirtieth, Paul Cambon, who had returned from his hurried and somewhat mysterious visit to Paris, made an appeal to Grey, who merely responded that he would see the French Ambassador on the following day after the Cabinet had met.[5] In the evening, Poincaré made a personal appeal to Sir Francis Bertie, arguing that a declaration of British solidarity with France and Russia would cause Germany to modify her

---

[1] Izvolsky to Sazonov, 1:00 A.M., August 1, *L.N.*, II, p. 294.
[2] Schmitt, II, p. 304.
[3] Schmitt, II, p. 54.
[4] Grey to Bertie, July 29, Schmitt, II, p. 284.
[5] Fay, II, pp. 487f.

attitude and avert war. Bertie was sympathetic but not reassuring. "The French, instead of putting pressure on the Russian Government to moderate their zeal, expect us to give the Germans to understand that we mean fighting if war breaks out. If we gave an assurance of armed assistance to France and Russia now, Russia would become more exacting and France would follow in her wake."[1] The British Cabinet was divided. The Cambon-Grey interview of the thirty-first was painful. The British Foreign Secretary said that his Government could give no pledge of support. Beneath an imperturbable exterior, Cambon was in an agony of anxiety. Sir Arthur Nicolson urged mobilization, but Grey persisted in his course. With the approval of the French Cabinet, Poincaré now addressed a plea to George V, conceding "complete liberty" to His Majesty's Government but urging vehemently that Great Britain declare her solidarity with France in the interest of peace. This was a last desperate appeal on the eve of the decision for war.[2] Shortly before midnight on July 31, at the same hour when the French Cabinet was taking the fatal step, Nicolson was awakened by an urgent message from the French Embassy reporting (incorrectly) that the French frontier had been violated.[3] The dark dawn of Saturday, August 1, saw the French Government still without assurance of British support. The "ten-kilometer withdrawal" and the various peace moves had been designed to placate British opinion and win a promise of support. But the decision for war was reached with no guaranty that that support would be forthcoming.

These considerations prompted the French Cabinet to leave to Germany the initiative in declaring war. This would also obviate the necessity of summoning the Chambers and risking the possible embarrassments of a parliamentary debate on the obligations of the Franco-Russian Alliance. The lessons of July 14, 1870, were not forgotten.[4] At 8:00 A.M., Saturday, August 1, Joffre demanded of Messimy the mobilization of the French Army, declining to assume responsibility in the case of further delay. The Cabinet met again at 9:00 and granted the request without protest or discussion.[5] Further pressure from the militarists was unnecessary, since mobilization was the logical sequence to the decision of the preceding evening. The mobilization order would be issued at 4:00 P.M. Late in the morning Bertie informed Poincaré of King George's belated telegram to the Tsar, prepared by Asquith and Tyrell late on July 31; consented to by the King at 1:30 A.M., August 1; dispatched by Grey to Buchanan at 3:30 A.M., but not acknowledged by Sazonov until late on August 2, after war had begun. It was (too late) a plea to refrain from action which would make peace impossible and an appeal to resume negotiations.[6] Poincaré replied that the Russian

---

[1] Bertie to Grey, July 30, B.D., 318, Schmitt, II, p. 285, note.
[2] Renouvin, pp. 256f.; Huddleston, *Poincaré*, pp. 66–67; Schmitt, II, pp. 294–295.
[3] Nicolson, *Portrait of a Diplomatist*, p. 303.
[4] *Supra*, p. 6.
[5] Schmitt, II, p. 334.
[6] Schmitt, II, p. 328.

general mobilization had followed that of Austria—a statement which can be interpreted as a deliberate misrepresentation or as a further indication that the President and the Cabinet had been misled by Paléologue or by the staff at the Quai d'Orsay and had failed to ascertain the facts from Dumaine at Vienna. He added that Germany "in effect" was mobilizing, that Russia was ready to continue negotiations, and that the French Government did not quite despair of war being avoided—all of which was again calculated to influence English opinion favorably rather than to state the facts of the situation.[1]

At 11:00 A.M., August 1, Schoen appeared at the Quai d'Orsay for the answer to the German ultimatum, which expired at 1:00. Viviani left the Cabinet meeting to see him. The ambassador again posed his question. "France will be guided by her interests," replied the Premier, in accordance with the formula agreed to by the Cabinet the night before, Schoen found this vague. "You have a treaty of alliance?" "*Parfaitement.*" Schoen correctly interpreted the reply to the neutrality query as a negative one. Viviani neither contradicted him nor offered explanations, save to say that the situation seemed to be improving since Russia had accepted the British proposals (which was untrue) and that Germany was assuming a serious responsibility if she took the initiative in breaking the peace. Schoen did not announce his departure nor ask for his passports.[2]

French mobilization followed, as planned. Viviani seems to have been hesitant and confused. Despite the decision for war which had already been reached, he told the ministers that peace could perhaps yet be preserved in view of Schoen's attitude. But Izvolsky emphasized the terms of the German ultimatum to Russia and the imminence of German mobilization and Poincaré had no qualms.[3] At 3:40 P.M. the Minister of War issued the order for mobilization to an officer of the general staff who telegraphed it throughout France fifteen minutes later. Immediately thereafter Viviani appealed to him to hold it up, on the ground that his interview with Schoen offered some hope of a pacific settlement. "It is too late," replied Messimy. "The mechanism is unleashed."[4] The military commanders were ordered not to permit the covering troops to cross the ten-kilometer line except in case of an attack. Poincaré intervened to emphasize these precautions "with a view to assuring for ourselves the collaboration of our English neighbors." At 10:30 P.M. strict orders were issued that "for serious diplomatic reasons" no soldier must be found east of the line indicated.[5] The mobilization order was accompanied by a public proclamation "To the French Nation," signed by Poincaré,

---

[1] Bertie to Grey, August 1, 2:30 P.M., *B.D.*, 403. *Cf.* Poincaré, IV, p. 489. Poincaré mistakenly places the interview in the evening.

[2] Schoen, pp. 194–195; Viviani, pp. 218–220.

[3] Poincaré, IV, p. 480.

[4] Renouvin pp. 217f.; *cf.* Pevet, *Les responsables*, pp. 445–454; Demartial, *op. cit.*, pp. 109–117; Fay, II, pp. 531–534; for the text of the mobilization order, *infra*, p. 346, Note 1.

[5] Renouvin, p. 217; Schmitt, II, p. 336.

Viviani, and most of the members of the Cabinet, which declared (erroneously) that the majority of the nations had mobilized, that their legislation permitted mobilization without a formal decree while French legislation did not, and that France had "multiplied her efforts to maintain peace" but was compelled to issue the decree which the situation demanded. The Government would continue its diplomatic efforts. The citizenry was exhorted to patriotism, calm, vigilance, and dignity. "Mobilization is not war. Under the existing circumstances, it appears, on the contrary, as the best means of preserving peace with honor."[1] A few French citizens may have believed this —but certainly not those who signed the appeal.

The policy of mobilizing and awaiting further developments was not open to Germany which was menaced on two fronts, as the Dual Alliance had contemplated from the outset, and which saw only too clearly the French intention of attacking Germany in the rear after mobilization should be completed. The German plan of campaign, moreover, was based upon the assumption of the necessity of fighting in the east and the west at the same time and contemplated crushing France by marching through Belgium before turning in force upon Russia. Nevertheless the declaration of war against France was postponed. As for Russia, no reply to the ultimatum of the thirty-first was received. At 12:52 P.M., August 1, the German declaration of war against Russia was dispatched to Pourtalès, who presented it to Sazonov at 7:00 P.M., burst into tears, and departed.[2] At 5:00 P.M. (Central European Time) the general mobilization of the Germany Army was ordered, twenty minutes after the corresponding measure had been taken in France and two days after general mobilization in Russia.[3] At 5:30 Schoen appeared again at the Quai d'Orsay. Viviani assured him that French mobilization was not indicative of aggressive intentions, that he could not abandon his hopes for peace, and that no reason existed for Schoen's departure.[4] Neither man knew, as yet, of the outbreak of war between Germany and Russia. The interview was inconclusive and futile. Izvolsky telegraphed the news of the French mobilization to Sazonov and reported that Messimy had urged that Serbia be encouraged to take the offensive as soon as possible and asked that he be kept informed daily of the German army corps directed against Russia and of the date of the commencement of the Russian offensive against East Prussia.[5] The Minister of War at least was free from illusions or pretenses regarding peace.

At 11:00 in the evening the Russian Ambassador in Paris received word from Sazonov of the German declaration of war on Russia. He went at once to Poincaré to ask him what France would do. The President at once summoned a meeting of the Cabinet, which supported him in responding that

[1] J.O., August 2, 1914, pp. 7053–7054.
[2] Schmitt, II, pp. 322–328.
[3] Fay II, pp. 531–534.
[4] L.N., II, p. 296.
[5] Izvolsky to Sazonov, August 1, L.N., II, p. 297.

France would fulfill her obligations "unreservedly." This implied a French declaration of war on Germany. But there were difficulties. The English attitude was by no means clear. A declaration of war, moreover, constitutionally required a vote by Parliament, which could not be assembled for two days. Poincaré shrank from a public debate on the application of the treaty of alliance and regarded it as strategically advantageous for France to commence military operations only after mobilization should be further developed.[1] The Cabinet session was long and troubled, lasting until 4:00 A.M., Sunday, August 2. It was rumored in the press that Delcassé was to be made Minister of War and that Clemenceau would be given a Cabinet post. Both men were apparently present.[2] It was finally decided that the Chambers should not be convoked for ten days, by which time mobilization would be completed. Izvolsky was somewhat discouraged,[3] but transmitted the decision to St. Petersburg in deepest secrecy.[4] Poincaré was hopeful that Germany would attack at once and thus solve the problem. He could afford to wait and throw the burden of the initiative on Berlin.

On the evening of August 1st the German military occupation of Luxembourg commenced, to the tune of false allegations of French violations of the neutrality of the Grand Duchy and assurances to Paris that this indicated no hostile action toward France.[5] Sunday and Monday, August 2 and 3, were spent in marking time, while each Government proceeded to charge the other with numerous violations of the frontier, all of which were either manufactured or were exaggerations of insignificant incidents. The French Government, like the German, had an eye to London and its own public opinion.[6] Izvolsky described these "incidents" as giving to the French Government the possibility of declaring to the Chambers that France was the victim of unprovoked aggression and thus escaping the constitutional necessity of a formal declaration of war.[7] At 2:10 P.M., August 2, the Cabinet gave Joffre complete liberty of movement in the execution of his plans and the ten-kilometer line was abolished, though Joffre emphasized the necessity "for imperative diplomatic reasons" of leaving the initiation of hostilities to the German forces and of refraining from crossing into German territory.[8] On the morning of August 3 the order was given that "if there are incidents, they must start and develop on French territory."[9] While the entire country was placed under a state of siege, mobilization proceeded apace.[10] Under a

---

[1] Izvolsky to Sazonov, August 1, L.N., II, pp. 297–298.
[2] Cf. New York Times, August 2, 1914.
[3] Poincaré, IV, p. 496.
[4] Izvolsky to Sazonov, August 1, L.N., II, p. 299.
[5] Schmitt, II, pp. 363–365.
[6] Cf. Schmitt, II, pp. 366–371; Renouvin, pp. 237f.
[7] L.N., II, p. 300.
[8] Schmitt, II, pp. 369–370.
[9] Schmitt, II, p. 370, citing Les armées françaises, I, pp. 84–87.
[10] J.O., August 3, pp. 7083–7088, Décret of the Minister of War.

law of April 3, 1878, the former measure automatically required the convocation of the Chambers within two days to consider its duration and the Chambers were therefore convoked into extraordinary session for August 4.[1]

In view of the anxiety of Poincaré and Viviani to postpone as long as possible a parliamentary discussion of the issue of war and of the obligations of the Alliance, it is probable that they had come to take the view by Sunday afternoon that the frontier incidents could be presented to the Chambers as already constituting a state of war by act of Germany. They certainly had no intention of submitting the question of peace or war to Parliament for its consideration. The Cabinet had already decided upon war on the night of July 31 (Friday) and, despite the official proclamation, the door to peace had been closed by general mobilization, understood to be signal for war by the terms of the Dual Alliance, which obligated France to attack Germany with all its forces in the event of a German attack upon Russia.[2] French mobilization was ordered five hours before the German declaration of war was delivered to Russia (allowing for the differences in times), but the German "attack" followed at once and made a resort to war mandatory on the part of the Republic. Article 2 of the Boisdeffre-Obruchev agreement obligated the Allies to mobilize immediately and simultaneously as soon as one of the Powers of the Triple Alliance had mobilized. In fact, as has been shown, the mobilization of Russia preceded that of Austria (4:00 P.M., July 30 and 12:23 P.M., July 31) and the French that of Germany (3:40 P.M., August 1, and 5:00 P.M., August 1). The mobilization of the Dual Alliance was thus not a reply to that of the Central Powers, as the military convention contemplated. Russia had mobilized her own initiative, without consulting France. Technically, the Republic was under no legal obligation to follow suit, unless the Austrian mobilization could be regarded as the *casus foederis*—a position scarcely tenable since Russia had mobilized first. But the German declaration of war on Russia, if interpreted as an "attack," involved the *casus foederis* under Article 1 and left the French Government no alternative. It may be recalled that both Poincaré and Viviani, on the basis of Paléologue's falsified dispatch of July 31, believed, or pretended to believe, that Russian mobilization had followed Austrian. In their view, therefore, the *casus foederis* was involved under both articles. But a public discussion of what had been a closely guarded secret for twenty years might prove embarrassing and Poincaré, at least, had no intention of permitting one. As early as 1912, while Premier, he had apparently persuaded his colleagues of the necessity of a brusque attack upon the Rhineland in the event of war and of the expediency of confronting Parliament with a *fait accompli*.[3] In the actual crisis, the uncertain attitude of England dictated a policy of refraining from taking the

---

[1] *Decret* of August 2, signed by Poincaré, Viviani, and Malvy, *J.O.*, August 3, p. 7077. Renouvin takes the view that the law of 1878 made this decree technically unnecessary, *op. cit.*, p. 92.

[2] Article 1 of the Boisdeffre-Obrouchev convention, *supra*, p. 146.

[3] Pevet, *op. cit.*, pp. 502-503.

offensive, even though the Dual Alliance envisaged an immediate attack with all available forces on both frontiers of Germany. The policy adopted was therefore one of waiting in the hope that frontier incidents or a German declaration of war or both would intervene and enable the Cabinet to gain its diplomatic objectives in London and escape the danger of a parliamentary debate on the issue.

Berlin, at the last moment, unwittingly rescued the French Cabinet from its diplomatic and constitutional embarrassments. At 1:05 P.M., Monday, August 3, instructions were sent to Schoen, asking him to inform the French Government at 6:00 P.M. that, while the Germans had everywhere respected the frontier, French troops had crossed the line the previous day at Altmün-sterol and in the Vosges. French airplanes, moreover, had crossed Belgian territory and had been seen in the region of Eifel and others had dropped bombs on the railways near Karlsruhe and Nuremberg. Schoen was therefore to inform the French Government of the existence of a state of war, demand his passports and leave, after turning over the protection of German interests in France to the American Embassy. This telegram was received by Schoen in mutilated form, the portions relating to frontier violations by French troops being indecipherable. The cause of the mutilation are still something of a mystery,[1] but Schoen decided to act on such portion of his instructions as were intelligible. At 6:15 P.M., the Ambassador of the United States, Myron T. Herrick (who was scheduled to sail for home on August 8 and be succeeded by William G. Sharp, but who remained at his post in view of the crisis),[2] telephoned the Quai d'Orsay to say that Schoen had asked him to raise the American flag over the German Embassy. Viviani warned Poincaré and waited alone for the inevitable sequel. Thirty minutes later Schoen appeared—for the last time. He was deeply moved and spoke at once of the threats and insults addressed to him by several unknown persons while he was on his way to the Quai d'Orsay. Viviani received him with icy composure and expressed his regrets. Schoen then read a prepared statement, reciting the airplane incidents and informing him of the existence of a state of war. The allegations were without foundation—"the product of highly overwrought imaginations" Schoen later said—and Viviani emphatically denied their truth, referring in turn to German violations of the frontier. Schoen had at the moment no means of determining the facts and no discretion in the matter in any case. This blunder of German diplomacy served the French Cabinet admirably in the days which followed, enabling it to present the war as thrust upon an innocent France by German brutality and duplicity. Nothing more remained to be said. Bows and courtesies. The German Ambassador took his leave and left Paris the same evening.[3]

[1] *Cf.* Schmitt, II, pp. 372–373 for the original and mutilated versions; Poincaré, IV, p. 525; *American Historical Review*, XXXV, pp. 78*f.*; *Revue de Paris*, XXIX, iii, pp. 33–41.

[2] New York *Times*, July 31, 1914.

[3] Schoen, pp. 200–204; Viviani, pp. 227–232.

The story may be closed with a brief consideration of the situation in London and the action of the Chambers in France on the following day. In spite of Poincaré's appeal to George V, the British Cabinet was still unwilling to grant the coveted promise of support. The King was obliged to respond, weakly, that His Government would "continue to discuss freely and frankly any point which might arise of interest to our two nations."[1] On the afternoon of August 1, Grey and Cambon met again. The British Foreign Secretary said that if France could not remain neutral in the Russo-German war, it was because of an alliance of which he did not know the terms and to which Great Britain was not a party. France must make her own decision without counting on British aid. The Cabinet had decided, he said, that it could not ask Parliament to send an expeditionary force to the continent. Cambon rejoined that the French Channel coast was defenseless. When Grey responded that Great Britain had no obligation to help France as Russia's ally, the Ambassador raised the question of a moral obligation of naval cooperation. Grey promised no more than to submit the question to the Cabinet. To Nicolson, who urged upon Grey the obligations implied in the naval entente, Cambon could only say "They want to desert us, they want to desert us!" It was the French Ambassador's darkest hour. He told Wickham Steed of the *Times* that he was waiting to learn whether the word "honor" had been stricken from the English vocabulary.[2] At 1:25 A.M., Sunday, August 2, Churchill ordered the mobilization of the British Navy. During the day, news arrived of frontier incidents and the German occupation of Luxembourg and Grey at last gave to Cambon a written assurance that Great Britain would protect the French coasts in the event of a naval attack.[3] Cambon was much relieved, feeling certain now of British cooperation against Germany whatever else happened.

In point of fact a German naval attack upon the French coasts was not contemplated in Berlin and the German Government hastened to give London assurances to this effect. The German plan of campaign called for an invasion of France through Belgium to escape the necessity of taking the strong border fortresses of Belfort, Toul, and Verdun. But the neutrality of Belgium had been guaranteed in 1839 by an international agreement to which Germany, France, and Great Britain were all parties. While Viviani had replied to the British query that France would respect the neutrality of Belgium if other Powers did so, Berlin made no response. On the evening of August 2, the Belgium Government received a twelve-hour ultimatum from Berlin, alleging French intentions of violating Belgian neutrality and demanding the right of passage for German troops. Early the following morning (the day of the German declaration of war on France) Belgium replied, protesting against the proposed violation of international law and expressing its inten-

[1] August 1, cited in Schmitt, II, p. 354.

[2] Nicolson, *op. cit.*, pp. 304–305.

[3] *Cf.* Schmitt, II, pp. 353–361.

tion to repel every attack upon its rights by all means at its disposal. King Albert at once appealed to George V for British aid in safeguarding Belgian integrity. "The lamps are going out all over Europe," said Grey to a friend. "I feel like a man who has wasted his life."[1] On the following morning German troops crossed the Belgian frontier to attack Liège and Bethmann declared before the Reichstag: "We are now in a state of necessity and necessity knows no law." When the British Cabinet met on the morning of August 3—minus Mr. Burns, Lord Morley, Sir John Simon, and Lord Beauchamp who had all resigned—it was decided to make the violation of Belgian neutrality the *casus belli*. The House of Commons approved and Cambon was delighted. The Belgian issue enabled Grey to commit Great Britain to war with the support of a united nation. On August 4, Grey sent an ultimatum to Berlin and at 4:00 P.M. the mobilization of the British Army was ordered. Bethmann bitterly reproved the British Ambassador for the action of his nation in going to war "just for a scrap of paper." At midnight, Great Britain declared war on Germany.[2] The cycle was complete. Except for Italy, whose faith in "scraps of paper" was no greater than Germany's, all the Powers of the continent were at war. On the Danube, along the frontiers of East Prussia, in the Vosges, and before Liège, rifles were already cracking and the advance guards of the great armies were already coming to grips in the most titanic conflict of nations in the history of the Western State System.

At 3:00 P.M., August 4, the Senate and the Chamber of Deputies assembled in Paris, confronted with a war which imperiled the very existence of France and in the initiation of which they had had no voice. The problem of the Cabinet was to present the situation in such fashion that Parliament would regard the country as the victim of unprovoked aggression and give its united support for the course which had been embarked upon. With the exception of the Socialists, the Senators and Deputies had watched the unrolling of the tragedy through the eyes of good patriots, confident of the honesty and pacific intentions of the ministry and convinced that the war was hatched in Wilhelmstrasse and not at the Quai d'Orsay. On July 29, some fifty Socialist Deputies had prepared a resolution opposing war over Serbia and demanding the immediate convocation of the chambers. Jaurès transmitted it to Bienvenu-Martin, who replied that the suggestion was pointless, since the Government had no statement to submit to Parliament.[3] On the thirtieth, Malvy had informally assured a number of Deputies that the diplomatic situation appeared more hopeful.[4] Except for this, there had been no direct contact between the Cabinet and the Chambers during the development of the crisis. Jaurès' funeral took place on the morning of August

[1] Schmitt, II, p. 409.
[2] *Ibid.*, II, pp. 383–409; *cf.* Nicolson, pp. 306–309.
[3] *Cf.* New York *Times*, July 29, 1914.
[4] *Ibid.*, July 31, 1914.

fourth. Viviani delivered a colorless address and the ceremony passed off without incident. In the afternoon the session opened. By Presidential decree, Senator Gaston Doumergue had been named Minister of Foreign Affairs, to relieve the Premier of this burden, and Deputy Albert Sarraut had been made Minister of Public Instruction to replace M. Augagneur who, in turn, was transferred to the Ministry of Marine in view of the resignation of M. Gautier.[1]

The proceedings began in both chambers in a mood of great excitement and enthusiasm. Viviani in the Chamber and Bienvenu-Martin in the Senate read a brief message from Poincaré, in which the war was presented as "a violent and premeditated attack, which is an insolent defiance of the law of nations. Before any declaration of war had been sent to us, even before the German Ambassador had asked for his passports, our territory had been violated." The Deputies and Senators were carried away by indignation and patriotic pride. Viviani then read a message of his own, first to the Deputies, and then, proceeding rapidly from the Palais Bourbon to the Palais Luxembourg, to the Senators, picturing the Entente Governments as having exhausted all possibilities of peace and as being the innocent victims of a German conspiracy to drown Europe in blood. The German statesmen were painted as the archplotters behind Vienna, and the efforts of Berlin to restrain Vienna, as well as the French encouragement to St. Petersburg, were ignored. Russia was portrayed as having agreed to the British mediation proposals and as having mobilized in response to an Austrian mobilization and declaration of war. Germany had begun "secret mobilization" on July 25 and had invaded France and Luxembourg and threatened Belgium on August 2. The Premier then explained the Grey-Cambon letters of 1912 and the British pledge to protect the French coast.

. . . Gentlemen, these are the facts . . . Germany can reproach us with nothing. Bearing in silence in our bosom for half a century the wound which Germany dealt us we have offered to peace an unprecedented sacrifice . . .

France, unjustly provoked, did not desire war, she has done everything to avert it. Since it has been forced upon her, she will defend herself against Germany . . . A free and strong nation, which fights for an ideal rooted in the centuries, and unites, in its entirety, to protect its existence; a democracy which has been able to keep its military strength within the bounds of discipline and did not fear, a year ago, to increase the burden of that strength in order to counter the arming of its neighbors; a nation in arms fighting for its very life and for the independence of Europe—these are the things we have the honor of showing to the witnesses of this tremendous struggle, for which preparations have been going on for days amid the greatest calm and in the most methodical manner. We are without reproach. We shall show ourselves to be without fear. France has often proved in less favorable circumstances that she is a most formidable adversary when she fights, as she does to-day, for liberty and for right.[2]

Viviani had carried with him to Parliament the texts of the Franco-Russian Alliance. They were unnecessary. No one asked to see them. No

[1] Decrees of August 3, *J.O.*, August 4, 1914.
[2] *J.O.*, August 5, 1914.

voices of dissent were raised. No discussion took place. The Premier's address, like that of Bethmann-Hollweg before the Reichstag at the same time, was not a statement of facts nor an explanation of what had occurred, but an appeal for support. As such, it was completely successful. Both Chambers hailed Viviani in an unprecedented demonstration of nationalistic fervor. Credits were opened and war legislation passed by acclamation. Both Chambers adjourned *sine die*, the Senate at 6:50 P.M. and the Deputies at 7:00, amid loud cries of "Vive la France!"[1] A month later, despite some protest, Poincaré signed a ministerial declaration closing the extraordinary session of Parliament, which had not been reconvened in the interval. The Chambers did not meet again until December 22, after which they remained in permanent session until the close of the war, to do the bidding of the executive.[2] Parliamentary control of French foreign policy was thus reduced to a nullity and played no rôle, save that of acquiescence, in the initiation of a conflict which was to cost the lives of over a million Frenchmen and make France the devastated battlefield of a world in arms.

* * * * * *

Questions of "responsibility," as that term has been used in the voluminous literature of "revisionism," are beyond the scope of the present study. Suffice it to note that the version of the outbreak of war presented to Parliament on August 2 remained substantially the version which was adhered to subsequently by Poincaré, Viviani, and the Quai d'Orsay. The *Livre Jaune* issued by the Ministry of Foreign Affairs was not designed to reveal the facts of the diplomatic situation which had led to war, but to conceal all that was damaging to the Entente thesis of sole German responsibility. It concealed the nature of Franco-Russian obligations, obscured the rôle of Poincaré and Paléologue in supporting Sazonov, veiled the significance of Russian mobilization, and repeated, verbatim, the falsified report of Russia's fatal action, which, as has been indicated, was perhaps accepted by the President, the Premier, and the Cabinet throughout the crisis as a true statement of the facts.[3] On July 5, 1922, both Poincaré and Viviani, in response to the accusations of Communist Deputies, publicly reaffirmed their "innocence" in Parliament and won the support of the Chamber by a vote of 532 to 65.[4] The nature of the accusations are sufficiently clear from the preceding narrative.[5] Poincaré has denied them as a whole and in detail and

---

[1] *Ibid.*

[2] P. Renouvin, *The Forms of War Government in France*, p. 98.

[3] *Cf.* Demartial, *op. cit., passim.;* A. von Wegerer, *A Refutation of the Versailles War Guilt Thesis*, pp. 25–29.

[4] "La Chambre, réprouvant et flétissant de toute la force de son méprise la campagne de calomnies organisée et developpée au profit de L'Allemagne pour imputer à la politique de la France la résponsibilité de la guerre, en dépit de l'évidence des faits et des aveux catégoriques consignés dans le traité de Versailles et formellement confirmés par le Reichstag dans sa séance du 10 mai 1921, repoussant toute addition, passe à l'ordre du jour." *J.O.Ch.*, July 5, 1922.

[5] *Cf.* Scott, *Five Weeks*, pp. 248–252.

has absolved all of the French statesmen of 1914 from any degree of responsibility in initiating the conflict.[1] The French "revisionists" have not hesitated to accuse him of hypocrisy and misrepresentation,[2] and their allegations have been received sympathetically in certain quarters abroad.[3] Certain aspects of these questions can be cleared up only when the French diplomatic archives for 1914 are thrown open, and others will probably always remain a mystery. The guilt-and-innocence dichotomy is meaningless to anyone interested in a realistic study of the functioning of the Western State System. Meanwhile the foregoing account of the facts which have been established speaks for itself and must stand as an accurate statement of the rôle of the French Government in the crisis of 1914.

As for the internal control of French policy during the crisis, the facts, here too, need little commentary. The pattern of the fabric is plain. In the warp one finds a helpless Parliament, not in session during the crisis, called too late to exercise its constitutional power over peace and war, and readily persuaded to acquiesce, since its only party, the Socialist, which might have stood firmly for peace, was helpless without its martyred leader and, in the test, placed national patriotism above revolutionary Marxism. One finds also a complacent and patriotic public opinion, uninformed of the facts, poisoned by a corrupt press, subsidized from abroad, and incapable of anything but shouting "Vive la France!" and thus supporting the position of the Government. Bankers, merchants, petty *bourgeoisie*, peasants, proletarians— all are fearful, undesirous of war, staunchly patriotic, confused, and at last compounded into a solid phalanx of militant nationalism supporting the Government dumbly in the conviction that *la patrie innocente* is being ravished by a brutal and scheming invader.

In the woof of the cloth are familiar figures. The President, no longer a constitutional puppet, but a past and future Premier and Minister of Foreign Affairs, is Poincaré the Lorrainer: *bourgeois*, conservative, ardently nationalist, completely committed to solidarity with Russia even at the cost of war, firmly opposed to any concessions to the Triplice, and equipped by his experience and powerful personality to dominate Viviani and his colleagues and give the Russian war makers the encouragement they crave. The Premier lacks such assurance and decisiveness. He is guided by the stronger man. His colleagues in the Cabinet play a passive rôle until the end, when the Minister of War, under pressure from the general staff, performs his part in confirming and precipitating the inevitable decision. The Quai d'Orsay is under the spell of the secret alliance and does not shrink from its implications. The diplomatic service strengthens its hand. Paléologue,

---

[1] *Cf.* Poincaré, IV, pp. 528–535.

[2] *Cf.* Works of Morhardt, Pevet, Demartial, cited above, *passim.*

[3] For example, H. E. Barnes, *The Genesis of the World War*, especially Chap. VII, "Poincaré and His Clique Incite the Russians in the Crisis of 1914," and Chap. III, "The Franco-Russian Plot That Produced the War." *Cf.* Frederick Baussman, *Let France Explain, passim.*

convinced of the irrepressibility of the conflict from the beginning, fails to keep Paris adequately informed of the fatal developments at St. Petersburg, while Izvolsky at Paris helps him to encourage Sazonov to find what he desires in the French capital. When the French Ambassador finally reports Russian mobilization belatedly, the news is falsified, apparently at the Quai d'Orsay, and gives to the President, the Premier, and the Cabinet a wholly erroneous view of the situation. But they have already decided for war.

Out of hysteria, confusion, the misrepresentations of bureaucracy, and the nerve-racking fatigue of sleepless nights the decision emerges. German blunders enable the Government to win over Great Britain and gain the unanimous support of its public for the combat. The tapestry is woven and the machine has reached its goal, albeit creakingly and with the weavers not willing the design but guiding it by a pattern which has but one ending. Diplomats are replaced by militarists at the levers of powers. Once the last fatal shuttle is cast, all else is forgotten in the *Union Sacrée* for the defense of the fatherland. The pattern is completed and the threads turn from diplomatic yellow and documentary grey into red and black and a chaotic horror of flames and blood.

Chapter XI

THE OCCUPATION OF THE RUHR

1. The Fruits of Victory

Article 231: The Allied and Associated Governments affirm and Germany accepts the responsibility of Germany and her allies for causing all the loss and damage to which the Allied and Associated Governments and their nationals have been subjected as a consequence of the war imposed upon them by the aggression of Germany and her allies.

Article 232: The Allied and Associated Governments recognize that the resources of Germany are not adequate, after taking into account permanent diminutions of such resources which will result from other provisions of the present Treaty, to make complete reparation for all such loss and damage.

The Allied and Associated Governments, however, require, and Germany undertakes, that she will make compensation for all damage done to the civilian population of the Allied and Associated Powers and to their property during the period of the belligerency of each as an Allied or Associated Power against Germany by such aggression by land, by sea and from the air, and in general all damage as defined in Annex I hereto.

IN these words the Treaty of Versailles, signed June 28, 1919, fixed moral responsibility for the Great War upon Germany and her allies and established the legal basis for the imposition of a pecuniary indemnity upon the vanquished in the form of reparations. In view of the obvious physical impossibility of collecting from the defeated States the entire financial cost of the war to the victorious Powers, the framers of the Treaty were obliged to limit their demands to civilian losses defined by certain specified categories. Germany was required to pay damages for all civilian injuries or deaths during the course of the conflict, for all maltreatment of prisoners of war, for all pensions paid to members of the Allied military, naval, and air forces or their dependents, for all financial assistance granted by the Allied and Associated Governments to prisoners of war and their dependents and to dependents of persons serving in their forces, for all forced labor of civilians for which just remuneration had not been paid, for all destruction, injury, or seizure of non-military property wherever situated belonging to the Allied and Associated Governments or their nationals, and for all levies, fines, or executions imposed upon the civilian populations under German military occupation during the conflict.[1] In the case of Belgium, Germany was required to pay the foregoing damages and, in addition, to repay, with 5 per cent interest, all sums borrowed by Belgium from the Allied and Associated Governments up to November 11, 1918.[2] The total German indebtedness

[1] Annex I to Part VIII of the Treaty of Versailles.
[2] Article 232, third paragraph, Part VIII.

was to be fixed by an interallied Reparation Commission and notified to Germany on or before May 1, 1921, along with a schedule of payments, subject to subsequent modification by the commission itself in accordance with its findings regarding the resources and capacity of Germany.[1] Meanwhile, Germany was to deliver, before May 1, 1921, in addition to deliveries in kind, 20,000,000,000 gold marks, out of which should be paid the expenses of the Allied armies of occupation on the Rhine and the costs of such supplies of food and raw materials as the Allied Governments might judge essential to enable Germany to meet her obligations.[2]

In case of default by Germany in the performance of any obligation under this Part of the present Treaty, the Commission will forthwith give notice of such default to each of the interested Powers and may make such recommendations as to the action to be taken in consequence of such default as it may think necessary.

The measures which the Allied and Associated Governments shall have the right to take, in case of voluntary default by Germany, and which Germany agrees not to regard as acts of wars may include economic and financial prohibitions and reprisals and in general such other measure, as the respective Governments may determine to be necessary in the circumstances.[3]

The peace settlements of 1919, in their financial, economic, and political aspects, were intended, like all such settlements, to legalize and perpetuate the new relationships of power in the Western State System which had resulted from the military verdict in the conflict preceding them. The armistice agreements of the autumn of 1918 were the outcome of the defeat on land and sea of the armed forces of Germany, Austria-Hungary, Bulgaria, and Turkey at the hands of the twenty-three States at war with the Central Powers. The Treaties of Versailles, St. Germain, Trianon, Neuilly, and Sèvres were imposed by the victors on the vanquished as the formal expression of the decision of the battlefields and as the basis for a new international public law which should henceforth govern the relations between the two groups of signatories in accordance with that decision. The settlement, like every dictated peace, was designed to consolidate the victory, to perpetuate its results, to realize the aspirations of the victors at the expense of the vanquished, to reduce the defeated States to a position of impotence, and to insure the military and political preponderance of the triumphant Powers in future world politics.

The international position of France at the close of the Great War may be analyzed briefly as a background for a treatment of the development of French policy toward Germany and the reparation question. The military collapse of Imperial Germany, following the dissolution of Austria-Hungary, placed the Quai d'Orsay in a position to achieve the objectives which it had

[1] Articles 232 and 234.

[2] Article 235.

[3] Paragraphs 17 and 18 of Annex II to Part VIII; cf. Annexes III–VII for a detailed statement of required deliveries of ships, live stock, coal, coke, chemicals, dyestuffs, and cables. On the framing of these clauses, see B. M. Baruch, *The Making of the Reparation and Economic Sections of the Treaty*, pp. 13–77; Moulton and Bass, *The Balance Sheet of Europe*, p. 161.

pursued through many vicissitudes ever since the Treaty of Frankfort. Within the limits imposed by British, Italian, and American interests, the French Government could now translate the *revanche* from a half-confessed aspiration into a diplomatic reality. The circumstances of the victory and of the Peace Conference, however, created a large gap between what was desired and what was obtainable. The collapse of Tsarist Russia into social revolution and civil war, the "Balkanization" of eastern and southeastern Europe in the name of "self-determination," the economic interest of Great Britain in the restoration of normal trade conditions on the Continent, the peace plans of President Wilson all represented stubborn and irreducible obstacles to the realization of the maximum program of the Quai d'Orsay. The final settlement was necessarily a compromise, satisfactory to no one.

French disappointment with the work of the Peace Conference was naturally increased by the ever present reflection that the cost of victory to the Republic had been appalling while Germany had emerged from the war relatively unscathed. No part of Germany, save a strip of East Prussia, had been invaded, devastated, or subjected to hostile military occupation during the conflict, while France, twice invaded within a generation, had furnished the theater for four years of the bloodiest and most destructive fighting in the history of warfare. Germany retained the major portion of her industries and economic resources intact and could still boast a large and growing population of 63,000,000, compared to France's decimated and stationary population of 39,000,000. The increment to French population, represented by the recovery of Alsace-Lorraine, barely compensated the nation for its war deaths. 1,427,800 French soldiers—"*mort pour la patrie*"—had lost their lives in the struggle. Seven-hundred thousand had been crippled or incapacitated, 2,344,000 more had been wounded, 453,000 had been taken prisoner or were reported missing.[1] The human losses of the war to France had been greater than those of any of her allies with the single exception of Russia. The money costs of the conflict had been so huge as to be incalculable. Estimates of the direct war expenditures of the French Government vary from 130,000,000,000 to 170,000,000,000 fr., *i.e.*, from twenty-six to almost thirty-four billion dollars.[2] The northeastern departments had been ravaged and blasted by fifty-two months of uninterrupted fighting. Once productive coal mines, factories, and farms, once thriving towns and cities were now in ruins, in some cases beyond all hope of restoration. Every home in the nation has in greater or lesser degree felt the terrific impact of these stupendous human and material losses. Every family in France had been encouraged to believe in the sole responsibility of Germany for the catastrophe and to rest assured that Allied victory would compel the aggressor to make restitution and reparation for all that had been endured.

[1] G. Jèze and H. Truchy, *The War Finance of France*, p. 5, New Haven, 1927.

[2] *Ibid.*, pp. 9–11 and 105. Jèze discusses the various bases of calculating monetary costs and concludes that no accurate figure of money costs can be arrived at.

Under these circumstances the final terms accorded to Germany appeared unjustifiably lenient to a large section of French opinion. The treaty seemed to fall far short of war time aspirations. In terms of territory the "lost provinces," to be sure, were recovered. In the Near East the Republic secured control of Syria and the Lebanon; and in Africa, of portions of the Togoland and Cameroons, but only as "mandated territories" under the terms of the compromise between Wilsonian idealism and the Allied designs of aggrandizement.[1] Many French leaders, including Clemenceau, Poincaré, and Foch had insisted upon the strategic necessity to France of the Rhine frontier. The Rhine had for centuries been regarded as the "natural" frontier which France must secure in order to feel safe from a German attack.[2] In February of 1917 a Franco-Russian agreement had envisaged the creation of an autonomous Rhineland State under French protection and military occupation, but at the Peace Conference this project had failed of adoption because of British and American opposition. In return for an Anglo-French-American security pact, Clemenceau had finally agreed to a compromise under which the Rhineland would be demilitarized and remain under Allied military occupation for a period of fifteen years. When the *quid pro quo* of the security agreement failed to materialize, as a result of American isolationism and British reluctance to accept military commitments on the continent, there were many French leaders who felt that the nation had been tricked.[3] Even the rich coal region of the Saar Valley, which the French Government had demanded in compensation for the destruction of the mines of northern France, was not transferred to the Republic, but merely internationalized, subject to a plebiscite and a German right of repurchase of the mines in 1935. In all of these respects, the settlement failed to realize French hopes—so much so that President Poincaré, who had regarded the armistice as premature and had insisted upon the invasion of Germany, used all his influence against the terms drawn up by Clemenceau and the Cabinet and threatened to resign when the French representatives attached their signatures to the treaty. He finally decided, after consultation with Foch and the presidents of the Chambers, that it was his constitutional duty to remain in office and sign the treaty, since Parliament had approved it, despite his opposition to it.[4]

[1] *Cf.* Quincy Wright, *Mandates under the League of Nations*, Chicago, 1930.

[2] *Cf.* Philip Sagnac, *Le Rhin français pendant la révolution et l'empire*, Paris, 1917; R. Recouly, *La barrière du Rhin: droits et devoirs de la France pour assurer sa sécurité*, Paris, 1923; J. Aulneau, *Le Rhin et la France*, Paris, 1921; Travaux du Comité d'Etudes, *L'Alsace-Lorraine et la frontière du nord-est*, Paris, 1918. For an interesting presentation of the view that under modern conditions of warfare forests, rather than rivers, are the best national defenses, see the address of M. Margaine before the Chamber of Deputies on May 22, 1923, *J.O.Ch.*, May 23, 1923.

[3] *Cf.* address of Maurice Barrès, Deputy and president of the League of Patriots at the dedication of the statue of Paul Déroulède at Metz, October 16, 1921; Maurice Barrès, *La politique rhenane*, Paris, 1922, pp. 11–14; *Cf.* Henry T. Allen, Introduction, to *The Rhineland Occupation*, Indianapolis, 1927.

[4] L. Duguit, *Traité de droit constitutionnel*, IV, pp. 553–554; S. Huddleston, *Poincaré, A Biographical Portrait*, pp. 89–97.

Once the treaty was signed and ratified, however, these regrets were put aside and the Government and the nation rallied to the cause of its effective execution. Despite its shortcomings, it constituted the legal instrument by which French hegemony over Germany was written into the public law of Europe and through which French "security," in the broadest sense of the term, could be guaranteed. Germany was indicted for having caused the war, disarmed on land and sea, saddled with a still indeterminate burden of reparation payments, economically crippled, and rendered politically helpless and strategically impotent. The Rhine was placed under Allied military occupation and France's allies in the conflict were pledged to cooperate in the enforcement of the treaty terms. The Covenant of the League of Nations, moreover, had been written into the treaties at Wilson's insistence and could perhaps be made to serve as the basis of international cooperation on a worldwide scale to preserve and safeguard the fruits of victory. Along with these guarantees, the Republic could rely upon its new alliances in Eastern Europe. Imperial Russia, unfortunately for the Quai d'Orsay, was gone and there could be only enmity between *bourgeois* France and the new proletarian dictatorship in Moscow. The Red régime had sanctioned Russian withdrawal from the war at Brest-Litovsk (March 3, 1918), had repudiated the nineteen billion franc debt owing to France, had published the secret treaties of the Tsarist Government, had confiscated the property of foreign investors along with that of the Russian nobility and *bourgeoisie*, and had summoned the workers of the world to revolt against capitalism and imperialism. With the support of conservative middle-class opinion throughout the country, the Cabinet and the Quai d'Orsay took the leadership in the imposition of the blockade and the intervention of 1918 to 1921, designed to overthrow the Soviet régime.[1] The effort failed. Communist Russia remained outside the pale and entered into the calculations of the Quai d'Orsay only as the potentially dangerous ally of a recalcitrant Germany and as a breeder of proletarian unrest throughout the world. The Dual Alliance was as incapable of resurrection as the Tsardom. But in the new Poland of Pilsudski and in the Little Entente countries of Czechoslovakia, Jugoslavia and Roumania[2] the Quai d'Orsay found warm friends and allies in the East, barriers to Bolshevism and to any restoration of the Hapsburgs or the Hohenzollerns and dedicated, like France herself, to the preservation of the *status quo*. These alignments, coupled with the war weariness of a bleeding world and

[1] For detailed figures of the Russian war debt to France, see *Rap. Budget, Ch.* 1925, No. 1961, p. 11, which gives 6,023,300,000 fr., out of a grand total of 15,133,074,000 fr. owing to France as a result of war and post-war loans. This figure, with interest and new advances to the White Armies in the Russian Civil War, was put at 7,389,202,217 fr. in 1927. *Cf. Rap. Budget, Ch.,* 1927, No. 4875. The private pre-war debt is estimated at about 11,300,000,000 fr. On French policy toward Soviet Russia, see Zaintchkovsky, Anders, Egoriev, *et al., Les Allies contre La Russie,* Delpeuch, Paris, 1929; Jean Xydias, *L'Intervention français en Russie,* 1918–1919, Paris, 1927; Frederick L. Schuman, *American Policy toward Russia since* 1917, Chaps. V–VIII, New York, 1928; Louis Fischer, *The Soviets in World Affairs,* Vol. I, *passim.* New York, 1930.

[2] *Cf.* John O. Crane, *The Little Entente,* The MacMillan Company, New York, 1931.

the cry for peace in all countries, meant that those responsible for French foreign policy could face the future with reasonable confidence in the adequacy of the Treaty of Versailles as a bulwark of French national interests in post-war Europe.

That the strict fulfilment of the letter of the treaty should be insisted upon by almost all French-opinion groups was a natural outcome of the circumstances which have been indicated. "Security" and "reparations" became the keynotes of French policy. Views might differ as to the means qo be adopted to achieve these objectives. There could be no division of ipinion regarding the objectives themselves. France must be permanently protected from the menace of future German invasion. France must be compensated, as far as possible, for the heavy burden of restoring her devastated departments. The two objectives are now conflicting, now in harmony, from one point of view irreconcilable, from another opposite facets of the same stone. "Security" depends upon the maintenance of the military preponderance of France and her allies over Germany, upon the permanent unilateral disarmament of Germany, upon the "moral" and "economic" disarmament of the Reich, upon the certainty of outside aid in the event of an attempt to upset the *status quo*. To a Poincaré, it requires the strict fulfilment of the treaty, plus a diminution of German economic strength and political unity as an additional safeguard. To a Briand, it requires the strict fulfilment of the treaty, plus close cooperation between the Allies and a reconciliation with Germany.[1] The payment of reparations, on the other hand, requires a restoration of German economic strength and prosperity, since no amount of pressure can produce returns from an economic vacuum. And yet, Germany becomes a threat to French security to the degree that she becomes economically strong. If by "reparations," payments in money and kind are meant to meet the needs of an almost bankrupt treasury, the necessary conditions of such payments are irreconcilable with the Poincaré version of security. If reparation claims, on the other hand, are pressed as a means of weakening Germany, politically and economically, they can be made to serve the cause of "security," but payments will not be forthcoming.

Post-war French foreign policy is intelligible only in terms of this paradox. No French statesman can accept either horn of the dilemma to the exclusion of the other, since, to the nation, security and reparations are equally important. No one can devise a program of attaining both, in a fashion not involving an apparent diminution of the one or the other which the nation, as yet, is unprepared to accept. Between 1920 and 1925 no French Premier dares to yield security in order to obtain reparations, nor to yield reparations in order to obtain security, since either policy will expose him to attack for surrendering French treaty rights or neglecting the vital interests

[1] See the interesting alternative theses regarding French Rhineland policy presented by Maurice Barrès and Albert Thomas during the debate on the ratification of the Treaty of Versailles, *J.O.Ch.*, August 30, 1919.

of the Republic. Neither can he attain both in the face of German recalcitrance and the inescapable facts of an economic order based upon national interdependence and a delicate coordination of international industry, commerce, and finance in production, distribution, and exchange. The problem is seemingly insoluble. With its far-reaching political and economic implications we are not here concerned. In the following pages an effort will be made to trace the development of French policy culminating in the occupation of the Ruhr in 1923 from the point of view of the domestic forces and influences operative at Paris.

2. VAE VICTIS

Among the numerous instances of economic dislocation resulting from the redrawing of frontiers by the Peace Conference on the basis of "self-determination," strategy, or political expediency, none was more striking than the disruption of the Western European steel industry as a consequence of the retrocession of Alsace-Lorraine to France. The following table of pig-iron and steel production, in thousands of tons, reveals the situation:[1]

State	Pig Iron			Steel		
	1913	1922	1924	1913	1922	1924
Germany	19,000	8,000	8,200	18,631	9,000	8,500
Great Britain	10,260	4,902	7,400	7,664	5,881	8,400
France	5,126	5,147	7,500	4,614	4,464	6,850
United States	30,653	26,851	31,000	31,301	33,603	37,800

One of the primary causes of the decline in German production was the political separation of the Lorraine iron-ore deposits from the coal basin of the Ruhr in which the German metallurgical industry is so heavily concentrated. The frontiers of 1871 had been drawn to include the major portion of the Lorraine ore fields within the boundaries of Germany, though the mistakes of Bismarck's geologists left over half the deposits in French territory. The balance, along with the coal mines of the Saar, became an indispensable adjunct to the whole Ruhr-Lorraine industrial system, with the Ruhr industrialists owning many of the mines and iron works of Lorraine. A few of the Ruhr and Saar mines, on the other hand, were owned by French ironmasters.[2] During the Great War, with Germany in possession not only of the Ruhr, the Saar, and Lorraine, but also of the coal mines of Belgium and most of those of northern France, the whole region, with all its rich industrial resources, became a more compact and highly organized economic unit than ever.

[1] Guy Greer, *The Ruhr-Lorraine Industrial Problem*, pp. 16–17, New York, 1925
[2] *Ibid.*, pp. 54–83.

This unity was completely shattered by the peace. The normal interchange of Ruhr coke and Lorraine iron ore came to a halt, despite efforts to continue it, as through the Luxembourg agreements of December 25, 1918. All of Lorraine, with its estimated iron ore reserve of 5,100,525,000 tons (about 47 per cent of the total iron ore reserves of the European continent) again became part of France, while the coal mines of the Saar also passed into French hands. In the east, Upper Silesia, with its mines and forges, was also cut off from German economy, at first by the institution of international control and later, in 1921, by the partition of the province between Germany and Poland on the basis of a plebiscite. It has been calculated that these territorial changes resulted in a loss to Germany of 26 per cent of her pit coal, 75 per cent of her iron ore, and 65 per cent of her zinc ore.[1] France, on the other hand, made a corresponding gain in the essential raw materials necessary for iron and steel production. The acquisition of Lorraine and the Saar increased the pig-iron production capacity of France from five to eleven million tons annually. In spite of the destruction during the war of many of the coal mines of northern France and the general coal shortage in Western Europe at the close of the conflict, the French metallurgical industries, represented by the *Comité des Forges*, could look forward to a profitable expansion of their activities. Two conditions were necessary, however, to reap the fruits of victory: an adequate supply of coal and coke, and export markets to absorb the surplus of production over domestic needs. The coke ovens of France, Lorraine, and the Saar had a maximum output of about six million tons annually, as compared with the thirteen million tons needed for the production of eleven million tons of pig iron. The French coal-mining interests, organized into the *Comité des Houillières de France*, were in a position to gain from this shortage in the coal and coke supply. But they could not supply the new demand. The balance could be secured most easily from the pre-war source of supply, the Ruhr Valley, either through reparations' payments, through special agreements between the French and German industrialists, or—through the forcible seizure and exploitation of the Ruhr mines by the French Government.[2] The further interest of the French metallurgists in hampering the activities of their German competitors in world markets is obvious. These considerations were factors of great importance in influencing the attitude of the French Government toward reparations and toward Franco-German relations.

The reparation provisions of the treaty were in part designed to meet the coal needs of the continental Allies. Article 236 required Germany to pay reparation in kind in the form of merchant shipping (Annex III), building materials and live stock (Annex IV), coal products, dyestuffs, and chemicals (Annex VI). Under the terms of Annex V, Germany agreed to

[1] *Cf. Current History*, May, 1924.

[2] *Cf.* article in *Clarté*, June 20, 1923, quoted in Cecil Street, *The Treachery of France*, pp. 92–98, London, 1924.

deliver to France seven million tons of coal annually for ten years, plus an additional quantity, not to exceed twenty million tons in any one year during the first five years, nor eight million tons in any one year during the succeeding five years, to make up for the difference between the production of the coal mines of the Nord and Pas de Calais and their pre-war production (Annex V, Article 2). Belgium was to receive eight million tons of coal annually for ten years (Annex V, Article 3). Italy thirty-four and one-half million tons over a period of five years, and eight and one-half million tons annually during the following five years (Article 4), and Luxembourg a quantity equal to its pre-war annual consumption of German coal (Article 5). Three tons of coke might be demanded in place of four tons of coal at the discretion of the Allied and Associated Governments (Article 7). For three years, Germany was to deliver annually to France 35,000 tons of benzol, 50,000 tons of coal tar, and 30,000 tons of ammonium sulphate (Article 8). The condition, time, and mode of delivery were left to the determination of the Reparation Commission, which might cancel or postpone deliveries if they seemed to interfere unduly with German industrial requirements (Article 10). The basis of payment for these commodities was indicated (Article 6) and all payments would of course be credited to Germany's reparation account.

These aspects of the reparation question were but one phase of a vast problem of enormous complexity. A discussion of the technical economic and financial aspects of the question as a whole would not be pertinent to the present study.[1] With the intricacies of foreign exchange and the difficulties of the taxation and transfer problems in Germany the French Government and French public opinion were not at first concerned. Germany must be made to pay the maximum sums obtainable. German offers in 1918 and 1919 to supply labor and materials for the direct reparation of war damage were rejected at Paris. Among these offers was a project for the restoration of the coal mines of northern France, which was discussed for a time by Loucheur, French Minister of Industrial Reconstruction, and the German Commission for Reconstruction.[2] The terms appeared unsatisfactory and economic nationalism dictated the employment of French labor by French contractors for this work. The necessary sums were charged in the national budget to "expenses recoverable in the execution of the peace treaty." Since payments in services were rejected and payments in kind were small, the bulk of payments must take a monetary form. The amount of the total remained to be determined. Since the peace was dictated and imposed by *force majeure*, it could be assumed, on the basis of all historical precedents, that the victim

[1] *Cf.* Moulton and Bass, *The Balance Sheet of Europe;* J. M. Keynes, *Economic Consequences of the Peace* and *A Revision of the Treaty;* Moulton and McGuire, *Germany's Capacity to Pay;* Angas, *Reparations, Trade, and Foreign Exchange* and *Germany and Her Debts;* Moulton, *The Reparation Plan,* etc., etc.

[2] Carl Bergmann, *The History of Reparations,* p. 25, London, 1927; *cf.* Loucheur's comments to the Senate on these proposals, *J.O.Sén.,* April 1, 1921.

would neglect no opportunity to evade payment, if this could be accomplished without exposing the country to new penalties and losses. This inevitable predisposition to evasion was fully appreciated at Paris—even to point of alarmist exaggeration—and constituted one of the basic assumptions of the French Government in dealing with Berlin. On the other hand, even if a will to pay were assumed, the question of capacity to pay remained. Just as the experiences of the past and the apparent insecurity of the present created in French nationalistic circles a propensity to underestimate German good faith in the execution of the treaty, so French war losses and the desperate needs of the French treasury created a propensity to overestimate the amount of money which could be extracted from the vanquished. The effects upon French policy of these tendencies will become apparent in the narrative which follows.[1]

The Treaty of Versailles came officially into force on January 10, 1920. As a result of agreements between the German Government, the German *Kohlensyndikat*, the largest organization of coal producers in the country, and Allied agents, deliveries of reparation coal had commenced in the preceding September and already amounted to 2,500,000 tons. On February 8, 1920, Millerand, Premier and Minister of Foreign Affairs, complained of the insufficiency of the German deliveries and two days later the Reparation Commission fixed future monthly deliveries at 2,234,000 tons. On March 31 the April quota was reduced to 1,440,000 tons in response to German protests and later the May, June, and July quotas were fixed respectively at 1,925,000, 2,062,000, and 2,175,000 tons. These figures were not attained in the actual deliveries and the Reparation Commission, presided over by Poincaré, was not disposed to listen sympathetically to German pleas of the impossibility of fulfilment. On May 29, the commission ordered an increase in deliveries of Upper Silesian coal to Poland from 200,000 tons to 450,000 tons per month, thereby reducing German receipts of coal from Upper Silesia. Pilsudski's invasion of the Ukraine had just been launched and France's eastern ally was desperately engaged in hostilities with Soviet Russia. The German Government challenged the commission's right to regulate coal deliveries from Upper Silesia and in retaliation ordered a 10,000-ton reduction in the daily deliveries of coal from the Ruhr. On July 30, 1920, the Reparation Commission informed the Allied Governments that Germany had voluntarily defaulted in her coal deliveries.[2]

[1] It should not be assumed that no one of authority in France was aware of the economic and financial difficulties in the way of reparation payments. French economists were as cognizant of them as their English and American colleagues, though of necessity less outspoken in their views which the state of public opinion rendered unpopular. M. Joseph Barthélemy presented to the Chamber of Deputies an excellent summary of the economic realities of the situation on February 21, 1922 (*cf. J.O.Ch.*, February 22, 1922). But in the French press and in French official circles all emphasis was placed upon the necessity of securing payments and upon the alleged bad faith of Germany in refusing them. In such an atmosphere the pleas of academic economists preaching sanity were voices in the wilderness.

[2] Bergmann, *op. cit.*, pp. 25-31.

Meanwhile steps had been taken to fix the total indebtedness of Germany. The treaty had contemplated that it should be fixed by the Reparation Commission itself. On May 19, Poincaré resigned as its chairman, being replaced by Louis Dubois, in protest against the decision of the interested Governments to deal with the question by independent negotiations. Germany had already been invited, on April 26, to a conference at which the whole problem should be discussed. At the same time the German Government was informed that it had not fulfilled its obligations, that further infractions of the treaty could not be tolerated, and that the Allied Governments were determined upon enforcement, even if this involved the occupation of additional German territory. The Ruhr Valley was not specifically mentioned, but isolated voices in the French Nationalist press were already mentioning this as among the possibilities. Germany was in the throes of civil disorder. The Kapp-Luttwitz *putsch* of the monarchists in March had been broken by a general strike, but had led to Communist uprisings in various parts of the country, including the Ruhr Valley. In the occupied Rhineland, various groups began agitating for the autonomy of the province and its separation from Prussia, a situation which led to the suspicion in Germany and England that the French Government was secretly supporting the separatist movement with a view toward fostering the political disintegration of the Reich.[1] In consequence of German troop movements to suppress the Red Army of the Ruhr workmen, French troops temporarily moved into Frankfurt and Darmstadt in April.[2] In this atmosphere, conversations continued between London, Paris, Brussels, and Rome in preparation for the forthcoming conference to which Germany had been invited. Between the British and French Governments sharp differences of views developed over the total amount of reparation to be demanded as well as over the division of the total among the Allies. Meetings took place at Hythe and Boulogne during May and June without agreement. Early in July, however, a tentative scale of partition was drawn up at Brussels and on July 5 the projected conference met at Spa.

The Spa Conference opened with a discussion of the disarmament of Germany and the proposed prosecution of "war criminals." Threats were made to occupy the Ruhr and other German territory if the military provisions of the treaty, limiting the German Army to 100,000 men, were not complied with. Following German explanations of the coal situation, Millerand challenged the good faith of Germany in the whole matter of reparations deliveries and Hugo Stinnes, the great German industrialist, waxed bitter over the "madness of the victors." The Allied Premiers at length offered to reduce coal deliveries to 2,000,000 tons per month and threatened to occupy the Ruhr when the Germans insisted upon a lower

---

[1] *Cf.* Jacques Bardoux, *De Paris à Spa*, pp. 259–265, Paris, 1921; and Jean Pange, *France et Allemagne*, pp. 9–24, Paris, 1928.

[2] *Cf.* H. T. Allen, *The Rhineland Occupation*, pp. 159–170.

figure. Stinnes favored defiance, arguing that even if the Ruhr were occupied the Allied forces would be compelled to withdraw empty-handed after a few months. But the German foreign minister, Dr. Simons, and his colleagues feared the economic and political effects of the coal famine which the occupation would cause in Germany and on July 16, 1920, signed the Spa Protocol, calling for 2,000,000 tons of coal monthly for six months. The German objection to a provision authorizing the Allies to occupy the Ruhr in the event of a default was met by a reservation to the agreement, and a delegation of the Reparation Commission was installed in Berlin to supervise coal deliveries. At the same time the Allied Premiers confirmed the Brussels scale of partition: France would receive 52 per cent of all reparation payments, Great Britain 22 per cent, Italy 10 per cent, Belgium 8 per cent, and all the other participants the remaining 8 per cent. No figures of total indebtedness were agreed upon or even discussed.[1]

It is clear from this summary of the early phases of the controversy that the Allied Premiers were disposed to dictate to Berlin rather than to negotiate, and that the occupation of the Ruhr Valley was mentioned from the beginning as a possible penalty to be imposed upon Germany in the event of defiance or a default of payments. Under the circumstances, the impression was created in France that large payments could be secured from Germany if only sufficient pressure were brought to bear and that the threat of occupying the Ruhr would suffice to break down German resistance. From August to October, Germany succeeded in delivering 2,000,000 tons of coal per month. From November to January the deliveries fell somewhat below the Spa schedule, but the Reparation Commission tacitly permitted a reduction of the monthly quota to 1,700,000 tons in view of the diminishing acuteness of the general coal shortage and the disturbances in Upper Silesia. In December, 1920, a conference of German and Allied experts met at Brussels to discuss German finances. The meeting reassembled at Paris in January of 1921 in the hope of arriving at an agreement as to the total German indebtedness. The French expert, M. Seydoux, proposed that Germany pay an annuity of three billion gold marks for five years, during which period the total should be fixed as soon as possible.[2] In the French press the view was generally taken that Germany's total indebtedness should not be fixed on the basis of present capacity to pay, determined at a time of German economic and financial prostration, but should be fixed later on the basis of potential capacity.[3] On instructions from Berlin, Herr Carl Bergmann discussed inconclusively the suggestion of a temporary settlement with Seydoux and Lord d'Abernon.

In the preceding September, Millerand had been elected President of the French Republic. Leygues succeeded him as Premier, only to be overthrown

[1] Bergmann, *op. cit.*, pp. 32–43; Bardoux, *op. cit., passim.*

[2] Bergmann, pp. 44–52.

[3] *Cf. Le Temps*, January 18, 1921.

and succeeded by Briand on January 16, 1921.[1] The latter, with the approval of the Chamber, was prepared to press for a provisional settlement in accordance with the recommendations of the Brussels experts made at Paris on January 18. But at the meeting of the Supreme Council on January 24, Lloyd George opposed Briand's plan and insisted upon a final settlement. In this he received a certain amount of sympathy from two of Briand's colleagues, Doumer, Minister of Finance, and Loucheur, Minister of the Liberated Regions, and also from the Belgian, Italian, and Japanese members of the council. As a result Briand was obliged to compromise and on January 29 the so-called Paris Resolutions were drawn up, ignoring the advice of the experts and reversing the position which the French Government had previously taken. They embodied a "final" settlement on the basis of a fixed scale of payments over a period of forty-two years, beginning at 2,000,000,000 gold marks and reaching 6,000,000,000 by the eleventh year, plus an additional annual payment equal to 12 per cent of the value of German exports. All foreign credit transactions of the Reich would be subject to the approval of the Reparation Commission which would also approve the appointment by the German Government of a General Receiver of Customs who would supervise the collection of German customs duties and hold the receipts as security for reparation payments. This plan was communicated by the Supreme Council to the German Government, which accepted the accompanying invitation to attend a conference in London at the end of February, despite the loud outcries against the Paris Resolutions in the German press, which, of course, provoked corresponding threats and alarms in the French press.[2]

The London Conference, which met on March 1, 1921, brought the first phase of the reparation controversy to a crisis. The German foreign minister, Dr. Simons, declared the Paris Resolutions unacceptable, asserted that Germany had already paid over 20,000,000,000 gold marks in cash, kind, and services, and suggested 30,000,000,000 marks as a proper total for the balance. At once Briand, Lloyd George, and almost the entire French and British press assailed the German offer as a challenge and a mockery of the Treaty of Versailles and demanded the imposition of penalties on the recalcitrant debtor. On March 3, Lloyd George informed the German delegation that it must accept the Paris Resolutions within four days or the Allies would occupy the towns of Duisburg, Ruhrort, and Düsseldorf (east of the Rhine, at the mouth of the Ruhr Valley), retain in Allied countries part of the purchase price of German imports, and establish a customs barrier between the occupied and the unoccupied regions of Germany. The threat was ineffective. At a private conference on March 5, Bergmann suggested a reversion to the suggestions of the Brussels experts for a provisional settlement, but Loucheur declared that the state of French public opinion made this impos-

---

[1] *J.O.Ch.*, January 17, 1921.
[2] Bergmann, pp. 53–58; J. Bardoux, *Lloyd George et la France*, pp. 149–174, Paris, 1923.

sible. Further German suggestions were rejected and the German delegation refused to accept any schedule of payments which it regarded as impossible of fulfilment. The conference ended in a rupture and on March 8 the threatened sanctions were put into effect. French and Belgian troops occupied the three towns mentioned and in France the class of 1919 was mobilized. The German contention that the 20,000,000,000 marks due, under the treaty, by May 1, 1921, had already been paid was rejected by the Reparation Commission, which, on March 15, demanded the payment of 1,000,000,000 gold marks in French, English, or American money within eight days and of 11,000,000,000 in addition within the next six weeks. When these payments were not forthcoming, the commission informed the Allied Governments that Germany had defaulted. On April 27, the commission completed its task of fixing the total German indebtedness—a function which had all but been taken out of its hands by the various unsuccessful efforts at a diplomatic agreement on the subject.[1]

The conclusions reached by the Reparation Commission were accepted by the Allied Governments and incorporated into the so-called London Schedule of May 5, 1921. They imposed upon Germany a total reparation debt of 132,000,000,000 gold marks (about $33,000,000,000). Germany was to be credited with the sums already paid, with the amounts which might be credited to the reparation account in respect of the value of German State property in ceded territory, and with any sums which might yet be received in reparation from Germany's former allies. The whole of the Belgian war debt, on the other hand, was to be added to this total. The commission decided that it had received from Germany thus far about 2,600,000,000 gold marks, a sum barely sufficient to pay the costs of the armies of occupation on the Rhine. The receipt of another 2,500,000,000 marks from Germany was acknowledged, including the Saar coal mines and the value of State property in territory ceded to the Allies, giving a total of somewhat more than 5,100,000,000 marks credited to Germany on reparation payments up to May 1, 1921. The Supreme Council met in London at the end of April and on the basis of the report of the Reparation Commission drew up the London Schedule of Payments which was presented to Berlin with an ultimatum threatening the occupation of the Ruhr unless Germany accepted the entire plan within six days. The German Government was called upon to deliver to the Reparation Commission 12,000,000,000 gold marks worth of "A" bonds by July 1, 1921; 38,000,000,000 in "B" bonds; and 82,000,000,000 in "C" bonds by November 1, 1921. Germany would pay annually 2,000,000,000 gold marks, plus 26 per cent of the value of German exports, until all the bonds should be redeemed. In the face of much opposition the Reichstag decided for acceptance by a small majority, and a new ministry, headed by Dr. Wirth, complied with the Allied ultimatum on May 11. The bonds were delivered on the dates specified and the required

[1] Bergmann, pp. 63–68.

initial payment of 1,000,000,000 gold marks within three months was effected by foreign borrowings, accompanied by an increasingly rapid depreciation of the currency within Germany and on the foreign exchanges.[1]

A period of comparative calm followed the acceptance of the London Schedule. The view of the situation taken by the Cabinet, the Parliament, the press, and the public in France was necessarily conditioned by the many months of diplomatic wrangling which have been reviewed. The economic and financial complexities of the problem, poorly understood at best by experts and professional economists, were in France and elsewhere beyond the ken of the great majority of journalists, parliamentarians, and ministers. These phases were difficult of simplification and dramatization and therefore beyond the sphere of public opinion. The political aspects of the situation, on the other hand, could be reduced to such simple, dramatic terms as to be intelligible to the veriest novice. To almost all Frenchmen, from the President of the Republic and the Premier down to the poorest shopkeeper, the most miserable artisan, and the most backward peasant, certain elementary "facts" were luminously clear: Germany had caused the war. Germany had inflicted grevious injuries upon *la Patrie* and all its children. Germany had been defeated and was pledged to make reparation. Germany was uninvaded, rich, populous, and prosperous, and was still dominated by the spirit of Prussian militarism. Germany was attempting to evade reparation payments and must be compelled to pay.

If Germany, encouraged by our patience, can treat in this fashion all the stipulations, all the most precise provisions of the Treaty, I must ask myself what remains of the obligations of Germany and of our legitimate hopes to see repaired the ruins of our unhappy provinces. No one is more disposed than I to maintain integrally our alliance and our friendship with those who have shed their blood along with ours on the fields of battle. I am disposed to do all—at least all that is honorable and worthy of France—to maintain this union which is still necessary at the present hour, and I hope with all my heart that it will be maintained and strengthened. But it is necessary that our allies and friends understand that such a situation is intolerable, that it cannot be prolonged. If we permit Germany to address to us veritable defiances—for they are defiances of the Treaty—nothing will remain tomorrow of the Treaty of Versailles, acquired so dearly at the cost of the blood of our children and the blood of our allies . . . [2]

In these words, enthusiastically applauded by the entire French Senate, the veteran statesman, Alexandre Ribot, expressed the view held everywhere in France with remarkable unanimity and strength of conviction. Briand fully shared this view, though insisting at all times upon the necessity of cooperation with the other allies in the solution of the problem. "I say that the problem is insoluble if France does not approach it with the will to resolve it in complete and cordial agreement with its allies."[3] In so far as this method involved concessions to the English point of view and a possible

[1] Bergmann, pp. 69–84; Bardoux, *op. cit.*, pp. 154–209, for a French nationalist view of the problem; Angas, *Reparations, Trade and Foreign Exchange*, pp. 15–22, containing Lloyd Georges' speech of May 5, 1921.

[2] *J.O.Sén.*, April 1, 1921.

[3] *J.O.Sén.*, April 7, 1921.

scaling down of French demands upon Germany, it exposed the Premier to criticism for excessive moderation and neglect of French interests.[1] His task as a diplomat, as he saw it, was to maintain Allied solidarity. His task as a parliamentarian, dictated by the exigencies of domestic politics and the temper of public opinion, was to convince the chambers and the country that this involved no diminution of French treaty rights and no toleration of German recalcitrance.

Success in the accomplishment of this double task became increasingly difficult in the autumn of 1921. For some months the enforcement of the London Schedule proceeded hopefully and the required reparation installments in money and in kind were made in full and on time, despite the continued fall of the mark and the growing financial embarrassment of the Reich. On October 1, the Rhine customs barrier and certain other sanctions of a commercial character were lifted. On October 6 and 7, Loucheur and Walter Rathenau signed the Wiesbaden Agreements to facilitate deliveries in kind to France on a basis which, after considerable argument and some modifications, was approved by the Reparation Commission the following March. But other straws in the wind pointed to future difficulties. During September and October the Committee on Guarantees created by the London Agreement met in Berlin and faced the prospect that the payments under the London Schedule might not be made in the months to come. In November, the Reparation Commission itself came to Berlin, considered the effects of the depreciation of the German currency, urged that the January and February maturities be paid without fail if serious consequences were to be avoided, and departed with somewhat futile admonitions to put the German budget in order and to cease increasing German note circulation.

These forebodings were reflected in renewed criticisms of Briand's policies in Parliament. In defense he could only dwell upon the difficulties of the transfer problem, deplore all tendencies toward Allied disunity, and insist upon the likelihood of German fulfilment in the face of a united Allied front. He felt obliged to answer the demands which were being made with growing vehemence for further sanctions in the form of the occupation of additional German territory. "I have said: 'If the ultimatum is not accepted, if the time limits fixed by the treaty expire without Germany having paid, without her having accepted the Allied terms of payment, we will make a new gesture of coercion and that will be the occupation of the Ruhr!'" But for France to occupy the Ruhr alone, against the wishes of the other Allies, would expose the Republic to diplomatic isolation, to worldwide criticism, to accusations of militarism entirely unjustified by her truly pacific intentions, lately manifested by the Government's acceptance of President Harding's invitation to participate in the Naval Disarmament Conference to be held in Washington.[2] Despite his arguments, suggestions were repeatedly

[1] Cf. J.O.Sén., April 7, 1921.
[2] J.O.Sén., October 28, 1921.

made in Parliament looking toward the occupation of more German territory as a means of pressure.[1] Briand returned hurriedly from the United States after the opening of the Washington Conference. Before a hostile Parliament, he defended his position, insisted that Germany would pay and was meeting the London Schedule, and threatened to resign if unilateral military action was insisted upon. "To-day, perhaps, the Government will fall. In that case, cause it to fall at once. But if it is to remain in office, grant it the necessary strength and authority!"[2] The Chambers refused to accept the challenge. Though numerous voices were raised in Parliament against Briand's position and in favor of further coercive measures, the majority seemed unwilling to take the initiative in overthrowing his Cabinet and precipitating the issue. The Senators and Deputies preferred that a change in policy should come from the executive rather than from the legislature, whose normal rôle in foreign affairs is to follow and criticize, but not to lead or to initiate.[3]

Meanwhile it became increasingly apparent that the London Schedule would not be met. Not only were the necessary sums not raised out of the German State budget, but the problem of transferring such sums as were raised into foreign currency defied solution. Efforts to secure an international loan failed and on December 14, 1921, the Chancellor notified the Reparation Commission that the German Government would be unable to secure the total amount of the installments falling due on January 15 and February 15, 1922. A moratorium was therefore requested. The commission expressed surprise and regret, while Rathenau sought to bargain directly with Lloyd George in London and the mark continued to decline.[4] The British Cabinet began considering the advisability of reducing the total cash payments for 1922 to 500,000,000 gold marks. On its suggestion a meeting of the Supreme Council was called at Cannes early in January, 1922, to consider the German request for a moratorium.[5]

The Cannes Conference produced a crisis at Paris and led to the fall of the Briand ministry under circumstances of unusual interest to the student of the control of foreign policy. Security and reparations remained more than ever the guides of the Quai d'Orsay. Briand was no less concerned with this double interest than the Right critics of his policies, but he felt that nothing could be gained on either score except through close cooperation between the Allies. But friction had developed between Paris and London at many points[6] and the opposition groups in Parliament and the press presented the Cabinet's

[1] Cf. J.O.Sén., December 7, 1921.

[2] J.O.Sén., December 7, 1921.

[3] Cf. comments of Joseph Barthélemy in address of December 19, 1929, Dotation Carnegie, Paris.

[4] The monthly average of the exchange rate was 62.5 marks to the dollar in January, 1921; 76.9 in July, 1921; 192.0 in January, 1922.

[5] Bergmann, pp. 99–112.

[6] Cf. A. Fabre-Luce, La crise des alliances, Paris, 1922.

supposedly Anglophile attitude as a sign of weakness, certain to endanger French security and to lead to new concessions to Germany. Early in December, Briand had proposed a conference of the British, French, and Italian foreign ministers at Paris to consider Anglo-French relations in general and to discuss terms of peace in the Near East with the Turks, who had torn up the Treaty of Sèvres and driven the Greeks out of Asia Minor.[1] Conversations followed on an Anglo-French Guarantee Pact or treaty of alliance and it was decided to discuss these proposals at Cannes.[2]

The conference opened on January 5, 1922. On its eve, Lloyd George dispatched to Briand a long memorandum, soliciting French cooperation in the reconstruction of Europe, recognizing the legitimacy of French insistence on reparation and security, and suggesting a renewal of the Entente of 1904 and a British guarantee of French soil against unprovoked German aggression. In return France would reduce her submarine forces and join Great Britain in a new conference at Genoa in seeking to restore normal trade relations between the European States, including Russia.[3] Briand replied that a unilateral guarantee, such as that proposed in 1919, was regarded as unsatisfactory by the French Government, which felt that the interests of peace could best be served by an offensive and defensive military alliance between the two countries.[4] Lloyd George insisted that British opinion would not sanction such an extensive commitment, but on January 11 presented a draft of a ten-year guaranty and consultative pact in accordance with the views he had already expressed.[5] The security issue thus dominated the conference at the outset, though, at Lloyd George's suggestion, a German delegation was invited to join in the reparations discussions. Rathenau arrived on the eleventh and was told by Loucheur and Sir Robert Horne that the position of the French Cabinet was precarious, that large concessions were impossible, and that nothing more than a one-year moratorium could be granted, with a reduction of cash payments for 1922 to 720,000,000 gold marks, plus deliveries in kind to the value of 1,450,000,000 gold marks. Rathenau, hoping for better terms, discussed German capacity to pay before the Reparation Commission, also meeting at Cannes, and on January 12 presented his views to the Supreme Council. In the midst of the debate news came from Paris of the fall of the French Cabinet and the conference was obliged to adjourn, throwing back upon the Reparation Commission once more the task of passing upon the German application for a moratorium. On January 13, the commission granted a provisional postponement of the installments due on January 15 and February 15, on condition that Germany deliver every ten days 31,000,000 gold marks and submit plans for the reform

[1] Briand to M. de Saint-Aulaire, French Ambassador in London, December 4, 1921, *L.J.Sécurité*, 1924, No. 17.

[2] Saint-Aulaire to Briand, December 14 and 31, 1921; *ibid.*, Nos. 18 and 19.

[3] Lloyd George to Briand, January 4, 1922; *ibid.*, No. 20.

[4] Briand to Lloyd George, January 8, 1922; *ibid.*, No. 21.

[5] Briand to the French Ambassadors Abroad, January 13, 1922, *ibid.*, No. 22.

of the budget and of note circulation. Payments for the balance of 1922 were left to later determination.[1]

At Paris, general hostility had developed in press and Parliament to the British attitude toward both reparations and security. It was felt in many quarters that Briand's participation in the discussions could lead only to new financial concessions to Germany and to increased military insecurity for the Republic. On Tuesday, January 10, Léon Daudet, Royalist and extreme Nationalist leader, accused the absent Premier of taking steps at Cannes contrary to his own declarations to the Chamber, as shown by his giving serious consideration to proposals for a 200,000,000 mark reduction in German payments for 1922, for the subordination of reparations to the economic reconstruction of Europe, and for "the admission of Lenin and Rathenau" to a new conference at Genoa. Daudet and his colleagues therefore demanded that the Chamber meet on the following day, Wednesday, instead of on Thursday, as originally planned. This suggestion was voted down, 312 to 199, but the large size of the minority was indicative of Briand's increasing unpopularity among the Deputies.[2] The Chamber Commission of Finance sent a message to the Premier, insisting that he consent to no new sacrifices and, on the eleventh, the ministers met under President Millerand to discuss the security proposals which Briand had sent from Cannes. The meeting had the appearance of a Cabinet Council called by the President to control the actions of the Premier, though Millerand denied that he had taken the initiative in convoking it and asserted, without contradiction, that it had been called by Briand himself *via* telegram.[3] On the same day the Senate Commission of Foreign Affairs, presided over by Poincaré, admonished the Premier not to conclude any accord with Lloyd George without the previous advice of Parliament.

On Thursday, January 12, Briand returned to Paris, conferred with the Cabinet, and went before the Chamber to defend his position. Raoul Peret, the newly reelected president of the Chamber, dealt with the general international situation of France, insisted upon a "reparatory peace with security, independence, and honor," and won the enthusiastic applause of all the Deputies by his implied criticisms of Briand's policies. The Premier was applauded only by the Left and extreme Left benches. Before a hostile Parliament, he appeared injured, depressed, disdainful. He sought to show that the criticisms which had been made were unjustified and that despite his insistence upon French collaboration with Great Britain no concessions had been made or would be made which could jeopardize French rights or interests. Anyone in his position, engaged in delicate negotiations with foreign Governments, had need of the support of the country. He could not continue his work if he was to be stabbed in the back. He felt that he did

[1] Bergmann, pp. 113*f.*
[2] *J.O.Ch.*, January 11, 1922.
[3] Address of Joseph Barthélemy at the Dotation Carnegie, December 12, 1929.

not have the confidence of the Chamber. Apparently on the spur of the moment, he decided to resign without permitting further discussion or waiting for a formal vote of confidence. "What I have done I have told you . . . Others may do better!" With that, he walked out of the hall, followed by his astonished colleagues in the ministry.[1]

Briand's resignation was at once interpreted in parliamentary and press circles as a result of his friction with President Millerand, who was supposed to have "recalled" the Premier from Cannes, exercised his "constitutional rights" over treaty making, and played a decisive rôle in foreign affairs in this fashion. The President's political sympathies were with the Right groups which had been most active in assailing Briand, and the whole situation, coupled with Millerand's personality, lent color to the theory that the titular chief executive had taken the initiative in repudiating the Cabinet and making the Premier's position untenable. Some attacked Millerand, others defended him. He and Briand remained silent and the controversy went on unabated. Seven years later, however, the former President denied that he had played the part attributed to him. "M. Aristide Briand was not recalled from Cannes by the Council of Ministers, nor by me, nor, that I know, by anyone."[2] It seems reasonably clear that Briand's resignation was in no sense forced by the Palais d'Élysée, though Briand resented Millerand's attitude and helped to force him out of the Presidency in 1924. Nor is there much reason to attribute it to opposition or obstruction on the part of the permanent staff at the Quai d'Orsay. The Premier simply felt that he lacked the confidence of the President, of his colleagues, and of public opinion, that the successful accomplishment of his diplomatic task was rendered impossible by this circumstance, and that his position in the future would be strengthened by stepping aside and transferring control to those whose conceptions of French interests, and of the best means of protecting them, seemed more popular at the moment than his own.

3. The Use of Force

Raymond Poincaré, pre-war Premier, war President, and post-war leader of militant French nationalism, became Premier and Minister of Foreign Affairs in the next Cabinet. Loucheur, author of the much criticized Wiesbaden Agreements, was dropped from the new slate. Barthou, Berard, Le Trocquer, Dior, and Maginot remained in the ministry, but their colleagues were picked with a view toward basing the Cabinet more definitely on the Right parties. The change, like most French Cabinet changes, did not signify a sharp break with the past, either in foreign or domestic policies. It signified rather the adoption of different methods in pursuit of the same general objectives—which, as has been indicated, were determined, here as always, less by parties and personalities than by the position of France in

[1] *J.O.Ch.*, January 13, 1922.
[2] Letter to Joseph Barthélemy, April 19, 1929.

the whole European situation. The new Government would strive to achieve security and reparation payments less by international cooperation, endless conferences, and perpetual concessions than by a vigorous and direct assertion of French rights and interests. The transition from Briand to Poincaré in 1922 would have the same effect upon Franco-German relations as the transition from Caillaux to Poincaré in 1911, except that the "enemy" across the Rhine was no longer a formidable military Power but a disarmed and helpless neighbor. Amid cries of "Down with war!" and "Long live Briand!" from the Left benches, the new Premier read his ministerial declaration on January 19:

Called by the President of the Republic to take power in a grave situation, the Cabinet which presents itself to you has no ambition other than to assure, in close collaboration with parliament, respect for the treaties which have fixed the conditions of peace. To define our program, we shall simply appropriate the good words which have been pronounced at the opening of your session by the president of the Senate and the president of the Chamber of Deputies . . . We can only be assured of saving French finances if Germany, to whose account we have already advanced so many billions, finally executes the engagements which she has undertaken and repairs the damage which she has caused. It would be the most scandalous of iniquities for a country which has had to submit to an inexcusable aggression and which had had ten of its departments ravaged by invasion, to be obliged, after the victory, to repair at its own expense the ruins which four years of war have accumulated on its territory and to make its own taxpayers support the burden of pensions and allotments due to the victims of the war, to the widows, to the orphans, to the discharged, to the wounded, to the families of civilians shot by the enemy . . . We demand only the payment of what is due us . . . Toward all our allies we have the constant preoccupation of employing only the language of moderation, of frankness, and of friendship, but we know that they will never resent our sustaining the interests of France with a courteous firmness, as they themselves sustain theirs. In this national task we can only succeed with the support of the Chambers. We make appeal to all among you who, feeling the gravity of the occasion, are ready to unite in respect for the laws of the Republic in order to safeguard the rights of France.[1]

In the discussion which ensued, Poincaré dwelt upon the necessity of guaranties and sanctions in connection with reparations and of perfect equality in any Anglo-French security pact. In the face of attacks from the extreme Left, he insisted upon French innocence in 1914, upon the imperative financial need of securing reparation payments in full, and upon the necessity of sanctions and penalties in case of default. It is noteworthy that the Left opposition speakers, with the exception of the Socialists, represented by Léon Blum, and of the Communists, represented by Marcel Cachin, found little to object to in Poincaré's views. Herriot, leader of the Radical Socialists, accepted as beyond discussion full enforcement of the treaty and full payment of reparations, urging only that a pacific and just solution of the problem be achieved by international action. This was, of course, Briand's position. At the end of the debate the Poincaré Cabinet was sustained by a vote of 434 to 85, with only the Socialists and the Communists voting in the opposition and the Radical Socialists abstaining.[2]

[1] *J.O.Ch.*, January 20, 1922.
[2] *Ibid.*

During the months which followed the Anglo-French security negotiations continued without success. Poincaré, even more than Briand, was opposed to any unilateral guarantee pact with Great Britain. He insisted upon a reciprocal alliance, implemented by a military convention and renewable at the end of thirty years.[1] Any German violation of Articles 42, 43, or 44 of the Treaty of Versailles, providing for the demilitarization of the Rhineland, would be treated as an act of aggression against both countries. Lord Curzon objected to any such clause and declared a military convention out of the question.[2] Desultory negotiations dragged on into the summer and then were discontinued without result.[3] Poincaré and the Quai d'Orsay were seeking British military aid in the event of future war with Germany. Since France would, at the outset, possess a great military preponderance over the disarmed enemy, the best defense against invasion would be a strategic offensive with British cooperation.[4] A mere guarantee pact against aggression would give no assurance of such cooperation. The British Government, on the other hand, sought to give France security against renewed invasion in order that French cooperation might be gained in efforts at European economic reconstruction. But here, as in the decade before 1914, it was unwilling to accept definite military commitments on the continent. The type of agreement which Poincaré proposed would pledge Great Britain to the indefinite maintenance of French military hegemony over Europe with no tangible *quid pro quo* which would render such an arrangement acceptable to British opinion. Under the existing circumstances no formula could be found to reconcile the divergent interests of the two parties. French "security" continued to depend upon French military power and upon the alliances in the east.

Meanwhile the reparations' controversy pursued its tortuous and troubled course. On January 14, a committee of Allied experts, meeting at Cannes, drew up a program for 1922, envisaging cash payments of 720,000,000 gold marks for the year, deliveries in kind to the value of 1,450,000,000 gold marks, a reduction of occupation costs to 220,000,000 gold marks, to be paid in future out of the deliveries in kind, and the control of German fiscal and financial legislation by the Reparation Commission's Committee of Guarantee. France was to receive the bulk of the deliveries in kind and 140,000,000 marks out of the cash payments from May 1, 1921, to the end of 1922, to cover occupation costs. Great Britain would receive 500,000,000 marks for the same purpose and the balance would go to Belgium. These proportions were accepted in the Interallied Financial Agreement of March 8, 1922. The German Government pressed for a reconsideration of the whole problem on

---

[1] *L.J.Sécurité*, 1924, No. 23, Poincaré to St. Aulaire, January 23, 1922.

[2] *Ibid.*, No. 24, St. Aulaire to Poincaré, January 26, 1922.

[3] *Ibid.*, Nos. 25–39.

[4] *Cf.* the illuminating debate in the Chamber on the army recruitment law, *J.O.Ch.*, March 11, 1922, in which the necessity for such tactics in the event of war was clearly set forth by the Minister of War, with no objection from the Deputies except on the extreme Left.

the ground that future payments could be assured only by long-term international credit operations, which, in turn, depended upon a restoration of confidence in German solvency—a contingency impossible of realization under pressure for large immediate payments. In the Reparation Commission the French delegates became increasingly hostile toward a moratorium, which they were disposed to grant only in return for "guarantees" in the form of extensive control of German finances by the Allied Governments. On March 21, the Reparation Commission, acting under the terms of the program indicated above, decided that Germany should pay 50,000,000 gold marks per month from May 15 to October 15 and installments of 60,000,000 gold marks on November 15 and December 15. Of the deliveries in kind, 950,000,000 marks should go to France and 500,000,000 marks to the other Allies. The German Government was ordered to impose new taxes and to put its budget in order to insure the raising of the necessary sums. On March 30, Chancellor Wirth attacked these decisions in the Reichstag, declaring the demands for new taxes impossible of acceptance and protesting, in the name of sovereignty and self-determination, against the proposals for control of German finances. Rathenau attributed these demands to the accession of Poincaré to power. The Reparation Commission was dismayed at this reaction to a decision which the British and Belgian members of the commission had almost wrested from their French colleagues, who at first had insisted upon the original London Schedule. In Paris, the German attitude naturally strengthened the prevalent suspicions of German bad faith and recalcitrance.

On April 10, 1922, the Genoa Conference opened.[1] At Poincaré's insistence all discussion of reparations was barred from the agenda, though the purpose of the conference was to discuss the general economic and financial conditions of the continent. This decision was due to Poincaré's own view that further discussion of reparations with a German delegation would be fruitless and to his realization that each new conference on the question increased the impatience and irritation of those of his followers in Parliament and the press who had attacked Briand for a similar policy and who were demanding vigorous measures to compel Germany to pay. Though most of the other Governments sent their Premiers or foreign ministers to Genoa, Poincaré remained in Paris and sent Barthou, Minister of Justice, to represent France. Despite the ban, unofficial and informal discussions of reparations took place, only to be rudely broken off with the signature, on April 16, of the Treaty of Rapallo by the heads of the German and Soviet delegations, Rathenau and Chicherin.[2] This agreement canceled all financial claims of the parties against one another and provided for the immediate resumption of diplomatic and consular relations. It was concluded behind the backs of the other delegates after the Germans had been excluded from the preliminary discussions between the Allies and the Russians, and after the latter had failed to

---

[1] *Cf.* J. Saxon Mills, *The Genoa Conference*, London, 1922.
[2] F. L. Schuman, *American Policy toward Russia since 1917*, pp. 217f.

reach any agreement regarding debts, claims, and counterclaims. Wirth and Rathenau feared that the Allied statesmen contemplated action under Article 116 of the Treaty of Versailles, which reserved all rights of Russia to reparation from Germany, and they therefore hastened to conclude an independent agreement which ended this danger. The news of this liaison of the outcasts threw the other delegates into an uproar. The Treaty of Rapallo was at once interpreted in Allied circles as a breach of faith, a fatal blow at the whole spirit of the conference, and a possible precursor of a Russian-German alliance against the Versailles Powers. French distrust of German honesty was greatly increased. All discussion of reparations ceased and the conference adjourned, empty-handed, after it had become apparent that an agreement between the Allied statesmen and the Soviet spokesmen was impossible.[1]

Under these circumstances an agreement regarding the terms of a moratorium became increasingly difficult of achievement. At the end of May an agreement was reached between the Reparation Commission and the German Government for a postponement of the London payments under the terms of the Cannes program. But the Loan Committee of the Reparation Commission, of which J. P. Morgan was a member, decided that the successful flotation of an international reparations' loan would be impossible without a rehabilitation of German credit and a definite settlement of the whole reparations question, fixing Germany's total indebtedness within the limits of German capacity to pay. The French member, M. Sargent, declared that this could not be discussed, since the French Government could consent to no reduction of its rights under the treaty and the London Schedule. Against the vote of Sargent, the committee decided to inquire into the scope of its competence from the Reparation Commission, which agreed, again against the vote of the French delegate, that the Loan Committee might study all conditions relevant to the issue of German foreign loans. When Poincaré intervened to make the dispute public and to instruct Sargent that no reduction of the French claims could be considered, the other members took the view that further discussion would be futile. The committee accordingly adjourned, after issuing a report, signed by all but the French member, declaring that no progress could be made without a definite settlement of the whole debt and reparation question on the basis of economic realities With the failure of this effort, the mark resumed its decline. At the same time Walter Rathenau was assassinated and the German Government lost its ablest leader.

On July 12, Berlin applied for a complete release from further cash payments during 1922, alleging that the desperate condition of German finances rendered such payments impossible during the current year and during 1923 and 1924 as well. Louis Dubois, French chairman of the Reparation Commission, refused to consider this request and was supported by Poincaré and the Paris press. The French Premier now adopted the plan originally suggested

[1] *Cf*. Bergmann, pp. 124–129.

by Seydoux—that of demanding "productive pledges" from Germany, in the form of the Ruhr coal mines, the national forests of the Rhineland, customs receipts in the occupied territory, etc.—except that in Poincaré's view these pledges were to be demanded not as a condition of a moratorium, but as a means of insuring continued payments.[1] At the London Conference of August, called by Lloyd George, Poincaré presented this program, which was unacceptable to Great Britain as well as to Germany and which caused the conference to adjourn without results. The Reparation Commission again took up the matter and finally, on August 31, resolved to defer a decision on the German request of July until it should have completed plans for the reform of German finances, for the issue of German internal and foreign loans, and "for the reduction of the burden of reparation, in so far as may be considered necessary in this connection." It agreed to accept, in lieu of the remaining payments for 1922, German treasury bills, payable in gold at the end of six months and guaranteed in such fashion as the German and Allied Governments might agree upon. This temporary respite was only a postponement of the issue for half a year and offered little promise for the future.[2]

In the light of these developments, the internal situation in France may be examined once more. The personal attitude of Poincaré toward Germany was a factor of major importance in shaping French policy. It was reinforced by the needs of the treasury and by considerations of political expediency. He could remain in office only so long as he reflected the views of his supporters and the temper of public opinion. Political leaders, journalists, industrialists, merchants, shopkeepers, taxpayers, peasants, artisans—all had been led to believe in the possibility of extracting large sums from Germany, all were insistent upon reparation payments, all were impatient with endless conferences and delays, all were demanding effective pressure upon Germany to insure the execution of the treaty. As leader and spokesman of these groups, Poincaré was under a practical compulsion of translating these feelings into concrete action. Like the fabled revolutionary agitator who was asked by a passer-by why he followed the mob to the barricade, he might say: "I must follow them. I am their leader!" Throughout the summer and fall, and with increasing frequency throughout 1923, he adopted the practice of making Sunday speeches in various parts of the country, assailing Germany for having caused the war and for seeking to cheat France of her just reparations. In his speech of August 21, 1922, delivered at his birthplace, Bar-le-Duc, Lorraine, he replied to the famous Balfour note of August 1 by insisting, as did the American State Department, that interallied debts, contracted in the common cause against the common enemy, could not be linked up in any way with Germany's obligation to pay damages for her war crimes. The bankruptcy of the German Government was a device to evade payment. France could relinquish none of her rights. A moratorium

[1] Bergmann, pp. 141–142.
[2] *Cf.* Bergmann, pp. 130–149.

could be considered only if specific guarantees were secured to insure payment from other sources. These speeches, all variations on the same theme, were always made available to correspondents in advance at the Quai d'Orsay and received wide circulation. All of them asserted that German resistance could be broken down and French rights safeguarded only by the seizure of "productive guarantees." This message, hammered home with almost monotonous reiteration,[1] was in accord with the basic prejudices and preconceptions of the overwhelming majority of French citizens and served to prepare French opinion for the inevitable sequel: the occupation of the Ruhr. The Ruhr became a catchword, a symbol, a magic panacea for all the ills the Republic had fallen heir to. Whether Poincaré sincerely believed that its seizure would be followed by reparation payments and by a satisfactory solution of the whole problem is perhaps questionable. But no statesman is a free agent and the French Premier was the slave of the opinion groups which supported him. Ultimately the political situation, coupled with the progressive breakdown of the London Schedule, left him no alternative but to carry out his threats and promises, for better or for worse.[2]

The forces which played upon him and pushed him along the course he had chosen are difficult to analyze and impossible to evaluate with any degree of precision. His political opponents in France and many foreign observers emphasized the influence of the French iron and steel magnates, represented in the *Comité des Forges*, and of the French mining interests, represented in the *Comité des Houillières de France*. Poincaré's policy was interpreted as one of economic imperialism, dictated less by considerations of national welfare than by these private business interests. As early as March of 1922 it was suggested in the Senate that a commission of bankers and industrialists be created to compel Germany to pay, under penalty of a capital levy on their own wealth and war profits. The Government must assist by occupying the Ruhr and destroying the economic unity of Germany.[3] The Stinnes-Lubersac agreement was assailed by the Left as a "monstrous and infamous alliance against the French war victims and against the workers of German industry," on the part of the *Bloc National*, the French industrialists, and the capitalists of Germany.[4] To the Communists it was clear that the occupation of the Ruhr was designed to enrich the French *bourgeoisie*, with the connivance

[1] See, for examples, his speeches of May 10, 1923, at Vichy; July 15, 1923, at Senlis; August 12, 1923, at Marville; September 9, 1923, at Damvillers; October 1, 1923, at Bar-le-Duc; October 7, 1923, at Ligny en Barrois; October 28, 1923, at Sampigny, etc., in R. Mortier et G. Roussel (ed.), *La Politique française en* 1923, pp. 31–85, Paris, 1924. Most of these addressed were dedication speeches to monuments to the war dead.

[2] *Cf.* Bergmann, pp. 148*f.*; Huddleston, *Poincaré*, pp. 157–161.

[3] Proposal of the Left Senator, M. Gaudin de Villaine, *J.O.Sén.*, March 28, 1922. He suggested that the Minister of Finance form such a group, composed of the Rothschild banking interests, the *Comité des Forges*, the Mirabeau Bank, the Creusot metallurgical interests, the *Banque de Paris et des Pays-Bas*, the *Crédit Lyonnais*, the *Union des metallurgistes et des houillières*, etc.

[4] *J.O.Ch.*, October 14, 1922, address of M. Jules Uhry.

of their German counterparts, at the expense of the proletariat of both countries.[1] Even less radical Deputies were prepared to give a certain credence to the theory that the French steel magnates, lacking the coke and coal which could be secured only in the Ruhr, were controlling the Cabinet's actions in their own interests.[2] German coke deliveries had increased from 3,082,000 tons in 1921 to 4,302,000 tons in 1922, but still constituted less than half of the supply necessary to operate the French furnaces at full capacity. On the other hand, Germany, which had absorbed 26,000,000 tons of the iron ore of German Lorraine in 1913, took only 32,000 tons from French Lorraine in 1922, securing the balance from Austria, Sweden, and Spain.[3]

While the influence of powerful business groups upon governmental policies, in France as in other *bourgeois* States, is undoubtedly very great, no convincing evidence has yet been adduced, to the writer's knowledge, which would substantiate the view that the policy of the Quai d'Orsay in regard to reparations was dictated by the Lorraine ironmasters and steel producers or even approved by them with anything approaching unanimity. Some of them, to be sure, envisaged the occupation of the Ruhr as a means of securing the necessary coke and coal which had not been gained through reparation deliveries nor through private agreements with the German industrialists.[4] These groups looked forward to a profitable expansion of the French metallurgical industries at the expense of the German which would enable them to compete with Great Britain in foreign markets. The policy of the authorities of occupation during 1923 gave credence to the view that they were acting, in part at least, as the agents of this group of industrialists.[5] The ramifications of the influence and power of these interests in French politics and journalism are difficult to trace, but it is scarcely to be doubted that they were in a position to influence public opinion and certain members of the Cabinet very effectively. Most of the French industrialists, however, seem to have realized that while coke and coal shipments might be temporarily increased by the occupation of the Ruhr, no permanent gain to themselves could result from the political conflict and economic disorganization which would ensue. Some of them, such as Loucheur and Lubersac, had already found it possible to make mutually advantageous arrangements with the German Government and the German industrialists on the basis of compromise instead of coercion. Few of them anticipated greater gains from political and military pressure than from business collaboration. The interests and influence of these groups were an important contributing factor to

[1] *J.O.Ch.*, January 19, 1923, address of M. Marcel Cachin.

[2] *J.O.Ch.*, May 23, 1923, address of M. Margaine.

[3] *Clarté*, June 20, 1923.

[4] *Cf.* M. Georges Levy in *La Front Unique*, Brussels, November 18, 1923, quoted in Street, *The Treachery of France*, pp. 98–99.

[5] *Cf.* W. R. Heatley, "German Coal Deliveries under the Treaty of Versailles," *Fortnightly Review*, April, 1923.

the final decision, but they can scarcely be regarded as the single and decisive cause behind the resort to force.[1]

More important than these private economic interests were the needs of the treasury, the burdens upon French taxpayers of the costs of reconstructing the devastated regions, the constant expectation of reimbursement from Germany, and the perpetual and ubiquitous feeling of uncertainty and insecurity in the face of a traditional foe, still populous and powerful despite defeat in the Great War. These considerations dominated all discussion of the question in the French Parliament. The stakes of French diplomacy which were involved were predetermined by the general political and economic position of the Republic in the European State System. These goals and interests were accepted as legitimate by all sections of French opinion, from the Royalists on the extreme Right to the Communists on the extreme Left. Opinions differed only as to the means by which these objectives could be attained. Extreme Nationalists favored the seizure of German territory and the forcible destruction of the political and economic unity of the Reich by the French Army—with or without the cooperation of the other Allies—before the defeated foe could recover strength for a counter-revanche. Extreme Socialists and Communists favored international proletarian revolution to overthrow the bourgeoisie of both countries, demolish capitalism, nationalism, and militarism at a blow, and thus prepare the way for pacific collaboration between the workers of the world in assuring peace and repairing the damage of war. Between these extremes all shades of opinion could be found. The great majority of Deputies and Senators were content to follow Poincaré's leadership and to support his policy of demanding "productive guarantees" to insure future reparation payments. If payments were not forthcoming, France would at least have secured a stranglehold on the economic life of Germany— "main au collet" in the popular phrase— and would presumably have gained military security if not monetary indemnification for war losses. Poincaré's personal predilections and past experience disposed him to favor strong executive leadership, with a minimum of contact with Parliament. He would not permit his hand to be forced by the Chambers, nor were they likely to insist on taking the initiative. On the other hand, he must safeguard the Government's majority by taking into consideration the views of the various political groups and by winning public opinion to his side through speeches and the press. He accomplished this task with his usual political astuteness.

A survey of the more important developments in the Chambers will suffice to substantiate the foregoing generalizations. Opportunities for discussion of reparations and of foreign policy generally were offered by the Premier's statements to Parliament, by interpellations, by the submission of diplomatic agreements for ratification, by the presentation of the budget of the Quai d'Orsay for approval, and by the debate on the "Special Budget

[1] Cf. Greer, The Ruhr-Lorraine Industrial Problem, pp. 178–183.

of Expenses Recoverable in the Execution of the Peace Treaties." The costs of reconstructing the devastated regions had been borne by the flotation of "Bonds of National Defense," the interest and principal of which were to be paid out of reparations installments. These costs did not appear in the ordinary budget, nor yet in the extraordinary budget, which was balanced with difficulty out of the proceeds of new loans, but in a special category of expenditures, representing an enormous deficit in the event that the anticipated reparation payments were not forthcoming. By a law of April 17, 1919, the right of war victims to compensation by the French Government was expressly recognized "without prejudice of the right of the French State to recover the payments from the enemy."[1] This Special Budget for the year 1922 totalled 10,718,534,377 fr. in its final form as approved by the Senate, 301 to 151, on March 29, 1922; and accepted by the Chamber without a recorded vote on March 31.[2] This total included the expenses of the Rhineland occupation and 190,000,000 fr. in addition for the expense of mobilizing the class of 1919.[3] In the debates which preceded the voting of this sum, it was clear that the majority of the Senators and Deputies expected the Cabinet to do its part in compelling payment by Germany. A few parliamentarians with economic training were disposed to recognize the difficulty of the transfer problem,[4] but many more were concerned with German recalcitrance, and frankly demanded coercive measures. The occupation of the Ruhr and the separation of the Rhineland from the Reich were mentioned most frequently.[5] In the Senate, Henry Bérenger bitterly assailed the thesis of the British

[1] *Cf. J.O.Sén.*, March 28, 1922.

[2] *J.O.Sén.*, March 30, 1922; and *J.O.Ch.*, April 1, 1922.

[3] In the Chamber debate on this item M. Ernest Lafont declared that the costs of the occupation had absorbed most of what Germany had paid, that the presence of French troops in the Rhineland gave no assurance of future payments, and that these sums should therefore not be regarded as "recoverable" expenses. The Minister of Liberated Regions asserted that under the treaty they were a proper charge against Germany. The item was approved by the Chamber, 492 to 67, *J.O.Ch.*, March 8, 1922. In gold francs the total of the Special Budget would represent about $2,143,706,000. In the spring of 1922 the exchange value of the franc fluctuated around 0.08, which would give about $857,480,000 as the dollar value of the sum appropriated. Even were the Cannes schedules fully carried out and occupation costs reduced to 220,000,000 gold marks, a total balance in cash and kind of only 1,950,000,000 gold marks ($487,500,000) would remain, and this would be partitioned among all the Allies. The French reconstruction appropriations for the years immediately following the war were, of course, to be paid out of reparation installments over a long period of years, but the comparative figures of prospective receipts and appropriated expenditures for the year 1922 serve to explain the refusal of the French Cabinet and Parliament to consent to any further reduction of German payments.

[4] *Cf.* Address of M. Joseph Barthélemy, *J.O.Ch.*, February 22, 1922.

[5] *Cf.* Address of M. Elisée Frouin, *J.O.Ch.*, February 22, 1922, On February 23 a somewhat amusing debate took place in the Chamber as a result of the objections of M. Alexandre Varenne to the policy of the Government in encouraging French patronage of the Rhineland spas, to the detriment of the French watering places, as part of the program of fostering Rhineland separatism. Poincaré recognized the validity of the complaint and declared that in the future French expositions in the Rhineland would be established in different towns, not competing with the French spas. *J.O.Ch.*, February 24, 1922.

economist, John Maynard Keynes, and insisted that Germany must be compelled to pay.[1] The Minister of Finance, Lastyrie, denied that the economic crisis in Europe was due to reparation difficulties and that German payments contributed to English unemployment, insisting that "this question of reparations is for us a question of life or death!"[2] André Tardieu called upon the Premier to enforce the treaty in full—an objective with which Poincaré declared himself to be in full accord. In the debate on the army recruitment bill, many Deputies expressed their anxiety regarding a German war of revenge and indicated their conviction that France must maintain a powerful military force ready to take the offensive at the first hint of hostilities.[3] Only the Communists and a few other extreme Left Deputies criticized this conception of Franco-German relations.[4] Even the Socialists were opposed to any economies at the expense of national defense, though opposing the occupation of the Ruhr, suggesting the establishment of an international credit agency under the auspices of the League of Nations to handle reparation payments, and demanding a capital levy and steeply graduated income and inheritance taxes to balance the French budget.[5] The great majority of the Senators and Deputies, it was apparent, were prepared to support Poincaré wholeheartedly in opposing any reduction of the German debt and in threatening punitive sanctions in the event of a default. "I should like to believe," he declared, "that the attitude of Germany will not push us to this extremity, but we are ready to use all our rights rather than not be paid. It is for us a question of salvation or ruin, I ought to say a question of life or death: France wishes to live, and she will live!"[6]

The autumn of the year brought new difficulties in the diplomatic realm and new German demand for a moratorium. The exchange value of the mark fell from 490.0 to the dollar in July, to 3,012.0 in October, and 7,353.0 in December.[7] Sir John Bradbury, British member of the Reparation Commission, sought in vain to devise a moratorium scheme acceptable to the Quai d'Orsay. Discord prevailed with the commission itself and even a trip to Berlin early in November was of no avail. On November 4, the German Government proposed international credit support for the mark and the summoning of a conference of financial experts to prepare plans for this

---

[1] *J.O.Sén.*, March 28, 1922; *Cf.* M. Guillaume Chastenet, *J.O.Sén.*, March 29, 1922; Louis Dausset, *J.O.Sén.*, March 30, 1922; François Albert, *J.O.Sén.*, June 30, 1922: "Ce n'est pas dans dix ans, dans vingt ans, qu'il faudra appliquer la méthode de l'occupation et de l'action militaire, c'est tout de suite! Allez à Berlin, ou alors vous n'irez jamais!" M. Dominique Delahaye, *J.O.Sén.*, June 30, 1922: "La marche sur la Ruhr et sur Berlin! . . . Vous ne pouvez aboutir que par l'emploi de la force!"

[2] *J.O.Ch.*, February 24, 1922.

[3] *Ibid.*, March 11, 1922.

[4] *Ibid.*, March 15, 1922.

[5] *Cf.*, address of M. Fourment, *J.O.Sén.*, March 29, 1922.

[6] *J.O.Sén.*, June 30, 1922.

[7] These are monthly averages from *U. S. Commerce Reports*. Wide fluctuations took place daily, the mark reaching 9000 to the dollar on November 8.

purpose. The Reparation Commission made no reply, but returned to Paris. On November 14, Berlin sent a supplementary note to the commission, asking to be relieved for three or four years of all payments under the treaty, except limited deliveries in kind, in return for which the German Government would issue internal and foreign bonds to balance the budget. This was accompanied by two reports on the stabilization of the mark, signed by J. M. Keynes, Gustav Cassel, Jeremiah Jenks, and Brand for the majority and by Vissering, Dubois, and Kamenka for the minority.[1] Again no reply was made, since a moratorium and the stabilization of the mark were inseparable from a reduction of the total German indebtedness, which the French Cabinet refused to consider. Poincaré's plans for a conference at Brussels to discuss both reparations and interallied debts were supported by Mussolini, who had just seized power in Italy, but opposed by Bonar Law, head of the new Conservative Cabinet in Great Britain. It was finally decided that a conference should be held in London. Meanwhile Poincaré decided to invite J. P. Morgan to come to Paris for a new bankers' conference, but when the American financier replied that all discussion would be fruitless, unless it were recognized that Germany must have a moratorium for several years, the matter was dropped.

The French Chambers had met in extraordinary session on October 12, 1922. The success of French policy in the Near East had enhanced the Government's prestige and Poincaré declared himself ready to discuss all interpellations. M. Margaine opened the discussion by declaring that during the parliamentary recess the defeat of the Greeks in Asia Minor by the Turkish Nationalists and the refusal of Germany to continue reparation payments had both had an adverse effect upon Anglo-French relations. The most important factor in the international situation, so far as France was concerned, was the persistence across the Rhine of Pan-Germanistic dreams of revenge. In view of this danger the great problem before the country was whether or not the Government's policy offered adequate security for the maintenance of the *status quo*. Margaine then launched into a general attack upon the Government's policy toward the disposition of the Saar coal and toward the import and export of steel, declaring that it was dictated by French capitalists and the *Comité des Forges*, contrary to the interests of French consumers.[2] In the debates which ensued, extending over several weeks, no less than thirty-seven interpellations were addressed to the Government Only a few of these related to foreign affairs, but these aroused most interest and led to the most extensive discussion. The Poincaré Cabinet was accused by the Left Deputies of endangering French security by alienating Great Britain, antagonizing Germany and Russia, constantly threatening Germany with military action but hesitating to act, and jeopardizing peace by its ineptitude.[3] The occupation of the Ruhr was discussed as a means of pressure

[1] *L.J.Demande de Moratorium, Conference, Londres, Paris*, Nos. 1 and 2, Paris, 1923.

[2] *J.O.Ch.*, October 13, 1922.

[3] *Ibid.*, address of M. Albert Favre.

on the German industrialists[1] and the Cabinet was alternately criticized by the Left for a policy of brutality and ruination toward Germany and assailed by the Right for tactics of bluff and weakness. On November 17, Poincaré explained the plan which he would present at the London Conference: France must keep her hands free and must act in accord with the Belgian if not with the British Government. The various proposals for private French and British participation in German industry must be rejected as impractical. The transfer problem was difficult, but a moratorium could be accorded only on condition of the seizure of productive guarantees. France would prefer the "tranquil and spontaneous execution" of the treaty, but it could not give up its right to resort to force in the face of German recalcitrance. "M. Loucheur," said the Premier, "declared the other day that if it ever became necessary to choose between our security and reparations, he would not hesitate: he would choose our security . . . If we are ever placed before this tragic choice, I also would choose our security without hesitation, but I do not wish to choose. For the rest, the guarantees which will assure our security are at this moment . . . the best guarantees of our reparations." Poincaré demanded the postponement of further discussion for one month and put the issue as a question of confidence. He was upheld, 418 to 70, with the Socialists and Communists in the opposition, and the Radical Socialists abstaining.[2]

The London Conference met December 9, 1922. The new Cuno Cabinet in Germany transmitted a plan for moratorium and the stabilization of the mark, coupled with a proposal for an international gold loan out of which reduced reparation payments should be continued. Bonar Law presented it to the conference and Poincaré moved its rejection as entirely unsatisfactory. A plan presented by Mussolini was likewise rejected. Poincaré insisted that the French Parliament would consent to no plan involving any reduction of the German indebtedness. He proposed the occupation of the Ruhr and the imposition of certain financial measures in the Ruhr and the Rhineland to compel Germany to make "serious propositions" and to insure their execution. The British and Italian Prime Ministers rejected this proposal and the conference ended on December 11 with a decision to reassemble in Paris on January 2.[3] On December 26, the Reparation Commission, on the basis of a French motion made October 20, declared unanimously that Germany had failed to make full deliveries of timber to France during 1922. Against the vote of the British member, it further declared that this constituted a voluntary default. On December 28, Barthou proposed that the same action be taken regarding coal deliveries.[4] Meanwhile the German Cabinet feverishly prepared new plans to be presented to the Paris Conference and it was apparent on all sides that a new and serious crisis was imminent.

---

[1] *Cf.* address of M. Paul Reynaud, *J.O.Ch.*, October 31, 1922.

[2] *J.O.Ch.*, November 18, 1922.

[3] *L.J.Demande de Moratorium*, etc., Nos. 3–6, pp. 23–73.

[4] Greer, *The Ruhr-Lorraine Industrial Problem*, pp. 292–301.

On December 15, Poincaré reported the results of the London Conference to the Chamber. He minimized Anglo-French differences and emphasized the desire of both Governments to reach an agreement. The Cabinet had not consented, and would not consent, to any unconditional reduction of German payments and it refused categorically to discuss any bargain involving a simultaneous consideration of war debts and reparations. Germany had the means of payment and had refused to pay. The sanction contemplated in Article 232 of the treaty must therefore be resorted to. But as regards their form, prudence dictated silence and caution for the time being. The Government demanded the support of the Chambers for the next conference.[1] Léon Daudet expressed himself as opposed to the occupation of the Ruhr on the ground that the preceding Cabinet, by its failure to compel the execution of the treaty, had rendered such a policy impractical. It would destroy the vestiges of Allied unity, leave France isolated, and provoke strikes and disturbances which would make the seizure of no productive value. Briand defended himself against the accusation and declared that he would support the Government in all its efforts to solve the problem in accord with the other Allies. A long and inconclusive discussion followed, in the course of which André Tardieu expressed his skepticism over the probable results of an occupation of the Ruhr and urged close collaboration with Great Britain in working out some alternative solution. New methods were needed. Poincaré replied by demanding an end of the discussion the same evening: "If you wish to change the method, you must change the Government." The debate withered away in wrangling over personalities and party politics. Five *ordres du jour* were presented. The first, proposed by the Socialists, censured the Government. The second, approving the acts and declarations of the Government, was withdrawn by its proposer in favor of the *ordre du jour* pure and simple. The remaining three expressed confidence in the Cabinet in various ways. When the Chamber finally voted closure of the debate, Poincaré demanded the *ordre du jour* pure and simple. It was approved, 486 to 66, with the Radical Socialists this time supporting the Government.[2] In the Senate debate of a week later, the Cabinet was supported by a unanimous vote.[3] No further discussion took place in either Chamber before the Paris Conference, except in connection with the debate on the budget of the Quai d'Orsay, marked by new attacks upon Prussian militarism and new demands for the occupation of the Ruhr.[4] The Government could thus proceed, secure in the support of all groups save the traditionally irreconcilable Socialists and Communists. With singular unanimity all other parties, with all shades of opinion, Right, Center, and Left, were prepared to stand behind the Cabinet in its determination to force a solution of the controversy which would protect the Republic's rights to reparations and security.

[1] *J.O.Ch.*, December 16, 1922.
[2] *Ibid.*
[3] *J.O.Sén.*, December 22, 1922; *cf.* November 9, 1922.
[4] *J.O.Ch.*, December 31, 1922.

The whole situation reveals clearly the inherent limitations of parliamentary control of foreign policy. The circumstances were favorable to the exercise of a large degree of control over the actions of the Cabinet by the Chambers. Notwithstanding his predilection for executive initiative and his disposition to chafe under all forms of parliamentary supervision, Poincaré, confident of his majority, was not especially reluctant to give the Chambers ample opportunity to discuss the problem, within the limits imposed by the diplomatic situation. Between the Cabinet and the great majority of parliamentarians there was complete agreement as to the goals to be pursued, the objectives to be attained. But as to methods all was confusion. The reparation controversy revolved about itself in what Briand called *une brume d'erreurs*. Discordant voices preached this, that, and the other solution. Here, as always, Parliament could criticize, it could demolish, it could overthrow, if it chose, but it could neither control nor construct. It must necessarily look to the ministry for leadership and direction. It had no other machinery for formulating policies or dealing with concrete situations. Its Commissions of Foreign Affairs could consult, advise, and admonish, but never initiate or execute. Many of the Deputies and Senators might distrust the Cabinet, but since none of them could offer any alternative plan or were prepared to assume responsibility themselves, they hesitated to overthrow it, just as they had hesitated to overthrow Briand. By the end of the year, the tension and anxiety had reached a point where decisive action was necessary, where any action would seem preferable to further discussion and procrastination. Parliament, anticipating action by the Cabinet, lent its support and permitted the Premier to dictate what form that action should take. Even the groups which opposed the occupation of the Ruhr voted to sustain in power the Cabinet which was certain to embark upon it. Poincaré was not forced into the occupation by Parliament. But his own tactics, his constant threats, his perpetual reiteration of the necessity of force had created a psychological situation in Parliament and in the nation which left him no avenue of retreat from a step which had thus become "inevitable."

The failure of the Paris Conference was almost a foregone conclusion. It met on January 2, 1923, at the Quai d'Orsay. It was in no sense a conference between the Allied Governments and Germany, since the latter's representative, Herr Bergmann, was given no opportunity to present his views, but one between the Allied Governments themselves. The conversations commenced with the acceptance of Poincaré's view that the hearing of the plan to be presented by Bergmann should be deferred. The French Premier declared that Herr Mayer, the German Ambassador, had asked him to receive Stinnes and Schriberg on the eve of the conference and that he had refused to consider this, as well as the further German suggestion, transmitted through the United States, of a Rhine security pact, which he regarded as "dangerous hypocrisy." Poincaré then presented to the delegates the reports of the Reparation Commission. Bonar Law asserted that British opinion had reacted unfavorably to French insistence on declaring Germany in default. After a brief exchange of sugared recriminations, Poincaré presented the French plan for the solution of the reparation problem. It permitted a reduction of the total of the London Schedule (132,000,000,000 gold marks) only if the Allies altered their share of the proceeds in favor of France or granted priority for the reconstruction of the devastated regions. Any moratorium must be partial, limited to two years, and subject to the following conditions: The establishment of an Interallied Coal Commission in Essen, under French chairmanship, to insure the continuation of coal deliveries; the Allied exploitation of the State forests of occupied Germany; the requisition of goods in the Rhineland and the Ruhr to make good any defaults; the seizure of customs receipts and the proceeds of the coal tax in the occupied area and the Ruhr, etc. Any defaults under this plan would be followed by the military occupation of Essen, Bochum, and such other parts of the Ruhr as Marshal Foch might designate, and by the drawing of a customs line east of the occupied territory. The Marquis della Toretta next presented the Italian scheme, which contemplated a reduction of German payments on condition of a corresponding reduction of the interallied debt to Great Britain and was as unacceptable to Bonar Laws as the French plan. The British proposal envisaged a reduction of the German debt to 50,000,000,000 gold marks, with a complete moratorium for four years, during which period the mark should be stabilized and German finances restored with the assistance of an Interallied Finance Committee in Berlin. Great Britain would cancel the war debts owing to her by the other Allies on condition of the waiving of Belgian priority in reparation payments and the forfeiture of the gold deposited in London during the war by the French and Italian Governments. These conditions were, of course, wholly unacceptable to the French, Belgian, and Italian delegates. Poincaré declared the British plan contrary to the Treaty of Versailles. Bonar Law opined that the French plan would completely destroy German credit and render all future reparation payments impossible. M. Theunis, the Belgian representative, took the same position as Poincaré. On January 4, the conference broke up in disagreement, amid polite expressions of regret and chagrin. A final note, submitted on January 7 to the Foreign Office by Ambassador Saint-Aulaire at Poincaré's instructions, made the disagreement complete.[1]

The breakup of the Paris Conference ended all hope of arriving at a new reparations' settlement by the method of interallied agreement. The diplomatic *impasse* confronted the French Premier with a desperate dilemma. To continue negotiations would be fruitless so long as the British and French Governments adhered to their irreconcilable positions and it would, moreover, expose Poincaré to the same charges of weakness which had under-

[1] For the details of these negotiations, see L.J. *Demande de Moratorium*, etc., pp. 74–199. A summary is given in Bergmann, pp. 163–169.

mined Briand a year before. To withdraw from the position he had taken would be a political impossibility and a surrender of diplomatic *amour propre* not to be contemplated. To adhere to it required immediate action of the kind that had been threatened and promised for so long as the ultimate solution of the whole problem and the final means of compelling Germany to pay. But the application of military sanctions against Germany, without the consent or cooperation of Great Britain, was a dangerous policy, bound to have far-reaching reverberations and by no means certain to have the results expected. Even Poincaré apparently hesitated, though he had decided upon the occupation at the time of the London Conference. But he was in a *cul-de-sac*, which had but one escape. According to one story, he conferred with President Millerand, who urged the occupation as a means of securing a constant supply of coal and coke for the Lorraine industrialists; and with the ardently nationalist Minister of Transport, M. Le Trocquer, who argued that the plan which had already been prepared for the French administration of the Ruhr under military protection was feasible and would lead to substantial reparation profits.[1] In any case, he decided to act forthwith.

Since foreign opinion could not be defied with impunity and since Poincaré had always championed the strict enforcement of the Treaty of Versailles, some means must be found of giving the projected occupation the appearance of legality. Paragraph 18 of Annex II of the reparations clauses offered an opportunity.[2] The occupation could be resorted to as a permissible sanction imposed upon Germany because of a voluntary default in payments, on the assumption, which was challenged in Germany, Great Britain, and the United States, that the phrase "such other measures" as used in the Annex included the occupation of additional German territory and that they might be resorted to by each of the "respective Governments" without a general agreement. The Reparation Commission had already declared Germany in default on timber deliveries. If a similar declaration could be secured regarding coal shipments, as Barthou had already proposed, the Cabinet's case would be greatly strengthened. The Reparation Commission accordingly met in Paris on January 9. Barthou, as chairman, pointed out that German coal deliveries had fallen below the specified quotas. Of 13,864,100 tons demanded during 1922, only 11,710,365 tons had been delivered, and some of this had been refused because of poor quality. Coal shipments throughout 1921 and 1922, in fact, were regularly below schedule, but few protests had been made since an oversupply of coal from Great Britain and from reparation sources had produced a decline of prices, to the detriment of French mine owners. But coke and coking-coal shipments were also below schedule and these products were indispensable to the Lorraine iron masters.[3] The German spokesmen pointed out that the deficit was small and alleged the physical

---

[1] Bergmann, p. 174.
[2] *Supra*, p. 254.
[3] *Cf.* Greer, *The Ruhr-Lorraine Industrial Problem*, pp. 120–176.

and financial impossibility of further deliveries, since Germany was already importing more coal from Great Britain than she was delivering in reparations. No discussion was permitted, however. Barthou emphasized the coke shortage and the resulting losses to the Lorraine metallurgical industry, and moved that Germany be declared in voluntary default. Sir John Bradbury presented counter arguments. Mr. Roland W. Boyden, unofficial American delegate, read a statement which accepted Barthou's legal reasoning, but declared that the conditions imposed by the treaty were impossible of fulfilment. It was received in silence. Barthou asked those in favor of declaring Germany in voluntary default to raise their right hands. He raised his own and was followed by Marquis Salvaga Raggi of Italy and M. Delacroix of Belgium. Sir John Bradbury voted in the negative. M. Barthou declared: "*La proposition est adoptée*." The decision was recorded and the commission adjourned.[1]

On January 10, the *Kohlensyndikat* moved its headquarters from Essen to Hamburg. On the same day, Poincaré requested the German Ambassador in Paris to inform his Government of the measures which the Government of the Republic "is compelled to take because of the lack of execution by Germany of the programs of the Reparation Commission concerning the deliveries of wood and coal to France. The measures in question are taken in virtue of Paragraph 18 of Annex II of Part VIII of the Treaty of Versailles; they do not imply, on the part of France, any thought of operations of a military order or of any occupation of a political character. I should be pleased to hope that the German Government will not impose any obstacles in the way of the execution of these measures which will be of a kind to aggravate them and, in consequence, render more difficult the task of the two Governments." Accompanying the note were three annexes in which it was stated that the French Government had decided to send into the Ruhr Valley a commission of control, composed of engineers, to supervise the operations of the *Kohlensyndikat* and insure the strict fulfilment of the program of deliveries. Military and political objectives were disclaimed and the German Government was asked to inform its local authorities of the powers of the commission of engineers and to facilitate its work. It purpose was "to insure respect by Germany of the obligations contained in the Treaty of Versailles." Troops would accompany the engineers only in sufficient numbers to protect the commission and guarantee the accomplishment of its task. German cooperation was expected, declared the communication. Coercion was threatened if it was not forthcoming. On January 11, 1923, French and Belgian troops entered the Ruhr and occupied its largest city, Essen. Bochum and Dortmund were occupied within a week. On the twelfth, the German Government withdrew its ambassador from Paris and its minister from Brussels, leaving *chargés d'affaires* in their places. It protested to the world against what it described as a military invasion in violation of

[1] *Ibid.*, pp. 295–301.

the Treaty of Versailles and announced its intention of refusing all further reparation payments until the illegal occupation of German territory should be terminated.[1]

4. EPILOGUE

The valley of the Ruhr is the most highly industrialized area of its size (3,400 square kilometers) on the European continent. Its mines and furnaces comprise the very heart of German industry. Its population exceeds 4,000,000, with fourteen towns with over 100,000 inhabitants each, Essen, Düsseldorf Dortmund, and Duisburg leading the list.[2] Its forcible occupation constitutes the only instance in the history of the modern State System of the seizure of a portion of the European territory of one Great Power by the military forces of another, against the will of the population and of the local government, without hostilities resulting. Except for the physical disarmament and the diplomatic isolation of Germany on the one hand and the overwhelming military preponderance of France on the other, war might have occurred in 1923. But since, under the circumstances, war would have been suicide, Germany could fight the "invader" only with such weapons as were available. A comprehensive policy of non-cooperation and "passive resistance" was embarked upon. All reparations deliveries in cash and kind to France and Belgium were discontinued and both workers and owners in the Ruhr were ordered to sabotage the occupation. The French and Belgian commanders responded with repressive measures which led to riots and acts of violence and gave the whole operation a military character. While the economic life of Germany became progressively paralyzed and the costs of passive resistance gradually pushed the German treasury into bankruptcy and the mark into oblivion, the British Government held aloof and the American Government withdrew all its troops of occupation from the Rhineland by the end of January. In the press of the world the occupation was either defended as a just and legitimate means of compelling Germany to pay or attacked as an outrageous violation of the treaty, certain to lead to catastrophe. In the Ruhr itself the occupying forces extended their control, took over the management of the railways and the local administration, and attempted to operate certain of the mines and factories. Scores of German civilians were killed in the sporadic clashes which were constantly taking place and tens of thousands were imprisoned or expelled from their homes for disobedience to orders.[3]

[1] For documents, see *Der französisch-belgische Einmarsch in das Ruhrgebiet*, Berlin, 1923 (56 pp.).

[2] *Cf.* L. Coupaye, *La Ruhr et l'Allemagne*, Paris, 1922; R. Recouly, *La Ruhr*, Paris, 1923.

[3] *Cf.* H. T. Allen, *The Rhineland Occupation*, pp. 266–295; Bulletins of the "British Bureau of Ruhr Information," headed by Oswald Mosley, beginning August 8, 1923, ending June 25, 1924, and presenting the views of the British Labour Party; *Die Verträge über Besetzung und Räumung des Rheinlandes und die Ordonnanzen der interalliierten Rheinlandsoberkommission in Coblenz* and *Die politischen Ordonnanzen der Rheinlandsoberkommission und ihre Anwendung in den Jahren* 1920–1924, Carl Heymanns, Berlin, 1925, both issued by the Reichsministerium für die besetzten Gebiete. For a

The details of these consequences of the occupation are not directly relevant to a consideration of the control of French policy. It will suffice to note the effect of the occupation within France. As in wartime, the nation rallied as a unit to the support of the Government. The heritage of hate in Franco-German relations, the universal fear of renewed German aggression, the general distrust of German good faith, all combined to condition the basic attitudes and predispositions of politically minded Frenchmen in such a way that the issue appeared a very simple one: *La Patrie vs.* the hereditary foe. The small Right minority of extreme nationalists and chauvinists hailed the occupation as the precursor of the destruction of Germany and the permanent annexation of the occupied regions. The great majority of *bourgeois* patriots regarded it as a necessary means of compelling Germany to pay reparations and of safeguarding the security of the Republic. A Left group, represented by the Radical Socialists and Socialists, regarded the occupation as a mistake, likely to alienate sympathy from France abroad and to destroy the source of future reparations' payments by disorganizing German economy. A small Left minority of extreme Socialists and Communists was irreconcilably opposed, in France as in Germany and everywhere, to all manifestations of what it regarded as *bourgeois* militarism and capitalistic greed. The protest of the Soviet Government at the occupation as an outrage against the international proletariat was indicative of the communist view. But in the Parliament, in the press, and, so far as can be judged, among the citizenry generally, those opposed to the occupation constituted a negligible minority without influence or power to obstruct Poincaré's policy. Everywhere in France patriotism dictated approval.[1]

Following the Christmas holidays the Chambers had reassembled on January 9, for the regular session of 1923. The first sitting was spent in organizing the two houses and despite the recognized imminence of the Ruhr occupation no mention of it was made in the public debates. In the Senate great applause greeted the reading of a letter from Léon Bourgeois, the absent president of that body, in which he expressed his warm approval of the policy of the Government in defending French rights and called upon his colleagues to unite in supporting the Cabinet. Except for this, the Government's foreign policy was not mentioned in any way. On the following day, January 10, the Chamber did not meet and the Senate engaged in a discussion of the relations between France and China. On Thursday, January 11, the occupation was already a *fait accompli* and both houses met in an atmosphere

---

propagandist account of acts of violence and atrocities which took place during the occupation see *Sammlung eidlicher Aussagen über Gewaltakte der französisch-belgischen Truppen im Ruhrgebiet*, 2 vols., Reichsdruckerei, Berlin, 1925. *Cf.* Tardieu's enumeration of acts of violence against the forces of occupation between January and May, *J.O.Ch.*, May 30, 1923. For a French view of the legality of the occupation see E. Poupard, *L'Occupation de la Ruhr et le droit des gens*, Paris, 1925.

[1] *Cf.* Henri Lichtenberger, *The Ruhr Conflict*, Carnegie Endowment for International Peace, Publication 19, 1923. *Cf.* Jacques Kayser, *Ruhr ou Plan Dawes?*, pp. 45–63, Paris, 1924.

suggestive of a war situation. The Premier was loudly cheered by the Deputies as soon as he appeared. The president of the Chamber, Raoul Peret, had scarcely said three words when he was interrupted by M. le Prevost de Launay who threw the entire house into an uproar by accusing the Communist leader, Marcel Cachin, of treason and by demanding his expulsion from the Chamber. Peret resumed his discourse, however, and made a patriotic appeal for national unity. Poincaré followed with a long exposition and defense of his policies. He concluded that the supervised delivery of coke and coal from the Ruhr and of wood from the German State forests would produce an annual income from the "productive guarantees" of about one billion gold marks. The Premier was wildly applauded by the Center and Right of the Chamber. The Left remained silent. Léon Blum, on behalf of the Socialists, demanded an immediate discussion of the various interpellations addressed to the Government and correctly interpreted the Premier's evasion of them as indicative of a desire to postpone consideration of them as long as possible. When he criticized the occupation of the Ruhr, he was assailed as a Jew and a traitor by Léon Daudet and the extreme Right, and the president, amid a tumult of attacks and recriminations, was obliged to suspend the session. The debate was resumed ten minutes later and Poincaré asked the postponement of all interpellations until the first Friday in February, by which time he hoped that the Chambers would have passed the budget. A scene of wild disorder followed, with the Communists and Royalists exchanging insults and accusations. Finally, by a vote of 452 to 72, the Deputies accepted the Premier's demand and thereby expressed their confidence in the Cabinet. Again, only the Socialists and Communists voted in the opposition, with most of the Radical Socialists abstaining.[1] Poincaré spoke before the more orderly and dignified upper house the same day and gained the confidence of the Senators without a formal vote.[2]

In accordance with these decisions no further debate on the Ruhr occupation took place in either Chamber during the balance of the month. Under date of January 10, however, the prosecuting attorney of the Paris Court of Appeals had presented a request for the suspension of the parliamentary immunities of Marcel Cachin in order that he might be proceeded against for having visited Essen on January 7 and for having attended a conference of the Communist International in Moscow in the preceding November for purposes alleged to be dangerous to the safety of the State. This request was certainly approved, if not instigated, by Poincaré and the Cabinet, doubtless with a view toward diverting public attention from the Ruhr occupation and stirring up against the Communists a storm of patriotic wrath which would inevitably strengthen the position of the ministry. Such tactics in times of crisis are familiar to all students of parliamentary procedure everywhere.

[1] *J.O.Ch.*, January 12, 1923.
[2] *J.O.Sén.*, January 12, 1923.

On January 18, the Chamber commission charged with examining the request reported favorably upon it. Cachin declared that the French Communist party assumed collective responsibility for his acts and those of his colleagues. He defended himself ably, exposing the inaccuracies in the charges and asserting that the process was motivated entirely by the opposition of the Communists to the Ruhr occupation. In a long, bitter, and tumultuous debate, marked by much disorder and several suspensions of the session, Cachin was defended by his comrades and by the Socialists, but the Deputies finally voted, 371 to 143, to suspend the immunities of the accused and to permit the prosecution to proceed. The Communists, Socialists and Radical Socialists this time combined against the Center and Right majority.[1] Cachin was accordingly arrested and imprisoned, pending his trial. On February 20, a Socialist resolution demanding his release was voted down, 337 to 176.[2] In the course of the trial it became apparent that the conspiracy charges rested in part upon falsified evidence. They were abandoned in favor of a criminal charge, which was in turn abandoned and Cachin was released and returned to the Chamber on May 8.[3] The incident is indicative of the degree to which the Ruhr conflict had introduced a war psychology into French political life.

Meanwhile the occupation itself had become a subject of increasingly acrimonious discussion in parliamentary circles, since it was clear that no immediately favorable results were forthcoming and that the seizure of "productive guarantees" had led to an expensive and unprotective war of attrition between the occupying forces and German passive resistance. On February 1, Poincaré demanded once more the adjournment of all interpellations on foreign policy. M. Lacotte declared that the Government was seeking to make dupes of the Deputies by confronting them with a forced choice between the partisans of law and order and the men with knives between their teeth (the Communists). He accused Poincaré of making only a pretense of action in the Ruhr, because of the exigencies of domestic politics, and of following Clemenceau's example of 1919 in seeking to cover up his own mistakes by imposing silence on the Parliament and the press. Herriot, on behalf of the Radical Socialists, condemned the occupation, but declared that out of considerations of patriotism his party would vote for the postponement of discussion. MM. Blum, Jean, and Lafont, for the Socialists, insisted upon an immediate debate, but the Deputies voted postponement *sine die*, 488 to 68, with only the Socialists and Communists in the opposition.[4] On February 15, the Chamber voted, 487 to 62, to approve a 400,000,000 fr. loan to Poland for military purposes and on the same day the question of the financial results of the Ruhr occupation was raised in the

[1] *J.O.Ch.*, January 19, 1923.
[2] *Ibid.*, February 21, 1923.
[3] *Ibid.*, May 9, 1923.
[4] *Ibid.*, February 2, 1923.

course of the debate on the renewal of the short-term treasury bonds. Again the Government triumphed, 477 to 71.[1]

In the various debates which ensued, the Government retained this large majority, with all the Center and Right parties solidly behind it, the Radical Socialists sometimes voting with the majority and sometimes abstaining, and only the Socialists and Communists consistently in the opposition. These were normal party alignments, quite apart from questions of foreign affairs, but the ability of the Cabinet to present the Ruhr issue in the patriotic guise of France *vs.* Germany unquestionably increased its majority in Parliament by giving opposition the appearance of treason to the nation. No incisive discussion of the Ruhr occupation took place for many months. Patriotism dictated approval in silence. Finally, on May 8, various demands for interpellations on the Ruhr again came up for consideration. Poincaré once more declared that an immediate discussion would be inopportune. He intimated that the debate on the budget of recoverable expenses would offer sufficient opportunity for an exchange of views. He made the issue a question of confidence and again triumphed, 487 to 71.[2] On May 22, however, a lengthy debate began on the credits demanded by the Government to meet the expenses of the Ruhr occupation. Louis Dubois, on behalf of the Government, defended the occupation in conventional terms and attempted to show that receipts had exceeded expenditures. He asked unanimous approval of the credits as a manifestation of national solidarity. Margaine suggested that the Ruhr occupation was, in effect, a continuation of the war which was futile and unproductive and must be brought to an end as soon as possible. The Premier, by his own admission before the Commission of Foreign Affairs, had made no adequate preparations for exploiting the Ruhr for fear of forewarning Germany of his plans. As a result no useful results had been attained and the Cabinet, as in wartime, took refuge in silence.[3] On the twenty-fourth, Vincent Auriol, for the Socialists, assailed the Government on similar grounds. Poincaré defended himself by new attacks upon Germany, accompanied by a lengthy reiteration of the old arguments, and by insisting that from a budgetary point of view the results of the occupation were quite satisfactory.[4] After further extensive discussion the credits, totalling 145,000,000 fr., were approved, 481 to 73.[5] The Senate gave its unanimous approval a month later.[6]

That the Poincaré Cabinet possessed the support of the overwhelming majority of the Deputies and Senators in its Ruhr policy is abundantly clear from this summary of the debates. The Premier's apparent anxiety to prevent discussion was due in part to the delicacy of the diplomatic situation and

[1] *Ibid.*, February 16, 1923.
[2] *Ibid.*, May 9, 1923.
[3] *Ibid.*, May 23, 1923.
[4] *Ibid.*, May 25, 1923.
[5] *Ibid.*, May 30, 1923.
[6] *J.O.Sén.*, June 30, 1923.

in part to his innate reluctance to share with Parliament as a whole the responsibility for the formulation and execution of policies. He was confronted with no necessity of deceiving Parliament as to his intentions, as was Ferry forty years previously, or of imposing a policy of military action upon a pacific and unresponsive public opinion. On the contrary, he was almost compelled to act as he did by the state of public and parliamentary sentiment. The action once taken could readily be presented in terms which appealed to all the emotions of ethnocentric nationalism and evoked all the stereotyped reactions associated with patriotic pride and loyalty to *la Patrie*. Patriotism was left no choice in a situation which resembled war. The occupation was, in fact, as Margaine had argued, a continuation of the war in a new form, except that the military action was taken under the cloak of the treaty and did not eventuate in armed hostilities because of the impotence of Germany. The unanimity with which all political groups and all classes of the population rallied to resist the invader in 1914 was paralleled by the almost equal degree of unanimity with which the nation supported the military and economic coercion of Germany in 1923 to compel the payment of reparations and guarantee French security. As soon as the issues involved were formulated in terms of the slogans and symbols of passionate patriotism, they ceased to be amenable to objective and logical treatment, involving the deliberate and reflective weighing of values and alternatives. In the heat of emotional nationalism, which reduces all international problems to simple terms of rectitude and villainy, a resort to force becomes the obvious solution of diplomatic difficulties when non-forcible measures fail to yield the desired results. The constitutional and administrative machinery for the handling of foreign affairs becomes the vehicle and instrument of a mass emotion which would doubtless translate itself into policy in much the same way under any scheme of control.

The ultimate consequences of the use of force in the reparations controversy are of small interest from the point of view of the present inquiry. They may be briefly summarized, however, by way of bringing down to date the narrative of a problem which has already had several "final" solutions, but which still remains unsolved at the time of writing. Since coal cannot be mined with bayonets nor factories and foundries operated profitably under the shadow of machine guns, the occupation of the Ruhr, coupled with German passive resistance, led to a substantial decrease in reparation receipts. The production of coal in the Ruhr district fell from a monthly average of 8,046 metric tons in 1922, to 1,564 metric tons in August of 1923. Coke production, which averaged 2,083 metric tons monthly during 1922, fell to 265 tons by September of 1923. During 1922 France, Belgium, Italy, and Luxembourg received approximately 18,062,00 tons of German coke and coal, while during 1923 they obtained only 7,626,000 tons.[1] The occupation was successful in disrupting the economic life of Germany but failed to

[1] Greer, *op. cit.*, pp. 194–201.

achieve for France either coal, reparation payments, or security. The mark declined from 14,285 to the dollar in January of 1923, to 2,950,000 in August, and 4,200,000,000,000 in December. The franc fell from 14.98 to the dollar in January of 1923, to 22.64 in February of 1924, while the index of French wholesale prices rose correspondingly.[1] Chancellor Cuno resigned in August, when it was clear that the continuation of passive resistance was financially impossible, and in September the policy of obstruction was officially abandoned by the Stresemann Cabinet. November brought the abortive Ludendorff-Hitler *putsch* in Munich, Stresemann's replacement by Marx, and the conclusion of a series of agreements between the Ruhr industrialists and the Micum (*Mission interalliée de controle des usines et des mines*). The end of the year left the French Government the "victor" in the sense that Germany was bankrupt and German resistance to the occupation was at an end. But the Poincaré Cabinet had achieved none of the tangible objectives which French opinion had been led to expect from the occupation. During the course of the year, goods and cash to the value of 1,621,310,000 Belgian fr. had been collected in the Ruhr and the Rhineland at a cost of 987,000,000 fr., leaving a net "profit" of 634,310,000 fr. (Belgian) or about 100,000,000 gold marks, of which 89,000,000 were owing to the United States for the still unpaid costs of the American army of occupation. Most of the balance went to Belgium because of her priority.[2] M. Lamoureux, of the Chamber Commission of Finance, estimated that the net deficit to the French treasury as a result of the occupation was 134,000,000 French fr.[3] Poincaré denied this, but the complexity of the budget and the juggling of the accounts make an accurate financial evaluation impossible. In any case, it was apparent that the proceeds of the occupation in cash and kind were not only far below the London Schedule, but were barely sufficient to pay expenses. Germany's capacity to make future payments had been obviously impaired. The imponderabilia of the situation, in terms of French security, German willingness to execute the treaty, the attitudes of other Governments, etc., were not such as to reassure even the most extreme of French nationalists. Under these circumstances a new departure at the Quai d'Orsay seemed not only expedient but imperative.[4]

Poincaré, in fact, had already lent an ear to overtures which seemed to promise a way out of the *impasse*. On May 2, 1923, the German Government had solicited from the Allied Governments a resumption of negotiations. Poincaré refused to consider it until passive resistance should be abandoned.[5] A new German offer of June 5 was also rejected as unsatisfactory and Anglo-French relations became more strained than ever as a result of unsuccessful

[1] *Cf. Ch. des Deps., Session Extraord. de* 1924, *Rapport, Commission des Finances*, No. 976.

[2] J. Kayser, *Ruhr ou Plan Dawes*, pp. 60–61.

[3] *Ibid.*, p. 61.

[4] The decline of Poincaré's majority in the Chamber is shown by the vote of confidence accorded him on February 7, 1924. The vote was 333 to 205. *J.O.Ch.*, February 8, 1924.

[5] *L.J. Documents relatifs aux notes allemandes des 2 mai et 5 juin*, 1924, Nos. 1–13.

efforts to agree upon a joint reply to Berlin.[1] In October the French Premier definitely refused to negotiate with the German Government, despite the cessation of passive resistance and the insistence of the British Foreign Office on new discussions looking toward a settlement. Finally, an acceptable formula for permitting a reconsideration of the whole problem was discovered in the suggestion which had been made by the American Secretary of State, Mr. Hughes, in December of 1922, for an international committee of experts. On October 26, Poincaré, in response to British inquiries, agreed to this procedure and on November 30 the Reparation Commission appointed two committees, the first, under the chairmanship of Charles G. Dawes of the United States, to consider means of balancing the German budget and stabilizing the currency; and the second, under Reginald McKenna of Great Britain, to discuss methods of estimating the amount of capital exported from Germany and of bringing it back.[2]

While the new Labor Cabinet of Ramsay MacDonald in Great Britain strove for a settlement and the committees began their work, Poincaré's parliamentary majority dissolved and on March 26, 1924, his Cabinet was overturned in the Chamber by a vote of 271 to 264.[3] He succeeded in constituting a new ministry, but the general elections on May 11 resulted in appreciable losses by the Center and Right parties which had supported him and corresponding gains by the Radical Socialists and other Left groups constituting the *Cartel des Gauches*. Meanwhile, On April 9, the committees of experts had issued their reports, which came to be known as the "Dawes Plan." Its complex technical details cannot be analyzed here. In order to avoid the appearance of a diplomatic rebuff for the Quai d'Orsay, it did not reduce the total German indebtedness, nor fix the number of annual payments, but provided that Germany should pay 1,000,000,000 gold marks during the first year following the adoption of the plan; 1,220,000,000, the second; 1,200,000,000, the third; 1,750,000,000, the fourth; and 2,500,000,000, the fifth and following years; plus an increment based upon an index of prosperity. These sums were to be raised out of taxes, railway bonds, and industrial debentures. A transfer committee would supervise the transference of the sums raised within Germany into foreign currency in such fashion as to safeguard the exchange rate and the stability of the German monetary system.[4] Poincaré resigned on June 1. President Millerand was forced out of office for alleged partisanship in the election and after various ministerial vicissitudes Edouard Herriot, leader of the Radical Socialists, formed a Left Cabinet on June 14. A new international conference met in London in July. On August 16, the experts' plan was officially adopted by all of the

[1] *Ibid.*, Nos. 17*ff.*

[2] Resolutions of the Reparation Commission of November 30, 1924; *cf.* Rufus C. Dawes, *The Dawes Plan in the Making*, Indianapolis, 1925, Appendix 2.

[3] *J.O.Ch.*, March 27, 1924.

[4] R. C. Dawes, *op. cit.*, pp. 299–509 for full texts of the reports.

interested Powers, on condition of the evacuation of the Ruhr within a year. Although Mr. Dawes, as chairman of the first committee, took pains to conciliate French opinion by presenting the Ruhr occupation as a step toward the solution of the problem, the new plan insisted upon the restoration of German economic and fiscal unity and the occupying forces were gradually withdrawn. The accords were approved by the Chamber, 336 to 204, on August 23, and by the Senate, 204 to 40, on August 26.[1]

The 1924 settlemént constituted the first move in the direction of removing the reparation problem from the sphere of international politics and power-and-prestige diplomacy into the realm of international economic and financial administration. By so doing it paved the way for the Briand-Stresemann period of Franco-German *rapprochement*, marked by the Locarno Agreements of 1925, the admission of Germany into the League of Nations in 1926, the formation of the Franco-German Steel Cartel, and the final complete evacuation of the Rhineland by Allied military forces on June 30, 1930. French financial solvency has been achieved through internal reforms, again under Poincaré's leadership, and through the stabilization of the franc in 1928 at 25.64 to the dollar. French security has been attained in a measure, at least temporarily, by international agreements providing for mutual assistance against aggression and by the renunciation by the Powers of war as an instrument of national policy in the Kellogg-Briand Pact of August 27, 1928. Meanwhile the Dawes Plan has been superseded by the Young Plan, signed on June 7, 1929, after arduous months of negotiations by a new committee of experts, headed by Owen D. Young of the United States, and intended to be a "complete and final" settlement of the reparations problem. Under its terms, Germany is required to pay fifty-nine annuities, derived from the taxes and railway revenues, gradually increasing from 1,707,900,000 gold marks in 1930–31 to 2,428,800,000 gold marks in 1965–66. Thereafter, Germany shall pay annuities of slightly more than 1,500,000,000 gold marks from 1966 to 1984, with three final payments, ending in 1988, totalling an additional 2,653,300,000 gold marks. Deliveries in kind, in decreasing amounts, are to terminate in ten years. The plan is to be administered by the new Bank for International Settlements which receives and distributes the payments. Germany recovers financial autonomy by the abolition of all the controls and guarantees provided for in the Dawes Plan, including the Transfer Committee, and by the imposition upon the German Government of full responsibility for making transfers into foreign currency, in which all payments are to be made. Germany may postpone transfers or payments for a period not exceeding two years, subject to investigation by a special advisory committee which shall report to the Bank and to the interested Governments. With slight modifications, the plan was approved by the representatives of the respective Governments at the Hague Conference of August, 1929, and incorporated into the Final Act, with its supplementary

[1] *J.O.Ch.*, August 24, 1924; *J.O.Sén.*, August 27, 1924.

agreements and annexes, signed at the Hague, January 20, 1930.[1] All future disputes are to be settled by arbitration and the reparations question is, at the time of writing, no longer a subject of acrimonious diplomatic controversy.

* * * * * *

While speculation regarding the future is always hazardous and is not directly germane to the present study, the opinion may be ventured that the reparations question is not likely, within the next decade, to become again the focus of Great Power politics, except as a phase of the broader problem of international debts in general. The world-wide financial crisis of 1931, which threatened the financial collapse of Central Europe along with the loss or partial default of the billions of dollars and pounds which have flowed into Germany from the financial centers of the United States and Great Britain since 1924, led President Hoover, on June 20, to propose a one year moratorium on reparations payments and inter-allied debts. The general acceptance of this program of palliation, despite French reluctance to acquiesce in its original terms, renders it entirely improbable that either the French or the American Governments will be able in the future to deal with reparations and inter-allied debts as separate problems. Neither does it seem likely that the Young Plan payments will be resumed in 1932 or in the following years. The successive credit crises in the summer of 1931, the steady fall of the world price level, the progressive paralysis of world trade, the abandonment by Great Britain of the gold standard, and the intensification of the world economic depression at the time of writing all render imperative a wholesale readjustment of international financial obligations during 1932. The French Government may be expected to make the most of its strong financial and military position for purposes of political bargaining, as it has already done in compelling the abandonment of the Austro-German customs-union project, but a new resort to violence is unlikely, except in the event of a repudiation of the Treaty of Versailles as a whole by the German Government. The devastated areas of France have been largely restored and the stability of the French Budget is no longer dependent upon German payments. Reparations are no longer for the French Government "a matter of life or death." While any French Cabinet would resist very vigorously any attempt on the part of Germany to repudiate her reparation obligations, even in such a crisis cooperative action on the part of the beneficiaries of the Treaty of Versailles would be more likely to be resorted to than another recourse to force on the part of the Quai d'Orsay.

[1] For full texts of the documents, see International Conciliation Pamphlets No. 253, October 1929, containing the report of the Committee of Experts, signed June 7, 1929, and No. 262, September, 1930, containing the Protocol and Annexes of August 31, 1929, the Final Act of January 20, 1930, the Agreements with Germany, Austria, Bulgaria, and Hungary, the Convention with Switzerland respecting the Bank for International Settlements, and the related annexes and arrangements.

At the same time, the broader issues of Franco-German relations remain sources of friction and the ultimate fate of reparations would seem to depend upon the outcome of future efforts at a *rapprochement*. Barring an entirely improbable reversal of German opinion and German foreign policy, such efforts appear unpromising so long as the military and political preponderance of France on the continent persists in a form which perpetuates the unilateral disarmament of Germany, the prohibition of the *Anschluss* or union between Germany and Austria, the maintenance of the present German-Polish frontiers, and the continued imposition upon Germany of a status of inferiority in power and prestige which German patriots regard as incompatible with the size, population, dignity, and honor of the Reich. On the other hand, the great majority of French patriots are likely to continue in the view that French "security" demands the maintenance of the existing territorial, military, and political *status quo*. Not even so conciliatory a statesman as Briand is disposed to consider any revision of the Treaty of Versailles nor to regard such assurances of peace as are contained in the League of Nations Covenant, the Locarno Treaties, the Kellogg-Briand Pact, etc., as adequate substitutes for the military preponderance of France and her eastern allies. Whether the French and German views can be pacifically reconciled remains to be seen. Much depends upon the outcome of the General Disarmament Conference of 1932, the disposition of the Saar Valley in 1935, the future of German relations with Poland, Czechoslovakia, and Austria, and the efficacy of the League machinery at Geneva for the pacific settlement of such disputes as may arise out of these matters. The course of future diplomatic developments is likely to be determined more by these problems than by any new developments in the reparations situation. Should French opinion become convinced that the interests of security can best be served by a partial acceptance of the German contentions and by a general political and territorial readjustment, the prospects of pacific Franco-German collaboration would be excellent. On the other hand, should the Quai d'Orsay, along with Poland and the Little Entente, remain obdurate in insisting upon the maintenance of the Versailles *status quo*, and should German opinion remain equally insistent upon treaty revision and become convinced that it is impossible of achievement through peaceful agreement, one may reasonably anticipate the secret or open rearming of Germany and the adoption by Berlin of a policy of seeking aid against the Versailles coalition from other malcontent States, such as Austria, Hungary, Bulgaria, Italy, and possibly the U.S.S.R. In the event of such realignment of the continental States into two hostile camps the prospects of permanent peace would obviously be jeopardized. The uncontrollable variables in the situation are too numerous to justify prediction at the time of writing as to which sequence of developments is most probable. It is enough to point out that the reparations problem has ceased to dominate the scene and to suggest that its future is inextricably bound up with the whole complex of continental politics.

The preceding analysis, it is hoped, clearly reveals the process by which French policy was formulated between 1919 and 1923 and the steps by which the decision to resort to force was reached. The post-war international situation translated the traditional power-and-prestige values of diplomacy into specific terms of Treaty enforcement, security, and reparations. The efforts of the Quai d'Orsay to achieve these goals were furthered by economic and financial considerations of a domestic character. Economic nationalism dictated the employment of French capital and labor in rapid reconstruction of the devastated areas. Financial pressure dictated payment of this expense out of loans which should be met from future German reparation payments. The national determination to compel Germany to assume this burden was strengthened by an almost hereditary animosity and suspicion of German designs, by the necessity of military "security," and by the economic interests of organized groups of politically influential industrialists. When payments were not forthcoming, force was resorted to. In the execution of this policy, all the constitutional organs for the conduct of foreign affairs worked in harmony, and the press and public opinion acquiesced. Patriots saw no reasonable alternative—until long after the step had been taken and its results had proved disappointing. The whole case would seem to justify the conclusion that when a diplomatic issue, however complex to the outside observer, can be presented in simple, dramatic terms of the political and economic interests of the nation *versus* those of the past and prospective enemy nation, when it can be shown to involve relationships of power in which a surrender or compromise obviously imperils the strength and prestige of the State, to the corresponding advantage of the other disputant, those who advocate a resort to force are easily able to put their policy into execution with the full and enthusiastic support of the great majority of the parties, groups, and classes controlling public opinion and expressing the national will.

PART III
THE DYNAMICS OF FOREIGN POLICY

CHAPTER XII

THE MAKING OF TREATIES

IN the preceding chapters an effort has been made to describe the agencies which exist within the governmental framework of the Third French Republic for the conduct of foreign affairs and to study the functioning of these agencies in the specific cases which have been examined. In the present and concluding portion of the inquiry, attention will be directed toward the procedures which have been developed in handling diplomatic problems. These procedures may be thought of as the more or less standardized and stereotyped patterns of action which the various constitutional and administrative agencies follow in dealing with foreign affairs. From the historical instances which have been studied, certain general conclusions emerge regarding the rôle of the various agencies and their interrelationship in operation. In this final section, these conclusions will be formulated with reference to the making of treaties, the waging of war, and the formulation of foreign policy generally. These broad categories would seem to cover the more important procedures through which French foreign affairs are directed and controlled.

1. NEGOTIATION

In the conduct of foreign affairs in any modern State, the process of treaty making is of fundamental importance since almost every phase of international relations is subject to written agreements between Governments and almost every international discussion is concluded sooner or later by a written understanding of one kind or another if it does not end in disagreement and a diplomatic rupture. In all of the cases examined in the preceding chapters, and in fact in every diplomatic episode in the history of France or of any other State, questions of the negotiation, the ratification, the interpretation, and the application of treaties are constantly recurring. Every loss or acquisition of territory receives formal expression in a treaty agreement, if the territory in question, as is almost always the case, is acquired from or ceded to another sovereign State or is partitioned as a result of international agreement. Every alliance, entente, or political understanding is necessarily embodied in written documents, defining the rights, interests, and obligations of the parties. Almost every resort to war, or to forcible measures short of war, involves questions of the interpretation or application of past treaties or the terms of proposed treaties or conventions regarding which the two parties are in dispute. In the present chapter an attempt will be made to analyze the process of treaty making as it has developed in the Third French Republic.

The French Constitution of 1875 vests in the executive branch of the Government exclusive control of the initiation and conduct of treaty negotiations. "The President of the Republic . . . names all of the civil and military officials . . . The envoys and ambassadors of foreign Powers are accredited to him."[1] "The President of the Republic negotiates and ratifies treaties. He gives cognizance of them to the Chambers as soon as the interest and the safety of the State permit."[2] The negotiation of international agreements, in France and elsewhere, is an executive function which could not, because of its nature, be exercised effectively by any other branch of the Government. The Constitution makes it clear that this power is vested in the President, acting through the ministry in accordance with the familiar constitutional requirement that all the President's acts must be countersigned.[3] In practice treaty negotiations are initiated and conducted by the Minister of Foreign Affairs or his subordinates and the Cabinet assumes collective responsibility to the Chambers for the result.

More specifically, the foreign minister, with or without the collaboration of the other members of the Cabinet, determines what States or Governments the Republic shall enter into diplomatic relations with; what matters shall constitute a subject of diplomatic negotiations; when, how, and by whom these negotiations shall be conducted; and what terms shall be accepted and embodied in agreements with other States. Neither in constitutional law nor in political practice does Parliament possess any direct control over questions of diplomatic recognition and the conduct of diplomatic negotiations. Diplomatic and consular appointments are not subject to legislative confirmation and Parliament's control over the budget of the Ministry of Foreign Affairs is not in practice used to control appointments, nor to determine to what foreign governments diplomatic and consular agents shall be sent.[4] Neither can Parliament determine whether diplomatic agents sent to

[1] Law of February 25, 1875, Article 3.

[2] Law of July 16, 1875, Article 8.

[3] The Constitution of the United States implies that the power of negotiating treaties shall be shared by the executive with the legislature, since the President is given power to make treaties, and to appoint ambassadors, public ministers, and consuls "by and with the advice and consent of the Senate" (Article II, Sec. 2, p. 2). In practice the "advice" of the Senate in treaty negotiations is given only at the time of "consent" in approving or disapproving ratification. Treaties are frequently negotiated, moreover, by special agents whose appointments are not submitted to the Senate for confirmation. Cf. Quincy Wright, The Control of American Foreign Relations, pp. 246–255, New York, 1922; and D. F. Fleming, The Treaty Veto of the American Senate, pp. 16–33, New York, 1930. The French Constitution does not admit of any interpretation which would give to either Chamber of Parliament a rôle in the making of treaties comparable to that which the American Senate has frequently claimed.

[4] Cf. S. R. Chow, Le contrôle parlementaire de la politique étrangère en Angleterre, en France, et aux États Unis, pp. 131–135, Paris, 1920. "Bref, le Parlement français, au point de vue constitutionnel, ne possède aucun droit de contrôle sur le pouvoir exécutif en ce que concerne la représentation extérieure" (p. 133).

Paris by a foreign State shall be received or refused reception. The initiation, the conduct, and the termination of diplomatic negotiations, as well as the personnel of the diplomatic service are questions for determination by the executive exclusively. Diplomatic recognition and the appointment and reception of diplomatic representatives are thus matters beyond the sphere of legislative action, unless Parliament (as it has never, in fact, done) chooses to resort to the extreme step of overturning the Cabinet in power as a means of exercising control in these fields.[1]

The question may next be raised as to whether Parliament can control the substance and the course of diplomatic negotiations, even if it is unable to determine with what governments they shall be carried on or through what agents. This question must also be answered in the negative, subject always, of course, to the qualification that the Chambers may turn the ministry out of office or make its position untenable and thereby modify or terminate particular diplomatic conversations.[2] This extreme measure, however, is scarcely an instrument through which the details of diplomatic conversations can be controlled by Parliament, though it may readily be used to guide the general foreign policy of the ministry, as will be shown below. Whatever control Parliament is able to exercise over treaty negotiations it normally exercises after the treaty has been signed and submitted for legislative approval.[3] Most authorities are agreed that Parliament may not surrender its constitutional power of approval by authorizing the Cabinet in advance to conclude a particular treaty, nor may it limit the government's freedom of action by specifying in advance what terms shall be incorporated in a particular treaty or what treaties shall be entered into with designated

[1] The Chambers may, of course, lay down general rules in statutory form governing the organization and recruitment of the foreign service. Cf. *supra*, pp. 40–45. But this power is not used to control diplomatic recognition and the personnel of particular embassies and legations. Parliament may pass resolutions recommending recognition of particular States or governments, but such action is not binding upon the Cabinet and would not ordinarily be taken if opposed by the Cabinet. No instance of this kind has come to the attention of the writer.

[2] The resignation of Briand in January, 1922, was due to parliamentary dissatisfaction with his attitude at the Cannes Conference (*supra*, pp. 269–272). Similarly, a new Cabinet may repudiate negotiations entered into by its predecessor, even though a draft treaty has already been signed (*supra*, pp. 82–83). On the other hand, when secret negotiations are in progress, they may easily be brought to a conclusion in accordance with the wishes of the Cabinet which initiated them, even after its overthrow by parliament (*supra*, pp. 95f.).

[3] The visit of the Chamber commission on international arbitration to London in 1903 is one of the few instances of action by a parliamentary committee which played a part in actual negotiations (*supra*, pp. 170f.). The Treaty of Frankfort of 1871 was negotiated by Thiers and Favre with the collaboration of a parliamentary commission of fifteen. On December 11, 1925, a resolution was introduced into the Chamber instructing the Government to engage at once in diplomatic negotiations with the Council of the League of Nations with a view toward giving up the French mandate over Syria. It was referred to the Commission of Foreign Affairs, but never reported out nor acted upon. The Government ignored it and it played no part in the stormy debates on the Syrian rebellion which ended on December 21, with the Cabinet upheld. *J.O.Ch.*, December 12 and 22, 1925.

foreign States.[1] This principle has repeatedly been insisted upon by ministers, parliamentarians, and constitutional lawyers, not merely as one which ought to guide Parliament because of considerations of political and administrative expediency but as one implicit in the very nature of the constitutional controls over foreign affairs.[2] To take a recent example, in the debates which preceded the fall of the Briand Cabinet on October 22, 1929, the Premier insisted, in his plea for a postponement of interpellations on foreign policy, that any parliamentary discussion of the reparation and debt negotiations then going on at The Hague would embarrass the Government diplomatically.[3] According to this view, which has been accepted in practice, with very few exceptions, throughout the history of the Third Republic, the Government alone is master of diplomatic negotiations and the Chambers may express their views only after they have been completed. In the instance mentioned, the Left Deputies, MM. Blum, Marin, and Montigny, presented the counter-thesis that since Parliament is ultimately responsible before the

[1] Cf. L. Michon, Les traités internationaux devant les chambres, pp. 208–221, Paris, 1901; H. Lefebvre, Du rôle réspectif du chef de l'état et des chambres dans les traités de commerce, pp. 120–146, Paris, 1910; P. Barisien, Le parlement et les traités, pp. 122–143, Paris, 1913. A law of December 29, 1891, authorized the Government to concede minimum tariff rates to certain countries under specified conditions. Some of the Deputies argued that this was an unconstitutional infringement upon the Cabinet's liberty of action. In practice, no Cabinet has ever regarded itself as bound by such limitations on its freedom to negotiate, nor has Parliament ever succeeded in compelling observance of such recommendations.

[2] At times the Chambers have transgressed upon the Cabinet's freedom of action in this respect by proferring advice or seeking to control the course of negotiations. For example, on January 23, and again on June 4, 1880, measures were introduced into the Chambers to limit the Government's discretion in the negotiation of commercial treaties. In both instances they were objected to and dropped on constitutional grounds. On March 21, and again on May 22, 1891, the Commission des Douanes of the Chamber of Deputies recognized that the establishment by law of a minimum tariff could not prevent the Cabinet from providing for lower rates by special international agreement. On April 3, 1919, M. Raynaud introduced into the Chamber a proposition inviting the Government to insist at the Peace Conference upon the complete disarmament of Germany. Both Déschanel, president of the Chamber, and Pichon, Minister of Foreign Affairs, took the view that such a proposal was unconstitutional and it was accordingly withdrawn. The same position was taken by the Senate Commission of Foreign Affairs in reporting on a proposal of April 17, 1919, regarding military guarantees in the treaty. The phraseology was changed from "réclame instamment du gouvernement" to "compte sur le gouvernement pour assuer." In this advisory form it received the unanimous approval of the upper Chamber. On July 8, 1895, the Chamber approved a resolution by which "La Chambre invite le gouvernement à négocier le plus tôt possible la conclusion d'un traité d'arbitrage entre la République Française et la République des États-Unis d'Amerique." No such treaty was concluded at the time. Since such resolutions may easily embarrass the Quai d'Orsay, they are usually frowned upon and seldom approved by Parliament. Cf. J.O.Ch., January 24, June 5, 1880; March 23, May 23, 1891; July 9, 1895; April 4, 1919; J.O.Sén., April 18, 1919. Cf. L. Duguit, Traité de droit constitutionnel, IV, pp. 795–798, Paris, 1924. Barisien, op. cit., pp. 6–7.

[3] Briand spoke as follows: "Lorsque les pourparlers seront terminés et les accords arrêtés, comme je l'ai promis, sous la réserve pleine et entière de la ratification du Parlement, vous serez alors libres de les discuter et de demander à leur sujet toutes explications que vous désirez obtenir. La voilà, la vraie interpellation. Mais discuter avant ce moment, là, c'est suspendre le mandat de confiance qui a été donné au Gouvernement . . . " J.O.Ch., October 23, 1929.

country for foreign policy, it is entitled to know its direction at all times and has a duty not only of control, but also, in Marin's phrase, of "orientation." On this occasion, the Chamber, contrary to past precedent, accepted the latter view and turned the Cabinet out, 287 to 277.[1] Ordinarily, however, Parliament itself recognizes the validity of the principle that it should intervene in the treaty process only after the conclusion of agreements and their submission for approval or disapproval. The degree to which the Cabinet takes Parliament into its confidence during the course of negotiations and the fullness and accuracy of its disclosures are matters for the determination of the Cabinet alone.[2]

Since it is clear, then, that for all practical purposes, the Cabinet initiates and directs the course of negotiations without interference or control from parliament, attention may next be turned to the actual processes of initiation and direction within the Cabinet. The flexibility of executive organization and procedure makes generalization difficult here, since, broadly speaking, each negotiation can be handled in such fashion and through such agents as circumstances render expedient. Certain uniformities of practice have developed, however. They may be dealt with first in terms of the direction of negotiations from Paris, and second, in terms of the field agents employed. The whole structure of the ministerial system is obviously based upon the assumption that the Minister of Foreign Affairs will assume personal responsibility for the initiation and conduct of negotiations with other States, just as each of his colleagues assumes responsibility in his particular sphere. The minister will work through the machinery provided for his use at the Quai d'Orsay and in the foreign service, while the Cabinet, under the leadership of the Premier, will assume collective responsibility before Parliament for the acts of its members. But the cases which have been analyzed make it apparent that the precise relationships between the Minister of Foreign Affairs, the Premier, and the other members of the Cabinet vary greatly with circumstances and personalities. Sometimes the Minister of Foreign Affairs is also Premier,[3] in which case he presides over his colleagues, seeks to harmonize their views, and directs the general policy of the entire Cabinet as well as of his own department. Even in this situation, the absence of the Premier may throw the burden of critical decisions on other ministers, as happened in 1914.[4] When the Premiership and the portfolio of foreign affairs are held by different persons, they may collaborate closely in directing the course of diplomatic negotiations or each may go his way with little

[1] *J.O.Ch.*, October 23, 1929; *cf.* comments of J. Barthélemy, lecture at Dotation Carnegie January 9, 1930.

[2] *Cf. supra*, Chaps. IV, VI, VII, VIII, *passim*.

[3] *Cf.* Appendix B, *infra*, pp. 427-431. Almost half of the total number of foreign ministers held the Premiership and the portfolio of the Quai d'Orsay simultaneously: Broglie, Waddington, Freycinet, Gambetta, Duclerc, Fallières, Ferry, Ribot, Casimir-Périer, Bourgeois, Rouvier, Poincaré, Doumergue, Viviani, Briand, Millerand, Leygues, and Herriot.

[4] *Supra*, pp. 216f.

cooperation between them. When a Minister of Foreign Affairs holds his post in many successive Cabinets, he is likely to enjoy a large degree of freedom of action with little control or direction by the Premier. Such was the position of Delcassé.[1] More recently Briand has become the "permanent" Minister of Foreign Affairs in many successive Cabinets, having held the office continuously from July, 1926, until the time of writing. If a diplomatic crisis emerges out of the minister's independent handling of negotiations, the Premier may intervene. If he disagrees with the minister, he may force him out of office[2] or the entire Cabinet may resign. On the other hand, the foreign minister may play a secondary rôle, with the Premier or even some other member of the Cabinet actually initiating and controlling negotiations. In the initiation of the Franco-Russian Alliance negotiations, the Premier, who was also Minister of War, dominated the scene with the foreign minister as a weak second.[3] The Minister of Marine,[4] the Minister of Finance,[5] the Ministers of Colonies, of Commerce, or of other departments may all have a hand in diplomatic negotiations in one way or another if a particular concatenation of circumstances and personalities does not concentrate power in the hands of one individual. In such cases, the Cabinet meetings may serve as a forum in which divergent views may be reconciled and a cooperative policy worked out under the Premier's direction, though instances are not lacking of continued disharmony between Cabinet members in dealing with negotiations.[6] The secrecy of Cabinet sessions makes it difficult to secure conclusive evidence of what takes place. Generally speaking, the initiation and direction of negotiations are controlled by the Minister of Foreign Affairs, subject to such control from, and collaboration with, the Premier and his colleagues as his personal and political relations with them require.

The rôle of the President of the Republic in the negotiation of treaties may be briefly described by saying that while his constitutional position ordinarily prevents him from exercising any direct control, he may nevertheless conduct himself in such fashion as to influence the course of diplomatic conversations.[7] If he is personally opposed to a particular treaty project or to the direction which the Minister of Foreign Affairs has taken in the course of negotiations, he may offer advice and admonitions, but he has no effective means at his disposal for obstructing a policy approved by the Cabinet.[8] If he steps outside the limits of his office to appeal to Parliament or to the public in opposition to the Government in power, he exposes himself to criticism on constitutional grounds and may even jeopardize his own con-

---

[1] *Supra*, pp. 160–184.

[2] *Cf.* Delcassé and Rouvier, *supra*, pp. 167–173.

[3] *Supra*, pp. 137–138.

[4] *Cf. supra*, pp. 109f.

[5] *Cf. supra*, pp. 139–140.

[6] *Cf. supra*, pp. 153f.

[7] On the general position of the President *cf.*, *supra*, pp. 18–20.

[8] *Cf.* Poincaré's attitude toward the Treaty of Versailles, *supra*, p. 256.

tinuation in office.[1] On the other hand, if he approves the course adopted by the Cabinet, he may, through a judicious exercise of his ceremonial functions and a careful use of his contacts with the public and with the heads of foreign States, do much to further the Cabinet's designs. The rôle of President Carnot in the formulation of the Dual Alliance and of President Loubet in the Anglo-French Entente are cases in point.[2] But, in general, the President's position gives him little opportunity to guide the action of the Cabinet in negotiating treaties. Here, as in other respects, he hunts rabbits and does not govern, though his influence over foreign affairs is somewhat greater than over matters of domestic concern.

Turning next to the field agents employed in negotiations, a great variety of alternatives is open to the Premier or foreign minister. Ordinarily he will utilize the services of the regular staff of the diplomatic corps, establishing contacts with foreign States either through the regularly accredited French diplomatic agents residing at the seat of the foreign Government or through the agents of that Government at Paris.[3] In the instances of treaty negotiations which have been analyzed in the preceding section this most obvious procedure has been the one most frequently employed.[4] The permanent officials at the Quai d'Orsay may likewise be designated to carry on negotiations. If he chooses, the Minister of Foreign Affairs may, of course, negotiate personally with foreign ambassadors or ministers or with the heads of foreign States, either at Paris or elsewhere.[5] The visits of Premier Laval and Minister Briand to London, Berlin and Washington in the summer and autumn of 1931 offer notable examples of this procedure. Such direct personal contacts have become more frequent in recent years and in the post-war period have been institutionalized in the Supreme Council and later in the Council of the League of Nations. The foreign minister is likely to participate directly in important international conferences, such as that at Paris in 1919, and in the regular meetings of the Council and Assembly of the League, though he may choose to have the Republic represented by diplomatic agents or by other persons designated by himself.[6] In the period of colonial expansion there were numerous instances of the Minister of Foreign Affairs naming consular rather than diplomatic representatives to conduct negotiations[7] or conducting negotiations in cooperation with the Ministers of War or Marine through military or naval commanders.[8] The foreign minister thus has the greatest possible latitude in his choice of instruments.

---

[1] Cf. the circumstances of Millerand's resignation, supra, p. 297.

[2] Supra, pp. 129f. and 167f.

[3] For examples, supra, pp. 58, 87f., 109f., 116f., 123, 141f., 163, 171, 193, etc.

[4] On the organization of the diplomatic service, cf. supra, pp. 40–45.

[5] Cf., supra, pp. 155–156, 174, 284, 286, etc.

[6] Poincaré sent the Minister of Justice to represent France at the Genoa Conference of 1922, supra, p. 275.

[7] Cf. supra, pp. 58, 109, etc.

[8] Cf. supra, pp. 70, 83–85, 90, 107, 109, 114, etc.

The occasional use of secret agents, sometimes only semiofficial in character, calls for special notice. Circumstances arise from time to time in which the foreign minister finds himself embarrassed or thwarted in his plans by the position taken by a diplomatic representative abroad. For reasons of State, he may not wish to remove, replace, or rebuke the agent in question and thereby provoke public controversy.[1] In such instances he can readily resort to the services of secret agents, taken from the diplomatic or consular corps, from the permanent staff of the Quai d'Orsay, or from unofficial circles. Ferry, for example, initiated treaty negotiations with the Chinese Government in 1885 quite outside of ordinary diplomatic channels through the Chinese Inspector-General of Customs and certain subordinate officials at the Ministry of Foreign Affairs.[2] Later, in the same year, Freycinet sent the French Consul-General at Beyrout on a secret mission to circumvent the activities of the regular diplomatic agent.[3] Sometimes the Premier himself will resort to such devices to frustrate the designs of his own foreign minister. Rouvier adopted this method in 1905 in dealing with Berlin through unofficial channels behind the back of Delcassé.[4] In the Moroccan crisis of 1911, Caillaux, in his anxiety to avoid provocation and preserve peace, acted upon the advice of Jules Cambon, French Ambassador in Berlin, in employing secret, unofficial agents who were answerable only to the Premier and not to the foreign minister, De Selves.[5] Caillaux regarded the latter as being under the domination of dangerous hotheads at the Quai d'Orsay. At an earlier period, in 1907 and 1908, Pichon, Minister of Foreign Affairs in the Clemenceau Cabinet, conducted negotiations with Berlin through Robert Raynaud, director of the *Dépêche Marocaine*, who was in contact with the German legation in Morocco. He later utilized the services of Tardieu, then editor of *Le Temps*, and of Baron Lancken, first secretary of the German Embassy in Paris.[6] In the unsuccessful negotiations of 1909 for a consortium between the N'Goko-Sangha Company, which enjoyed a concession from the French Government in Central Africa, and the German Company of South Cameroon, all the conversations were handled by business men and journalists in Paris and Berlin. The whole scheme was apparently devised to enable the French company to secure the financial indemnity to which it claimed it was entitled and which the Minister of Colonies, the Minister of Foreign Affairs, and the Premier had refused to grant. The Monis Cabinet rejected the consortium arrangements, despite the efforts of Conti, assistant director of political affairs at the Quai d'Orsay, to present them as essential for continued friendly relations between France and Germany. When the German Ambassador expressed his regrets, Caillaux, then Minister of

[1] *Cf.* the Georges Louis affair, *supra*, p. 194.

[2] *Supra*, pp. 93f.

[3] *Supra*, pp. 115–116.

[4] *Supra*, p. 180.

[5] *Supra*, p. 185; *cf.* Caillaux, *Agadir*, pp. 155–178.

[6] Caillaux, *Agadir*, pp. 31–32.

Finance, resumed negotiations with the authorization of the Cabinet, using the services of one M. Fondère, a French business man interested in the Congo. Here again no agreement was concluded, since the Cabinet, on Caillaux's advice, decided against the terms offered by the German business groups.[1]

These examples, which might easily be multiplied, reveal the flexibility and adaptability of the means available to the Cabinet in the initiation and conduct of treaty negotiations. In one situation the Minister of Foreign Affairs employs the regularly accredited diplomatic agents of the Republic in dealing with foreign Powers. In another a minister who nominally has little or nothing to do with foreign affairs secretly utilizes the services of journalists, investors, and concessionnaires to communicate with diplomats, ministers, or business groups in other countries. Between these extremes, all possible variations of plot and counterplot are found, with the Premier circumventing his own foreign minister or *vice versa*, the foreign minister employing, avoiding, or deceiving his field agents, cooperating with, or circumventing, his staff at the Quai d'Orsay, and the other ministers playing such rôles as opportunity provides through such official or unofficial agents as come to hand. The complex interplay of political expediency, personal ambitions, economic pressures, and considerations of power and diplomatic prestige combine in all the subtleties of high politics, with its duplicity, its bold strokes, and its secret machinations, to produce a rich counter-point to the main *motif*. So intricate and deceptive are these harmonies and dissonances, suggestive of the music of Honnegger, Milhaud, or Ravel, that their unravelling and comprehension require all the skill of the critic and analyst. The meddling in diplomacy of Ministers of Finance, of Colonies, or of Commerce, each with his own public or secret agents, may at times assume the appearance of a devolution of power in the handling of negotiations, leading perhaps to a consideration of problems by technical experts on an administrative level rather than by diplomats on a political level. At other times a dangerous irresponsibility and confusion may result, with the foreign minister and the Quai d'Orsay no longer in control of the course of conversations and sometimes not even aware of them. The tracing out of the tangled threads should reveal the forces at work below the surface in the formulation of foreign policy. For the moment it is enough to emphasize the complexity and the kaleidoscopic character of the pattern which overlays the conduct of treaty negotiations.

2. THE CHAMBERS IN RATIFICATION

If the formulation of international agreements through diplomatic negotiations is a task which is in practice undertaken by the executive agencies of the government, the process of ratification by which such agreements are made binding obligations upon the State is generally regarded as a

[1] *Ibid.*, pp. 57–94.

matter in which the legislature should possess the controlling voice. Most modern Constitutions provide for a greater or lesser degree of legislative participation in treaty ratification. The various nineteenth-century Constitutions of France are no exception to this general practice. Even in the *ancien régime* the King sometimes secured the assent of the Estates General for treaties affecting territory, though this was never regarded as a constitutional requirement. Later, treaties were often "registered" with the *Parlement de Paris,* though again their constitutional and international validity was apparently not dependent upon such action. Under the short-lived limited monarchy of 1791 no treaty of peace, alliance, or commerce was effective without the ratification of the Legislative Body. The Constitution of the First Republic of 1793 also made mention of legislative ratification of treaties, but the matter was left in doubt and treaties were usually ratified as well as negotiated by the Executive Council, whose powers were assumed by the Committee of Public Safety. The Directorate Constitution of 1795 required the consent of the Legislative Body for treaties, though it permitted the Directorate to put secret articles into execution at once. The Constitution of the year VIII placed treaties of peace, alliance, and commerce in the same category as laws, but the Constitution of the year X and the practice of the First Empire vested in Napoleon and his ministers all power over both ratification and negotiation. The 1815 Charter similarly gave the King complete control of the treaty process, as did the Constitution of 1830. The 1848 Constitution of the Second Republic, on the other hand, required the consent of the National Assembly for all treaties, while the Constitution of 1852, which preceded the establishment of the Second Empire, once more vested all power in the chief executive.[1]

The constitutional history of France had thus established an association between republicanism and legislative participation in treaty making. During the period of the National Assembly (1871 to 1875) most treaties were ratified by the President with the approval of the Assembly, which was both a parliament and a constitutional convention.[2] In the debates over the terms of the new Constitution, some members urged that treaty making should be exclusively an executive function while others insisted upon the desirability of legislative approval for all treaties and still others, including MacMahon and the Duc de Broglie, wished to follow the American example by requiring the ratification of treaties by the upper house of the legislature. Article 8 of the Law of July 16, 1875, was a compromise between these conflicting views:[3]

The President of the Republic negotiates and ratifies treaties. He gives cognizance of them to the Chambers as soon as the interest and the safety of the State permit. Treaties of peace and of

---

[1] For a detailed analysis of these provisions and practice under them, see L. Michon, *Les traités internationaux devant les chambres,* pp. 17–154.

[2] *Ibid.,* pp. 168–193.

[3] *Cf.* Lefebvre, *op. cit.,* pp. 98–103, and Michon, *op. cit.,* pp. 194–199.

commerce, treaties which affect the finances of the State, those which relate to the status of persons and the property rights of French nationals abroad are binding (*définitifs*) only after having been voted by the two Chambers. No cession, no exchange, no addition of territory may take place except by virtue of a law.

This article has provided the constitutional basis for legislative consideration of treaties throughout the whole period of the Third French Republic.[1] In practice, ratification is effected by the attachment to the text of the treaty of the signature of the President of the Republic, with the counter-signature of the Minister of Foreign Affairs. For treaties in the categories specified in Article 8 this action follows approval by the Chambers of a *projet de loi* authorizing the President to ratify and put the treaty into execution. The first step in the process is the introduction of the *projet* into Parliament by a member of the Cabinet—usually the Minister of Foreign Affairs—who may introduce it into both houses simultaneously or into either Chamber first at the discretion of the Government. The *projet* is submitted in the name of the President of the Republic, the Premier, the Minister of Foreign Affairs, and sometimes of other ministers. Its introduction may be a simple formality or may be accompanied by a defense of the treaty on the part of the Premier or foreign minister.[2] In either case the treaty *projet* will be referred as a matter of course to the Commission of Foreign Affairs for consideration. Prior to the creation of the permanent commissions in 1914 and 1915[3] such *projets* were, of course, referred to a "bureau" or to a special commission chosen for the purpose, after the first reading (*première délibération*) and the printing and distribution of the *projet* and accompanying treaty text to the parliamentarians. The first reading was usually a formality, not followed by

[1] On March 1, 1912, the Chamber discussed and rejected the proposal of M. Piou for the revision of Article 8 and the creation of an elective council to assist the President in the negotiation and ratification of treaties. *J.O.Ch.*, March 2, 1912. Duguit observes: "Si la proposition Piou avait été adoptée, le traité de Versailles ne serait peut-être pas ce qu'il est," *op. cit.*, IV, p. 802.

[2] A typical example of such a *projet* follows: "Article unique—Le Président de la République Française est autorisé à ratifier et, s'il y a lieu, à faire exécuter la convention de poste conclue, le 29 septembre 1874, Entre la France et le Pérou et dont une copie authentique demeure annexée à la presente loi," *J.O.Ch.*, July 4, 1876. Two days after the Chamber had voted its approval, the same *projet* was introduced into the Senate:

"*M. le président:* La parole est à M. le ministre des affaires étrangères.

"*M. le duc Décazes*, ministre des affaires étrangères: J'ai l'honneur de déposer sur le bureau du Sénat un projet de loi portant autorisation de ratifier et, s'il y a lieu, de faire exécuter la convention postale conclue, le 29 septembre 1874, entre la France et la Pérou.

"J'ai également l'honneur de déposer sur le bureau du Sénat un projet de loi portant autorisation de ratifier la convention conclue, le 22 avril 1876, entre la France et les Pays-Bas, pour l'échange des mandats de poste.

"Ces deux projects ont été soumis à la Chambre des Députés et adoptés par elle.

"*M. le président:* Les projets de lois seront imprimés et renvoyés aux bureaux," *J.O.Sén.*, July 6, 1876. *Cf. ibid.*, December 2, 1876.

When Ferry submitted the Tunisian treaty of 1881 to the chambers, it was accompanied by a *Livre Jaune*, prepared by the Quai d'Orsay, in justification of the Government's policy (*supra*, pp. 70–71).

[3] *Supra*, pp. 25–26.

debate. Between the first and second readings the bureau or special commission would prepare a report upon the treaty, with recommendations for legislative action. The second reading followed the presentation of the report, which, if favorable, was usually accepted and acted upon with little discussion.[1] In the event of extended debate the *rapporteur* or the Minister of Foreign Affairs, or both, sought to explain away objections and secure the consent of the Senators and Deputies.[2] The present procedure varies little from this, except that since the creation of the permanent Commissions of Foreign Affairs all treaty *projets* are referred to them and often made the subject of intensive investigation and detailed reports.[3]

When treaties receive careful study in Parliament, the Commissions of Foreign Affairs, sometimes in cooperation with other commissions, such as those of Commerce and Finance, act as the agencies through which investigations are conducted and conclusions reached. The same might be said of all *projets* or *propositions de loi*. The French Parliament, like every legislative body, does most of its work through committees. But by its very nature a treaty is not subject to amendment or modification, as is an ordinary law. The rules of both Chambers require that a treaty *projet* be accepted or rejected as a whole or "tabled," in the English phrase, *i.e.*, postponed for future

---

[1] The following is an example of a first reading:

"*M. le président:* L'ordre du jour appelle la première délibération sur le projet de loi portant approbation du traité d'extradition conclue, le 28 mars 1877, entre la France et le Danemark . . .

"Personne ne demande la parole sur la discussion générale? . . .

"Je donne lecture de l'article unique:

" ' *Article unique*—Le Président de la République Française est autorisé à ratifier et, s'il y a lieu, à faire exécuter la convention d'extradition conclue, le mars 1877, entre la France et le Danemark, et dont une copie authentique demeure annexée à la présente loi.'

"L'article unique, mis aux voix, est adopté.

"*M. le président:* Je consulte le Sénat sur la question de savoir s'il entend passer à la seconde délibération (assentiment)" *J.O.Sén.*, November 8, 1877. The second reading took place in this instance on November 16 and the *projet* was approved without discussion, 213 to 1.

The following is an example of a second reading, with *urgence:*

"*M. le comte de Saint-Vallier, rapporteur:* (He declares that he has the honor of placing two reports before the Senate, in the name of the commission charged with examining the *projets* approving the postal conventions of April 22, 1874, and September 29, 1874, with the Netherlands and Peru respectively.) . . . Ces deux projets ont été approuvés par la Chambre des Députés avec le caractère d'urgence. La commission, conformément au voeu exprimé par le Gouvernement, sollicite du Sénat une déclaration d'urgence. Le Sénat veut-il autoriser la lecture pour que l'urgence puisse être demandée?

"*Voix nombreuses:* Oui! Oui! Lisez! Lisez!

"*M. le comte de Saint Vallier:* (He cites the advantages of facilitating postal communication and explains and summarizes the terms of the conventions.)

"(L'urgence est adoptee.)" The President of the Senate then reads the *projets* and each is approved unanimously without discussion. *J.O.Sén.*, July 31, 1876.

[2] *Cf.* the comments of Décazes, *J.O.Sén.*, May 7, 1877.

[3] *Cf.* Duguit, *op. cit.*, IV, pp. 798–802; L. Michon, *op. cit.*, pp. 202–207 and 228–235; Barisien, *op. cit.*, pp. 103–121; Lefebvre, *op. cit.*, pp. 117–120; J. Barthélemy, *Démocratie et politique étrangère*, pp. 103–104, Paris, 1917.

reconsideration.[1] The commissions, therefore (following the example of the bureaus in the earlier period), do not in their reports attach "reservations" to treaties in the fashion so popular with the American Senate, except in rare instances. A recommendation of postponement (*ajournement*), however, may be *motivé*, *i.e.*, it may indicate specific objections to the treaty and request the Government to resume negotiations for the purpose of meeting them.[2] Occasionally partial ratification has been resorted to when the terms of an agreement make this permissible, as in the case of the Brussels Slave Trade Convention of July 2, 1890, which was ratified by the Chambers with the exception of five articles.[3] The commission may likewise attach to the *projet* an amendment or an interpretative article, which may have the practical effect of a reservation, though this is rarely done. In general the Chambers approve or disapprove treaties as a whole and the commissions act accordingly in preparing their recommendations.[4]

The amount of time and attention which the commissions devote to considering treaties varies greatly with circumstances. It is safe to say, however, that treaty *projets* usually receive much more detailed study from the commissions than they did from the old bureaus, since the latter were temporary bodies chosen by lot while the former are permanent and specialized agencies. The generalization may also be ventured that the commissions have exhibited a tendency to subject treaties to closer scrutiny in recent years than was formerly the case. The Premier, the Minister of Foreign Affairs, or one or more of the permanent officials at the Quai d'Orsay, accompanying the foreign minister, may be called in for explanations. Proceedings are secret. On at least one occasion the indiscretion of the head of the Government in the course of such a hearing led to the fall of the Cabinet.[5] If, as rarely happens, the Government encounters serious opposition from the

---

[1] "Si le Sénat, après débats, a décidé le renvoi, la Commission, avant le vote définitif, fait un report d'ensemble, qui doit être imprimé et distribué, sur les différentes clauses contestées et renvoyées à son examen, elle conclut à l'adoption, au rejet ou à l'ajournement du projet de loi," *Reglement du Sénat*, Article 73. "Si après le débat, la Chambre prend en consideration, elle prononce le renvoi. Lors de la seconde déliberation, la Commission fait un rapport d'ensemble qui doit être imprimé et distribué, sur les différentes clauses contestées et renvoyées à son examen. Elle conclut à l'adoption, au rejet ou à l'ajournement du projet de loi," *Réglement de la Chambre des députés*, Article 32. Cited in Lefebvre, *op. cit.*, pp. 109–110. This phraseology, which has not been changed in subsequent modifications of the rules of the two Chambers, implies that treaties may be approved without submission to the commissions. At the present time, however, all treaty *projets* are submitted to the commissions as a matter of course.

[2] *Cf. J.O.Sén.*, May 2, 1877. As Duguit puts it: "Elle conclut à l'adoption, au rejet ou à l'ajournement du projet de loi. L'ajournement est motivé en ces termes: La Chambre, appelant de nouveau l'attention du gouvernement sur telle clause du traité . . . surseoit à donner l'autorisation de ratifier," *op. cit.*, IV, p. 802, citing *Rég.Ch.*, Article 93, and *Rég.Sén.*, Article 73.

[3] *J.O.Ch.*, June 25 and December 23, 1891.

[4] Poincaré once declared, in response to the leader of the socialists, "Vous savez, M. Jaurès, qu'on ne vote pas les traités disposition par disposition, clause par clause," *J.O.Ch.*, March 2, 1912.

[5] Caillaux in 1911, *supra*, pp. 185–186.

commission to the terms of a treaty, and if it does not choose to risk being overthrown by making the *projet* a question of confidence, it may drop the treaty entirely, as did Delcassé with the Siamese treaty of October 7, 1902,[1] or it may accept certain modifications of the terms, as did Ferry in the case of the Annam treaty of August 25, 1883.[2] The latter step, however, may easily lead to diplomatic embarrassment abroad and the foreign minister will usually exert himself to secure a favorable report on the treaty as submitted. At the end of their deliberations the members of the commission prepare their recommendations, sometimes accompanied by elaborate explanations written by the *rapporteur*. The reports represent the views of the majority of the members of the commissions. Dissenting minority reports are rarely submitted.

Neither the hearings of the commissions nor the discussion of their reports in the Chambers are likely to lead to sharp and penetrating debate, clarifying the issues at stake and possibly jeopardizing the Cabinet's position. If the Premier has deceived Parliament as to the policy of the government during the course of negotiations, as did Ferry with regard to Tunis,[3] he may arouse resentment and his majority may be endangered in the treaty debate. But even here, if he is able to confront the Chambers with an acceptable *fait accompli*, he may easily escape unscathed because of the tradition of national unity in foreign affairs and the reluctance of the parliamentary groups to make a treaty a party issue. If the party composition of the Cabinet and its position on domestic issues assure it a stable majority, it need not fear overthrow on a treaty *projet*. The Commissions of Foreign Affairs are chosen from among the Deputies and Senators on the basis of proportional representation and therefore reflect the positions and relative strength of the parties in Parliament as a whole. While only the cynic would suggest that their members are influenced exclusively by partisan considerations, it is nevertheless true that when disagreements arise which threaten the maintenance of the Government in power, the decision will tend to follow party lines. The same is true on the floor of the Chamber and the Senate. Party ties usually insure complete harmony between the Cabinet, the commissions, and the Chambers. The great debates over foreign affairs seldom center about the reports of the commissions on specific treaties, but arise out of interpellations addressed to the Government on its foreign policy in general. Under these circumstances it is not surprising that the reports themselves very infrequently propose modification or disapproval of treaties nor that the consideration given to such reports by Parliament as a whole is often rapid, superficial, and confused, with no adequate presentation of the precise significance of the treaty and no clear understanding on the part of the parliamentarians of the legal and political problems involved. The important

[1] G. Stuart, *French Foreign Policy*, pp. 71–74.
[2] *Supra*, pp. 83–84.
[3] *Supra*, pp. 69–71.

Treaty of Berlin of February 26, 1885, was approved by the Chamber almost without discussion.[1] The treaty of March 15, 1874, establishing a protectorate over Annam, was voted without debate.[2] The Madagascar protectorate was ratified with no comprehension of its legal implications.[3] It is the exception rather than the rule for the Chambers to debate a treaty *projet* at length and to arrive at a mature and well-reasoned judgment regarding it. And it is exceptional for a Premier or foreign minister to feel regret over this situation and exert himself to enlighten Parliament. In some instances an incisive and illuminating discussion may have taken place before the commission, which may indicate as much in its report. More frequently this is not the case. The executive usually secures parliamentary acquiescence with little difficulty and it may, at any stage in the proceedings, even after Parliament has voted approval, drop a treaty entirely by withholding the final act of Presidential ratification which the Chambers have advised. The overwhelming majority of treaties submitted are approved and the average time required by the Chambers to act upon treaty *projets* is, on a rough estimate, about eight months.[4]

For the purpose of throwing further light upon the procedures which have been summarized, it may be useful to notice the character of parliamentary action on a few recent international agreements of major political importance. The Washington Conference treaties of 1921 and 1922 were made the objects of detailed study by the Chamber Commission of Foreign Affairs. Its report on the Five-Power Naval Disarmament Treaty of February 6, 1922, was an exhaustive fifty-page résumé of the naval policies of the various signatories and included an exchange of letters between the *rapporteur* and Poincaré on the points to which the commission raised objection. It concluded that the treaty was defective in making no provision for freedom of the seas and the abolition of the right of prize in naval warfare, that the 1.75 ratio in capital ships granted to both France and Italy was not to be construed as recognizing the principle of naval parity between the two Mediterranean Powers, and that the ratios adopted were not susceptible of extension to other categories of war vessels. But since France was left free to construct as many cruisers and submarines as she desired, the commission recommended ratification. The report was submitted on June 7, 1923, over a year after the submission of the *projet* for ratification. The Four-Power Pacific Pact of December 13, 1921, was submitted for ratification on May 30, 1922. On January 22, 1923, the Chamber commission, in an eight-page report, recommended approval, with a second article attached to the *projet*, declaring, after the example of the American Senate, that the treaty was understood to impose upon France no obligations of military assistance to the other

[1] *J.O.Ch.*, August 4, 1885.

[2] *Ibid.*, July 8, 1875; *supra*, p. 83.

[3] *Supra*, pp. 117–118.

[4] *Cf.* Barthélemy, *op cit.*, pp. 104–105, 131–132, and Lefebvre, *op. cit.*, pp. 108–118.

signatories.[1] In the Chamber discussion of these reports reservations were suggested to both of them. Poincaré vigorously opposed these suggestions and after further discussion the Deputies approved ratification of the naval treaty, without reservations, by a vote of 411 to 96 on July 7, 1923. On July 9, by a vote of 437 to 0, they also approved ratification of the Pacific Pact. The Senate, after some discussion, approved ratification of both agreements on July 9, 1923, by a vote of 281 to 3. The Presidential act of ratification followed immediately and ratifications were exchanged on August 17, 1923. Slightly more than a year and one-half thus elapsed between signature and exchange of ratifications, this delay being due primarily to the action of the Chamber commission and being much longer than usually occurs in the case of engagements of a less controversial character.[2]

A much shorter time was required for parliamentary action on the four Locarno treaties signed on October 16, 1925. The Chamber commission acted favorably upon them in a thirty-five page report submitted on February 23, 1926. A long debate followed in the Chamber, during the course of which Tardieu and others attacked the accords as affording no guarantee against an Austro-German *Anschluss*, but they were approved 413 to 71 on March 2 and ratifications were exchanged on September 14, 1926, following Germany's admission to the League of Nations.[3] The Mellon-Berenger debt accord of April 29, 1926, on the other hand, led to acrimonious controversy and a delay of three years in ratification. The agreement obligates France to pay $4,025,000,000 to the United States in sixty-two annuities. The *projet* of ratification was submitted by the Government to the Chambers on May 27, 1926, accompanied by a twenty-one-page defense of its terms. It was considered in the Chamber both by the Commission of Finance and by the Commission of Foreign Affairs. Their reports suggested reservations which would make French fulfilment of the terms contingent upon the receipt of reparations' payments from Germany. A furor of opposition arose in Parliament and the press to the agreement, as well as to the Caillaux-Churchill accord of July 12, 1926, for the settlement of the French war debt to Great Britain. In view of this, Poincaré sought to reopen negotiations in October of 1927, but without success. The final debates of July, 1929, were long and

---

[1] "Article 2. Les textes ci-joint n'obligent la France à aucun concours armé. Ils ne comportent aucune alliance ni aucun obligation de participer à une action défensive." *Rapport, Chambre des Députés*, session de 1923, No. 5467.

[2] The Five-Power Naval Pact was signed February 6, 1922, submitted to the Chambers on May 30, 1922, reported on by the commission on June 7, 1923, approved by the Chamber, July 7, 1923, approved by the Senate, July 11, 1923, and put into force with the exchange of ratifications on August 17, 1923. The corresponding dates for the Four-Power Pacific Pact were December 3, 1921; May 30, 1922; January 22, 1923; July 9, 1923; July 11, 1923; and August 17, 1923. *Cf. J.O.Ch.*, July 8 and 10, 1923, *J.O.Sén.*, July 12, 1923, *Rapport fait au nom de la Commission des Affaires Étrangères*, June 7, 1923, Chambre des Députés, session de 1923, No. 6109; *ibid.*, Jan. 22, 1923, Chambre des Députés, session de 1923, No. 5467.

[3] *J.O.Ch.*, March 3, 1926, *Rapport*, February 23, 1926, Chambre des Députés, session de 1926. No. 2615.

stormy. Many *contre-projets* were proposed, with various kinds of reservations in addition to those suggested by the commissions. None was sent back to the commissions for reconsideration. The Government insisted upon one which recommended simple and unconditional ratification. The issue was made a question of confidence and the Cabinet was upheld on July 20, 1929, by the narrow margin of eight votes. The Senate followed suit on July 26, 1929, after further debate, with the Government upheld by a large majority.[1]

These controversial political agreements are, of course, not representative of the larger number of treaties, and parliamentary action upon them cannot properly be made the basis of generalizations regarding the rôle of the Chambers in dealing with other types of engagements. Such political agreements are likely to provoke more incisive debate on the floor of the Chambers, to require a longer time for parliamentary approval, and to be made the object of more detailed commission reports than are other international accords. Generalization on these points would be justified for various types of treaties only after an exhaustive survey had been made of parliamentary action on all treaties submitted to the Chambers during the life of the Third Republic. To the best of the writer's knowledge, no such survey has ever been made[2] and the task is so large in itself as to be beyond the scope of the present inquiry. The cases cited here, and in the preceding chapters, are sufficient to indicate the rôle of parliament and the scope and method of parliamentary procedure in handling *projets* of ratification. International agreements which are outside the realm of Great Power politics and are confined to routine administrative or commercial matters are not likely to receive detailed study or careful consideration, unless, as sometimes happens, they involve important economic interests in the constituencies of the members of Parliament. The commercial convention of August 7, 1921, for example, regulating the trade of Haute-Savoie and Gex with the neighboring Swiss cantons, was the object of a lively debate, not because it possessed any international political significance but because the Deputies from the affected departments were much interested in wine, shoes, chocolate, and bon-bons.[3] On the other hand, as has been shown, important political engagements are frequently ratified with little study or discussion by the Deputies and Senators. The Franco-Italian accord of September 12, 1919, granting to Italy territorial concessions along the frontier between Algeria and Tripoli, under the terms of the secret Treaty of London of December 1, 1915, was approved by the Chamber on January 31, 1923, without a formal vote and with no discussion whatever.[4] What action the Chambers and their commis-

[1] *Cf. Projet de loi*, Chambre des Députés, session de 1926, No. 2915, May 27, 1926; *J.O.Ch.*, July 21, 1929. The Chamber vote was 300 to 292. *J.O.Sén.*, July 27, 1929. The Senate vote was 234 to 29.

[2] *Cf. infra*, p. 322, Note 2.

[3] *J.O.Ch.*, February 3, 1923.

[4] *Ibid.*, February 1, 1923.

sions will take on a particular treaty depends upon a great variety of un-controllable factors which make generalization and prediction difficult.

It should be noted, however, before leaving the subject, that throughout the entire sixty years of parliamentary life of the Third French Republic no Cabinet has ever fallen because of the refusal of the Chambers to approve ratification of a treaty submitted to them by the Government. The nearest approaches to such a situation occurred on March 13, 1890, when the Senate, by a vote of 129 to 117, rejected the *ordre du jour pur et simple* insisted upon by the Tirard Cabinet, following a discussion of the expiration of the commercial treaty of 1802 with Turkey, and again on January 11, 1911, when the Caillaux Cabinet resigned following an incident before the Chamber Commission of Foreign Affairs.[1] In the first instance the Government fell on its tariff policy. In the second, the Premier's diplomatic methods were the object of attack, but the treaties involved were accepted by the succeeding Cabinet and ratified by the Chambers. Parliamentary opposition to treaties may influence the Government in negotiations and in its handling of treaties after they have been signed, but it has never produced a ministerial overturn in the course of consideration of a *projet* for ratification.

All of the foregoing discussion has relevance only to those treaties which constitutionally require the assent of Parliament, *i.e.*, treaties of peace, and of commerce, those modifying title to territory, those affecting the finances of the State, and those relating to the personal or property rights of French nationals abroad. In practice, this list has been narrowly construed and, properly so, in the opinion of most authorities. These treaties are exceptions to the general rule that the President, *i.e.*, the Cabinet, negotiates and ratifies treaties without legislative participation. All treaties not specified may be ratified by the executive without submission to the Chambers in any form, although the Cabinet does from time to time submit treaties outside of the specified categories as a means of avoiding criticism and strengthening its political position. If a treaty is obviously within one of the categories mentioned the Cabinet has no discretion about submitting it. But if there is controversy over its character, the Government usually gives itself the benefit of the doubt and avoids legislative action.[2]

[1] *J.O.Sén.*, March 14, 1890 and January 12, 1911.

[2] *Cf. Rapport*, July 6, 1921, Chambre des Députés, session de 1921, No. 3025, on the protocol of December 16, 1920, for the establishment of the Permanent Court of International Justice. The *rapporteur*, M. Joseph Barthélemy, expresses doubt as to whether the protocol constitutionally requires approval by the chambers, but attributes the scruples of the government to the fact that the protocol might be considered as a supplement to the peace treaties.

So far as the writer has been able to discover, there is nowhere available in tabulated form a compilation of all the treaties of the Third Republic showing the action taken by Parliament on those submitted to it. The nearest approach to such a list is to be found in Barisien's study. He fails to list the treaties and conventions not submitted to Parliament. Of those submitted, sixty-four were treaties of commerce submitted between 1877 and 1911, of which only two were not approved (with Italy of July 6, 1877, and with the United States of July 24, 1899); fifty-six treaties involving the finances of the State were submitted between 1876 and 1908, most of them

As regards treaties affecting title to territory, Article 8 of the Law of July 16, 1875, declares that no cession, exchange, or addition of territory may take place except by virtue of a law. Many treaties of protectorate with semicivilized chieftains in Africa have not been submitted to Parliament, although those relating to Tunis and Madagascar were presented to and approved by the Chambers.[1] The retrocession of the West Indies island of St. Barthélemy by Sweden to France was sanctioned by a law of March 2, 1878, authorizing the President to ratify the treaty of August 10, 1877. In 1880 ·Tahiti was annexed by simple statutory enactment with no treaty involved and in the same way the Senate and the Chamber proclaimed the annexation of Madagascar in 1896.[2] Treaties with other colonial Powers delimiting possessions have always been submitted, with the exception of the Anglo-French Agreement of August 10, 1889, relating to the east coast of Africa.[3] All formal treaties of peace have been submitted, but many treaties for the prevention of war or the pacific settlement of international disputes have not been submitted, though the Kellogg-Briand Pact of 1928, the Locarno Treaties of 1925, and many recent arbitration treaties are exceptions. The Treaty of Berlin of 1878, closing a war in which France was not a belligerent, and the Hague Conventions of 1899 and 1907 were ratified by the executive alone.[4] Almost all treaties of commerce, including navigation agreements, trade-mark conventions, and arrangements for the protection of industrial or esthetic property rights, have been submitted to parliament.[5] Most naturalization and extradition treaties have been submitted, as agreements affecting personal and property rights.[6] As for treaties involving the finances of the State, only those have been submitted which require a direct and immediate appropriation to execute them, such as agreements for loans extended or guaranteed by the State, conventions for the settlement of financial claims, and multilateral arrangements for the establishment of

---

postal and telegraph conventions, all of which were approved; eight treaties relative to the status of persons were submitted between 1879 and 1908 and all were approved; ten extradition treaties between 1876 and 1908 and all approved; sixteen treaties for the protection of industrial, artistic, or industrial property and all approved; fourteen trade-mark agreements between 1882 and 1909 and all approved; sixteen boundary treaties between 1885 and 1911 and all approved; six arbitration conventions between 1880 and 1909 and all approved. Among the treaties not submitted to the Chambers were forty-three treaties of protectorate with African chieftains concluded between 1880 and 1884, eight specific arbitration agreements between 1879 and 1909, and twelve general arbitration conventions between 1903 and 1911 (Barisien, *op. cit.*, pp. 146–157). It is noteworthy that out of a total of 190 treaties mentioned by Barisien as being submitted to parliament during this period, only two failed of ratification as a result of the disapproval of the chambers.

[1] *Supra*, pp. 71–72 and 118.
[2] *Supra*, p. 126.
[3] Michon, pp. 240–252.
[4] Michon, pp. 252–254; Barisien, pp. 26–28; Michon, pp. 285–292.
[5] Michon, pp. 254–261.
[6] *Ibid.*, pp. 266–285.

international unions or bureaus.[1] All other treaties are both negotiated and ratified by the executive alone, although some commentators have argued that any treaty requiring legislative action by Parliament should be submitted to the Chambers for approval and the Government has occasionally taken this view.[2]

A moment's reflection will indicate that those international engagements which are of the most far-reaching political importance and which may have the most decisive effects upon the destinies of the nation need not constitutionally be submitted to Parliament and are in practice concluded by the Cabinet alone.[3] In France there does not exist, as is the case in the United States, a clear distinction between treaties which bind the State, and "executive agreements" which bind only the Cabinet or President concluding them, since, from a constitutional point of view, legislative approval is necessary to create binding State obligations only for those categories of treaties which have been enumerated. One might perhaps say that only agreements which have been ratified by the President of the Republic, in conformity to the provisions of the Constitution, bind the State, but the Franco-Russian Alliance agreements, which in practice were regarded as fully binding, were neither signed nor formally ratified by the President of the Republic.[4] In fact, none of the great international agreements which have affected the balance of power and marked definite turning points in the diplomatic history of Europe have ever been submitted to, or even revealed to, Parliament and some of them have not even been ratified by the chief executive. Neither the Franco-Russian Alliance conventions, the Franco-Italian exchange of notes of 1902,[5] the Franco-Spanish Moroccan Convention of 1904, the secret articles of the Anglo-French Entente of 1904,[6] the Grey-Cambon letters of 1912, the Interallied Agreement of September 5, 1914, nor the post-Versailles alliances with Poland and the Little Entente were submitted to Parliament.[7] The letters and exchanges of notes mentioned were not formally ratified by the President. Every student of diplomacy would at once recognize that engagements of this type, as judged by their fruits, are infinitely more significant for the nation than any number of commercial treaties, arbitration conventions, or trade-mark agreements. These international understandings in the realm of high politics, whether consummated through exchanges of unratified diplomatic notes or embodied in formal written agreements signed by the President, have in practice been treated as solemn obligations binding upon the French State. They have been the

[1] *Ibid.*, pp. 261–266.

[2] *Ibid.*, pp. 293–303; Barisien, pp. 78–87.

[3] "C'est le gouvernement seul qui fait la grande politique internationale," Barthélemy, *Démocratie et politique étrangère*, p. 111.

[4] *Supra*, pp. 149, 158–159.

[5] *Supra*, pp. 162–163.

[6] *Supra*, p. 172.

[7] Barthélemy, *op. cit.*, pp. 109–118; Michon, *op. cit.*, pp. 303–308.

instrumentalities of imperialism, war, and "security." They have safeguarded the Republic from diplomatic isolation, made it a party to the greatest of all international conflicts, protected it from military disaster, and helped to maintain the post-Versailles *status quo*. In no case has Parliament had a voice in their making. As judged by the pragmatic test of results, the rôle of Parliament in the conclusion of treaties is even smaller than the language of the Constitution would imply.

In the application, interpretation, and termination of treaties, the executive enjoys even greater freedom from parliamentary control than in their negotiation and ratification. On these points the Constitution is silent. But all authorities are agreed that the Government may interpret and apply a treaty as it chooses without consulting the legislature. The early seventeenth-century treaties with Madagascar, for example, were interpreted by the Premier to give France a protectorate over the north coast of the island without consultation with the Chambers and with no expression of opinion from them.[1] The Chambers may, of course, pass resolutions calling upon the Government to enforce existing treaties.[2] They may express their views regarding the interpretation of a treaty through an *ordre du jour motivé*. They may request the denunciation of a treaty by the Cabinet. But such expressions of parliamentary opinion are of no significance so far as foreign Governments are concerned and cannot modify the international obligations of the Republic. From a constitutional point of view, the Cabinet may ignore them. In doing so it may run the political risk of losing its majority.[3] But even in this case the parliamentary action in itself would effect no change in the legal status of a treaty, either from the point of view of international law nor of French public law. Parliament could presumably nullify a treaty in practice by passing legislation in violation of it or failing to enact laws or make appropriations required by its terms, but this would involve either the fall of the Government or its acceptance of Parliament's position. In either case the formal act of abrogation or denunciation would be taken by the executive. No instance of this kind has come to the writer's attention. In law and in practice treaties can be terminated only by the action of the Minister of Foreign Affairs, acting in the name of the President of the Republic. Similarly the Government itself passes upon questions of interpretation and application. Neither the legislature nor the judiciary[4] has any voice in these matters. The Cabinet may—and it frequently does—consult the Chambers as a matter of political expediency. It is under no obligation to do so. Parliament may influence executive decisions through the give and take of partisan politics, but the Chambers have no legal power to make the decisions themselves. Their rôle here, as in negotiation and ratification, is

---

[1] *Supra*, pp. 105–106.
[2] *Supra*, p. 92, for an example.
[3] *Cf. supra*, pp. 272*f*.
[4] On the position of the Courts, *cf. supra*, pp. 26–27.

not one of control but one of admonition, supervision, and review. It is exercised so infrequently and sporadically that under ordinary circumstances the Cabinet possesses a free hand.[1]

3. SECRET DIPLOMACY

Article 8 of the Constitutional Law of July 15, 1875, provides that the President shall give cognizance of treaties to the Chambers as soon as the interest and the safety of the State permit. In the case of treaties requiring legislative approval prior to ratification, this provision is of little significance, since the text of the treaty is always submitted to Parliament along with the ratification *projet*. Such treaties are usually published in the reports of the Chamber commissions, in the annexes to the *Journal Officiel*, and sometimes also in explanatory *Livres Jaunes* issued by the Quai d'Orsay. Such agreements might conceivably be kept secret from the press and the general public by common consent of the Cabinet and the chambers. This has apparently never been done, however, and such secrecy would be very difficult to maintain. In general, secret treaties cannot be concluded by the Minister of Foreign Affairs if their subject matter requires their submission to Parliament for approval. But even public treaties, ratified by the Chambers, may contain secret articles which are neither revealed nor submitted to Parliament. From a constitutional point of view it can be argued that when a treaty contains any clause which requires legislative approval for ratification, the entire treaty should be submitted.[2] On the other hand, if, as is the case in practice, a narrow construction is given to the categories of treaties requiring legislative consent, an equally good argument can be presented in favor of regarding agreements which do not, as a whole, fall within these categories, as outside the limits of parliamentary supervision. When the Cabinet is confronted with this problem, it usually concludes several agreements, some of which are kept secret and not submitted to Parliament, or it concludes secret articles which are not published nor placed before the Chambers.[3] Parliament may object to this procedure,[4] but its objectives are seldom effective in preventing resort to this device by the ministry. As for treaties, or articles of treaties, which are submitted to Parliament for approval, the Cabinet gives cognizance of their terms to the Chambers through the process of submission itself.

[1] Lefebvre, *op. cit.*, pp. 158–161.

[2] Barthélemy, *op. cit.*, pp. 204–209.

[3] *Supra*, p. 172.

[4] The Senate commission charged with examining the Franco-German convention of November 4, 1911, declared: "La Commission estime qu'il a été fait, pendant les dernières années, un abus des traités secrets. Sans doute, la Constitution de 1875 laisse au Président de la République la faculté d'apprécier à quel moment un traité peut être communiqué aux Chambres sans dommage pour la sécurité et les intérêts du pays; mais elle n'autorise pas l'addition à un traité public de clauses secrètes qui en modifient l'esprit et les dispositions." *Cf. supra*, pp. 185f.

A different situation obviously exists with respect to those treaties which are not submitted to the Chambers for approval. The Government gives cognizance of such agreements to Parliament as soon as it regards publicity as compatible with the interests and the safety of the State. Both the language of the Constitution and the accepted parliamentary conventions leave the determination of this moment to the Cabinet rather than to the legislature—and in the case of secret political engagements affecting the balance of power and contemplating cooperation in the event of war many years or even decades may elapse before the Cabinet regards publicity as permissible. The terms of the Franco-Russian conventions and understandings were kept rigidly secret during the entire life of the Dual Alliance.[1] Viviani carried the texts before the Chambers on August 4, 1914, but they were neither asked for by the Deputies and Senators nor revealed by the Premier on his own initiative.[2] Only after the Soviet authorities in Russia published them, following the revolution of 1917, did they become known to the French Parliament and public. All earlier efforts to discover the precise nature of the Republic's obligations to Imperial Russia were unsuccessful in the face of the insistence of successive Cabinets on the diplomatic necessity of secrecy. A majority of both chambers acquiesced at all times in the Cabinet's position. The most significant terms of the Anglo-French Entente of 1904 were similarly guarded from public view and the French-Spanish Agreements of the same year for the partition of Morocco were not only not revealed to Parliament by Delcassé but kept secret from his colleagues in the Cabinet.[3] Such treaties may be kept secret indefinitely, since the Quai d'Orsay publishes no complete French treaty series and the Cabinet alone determines whether particular treaties shall be published in the *Livres Jaunes* or revealed to Parliament in other ways.[4] In 1912, during the parliamentary discussion of the Franco-German African accords of November 4, 1911, M. Piou proposed in the Chamber that secret treaties should be communicated to a special council, composed of six Deputies, three Senators, and other members drawn from non-parliamentary circles. He also proposed a modification of Article 8 of the Law of July 16, 1875, which would limit secrecy of negotiations, but Poincaré, despite his declared intention of giving greater publicity to treaties and to foreign affairs in general, opposed these suggestions as unacceptable and paralyzing to the Quai d'Orsay, and they were rejected.[5]

[1] *Supra*, Chap. VII, *passim*, pp. 129*f*.

[2] *Supra*, pp. 249–250.

[3] *Supra*, pp. 172–174.

[4] "Bref, tous les grandes résultats de la diplomatie française, tous ceux qui marquent un tourant de notre histoire, sont l'oevre du gouvernement seul; et il n'en a informé les assemblées et l'opinion qu'à l'heure qu'il a lui-même fixée et dans le mesure qu'il a lui seul jugée bonne." Barthélemy, *op. cit.*, pp. 223–224. *Cf. ibid.*, pp. 188–204.

[5] *J.O.Ch.*, March 2 and March 16, 1912. *Cf.* Gaston Jèze, "Le pouvoir de conclure les traités internationaux, et les traités secrètes," *Revue de Droit Public*, XXIX, 1912, pp. 313–329. Jèze argues that the implications of Article 8 are that (1) secret treaties should be exceptional; (2) secrecy

During the period since the establishment of the League of Nations it has been more difficult for the Cabinet to conceal treaties from parliament and the public. The universal condemnation of "secret diplomacy" during the Great War, the pleas of President Wilson at the Peace Conference for "open covenants, openly arrived at," and the determination of large opinion groups in France and elsewhere to democratize foreign affairs through full publicity led to the incorporation into the Covenant of the League of Article XVIII:

> Every treaty or international engagement entered into hereafter by any Member of the League shall be forthwith registered with Secretariat and shall as soon as possible be published by it. No such treaty or international engagement shall be binding until so registered.

Up to June, 1930, the Secretariat had published ninety-four volumes of the *League of Nations Treaty Series*, containing the texts of 2,160 treaties. It is impossible to ascertain at the time of writing how effective these arrangements have actually been in preventing the conclusion of secret international engagements. Article XVIII of the Covenant has never received any authoritative and generally accepted interpretation. Whether France has concluded any secret treaties since 1920 not registered at Geneva is doubtful, though no outside observer can answer this question conclusively. If any such treaties exist and both parties treat them as binding obligations, it is difficult to see how they can be invalidated in practice by Article XVIII, whatever their legal status may be in consequence of its terms. It is perfectly clear, moreover, that international bargains which involve the State in extensive commitments may still be concluded in secret through exchanges of diplomatic notes or administrative agreements between military authorities which do not require registration. It is probable that a number of secret and unregistered military and political engagements, in addition to the registered treaties of alliance, have been entered into by France with Belgium, Poland, Czechoslovakia, Jugoslavia, and Roumania.[1] A committee of the Second Assembly took the view that such agreements did not need to be registered under Article XVIII. This report was not accepted by the Assembly

---

should be temporary; (3) a minister should not deceive or confuse Parliament when interrogated regarding the terms of a secret treaty; (4) no treaties enumerated in Article 8 may be secret and (5) no treaties submitted to Parliament should contain secret clauses. He concluded that in these respects the Constitution is in no need of modification but only in need of enforcement. The flexibility of its provisions, however, renders this position questionable. Few Cabinets have accepted these "implications" of Article 8 in practice and it can scarcely be argued that their failure to do so has constituted a violation of the Constitution.

[1] *Cf. League of Nations Treaty Series*, Vol. II, pp. 128–130, No. 56, Exchange of Letters between France and Belgium, September 10 and 15, 1920, confirming the Franco-Belgian military understanding of September 7, 1920, which was *not* registered. *Cf.* Vol. XVII, pp. 12–13, No. 449: Treaty between France and Poland of February 19, 1921; Vol. XXIII, pp. 163–170, No. 588: Treaty between France and Czechoslovakia of January 25, 1924; Vol. LVIII, pp. 225–232, No. 1373; Treaty between France and Roumania of June 10, 1926; Vol. LXVIII, pp. 373–392, No. 1592: Treaty between France and Jugoslavia of November 11, 1926.

and the exact nature of the obligation in question remains doubtful.[1] So long as the provisions of the French Constitution remain unchanged and so long as secret international agreements appear desirable and expedient to French diplomats, ways will probably be found of concluding them in spite of Covenants and Pacts to the contrary.

Secret treaties constitute, of course, only one aspect of secret diplomacy. If the final results of treaty negotiations are often kept secret, the course of the negotiations themselves are veiled from the eyes of the curious much more frequently. As has been shown in the preceding pages, the Cabinet is released both by the terms of the Constitution and by accepted political practice from any obligation to take Parliament or the public into its confidence during the course of diplomatic conversations. The Franco-Russian Alliance negotiations were shrouded in deepest secrecy from beginning to end—so much so that the threat of publicity was more or less effectively used as a bargaining weapon to secure Russian consent to the French demands.[2] Whether negotiations are conducted through regular diplomatic channels, or through secret agents, whether they culminate in secret treaties or in public agreements, their conduct is likely to be kept secret both at the time during which they are in progress and for a longer or shorter interval afterwards. Sometimes the government may submit a detailed report to the Chambers along with *project* of ratification.[3] More frequently the Minister of Foreign Affairs will simply offer verbal explanations to the commissions. His honesty and accuracy must be taken on faith by the parliamentarians.[4] In the case of important political engagements, the instructions to the delegates, the exchange of views, the positions taken, and the compromises reached are often concealed for years, decades, or even generations after the event. In other instances the foreign minister, the director of political affairs, or subordinate officials at the Quai d'Orsay may summarize the course of conversations in general press releases or in statements to the semiofficial papers, such as *Le Temps* or *Le Journal des Débats*. Statements may be transmitted to the chambers publicly or given in confidence before the commissions. The diplomatic correspondence itself may be published in whole or in part in a *Livre Jaune*. The institution of the *Livres Jaunes* was established under the Second Empire as an annual selection and compilation of diplomatic documents. The regular volumes were sometimes supplemented by special publications on important negotiations. In 1870 the *Livres Jaunes* lost their annual character. From 1873 to 1877 none was published, and they have since appeared sporadically at the discretion of the Minister of Foreign Affairs. They constitute an incomplete, fragmentary, and unbalanced series with much of the material on matters of secondary importance

---

[1] *Records of the Second Assembly*, Plenary Meetings, p. 704.
[2] *Supra*, pp. 145–146.
[3] *Supra*, p. 71.
[4] *Cf. supra*, pp. 69f., 117, 118, 185–186, 193, etc.

and the remainder carefully and sometimes dishonestly[1] edited. Their purpose is less to provide publicity than to justify the Government's policies and strengthen its position. For some years prior to 1914 the Ministry of Foreign Affairs published *Livres Jaunes* with decreasing frequency, taking the view that they should be issued only at the demand of Parliament and often delaying publication even when such demands were made.[2] Occasionally the contents of a *Livre Jaune* is made the object of a special investigation by the Chamber Commissions of Foreign Affairs. When this occurs, the members of the commissions are not granted access to the diplomatic archives, but are dependent upon such documents as the Quai d'Orsay may be willing to supply. The Margaine report on the Franco-Russian Alliance complained of the evasive and obstructive tactics of the Minister of Foreign Affairs in dealing with the commission.[3] The diplomatic archives are, with rare exceptions, closed to parliamentarians and to historians alike. They were open only up to the year 1791, prior to 1909. In the latter year they were partially opened to 1848. Current and recent correspondence is always closed to investigators and the French Government has been one of the last of those participating in the Great War to commence a comprehensive publication of its correspondence between 1871 and 1914 under the supervision of a committee of historians. At the time of writing it is as yet impossible to venture a judgment as to the honesty and accuracy of the projected series.[4]

It is clear, then, that the content of diplomatic correspondence, both at the time of negotiations and for a long period subsequent thereto, remains a secret of the Quai d'Orsay. French practice in this respect is similar to that in other countries. The arguments against this practice presented by champions of democratic control of foreign policy are obvious. The reasons advanced in favor of it are equally familiar. The constant give-and-take of compromise which characterizes successful diplomatic negotiations would be impossible if the position assumed by each participant on every moot question was at once made public. The diplomat who has openly committed himself to a given position usually finds a recession from it in the interest of agreement a political impossibility. Diplomatic crises, moreover, may sometimes be settled peacefully through secret channels, whereas full publicity might inflame public opinion and render a pacific settlement

---

[1] *Supra*, pp. 233–234.

[2] *Cf. Rap. Budget, Ch.*, session extraord., 1913, No. 3318: "Il est indispensable dans l'intérêt du pays que ces méthodes d'obscurité et de crainte des résponsibilités prennent fin. Il faut que le pays et le Parlement soient tenus periodiquement au courant de tous les faits diplomatiques qui l'intéressent" (p. 53).

[3] M. Margaine, *Rapport . . . sur le Livre Jaune rélatif à l'Alliance Franco-Russe*, Chambre des Députés, session de 1919, No. 6036, p. 106.

[4] *Cf.* Commission de publication des documents rélatifs aux origines de la guerre de 1914, *Documents Diplomatiques Français* (1871–1914), Imprimerie Nationale, Paris, 1929 to —. At the time of writing three volumes have appeared: first series, vol. I: May 10, 1871, to June 30, 1875; vol. II: July 1, 1875, to December 31, 1879; third series, vol. III, November 4, 1911, to February 7, 1912.

difficult of attainment. Again, the diplomatic game can usually be played more successfully, from the point of view of "national interests," if the players conceal their cards from one another.[1] Full publicity of pending negotiations may also give offense to foreign Governments. These considerations are by no means negligible. Even such a redoubtable champion of "open diplomacy" as President Wilson felt obliged to acquiesce in the secrecy of the proceedings of the Paris Peace Conference, and the United States, which is popularly supposed to be less given to secrecy in its diplomatic relations than other Powers, would perhaps have never come into existence as a nation if the Constitutional Convention of 1787 had not conducted its work in quiet, behind closed doors, away from the tumult and shouting of the market-place.[2]

The use of "secret funds" by the Quai d'Orsay may also be considered in this connection. The annual voting by the Chambers of the budget of the Ministry of Foreign Affairs offers an oportunity for parliamentary investigation into current diplomatic negotiations and might conceivably give to Parliament an opportunity not merely to give publicity to them but to control or influence their conduct as well. In practice the power of the purse is not utilized for such purposes. Far from exhibiting undue inquisitiveness into the purposes for which appropriated sums are expended by the Quai d'Orsay, Parliament follows the traditional and well-established practice of granting to the Ministry of Foreign Affairs each year certain sums which are specifically "secret" and which may, therefore, be expended in such fashion and for such purposes as the minister may deem advisable, with no accounting to any outside agency. The Ministries of War and Marine also enjoy the use of secret funds.[3] The report of the Chamber Budget Commission in 1913 complained that the sums made available to the Quai d'Orsay in this fashion were smaller than the corresponding sums in Germany. It recommended that they should be increased and that their expenditure be supervised by a parliamentary commission.[4] None of the efforts at parliamentary supervision of the use of such funds have been effective, since it is difficult to reconcile secrecy and legislative control. It is interesting to notice that under Napoleon I over 1,000,000 fr. a year were made available to the

[1] "Ce qui serait folie dans les affaires privées ne peut être sagesse dans les affaires publiques," Barthélemy, *op. cit.*, pp. 179–180.

[2] "La conclusion la plus nette à laquelle on puisse aboutir, c'est donc que le gouvernement doit publier ses négociations toutes les fois qu'il n'y voit pas d'inconvénients, et aussitôt qu'il lui paraît que cette publicité est compatible avec les intérêts et avec la sureté de l'État," *ibid.*, p. 181.

[3] On September 22, 1916, a Socialist Deputy proposed that the Minister of Foreign Affairs be given control over the expenditure of secret funds by all the other Ministries having such items in their budgets, but the proposal was rejected. Various efforts at supervising the use of such funds through commissions have also been ineffective. Barthélemy regards this as inevitable and goes so far as to say: "Le plus grand reproche que l'on puisse adresser aux fonds secrets votés par le Parlement français, c'est leur insuffisance: 1 million en temps de paix, 25 millions depuis la guerre," *op. cit.*, p. 187.

[4] *Rap. Budget, Ch.*, session extraord. de 1913, No. 3318, pp. 53–65.

Quai d'Orsay for secret use. These annual appropriations were usually about 500,000 fr. under the Second Republic, the Second Empire, and the Third Republic until 1891, when the Chamber Budget Commission, then headed by Pichon, took the initiative in increasing them once more to 1,000,000 fr. a year. They were maintained at this level until the outbreak of the Great War, when they were increased to 5,000,000 fr. in 1915, 8,000,000 in 1915, and 25,000,000 in 1917. In 1921 and 1922 they were reduced to 2,000,000 fr. In 1924 they rose again to 21,000,000 fr. The annual appropriation has since been 2,000,000 fr., but this has been supplemented by another chapter of the budget of the Quai d'Orsay, entitled "*Fonds Speciaux pour Dépenses à l'Étranger,*" out of which the Minister of Foreign Affairs can also make secret expenditures. This item totalled 34,000,000 fr. in 1919; 20,000,000 in 1920; and about 13,500,000 annually since 1923.[1]

The exact uses to which these secret funds are put is, of course, a matter of conjecture, but their general purpose is to provide money for propaganda purposes abroad. They are apparently not utilized directly in negotiations, but are employed to create a public opinion favorable to France in foreign countries. This objective is achieved by "subventions"—in plainer language, bribes—to foreign newspapers, in exactly the same fashion, it may be presumed, as the French press itself was subsidized by the Imperial Russian Government before 1917 and by other Governments in the post-war period. The Minister of Foreign Affairs is theoretically expected to report to the President of the Republic on the use which has been made of secret funds. In fact, this control is entirely illusory, so much so that at times the practice is followed of having the minister dispatch to the President, in lieu of a report, blank slips of paper which the President destroys in his presence.[2] Since the distribution of the money is secret and the distributors are answerable to no one, abuses frequently develop which admit of no remedy save such as may be furnished by the foreign minister himself. Not only it is often suspected that the funds go into the pockets of owners, editors, or reporters of foreign newspapers with no compensatory service rendered, but it is usually admitted that a portion of them find their way into the coffers of French newspapers as well. Ministers and Cabinets may in this way seek to counteract the effect of foreign bribery of the French press or to strengthen their own power and position before the public. The whole system is more suggestive of legalized corruption, graft, and racketeering than of the refine-

[1] *Ibid.*, 1921, No. 3131, p. 145; 1924, No. 509, p. 93; 1926, No. 3391, pp. 150–151; 1925, No, 1961, pp. 50–52. In 1917 a resolution was introduced into the Chamber by M. Émile Constant, condemning the Premier (Clemenceau) for having flouted the law by transferring the propaganda service from the Ministry of Foreign Affairs to the Ministry of War. The Budget Commission took the view, however, that the Premier had not acted improperly, since the service for which he transferred funds was attached to the Premier's office. When he gave up the portfolio of foreign affairs and took that of war he transferred the service at the same time. *Cf. Rap. Budget Ch.*, 1917, No. 3982 and No. 4084.

[2] Barthélemy, *op. cit.*, pp. 187–188.

ments of diplomacy. While no means exist of measuring their effects in precise terms, "secret funds" certainly constitute a political weapon of major importance in both foreign and domestic politics.

In summary, "secret diplomacy" has always played and continues to play a significant rôle in the international relations of the Third French Republic. Increasing popular realization since the Great War of the dangers of hidden diplomatic intrigues, coupled with increasing interest in foreign affairs on the part of Parliament, the public, and the press, has probably led to increased publicity in recent years. The League of Nations has been instrumental in limiting the number of secret international engagements. The attitudes of the Chamber Commissions of Foreign Affairs have also contributed to the same result. But only the historian of the future will be able to ascertain how effective these pressures have been and to what degree full publicity has been achieved. There are still ample opportunities for secrecy for a Minister of Foreign Affairs who regards such methods as necessary. Whatever pressure for publicity he may feel from Parliament and the world of journalism and politics will tend to be counterbalanced by pressure for secrecy from the tradition-bound bureaucracy in the diplomatic and consular services and at the Quai d'Orsay. Negotiations may still be initiated behind the scenes. They may be conducted through secret agents of the minister or the Premier, with the use of secret funds to pay for such services or to influence foreign or domestic opinion. Their course may be kept secret and the written records of what transpired may be guarded from public view for many years. Written international engagements of the greatest political importance may be withheld from Parliament if the Cabinet feels that the interest and the safety of the State require secrecy. The same considerations may cause the Government to neglect to register such engagements at Geneva. Neither the constitutional provisions nor the political traditions of the French Republic forbid these practices. In the last analysis, the scope of secret diplomacy is limited only by the views of the foreign minister and of the Cabinet as a whole. In this, as in all aspects of treaty making, initiative and control rests in the hands of the ministers whose decisions are shaped by pressure, on the one hand, from the permanent bureaucracy and, on the other, from the intangible though powerful forces of public opinion, but whose own views are ultimately conclusive.

Chapter XIII

THE INITIATION OF WAR

1. The Rôle of Parliament

IN defining the relations between the legislature and the executive, the framers of the Constitution of 1875 were even more anxious to subject executive discretion to legislative control in the initiative of war than in the making of treaties, since, under the terms of the instrument which they drew up, the Cabinet is required to submit only certain specified categories of treaties to Parliament prior to ratification whereas all declarations of war must be approved by the Chambers. "The President of the Republic may not declare war without the previous assent of the two Chambers," declares the Constitution.[1] Here, as in the case of legislative participation in treaty making, the historical antecedents of the article in question had established an association between republicanism and parliamentary approval of executive action. In the *ancien régime* the war power was vested exclusively in the Crown. Mirabeau secured the insertion in the Constitution of the limited monarchy of 1791 of a provision for legislative consultation prior to a declaration of war. The initiative was to rest with the King, but a *décret* of the Legislative Body was to be required before war could be embarked upon.[2] This arrangement does not differ essentially from corresponding provisions in the Constitution of the year III, that of the Second Republic of 1848, and that of the Third Republic of 1875.[3] The extreme of democratic control of the war power was reached in Article 54 of the Constitution of the First Republic of June 24, 1793, which vested the initiative in the members of the Legislative Body, required a fifteen-day delay between a proposal for a declaration of war and a vote upon it, and specified that a declaration of war should become definitive only if approved within forty days by popular assemblies in the communes. This utopian scheme was never applied in practice, nor did it receive any serious consideration from the National Assembly of 1871 to 1875.[4] The Constitution of the Third Republic simply repeated the

[1] "Le président de la République ne peut déclarer la guerre sans l'assentiment préalable des deux Chambres," Law of July 16, 1875, Article 9. *Cf.* Chow, *op. cit.*, pp. 135f.

[2] "La guerre ne peut être décidée que par un décret du Corps Législatif rendu sur la proposition formelle et nécessaire du roi et sanctionné par lui." Constitution of 1791, Title III, Chap. III, Section 1, Article 2.

[3] *Cf.* Barthélemy, *Démocratie et politique étrangère*, pp. 310f.

[4] In Barthélemy's opinion, "L'idée d'une consultation positive et formelle des citoyens an moment de la déclaration de guerre est une idée chimérique, anarchique, antinationale," *op. cit.*, p. 310.

provisions of the earlier republican Constitutions requiring legislative assent for a declaration of war.

The precise legal meaning of Article 9 of the Constitutional Law of July 16, 1875, has been a subject of extensive commentary by lawyers and publicists. It is clear that the initiative in a declaration of war must come from the Cabinet. The Chambers might conceivably recommend a declaration of war to the Cabinet by passing a resolution to this effect—but no such instance has ever occurred. The Cabinet proposes and Parliament approves or disapproves. The most significant question which the article raises is whether the Cabinet may under certain circumstances resort to war without the preliminary formal assent of the Chambers. The answer must be an emphatic affirmative on the basis both of the opinions of authorities and of actual practice.[1] Barthélemy suggests that at least three categories of cases exist in which the constitutional necessity for parliamentary authorization of belligerent measures is doubtful: (1) hostilities against people who do not constitute a State in the legal sense; (2) hostilities of a defensive character in resistance to external aggression; (3) hostilities resulting from external aggression against an ally of France.[2] The first category would, of course, include colonial expeditions against "backward" peoples. The second would comprise all "wars of defense"—and under modern conditions almost all wars can be more or less persuasively presented in this guise. The Constitution of 1791 contained elaborate provisions to prevent the executive from escaping parliamentary control under this pretext, but later Constitutions have recognized, either expressly or by implication, not only the right but the duty of the executive to resist attack without waiting for parliamentary authorization. The Constitution of 1875 is silent upon this point, but since the executive controls the armed forces of the Republic and since invasion may obviously be resisted without legislative action, it follows that wars in resistance to aggression may be embarked upon without parliamentary approval.[3] As for defense of an ally, even the Constitution of 1791 allowed the King wide discretion here with no constitutional limitation on his power save the duty of informing the legislature. Under the Constitution of 1875 an attack upon an ally of the Republic apparently authorizes the Cabinet to recognize the existence of a state of war between France and the alleged aggressor with no necessity for a formal declaration by Parliament. In a diplomatic note of November 5, 1914, the Minister of Foreign Affairs informed the Powers that the country was at war with Turkey in consequence of the hostile acts of the Turkish fleet, under German command, against Russia.[4] Parliament was not in session and took no action on the matter.

[1] Chow, *op. cit.*, pp. 137–149.

[2] *Op. cit.*, pp. 311–313.

[3] Duguit, *op. cit.*, IV, pp. 802*f*.

[4] The French Prize Court held that war began at 3:00 A.M., October 29, 1914, with the killing of two French nationals on a French vessel when a Turkish squadron bombarded the port of

On October 17, 1915, the Quai d'Orsay issued a press release announcing that a state of war existed between the Republic and Bulgaria from 6:00 A.M., October 16, by the action of Bulgaria in attacking Serbia. Parliament was neither consulted nor even informed.

When all of the exceptions to the principle of Article 9 have been enumerated, very little remains of the power of Parliament to control the initiation of war. In the course of sixty years the French Chambers have never once voted a formal declaration of war upon the recommendation of the Cabinet, either for colonial expeditions and distant operations or for conflicts with other Great Powers.[1] In 1914, at the outbreak of the greatest of wars, the Cabinet informed the Chambers on August 3 that war already existed by act of Germany. Parliament agreed and voted war credits with no discussion whatever of its supposed constitutional right to determine when war shall be embarked upon.[2] No formal declaration of war was submitted for approval, since the Cabinet had so shaped the diplomatic situation that the declaration of war came from Germany. The existence of a state of war with Austria-Hungary was recognized by executive *décrets* on August 12, 1914, with no consultation of the Chambers in any way. The instances of Turkey and Bulgaria have already been noted. In every other instance of a resort to military force by the Cabinet in its handling of diplomatic relations with other States —and the number of such instances is legion—war was not formally declared or recognized as existing and no question of parliamentary authorization arose. Both overt acts and an intention to wage war are necessary to create a legal state of war. The intention has usually been denied by the Cabinet in explaining to Parliament the necessity for resorting to forcible measures. In the conquest of Madagascar, to be sure, Ferry admitted to Parliament that he was waging an undeclared war upon the Hovas[3] and the Chambers supported him in his policy without raising embarrassing questions of the constitutionality of such procedure. But such admissions are dangerous and Cabinets seldom make them.

Instead of asking the Chambers to declare war it is easier for the Cabinet from a political point of view and simpler from a constitutional point of view to present warlike operations to Parliament and the nation as "reprisals," as steps essential to enforce treaties or to protect the security of the Republic of its possessions, as police activities against "bandits" or "pirates," or as defensive measures forced upon the Government by the aggressive acts of other States. Such procedures have been adopted by the Cabinet in every single instance of a resort to force against other States

---

Odessa. The diplomatic note also cited this as the technical ground for war, though actually the Turkish attack upon Russia was the real *casus belli*.

[1] "Pratiquement . . . l'Article 9 est inapplicable pour les guerres véritables comme pour les expéditions," Duguit, *op. cit.*, p. 806.

[2] *Supra*, pp. 249f.

[3] *Supra*, p. 111.

during the period of the Third Republic. No French Ministry, since the fatal July 14, 1870, has gone before Parliament with a proposal for a declaration of war. During the sixty years of its existence the Government of the Republic has been engaged in war with the formal authorization of Parliament only between August 3, 1914 and November 11, 1918—and even here Parliament did not give its prior assent to any formal declaration of war but merely acquiesced, after the outbreak of hostilities, in the Cabinet's view that war existed by act of the enemy. But the other fifty-four years of the Third Republic have been years of "peace" only in a narrowly legalistic sense. French military and naval forces have fought the armies and fleets of China,[1] occupied the territory of disarmed Germany,[2] blockaded Soviet Russia, invaded its territory, and fostered civil war among its inhabitants,[3] conquered Tunis, Madagascar, Indo-China, and Morocco,[4] engaged in bloody fighting to suppress insurrections in Syria, Algeria, Morocco, and elsewhere, and used coercive measures against small and weak States in various parts of the world—all in periods of formal "peace." A full catalogue of such activities would probably show very few years during which French soldiers, sailors, or marines were not fighting hostile forces somewhere on one ground or another—and all without a declaration of war or prior parliamentary authorization of any kind.[5] So conclusive and uniform is the evidence that one might almost venture the prediction that if and when the "next war" comes, the French Cabinet, like all of its predecessors and its counterparts in other States, will again go before Parliament not to ask its approval in advance for a declaration of war, but to explain after the event how war has been thrust upon the Republic by the acts of other States in violating treaties or threatening the security of France or its allies. And in minor "wars" or interventions Parliament will, as usual, not be consulted at all—or, if consulted, will be hoodwinked until military operations are already well under way on orders from the Cabinet.

[1] *Supra*, pp. 87f.

[2] *Supra*, pp. 286f.

[3] *Supra*, pp. 257, 258.

[4] *Supra*, pp. 65f., 78f., 105f.

[5] Between 1901 and 1914 not a single year passed without French military operations in Morocco. These operations have been analyzed by Miss Edna Wallace in an unpublished M.A. thesis prepared at the University of Chicago, entitled *French Military Operations in the Western Sahara and Morocco*, Chicago, March, 1931. Such situations are not, of course, peculiar to the French Republic. Exact parallels can be found in the diplomatic history of all the other Great Powers. In the case of the supposedly peace-loving United States, it has been estimated that between 1789 and 1929 the American Government launched seventy-one military interventions in Latin America, thirty in Asia and Africa, and thirteen involving European Powers. Active military operations were under way during 92 out of the 126 years of "peace" between the United States and other countries. *Cf.* Miss Lulu Caine, *Conditions Underlying the Minor Wars and Interventions of the United States*, p. 507, unpublished Ph.D. thesis, University of Chicago, August, 1929. On Great Britain, *cf.* F. R. Flournoy, *Parliament and War*, London, 1927, *passim.* and Mary Jane Brumley, *Minor Wars and Interventions of the British Empire*, 1900–1926, unpublished M.A. thesis, University of Chicago, August, 1928.

A few references to the episodes analyzed in the preceding chapters will substantiate these generalizations. In the conquest of Tunis, the Chamber of Deputies voted credits for military action without knowing the real purpose of the expedition which the Cabinet had proposed. No war was declared and suggestions that the Government could not wage war without parliamentary approval were ignored.[1] Following the conquest and the establishment of the protectorate, Ferry argued that parliamentary approval of a treaty authorized the Government to use force in insuring its execution[2]— an argument which could be used with equal facility to justify the occupation of the Ruhr in 1923.[3] The same logic was successfully used by the Cabinet to secure legislative approval of credits for the military expedition against Annam.[4] The war with China, which followed, was embarked upon the Government without "l'assentiment préalable des deux Chambres." The military operations of 1893 against Siam were similarly conducted without prior parliamentary authorization of any declaration of war, though the Chambers sanctioned the use of force to protect French "rights."[5] The same was true of the conquest of Madagascar.[6] Similarly in the crisis of 1914 and in the use of force in the reparations controversy, troop movements did not follow but preceded parliamentary action, which in both cases took the form not of express *a priori* approval of warlike measures but of *a posteriori* acquiescence in the policy with which the Cabinet confronted the Chambers. In none of these cases, nor in any others that can be discovered, have the executive and the legislature in initiating military action followed the procedure apparently intended by Article 9 of the Law of July 16, 1875.

While Parliament does not initiate war, it does vote credits to carry it on after it has been precipitated by the Cabinet. Any control which it may exercise over the making of war it must therefore exercise through the power of the purse. Without money to carry it on, war is impossible. Money, in the large quantities usually needed to finance military and naval action, can be secured only by special parliamentary appropriations, since it is a well-established principle that the Cabinet may not withdraw funds from the treasury without legislative authorization. The Premier may raise small sums for limited periods by juggling the budget and transferring to military uses items appropriated for other purposes,[7] but this procedure may subject him to attack on legal grounds and is at best a poor expedient for financing military operations. When such operations are contemplated the Cabinet must base its decision quite as much upon the prospects of securing financial support from Parliament as upon the opportunities and dangers inherent

[1] *Supra*, pp. 67–70.
[2] *Supra*, pp. 74f.
[3] *Supra*, pp. 286f.
[4] *Supra*, pp. 79–80.
[5] *Supra*, pp. 101–102.
[6] *Supra*, pp. 111, 120–123.
[7] *Cf.* Ferry's tactics in 1881, *supra*, p. 72.

in the diplomatic situation. The ministers need seldom ask themselves: Will the Chambers declare war on the Cabinet's recommendation? Their problem is to shape the diplomatic situation in such fashion that the other State in the dispute will declare war or that the hostilities will appear "defensive" even if there is no declaration of war on either side. The manner in which such considerations influenced diplomatic and military action in July, 1914, has been analyzed in some detail above.[1] But the ministers must always ask themselves: Will the Chambers vote money for expenses to be incurred in military and naval operations? Opposition may be encountered unless the hostilities seem to be imposed upon the nation by its "security," its "national honor," its "vital interests," or some other cherished value. Here again the diplomatic issue must be presented in such form that the patriotic parliamentarians will be left with no reasonable alternative save support of the Government's policy. If the Cabinet asks for credits for military purposes without taking this precaution, it risks its majority and may be overthrown.[2]

When political expediency counsels deception, the Premier and foreign minister may make unauthorized expenditures and trust Parliament to approve them later;[3] they may postpone the opening of the session of the Chambers in order to avoid premature discussion of embarrassing questions;[4] they may disguise their purposes in order to secure credits in the hope that Parliament will ultimately approve if the venture is a success;[5] they may present a military reverse as a slight upon the national dignity, demanding revenge;[6] or they may soothe parliamentary anxiety by asking for only small quantities of money at frequent intervals.[7] Examples of all these devices, and others as well, may be found in the episodes which have been dealt with above. In the period of French diplomatic isolation and anxiety in the face of powerful foes, Cabinets were obliged to act cautiously in presenting demands for military credits to the Chambers. Not only were such demands sometimes rejected with a consequent curtailment or postponement of military plans by the Cabinet,[8] but governments were sometimes turned out of office when their policies appeared to be dangerous or unsuccessful.[9] Ferry's dramatic overthrow on March 31, 1885, is an instance of such action. In recent years, with the Republic once more the strongest of military Powers and exercising a more or less successful diplomatic hegemony over Western Europe, the Chambers have been less critical of demands for credits for warlike operations.

[1] *Supra,* pp. 216*f.*
[2] *Supra,* p. 82.
[3] *Supra,* pp. 74–75.
[4] *Supra,* p. 72.
[5] *Supra,* p. 80.
[6] *Supra,* p. 83.
[7] *Supra,* pp. 91–92.
[8] *Supra,* pp. 109*f.*
[9] *Supra,* pp. 82, 94–95, 125*f.*

Parliament's power of the purse may be used to control and restrain bellivolent Cabinets in a variety of ways. It may be exercised at the time of the voting of the regular budgets of the Ministries of War and Marine, though when discussion takes place on these items it usually centers about problems of the internal organization and efficiency of the military and naval forces, rather than about the uses to which they shall be put.[1] More frequently the Chambers exercise their power in connection with requests from the ministers for supplementary credits in addition to the regular budget—since such special credits are almost always required by military and naval operations. Requests of this kind occasionally give rise to extensive debates of the type reviewed in the cases of Tunis,[2] Tonkin,[3] and Madagascar.[4] More frequently demands for supplementary credits are granted without discussion.[5] In numerous instances, the Cabinet has resorted to the device of opening supplementary credits prior to their submission to Parliament for approval. While the abuses of this practice have at times been sharply criticized, no minister has ever been held civilly responsible for such action and the Senators and Deputies have usually acquiesced.[6] When this procedure is followed the Chambers are given no opportunity to pass upon the merits of the demands for money, since the expenditures have already been made. They must accept the Cabinet's *fait accompli* with good grace or turn the Government out of office. Even in the latter case, what has been done cannot readily be undone and it is too late, usually, to change the direction of policy.[7]

[1] *Cf.* Annual Budget Debates in *J.O.*

[2] *Supra*, pp. 67–70, 74f.

[3] *Supra*, pp. 79–80, 91–92, 101.

[4] *Supra*, pp. 122–123. In the Chamber debate of July 2, 1900, on the supplementary credits asked by the Minister of War for the expenses of the expedition south of Algeria, André Berthelot assailed the whole military policy of the government as unconstitutional. The Premier sought to refute such accusations and finally won the support of the Deputies. Berthelot proposed an *ordre du jour motivé*, thus conceived: "La Chambre, considérant que l'expédition d'Igli a été engagée pendant la session des Chambres et sans qu'elles aient été préalablement consultées, regrette l'illégalité commise et pass à l'ordre du jour." The Deputies, however, approved, 458 to 60, the *ordre du jour pur et simple* demanded by Waldeck-Rousseau, *J.O.Ch.*, July 3, 1900.

[5] For example, *cf. J.O.Ch.*, June 17, 1877; *J.O.Sén.*, June 23, 1877, etc.

[6] This practice is, of course, an exception to the general constitutional principle that the opening of credits is a legislative act. The Government is authorized, however, to open extraordinary or supplementary credits in emergencies by Presidential decree, while Parliament is not in session. A law of August 5, 1914, extended this right for the period of the war, but was abrogated by a law of November 30, 1915, which restored the original law of December 14, 1879, requiring that all such credits must be discussed and approved by the Council of Ministers and placed before the Council of State, and that they indicate the purpose and the method of the proposed expenditure. A law of August 10, 1922, permits the Government to make exceptional and unauthorized expenditures for national defense or for external or internal security, even while parliament is in session. If the Chambers do not approve subsequently and the expenditures thus remain illegal, the ministers and officials may be held civilly responsible. As Duguit points out, however, this remedy is wholly illusory, *op. cit.*, IV, pp. 617–623.

[7] *Cf. supra*, pp. 125f.

In summary, Parliament's control over the initiation of war is almost negligible. The Cabinet can always avoid a formal parliamentary declaration of war, or can shape the diplomatic and military situation in such fashion as to leave the Chambers no genuine choice. The Parliament's control over the budget is more impressive as a means of influencing the Cabinet's policies, but it is less important in practice than in theory because of the exceptions and deceptions which have been indicated. In the actual conduct of war, Parliament can have little voice, since deliberative bodies cannot plan campaigns nor fight battles. Only when wars are terminated by formal treaties of peace does Parliament have a real rôle—and even here, as has been shown in the preceding chapter, legislative control is often illusory.[1] The initiation and the waging of war are executive functions in the exercise of which the Cabinet enjoys a very large degree of freedom from parliamentary supervision.

2. THE MASTERS OF FORCE

In turning to problems of executive organization and procedure with reference to the commencement and the conduct of warfare, it is at once apparent that in France, as in most countries, control of the armed forces of the nation is vested in the chief executive. Article 3 of the Constitutional Law of February 25, 1875, declares that "the President of the Republic disposes of the armed forces." This provision has been broadly interpreted to include all of the active and reserve military, naval, and air forces of the Republic and to confer upon the President the power not only to order these forces into action but to assume command of them. Here, as in all things, the President acts only through the ministers and he is generally regarded as having no inherent right to assume military command in person. While he could perhaps be given such a right by decree there has been no instance of this kind. Such an assumption of personal command would, in any case, be flatly contrary to republican traditions, predicated as they are on fear of the man on horseback in view of the fate of the Second Republic.[2] The President therefore controls the armed forces only in a nominal sense, with the ministerial counter-signatures indicating the actual sources of power. The Cabinet thus controls the uses to which the armed forces of the Republic shall be put and may even control the details of their movements and organization, though the latter is largely fixed by statutes and decrees and the former is a matter for the determination of the military officers themselves.

Within the Cabinet, the Ministers of War, Marine, and Air have jurisdiction over their respective branches of the armed forces of the Republic. Both the metropolitan and colonial armies are under the control of the war minister, though the expenses of the colonial troops are assessed against the Ministry of Colonies, with the exception of the forces in Algeria, Tunis,

[1] Barthélemy, *Démocratie et politique étrangère*, pp. 314–316.
[2] Duguit, *op. cit.*, IV, pp. 602–606.

and Morocco. The total number of soldiers enrolled in the standing army of the Republic is about 578,000 at the time of writing,[1] but they constitute the skeleton of the nation in arms rather than a small, professional fighting force. Over 8,000,000 men were mobilized during the Great War. All questions of strategy and high military policy are dealt with by the *Conseil Supérieure de la Guerre* which was created by a law of July 27, 1872. This body is presided over by the Minister of War and consists of the twelve marshals of France and twelve selected generals, including the Chief of the General Staff. Its Vice President is Commander-in-Chief of the French Armiès in time of war. Naval strategy and policy are similarly in the hands of the *Conseil Supérieure de la Marine*, headed by the Minister of Marine and including the Chief of the Naval Staff. The Minister of Air has under his control the Directorates of the Army Air Services, of the Naval Air Forces, and of Civil Aviation, as well as the central air departments of the colonies. The disposition of the Republic's 1,700 fighting planes[2] is subject to the general plans of the military and naval councils,[3] which now collaborate with the newly created air council. These agencies are coordinated through the *Conseil Supérieure de la Défense Nationale*, composed of the President of the Republic, as chairman, the Premier, the Ministers of War, Marine, Air, Colonies, Foreign Affairs, Finance, Interior, and Public Works, and the Vice President of the *Conseil Supérieure de la Guerre* and of the *Conseil Supérieure de la Marine*. This body was created by a decree of April 3, 1906, and reorganized by decree of November 17, 1921.[4] Below these directing and coordinating boards is the usual hierarchy of military and naval officials and officers.

The problem of the location of control and responsibility in connection with the war power may be thought of in terms of the relationships between Parliament, the Cabinet, and the military command. As for the first of these, its limited rôle has already been indicated. The Chambers vote the annual budgets of the Ministries of War, of Marine, and of Air. In doing so they may determine the size and equipment of the military, naval, and air forces and review the conduct of administration in the respective departments. The Budget Commissions of the two chambers do, in fact, discuss such problems in consultation with the ministers in preparing their reports and recommendations to Parliament. But the ministers themselves make their own estimates of the financial needs of their departments on the basis of the technical advice of their subordinates and the Cabinet as a whole must in

---

[1] French memorandum to the League of Nations on disarmament, July 21, 1931.

[2] The memorandum cited above lists a total of 1,713 planes, "exclusive of those in immediate reserves," which would perhaps double the total number available for war purposes.

[3] *Cf.* J. Monteilhet, *Les institutions militaires de la France*, Paris, 1926; A. Thomazi, *La marine français dans la grande guerre*, Paris, 1925; Ministère de la Guerre, *Les armées françaises dans la grande guerre*, Vol. I, Chaps. I and II, Paris, 1923.

[4] For a useful short sketch of these agencies, see C. J. H. Hayes, *France—A Nation of Patriots*, pp. 64–93, New York, 1930.

every case formulate the military, naval, and air policy of the Government. Since its members represent the majority groups in the Chamber, its decisions are almost certain of acceptance, though active debate may take place in the commissions and on the floor of the Chambers and, in extreme cases, such problems may become questions of confidence and lead to the fall of the Cabinet. In practice, however, no Cabinet has ever been overthrown on a clear-cut issue of military or naval policy with the possible exception of the Ribot ministry of June, 1914. Universal compulsory military service has been required by parliamentary enactment throughout the entire history of the Third Republic. The principle of conscription has never been an issue between Cabinet and Parliament nor even between the principal party groups in the chambers. The conditions and the length of the required service, however, have frequently given rise to sharp differences of opinion. The whole nation was rocked by the three-year service law of 1913, to which, it will be recalled, successive Cabinets were pledged and which provoked vehement opposition from the Left in Parliament. When it appeared possible, as a result of the elections in which the parties opposed to the law made heavy gains, that a Cabinet might be created which would propose the repeal of the law or fail to enforce it, President Poincaré, in his anxiety to avoid such a calamity, almost overstepped the constitutional bounds of his office. Great pressure was brought to bear upon Viviani to retain the law in force, even though the prevailing sentiment in the Chambers and throughout the country seemed to be unfavorable to it. The pressure was effective and, as usual, parliamentary opposition was impotent before executive determination to carry through the military policy which had been adopted.[1] Nevertheless, Parliament ultimately determines not only the size and general organization of the war forces of the nation, but the length and conditions of service as well. To say that its decisions in these matters are largely guided and controlled by the Cabinet is merely to restate the normal relations between executive and legislature everywhere in parliamentary governments.[2]

From the point of view of many parliamentarians, the Chambers are policy-determining agencies with reference to military, as well as to civil, affairs and the ministers are the executive agents which carry out the policies which Parliament has formulated and adopted. But the ministers regard themselves (and properly so) not as administrators exclusively, but also as framers of policies which they count upon Parliament to approve so long as the Cabinet possesses the confidence of the Chambers. The typical minister is a not a technical administrator, but a political amateur who carries out the policies which the Cabinet has formulated and the Parliament has adopted through the services of the permanent staff of *fonctionnaires* under his direction. These permanent expert officials are the actual administrators,

---

[1] *Supra*, pp. 207–209; *cf*. Montheilhet, *op. cit.*, pp. 267f.

[2] The law of 1928 provides for a one-year period of active service, three years in the *disponsibilité*, sixteen years in the first reserve, and eight years in the second reserve.

entrusted with the duty of putting into execution the orders of the ministers and the acts of Parliament.   A sharp line between the determination of policy and the administrative execution of policy is admittedly difficult to draw, in military as in non-military matters. But from the point of view of the procedure of initiating war and of controlling the armed forces of the nation, it is important to bear in mind the general theory of the distribution of governmental functions which underlies the whole parliamentary system. This theory differs radically from the American conception of a separation of powers between independent executive, legislative, and judicial departments. It can better be couched in the terms already suggested. Governmental functions from this point of view consist of formulating policies and programs of action on the one hand, and in putting such policies and programs into practical execution on the other. Parliament determines policies. The permanent civil service carries them out. The ministers constituting the Cabinet are the agents of *liaison* who guide Parliament in its task of formulating policies and at the same time direct the permanent staff in the administration and execution of the policies which have been incorporated into law.

The most significant feature of these relationships is that the permanent officials play a much more important rôle in practice than they appear to enjoy in theory. The war staffs themselves presumably have no control over such questions of public policy as the size, general organization, and recruitment of the army, the navy, and the air services, all of which fall within the scope of legislative determination, but are limited to the technical details of administering such programs as Parliament establishes. In practice this distinction tends to break down. The permanent staff—including both the civilian and professional military officials in the three war ministries— actually assumes the functions of policy determination through its inevitable pressure upon the ministers who are temporarily in charge of their activities. When the ministers are civilian amateurs they must necessarily rely upon the advice of technical experts and professional military men in formulating their programs and preparing recommendations to Parliament for legislation and appropriations. When they are themselves professional military officers or naval commanders, as is the case in about half of the Cabinets,[1] their outlook is necessarily more or less identical with that of their professional subordinates. In either case the real source of initiative and control would seem to lie with the permanent staffs of the army, navy, and air forces rather

[1] Of forty-five Ministers of War, who served between February 19, 1871, and October 22, 1929, twenty-seven were army officers, two were engineers, and one was an army instructor. Of forty-eight Ministers of Marine who served during the same period, sixteen were naval commanders. These posts have been held less frequently in recent Cabinets by professional naval and military men than was formerly the case, but it is obvious that the heads of the war ministries are less often "amateurs" as regards the work of their departments than their colleagues in the Cabinet. The writer is indebted for the above figures to a series of tables on the personnel of French Cabinets prepared by Professor J. Gilbert Heinberg of the University of Missouri. *Cf.* his "The Personnel of French Cabinets, 1871-1930," *American Political Science Review*, XXV, pp. 389–396, May, 1931.

than with Parliament or the Cabinet. The subjection of military authority
to civilian control has often been an important political issue in French
politics, but only because of fear of Bonapartism and dictatorship. The
efforts of Parliament to control the use of the armed forces in foreign affairs,
and even to shape the general military policy of the Government, have been
feeble and ineffective. Real power over these matters rests with the professional war makers who are in fact able to determine policies through their
daily pressure upon the ministers in the routine of administration and
through the prestige of technical knowledge which they enjoy in the
deliberations of the *Conseil Supérieure de la Défense Nationale* and of the subsidiary military, marine, and air councils. The war ministers are the focal
points of pressures brought to bear by their colleagues in the Cabinet, by the
Senators and Deputies, and by their professional subordinates in their
departments.   The last mentioned source of pressure would appear to be the
most significant and decisive from a long-run point of view.

While it is obvious that, in war time, control of military policy passes
to the professional military authorities, it is not commonly realized that they
frequently exert an almost equally effective, if less open, control in times of
peace. Under ordinary circumstances the Ministers of War, Marine, and Air,
in collaboration with the Premier, the Minister of Foreign Affairs, and sometimes of other members of the Cabinet, make such disposition of the armed
forces of the Republic as is required by considerations of efficiency, economy,
and national security. The movements, location, and concentration of army
divisions, war fleets, and air squadrons are under their direction and the
general terms of statutes passed by Parliament seldom limit their discretion
in these respects.[1] But their discretion can be exercised intelligently only
on the basis of the technical advice of the professional war makers. This
advice need not be followed, it is true, since the ministers direct the permanent staff under their control rather than take orders from it. But a
minister who has himself had a career in the army or navy will be inclined
to take such advice, which is likely to coincide with his own views, and
one who is an amateur will be almost compelled to do so by his own ignorance. The orders which are finally given are issued in the name of the President of the Republic over the signature of the minister in question.[2] This
procedure is followed even in the extreme case of general mobilization, which
has been ordered only once during the life of the Third Republic—on the
fatal first of August, 1914, and at the demand, be it noted, of the Chief of the

---

[1] "En temps de paix . . . la gouvernement est libre sans réserve d'ordonner les mouvements
et les concentrations de troupes qu'il juge à propos pour assurer la sécurité extérieure et intérieure
du pays. Il peut déterminer librement les emplacements des forces militaires," Duguit, *op. cit.*,
IV, p. 598.

[2] In Duguit's opinion, military commanders may not refuse to obey the orders of the ministers
even if they are contrary to law, *ibid.*, IV, p. 597. But since the orders are usually issued by the
Ministers on the advice of the high military command, such situations seldom arise.

General Staff.[1] Mobilization usually means war. But Parliament is not consulted. Here, as in the case of smaller movements and concentrations of troops or war vessels, the order will be issued by the appropriate minister, after consultation with the Premier and usually with the Cabinet as a whole, and again, in most cases, on the basis of the advice of the professional warriors.

After military operations have been embarked upon, whether or not they involve the nation in a legal state of war, the ministers directing action must necessarily subordinate themselves more or less completely, on technical questions of strategy and tactics, to the advice of the professional military experts who are supposedly under their control. If the operations are of

[1] "Le Président de la République Française,

"Vu l'article de la loi constitutionnelle du 25 février 1875, relative à l'organisation des pouvoirs publics;

"Vu les titres III et IV de la loi du 24 juillet 1873, relative à l'organisation générale de l'armée;

"Vu la loi du 19 mars 1875, relative à la mobilisation par voie d'affiches et de publication sur la voie publique;

"Vu la loi du 3 juillet 1877 sur les réquisitions militaires, modifiée par les lois des 5 mars 1890, 27 mars 1906 et 23 juillet 1911;

"Vu la loi du 22 juillet 1909, relative à la réquisition des voitures automobiles;

"Vu la loi du 28 décembre 1888, modifiant les articles 22 à 27 (service militaire des chemins de fer) de la loi du 13 mars 1875;

"Vu la loi du 21 mars 1905, modifiée par la loi du 7 août 1913 sur le recrutement de l'armée:

"Vu l'avis du conseil des ministres,

"Décrète:

"Art. 1.er—La mobilisation des armées françaises de terre et de mer est ordonnée sur toute l'étendue du territoire français, en Algérie, dans les autres colonies et dans les pays de protectorat.

"Art. 2.—En France, en Corse, en Algérie et en Tunisie, la mobilisation sera portée à la connaissance des populations au moyen d'affiches qui seront immédiatement placardées sur la voie publique.

"Art. 3.—Dans les colonies (autre que l'Algérie), la mobilisation sera portée à la connaissance des populations par les soins des gouverneurs.

"Dans les pays de protectorat (autres que la Tunisie), elle sera portée à la connaissance des Français soumis aux obligations militaires par les soins des résidents généraux.

"Art. 4.—Le présent décret entraine l'appel a l'activité des hommes qui ont été designés, dès le temps de paix, pour constituer les unités de douaniers ou de chasseurs forestiers ainsi que les services accessoires de l'armée (trésorerie et postes, télégraphie militaire, sections de chemins de fer de campagne, etc.) et qui ont reçu, en conséquence, une affection spéciale.

"Art. 5.—Le droit de réquisition est ouvert sur tout le territoire français, en Algérie et aux colonies. Il s'exercera conformément aux lois et décrets en vigeur.

"Dans les pays de protectorat, les réquisitions s'opéront d'après les conventions arrêtées avec les gouvernements de ces pays de protectorat.

"Art. 6.—Les autorités civiles, militaires, maritimes et coloniales sont chargées, sous leur responsabilité, de veiller à l'exécution des dispositions du présent décret.

"Fait à Paris, le 1er août 1914.

"R. Poincaré.

"Par le Président de la République:

"*Le ministre de la guerre,*   *Le ministre de la marine,*
MESSIMY.   GAUTHIER."

J.O., *Partie Offic· 'le,* August 2, 1914.

major proportions, as in a war with another Great Power, the usual rôles of minister and permanent staff will be reversed, since the most elementary considerations of defense require that the military and naval high command shall have a free hand in directing the campaign. A decree of October 28, 1913, declared that in time of war the Cabinet is limited to determining the political ends of military operations, involving the allocation of effort between various theaters of war, but not extending to technical questions of the conduct of hostilities. On December 5, 1915, General Joffre was made generalissimo of the French armies by a decree which gave him full control of war operations, even to the extent of allocating forces between various fronts—a power expressly reserved to the Government by the 1913 decree. This led to criticism in the Chamber, but the Government refused to discuss the matter and was upheld by the Deputies, 394 to 169.[1] In war the determination of policy and its practical administration both pass into the hands of professional strategists, since war cannot be waged effectively by civilian politicians. The latter may consult, cajole, offer advice, and even insist upon the acceptance of their own views, and the pressures brought to bear in this fashion may be determining, but usually the military officials will have the deciding voice. This situation may easily arise even in the absence of a recognized state of war under circumstances in which war seems imminent or in which military operations are under way. The professional military authorities are thus in a position to influence the course of diplomacy itself before it gives way to war—and, in view of their vocation, their influence will ordinarily be exerted in favor of forcible measures.

The foregoing analysis can again be readily substantiated by reference to the concrete situations which have been reviewed in the preceding chapters. In practically all of the instances cited, the resort to force followed upon a decision of the Premier or Minister of Foreign Affairs to have recourse to warlike measures to achieve a diplomatic objective, often on the advice of the military authorities. Once military action gets under way, control of the whole diplomatic situation tends to pass into the hands of generals or admirals, usually with the acquiescence of the ministers. In the conquest of Tunis the first recommendations for the use of force apparently came from the diplomatic agent on the scene.[2] The Governor-General of Algeria at first dissented and later agreed on the advisability of military action, after learning of the ambitious plan of the Cabinet. The foreign minister transmitted the diplomatic dispatches to the war minister who was a professional army officer and who urged the use of force as the best means of achieving the objective in view.[3] The same advice was tendered by the director of

---

[1] *J.O.Ch.*, February 19, 1916. *Cf.* Duguit, *op. cit.*, IV, pp. 599–601. After Verdun the Cabinet conceded the right of the Deputies to discuss the question in secret session but the decree was not modified.

[2] *Supra*, p. 64.

[3] *Supra*, p. 66.

political affairs at the Quai d'Orsay. After the Cabinet had decided upon military action the Minister of War went before the Chamber to ask for credits which the Deputies voted without knowing the real purposes in the minds of the ministers. The final treaty was imposed upon the Bey by the French military commanders, at the order of the foreign minister.[1]

In the conquest of Tonkin, the Premier seemingly took the initiative in asking the Minister of Marine to prepare plans for an expeditionary force.[2] Following a Cabinet upset, the new Minister of Marine stopped all movements of ships and troops much to the disgust of the local commander, the Governor of Cochin-China. The next Cabinet acted upon the original plan, but the troops acted under orders from the Governor, and the Premier professed ignorance as to their movements.[3] The situation which resulted permitted the local military and naval commanders, with the connivance of the diplomatic agents on the scene, to shape events in such fashion as to make war with China inevitable, despite the apparently pacific inclinations of the Cabinet in Paris.[4] In the hostilities which followed, the Minister of Marine sought to direct the strategy of the admirals, but actual power had passed into the hands of the professional war makers who acted in accordance with their own views, again with the support of the local diplomatic representative. The ministers in Paris were in no position to ignore their advice and in the ensuing confusion of diplomacy and strategy, of policy formulation and policy administration, effective control was exercised by the strategist-administrators rather than by the diplomat-politicians,[5] even though the Minister of War, the Paris spokesman for the former group, resigned because of the criticism of his recommendations expressed by the Premier and other members of the Cabinet.[6] In the hostilities with Siam, the Cabinet decided upon a policy of force and a military and naval program was formulated by the Minister of Foreign Affairs in consultation with the Minister of War and Marine and the under-secretary of state for the Colonies.[7] But the local naval commander received conflicting orders from the Quai d'Orsay and from his immediate superiors in the Navy. He obeyed the latter and thus precipitated hostilities, contrary to the wishes of the Minister of Foreign Affairs.[8] Subsequently the admirals imposed a war blockade against the "enemy," even though no war had been declared and the Quai d'Orsay had not sanctioned such a measure. A grave diplomatic crisis with Great Britain resulted, due entirely to the actions of the military and naval commanders on the scene of action.[9]

[1] *Supra*, pp. 68–71.
[2] *Supra*, p. 80.
[3] *Supra*, p. 81.
[4] *Supra*, pp. 85–86.
[5] *Supra*, pp, 89f.
[6] *Supra*, p. 92.
[7] *Supra*, pp. 98–99.
[8] *Supra*, p. 101.
[9] *Supra*, p. 102.

In the case of Madagascar, a resort to force was urged by the local diplomatic agent. The Premier at first refused to consent, but intrusted negotiations with the Hova mission in Paris to the Chief of the General Staff and finally decided that forcible measures were necessary.[1] The Minister of Foreign Affairs and the Minister of Marine sent identical instructions to the admiral and to the diplomatic representative on the scene.[2] Later the diplomatic agent appeared, paradoxically, as the advocate of force, while the admiral urged pacific negotiations. The latter's recommendations were transmitted to the foreign minister by the Minister of Marine and acted upon.[3] In the final contest the commanding generals became agents of the diplomacy of the bayonet and later crushed the rebellion, organized French control of the island, and became colonial administrators.[4]

This extension of the power of the military bureaucracy into the spheres of diplomacy and high politics is strikingly apparent in the interplay of the European balance of power prior to and during the explosion of 1914. In the Franco-Russian Alliance negotiations, the initiative came entirely from the Minister of War (who was also Premier) and the Minister of Marine.[5] The former, Freycinet, was a military engineer by profession. The military agreement of 1892 was signed, on behalf of the French Government, by the Chief Adjoint of the General Staff[6] and the naval convention of 1912 by the Minister of Marine and an admiral.[7] The real substance of the Anglo-French Entente was similarly not to be found in diplomatic notes and agreements, but in the intimate contacts established between the military and naval authorities of the two countries.[8] In the final crisis, differences of opinion as to policy developed between the Cabinet and the Chief of the General Staff as soon as diplomatic problems became confused with problems of military strategy. The result was the temporary compromise of the "ten-kilometer withdrawal," followed at once by renewed pressure from the army commanders for further preparations for war. Their misrepresentations of the military danger from Germany alarmed the Cabinet and hastened the decision to resort to arms.[9] The eager anxiety of the strategists to take the last irrevocable step was thwarted by diplomatic considerations, but only for a moment. Finally, the Chief of the General Staff, General Joffre, demanded mobilization. The Minister of War agreed and the Cabinet consented.[10] When the unleashing of the military mechanism ended all reasonable

[1] *Supra*, pp. 106–108.
[2] *Supra*, pp. 108–109.
[3] *Supra*, p. 114.
[4] *Supra*, pp. 123–127.
[5] *Supra*, pp. 137f.
[6] *Supra*, pp. 145–146.
[7] *Supra*, p. 157.
[8] *Supra*, pp. 191–194.
[9] *Supra*, pp. 234–236.
[10] *Supra*, p. 241.

hope of a pacific settlement, Joffre was given complete liberty of action by the Cabinet.[1]

In the occupation of the Ruhr, the military forces always remained under the control of the Premier and Minister of Foreign Affairs, since the situation was not one threatening open hostilities, but even here diplomatic decisions were influenced to no small degree by the advice of Foch and the strategists. The substance of the post-war alliances between France on the one hand, and Belgium, Poland, and the Little Entente States on the other, is to be found not in the published treaties and conventions, but in the secret plans for military cooperation worked out by the general staffs of the countries involved. Diplomacy here again is in the hands of the military authorities. Similarly, the break-down of the Anglo-French-Italian naval negotiations in the spring of 1931, after a tentative agreement had been announced, appears to have been due in part to French naval policy having been determined by professional navy officials, such as Admiral Darlan and René Massigli, chief naval expert at the Quai d'Orsay. These officials, with the acquiescence of the foreign minister, Briand, took the view that France must reserve the right to increase by 66,000 tons, to be laid down between 1934 and 1936, the allotment of 136,000 tons of war vessels accorded to her in the Franco-Italian agreement of March 1, 1931. This agreement forbade further new naval constuction by France and Italy after the completion of the 1930 program until December 1, 1936. The French position, however, was that the construction of new war vessels to replace others becoming obsolete might be begun during the *interim* providing that they were not launched before its expiration. This insistence on replacement rights was based upon an interpretation of the original accord wholly unacceptable to both the British and Italian Governments. The agreement therefore failed of acceptance and a diplomatic deadlock resulted—due evidently to the acceptance by Briand of the policy advocated by the naval technicians.[2] This is simply another instance of policy determination passing into the hands of professional warriors instead of remaining under the control of the civilian ministers.

In summary, the views of generals and admirals often become decisive factors in diplomatic negotiations, since war and diplomacy are inseparable when force is employed as a diplomatic weapon. What is perhaps more significant, such officials are frequently in a position to influence decisions as to when, how, and under what circumstances forcible measures shall be resorted to. To be sure, the Minister of Foreign Affairs, in consulation with his colleagues and under the direction of the Premier, supposedly determines whether military and naval forces shall be employed in diplomatic disputes and what political objectives they shall pursue. But he will in most cases be relatively ignorant of strategy and of the tactical dangers and opportunities of a given situation. Unless he rejects outright all utilization of armed

---

[1] *Supra*, pp. 242–244. *Cf. Les armées françaises dans la grande guerre*, I, pp. 68–90.

[2] *Cf.* New York *Times*, March 11 and 12; April 14 and 27, 1931.

force, he is under the necessity of heeding the advice of the Ministers of War, Marine, and Air, who, in turn, are dependent for technical information upon their professional subordinates in the army, navy, and air forces. It is, therefore, inevitable that diplomatic decisions should be shaped and in some cases even dictated by military rather than by civilian authorities. The servants become masters by virtue of the dependence of their nominal masters upon them for information and guidance. This is perhaps the normal relationship between amateurs and professionals within an administrative organization which of necessity places a higher premium upon the efficiency, speed, and success of military action than upon civilian restraints which might lead to confusion of counsels and to disaster in a national emergency. In consequence, the military and naval high commands are not purely administrative agencies at the disposal of the policy-determining organs of the Government, but are frequently in a position to determine policies themselves by bringing to bear upon the ministers pressures and influences which may be hidden and imponderable, but which are nevertheless substantial and effective.

3. POUR LA PATRIE!

When war has been embarked upon on a grand scale, most of the normal operations of the political process in peace time come to an end and the Government ceases to be a forum of debate and a referee between conflicting groups. It becomes instead a directing and planning agency for the mobilization of all the human and material resources of the State against the enemy. All domestic contests for power are subordinated to the exigencies of a combat between Great Powers for mastery. This usually involves, in greater or lesser degree, a suspension of the deliberative functions of the legislature and a more or less complete transfer of control to the executive authorities. As one observer described the situation in 1914, "The Chamber and the Senate had disappeared; the Cabinet had become so intimately united with the military authorities that the war office seemed to be the only seat of government."[1] In a war of major proportions, waged under the technological and psychological conditions imposed by the machine age, a whole series of administrative and legal changes in the peace-time organization and operation of government become necessary.[2] But these problems have little direct relation to the conduct of foreign affairs and need not be discussed as part of the present inquiry.

There is one aspect of the actual conduct of hostilities, however, which has an immediate bearing upon the formulation of foreign policies preceding a resort to war. A Premier, foreign minister, or diplomat, in making his

[1] Abbé Dimnet, *France Herself Again*, p. 497, Chatto and Windus, London, 1914.

[2] *Cf.* P. Renouvin, *The Forms of War Government in France*, pp. 1–26, New Haven, 1927; A. Bosc, "Les actes de gouvernement et la théorie des pouvoirs de guerre," *Revue de droit public et de la science politique*, Vol. 43, pp. 186–257, 1926.

calculations as to the probable reception on the part of Parliament, the press, and the public, of a decision to resort to forcible measures in an international controversy, may usually assume that if the issues at stake can be presented in terms of "national honor," "vital interests," "security," or other shibboleths of patriotism, he can draw for support upon a vast reservoir of power which can seldom be tapped in any effective way in dealing with domestic affairs. This source of power flows from the complex of group emotions, social attitudes, and mass-behavior patterns which compose the fabric of ethnocentric nationalism.

France, like all other States in the Western State System, is a "nation of patriots."[1] The patriotism of its people is possibly more ardent and active than that of any other national community.[2] National patriotism in its modern aspect, in France as elsewhere in Western civilization, was originally part and parcel of the ideology of the rising *bourgeoisie* in the period between the fifteenth and nineteenth centuries. But with the industrial revolution and the triumph of middle-class democracy it became the heritage of all groups and classes of the population until, in the period of the Third Republic, it is a universal and all-pervasive loyalty to *la Patrie*, inspiring the thought and action of all French citizens. The only group which must perhaps be excepted from this generalization is that portion of the urban proletariat which, as a result of its status of economic inferiority and relative impotence in capitalistic society, rejects the established social and political order and derives the emotional satisfactions which patriotism furnishes to others from a consciousness of solidarity with the world proletariat and from dreams of social revolution. But this group and its political leaders are beyond the pale of republican respectability and—being always in the opposition on every question—need scarcely be reckoned with by the Government save as a possible source of parliamentary obstructionism or of extra-parliamentary subversive activities.[3] The great mass of Frenchmen, including the major portion of the proletariat itself, as well as the *grande* and *petite bourgeoisie*, and the peasantry, is solidly patriotic, with a loyalty which is capable of releasing enormous stores of national energy for whatever heroic sacrifices or deeds of valor may be required. The million and a half sons of France—"*mort pour la patrie*"—lying in the battlefield cemeteries of the Great War, are eloquent, if silent, witnesses to the patriotic devotion of a people to whom nothing is dearer than its national culture and traditions and its sense of common allegiance to *la belle France*.

The close association between the emotional responses of patriotism and the stimuli furnished by war situations scarcely needs to be emphasized.[4]

[1] *Cf.* Carlton J. H. Hayes, *France—A Nation of Patriots*, New York, 1929.

[2] "Indeed, no other modern nationality (save, perhaps, the English) possesses a common consciousness more deeply rooted or more stubbornly enduring than the French," *ibid.*, p. 1.

[3] *Ibid.*, pp. 318f.

[4] *Ibid.*, pp. 343–400, containing a digest of French history textbooks and revealing clearly the predominance of war ideology in French national psychology.

The French Nation-state, like its neighbors, was born of war. The French Republic was the creation of patriots resisting foreign invasion. Its flag shines with the white heat of devotion, the red blood of courage, the true blue of loyalty—the virtues of a thousand fields of strife and victory. Its national anthem is a battle hymn. Its physical symbols of national power are the army, the fleet, the air squadrons of the Republic. Among the monuments of the mighty past are the *Arc de Triomphe*, the tomb of Napoleon, *l'École Militaire*, and the *Champ de Mars*, all reminiscent of warriors and war. The "Gallery of Battles" in the great palace at Versailles is one of the most cherished shrines of patriots. National patriotism, in France as everywhere, derives much of its inspiration from the sacrifice of battle and the glory of combat.[1] Prowess in war and the pride of power are its supreme values. Death for *la Patrie* is its supreme act of devotion. Immediately after a bloody and costly international conflict these enthusiasms and associations may be weakened in the popular mind. But memories are short and the "glory" of war is recalled long after its horrors are forgotten. The systematic teaching of the duties of patriotism to each new generation, and the inculcation of reverence for the war-dead of the past, soon reestablish sacrifice in war as the noblest expression of national loyalty.[2] The wartime responses of patriotism always involve uncritical allegiance and obedience to the Government of the day, unhesitating acceptance of the exigencies of the conflict, whole-hearted support of the armed forces of the Republic, and the condemnation, as "traitors," of all who venture to attack the policies of the Cabinet or to give aid or encouragement to the real or potential foe beyond the frontier. In war, popular acquiescence in the acts of the State is transformed into enthusiastic support of the Cabinet in power as the living symbol of national strength.

Every Premier and Minister of Foreign Affairs can safely calculate that a major war, embarked upon under circumstances giving the appearance of foreign aggression, will win for the Cabinet the almost unanimous support of patriotic opinion in the Chambers, the press, and throughout the country. All groups, parties, and classes of the electorate, with the occasional exception of the irreconcilable revolutionaries of the extreme Left, rally to the defense of *la Patrie* and to the support of its representatives and leaders in the Government in office. The striking unanimity of French opinion in August, 1914, later expressed in the *Union sacrée*, reveals the ease with which patriotic sentiment can be mobilized by the Government for a resort to arms.[3] The

[1] Maurice Barrès, the great patriot of the *révanche*, wrote as follows in 1884: "Certainly they have a terrible anger, those of our forefathers who love us most! And we ourselves, who look back to the dark year (1870) in the vague mist of our childhood, feel that the honor of *la Patrie* is embodied in the marching ranks of a regiment; all the military fanfares carry us back to the conquered soil; the waving of the flags seems to us a distant signal to the exiles; our fists clench; and we have only to make ourselves provocative agents." *Les taches d'encre*, November 5, 1884, quoted in Carlton Hayes, *The Historical Evolution of Modern Nationalism*, p. 185, New York, 1931.

[2] For an interesting study of the attitudes of school children toward war, see Alice Descoeudres, *Ce que pensent les enfants*, III, *Le Militaire*, Neuchatel et Genève, 1924, *passim*.

[3] *Supra*, pp. 248f.

same possibility exists to a lesser degree in situations not constituting an open state of war, but involving the employment of force on a smaller scale for other purposes. The extent to which the Cabinet can reply upon patriotic emotionalism to win it the support of Parliament and the nation in warlike policies obviously depends upon the degree to which a conflict situation in foreign affairs can be presented to the nation in terms which seem to involve values cherished by the entire national community. A contest of strength with another Great Power which requires every ounce of national energy and endurance to protect the integrity and the existence of the nation will silence all opposition. Minor wars, interventions, and distant military or naval expeditions, which involve only a small fraction of the power of the nation, will not have this result, and may, indeed, increase criticism of the Government. Between these two extremes many variations are possible. A shrewd Premier or foreign minister, can, within limits, turn on or off at will the dynamo of patriotic fervor by skillful handling of the controls. If he succeeds in presenting a conflict situation as a national cause, in his contacts with the Deputies, Senators, journalists, politicians, and other formulators of opinion, he will win the support of all patriots. If he fails to do this, patriots will not hesitate to attack his policies and even to turn him out of office.

Foreign war has frequently furnished statesmen with an escape from domestic embarrassments and with an effective means of silencing domestic opposition. The effectiveness of the means is dependent upon the proportions of the war, which also fixes the limits of ultimate danger to the war makers and to the nation. In the summer of 1870 Louis Napoleon staked his all in the game—and lost.[1] In the history of the Third Republic there is no clear instance of a government deliberately embarking upon a war as a means of escaping internal difficulties and winning the united support of the nation. Arguments of patriotic duty to the obligations of the Dual Alliance, however, were used at times against the Left opposition and made weapons of domestic politics.[2] On numerous occasions when force has been resorted to in diplomatic controversies, the Cabinet has made political capital out of the patriotism of Parliament and the nation, and has countered the criticism of its opponents by wrapping itself in the flag and presenting its policies as essential to protect the interest and safety of the State. In the Tunis episode, Ferry confronted the Chambers with a *fait accompli* and insisted, successfully, that parliamentary and public approval of the Government's course was an obligation of patriotism.[3] In the Tonkin operations, the news of a military reverse and the death of a French commander at the hands of the "enemy" led the Chambers to vote war credits in a great outburst of patriotic enthusiasm to avenge the national honor.[4] Parliament was equally willing,

[1] *Supra*, pp. 5–6.
[2] *Supra*, Chap. VII, *passim*.
[3] *Supra*, pp. 69, 75–76.
[4] *Supra*, p. 83.

on patriotic grounds, to approve the use of force against Siam.[1] In the conquest of Madagascar, the Chambers similarly approved forcible measures for patriotic reasons,[2] although at one time the Cabinet hesitated to act out of fear of parliamentary criticism,[3] and a later Cabinet was overturned when the war led to a stalemate.[4] The Ruhr occupation, in its early phases, also enabled the Cabinet to present the issue in terms of *la Patrie versus* the hereditary foe, and the opposition was accordingly silenced.[5] On the other hand, instances can be found of Parliament and the public repudiating a Cabinet which proposes to embark on military measures not having the appearance of involving the national honor, prestige, or security[6] or threatening disaster or serious diplomatic embarrassments.[7] In general, however, when a resort to force can be presented in patriotic guise, when it leads to success in attaining ends regarded as desirable by patriots, the Government can be reasonably certain that patriotic sentiment and loyalty will cause the nation to follow it in the course which it proposes to pursue.

This political calculation, whether made deliberately or assumed unconsciously by those responsible for the formulation of foreign policy, is patently a factor of major significance in situations which lead to war. The uncritical devotion and unhesitating allegiance of all Frenchmen to France when the security, honor, or prestige of the nation seem to be at stake, can be relied upon by all French statesmen in their handling of foreign affairs. Before military measures are adopted, the Government's foreign policy may be subjected to the same criticisms and attacks as are made on its domestic policies in the customary thrust and parry of party politics. But once war is resorted to—or forcible measures approximating war—criticism of the Government becomes treason. The Cabinet is, in a sense, released from responsibility and can proceed with its task, assured of the support of a united nation. The degree to which this assurance makes Cabinets less reluctant than they might otherwise be to resort to force is obviously not reducible to measurable terms. That it has had such an effect at times is scarcely open to doubt. National patriotism, in its bearing upon the relations between rulers and ruled, may thus be regarded as a contributing cause of war in so far as it encourages the Cabinet in power to resort to violence in international controversies, confident that such measures, far from subjecting it to criticism, will tend to smother opposition and give the Government the enthusiastic support of all good patriots throughout the nation. All patriots are not warlike. But all wars are patriotic.

[1] *Supra*, pp. 101–102.
[2] *Supra*, pp. 119f.
[3] *Supra*, p. 110.
[4] *Supra*, pp. 125f.
[5] *Supra*, pp. 291f.
[6] *Supra*, p. 82.
[7] *Supra*, pp. 94–95.

Chapter XIV

THE FORMULATION OF FOREIGN POLICY

1. Patriotism and the Past

THAT nationalism is the most dynamic social force determining the goals and the direction of foreign policy in every national State is a truism so obvious that it would scarcely be in need of restatement except that its implications are frequently forgotten in discussions of international problems. National patriotism is the most distinctive characteristic of the State System of contemporary Western civilization. It has asserted its predominance over all other forms of group loyalty and allegiance so successfully that citizens everywhere accept it as a matter of course that their governments, symbolizing the power of their nations, should expect them to renounce all they possess—their money, their property, and, if need be, their lives—in the service of the national State. The nation has become the final repository of atavistic ethnocentrism and the most highly developed manifestation of the social-behavior patterns of the human animal. The controlling rôle of nationalism as a determinant of French foreign policy has been apparent in every phase of the present inquiry.

With the historical origins and the psychological aspects of national patriotism in France this study cannot legitimately concern itself. A summary of the conclusions of scientific investigators regarding nationalism as a general social phenomenon, however, would be distinctly pertinent to an attempt to analyze and evaluate its place in French foreign policy, since French national patriotism is similar to patriotism everywhere throughout the Western world, differing from its counterparts elsewhere only in its longer history, its more solid foundations, and the distinctive attributes and idiosyncrasies stamped upon it by the Gallic temperament and by the geographical *milieu* in which it has developed. Unfortunately, nationalism is one of the many objects of investigation by social scientists regarding which there has been more heat than light.[1] Oceans of ink and tons of print paper have been utilized in discussing it, but the residue of valid scientific conclusions is extremely small. The most that can be said is that there is general

---

[1] Among the few illuminating analyses of nationalism, treated from a point of view with which the present writer is in sympathy, are Hans Kohn, *A History of Nationalism in the East*, (Harcourt, Brace & Company, New York, 1929), Robert Michels, "Zur historischen Analyse des Patriotismus," *Archiv für Sozialwissenschaften und Sozialpolitik*, vol. 36, pp. 14–43, 394–449, and *Der Patriotismus, Prolegomena zu seiner soziologischen Analyse* (Duncker und Humblot, München und Leipzig, 1929).

agreement that nationalism, while it has deep roots in the instinctive springs of human action, consists of a series of learned rather than unlearned responses, and that its general prevalence and potency at the present time are due to its systematic inculcation into each new generation through elaborate agencies of civic education, employing suggestion, imitation, persuasion, and all the other devices of propaganda and pedagogy.[1] These agencies have recently been analyzed in detail in a number of countries—France among them.[2] The more fundamental questions as to why, when, and how nationalism emerged as the predominant expression of social solidarity, taking precedence over the allegiances claimed by the church, the guilds, the feudal overlords, and the classes or Estates of the middle ages remain largely unanswered. The psychological process through which it played its part in transforming the "medieval" into the "modern" mind is, at best, ill understood. The causes of its becoming the omnipotent form of political loyalty, tending to efface provincialism and particularism, remain shrouded in mystery and speculation.

While these difficult problems of social causation are as fascinating as they are intricate, their solution can scarcely be undertaken here. The tentative hypothesis may be advanced, however, as suggested in the opening pages of this volume, that national-group consciousness bears much the same relation to communities as the "self" or personality bears to the individual. Social psychologists are generally agreed that the ego of the individual is a product of his contacts with others, that man, as a social animal, becomes aware of himself as a psycho-physical entity by "taking the rôle of the other."[3] The unique traits of the individual personality unfold and develop on the basis of inherited characteristics and propensities only through social contacts. While argument by analogy is always danger-

[1] At the close of his scholarly and stimulating survey of the doctrinal schools of nationalism, Professor Carlton Hayes attempts to explain its prevalence in modern times, only to arrive at a somewhat weak and disappointing conclusion. "What has given great vogue to nationalism in modern times? We really do not know. It is a pity that we do not know, for if we did, we could probably make some fairly accurate guess as to the future of nationalism. As it is we have to content ourselves with hypotheses and suggestions. Of these the most plausible would appear to be the underlying tendency in modern times to regard the national state as the medium through which civilization is best assured and advanced." *The Historical Evolution of Modern Nationalism*, p. 302, Richard R. Smith, New York, 1931.

[2] C. J. H. Hayes, *France—A Nation of Patriots*, Columbia University Press, New York, 1930. This volume is part of a series in methods of civic training under the general editorship of Professor Charles E. Merriam of the University of Chicago. The other volumes which have thus far appeared have been published by The University of Chicago Press and include Samuel N. Harper, *Civic Training in Soviet Russia;* John M. Gauss, *Great Britain;* Oscar Jászi, *The Dissolution of the Hapsburg Monarchy;* Elizabeth A. Weber, *The Duks-Duks;* H. W. Schneider and S. B. Clough, *Making Fascists;* B. L. Pierce, *Civic Attitudes in American Text-Books;* R. C. Brooks, *Civic Training in Switzerland;* etc. Cf. the concluding volume, *The Making of Citizens* by Chas. E. Merriam, Chicago, 1931.

[3] This phrase was frequently used in his lectures on social psychology by the late Professor George H. Mead of The University of Chicago.

ous, it seems permissible to view the sense of identity and solidarity which social groups develop similarly in terms of intergroup contacts.[1] A completely isolated community, having no contacts whatever with other and different communities, would probably never develop within itself any sense of communal identity and loyalty comparable to nationalism or even to less mature forms of ethnocentrism. The group becomes aware of itself through contacts with other groups—and in the early period of every culture these contacts are likely to be those of hostility and conflict which threaten the existence of the group and foster those qualities of group allegiance, loyalty to leaders, courage in battle, willingness to sacrifice life or limb in defense of the community, and enmity for the alien beyond the frontier which are the bases of all patriotism. Between the eleventh and sixteenth centuries in Western Europe a large number of communities, occupying fairly well-defined territories and having different languages and institutions, were thrown constantly in contact and conflict with one another in a relatively restricted geographical area. In consequence, each community tended to develop a keen sense of its identity as a "nation," distinct from neighboring "nations." This sense of national solidarity centered at first about the person of the national monarch and later became associated with the State as a whole—with its national flag, its armed forces, its political institutions, its distinctive culture and traditions. This process took place earliest, perhaps, in England. In France it emerges clearly during the Hundred Years' War, when resistance to foreign invasion becomes for the first time a "national" cause, expressed in the fervor and enthusiasm evoked by the first "national" figure of France, Jeanne d'Arc, the Maid of Orleans.[2] The development of this process remains to be traced out by historians with training in social psychology.

Here it is sufficient to emphasize again certain obvious but often forgotten facts—that "France" has no existence as a political community save as national patriotism gives to its members a sense of common Frenchness and that French foreign policy is but the political expression of French nationality in its contacts with other national groups. French nationalism, like all others, developed out of contacts and conflicts between the French national community and its neighbors. Inevitably it has been nourished by the continuation of such contacts. If it is more intense, more dynamic, more potent as a control of group behavior than other nationalisms, the cause is doubtless to be found in the fact that France, because of its geographical position, has had more frequent and more intimate contacts with more outside national groups than most other States and these contacts have been more often those of war. National patriotism and foreign affairs are thus inseparable—now as in the past. The object of foreign policy is

[1] Cf. the writer's review of Hayes, "The Historical Evolution of Modern Nationalism," in *The International Journal of Ethics*, June, 1931.

[2] *Supra*, pp. 3–4.

the more adequate realization of national personality, which obviously involves the stimulation of patriotism. An "unpatriotic" foreign policy is therefore a contradiction in terms. All in French foreign policy which promises to increase the territory, the power, the prestige, the glory of France is *ipso facto* good to the patriot so long as these things remain the most cherished values and symbols of nationalism. All that threatens weakness, defeat, or disgrace is bad. Upon these premises of patriotism foreign policy must rest. They prescribe rigidly the limits within which it may move. The foreign minister who forgets this is doomed. He who remembers it and uses patriotic sentiment as a firm foundation upon which to stand in his quest for power—for himself or for his State—becomes the great statesman. In every diplomatic episode examined in the preceding chapters, the omnipresent and all-pervasive relationship between patriotism and foreign policy stands forth with striking clarity.

National patriotism is, of course, but one phase of the whole culture-complex of the past which preceding generations have transmitted to the present. Through the various processes of general and civic education as they operate in normal times, the social heritage predetermines individual and group organization and behavior almost as absolutely as the biological heritage of a species predetermines the anatomy and physiology of its members. The tyranny of time weighs heavily upon human societies everywhere, even in periods of rapid social change.[1] French foreign policy, like all manifestations of group action and attitudes, is comprehensible only in terms of the past. It has been the assumption of the present study that the controls of French foreign affairs are understandable in the present, and predictable to a degree in the future, through an analysis of their operations in the past. But the precedents, the traditions, the socially inherited habits and customs which shape and guide French foreign policy are older than the Third Republic and older than the nineteenth century. Viewed in the broadest perspective, they extend back to the remotest origins of French nationality, of French political institutions, of the whole European State System of which France is a part. Any adequate analysis of these legacies of bygone ages would involve a dissection and evaluation of the entire history of Western civilization, since even such a small segment of that civilization as French foreign policy represents is intimately connected by a thousand ties with all other phases of the whole culture complex out of which it has grown. The astute and erudite morphologist of history could doubtless reveal in glowing colors the relationships between the actions of the Quai d'Orsay on the one hand, and on the other, the rose windows of Chartres, the politics

---

[1] M. Rénaud Jean, Socialist Deputy, once sought to explain the failure of all efforts to insure peace in these terms. ". . . je disais que vous ne pouviez pas travailler à la paix parce que vous êtes prisonniers du passé et parce que vous êtes dominés par les lois économiques du régime présent. Le passé vous tient avec les haines qu'il vous a transmises. Votre patriotisme est à base de haine," *J.O.Ch.*, March 16, 1922.

of Richelieu, the *bouillabaisse* of Marseilles, the paintings of Cézanne, the ideology of the Jacobins, the *cidres* of Normandy, and the music of César Franck. But the task of illuminating French foreign policy against the rich profusion of its entire cultural background must be left to the Buckles, the Comtes, and the Spenglers.[1] Such efforts remain impressionistic, since the social sciences have not yet evolved a technique of synthesis and interpretation which can claim to be a scientific tool for the understanding of cultural interrelationships. In place of such an all-inclusive interpretation, a few of the more obvious relationships between contemporary French foreign policy and the social heritage of the past may be pointed out.

The aspects of that heritage which are distinguishable as definitely political may be conveniently considered in terms of the State system of Western European civilization as a whole, in the operations of which France has always played a major rôle, and in terms of the political traditions of France itself. As for the former, it is clear that the independent sovereign States of Western Europe, in their dealings with one another, have evolved a system which can be depicted in reasonably precise language. Their interrelationships must be described as a system rather than as an organization, since each unit is free from outside control and, until very recently, no central institutions and agencies of cooperation have existed for coordinating the activities of each of the units in the interest of the whole. The Western European State System might be said to have originated in the Italy of the Renaissance and to have received its first clear description in the writings of Niccolo Machiavelli.[2] The principles which the great Florentine set forth as governing State and inter-State action in the Italy of his day later became predominant in the relations of the larger Nation-states of Western Europe, not by virtue of his advocacy of them, but because they described behavioristically the State System in which he lived and worked—a system which was a miniature of the larger State System of Western Europe as a whole. In the evolution of this system the goals and values of foreign policy became crystalized simultaneously with the growth of the sentiment of nationality. Each State in its contacts with its neighbors strove for power, *i.e.*, for territory, for material advantages, for diplomatic, military, and economic predominance. These objectives of foreign policy emerged as inevitable concomitants of the State System in which they developed. In France, as elsewhere, they have been accepted as axiomatic from Louis XI to Paul Doumer, and they have dominated the formulation of French foreign policy. In course of time, the members of the State System also developed certain norms of conduct in their relations with one another to which each member was expected to conform and certain agencies and procedures of international

---

[1] *Cf.* Oswald Spengler, *The Decline of the West* (Der Untergang des Abendlandes), Alfred A. Knopf, Inc., New York, 1929, Berlin, 1918 and 1922, Vol. I, *Form and Actuality*, Chap. I and *passim.*

[2] *Cf. The Prince*, 1513; *The History of Florence*, 1525.

intercourse which all were expected to adopt. The former have given rise to public international law and the latter to the practices of diplomacy. These features of the Western State System predetermine the legal and institutional framework within which the international relations of France are confined, just as the goals of State action which have come to be generally accepted as desirable in the dealings of States with one another, predetermine the values and objectives pursued by the Quai d'Orsay. These are limiting and controlling factors governing the formulation of French foreign policy which are almost as permanent and fixed as those arising from national patriotism, with which they are so closely associated.

Within the French nation, the political heritage of the past has also played its rôle in predetermining the political institutions and procedures through which foreign affairs are carried on. Here again a genetic treatment of the factors involved would carry the investigator far behind the establishment of the Third Republic into the earliest origins of French political institutions. These origins have been referred to incidentally in the preceding chapters. But from the point of view of the domestic conduct of foreign affairs in the contemporary period, it has been sufficient to review French political organization and practice under the Constitution of 1875. Written Constitutions are intended to lay down general principles of government which shall furnish the legal framework of the State within which politics and administration are confined. They achieve this objective to the degree to which they incorporate into their provisions the political traditions and experience of the past, and to the extent to which they admit of modifications to meet the needs of changing situations and changing relationships of power between groups and classes. As judged by this pragmatic test the Constitution of the Third French Republic has been an adequate instrument of government during the past half century. Its general provisions establish the legal and political framework within which French foreign and domestic politics move and have their being. But the provisions of written Constitutions admit of amendment, of development, of interpretation, even of abolition, much more readily than do the traditions of national patriotism and of the Western State System as a whole. They predetermine the ends and means of political action in a less absolute sense. Within the sphere of their operation, they obviously admit of greater variation from established norms, of more numerous alternatives, of great freedom of action—the more so when they are as general, fragmentary, and vague as the French Constitutional Laws of 1875. The chapters on the war power and the treaty power offer ample evidence of their flexibility and adaptibility. Nevertheless the Constitution does obviously impose certain restraints and limits upon the action that may be taken by a particular government or foreign minister.

If a Ptolemaic simile is permissible, the factors which have been dealt with may be thought of as constituting a series of concentric circles, each imposing limits upon freedom of governmental action which more or less predetermine the course of policy. The largest and outermost circle—that of the basic traditions of French nationalism—is never transgressed by the officials at the center. This is the *ne plus ultra* of the political cosmos, accepted on faith without thought or question. The next circle—that of the habitual-behavior patterns, legal principles, and diplomatic practices of the Western State System—is rarely broken through, though occasionally statesmen may venture beyond its periphery at their peril. The terms of the written Constitution comprise a smaller circle, more confining in its scope because narrower in its radius, but more flexible and with more freedom of action within its confines. The smallest circle, immediately surrounding the central officialdom, is that of the day-to-day practice of politics. Here, again within the area marked out by the perimeter, one finds an even greater degree of flexibility and adaptibility with even greater opportunities for the exercise of "free will," unrestrained by the barriers of the past. Even here, however, freedom of action is limited by habit, custom, and tradition. The traditions of the French party system and of established legislative and executive organization and procedure cannot be defied with impunity by any statesman, however powerful and respected he may be. These limitations on his freedom of action are somewhat nebulous and intangible. They may be exceeded, modified, or even disregarded under extraordinary circumstances. But they are none the less present at all times and must enter into the reckoning of all who deal with foreign affairs. The successful statesman is he who can fit his specific purposes into this limiting framework, who can weigh nicely in the balance the exigencies of his own objectives and the confining bonds of custom which he may manipulate and adjust, but which he may never transgress. Even his purposes and objectives are in large part predetermined and conditioned by the influence of the past in the environment in which he moves. In the formulation of foreign policy these various factors, in their complex interrelationships, delimit in subtle ways too intricate to be measured or even accurately described the lines between Destiny and Freedom, Inevitability and Control. Statesmanship is the art of knowing what is politically possible.

2. THE PUBLIC AND POLITICAL PARTIES

Among the political traditions of contemporary France, none is more universally accepted and insisted upon than "democracy." Popular sovereignty and representative government are the alpha and omega of the theory of the French parliamentary system, echoing the revolutionary battle cry of "Liberté, Égalité, Fraternité," and constituting in France, as in other *bourgeois* States, the ideological foundations stones of the whole political framework of the State. In nineteenth-century France, as elsewhere in Western Europe, the political theory of democracy came to be generally accepted during the period in which the *bourgeoisie* displaced the nobility of the *ancien régime* as the holders of economic and political power. The theory has persisted in France down to the present time and continues to receive general acceptance and respect, in the face of doubtings from the extreme Right and the extreme Left. Stated succinctly, it assumes that all citizens are entitled to a voice in government; that this voice is to be heard in free elections, in which the citizenry elects representatives to formulate policies in legislation and to direct their administration; that government rests upon the consent of the governed; that this consent is given through political parties which vie for popular support; that the party or group of parties which secures the support of a numerical majority of the electorate is entitled to wield the power of the State, with the minority acquiescing; that all legislation shall be passed by a majority of the elected members of parliament; and, finally, that the executive branch of the government shall hold office only so long as a majority of the legislators support it. The electorate, consisting of all male citizens over twenty-one years of age, is thus the final arbiter and source of sovereignty, and government is a process of counting noses. Each citizen is presumed to have power equal to his fellows and he receives representation in the national legislature in territorial blocs—departments under *scrutin de liste* and smaller areas under *scrutin d'arrondissement*.[1]

Without launching upon a criticism of the democratic dogma, it may be pointed out without much fear of contradiction that voters in France, or in any country, are not all as alike as so many peas in a pod, but obviously divide themselves into groups on the basis of their economic status, their social position, their religious views, and a great variety of other interests. All Frenchmen, by definition, are expected to acknowledge primary allegiance to the French national community. As voters they presumably act in accordance with their mature judgment as to what will be most conducive to the welfare of the whole national community. But in practice they have, of course, a vast number of lesser interests and allegiances, and are often moved more by the dictates of these lesser loyalties than by reasoned consideration of the more abstract interests of the nation as a whole. While one cannot overlook the common consensus of all members of the "public," without which divergencies of interest and views would lead to conflict and coercion rather than to the orderly establishment of an equilibrium of forces, a realistic treatment of politics in all modern democracies must necessarily be pluralistic in the sense of making its analyses and evaluations on the basis of the separate and diversified interests which dictate political behavior in a

---

[1] In the election of April, 1928, 10,912,438 French citizens were enrolled voters, as compared with 11,177,499 in April, 1914, and 9,961,261 in February, 1876. In these elections, 83.6 per cent, 77.1 per cent, and 74.0 per cent of the enrolled voters actually voted. *Cf.* H. F. Gosnell, *Why Europe Votes*, pp. 41 and 196, The University of Chicago Press, 1930.

very direct and immediate fashion.[1] The complex of factors which shape French foreign policy is conditioned by these divergencies of interest to almost the same degree as is the case with domestic politics.

It is impossible, within the limits of the present study, to enter upon the herculean task of analyzing all these sources of political pressure, even though such an analysis might seem essential to the attainment of the objectives of the investigation.[2] It can only be suggested that a full understanding of the process of French politics must begin with a consideration of the manifold ways in which the various groupings of French citizens express their views and promote their interests through political action.[3] These groupings are almost infinite in number and complexity, ranging from the family and other primary groups to religious congregations, vocational and professional associations, economic organizations, learned societies, and the like, all overlapping in complicated interpenetration and all being overlaid with various types of territorial loyalties, extending from the commune and the province to the nation and even to international society. These groupings are obviously not all of equal political significance, nor is their relation to one another fixed and permanent. It seems clear from the analysis of the political process attempted in the preceding chapters that in France, as elsewhere, the social groupings which play the largest rôle in shaping the course of politics are those which arise out of the vocational and economic stratifications of society. Attention may therefore be usefully directed toward the more important socio-economic aggregations of French citizens under the

[1] In this connection it may not be inappropriate to recall the words of the "Father of the American Constitution," James Madison. He found the source of political parties in the fact of "the various and unequal distribution of property. Those who hold and those who are without property have ever formed distinct interests in society. Those who are creditors and those who are debtors fall under a like distinction. A landed interest, a manufacturing interest, a mercantile interest, with many lesser interests, grow up of necessity in civilized nations and divide them into different classes actuated by different sentiment and views. The regulation of these various and interfering interests forms the principal task of modern legislation and involves the spirit of party and faction in the necessary and ordinary operations of government." *The Federalist*, No. 10, 1788.

[2] An interesting, though partial and now somewhat obsolete, effort at such an analysis for the western provinces of France is to be found in A. Siegfried, *Tableau politique de la France de l'ouest*, Paris, 1913.

[3] "People who act together get emotionally bound together. This process of becoming emotionally bound is dependent on no conscious process . . . People who are emotionally bound together are not yet involved in a political movement. Politics begins when they achieve a symbolic definition of themselves in relation to demands upon the world . . . Acts cease to be merely private acts; they have become related to remote social objects. The conception of the self has new points of reference which interlock with those of others. It is of the utmost importance to political science to examine in detail, not only the factors which contribute to the raising or lowering of the tension level, but the processes of symbolization." H. D. Lasswell, *Psychopathology and Politics*, pp. 185–186, The University of Chicago Press, 1930. This work is a suggestive effort to analyze in Freudian terms the relationship between the inner springs of private action and collective political behavior.

Third Republic, with emphasis upon their political activities as affecting foreign affairs.

It may be pointed out at the commencement of such an analysis that the social groupings in France which at once strike the observer as constituting fairly well-defined classes, whose members feel a sense of group solidarity and which are more or less organized for the protection of their economic interests through political action, are historical derivatives of the "third estate" of the *ancien régime*. For purposes of representation in the Estates General the political community of medieval and early modern France was divided into the three categories of the clergy, the nobility, and the Third Estate, the latter consisting of all groups not included in the first two— primarily, of course, of the burghers or town dwellers who constituted corporate entities with a legal status of their own, relatively early in the feudal period. This group was regarded by the government as worthy of representation in the deliberative, quasi-legislative body upon which the King relied for counsel, along with the clergy and the landed aristocracy, who constituted the ruling classes of feudal society.[1] So long as the peasantry remained in a state of serfdom and so long as industry remained in the handicraft stage, the third estate was composed chiefly of the representatives of the merchants, the money-lenders, the wealthier guildsmen, and such landowners as were not members of the nobility. With the economic changes of the seventeenth and eighteenth centuries, land ceased to be the most important source of economic power and the commercial and industrial *bourgeoisie* displaced the agrarian nobility as the wealthiest group in French society. A corresponding transfer of political power followed. The whole course of the French Revolution as a European movement is intelligible only when viewed as an effort of the *bourgeoisie* to wrest the control of the machinery of State out of the hands of the decadent nobility and its symbol and protector, the Absolute Monarch, and to exercise political power on its own behalf. The nobility was demolished. The clergy ceased to be politically significant with the secularization of society, though the last echoes of the struggle of the liberal *bourgeoisie* against it reverberated down into the early years of the twentieth century. The *bourgeoisie* emerged triumphant and undisputed, challenged only by a new giant slowly awakening to consciousness of economic and political power—the Fourth Estate of the urban proletariat, born of capitalistic industrialism, having no vested interest in the *bourgeois* social order, with its combination of political liberty, legal equality, and economic exploitation, and finding its political voice in Marxian socialism.

The details of this social process are irrevelant to the present enterprise. But its results are enormously significant in any consideration of contem-

---

[1] The Estates General met for the last time in 1614, prior to its final reassembling in 1789.

porary French politics. French society under the Third Republic, like society everywhere, is replete with vestiges of the past and anticipations of the future. Among the former are the Catholic clergy, still exerting a political influence of no small proportions over the backward and devout peasantry, and the fragments of the old nobility, still boasting a few estates and chateaux not lost in revolution nor sold to the *nouveaux-riches*, still taking pride in a noble lineage, and still exercising such political influence as the remnants of the aristocratic tradition vouchsafe them in a democratic republic. Among the foreshadowings of the days to come are, perhaps, the militant trade unions of the city wage earners and their political organs, the Socialist and Communist parties. Between the two is the present: the era of the *bourgeoisie*. The Third French Republic rests securely on a social and political foundation of business men, merchants, manufacturers, and all the petty proprietors and tradesmen who constitute, along with the professional classes and the *fonctionnaires*, the bulwarks of *bourgeois* respectability and conservative republicanism. Other classes there are—and they are by no means politically negligible: the ghosts of the old aristocracy; the religious and tradition-bound peasantry, still cherishing, colorfully, the provincial customs and costumes of the medieval past and constituting, by count, a good half of the population—sturdy, deliberate, content to till the rich soil of France, and ever hopeful of making good *bourgeois* of its favored sons; the workers of the factories, mills, and mines, often sullen, resentful, clinging to the red memories of '93, '48, and '71, and hoping and planning for the new revolution which is to transmit power to the proletariat. These groups are all alive and vital in the political life of *bourgeois* France. But the largest share of political power rests with the beneficiaries and masters of the economic order of capitalism, based, as it is, upon private property, personal and individualistic economic initiative, the profit motive to productivity, the employment and control of labor by the owners of the means of production, and relatively unrestricted competition between large numbers of producers and traders.

From the point of view of foreign affairs, little need be said concerning the peasantry and the proletariat. The former is under the spell of tradition and custom to a greater degree than any other group in French society. It is scarcely political-minded in a nation where all city-dwellers pursue politics as a sport and avocation. It furnishes support, especially in the western provinces, to the *Action Française* and the antirepublican royalists who dream dreams of restoring the monarchy. But no "peasant party" exists. The peasantry is content enough to accept the political leadership of the *bourgeois* parties. Its economic interests are not those of an integrated and well-organized economic group, but those of individual proprietors, each with his small family, his live stock, his plot of land, and his savings gleaned from the sale of his produce to the towns. The peasant is conservative, religious, patriotic, under less pressure than other groups to organize and cooperate with his fellows to further his interests. He is less disposed to view those interests rationally and less inclined to political action to protect them. He has few interests in foreign affairs save the security and glory of *la Patrie*, the protection of his farm from invasion, and the safeguarding of the home market for the produce which he wrests from the soil. He is sometimes a "regionalist," insisting upon the identity of his home province and his native *patois*, whether it be Breton, Corsican, Provençal, or Flemish. But his particularism is cultural rather than political and counts for little in foreign affairs.[1]

The urban worker, on the other hand, under the stimuli of the conditions of machine industry, is much more keenly aware of his economic interests and has joined freely with his fellows in forming powerful organizations for collective bargaining with employers as to wages, hours, and conditions of labor. The proletariat has exercised an important political influence through the Socialist and Communist parties. In the economic sphere the establishment of trade unions or syndicates has proceeded apace since the recovery which followed upon despair and impotence after the crushing of the Paris Commune. The *Confédération Générale du Travail*, the great central federation of trade unions affiliated with the Amsterdam International, had 500,000 members of 1914 and 1,200,000 in 1919. Its leaders have long been committed to a program of political action contemplating the overthrow of the social order of capitalism and the establishment of socialism, with political and economic power in the hands of the workers. After the Russian Revolution, the organization split, with the ultra-revolutionary radicals forming, in 1922, the *Confédération Générale du Travail Unitaire*, communist in sympathy and allied with the Red Trade Union International of Moscow. This organization began its career with an estimated membership of 350,000. In the political realm, the Communists similarly split off from the United Socialists at the same time.[2] Other small groups exist within the French labor movement, acknowledging allegiance to the doctrines of syndicalism or anarchism and repudiating political action. A large part of French proletariat, moreover, is unorganized either for economic or political purposes. But, in general, French labor is politically minded and revolutionary. In the sphere of foreign affairs it is international rather than national, viewing its interests as being common to those of the working classes everywhere in opposition to the *bourgeoisie* of all countries. In 1914, however, its nationalism proved stronger than its internationalism. It is usually without effective influence on foreign affairs. In domestic politics it has been able to achieve protective legislation, social insurance, and other reforms, with the aid of the sympathies and

---

[1] C. J. H. Hayes, *France—A Nation of Patriots*, pp. 292–317.

[2] A useful survey of these developments will be found in Charles W. Pipkin, *Social Politics and Modern Democracies*, Vol. II, pp. 314–334, New York, 1931.

apprehensions of *bourgeois* groups.[1] Its influence in shaping the foreign policies of the Government, however, has been almost as negligible as that of the peasantry—or perhaps more so, since the peasant is at least a patriot while the patriotism of the proletarian is often dubious.

The *bourgeoisie* remains as the dominant socio-economic group which effectively wields political power and largely dominates both the foreign and domestic policies of the Third French Republic. Certain general economic and political interests all members of the group have in common: the preservation of the institution of private property, the maintenance of an economic order based upon private profit and private ownership of the means of production and distribution, the continuation of a form of government and a system of law which afford protection to property rights and the assistance of the State to economic enterprises, with a maximum of aid and a minimum of regulation and interference. The Constitution of 1875 and the parliamentary system which has developed under it are acceptable and satisfactory to the French *bourgeoisie* because they assure protection to these interests. But aside from these fundamentals, there are numerous divergencies of interests and viewpoints in both the economic and the political spheres. *Bourgeois* society is individualistic and competitive—more so, perhaps, in France than in the more highly industrialized States where trusts, cartels, and monopolies have come to dominate the economic scene. The *bourgeoisie* cannot be thought of as a compact, completely integrated, powerfully organized social entity which thinks, feels, and acts as a unit. Like all social classes, it is composed of individuals who form themselves into many subclasses and groups on the basis of special interests. These interests are reflected in a large number of organizations, the mere listing of which would require many pages. Some of these are primarily economic in character and purpose, such as the *Union des Industries Textiles* or the *Union des Industries Metallurgique et Minières*. The latter, under its more popular name of the *Comité des Forges*, is not above political action. Among associations of a more definitely political type, designed to influence public opinion and governmental action, are the *Association Nationale d'Expansion Économique* and the *Union des Intérêts Économiques*. The latter was established in 1910 as an association of insurance companies to fight proposals for a government monopoly of insurance and later drew unto itself representatives of heavy industry, commerce, and finance, under the leadership of Senator Paul-Ernest Billiet.[2] Sometimes organizations of this kind are recognized by law as public agencies and become consultative and advisory bodies to govern-

---

[1] *Ibid.*, Vol. II, *passim*. On the French labor movement in general see Lewis Lorwin, *Syndicalism in France*, Longmans, Green and Co., New York, 1914; and *Labor and Internationalism*, The Macmillan Company, New York, 1929; David Saposs, *The Labor Movement in Post-war France*, Columbia University Press, 1931.

[2] J. Carrère, G. Bourgin et A. Guerin, *Manuel des partis politiques en France*, pp. 237–246, Paris, 1924. For a list of similar organizations, see pp. 246–248.

mental institutions. A statute of April 9, 1898, for example, made chambers of commerce public institutions established by governmental decree, one in each department. They are supported out of public funds and are authorized to engage in technical education and in the operation of certain public works and services. The National Assembly of Chambers of Commerce meets every two months in Paris and the Government is required by law to consult it as an advisory agency on all questions of economic legislation and on all tariff and commercial matters.[1]

The most significant effort to integrate and coordinate such organizations on a national scale and to "put business in government" (to use an American phrase in a more literal sense than that usually intended) is to be found in the establishment of the National Economic Council (*Conseil National Économique*). The first steps toward the formation of this body were taken in 1919, but it was not finally established until 1925, by a decree of January 16, supplemented by other decrees and orders of June 19. On November 18, 1927, a *projet* was introduced into the Chamber to provide a statutory basis for the council, but it has not yet been approved at the time of writing. The expenses of the council, which is attached to the office of the Premier, are met out of the budget of the Ministry of Labor. In spite of this, and in spite of the fact that the initiative toward its creation came from the C.G.T., the *Cartel des Gauches*, and other labor groups rather than from business organizations, the latter would appear to have a predominant voice in its deliberations. It is composed of forty-seven members and ninety-four deputy members: nine members represent the consuming public and are selected from consumers' cooperative societies and leagues, mayors' associations, users of the public utilities, and heads of families; thirty represent labor and industry, *i.e.*, intellectual labor and education, management, salaried employees, and artisans; eight represent capital, industrial, commercial, real estate, banks, stock exchanges, and insurance. The members, who must be citizens over twenty-five years of age and who hold office for two years, are chosen in each class by the most representative organizations, as determined by the Government, subject to appeal to the council itself. The council meets four times a year and acts as an advisory agency to the Government on economic legislation.[2] A series of subsidiary councils and committees[3] assists the National Economic Council in its work. The council itself may act on its own initative or at the request of the Government, but it is far from being an "economic parliament." It does not yet prepare *projets* of legislation and its only contact

[1] *Cf.* R. L. Buell, *Contemporary French Politics*, pp. 344–349.

[2] The proposed bill provides for 150 members: 80 representing "production" (10 real estate; 30 raw materials, machinery, and motive power; and 40 labor); 48 representing "distribution" (9 money and credit; 12 transportation and communication; 9 commerce; and 18 labor in distribution); and 21 representing "consumption" (7 for the general interests of consumers; 6 for private organizations of consumers; 8 for savings and insurance); and 2 for State finance. *Cf.* Pipkin, *op. cit.*, II, pp. 84–91.

[3] *Ibid.*, II, pp. 91–92 for a list and brief description of these.

with the Chambers is through the ministers. Its chief rôle in international affairs is played through its contacts with the economic and technical organizations of the League of Nations, to which it is in a position to present a reasoned consensus of opinion on French economic interests in all pending international questions.[1]

While eventually such bodies may become genuine channels of political pressure and may even take over certain "political" functions, as has happened under *bourgeois* auspices in Fascist Italy and under proletarian auspices in Soviet Russia, they still remain on the periphery of the political process in republican France. Socio-economic groups continue to function as political entities through the established structure of the French party system. That system, as compared with the American or English party systems, reflects with reasonable clarity the lines of politico-economic cleavage in French society, even though to a German observer French politics may appear to be less influenced by economic interests than in his own country.[2] All generalizations regarding the relationship between political parties and socio-economic groups are necessarily questionable, since no mathematically precise correlation exists. But no observer would dispute the statement that the extreme Right parties represent primarily the remnants of the old nobility, the more reactionary sections of the clergy, the tradition-bound peasantry, and a portion of the *haute bourgeoisie*. Similarly, the extreme Left parties (Communist and Socialist) represent the urban proletariat. The Left Center groups, especially the Radical Socialists, represent the *petite bourgeoisie* and the more conservative section of the working classes, while the Right Center speaks for heavy industry, big business, commerce, and finance. The Center itself is solidly grounded in the middle classes and the peasantry, even though it possesses no strongly organized party machines.[3] Exceptions and qualifications to such statements will come to mind at once. But it is scarcely open to question that economic groups do exert political pressure through political parties along the lines suggested.

These pressures are exerted, in France as in all States, in the electoral process and through "lobbying" in the broadest sense. French campaign funds are relatively small and elections are inexpensive. Nevertheless, money is required by candidates and by party organizations and when it cannot be

---

[1] The writer is indebted for much of this data to M. Georges Cahen-Salvador, secretary-general of the *Conseil National Économique*.

[2] "In ihrem Kern ist die französische Politik ausserwirtschaftlich," Richard Lewinsohn, *Das Geld in der Politik*, p. 242, Berlin, 1931. This commentator suggests that politics in France is more frequently a method of personal enrichment than a reflection of economic interests and that the normal sequence is from power to money rather than from money to power. By way of substantiating this interpretation, he points out that no under-secretariat for national economy was created in France until the spring of 1930 in the second Tardieu Cabinet, that French politics is intensely "individualized," and that "economy" in French means only parsimony. These observations do not invalidate the general interpretaion attempted here, however.

[3] *Supra*, pp. 14–17 for a general discussion of the French party system and a list of the parties.

raised out of personal means, which are usually meager, nor out of party dues, which are unimportant save for the extreme Left groups, it must come out of trade-union treasuries, corporation resources, or private contributions by persons of wealth. In France, as everywhere, such contributions are ordinarily made not in a spirit of charity, but for goods or services received or anticipated. Business groups, by virtue of their economic status, are obviously better able to make such contributions than any others. As a result, most successful candidates for Parliament and local elective offices are more or less indebted to contributors of this type, and are themselves *bourgeois* in outlook, origins, or sympathies.[1] Such organizations as the *Union des Intérêts Économiques* intervene actively in elections to insure the election of acceptable candidates. Ernest Billiet, head of the organization named, was fined 300 fr. by the Chamber commission investigating the origin of electoral funds because of his refusal to reveal the source of the money which his group contributed to the *Bloc National* in the elections of 1919 and 1924. In the former year his organization was supposed to have furnished 30,000,000 fr. to the Right parties and in 1924 it spent large sums in fighting the *Cartel des Gauches*. The investigating commission discovered that M. Pinot, vice-president of the *Comité des Forges*, had contributed to the funds collected for such purposes by Billiet.[2] Precise information on such questions is, of course, difficult to secure, but where there is much smoke there is certain to be some fire.

In the intervals between elections, pressure groups of all kinds lobby incessantly for and against legislative and administrative measures. Business interests frequently retain parliamentarians as attorneys or appoint them to lucrative positions in corporations.[3] Prominent business men, such as Louis Loucheur and François de Wendel, often sit in Parliament themselves, usually bringing with them a large number of lucrative positions for distribution among their colleagues. While public officials are forbidden to hold parliamentary seats, the agents of private corporations are under no such disability.[4] Lobbying of a less effective variety, because less directly

[1] *L'Intransigeant* of April 21, 1928, calculated that out of 1411 candidates for Parliament in the elections of May, 1928, 385 were lawyers; 266 journalists; 225 workers; 186 farmers; 128 industrialists; 67 merchants; 98 railway workers; 41 postal officials; 8 bankers; and 7 clergymen. However these professions may be allocated among the peasantry, proletariat and *bourgeoisie*, it is clear that well over half belong to the latter group. An even larger proportion of the successful candidates would doubtless be found in this group.

[2] Lewinsohn, *op. cit.*, pp. 245f.; Carrère, *op. cit.*, pp. 241f.

[3] Prior to the election of 1924 about 300 Senators and Deputies were retained in this fashion. Under the régime of the *Cartel des Gauches*, the number fell to 201—(104 Deputies and 97 Senators). Early in 1930 it was estimated that 144 Deputies and 118 Senators held a total of 1,019 positions as corporation lawyers, members of boards of directors and the like. Lewinsohn, *op. cit.*, pp. 250-253, citing R. Mennevée, *Les documents politiques: Parlementaires et financiers*, Paris, 1930.

[4] In 1921, Herriot introduced a resolution into the Chamber, which was approved 435 to 15 condemning the holding of places on boards of directors of credit companies by parliamentarians, ministers, or officials, but this proposal was never enacted into law, and would perhaps be of doubtful efficacy in any case.

based upon the pecuniary interests of the parliamentarians, is conducted by workers, farmers, religious congregations, veterans' associations, professional patriots, pacifists, militarists, feminists, regionalists, reformers, and many other pressure groups.[1] Out of the kaleidoscopic and confused interplay of these organized minorities emerges the pattern of contemporary French politics and the temper of "public opinion."

The incidence of this process in foreign affairs is difficult to trace. In dealing with foreign States, the Government is supposed to represent not organized minorities, but the "national interest"—the welfare, the security, the safety, and the prosperity of "France." But the abstract "general interest" is at all times compounded with particular and special interests and foreign policy, almost as much as domestic policy, is inextricably bound up with the pressures of interested groups. As for the political parties themselves, their divisions and feuds seldom arise out of questions of foreign affairs, though such questions may be, and frequently are, drawn into the arena of party combat. Throughout the entire history of the Third Republic there have existed, in popular parlance, foreign policies of the Right and of the Left, the former implying alliances, military preparedness, and an exclusive pursuit of national interests, and the latter presumably involving international cooperation, pacific means of settling disputes, disarmament and the like. That these categories have some reality is not open to doubt in view of the instances which have been reviewed, but they are obviously loose and inexact and correspond only to the general cleavages between Right and Left on all political issues.[2] The parties themselves, in their resolutions and in the addresses of their leaders, are usually little concerned with foreign affairs. To take but a single example—and that of a party whose members are probably more keenly interested in foreign affairs than most others—the Radical Socialist party, which supposedly represented a "Left" foreign policy, vigorously repudiated all accusations of lack of patriotism in the pre-war period, urged the peaceful penetration of Morocco by France, and stood for the strong defense of French interests everywhere, while it advocated at the same time, without any sense of inconsistency, disarma-

---

[1] Carrère, in his attempt to list such lobbying agencies, mentions, among others, *Les vétérans des armées de terre et de mer, les soldats de la grande guerre, l'association républicaine des anciens combatants, l'association pour la Societé des Nations, l'union populaire pour la paix universelle, l'association de la paix par le droit, la volunté de paix, l'union française pour le suffrage des femmes, la ligue française pour le droit de femmes, l'union nationale pour le vote des femmes, fédération régionaliste française, l'union populaire alsacienne, l'union républicaine lorraine, parti paysan* (established 1928, not as a party but as a lobbying organization), *l'union française des paysans, comité Dupleix, la ligue des familles nombreuses, le comité de la rive gauche du Rhin, la ligue naval, la ligue maritime et coloniale, l'union française, l'alliance française, la mission laïque, les amis de France, fédération nationale protestante, la ligue contre l'alcoolisme, l'union universelle de la jeunesse juive, ligue national Catholique*, etc., etc., Carrère, *op. cit.*, pp. 277–290.

[2] In a lecture delivered at the Dotation Carnegie on December 19, 1929, Professor J. Barthélemy called attention to the fact that the Combes Cabinet was internally "Left," while its foreign minister, Delcassé, pursued a "Right" foreign policy. Similarly, the recent Cabinets in which Briand has been foreign minister have been "Right" internally and "Left" in foreign policy.

ment, international arbitration, and a more active participation by Parliament in foreign affairs.[1] At the thirteenth congress of the party at Pau, October 16–19, 1913, M. Lucien Le Foyer presented an extensive report on foreign affairs, excusing its length by the long silence which the party had maintained on the subject.[2] The resolutions of the party congresses since the war have devoted more attention to foreign affairs than formerly, but even now little attempt is made to formulate a comprehensive and clearly defined program and to bind the party members to it. The other parties neglect foreign policy to an even greater degree, with the possible exception of the Socialist and Communist parties, with their internationalist orientation, and a few of the extreme Right advocates of "integral nationalism." Group pressures in foreign affairs are thus exerted not directly and obviously through the party system, but subtly and often secretly through indirect means of influence—some of which will be examined below—and through the manipulation of "public opinion."

3. THE PRESS

The nature and operation of public opinion in modern democracies have been, in recent years, a subject of intensive investigation and much controversy.[3] Suffice it to note here that the enthusiasm of early democrats for the submission of all political questions to the popular judgment and their implicit confidence in the efficacy of free discussion as the road to political wisdom have, of late, been sicklied o'er with the pale cast of pessimistic reflections which begin by doubting the intelligence of public opinion and end by questioning its very existence. Early commentaries dwelt on the common interest of all citizens in the welfare of the community and in the economical and honest management of the affairs of State and on their ability by processes of reason to arrive at truth in things political. Later writers, such as Lippmann, Laski, Wallace, Duguit and the like, tend to emphasize the diversity of interests between various groups of

---

[1] A. Charpentier, *Le parti radical et radical-socialiste à travers ses congrès*, Paris, 1913. It is not without significance that out of eighteen chapters which the author devotes to the views and programs of the party, only one deals with foreign affairs—seventeen pages out of 468. *Cf.* Chap. XVI, "Le patriotisme et le pacifisme," pp. 407–424.

[2] *Treizième Congrès—Parti Radical et Radical Socialististe*, pp. 80–141. *Cf.* reports of later annual congresses.

[3] The voluminosity of the literature on public opinion is equaled only by the diversity of viewpoints and conclusions which it presents. Among the better known contributions are G. de Tarde, *L'Opinion et la foule*, Paris, 1901; R. Chasseriaud, *La Formation de l'opinion publique*, Paris, 1914; G. Le Bon, *Les opinions et les croyances*, Paris, 1911; A. L. Lowell, *Public Opinion and Popular Government*, New York, 1913; Ferdinand Tönnies, *Kritik der öffentlichen Meinung*, Berlin, 1922; Walter Lippman, *Public Opinion*, New York, 1922, and *The Phantom Public*, New York, 1925; Norman Angell, *The Public Mind*, New York, 1927; C. E. Playne, *The Pre-War Mind in Britain*, London, 1928; Stuart A. Rice, *Quantitative Methods in Politics*, New York, 1928; Peter Odegard, *The American Public Mind*, New York, 1930; etc. *Cf.* the bibliographies in H. D. Lasswell, *Propaganda Technique in the World War*, New York, 1928, and *Psychopathology and Politics*, Chicago, 1930.

citizens, non-rational factors in the formation of opinion, and the non-existence of the abstract "good citizen" who has only the general interest at heart in his political behavior. It is clear that while the divergent interest of groups and classes are among the prime moving factors in the creation of public opinion, no opinion is possible without what Lowell aptly called a "constitutional consensus" among all the groups involved, implying willingness to follow established procedures and to acquiesce in the results to which they lead. Putting it differently, public opinion arises through discussion of "debatable demands for action"[1]—and demands can be debatable only by reference to certain fundamental values accepted as premises by all the debaters.[2] The French political public, by definition, consists of all who accept the established constitutional order, at least for the purpose of presenting their demands, and who seek to influence the policies of the French Government. The major economic groupings which participate in the process of formulating opinion have been indicated. Since the analysis and measurement of public opinion are still in an experimental stage, no useful purpose would be served by embarking upon a consideration of these problems here. All commentators are agreed that the most important single factor in the formation of opinion, however it may be defined, is the daily press, and no survey of the factors influencing French foreign policy would be complete without some attention to the rôle of journalism.

French newspapers, in general, are notable for their small size, their great number, their cheapness, effusiveness, variety and intense partisanship. Paris alone has thirty-four daily papers and the provincial papers are numbered by the hundreds. The typical newspaper (if anything can be typical in such a welter of variegated sheets) consists of four to eight pages, of smaller size than its English or American counterparts with relatively little advertising, few pictures or cartoons, much political news, and such a constant mingling of fact and comment that all pretension of a separation between news and editorial interpretation vanishes. It sells for twenty-five centimes in post-war currency (about one cent in American money), with the exception of Le Temps which costs forty centimes and l'Ami du Peuple which costs only ten, and it is usually the personal voice of its owner or the organ of a political party.[3] Papers are easily established at small expense and the market, at least in the vicinity of the capital, seems inexhaustible. French readers almost invariably read several papers and circulation depends to a large extent on vivacity, originality, literary brilliance, penetrating criticism, and incisive or even devastating comment on contemporary politics. In view of the political-mindedness of the French public, "yellow" journalism leans less toward crime, personal scandal, pseudoscientific

[1] H. D. Lasswell, "The Measurement of Public Opinion," *American Political Science Review*, XXV, pp. 311–326, May, 1931.

[2] *Cf.* John Dewey, *The Public and Its Problems*, New York, 1927.

[3] "A French paper is not an institution, it is a personality," Buell, *op. cit.*, p. 271.

sensationalism, and advice to the lovelorn than to political effervescence, revelations about politicians, and bitter invective against those of differing political views.

The number of newspapers and periodicals runs into the thousands.[1] Of the better known papers of Paris those with the largest circulation are *Le Petit Parisien* (1,700,000, sensational but politically moderate, established 1876); *Le Journal* (1,000,000, literary, non-political, established 1892); *Le Matin* (750,000, chauvinistic, anti-German, anti-Bolshevik, conservative, established 1884); *Le Petit Journal* (500,000, owned by Louis Loucheur, *bourgeois*, moderate, patriotic, established 1900); and *L'Écho de Paris* (200,000, conservative, *bourgeois*, ultra-patriotic, established 1884). All of these are morning papers which have formed a consortium for advertising and other purposes. All are rather moderate politically, with only the *Écho de Paris* a political propagandist sheet, and all are semiofficial organs of the Government in the sense of serving as channels of communication from the ministries to the public. Among the evening papers, those of largest circulation are *L'Intransigeant* (450,000), *Excelsior* (250,000, owned by *Le Petit Parisien*), *L'Humanité* (200,000, organ of the Communist party), *Le Quotidien* (200,000, organ of the Radical Left), and the royalist *Action Française* (200,000, occasionally). Aside from the great "journals of information," such as the "Big Five" and *L'Intransigeant*, which sway opinion subtly because of their apparently non-political complexion, papers are organs of parties or groups, propagandist and highly controversial in style and content. Among the older papers, each with a small and select circulation, are the eminently respectable and dignified *Le Temps* (established 1861, circulation about 65,000), *Le Figaro* (1826), and *Le Journal des Débats* (1789). The 240 odd newspapers of provincial France exhibit almost the same rich variety of form and of political views as do those of the capital. All are solidly patriotic, with the exception of the organs of the extreme Left. All are cheap and widely read and almost all serve as the political weapons of their owners, who use them for prestige, political power, and economic gain, as conscience and expediency dictate.[2]

It is clear that the relationship between politics and journalism in France is at all times very intimate. Indeed, there are few prominent French politicians who have not at one time or another been journalists and few journalists without political ambitions. The press is the path to public recognition and political power. A constant interchange of personnel takes place between the Chambers of Parliament and the editorial offices of papers.[3] The great

---

[1] Hayes, *France*, pp. 125–126, in commenting on the *Annuaire de la presse française et étrangère*, calculates that there are no less than 5,000 newspapers and periodicals published in France and her colonies, of which at least two-thirds were actually published and circulated as separate journals in 1926.

[2] *Cf.* the excellent survey of the French press in Hayes' *France*, pp. 124–171, 431–470.

[3] "New men are constantly stepping in and out, carrying programs from outside into the drowsy arcana of the ministries, and returning to their newspapers with a riper knowledge of

papers seek to bend politicians to their own views and interests. The ministers and parliamentarians, rather more successfully, seek to utilize the press as a means of promoting their political careers and of justifying official action to a critical and impatient public. Certain papers, such as *Le Temps* and *Le Journal des Débats*, are supposedly "official" in the sense of reflecting the views and having the ear of the Government in power. Others, such as the organs of the extreme Left and Right, *L'Humanité* and *L'Action Française*, are always in opposition to the Government. Between these two extremes all possible variations of attitude exist. But, in general, the Cabinet in office has ample means at its disposal for insuring a "favorable press" through contacts between officials and journalists, through the press departments of each ministry and under-secretariat, through the surveillance exercised over the press by the Ministries of Justice and of the Interior, and, if need be, through bribery.

The venality of the French Press has been commented upon by many observers. To paraphrase Walpole, every editor has his price, and papers are sold to the highest bidders. Among the bidders are all who have money and who can use the press to their own advantage—bankers, industrialists, corporations, sundry propagandist organizations, foreign governments, and the French Government itself. Daily newspapers in Great Britain, Germany, and the United States are perhaps more frequently bought and managed by powerful business interests than in France. But in the French Republic, as in other *bourgeois* States, those individuals and groups possessed of wealth and economic power inevitably seek to use the press to serve their own ends. In addition to sponsoring innumerable trade journals, circulated among professional financiers, merchants, industrial entrepreneurs and the like, they seek to influence or control the great metropolitan dailies of wide circulation as a means of exerting political pressure through public opinion. Most French papers, like others elsewhere, depend for the major portion of their revenue on advertising and the pressure of the advertiser on the editor and reporter is constant and effective, even though it may be subtle and not apparent to the casual observer. The captains of industry often control papers directly. Loucheur, for example, owns *Le Petit Journal* of Paris and the *Progrès du Nord* of Lille. The *Comité des Forges* issues *La Journée Industrielle*. François Coty, the great Corsican perfume magnate, owns *Figaro* and in 1928 established *L'Ami du Peuple* as a popular sheet selling at less than half the price of its competitors. Owing to the latter circumstance, the new paper won the enmity of all others and was boycotted by the publishing firm of Hachette which owns most of the newspaper kiosks in the metropolis. Coty, by

facts and conditions, which enables them to spread a greater spirit of moderation among an impatient democracy. The result has been a popular understanding of the national interests and requirements at home and abroad, especially throughout the provinces, which, I venture to think, exists in no other country to the same extent." T. Barclay, *Thirty Years* (Anglo-French Reminiscences, 1876–1906), p. 323, London, 1914.

reason of his wealth, was able to defy the monopoly and to establish his own distributing agencies. His paper has achieved wide circulation and is used to further its owner's political ambitions and to popularize his reactionary political views.[1] Many papers are subsidized by foreign governments. The wholesale bribery of French papers by the Imperial Russian Government has been dealt with above.[2] In 1917, M. Duval, of *Le Bonnet Rouge*, was sentenced to death and executed for receiving funds from Germany for defeatist propaganda. At the same time, *Le Populaire*, the minority Socialist organ, was suspected of being supported by German funds. Many papers, in peace more frequently than in war, are known to receive subsidies from foreign States. To counteract these influences and to strengthen its own position with the public the French Government itself resorts to the same tactics. The secret funds of the Ministry of the Interior and of other Ministries are often devoted to purchasing a good press. The conversion of Gustav Hervé, editor of *La Victoire*, from revolutionary Socialism to extreme Nationalism, was popularly attributed to such causes. The Ministry of Foreign Affairs similarly devotes a portion of its secret funds to such purposes, in addition to bribing foreign newspapers, despite the view frequently expressed in Parliament that this practice should be confined to the press of other countries.[3]

Under these circumstances it is clear that the press is more frequently than not a powerful tool in the hands of those who control it, whether they be public officials, politicians, party groups, or private individuals or organizations with special interests to serve. The "public," being more or less aware of these facts, tends to discount what it reads and is unquestionably less docile and gullible in its reactions to newspapers than is the case in the United States. Circulation, therefore, is no adequate index to the political influence of a paper though circulation figures are doubtless more significant than in the United States, where no genuine political press exists. At the same time, the public expresses itself between elections chiefly through newspapers and is, in itself, little more than the sum of the organized minorities striving for power. The Quai d'Orsay, in recent years at least, is as keenly sensitive to the attitude of the press as any other ministry. Its Information and Press Service issues releases more or less regularly to the representatives of French and foreign newspapers and seeks to control opinion on foreign policy through certain papers which it subsidizes or gains control of through

---

[1] Lewinsohn, *op. cit.*, pp. 262–266. *Cf.* pp. 254–257.

[2] *Supra*, pp. 203–205.

[3] "On doit faire remarquer à ce sujet, que s'il peut être nécessaire de subventionner la presse étrangère, la patriotisme de notre presse est certainement suffisant, quelque soit le parti du journal intéressé, pour obtenir sans rétribution spéciale, une collaboration utile pour tous les cas supérieurs d'intérêt national. L'histoire a montré dans cet ordre d'idées que les encouragements accordés à une certain presse avaient eu plutôt pour objet non de garantir les intérêts généraux du pays, mais, à des époques de crises graves, de tromper celui-ci en faisant l'apologie personnelle de quelques hommes politiques." *Rap. Budget, Ch.*, session extraord. de 1913, No. 3318, Tome II, p. 61.

special favors. The leading newspaper of France, *Le Temps*, is generally regarded as the mouthpiece of the Quai d'Orsay. The press is patriotic—by inclination, and because the profits of patriotism, as measured by circulation, by access to the official sources of news, and by governmental subsidies, are sufficiently substantial not to be ignored. It is not too much to say, perhaps, that the French Press, in its influence on foreign as well as on domestic politics, is less an independent agency, exerting pressure of its own, than one of the channels through which other forces seek to mold and shape opinion to suit their own ends.

4. Parliamentarians, Politicians, and Bureaucrats

The final result of the pressures which control the process of politics is reflected in the day-to-day operations of Government, in the formulation of programs of action by the executive agencies of the State, in the course of legislation, and in the formulation and execution of administrative orders and decrees. An adequate examination of the relation of government to the other types of social groupings which have been surveyed would obviously require a detailed examination of the nature of the State and a series of adventures in political theory for which space is lacking in the present inquiry and which might appear irrelevant to its main purposes. It is the writer's conviction that the future progress of the science of politics is largely dependent upon the formulation of adequate hypotheses regarding the rôle of the State and of political behavior in the social process. Such studies as the present one may make some small contribution to the attainment of that objective. But the labyrinth of political speculation can be entered here only to the extent required to synthesize and interpret the material which has been presented in the light of a self-consistent and, it is hoped, illuminating perspective.

Without professing unqualified allegiance to pluralism, pragmatism, economic determinism, or to any other school of political interpretation, it has been assumed throughout the present volume that the significance of government and politics in contemporary Western civilization—in France as in other countries—can be best appreciated by viewing the political process as one through which organized groups or classes, striving to control the machinery of the State for the promotion of their own interests, are coordinated and brought together in equilibrium on the basis of the general values or ends regarded as good by the entire political community. Few phases of political and governmental activity are comprehensible save in terms of the interaction of group pressures. This is true of foreign as of domestic affairs. These pressures are in all save revolutionary situations canalized by the habits and traditions of the past. These habits and traditions are incorporated in current political practices and crystallized in statutes and in the accepted concepts and principles of constitutional and administrative law. In the field of foreign policy, the channels of political pressure are defined not only by these domestic traditions of law and politics, but also by the established principles of international law, the accepted procedures of diplomatic practice, and the universal values of international politics in the Western State System as a whole. If public opinion and group pressures seem to exercise less effective control over foreign policy than over domestic affairs of State, the explanation is to be found, in part, in the greater weight of habit and tradition and the narrower confines of the channels in which the political process moves.[1]

The chief custodians of habit and tradition in every State are to be found in the permanent staff of the civil service among the bureaucrats who constitute the rank and file of the whole army of officialdom.[2] Since foreign affairs, by their nature, are dominated by historical precedents, established values, and traditional procedures to a greater degree than domestic affairs, it is but natural that the bureaucrats who are entrusted with their administration should exert more influence in the determination and execution of policy, as compared with the parliamentary politicians who direct their activities, than is the case with other governmental functions. That policies are often formulated by those who, in theory, are entrusted only with their administration has been pointed out repeatedly in the preceding chapters. The day-to-day conduct of foreign relations in France is in the hands of the permanent officials at the Quai d'Orsay and of the representatives of the Republic abroad—diplomats, consuls, commercial agents, army officers, naval commanders and the like. These officials work under the supervision and direction of their respective ministers, but ministers come and go while the bureaucracy goes on forever, undisturbed for the most part by political upheavals, shifts of public opinion, or even by revolutions. The bureaucracy furnishes the element of stability and continuity without which the French Government would be in constant confusion. In foreign affairs its rôle as the conservator of tradition is strengthened by the fact that even politicians and parliamentarians act much of the time on the assumption that foreign policy should be affected as little as possible by partisan considerations and changes of political alignments. The permanent officials in the foreign office and in the foreign service are thus the high priests of precedent to a greater extent

---

[1] "C'est en trait remarquable de l'évolution constitutionnelle dans tous les pays que le progrès démocratique est infiniment plus lent et toujours moins complet en ce qui concerne la direction de la politique étrangère que pour ce qui touche à la politique interne. La démocratie a cru jusqu'ici qu'elle n'était pas intéressée à la diplomatie: 'Ce qui importe essentiellement à chaque citoyen, écrit Rousseau dans les *Lettres écrites de la Montagne*, c'est l'observation des lois au-dedans, la propriété des biens et la sureté des particulars. Tant que tout ira bien sur ces trois, laissez les conseils négocier et traiter avec l'étranger; ce n'est pas de là que viendront les dangers le plus a craindre.' La démocratie est, avant tout, avide d'égalité, de liberté et de réformes sociales; le gout lui manque pour la politique étrangère." J. Barthélemy, *Le Gouvernment de la France*, p. 123, Paris, 1919.

[2] *Cf.* Walter R. Sharp, *The French Civil Service: Bureaucracy in Transition*, New York, 1931; Leonard D. White, *The Civil Service in the Modern State*, pp. 230–279, The University of Chicago Press, 1930.

than their colleagues in other branches of the national administration. They enjoy greater prestige and more of the pride and pomp of power which surrounds the highest affairs of State. They are the guardians of patriotism and of the past and they are, to a large degree, insulated from the fever and furor of public opinion, from the control of political parties, from the pressures of interested groups and organizations seeking to bend them toward courses other than those dictated by the habits and traditions which they have followed so long and preserved so carefully. They constitute, in short, the great conservative force which keeps the machinery for the administration of foreign affairs in its accustomed grooves and traveling in its habitual direction.

The various channels of influence through which the formulation of policy is shaped by the professional diplomats at the Quai d'Orsay and in the field services are difficult to trace from written records and do not appear obvious to the casual observer. They range all the way from direct and open recommendations to subtle suggestions and the insidious daily pressure of experts on amateurs. The officials at the Quai d'Orsay, who have been dealing for many years with long-drawn-out diplomatic problems or with types of problems which recur periodically, must necessarily be the main reliance of the foreign minister who holds office temporarily and who is likely to be unfamiliar with precedents and technical details. M. Philippe Berthelot, for example, has held the important post of Secretary-General almost continuously for a decade, following distinguished service in other posts at home and abroad for thirty years before. To say that every foreign minister is more or less dependent on his experience and sagacity in reaching decisions is to state what is obvious. Similarly, those agents who are on the scene of diplomatic action are necessarily better informed regarding current controversies and in a better position, therefore, to influence the formulation of policy than the minister at Paris, even in an age of rapid transportation and communication. These pressures of the professional bureaucracy are steady, continuous, and to be resisted only with the greatest difficulty. They emerge to the surface only occasionally. At times it may be obvious that a diplomatic or consular agent is deliberately protecting investors and concessionnaires in a backward area largely on his own initiative,[1] that a high official at the Quai d'Orsay is urging a definite course of action on doubting ministers,[2] that military commanders, with the acquiescence of diplomatic agents, are precipitating hostilities with foreign States,[3] that a diplomatic agent is embarrassing the Government in power to such a degree that he must be circumvented or removed.[4] The important rôle of the diplomatic and military bureaucracy in the formulation of policy in the crisis of 1914 has been noted

---

[1] *Supra*, pp. 61*f.*
[2] *Supra*, pp. 93*f.*, 112*f.*, 142*f.*
[3] *Supra*, pp. 84-87.
[4] *Supra*, pp. 114*f.*, 193*f.*

above.[1] The fashion in which professional soldiers control foreign policy has been analyzed at some length.[2] But quite apart from these special situations the permanent bureaucracy is always in the background and is always exerting pressure in directions dictated by precedent, tradition, special interests, and its own *esprit de corps*.

This pressure is effective only in so far as it controls the actions of those who hold ministerial posts and are actually responsible for the formulation of foreign policy. The Minister of Foreign Affairs, under the supervision of the Premier and in collaboration with his colleagues in the Cabinet, is obviously the ultimate source of authority and action.[3] His office in the Quai d'Orsay is the focal point at which the various pressures which shape and determine foreign policy converge. His permanent staff is, in theory, at his command, and it translates into action such policies as it receives through his orders. But, as already suggested, it is no mere passive instrument to be wielded as its temporary master wishes. It may cooperate. It may obstruct. It may advise, admonish, or warn. It may bend the minister to its own views. It may even thwart his express commands. In every case it constitutes a professional, expert bureaucracy, resisting subtly but often effectively all efforts of politicians or parliamentarians to adopt new courses toward new destinations.

Between this internal pressure from his own subordinates and the outside pressures coming, on the one hand, from the President, the Premier, the Cabinet, and the Chambers, and, on the other, from the press, political parties, public opinion, and innumerable groups, organizations, and individuals interested in controlling foreign policy, the foreign minister would appear to have but little room within which to exercise his personal judgment. The limits of the sphere of his freedom of action are largely determined by his own skill and astuteness as a politician and an administrator. Under favorable circumstances, such a statesman as Delcassé can pursue successfully an almost personal policy, even though he never holds the premiership.[4] Such veteran political leaders as Poincaré or Briand can largely steer their own course, so long as they bear in mind the structure of the vessel and the temper of the crew as well as the shoals and tempests which dot the sea of international politics. Lesser figures find themselves narrowly circumscribed by the machinery, in which they are neither the engine nor the rudder but only a wheel among many wheels. The Premier may wield effective power himself, whatever portfolio he holds.[5] Other ministers may play the major rôle.[6] The Cabinet as a whole may act under the leadership of its dominant

[1] On Berthelot, *supra*, pp. 216, 222. Paléologue, pp. 219, 226-227, 231-232. Messimy and Joffre, pp. 227, 234, 242; also p. 232.

[2] *Supra*, pp. 341-351.

[3] *Supra*, pp. 28-30, 305*f*., 334*f*.

[4] *Supra*, pp. 160*f*.

[5] *Supra*, pp. 65*f*., 80-82, 186*f*.

[6] *Supra*, pp. 137*f*., 228*f*.

members and divisions of opinion among them may lead to shifts of policy, both as to goals and methods.[1] Within the Cabinet the reins of control over foreign as over domestic affairs are held by those whose prestige, political influence, and personal leadership give them power—and the hands which guide diplomacy are not always those of the foreign minister. At all times the ministers as a body seek to preserve the appearance of unity in dealing with Parliament and the public in accordance with the well-established practice of collective ministerial responsibility.

As for parliamentary pressure on the foreign minister and on the Cabinet in general, the earlier chapters have been sufficient to indicate the tenuous and theoretical nature of the Chambers' control over foreign affairs.[2] It is almost an axiom of the French parliamentary system that Cabinets do not fall on foreign policy. Occasionally, to be sure, ministries are turned out of office because of parliamentary opposition to the international commitments which they have made or are about to make. Even here, however, the circumstances are almost always confused by considerations of domestic partisan politics and the policy which has been supposedly repudiated is frequently carried out by the succeeding Cabinet with little change.[3] Indeed it is a commonplace to say that the resignation of a French Cabinet ordinarily involves little change either in the composition or in the policies of the ministry, since a party leader's chances of getting back into office when he is out are almost as good as his chances of being put out when he is in.

[1] *Supra*, pp. 264-265, 237-240.

[2] *Supra*, pp. 305-355.

[3] Of the seventy-odd Cabinets of the Third French Republic, scarcely a dozen can be regarded as having fallen from power on clear-cut issues of foreign policy between the Government and the Chambers. To cite the outstanding instances, Ferry resigned on November 9, 1881, because of parliamentary criticism of his Tunisian policy. The policy, however, was alreay a *fait accompli* not to be undone by Parliament. Freycinet fell on July 29, 1882, because of the Chamber's rejection of his demand for credits for an expedition to Egypt. On March 30, 1885, Ferry was again turned out of office as a result of popular indignation and alarm over military reverses in Tonkin when Parliament refused his demands for credits—but his Tonkin policy was nevertheless carried to a conclusion. On December 29, 1885, the Brisson Cabinet fell, again over Tonkin, and again without any substantial change of policy at the Quai d'Orsay. On March 13, 1890, Tirard fell, following a debate on the commercial treaty with Turkey. On April 21, 1896, the Bourgeois Cabinet resigned after the Senate's rejection of its demands for credits for military operations in Madagascar. Again no change of policy ensued. On January 11, 1911, Caillaux resigned following an embarrassing incident before a Senate commission, and Poincaré introduced a new spirit at the Quai d'Orsay, without reversing anything done by his predecessor, however. On June 12, 1913, Ribot fell because of his insistence on enforcing the three-year military service law. His successor, Viviani, was at first opposed to it, but the law was nevertheless enforced. The Cabinet changes of the war years are, of course, of little value in revealing the normal relations between the Government and the Chambers as regards foreign affairs because of the practical suspension of the deliberative functions of Parliament and the cessation of party conflict. The fall of Briand on January 15, 1922, was due to parliamentary opposition to his policy at Cannes. The fall of his twelfth Cabinet, on October 22, 1929, was similarly due to opposition to his foreign policy, but the policy was unchanged and he remained foreign minister in the Tardieu Cabinet. *Cf. J.O.Ch.* and *Sén.* for dates immediately following those given above.

Briand once exclaimed, when asked by an admirer whether it was disagreeable to fall: "But, madame, one does not fall. One sits down at the road side, lights a cigarette, and waits to see the body of one's successor pass by."[1] Only when a national election turns on questions of foreign affairs, as is rarely the case, and when it results in marked changes in the party composition of the Chamber, is a change of government likely to mean a change in foreign policy, and even here the change is usually more apparent than real.

Apart from its ability to turn the Government out of office, Parliament can, of course, attempt to control foreign policy through less drastic means.[2] Its control over the purse with reference to diplomatic negotiations, its power of ratifying treaties, and its prerogative of declaring war have already been discussed and evaluated.[3] The interpellation is also a general means of control, the efficacy of which as an instrument for embarrassing the Cabinet in office can perhaps be judged by the anxiety of almost all Cabinets to avoid or postpone as long as possible its use in foreign affairs.[4] Interpellations are intended to compel the ministers to give information as to their policies to their fellow parliamentarians. In practice, they are used (or abused) to inaugurate general debates in which the opposition seeks to unseat the Cabinet and in which personal and partisan considerations push the real issues of foreign policy into the background. Written questions to the ministers are even less important as a means of parliamentary control. Such control as parliament exercises effectively over the Quai d'Orsay is wielded through the Commissions of Foreign Affairs,[5] although the minister is, of course, guided to some extent by the exchange of views which takes place in every debate on foreign affairs.

Although these commissions are of limited efficacy as instruments of control, they are perhaps the most important and imposing agencies of Parliament and are frequently presided over by former Premiers. They discuss and report on treaty *projets* and consider resolutions submitted in the Chambers relating to foreign affairs,[6] but their most important function is

---

[1] Story related by Professor J. Barthélemy in a lecture at the Dotation Carnegie in Paris, January 9, 1930.

[2] Cf. S. R. Chow, *Le contrôle parlementaire*, etc., Paris, 1920, and Jean Sapira, *Le Rôle des chambres au point de vue diplomatique dans un régime parlementaire*, Paris, 1920.

[3] *Supra*, pp. 305f., 313-325, 334-341.

[4] Cf. Pierre de Saint-Mart, *Étude historique et critique sur les interpellations en France*, Paris, 1912.

[5] Other commissions of the Chambers sometimes have occasion to review the activities of the Quai d'Orsay, though they seldom take up questions of policy. The Commissions of Finance, for example, review the budget of the Ministry of Foreign Affairs, but their reports are usually confined to a consideration of questions of expenditures and of internal organization and administration.

[6] See, for an example, *Proposition de résolution* invitant le Gouvernement a prendre les mesures nécessaires pour demander et pour obtenir de l'Allemagne le payement de toutes les réparations qui lui incombent, etc., December 29, 1922, *Ch. des Dép.*, Session Extraord. de 1922, No. 5381, Renvoyée à la Commission des Affaires Étrangères. No action on this resolution by the commission is recorded. Many such resolutions are buried in this fashion. Cf. *supra*, pp. 306-309.

that of controlling, or attempting to control, the general foreign policy of the Cabinet. The Senate and Chamber commissions act independently of one another and publish their reports separately in the annexes to the *Journal Officiel* and also in a separate series. The reports deal almost exclusively with treaties submitted for ratification and with demands for credits and are prepared on the basis of the hearings held before the commissions. Private individuals and representatives of economic or other pressure groups are never called in as witnesses. Information is secured entirely from the Quai d'Orsay or other official sources. Such information may be secured in writing at the request of the presidents of the commissions or it may be obtained by putting oral questions to the Premier, Minister of Foreign Affairs, or other officials who appear for interrogation. On such occasions the commissions sometimes meet jointly with other commissions of their respective houses.[1] The commissions never engage in discussions before a minister or high official and seldom engage in debates after the departure of such persons. This practice, coupled with the fact that months or years may pass without a single formal vote or decision on the part of the commissions and the further fact that they take no part as such in interpellations on foreign policy on the floors of the Chambers, means that they serve chiefly as organs of information rather than as organs of action.

Even as organs of information their utility is limited by the unsympathetic and secretive attitude often adopted by the foreign minister or Premier who appears before them. Unlike the corresponding committee of the German Reichstag, which is created by the Constitution instead of by the rules of the Chamber, the French commissions do not sit permanently between sessions of Parliament and have no general powers of investigation. The chambers may authorize the commissions to act as Commissions of Inquiry on particular questions and to report thereon, but this is seldom done. The ministers are under no obligation to appear in response to a request. During eight months prior to his resignation at the time of the Cannes Conference in 1922, Briand never once appeared before the commissions. The commissions, moreover, may never summon the permanent officials at the Quai d'Orsay or other higher officials of the Government before them without the consent of the minister, who may refuse to permit this. In the spring of 1920, the Chamber commission repeatedly expressed a desire to question General Franchet d'Espery, but permission was never granted. When the Premier or foreign minister consents to appear in person, he may come alone or bring with him such subordinates as he desires. Millerand, who among recent Premiers came most frequently and most willingly before the commissions, was always accompanied by Philippe Berthelot or some other

---

[1] The Chamber commission met with the Commission of Finance to hear Millerand on the Spa accords and Leygues on Syrian affairs, with the Army Commission to hear Millerand on German disarmament, and with the Commission of the Marine to hear Sarraut on the Washington Conference agreements.

high official in the ministry. The distinguished Secretary-General of the Quai d'Orsay, according to a member of the Chamber commission, was invariably suave, dignified, distant, charming, and always fully informed regarding the smallest details of current negotiations. But he conveyed the impression of disliking to appear before the Deputies. Reluctance to testify before a legislative committee is manifested quite as frequently by the ministers themselves as by their subordinates. Poincaré particularly expressed his irritation at this duty and his dissatisfaction with the whole commission system.[1] Even Millerand was often evasive and deceptive in his answers, sometimes eluding embarrassing questions by alleging pressing engagements elsewhere or asking the completest secrecy for some communication which appeared in the evening papers of the same day. Once, in response to a question, he read an extract from Le Temps. When asked what support the French Government had given to the anti-Soviet White Armies in the Russian civil war, he replied: "Un certain appui, dans certaines limites, à certaines moments." In response to a question by Marcel Cachin, he preserved dead silence. On April 20, 1920, Barthou, president of the Chamber commission, complained that he had been refused the text of the Treaty of Sèvres which was given to the press at the same hour. Later in the same year Paul-Boncour cited documents which he had gotten in confidence from the Quai d'Orsay two days previously but of which he had found the full texts in foreign newspapers of four months before. When the commissions are treated in this fashion, they have no recourse, since every minister or official who appears before them is necessarily in a delicate position and any indiscreet questioning or complaints may close future sources of information. Under these circumstances the limited value of the commissions as organs of parliamentary control of foreign policy is obvious.[2]

Inasmuch as the foregoing analysis of the relations between the Cabinet, the Chambers, and the bureaucracy leads to the conclusion that initiation and control of foreign policy rest almost exclusively with the executive, some further mention may appropriately be made of the rôle of the President of the Republic who is, in name at least, the highest source of executive authority. Earlier discussions of the part played by the President in particular diplomatic controversies have indicated, on the one hand, his generally feeble position; and, on the other, his opportunities to influence foreign affairs by shaping public opinion and maintaining contacts with foreign

---

[1] Cf. Avis Supplémentaire (on the project for opening credits to send an embassy to Moscow), Ch. des Dép. session de 1925, No. 1079, in which the Chamber commissions complain that Poincaré failed to transmit to it the correspondence with the Soviet Government regarding the disposition of Wrangel's fleet. The commission concluded that it should formulate no opinions on this controversy, but leave it entirely to the government.

[2] The writer is indebted to Professor Joseph Barthélemy, former member of the Chamber commission, for information regarding several of the incidents recounted above and for valuable insights into the functions of the commissions generally.

sovereigns or representatives of foreign governments.[1] His position as a symbol of the authority of the State and representative of the national interest, above political parties, should make him peculiarly influential in foreign affairs.[2] His constitutional powers afford him a wide field for action in the realm of diplomacy. But the requirement that all his acts must be counter-signed by a responsible minister leaves him in practice with few powers and small influence. His actual influence depends upon personalities and circum-stances. Out of deference to the dignity of his office, the Premier and foreign minister usually keep him informed regarding their goals and methods in foreign affairs, but they may prefer not to do so. In 1921 Tardieu, in his controversy with Poincaré over the terms of the Treaty of Versailles, asserted, correctly, that a President could never have first-hand knowledge of treaty negotiations. During the actual negotiations in question, when Poincaré and Clemenceau were at loggerheads, the President's notes of complaint often did not reach their destination and were as often unread or ignored when they did. The President under such circumstances may appeal to the Chambers or to the country, but only if authorized to do so by the Premier. If the latter refuses, he may ask for the Premier's resignation, but if the Premier has the confidence of a majority in the Chambers this action will not only be ignored but will savor of overstepping the constitutional bounds of the Presidential office. It may subject the President to sharp criticism and even endanger his position as chief of State.

Nevertheless, the President, like the bureaucracy, represents continuity in foreign policy and he has often exerted an appreciable influence on the course of diplomatic developments. Carnot was one of the makers of the Dual Alliance. Loubet's rôle in the Anglo-French Entente is well known. Poincaré's rôle before and during the crisis of 1914 needs no emphasis. The prestige of the highest office in the French Government also makes Presi-dential elections a test of political strength as between the rival candidates and the outcome may have serious reverberations in foreign affairs. Russian satisfaction at Poincaré's elevation to the Presidency in 1913 has been noted above. Clemenceau's defeat by Deschanel in 1920 and that of Painlevé by Doumergue in 1924 were not without their implications as to the attitudes of the parliamentarians toward the views on foreign policy of the candidates in question. In the election of May 13, 1931, Aristide Briand was defeated by Paul Doumer for the chief magistracy of the Republic. Despite the strong support accorded to the veteran foreign minister by the Chamber and the Senate meeting separately as legislative bodies, when the members of Parlia-ment met together as a National Assembly at Versailles they apparently

[1] *Supra*, pp. 18–20, 207–209, 211f., 267–272, etc.

[2] "Il semblait, en théorie, que la politique extérieure dût être le domaine de choix ou s'exerce l'influence présidentielle. Le Président peut, en se tenant au-dessus des partis ainsi que c'est la règle, s'occuper des intérêts supérieures du pays dans le monde," lecture of Joseph Barthélemy, Dotation Carnegie, December 12, 1929.

seized upon the opportunity which they had long been seeking to express their disapproval of the policy of Franco-German *rapprochement* and conciliation so consistently pursued by Briand. He was deserted by many of his Left supporters and received only 401 votes on the first ballot to his rival's 442, with 15 votes for Hennesy, 10 for Cachin, and the balance scattered. In chagrin, Briand then dropped out of the race, along with Hennesy and other minor candidates, and on the second ballot Doumer received a clear majority, with 504 votes to 334 for the new candidate of the Left, Senator Pierre Marraud. Briand's defeat was attributed to popular and parliamentary dissatisfaction with the results of his peace policy, such as the rise of Hitlerism in Germany following the evacuation of the Rhineland and the announcement of the proposed Austro-German customs union in March, 1931. On the other hand, many Senators who doubtless voted for Doumer on the first ballot to show honor to the president of the upper Chamber, might have shifted to Briand on the second had he not withdrawn, while a good many supporters of Briand's foreign policy among the Deputies may have voted against him deliberately in order to prevent his withdrawal from the Quai d'Orsay. The defeat of the "Minister of Peace" was nevertheless regarded as such a severe blow to his prestige that he tendered his resignation to Premier Laval, though it was rejected and he proceeded to Geneva, leaving the eventual disposition of his portfolio, which he had held longer than any of his predecessors, for future determination. Upon his return to Paris he decided to remain Minister of Foreign Affairs in spite of his humiliation.[1] Presidential elections may thus serve as an additional means through which Parliament may register its approval or disapproval of the foreign policy of the executive, though here again the issues are always confused and the control, like all others, is *ex post facto* in nature in the sense of censuring what has been done rather than indicating clearly what should be done in the future.

5. The Politics of Power

While few observers of contemporary French politics would challenge the facts which have been surveyed and the generalizations which have been drawn from them with reference to the constitutional controls of foreign affairs, any effort to interpret these data in psychological and sociological terms will at once lead to sharp differences of opinion. Some will explain the political process as a reflection of the economic interests of individuals, groups, and classes. Others will prefer to regard the political process in terms of the rôle of great personalities. Still others will treat politics as a mirror of political ideas and social theories, which are the creation of thinkers,

---

[1] *Cf. Le Temps*, May 13, 14, 15; New York *Times*, May 14, 15, 16, 1931. Briand's tactics at the European Union Committee and at the session of the Council of the League of Nations, both held immediately after the election, suggest that he may have used the threat of resignation as a bargaining weapon to win support and concessions from foreign governments.

the heritage of organized groups of apostles, and the dynamic forces controlling political action. Another school may regard the French State and the practice of French politics in the light of the spiritual qualities of the French people, or as expressions of the inner reality of French culture. The historian to whom history is past politics and politics present history will attempt to explain every situation in terms of its causal antecedents. The psychologist emphasizes the relationship between the hidden springs of individual behavior and the collective action of groups in dealing with the affairs of State.

All these various ways of viewing the process of politics, along with many others too numerous to mention, make valuable contributions to a clearer understanding of man as a social and political animal. The social sciences have not yet reached a point of development at which it is possible to attempt a valid synthesis of these various approaches and to present a final formulation of social and political theory which can be generally accepted as conclusive in dealing with concrete problems. At the same time the fundamental questions as to the nature of politics and of society which this study raises cannot well be evaded. It is usually desirable, moreover, that inferences be drawn from freshly assembled materials by those who have assembled them rather than by outsiders, even though the conclusions be tentative and open to attack from many angles. In view of these considerations it appears not only permissible but desirable to endeavor to describe as clearly as words permit the process of politics in the French Republic as it affects the formulation of foreign policy in the light of the data which have been reviewed.

It may be suggested at the outset, as has already been implied in the foregoing discussion, that the process of politics in Western civilization as a whole is intelligible and significant chiefly as an expression of the will to power. This hypothesis does not rest upon an acceptance of the philosophical premises of Nietzsche, nor upon any revolutionary assumptions regarding human nature, nor yet upon any *a priori* theory of the State. It is merely intended to emphasize the obvious fact that almost all political behavior is motivated, in one way or another, by a desire of one set of individuals to achieve, to retain, or to escape the control of another set. Private aspirations toward self-assertion, subordination, aggressiveness, submissiveness, recognition, new experience, security, response (a score of categories of instinctive or quasi-instinctive wants at once suggests itself) become politicalized when they achieve expression in actions centering around the institutions and procedures of the State. The State itself may usefully be viewed as an institutionalization of power relationships, implying, on the one side, control, rule making, direction, "government" in the broadest sense; and, on the other, acquiescence, allegiance, obedience, and acceptance of the will of those who have power by those over whom it is exercised. The dynamic realities of politics are to be found in relationships of power between individuals, parties, groups, organizations, social classes, or nations themselves. All politics may be regarded as essentially a struggle for power, on whatever level, for whatever specific goals, or by whatever means it may be conducted. The political process is one through which power relationships are modified, adjusted, and crystallized.[1]

This view is not new and need not be elaborated or defended here. It will simply be used as a means of clarifying the problems with which the present study is concerned, since it seems to the writer to furnish the most adequate basis for interpretation of the material which has been presented. Viewed in this light, French society is a manifold of interests, each of which is the *raison d'être* of the organized groups which are constantly forming and reforming to strive for power. Within each group there are leaders and led, officials and subordinates, hierarchies and laymen, bureaucrats and electorates, each with its own interests within the larger group. These groups are varied, multitudinous, almost infinite in their complexities and interrelationships—competing, cooperating, conflicting, coalescing, disintegrating. There is the all-embracing group of "France," comprising all Frenchmen and claiming, through the authority of the State, precedence over all others. The French State presides over a welter of lesser groups, but presumably exists to serve the interests of all. But its servants have interests of their own to serve as politicians, parliamentarians, and bureaucrats. The general interest, moreover, is a composite of lesser interests, territorial, economic, vocational, ecclesiastical and the like, and each of these lesser interests is constantly competing with others to impress the stamp of its own views on the prevalent conception of the general interest and to secure from the State benefits and favors of various kinds, sometimes for their own sake, more often for their effect on the relations of the group to other groups. Each member of the French community—patriot, pacifist, conservative, revolutionist, *bourgeois*, proletarian, peasant, Catholic, Protestant, Jew, or atheist— belongs to numerous lesser communities and has political significance only as he expresses his will through group action of a political character. Each group, whatever its composition, organization, or objectives, whatever the interests which it serves, strives for power. The course of politics is determined by the interaction of the resulting pulls and pressures.

In foreign affairs, as in all others, policies are formulated and executed as group pressures dictate. These pressures are too numerous, too variable, too complex in their interactions to make prediction and control possible.

[1] *Cf.* Harold Laski, *Politics*, New York, 1931, and *A Grammar of Politics*, London, 1925; Franz Oppenheimer, *The State*, Berlin, 1908, New York, 1914 and 1922; L. Duguit, *Law in the Modern State;* H. Kelsen, *Allgemeine Staatslehre*, etc. The analysis of politics in terms of power which is attempted in the present and in the following chapter is in no sense intended as an adequate formulation of the nature of the political process and of the State, but merely as a useful and valid frame of orientation for the consideration of the problems with which the present study is concerned. An adequate analysis would require a critical examination of many phases of the situation which are obviously neglected here for lack of space.

But the major sources of effective pressures are apparent and the patterns of their interactions emerge clearly enough to reveal the dynamics of policy formulation. These patterns are many and they are overlaid one upon another in intricate and fascinating rhythm and counter-point. International law and diplomatic practice, constitutional principles, statutory regulations, administrative rules and precedents, the fixed conditioned reflexes of politicians and bureaucrats, and the established stereotypes of political thought and action constitute the formal framework within which group pressures operate. Within this framework the struggle for power goes on between the representatives of lesser groups whose relations are less clearly defined and crystallized. Out of this process emerges the foreign policy of the French Republic. The content of that policy, at any given moment of time, is a result of the interaction between the consensus of the internal pressures which have operated upon it and the position of France with relation to other States in terms of power relationships. It serves those interests among the internal pressures which have been most successful in imposing their will upon the final result.

Each of the historical chapters of the present study is an attempted analysis of the forces which have controlled French foreign policy in particular diplomatic situations. If it has not always been possible to get fully behind the scenes at the Quai d'Orsay, it has at least been possible to uncover the major sources of influence and pressure on foreign policy and to suggest the probable motivations of statesmen and diplomats. In the episodes selected from the history of French imperialism, the interplay of forces which led to territorial acquisitions and to the coercion or conquest of weak and distant States have been analyzed with such care as the available records permitted. Those responsible for the formulation of the policies which led to these results were obviously moved by the usual considerations of national power and prestige which underlie all diplomatic action throughout the Western State System. Their goals were approved by patriotic opinion whenever they could be presented in terms which evoked favorable emotions and behavior patterns. These terms had no necessary relation to reality. Indeed, parliamentary and public apprehension frequently dictated deception, subterfuge, and evasions of constitutional principles and procedures, just as considerations of strategy and high politics at times required a somewhat cavalier treatment of the rights of other States as determined by international law and diplomatic amenities. The professional diplomatic service and the professional wagers of war were, for the most part, willing instruments in the hands of the executive agencies of the Government—if not prime movers in the drama—since they properly regarded themselves as the apostles and custodians of national honor, diplomatic prestige, and State power. The economic interests of French investors, concessionnaires, merchants, and property owners furnished both pretexts for action and sources of pressure for their own defense. Balance-of-power considerations, arising out of the juxtaposition of Powers in the whole European diplomatic arena, contributed to the final decisions. The Press, on the whole, was patriotic and insistent upon power and glory for *la patrie* through the vigorous protection of citizens abroad, except on those infrequent occasions when military reverses or disasters increased parliamentary anxiety and furnished opportunity for making political capital by assailing the policies of the Government. Out of these pressures policies emerged and were put into execution with such success as the skill of the directors and administrators permitted.

In the shaping of the policies which led to the formation of the great coalitions, the situation was less complicated by incalculable factors, since the reins of power were more firmly held by the politicians and professional diplomats, who accomplished their purposes secretly and subtly with the tacit approval of all good patriots and with little interest in their proceedings on the part of powerful economic groups. Investors, merchants, and entrepreneurs were by no means negligible factors. They sometimes pushed the Government into action, as was partially the case in the preparation of the Anglo-French Entente. They were sometimes used by the Government for its own purposes, as was the case with the loans to Russia. In both instances they acquiesced in the pursuit of policies dictated less by their own economic interests than by the more intangible values of *Realpolitik*. The servile press applauded and patriotic public opinion approved. The opposition of a portion of the proletariat and of certain sections of the *bourgeoisie*, expressed through the parties of the Left, was unable to turn the diplomatic machine from the course chosen for it by those at the throttle. The implications of that course, and the destination at its end were seen but dimly, even by many of the drivers themselves. Professional diplomats and warriors pursued their way with such objectives and by such methods as the creed of their trade dictated. In the catastrophe of 1914, French policy, like that of all the other belligerents, was still controlled by this same group, with results which seemed appalling to those unfamiliar with their secret antecedents, but which were accepted by all good patriots throughout the nation as inevitable or as the work of foreign devils beyond the frontier. In the post-war reparations controversy patriotic public opinion and the pressures of interested economic groups played a more direct rôle in pushing the Government forward along a path dictated by the exigencies of financial needs and of Great Power politics.

Most discussions of the control of foreign policy tend to center about the question of whether statesmen and diplomats are moved to action by considerations of public welfare and national interests or by the influence of private groups seeking profit or prestige by using the State on their own behalf. It is frequently charged, particularly by socialists and other economic determinists, that modern diplomacy in France, as in other *bourgeois* States, is a process whereby the nation as a whole is called upon to make sacrifices at the behest of entrepreneurs, investors, and profiteers who use the machinery of government for their own private advantage. Much evidence can be found in the foregoing pages to support such an interpretation of French foreign policy. The interplay of rival economic interests in Tunis and their influence on the Quai d'Orsay has been noted.[1] The importance of commercial considerations in the formulation of French policy toward Annam, China, and Siam is obvious.[2] The rôle of property owners and investors in Madagascar has also been pointed out,[3] along with that of money-lenders in the Franco-Russian Alliance[4] and that of the *Comité des Forges* and of French mining and manufacturing interests in the Ruhr occupation.[5] The influence of priveleged and protected economic groups on French tariff and commercial policies scarcely calls for demonstration.[6] Innumerable other instances of a like nature could be cited if space permitted, since French politics is replete with scandals and secret manipulations of politicians by the holders of economic power, reaching down into the smallest communes and up into the highest offices of the Republic. Among recent cases of this kind there comes to mind at once the trial before the Senate of Senator Raoul Peret, former president of the Chamber of Deputies, several times a minister, and a candidate for the Presidency, on charges of complicity in the failure of the Oustric Bank in the autumn of 1930.[7] Before the war no less eminent a statesman than André Tardieu, then an editor of *Le Temps*, a politician of influence, and an official in the Ministry of the Interior, apparently acted as the tool of private business interests, with appropriate compensation to himself, in the N'Goka Sangha and the Homs-Bagdad Railway affairs, using his power in politics and journalism to advance the pecuniary claims of his retainers.[8] In 1921

[1] *Supra*, pp. 62f.

[2] *Supra*, pp. 81f., 97f.

[3] *Supra*, pp. 105f., 118f.

[4] *Supra*, pp. 135f.

[5] *Supra*, pp. 260f., 278–279.

[6] *Cf.*, for a sketch of French tariff policy, C. Augier et A. Marvaud, *La politique douanière de la France*, Paris, 1911, and C. Augier, *La France et les traités de commerce*, Paris, 1906.

[7] *Cf.* New York *Times*, May 20, 1931. Peret received an acquittal, though the testimony made it clear that he had been indiscreet.

[8] The former of these interesting scandals involved the claims of the N'Goko-Sangha, a French concession company in the Congo, to an indemnity of 12,675,000 fr. from the French Government, on the ground that German merchants had infringed on its concessions and that frontier changes had altered disadvantageously the limits of its domain. This claim, which was evidently specious, was rejected by successive Premiers, foreign ministers, and colonial ministers, with the result that the company sought to bring political pressure to bear upon the Cabinet through the press. In the winter of 1907 to 1908 Tardieu began publishing questionable reports in *Le Temps* regarding the company's situation in Africa and alleged agreements between the French and German Governments for compensation to their nationals. Pichon then offered to pay the company its indemnity on condition that it enter into the projected Franco-German Congo-Cameroon consortium, which had been devised by M. Roels, Berlin correspondent of *Le Temps* and Herr Semler of the Reichstag, apparently as a means of securing the indemnity by a flank attack. Tardieu represented the company before the arbitral commission appointed to examine its claims, even though he was an official of the Ministry of the Interior. When the effort failed and the Chamber Commission of the Budget rejected the claims, Tardieu violently attacked

Philippe Berthelot was forced out of his post as Secretary-General at the Quai d'Orsay when it became apparent that in the interest of his brother, André, member of the board of directors of the *Banque Industrielle de Chine*, he misused his diplomatic powers, without informing the foreign minister, in order to strengthen the position of the bank in the Far East by misrepresenting the intentions of the French Government regarding it.[1] Such incidents are numerous and others like them which never come to light probably more so. They tend to confirm the view that politics is but the handmaiden of privileged business interests in foreign affairs as in other respects.

But the interrelationships involved here cannot accurately be expressed in any simple and obvious formula, suggesting that journalists, parliamentarians, and *fonctionnaires* are moved to action exclusively by the pressures of private economic interests or by desire for pecuniary gain to themselves. Granting that politics and economics are inseparable in all States, it does not follow that politicians are always moved to action by the demands of business groups. Economics is controlled by politics quite as frequently as politics is controlled by economics. The precise relationship between these two sets of pressures varies so greatly from time to time and from place to place that dogmatic insistence upon any single scheme of interpretation is scarcely conducive to a clear understanding of complex social situations.

Pichon and the Minister of Colonies through the columns of his paper during the winter of 1910 to 1911. Tardieu himself later blamed the socialists and presented the matter as one of high politics, attributing the diplomatic humiliation of 1911 to German resentment at French rejection of the consortium arrangement. There can be little doubt, however, that he hoped to profit, either personally or through subsidies to *Le Temps*, from the realization of the company's aspirations. On the details of this affair see M. Violette, *Á la Veille d'Agadir, la N'Goko-Sangha*, Paris, 1914; F. Challaye, "Politique international et journalisme d'affaires," *La revue du mois*, XI, pp. 749–757, June 10, 1911; A. Tardieu, *Agadir*, pp. 163–209, 288–365, Paris, 1912. Also *cf. supra*, p. 312.

In the Homs-Bagdad Railway affair of 1910, Tardieu was offered 1,000,000 fr. to bring pressure to bear upon the appropriate officials to secure French governmental pressure on Turkey on behalf of a railway concession to an Anglo-French-Turkish financial group which the Turkish Government seemed reluctant to grant. He won the sympathy of Pichon, the foreign minister, but was opposed by Paul Cambon and by Bompard, French Ambassadors, respectively, at London and Constantinople. Tardieu planned to head the French group himself and publicly announced his intention of quitting journalism for finance. When his hopes were dashed, he launched a vigorous press attack in *Le Temps* against Bompard and the Turkish Government, and published documents stolen from the French Embassy in Constantinople as proof of the incompetence of the ambassador. His English accomplice in the affair was tried for theft and sentenced to two years' imprisonment, but Tardieu went unscathed, due perhaps to Pichon's intervention. *Cf.* Challaye, *loc. cit.*, pp. 749–753; C. Paix-Seailles, *La diplomatie sécrète sous la troisième République, 1910–1911; Homs-Bagdad; Du Quai d'Orsay à la correctionnelle; Recueil documentaire*, Paris, 1911.

[1] In this affair Berthelot instructed the French diplomatic agents in China and Japan to deny all unfavorable rumors regarding the bank and to declare, falsely, that the French Government would arrange a consortium to come to its assistance. This fact leaked out to the chambers and created an uproar in which the Socialists demanded a full investigation. Poincaré sought to have Berthelot disciplined and also forced out of office his supporter, Jean Giraudoux, press chief at the Quai d'Orsay. In 1925 Berthelot was again received into the good graces of the Government and returned to his post. Lewinsohn, *op. cit.*, pp. 253–254.

If those who hold economic power in the French Republic frequently seek to control the actions of the holders of public office in their own interests, it is equally true that politicians and bureaucrats often strive to control and direct the activities of merchants, business men, and bankers for political purposes.

This is particularly true in the formulation of foreign policy, which is dominated by traditions far older than the industrial revolution and the rise to political predominance of the *bourgeoisie*. The power-and-prestige teleology of the Western State System antedates the machine age and capitalism by many centuries. Its values are buttressed in France, as in every State, by the sentiments and ideology of patriotism and are associated, rightly or wrongly, with the interests of the national community rather than with those of any group or class. Not only can the statesman and the bureaucrat not ignore the dictates of high politics in the international arena, but he is, by his very position, the custodian and conservator of the values which he has inherited from a long line of predecessors. These values are pursued through the arts of diplomacy and war and express themselves in the tangible and concrete objectives which are regarded as desirable from the point of view of the power and prestige of the State in its dealings with other States. While the ultimate values of foreign policy remain relatively constant, so long as the State System out of which they have evolved persists, the specific objectives are conditioned by the pressures of those interests which control the domestic machinery of government. At one period foreign policy is shaped by the interests of the feudal baronage which wields the power of the State. Later the personal and dynastic interests of the absolute monarch and of the aristocracy which supports him fix the goals of diplomatic action. In the period under discussion, the State is presumed to represent the entire national community in its contacts with other national communities and to act in such fashion as to protect the welfare and security of all its citizens. But despite the pretense of a classless State, those who dominate politics are still those who wield economic power. Under such conditions, foreign policy is still directed toward the unchanging ends of national power and prestige, but these goals are expressed in terms which reflect the interests of the dominant classes within the State. Business interests do not control the administration of foreign affairs. But those who administer foreign affairs have pressure brought to bear upon them by business interests, seeking economic gains through diplomatic action, and they in turn bring pressure to bear upon business interests to enlist their services in the pursuit of the objectives of high policy. This relationship is reciprocal and mutually advantageous. But the broad political objectives of French foreign policy are as ancient as France itself and are deeply rooted in patriotism and the past, while the economic gains of particular business groups are relatively transitory and temporary.

This fact, viewed in the light of the assembled data on the actual formulation of foreign policy in concrete situations, would seem to justify the conclusion that diplomacy bends business to its purposes quite as often as business controls diplomacy for objectives of its own. In none of the episodes analyzed in the preceding chapters could it be said that private business interests pushed the Quai d'Orsay into a course of action which bore no relationship to considerations of national power *vis-à-vis* other States, and which was adopted exclusively for the benefit of the business groups. In every case—even in that of the imperialism of Ferry[1]—patriotism and profits went hand in hand and it is naïve to assume that the values of patriotism are mere rationalizations of the economic interests of private groups or individuals. The diplomat inevitably views economic interests in terms of national power. If the desires of profit-seekers dictate action which coincides with the dictates of power considerations, the diplomat may yield to pressures initiated by the profit-seekers themselves. On the other hand, if power considerations dictate action which will be definitely disadvantageous to those who hold economic power, it is unlikely that it will be embarked upon, given a political system in which the holders of economic power can usually check action which they oppose even if they are not always able to induce action which they favor. More frequently the diplomat utilizes the acquisitiveness of profit-seekers to serve the ends of power and prestige. It goes without saying that imperialism, war, tariff bargaining, commercial treaties and the like are profitable to private interests—often at the expense of groups within the nation which are numerically larger but less articulate and less well organized for their own protection.[2] But it does not follow that the policies which lead to these profitable results are initiated in the first instance by the profit-seekers themselves. The profits may be incidental to the pursuit of much broader political objectives.

In no phase of modern diplomacy does this appear more clearly than in the much discussed relationship between high finance and high politics. Among the most powerful groups of capitalistic entrepreneurs in France, as

---

[1] *Supra*, pp. 67–68.

[2] "Power depends for its habits upon a consciousness of possession, a habit of organization, an ability to produce an immediate effect. In a democratic state, where there are great inequalities of economic power, the main characteristics of the poor are exactly the want of these. They do not know the power that they possess. They hardly realise what can be effected by organising their interests. They lack direct access to those who govern them. Any action by the working classes, even in a democratic State, involves risks to their economic security out of all proportion to the certainty of the gain. They have rarely in their hands the instruments necessary to secure their desires. They have seldom even learned how these may best be formulated and defended. They labour under the sense of inferiority which comes from perpetual obedience to orders without any full experience of the confidence which comes from the habit of command. They tend to confound the institutions they have inherited with the inescapable foundations of society. There is, in fact, every reason to expect that a State built upon universal suffrage will be responsible for wider concessions to the multitude than will be granted under any alternative form; but there is no historic reason to suppose that such a State will be able of itself directly to alter at the root the social results of an economically unequal society." H. Laski, *Politics*, pp. 26–27, Philadelphia and London, 1931.

elsewhere, are the banking and investing groups who act as the servants (or more often, perhaps, as the masters) of the millions of frugal French families whose combined annual savings available for foreign investment mounted from some two billion francs in the seventies and eighties of the last century to five billions by 1914. These savings flowed outward from a nation with a fairly stationary population and a stable, if not static, economic system into the undeveloped areas of the earth where population and resources were abundant but capital was scarce, until French lenders had in 1900 some twenty-eight billion francs invested abroad, as compared with only twelve billions in 1870. At the outbreak of the Great War the total had reached about forty-five billions, similarly invested in government bonds, in railway, commercial and industrial securities, and in all manner of economic enterprises in other countries. These investments were handled by the great industrial banks, such as the *Banque de Paris et Pays Bas*, the *Banque de l'Union Parisienne*, and the *Banque Française pour le Commerce et l'Industrie*. They were distributed throughout the country through the great deposit banks, such as the *Crédit Lyonnais*, the *Comptoir Nationale d'Escompte*, the *Société Générale*, and the *Crédit Industriel et Commercial*. Through these banking agencies the sous and francs in the deep stockings of burghers, peasants, and artisans were sent to the four quarters of the globe to develop industry and commerce and to send back a rich harvest in interest, premiums, and commissions to the bankers and the lenders.[1]

[1] The best available estimate of the geographical distribution of French long-term investments prior to the war is to be found in Herbert Feis, *Europe, The World's Banker*, 1870–1914, Yale University Press, New Haven, 1930. The table on p. 51 in billions of francs follows:

Geographical division	1900	1914
Russia	7.0	11.3
Turkey (in Asia and Europe)	2.0	3.3
Spain and Portugal	4.5	3.9
Austria-Hungary	2.5	2.2
Balkan States	0.7	2.5
Italy	1.3	1.3
Switzerland, Belgium, and the Netherlands	1.0	1.5
Rest of Europe	0.5	1.5
Total Europe	19.9	27.5
French Colonies	1.5	4.0
Egypt, Suez, and South Africa	3.0	3.3
United States and Canada	0.8	(plus Australia) 2.0
Latin America	2.0	6.0
Asia	0.8	2.2
Grand Total	28.0	45.0

Cf. supra, p. 154, for a different estimate of French investments in Russia.

Financial nationalism and imperialism are frequently cited as causes of war and determinants of foreign policy. In France, more so perhaps than in the other Great Powers, foreign investment and diplomacy have marched hand in hand. The assumption is often made that the Bourse controls the Quai d'Orsay, that the wealth and political power of the bankers enables them to control official action and bend the machinery of government to their own ends in protecting and extending the fields of capital investment. While this may at times be true, the weight of evidence would seem to indicate that in the long run the Quai d'Orsay has controlled the Bourse and has determined the fields and forms of investment on the basis of political considerations. The expansion and contraction of French investments in various countries between 1900 and 1914, as shown in the accompanying table, cannot be explained in terms of the profit motivations of French lenders, but only in terms of the use of investments by the French Government as a weapon of diplomacy. As early as 1823 foreign government securities were listed on the official Bourse only with the consent of the Minister of Finance. This right of the State to control the flotation of foreign securities was reaffirmed in 1873 and many times since.[1] The marketing of foreign bonds and stocks in France is controlled jointly by the stock exchanges and the Minister of Finance, with the advice of the Minister of Foreign Affairs.[2] Export industries bring pressure to bear in order to secure contracts and favors as conditions for the flotation of foreign securities. The Quai d'Orsay responds and foreign investment becomes a grave concern of diplomats.[3] What is more significant, the Quai d'Orsay seeks to make investment serve political ends by attaching political conditions to the official listing of securities, by barring loans to countries deemed to be unfriendly or potential enemies, and by encouraging loans to friendly or allied countries.[4] The investment of enormous sums of French capital in Tsarist Russia was a result of political considerations having little or nothing to do with economic interests. The bankers and investors profited, to be sure, until they lost all in the final debâcle of revolution, but they were the pushed rather than the pushers in entering the Russian investment market, the pressure coming from the French

[1] A letter of the Minister of Finance of August 12, 1873, declared: "It is necessary that the Minister of Finance and the Minister of Foreign Affairs judge, one from the point of view of the treasury, the other from the point of view of political interest, whether there is any reason for opposing the official listing of foreign government securities while the stock exchange has the duty of forming a judgment as to whether the negotiation is useful and opportune considering the public interest." Quoted in Feis, p. 120.

[2] "The Minister of Finance can always forbid the negotiation in France of a foreign security," Article V of the decree of 1880, cited in Feis, p. 120.

[3] In 1911, Pichon, Minister of Foreign Affairs, informed the Chamber that "it is a tradition to which we conform in the Ministry of Foreign Affairs. It is clear from the statistics that we have obtained valuable results in this respect, especially for our metallurgical industries; it is generally due to the intervention of our Minister of Foreign Affairs in accord with the Ministers of Finance and Commerce that we have been able to secure important orders," *J.O.Ch.*, January 13, 1911.

[4] Feis, pp. 133–134, 196–209.

Government and from the Russian Government as well.[1] Similarly, in the relations between capital investments and colonial imperialism, the investors would appear, on the whole, to have been induced by the Government to enter fields of activity they might otherwise have avoided.[2] Once the policy of controlling capital movements for political reasons is embarked upon, however, the beneficiaries acquire a vested interest in the fields which they have been invited to enter. They expect diplomatic protection and receive it. They exert pressure to control policy in order that the security of their investments may be assured. The drivers of the governmental cart steer the dray horse of international finance along the road to power in *Weltpolitik*. Having taken the road and found it good, the horse continues to pull the cart behind it whether the drivers have doubts or not as to the wisdom of the course.[3]

These relations between foreign investment and foreign policy have been no less intimate since 1919 than before the Great War. Now, as always, borrowing and lending are matters of prime importance to the Quai d'Orsay in the calculations of power-and-prestige diplomacy. High finance is, as always, the mistress of high policy, each using the other for mutually advantageous ends. The mechanisms of control are much the same, although there have been no flotations of foreign securities in France since the war comparable in size to those of pre-war days. The 25 per cent tax imposed in 1916 on all foreign securities sold in France as a measure designed to prevent the outflow of French capital during the war was retained, along with other restrictions, for some years after the armistice. The repudiation of the vast Russian debts, the depreciation of currencies, and the generally disorganized condition of the money markets of the world have also contributed to a decline of French investments abroad, which were estimated in 1929 to be about 40 per cent less in realizable values than in 1913. The Government, in cooperation with the *Association Nationale des Porteurs Français de Valeurs Mobilières* (established in 1898 and recognized by decree as a public utility in 1919) continues to protect the interests of French bondholders and the latter are still in a position to influence diplomacy in their own interests. This influence is normally exercised to secure protection for investments already made. The determination of what foreign securities shall be purchased, *i.e.*, of the countries into which French capital shall flow, remains in the hands of the Government, since the listing of foreign stocks and bonds on the Bourse is still subject to the approval of the Minister of Finance.[4]

[1] *Ibid.*, pp. 210–234. *Cf.* Paix-Seailles, *Homs-Bagdad*, pp. 6*f.* on Russian objections to French participation in the financing of the Bagdad railway project. Delcassé yielded to Russian pressure while Rouvier sought to make France a participant, but Russo-German political friction led to the abandonment of the scheme.

[2] *Supra*, pp. 57*f.*, on Tunis; Feis, pp. 397–409, on Morocco.

[3] *Supra*, pp. 257–258, on the effects upon French policy toward Soviet Russia of these financial commitments.

[4] *Cf.* H. Merle Cochrane, *French Experience with Defaulted Foreign Bonds*, U. S. Department of Commerce, Trade Information *Bulletin* 656, 1929.

The great objective of this political control is now, as before 1914, to strengthen French influence abroad, to aid France's allies, to enhance French power and prestige, and to weaken past and future foes. Loans to Germany are discouraged or limited.[1] One of the first effects of the announcement of the projected Austro-German customs union in March of 1931 was to "freeze" the French money market for further credits to Germany—not so much, apparently, as a result of any direct governmental veto as of the outcry of the French nationalist press and the realization among bankers and brokers that French loans to Germany would not obtain official sanction in a period of Franco-German friction. At the same time, at the meeting of bankers at the headquarters of the Bank for International Settlements, M. Moret, head of the Bank of France, expressed his approval of French participation in the proposed $21,000,000 loan to Austria to rescue the *Oesterreichische Creditanstalt* from its difficulties, provided that Austria definitely renounced all future attempts to form a customs union with Germany.[2] The abandonment of this project, immediately prior to the advisory opinion of the Permanent Court of International Justice of September 5, 1931, holding it to be a violation of the financial protocol of 1922, was due in large part to effective use of French financial power by the Quai d'Orsay in the face of the weak financial and diplomatic position of Austria and Germany.[3] On the other hand, millions of francs are available for loans to governments or private enterprises in France's eastern satellites. At the end of March, 1931, a $40,000,000 loan was arranged by the Schneider-Creusot steel interests and the *Banque des Pays du Nord* with the Polish Government, with the Quai d'Orsay and the polish foreign minister, Zaleski, playing a prominent part in the negotiations. Simultaneously, a Franco-Polish railway company was formed to use the proceeds of the loan to complete the strategically important line from Polish Upper Silesia to Gdynia, the new Polish port on the Baltic.[4] A $50,000,000 loan to Czechoslovakia, arranged in April of 1931, also has an obvious political significance. Investment and diplomacy march as closely together since Versailles as they did before Sarajevo. The financial historian of the future can say for the present, as for the past,

Capital was called upon to abstain from investment in the lands of potential enemies. It was urged or commanded into the service of allies. It was encouraged to develop the areas that were within the political system of the country where it accumulated. It was upheld in ventures which sustained a national political ambition or hope. In France and Germany, and within the alliances which they headed it came to be commonly regarded as a servant of national purposes rather than as ordinary private possession to be disposed of in accordance with the private judgment and on the private risk of the owner.[5]

* * * * * *

[1] *Cf.* New York *Times*, October 16, 1930; February 6, 10, 1931.
[2] *Cf. Ibid.*, May 18, 1931.
[3] *Cf. Ibid.*, September, 4, 6, 13, 1931.
[4] *Ibid.*, April 1, March 14, April 24, 1931.
[5] Feis, *op. cit.*, pp. 465–466.

In summary, French foreign policy is at all times the function of the complex manifold of pressures which the preceding pages have attempted to analyze. These pressures operate one upon another and upon governmental decisions along lines marked out by the institutions, practices, and traditions of the past. Their efficacy, in any given case, depends upon the relative power wielded by those who exercise them with respect to other group pressures, with respect to the whole fabric of French political life, and with respect to the State System of which France is a part. Constitutional and legal principles and the structure of administration are but the skeleton framework of policy formulation. The flesh and blood are supplied by the pressure groups in French society which operate within and upon official governmental circles. These interrelationships, in the present state of social and political investigation, cannot be reduced to a mathematical equation nor to anything susceptible of precise measurement and evaluation for purposes of control and prediction. This is unfortunate, since verbal formulations are always clouded with associations and connotations having little relationship to the realities which they purport to describe. This is no less true of the polysyllabic laryngeal patterns of the political scientist, to which he tries (not too successfully) to give precise meanings than of the simpler and more moving symbols which sway the thought and action of the masses: "L'État," "la Patrie," la Paix," "la Guerre," "Sécurité," etc. The keywords of the present formulation have at any rate been used throughout the present volume with what are intended to be clear and consistent meanings and it is hoped that they not only describe the facts and situations of which they are symbols, but they make some contribution to an understanding of the dynamics of foreign policy and Great Power politics.

Without digressing into problems of terminology and of the mechanisms of thought, it is clear that the forces which are most effective in determining the course of French foreign policy are those generally described by the generic terms, Nationalism and Capitalism. Patriots thirst for national power and prestige—and almost all Frenchmen are patriots. Business men, merchants, bankers, and entrepreneurs hunger for profits—and these groups are more influential than all others in French political life. Profits and patriotism go hand in hand. "Liberté, Égalité, Fraternité"—these are the magic words of the Third French Republic, emblazoned over the doors of the Palais Bourbon and other public buildings in Paris. In domestic politics, this formula may have reality. Upon this point the present writer does not venture a judgment. But over the portals of the Quai d'Orsay no such symbols are to be found. Perhaps some day a realistic stonemason may carve there the words which best epitomize the motivations of French foreign policy: "Patriotism, Power, Profits." French statesmen and soldiers may then depict the new Trinity on their banners and say to their followers, as they lead them forth to the fields of diplomacy and war, *In hoc signo vinces.*

CHAPTER XV

REFLECTIONS ON VIOLENCE

1. GREAT POWER POLITICS

FROM the earliest origins of the Western State System, its history has been largely the story of the struggle for power between its sovereign units. The interpretation of domestic politics in terms of the will to power may be challenged by certain schools of political thought. But the interpretation of international politics in terms of power can be challenged by no one familiar with the elementals of the historic relations between States. Not only does every State strive for power, but the State *is* power—so obviously that it is recognized as such in common parlance everywhere. States are everywhere classified as "Great Powers," "Secondary Powers," and "Minor Powers." Those with extensive colonial possessions are "World Powers." Those with large maritime armaments are "Naval Powers" and those with numerous battalions are "Land Powers." Their efforts at cooperation is the "Concert of Powers." The equilibrium of forces which States establish in their dealings with one another is the "Balance of Power." So deeply rooted and widely recognized is the power concept in international affairs that it must be the starting point of any realistic consideration of Great Power politics. All the phases of that politics which have been dealt with in the foregoing pages are meaningless save as an expression of the will to power of the French nation in its relations with other sovereign political entities.[1]

So much being granted, it may be useful to conclude the present inquiry with a brief examination of the problems of war and peace, and of the essential nature of a State System in which war and peace are alternating intervals, in the light of the power concept as it appears in the diplomatic history and political practices of the Third French Republic. To the social philosopher power is but a means to an end. To the statesman it becomes an end in itself. To the former power implies control, direction, "government," capacity for manipulation, ability to impose a will upon other wills—for purposes which may be adjudged good, bad, or indifferent, but always for purposes beyond itself. To those who actually rule, power is often pursued as the hungry pursue food—not as a means to other goods, but as a good *per se*. There is involved in the divergence between these two

[1] W. Morton Fullerton aptly entitles his survey of pre-war diplomacy, *Problems of Power*, London, 1914.

viewpoints a profound philosophical and psychological problem of human motivations. Power as a goal of individual or group action may be viewed logically as an instrument through which those who wield it may acquire more tangible and immediate benefits. Conversely, such benefits may be regarded as having value to individuals or groups only in so far as they contribute to prestige, to distinction, to recognition, to self-satisfaction—in short, to a sense of power which puts its holder at peace with himself and the world. These two phases of the power complex are inseparable in diplomacy. In none of the episodes which have been analyzed in the present volume have the representatives of the French State striven for an empty power, devoid of present or future tangible advantages of some kind to influential persons or organizations. In none of them have they striven for such advantages when they had no bearing on the power relationships of the States of the European State System. But it is scarcely necessary either to dwell upon logical distinctions or to embark upon a philosophical debate regarding the whole problem of values. It is enough to emphasize once more that State action in the international arena has been, is, and perhaps must always be, directed toward an end which is viewed as a value in itself: the acquisition and enhancement of the power of the State in its relations with other States.

The incidents and the forms of this quest are numerous and various. Each State, if left to itself, strives to extend its power over all others—even to the extent of suppressing their independence and incorporating their territory into the national domain. So universal and constant has been this propensity in the behavior of the States comprising Western European civilization that it might almost be regarded as an inherent characteristic of all inter-State relations. State power, like volcanic lava, tends to flow out in all directions from a central nucleus, taking the course of least resistance, crushing all in its path which can be broken, and stopping in its progress only when distance has cooled its energies or when it meets with immovable obstacles. These obstacles are frequently other States, seeking to preserve their independence or to expand their own power. If a great State, in the extension of its power, is able, as was Rome in the later centuries of classical civilization, to deal piecemeal with its rivals and to dispose of each separately, it will end its course by the establishment of universal dominion. But no State since Rome has been able to achieve this consummation in Western Europe because of the tendency of all States which are threatened by a stronger rival to combine against the common menace. In the resulting balance of power each State preserves its independence by throwing its weight against the stronger of its potential enemies. In the Western State System, the balance-of-power principle has always operated with almost mechanical precision. Every Power which has aspired to universal dominion has been checkmated by coalitions against it which have been powerful and many-membered in proportion to the size and scope of the menace to the weaker States from the stronger. The House of Hapsburg under Charles V and France under Louis XIV and again under Napoleon I were successively frustrated in their efforts to impose their will on all Europe by a series of "defensive" or "preventive" wars waged against them by coalitions of the threatened States, with England always on the side of the weaker continental group. After 1870 France was displaced from its position as the most powerful of the continental States by Imperial Germany and became, in turn, the nucleus of a combination against the new potential menace. The balance of power recrystallized in the rival coalitions which clashed in 1914. In the sequel, Germany proved more powerful than anyone had anticipated, with the result (seemingly inevitable on the basis of the historical operations of the State System) that State after State joined the coalition against her, from Japan and her own "ally," Italy, to the colossus beyond the Atlantic and its Latin-American satellites, until twenty-three Powers were leagued together to crush one whose might seemed a menace to all.

The relations of the so-called Great Powers to the lesser Powers in this process is conditioned by the exigencies of the rivalries between the Great Powers themselves. Under ordinary circumstances small and weak States cannot aspire to hegemony, but can only hope to preserve their independence and existence against the encroachments of their stronger neighbors. Salvation is often found in the fact that no one of the Great Powers can afford to permit another to acquire territory or power at the expense of a third State, since these values are always relative and an accretion to one State means a diminution for others. Each of the Great Powers *vis-à-vis* its rivals thus has an interest in preserving the independence of small States. This interest is frequently expressed in multilateral neutralization conventions or in arrangements of mutual guarantee, which may, however, become mere scraps of paper in a desperate contest for power. It is only by playing off one Great Power against another, *i.e.*, by finding their logical place in the balance-of-power system, that the lesser States of Europe have saved themselves from political destruction. When a weak State is unable to do this it is in imminent danger of its life. The formerly independent States of Asia and Africa lost their statehood because particular Powers were left free by their European rivals to annex them or because they were partitioned as part of the bargains between the Great Powers. The latter process is strikingly exemplified on the European continent by the partition of Poland between Austria, Russia, and Prussia at the end of the eighteenth century in order to preserve a "balance of power" which would have been upset had any one of the three Powers secured Polish territory without compensation to the other two. In general small and weak States maintain their independence only when the mutual jealousies between the great States cannot be composed by bargains of this kind.

War has always been the decisive incident in the quest of States for power. Armed violence and coercion have ever been the ultimate arbiters between rival political communities. Throughout the entire history of the Western State System all fundamental readjustments of power relationships between its members have come about through the test of battle. This intimate relationship between diplomacy and war has been repeatedly pointed out by numerous observers and statesmen and has appeared in every phase of the foreign affairs of the French Republic. Whatever the subsidiary objects of foreign policy in any State may be, whatever specific purposes or rationalizations of purposes are given to foreign policy, its object is always the same: to enhance the relative power of the State with, respect to other States, to increase its prestige, which is reputation for power, to place it in a position where it will be able to impose its will on its rivals in future contests for power. War and diplomacy are the methods of achieving this object. Historically considered, they are not alternative methods but rather different aspects of the same political technique.[1] Diplomacy unsupported by armed force, *i.e.*, by an actual or prospective ability to apply effective coercive measures in a contest of wills, is impotent. War waged without concrete diplomatic objectives is unthinkable. War is the diplomacy of the sword, just as diplomacy is war of the pen. But here the pen cannot be mightier than the sword, for it *is* the sword, albeit sheathed and kept in the background.[2]

If war be viewed in the light here suggested, international conflict cannot helpfully be regarded as an act of God, nor as a result of the machinations of wicked statesmen, nor yet as a consequence of the vices and imperfections of human nature. These alternative views would seem to be based upon an inadequate comprehension of the situations out of which wars arise. To the civilian and the layman the incidentals of war necessarily loom largest and condition all thinking as to its cause and cure. These incidentals, comprising all the episodes of organized and wholesale slaughter and destruction, tend to obscure the basic fact that every war is a contest between States for power. With their eyes on the incidentals, the victims of international conflict and their sympathizers everywhere are often disposed to regard war as a mysterious and inscrutable visitation. Those who are fatalists treat it as an inevitable scourge of Divine Providence, which periodically and capriciously unleashes the Four Horsemen of the Apocalypse to ravage the earth. Such a conception obviously precludes the possibility of a science of society and renders all study of the causes of war pointless. If war, on the other hand, is viewed as a disaster visited upon peoples through the selfish

[1] "La politique étrangère suppose deux éléments qu'il est aussi impossible de séparer dans la pratique qui dans une étude théorique: la diplomatie, la guerre. Un peuple fait la diplomatie de sa force militaire, l'armée est l'encaisse sur laquelle s'appuient les opérations de la politique étrangère; la guerre, c'est la diplomatie qui se continue; jamais, d'ailleurs, la diplomatie n'est plus active que pendent la guerre, les deux doivent aller de pair." J. Barthélemy, *Démocratie et politique étrangère*, p. 4.

[2] For a lucid and suggestive statement of this thesis see R. G. Hawtrey, *Economic Aspects of Sovereignty*, London, 1930.

and dastardly machinations of their political leaders, the problem is brought no nearer to a solution, since any assumption of uncontrolled and undirected freedom of action on the part of statesmen and diplomats makes futile all scientific study of their behavior. The assumption, however, is widely at variance with the facts. The sterility of the seemingly endless controversy over "responsibility" for the initiation of the Great War reveals the uselessness of applying the moral criteria of individual action in an organized society to State action in an anarchic State System. "Guilt" and "innocence" are relatively meaningless values in international relations.[1] Still another school òf interpretation lays major emphasis upon the innate and acquired behavior patterns of *homo sapiens* which predispose him to conflict with his fellows. These commentators seek to explain war in psychological terms. Such efforts range all the way from crude insistence upon the "inevitable" consequences of a postulated instinct of pugnacity to discussions of the motivations to belligerent action[2] or of the effects upon international relations of psycho-pathological types of behavior.[3] The psychological approach may well make contributions of incalculable value to a better understanding of war and it is far from the present writer's intention to disparage the utility of this orientation. But it is likely that this method will be useful only in proportion as it is imployed as a means of analyzing the psychological foundations of the State and of the State System which breeds war. All explanations of war which fail to view the Western State System in its historical perspective and fail to consider the social-behavior patterns which it has developed and fostered must remain partial and inadequate.

[1] During and after the Great War, many people, including the framers of the Treaty of Versailles, insisted upon the "guilt" of Germany. Later "revisionists" have insisted upon the "guilt" of the Allies. Among American historical scholars who have dealt with the origins of the Great War, Harry Elmer Barnes is perhaps the outstanding writer among the revisionists who insists upon treating the problem in accordance with the dictates of the guilt-and-innocence dichotomy. (*Cf.* his *Genesis of the World War* and *World Politics in Modern Civilization*, and the writer's review of the latter in the *International Journal of Ethics*, XLI, pp. 369–371, April, 1931.) Barnes does not quite descend to the level of Frederick Bausman (*Let France Explain*) or to that of the equally puerile defenders of the thesis of sole German responsibility for 1914, but he insists upon viewing the relations of States in terms of the standards of private morality. This propensity, which is encountered also in the writings of Sidney B. Fay (*The Origins of the World War*) and, to a lesser degree, in those of Bernadotte E. Schmitt (*The Coming of the War, 1914*), constitutes a serious obstacle to scientific detachment and, in the writer's opinion, confuses rather than clarifies the essential nature of the problem.

[2] *Cf.* Bertrand Russell, *Why Men Fight*, London, 1917, and G. M. Stratton, *Social Psychology of International Conduct*, New York, 1929.

[3] *Cf.* Caroline E. Playne, *The Neuroses of the Nations*, London, 1925, and *The Pre-War Mind in Britain*, London, 1929. Both of these suggestive volumes advance the thesis that the war of 1914 was a consequence of the general prevalence within the European States of a neurotic state of mind resulting from inhibitions and repressions on normal outlets of psychic energy which finally burst forth and found release in mass butchery and destruction. A somewhat similar, though less definitely psychological viewpoint is presented in H. Fielding Hall, *The Nature of War and Its Causes*, London, 1917.

To return to the point of view to which the present inquiry has led, the State is an embodiment of power and, in its political relations with other States, power considerations are necessarily foremost and controlling. The political process within each State is a struggle for power between groups competing for public attention and for the control of the machinery of government in order that they may put into action the demands which are expressive of their divergent views and interests. The political process between States is even more obviously a struggle for power— and one which differs chiefly from the corresponding process in domestic politics in that it is more frequently characterized by efforts at violent coercion and is, in fact, based upon the assumption that power relations are always fixed ultimately by an actual or threatened recourse to armed force. War is primarily a political phenomenon, since it is always carried on in civilized societies by groups organized for political action, whether they be classes, parties, factions, geographical divisions within a State, or the Nation-states themselves. War is the most important function of the State in international relations, since almost all of the States in the Western State System have been created, advanced, retarded, or destroyed through war and have always devoted the major portion of their public revenue to war purposes. Some cultural anthropologists would go so far as to insist that the State emerged as an institution in all societies out of war situations.[1]

The series of technological and economic changes which are usually described by the phrase, "The Industrial Revolution," worked profound and revolutionary modifications in the social and political organization of the major States of Western civilization, but it did not modify the process of politics either within States or between States. War has therefore persisted into the machine age and just as machinery has enormously enhanced the power and productivity of peoples within States, it has likewise increased to an equal degree the power of States in their relations with one another. It has correspondingly increased the destructiveness of war as an exercise of that power. The effectiveness of any exercise of State power is dependent upon its intensity and mobility with reference to time and space. Industrial States can wield power in distant areas and can concentrate their power in a small space during a short time interval with enormously greater efficacy than could the pre-industrial European societies of the eighteenth, seventeenth, and earlier centuries. Industrial technology has annihilated distance and made possible the achievement of greater results in several weeks or months than could be achieved formerly in as many years.[2] This has enabled

[1] "The State . . . owes its origin to war . . . Agriculture, slavery, and territoriality are the primary factors underlying State formation, but the force which actually welded them together to produce the State was war." M. R. Davie, *The Evolution of War*, pp. 174–175, Yale University Press, New Haven, 1929.

[2] "Power is local. A country which has become powerful enough to overawe all its near neighbors, may yet be unable to impose its will upon a distant country, no more powerful than they, which is out of reach of a successful attack. The economic effort required to maintain a

the Great Powers of Europe, and their new rivals in North America and Eastern Asia, to become "World Powers." The colonial empires of the sixteenth and seventeenth centuries were relatively feeble and fragile structures, requiring generations for their consummation. The imperialisms of the twentieth century wield power undreamed of at the time of their earlier counterparts. The creation of the French colonial empire, and of those of the other Great Powers, during the thirty years between 1880 and 1910 would have been impossible in a non-industrial age. Wars, meanwhile, have become briefer, more intense, more destructive to life and property, and more disruptive to the social life of the communities which engage in them. While States once pursued power through puny professional standing armies, they now fight by mobilizing all the human and material resources at their command. They employ all the intricate and amazing mechanism of wholesale destruction which scientific ingenuity can devise. So appalling are the results in terms of social welfare, and so menacing has the science of war become to the whole fabric of civilization that peace, for the first time in human history, appears to many not merely a desirable condition, but an imperative necessity. And yet, tragically, while the technique of war has been revolutionized by industrialism and while the incidental effects of war have been transformed from pain and suffering endured by a small fraction of the population to overwhelming disaster to entire national communities, the whole State system which breeds war has undergone no corresponding transformation.

The problem which results from this circumstance can be dealt with constructively only if the causal factors which have given rise to it are clearly borne in mind. On the one hand, war remains what it has always been in the Western State System—an incident in the struggle for power, a means by which States seek to impose their wills forcibly upon one another. War is perhaps more efficacious than ever as an instrument of national policy, as it is utilized by the great industrial States in their contacts with States which are technologically more backward. On the other hand, war between the great States becomes a nightmare to all participants, an unparalleled disaster for victors and vanquished alike for the very reasons which have made it a more effective means to power in imperialistic expansion. The surviving victors in the Great War gained more in power and prestige than the victors in any previous struggle. But the cost was appalling—more so, even, to the Allies than to the Central Powers, since the combat was waged on the territory of the former by the forces of the latter with a ruthlessness, a *Schrecklichkeit*, an efficiency in dealing death and destruction

given force grows rapidly greater as the distance of the force from its base is increased. Or, in other words, the amount of force that can be maintained by a given amount of economic power grows rapidly less as the distance increases. The hegemony of the Great Power will be effective within the distance at which it can make its threat of force effective." Hawtrey, *op. cit.*, pp. 108–109.

which the Allied armies were never capable of attaining and which they were enabled to overcome at the end by the weight of overwhelming numbers and resources. The contest brought ruin, in various degrees, to each of the participants. The Great Power which took the lead in marching its troops forth to battle in 1914 in the name of its integrity was utterly destroyed as a political entity. Another was defeated so crushingly that its entire economic, political, and social organization collapsed into chaos in the most stupendous revolutionary upheaval of modern times. A third lost all of its colonies and much of its European territory and suffered the misery of starvation, bankruptcy, economic and fiscal collapse, and political revolution. Still another, one of the "victors," was so disorganized by the sequel that political democracy gave way to incipient civil war and dictatorship. The enormous cost of the war to France has been noted and Great Britain's difficulties need no description. Only the United States and Japan remained relatively unscathed. The total casualties exceeded the combined casualties of all previous European and American wars between 1500 and 1914. The destruction of property can scarcely be measured in monetary terms. At the time of writing thirteen years have passed since the armistice and the world is still reeling from the effects of the conflict.

In view of these fruits of war, the diplomat and statesmen, while he pursues power as of yore, can no longer formulate policies in the language of Machiavelli, Richelieu, or Frederick the Great. Any support of diplomatic action by military force which threatens a conflict between Great Powers must be resorted to with the utmost circumspection in order that it may be apparent to the war-weary public that the hostilities which may possibly ensue are due entirely to the aggression of the enemy. Even in 1914 the Quai d'Orsay, like other foreign offices, shrank from embarking boldly on armed action, not only because of consideration of its effects upon the British attitude, but also because of a realization that national unity in prosecuting the struggle would be assured only if the war appeared defensive. Even then the calculation of prospective costs and losses served as a deterrent—not to war, but to giving to war the appearance of an enterprise lightly embarked upon without due provocation. In the bruised and shattered post-war world the same calculation, buttressed by bitter experience, necessarily serves as an even stronger deterrent. No statesman in France dares to order military action in a diplomatic controversy under circumstances which would give the appearance of aggression, for he knows that his political future would be thereby jeopardized in view of the persistent cry for peace from all classes of citizens. "Punitive" expeditions against colonial rebels in Morocco, Syria, or Indo-China, or the military occupation of the territory of a disarmed and impotent enemy, do not, of course, fall within this category, since such actions, though they may lead to serious complications, contain at the outset no obvious threat of prolonged hostilities. In all other cases, "Peace" must be the slogan of the Quai d'Orsay.

It would be naïve to assume, however, that this lip service to peace, even if it be quite sincere and if faith be accompanied by works, involves any fundamental modifications of the politics of power in the Western State system. Peace must be professed in Paris and in most other capitals because the public sentiment of the generation which lived through the Great War and which has not yet had time to forget, demands it. This sentiment is one of the imponderables of diplomacy which no statesmen can afford to ignore. Gestures toward peace, guarantees of peace, agreements to preserve peace, security for peace are imperative in such a situation. Active participation in the League of Nations, the conclusion of agreements for the arbitration or adjudication of diplomatic controversies, the holding of successive disarmament conferences, the Locarno treaties, and the Kellogg-Briand Pact are all reflections of this necessity. In the case of France, however, the politics of peace is reinforced by the politics of power. France emerged from the war as the dominant Power of the continent, with the fruits of victory firmly grasped and the terms of a conqueror's peace buttressed by the reduction of Germany to military impotence, and by the support of France's erstwhile Allies and of her new allies in the East in maintaining the present frontiers and the present equilibrium of power. Any new war would almost necessarily involve an upset of a *status quo* which is regarded as highly advantageous by the power-and-prestige diplomats of the French Republic. All French statesmen, without exception, place the maintenance of that *status quo* above peace. They would, paradoxically, fight without hesitation to preserve peace—the Peace of Versailles. The France of Poincaré and Briand desires peace as Bismark desired peace after 1871—as an indispensable condition for the maintenance of a political hegemony won by war. "Satiated" States are never disturbers of the peace until their dominance is threatened. "Security" is the great goal of the foreign policy of such States. Here, as always, power considerations are controlling. The implications of this situation will be examined below. Meanwhile the cry for peace continues.

2. The Democratic Illusion

The literature of peace continues to be filled with discussions of the democratic control of foreign policy as the great panacea for war—less so in France, perhaps, than elsewhere, since Frenchmen are usually realists and logicians, but to an extent sufficient to justify some further consideration of this phase of the problem. The present writer has no desire to suggest panaceas of any kind, nor yet to pass judgment on the abstract desirability of subjecting foreign affairs to democratic supervision. The assumption that democracy in foreign policy is conducive to peace nevertheless deserves critical examination both because of its wide prevalence and because of its bearing upon the objects of the present investigation. The assumption, reduced to its simplest terms, is that the "people" of France, or of any State, are never desirous of war; that a popularly controlled foreign policy would therefore be pacific; that the administration of foreign policy is not, in fact, democratic, though almost all other governmental functions have been subjected to democratic control; that, because of this circumstance, diplomats, moved by considerations having nothing in common with the welfare of the masses, pursue bellivolent policies in an irresponsible fashion; and, finally, that peace would be assured if those who framed foreign policy were genuinely representative of the masses, in touch with public opinion, and accountable to the nation as a whole for their conduct.

The first question which this line of reasoning raises is the meaning of "democratic control." Democracy, literally construed, means the rule of the people. A democratic government is, presumably, one in which all citizens are legally and politically equal and in which political power is, in theory, transferred to the whole mass of the citizenry. But the people of a national community, as an unorganized and undifferentiated mass, do not exercise political power over either domestic or foreign affairs. Any assumption that this is possible on a national scale is based upon a misconception of the motivations of political action and of the nature of the political process. Popular sovereignty can be exercised only through political organizations, *i.e.*, through parties which compete for public office by appealing to the electorate with a variety of programs of action. That party or group of parties which wins the support of a numerical majority of the voters is granted an opportunity to exercise power through the acquiescence of the minority. In this process effective control is exercised by those who are organized to wield power—usually by those whose wealth and economic status enable them to obtain political power through all the means known to propaganda and pressure groups. Power is actually exercised not by the "people" but by those groups among the people who have the will to power and the means of instrumenting their will. The essence of democracy lies not in any revolution in the sources of political power nor in the political process, but in the opportunity for free discussion and free organization for political purposes, unaccompanied by coercion and dictation of one group to another. How this opportunity will be used, and what results it will lead to in terms of the groups which actually secure power, depends upon the whole economic and social structure of society, as suggested in the preceding chapter.

If democracy be thought of in these terms, it is difficult to perceive in France any fundamental difference in the structure of the democratic process as it relates to foreign affairs and to domestic affairs. There is, it is true, less interest in foreign affairs than in domestic, and without interest or a will to power, opportunities for its exercise are not utilized. It is likewise true that in domestic politics, democracy affords an opportunity to all affected by an issue to make themselves heard, while in foreign affairs the millions across the frontier, who are no less affected by foreign policy than those within the State, have little or no voice in policy determination. At the same time in both foreign and domestic affairs within the French State, equal opportunity exists under the law for free discussion and free organization for purposes of influencing the formulation and administration of policy. The permanent bureaucracy, to be sure, perhaps acts as a more effective brake upon the precipitate translation of changes of public opinion into action in the case of foreign policy than in the case of domestic policy, for reasons which have been noticed. But if politically organized groups are sufficiently determined to change foreign policy, and if they win the support of the electorate, they may put their views into action with relatively little difficulty. This has sometimes happened in France with shifts of political power from Right to Left or *vice versa*. If the resulting change in foreign policy has often appeared slight, the cause is not to be found primarily in any lack of opportunity to effect a change on the part of the new Government, but rather in the lack of a will to change, in the absence of an interest in change, in the inertia of tradition and precedents, in the tyranny of the past. In the Presidential form of democratic government, best exemplified by the United States, with its separation of powers and its check and balance arrangements, with its diffusion of responsibility and its incessant starts and stops, the stuctural forms of democracy may not provide an adequate opportunity to translate the popular will into action in foreign policy. The American President is responsible to the electorate, but he administers foreign affairs with the cooperation or obstruction of the Senate and of Congress as a whole. But in the French parliamentary system the lines of responsibility are clear: from the bureaucracy to the foreign minister; from the foreign minister to the Premier; from the Premier to the Cabinet; from the Cabinet to the Chambers; from the Chambers to the voters. If the voters are apathetic, if public opinion is uninterested in foreign affairs, if the party leaders are uninformed regarding diplomatic problems, if the Chambers exercise no effective surveillance over the administration of foreign policy, the fault is less with the theory of democracy or the structure of the governmental machine than with the voters themselves.[1] Any discussion of the democratic control of foreign affairs which ignores these considerations is bound to go astray amid false premises and false deductions.

Nevertheless, discussion continues in terms of the mechanics of the parliamentary system, and particularly in terms of the legislative controls over the Quai d'Orsay. Almost all commentators concede the impossibility of referring decisions in foreign affairs to the electorate directly. The plea, therefore, is that the Chambers, as direct representatives of the voters, should be in a position to exercise a more effective restraining and directing influence over the Ministry of Foreign Affairs. That they do not in fact exercise such

---

[1] "La raison d'être de la démocratie, c'est la liberté, la justice, l'égalité à l'intérieur. Aussi, passionée de réformes politiques et sociales, la démocratie a-t-elle une tendance a réliguer au second plan les questions de politique extérieure, elle abdique volontiers entre les mains de ses governants la direction de cette partie si importante de ses destinées." Barthélemy, *op. cit.*, p. 125.

an influence is obvious from the material presented in the preceding pages. It can be argued that changes in the provisions of the Constitution, changes in the organization of the Chambers for dealing with foreign policy, and changes in the relation between the Chambers and the ministry would enable the Deputies and Senators to exercise pressure more successfully. If all treaties required ratification by the Chambers, or by more than a majority of the Chambers, if all diplomatic appointments were subject to legislative confirmation, if every use of military force required specific legislative authorization, then, it may be contended, democratic control of foreign affairs would be achieved. But the contention again overlooks political realities. Power is never exercised where there is no will to exercise it. Where the will exists, it will be exercised if opportunity permits. In the French parliamentary system, the Chambers have ample opportunity to exercise effective power over the formulation of foreign policy. The Constitution can be amended by a simple process. The statutes relating to the organization of the Quai d'Orsay can readily be modified by a process which is even simpler. The organization and the rules of the two houses can be amended without difficulty if a majority of the members desire to do so. The Chambers are under no legal or political compulsion to tolerate secret diplomacy, the obscure machinations of war makers, or the pursuit of power politics in foreign affairs. If they do so it is by their own will, by their own recognition that the administration of foreign affairs is not, and cannot in the nature of things, be handled by a deliberative assembly. Such changes as those suggested have been made only to the extent dictated by the interest of the parliamentarians in foreign affairs. The cause lies not in mechanical and legal obstructions to action, but in a relative lack of interest in action. Without interest, there can be no desire. If the Senators and Deputies fail to subject the foreign affairs of the Republic to the same careful scrutiny and supervision which they exercise over domestic affairs, it is because they are content to leave foreign affairs to the Quai d'Orsay. This, again, is a problem of social and political psychology, not of governmental machinery. The opportunity exists for the achievement of democratic control if only sufficient interest can be created.

To return to the premises of the argument, the assumption that democratic control of foreign policy is necessarily conducive to peace is as questionable as the assumption that democratic control is non-existent. If democracy means opportunity for free debate and for the exercise of power by those with the interest, the will, and the organization to exercise it, the control of foreign affairs in France is as democratic as the control of internal policies. The further postulate that democracy results in the pursuit of policies which lead to peace is of questionable validity. Democracy merely means that pacifists and others who urge pacific foreign policies have an opportunity to make themselves heard. It does not insure that they will thereby gain political power or that their influence, if they possess any, will result in the adoption of pacific policies by the Government in office.[1] Foreign policy is never pursued in any State with war or peace as ultimate objectives. These conditions of international intercourse merely offer different types of opportunities for the attainment of other goals which are usually valued more highly than either war or peace. During peace, power is pursued through diplomacy, negotiation, discussion, compromise, and bargaining. During war, it is pursued by the application of force to compel the weaker party to yield to the will of the stronger. Wars do not ordinarily result from the conspiracies of statesmen to bring them about. Except in those rare instances when war is resorted to as a solution of domestic difficulties, it is usually an incident in the struggle between States for power. All discussion of democracy in foreign affairs is futile if it fails to deal with the problem in terms of the power-and-prestige objectives of State action in the international arena.

From this point of view the historical coincidence of Democracy and Nationalism is of great significance. Democracy, on a national scale, assumes a common consciousness of general interests on the part of all members of the national community. Without such a consensus of values democracy is an impossibility. So long as men regarded as paramount their interests as members of local areas, provinces, or organized classes or Estates, democracy was feasible only within such areas, provinces, or groups as furnished their members with values and points of reference for the free discussion of divergent views, without efforts at violent coercion. Nationalism emerged out of the fusion of such local and particularistic loyalties into a broader consciousness of common interests over wider areas, comprising all peoples speaking a similar tongue and acknowledging common allegiance to a single government. The process through which this common allegiance was established was scarcely a pacific one in France—nor in any other modern State. It involved violence and coercion at many points. The wars of national unification in Italy, Germany, and the United States are of recent memory. The intestine conflicts of the Capetian and Bourbon kings in France with the feudal nobility and the provinces were scarcely different. The Fronde was more than the triumph of royal absolutism over feudal anarchy. It marked the victory of French nationalism over particularism. National democracy was unthinkable without national patriotism. Without a general consensus of common interests among all sections and classes of the French National State, no common values existed with reference to which particular divergencies of interests and views could be discussed pacifically and adjusted peaceably on the basis of common acquiescence in the result. In this sense, nationalism was the prerequisite of democracy.

---

[1] "C'est une illusion assez semblable à celle qui a fait croire, à la suite de Spencer, à la vertu pacificatrice, par elle seule, de l'évolution industrielle ou du libre échange." G. Guy-Grand, *La démocratie et l'après guerre*, p. 257, Paris, 1922.

The implications of this relationship on democratic control of foreign policy are so palpable as to require no labored presentation. Nationalism is a set of emotions and behavior patterns resting upon a sense of common membership in, and allegiance to, a community occupying a definite territory, enjoying a large degree of linguistic homogeneity, and having social customs and institutions derived from a common cultural background. It is apparently the result of contacts and conflicts between communities which induce in each a common sense of identity and solidarity. Nationalism is bred of war and is a breeder of war, for it stamps upon each national community not merely a consciousness of distinctiveness and individuality but also such a feeling of hostility to the out-group, to the alien, to the rival national community across the border that common ground between the two is difficult to find and mutual understanding difficult to achieve. "Difficult" becomes "impossible" when each national State pursues power and looks at its own interests in exclusive terms. In the pursuit of power in the Western State System, the ambitions of oligarchies and dynasties have been replaced as motive forces by the aspirations of national patriots. Democracy in national communities is possible only to the degree that national patriotism has permeated all levels of the population. At the same time, the processes of democratic government, in which the representatives of local areas are sent to a capital in which the political life of the entire national community is centered, foster the inculcation in each local area of the sentiments and ideologies of the whole nation. Democratic control of foreign policy can mean only patriotic control. And patriotism, in the form in which it has manifested itself most frequently in France and in all modern States, is scarcely conducive to peace.[1]

3. The Problem of Peace

The causes of war are deeply rooted in the very nature of the Western State System and in the whole fabric of contemporary Western civilization. To forget this fact is to deal with the problem of peace through illusions and chimeras which can lead only to quack panaceas. To recognize it is not to despair of a solution nor to accept, fatalistically, the inevitability of war. It is rather to deal with the problem in terms of political realities which are at once simpler than those usually employed in the literature of peace and which at the same time take cognizance of the enormous difficulties in the way of the suppression of armed conflict between States. If war were a result of the plotting of diplomats, of the lack of democratic control of foreign policy, of the conspiracies of militarists, of the greed of capitalists, or of any other of the thousand and one causes so glibly and uncritically cited in popular treatments of war and peace, the problem would admit of a relatively simple solution. The present analysis of the formulation of French

[1] For a suggestive discussion of the relationship between domestic politics and the power interests of States see Oswald Spengler, *The Decline of the West*, II, pp. 447f.

foreign policy has led to the conviction that such explanations are widely at variance with the facts and are therefore worthless as starting points for constructive proposals. It is the writer's opinion that similar analyses of foreign policy in any of the other Great Powers would strengthen this conviction. There would seem to be no necessity for launching upon an extended discussion of the various aspects of the problem here nor for examining and criticizing in detail the various paths to peace which have been proposed. But it may prove useful to conclude the present investigation with a brief restatement of the inferences which have been drawn from the material presented. Such "conclusions" as may emerge must, of course, be regarded as purely tentative and provisional, pending further detailed studies of the type here suggested and further social and political investigation into hitherto neglected fields of inquiry. The ultimate test of any hypothesis is the logic of history. The coming years should reveal to the generation now alive the truth or falsity of any conclusions which contemporary students of war may formulate.

If war is to be regarded as an aspect of the struggle between States for power, and if the Western State System is to be viewed as one in which sovereign units inevitably strive with one another for power, then it is obviously futile to deal with war as a social evil demanding eradication in any terms other than those implicit in the concept of the politics of power. Those who ignore the premises of that conception of inter-State relations seek peace through a variety of expedients which have little or no bearing upon the nature of the political process between States out of which war comes.[1] The number of such expedients is legion: the "outlawry of (aggressive) war," which places faith in verbal commitments which have no relation to power interests and which assumes that a line can be drawn between "defensive" and "offensive" wars; "disarmament," which assumes that States can be induced to give up the means through which they have always pursued power and that violent coercion will cease to be a means of power if its instrumentalities can be limited or abolished; "arbitration and adjudication," which assume that disputes over power between States are always reducible to justiciable terms and that agreements on methods of settling diplomatic controversies exclude the possibility of the use of force to gain power; "taking the profits out of war," which confuses power with tangible advantages to special groups and which assumes that national communities fight for the profits of privileged minorities or for general interests which are measurable in pecuniary terms; "economic internationalism," which assumes that men as political animals are rational beings who will necessarily behave in accordance with their own economic interests. These panaceas and many others, all of which are not without utility within the limited sphere of their own perspectives, fail to reach the heart of the problem, which lies in relationships of power. For the same reason, discus-

[1] *Cf.* A. C. F. Beales, *The History of Peace*, The Dial Press, New York, 1931.

sions of the economic causes of war are for the most part misleading in so far as they assume that competing economic groups on opposite sides of national frontiers push their governments into war for their private ends. It would be more accurate to say that States utilize the economic interests of their nationals as weapons in the struggle for power. War is an incident of this struggle. Its goal is a political value which must be served, to be sure, through economic means, but which uses such means for a political end.[1] Similarly much discussion of the ethnological, cultural, demographic, or other specific causes of war is irrelevant—not because these aspects of human competition and conflict do not condition the situations out of which wars arise, but because they have relation to war only as they affect the struggle of States for power.

In the pursuit of power, peace is a negative condition of affairs in which it is possible for sovereign States to deal with one another through the established procedures of diplomacy in such fashion that conflicting interests may be adjusted by discussion and compromise. The art of diplomacy in modern States is the art of so handling these contacts that the State may derive the maximum advantages in power and prestige at a minimum cost. Its object is not to preserve peace, but to serve the interests of the State. These interests are habitually conceived of by diplomats and patriots as having a unique and paramount value which is beyond good and evil and which often transcends in importance the desirability of maintaining the conditions under which interests may be served without recourse to force. This conception of State interests would seem to be inherent in the idea of sovereignty and in the emotions and dogmas of nationalism which underly the political fragmentation of Western civilization. War occurs whenever statesmen envisage international controversies in terms which make it appear that national interests can be better served, or more swiftly served, by a recourse to violent coercion, or by forcible resistance to outside coercion, than by a continuation of the conditions of discussion and compromise prevailing during peace.

The problem, then, is one of discovering the circumstances under which power is pursued by organized political groups through non-violent means and the differences in circumstances which lead to a resort to violent coercion. The pursuit of power does not in itself require any recourse to force on the part of the pursuers. Within national communities organized political groups pursue power over long periods of time with no resulting disturbance of the peace. This pursuit is characterized by discussion, compromise, and acquiescence on the part of those who fail to achieve power to the will of

---

[1] "The distinction between political and economic causes of war is an unreal one. The political motives at work can only be expressed in terms of the economic. Every conflict is one of power, and power depends on resources," p. 120, R. G. Hawtrey's *Economic Aspects of Sovereignty*. Cf. his chapter on "Economic Causes of War," pp. 105–129, for an excellent discussion of this phase of the problem.

those who succeed. The process is pacific, less because of the ability of the State to coerce and restrain all who resort to forcible measures, than because of the general recognition of a common consensus of values on the part of all groups who strive for power. All the conflicting demands made by these groups, whatever divergencies of views and interests they may manifest, are made within a frame of reference furnished by the common consensus. So long as the specific objectives and methods of the pursuit of power remain confined within the limits of the values accepted as good by the entire community, the process of politics remains pacific and the occasional individuals who repudiate the established values are treated as criminals and subjected to the coercion of the State with the approval of the community. The laws of the State—if they are to be enforceable—must reflect the values held in common by the community as a whole. They are enforced against individual offenders through the process of adjudication. The established machinery of legislation and administration, on the other hand, furnishes opportunities for the constant readjustment of power relationships within the limits of the values held in common. Politics is the dynamics of law, while adjudication is its statics. So long as particular goods are conceived of and presented as aspects of the general good, so long as each group pursues power without challenging the postulates of the common values, so long as the institutions and procedures of government function effectively in readjusting competing claims for power by reference to the collective interests and power of the entire community, peace is preserved and no group finds it necessary or expedient to resort to forcible action.

But from time to time in every national community, however stable and orderly it may be, the pacific processes of politics break down in revolution. From a juristic point of view, a revolution is an effort to change power relations by illegal methods, *i.e.*, by methods which repudiate the procedures provided for in established law. From a political point of view, revolution arises whenever groups, in their striving for power, resort to forcible coercion of other groups instead of to discussion and acquiescence in its results. In such situations, the State is almost always an object of attack, since revolutionists represent groups out of power striving to wrest control of the machinery of government out of the hands of those who are in power. If the groups fighting for control are merely factions of the same stratum of society, contesting as to who shall represent the ruling classes, the revolution is "political." If, however, the contending groups represent conflicting social classes and the issue is one of a fundamental modification of economic status, the ensuing upheaval becomes a "social" revolution. A political revolution may be consummated without actual violence or coercion, but merely by the threat of it, if the groups in power are willing to surrender without a struggle or if the groups out of power are enabled to achieve it without the employment of naked force. The same may be said of social revolutions, except that pacific surrender or acquiescence is less probable in view of the fact that the conflicting interests involved are much larger and the threatened transfer of power is likely to be permanent and to have far-reaching effects. France, during the last century and a half, has had one great social revolution (1789 to 1815) which was successful in transferring political power from one social class to another, several abortive social revolutions in which the classes in power crushed the efforts of the classes out of power to displace them (1793, 1848, 1871), and many political revolutions involving a shift in power as between leaders or factions representing essentially the same classes (1794, 1799, 1815, 1830, 1848, 1852, 1870). A detailed analysis by the social psychologist of any of these situations would reveal the circumstances under which the pursuit of power within the national community assumes violent forms.

The causes of revolution have an important bearing upon the causes of war. Revolution is war within the State. War is revolution against the established international order. In both cases power is pursued by force. The tentative hypothesis may be advanced that revolutionary situations arise within national communities whenever groups striving for power envisage their interests in relation to other groups in terms which preclude discussion, compromise, acquiescence. This occurs when particular interests become paramount over general interests in the eyes of those pursuing them, when the common consensus of values breaks down in the face of divergencies and can no longer serve as a frame of reference for the resolution of tensions and conflicts. If all groups accept common criteria of what is politically desirable and if the groups out of power acquiesce in the will of those in power, on the assumption that while views and interests may diverge all are nevertheless acting for the common good, or on the alternative assumption, which leads to the same result, that those in power possess such overwhelming force that any violent effort to displace them would be futile, revolution is impossible. But if, conversely, powerful groups regard other powerful groups as constituting such a menace to their interests that these interests are given precedence over what has been the common interest, revolution is inevitable. In revolutionary situations, to be sure, each group claims to be acting in the common interest in order to win over doubters among the non-partisans. But the genuine community of interests, which serves as the basis upon which particular differences of interests can be lawfully and pacifically reconciled, has in fact disappeared for the time being. With its disappearance, the political process becomes one in which power is pursued by violence, with victory going to the groups which are strong enough to impose their will upon their rivals.

Now if the community in question is the community of nations, and if the groups striving for power are sovereign States themselves, the problem may be posed in exactly the same terms in the larger arena of Great Power politics. War is comparable to revolution in that it involves a cessation of discussion, compromise, and acquiescence in the pursuit of power and a resort to forcible coercion. The bargaining and the adjustments of diplomacy give way to the organized violence of armies and fleets, just as in revolution the pacific procedures of legislation and administration, which keep divergent interests in equilibrium, give way to rioting, street fighting, mob violence, and *coups d'état*. The common consensus or the community values give way to the exigencies of particular interests, and peace is restored only when a new equilibrium is established in accordance with the verdict of force.

The difference in the two situations lies primarily in the fact that the consensus of values in the international community is more tenuous and fleeting and the equilibrium of power is more delicate and unstable than is ever the case within a national community. Particular interests are therefore conceived of, almost always, in terms which place them above the general interest—so much so that patriotism and sovereignty almost preclude the possibility of the submission of disputes to any institution occupying the same relations to competing Powers in the international sphere as the national State occupies to competing power groups within its own jurisdiction. The result is international anarchy, *i.e.*, a situation in which each Power is free from any higher control and pursues its own interests, as its highest values, without reference to the general interests of all Powers. Each sovereign State may find it useful and expedient to observe international law and to accept the established institutions and procedures of international intercourse. But no State concedes the right of another, or of all others, to control its actions in the common interest, since no State places the common good above its own quest for power. All pursue power competitively in so open a fashion that even in peace the political process between them tends to achieve adjustment and equilibrium only through threats and displays of violence and through calculations of the probable results of appeals to force. The balance of power which ensues is easily upset, since power is relative and all States are at all times extremely sensitive to changes in power relationships. An accretion of power by one State involves a diminution of power enjoyed by others. "Compensations" and "guarantees" are demanded, alliances and coalitions are formed against a potential menace, and ultimately war is resorted to, to prevent the balance from being completely upset.[1]

If the problem of international peace is viewed in these terms, it is seen to be a problem of creating a situation in which each member of the community of nations will envisage its power interests not as exclusive and paramount values but as aspects of a consensus of values which may serve

[1] Hawtrey puts the matter thus: "When I say that the principal cause of war is war itself, I mean that the aim for which war is judged worth while is most often something which itself affects military power. Just as in military operations each side aims at getting anything which will give it a military advantage, so in diplomacy each side aims at getting anything which will enhance its power. Diplomacy is potential war. It is permeated by the struggle for power and, when potential breaks out into actual war, that is usually because irreconcilable claims have been made to some element of power, and neither side can claim such preponderance as to compel the other to give way by a mere threat," *op. cit.*, p. 107.

as a frame of reference for the pacific adjustment of particular divergencies. If France and other States have no conception of such a consensus, no disposition to discuss, compromise, and acquiesce where national interests are at stake, no willingness to integrate the particular formulations of their quest for power into a broader common good, then periodical resorts to violence in the pursuit of power would seem to be inevitable, all professions to the contrary notwithstanding. International institutions and procedures for the pacific settlement of disputes can have only such efficacy as their member States are willing to give them through the modification or renunciation of their special interests in favor of general interests. Without a consensus of common values which, in the eyes of the governments and peoples of the Great Powers, take precedence over special values and national interests, international institutions for the maintenance of peace can rest only on the potential force of those States which are dominant at a given moment of time. Such a foundation is one of quicksand, for in the history of the Western State System no Power or group of Powers has ever been able to impose its will permanently on another Power or group of Powers if the latter acquiesce only before *force majeure*. This aspect of power relationships is not likely to be different in the future. Permanent peace and security are possible, not through preparedness for war, not through the coercion of States by States, not even through pious aspirations, efforts to limit or reduce the size or destructiveness of the instrumentalities of warfare, or written engagements renouncing force as an instrument of national policy. These cures for war can be effective only in so far as they contribute to the subordination within each State of national interests to general interests, the development of a will to peace to supplement and restrain the will to power, and the creation of international institutions and procedures for the maintenance of peace which rest firmly on a general consensus of common values in all States and which, if need be, may restrain the breaker of the peace through the collective force of the international community, as the State itself restrains the criminal and the peace breaker through the collective force of the smaller community which it represents.

In view of the enormous difficulties in the way of achieving this goal, in view of the enormous inertia of history standing in its path, it is scarcely surprising that few statesmen have had the vision to analyze the situation in terms of its fundamentals and the courage to accept the implications of their analysis. Among recent political leaders, Wilson, Briand, MacDonald, and Stresemann have perhaps sensed most accurately the essence of the problem. But even these builders of peace have never stood for peace at any price. They have seldom placed peace above the national interests and power of their respective States, even in an age when the abolition of war seems imperative to save Western civilization from its own destruction. Peace has been desired in proportion as it serves national power, though in the creation of the League of Nations an institution has perhaps been established which may place peace above power by building a consensus of common values which will supersede special national interests. The statesmen of peace, no less than the statesmen of war, are hedged about by the forces which have elevated them to their positions. They are in no sense free agents. Their art is the art of the possible. And so long as the sentiment of nationalism persists in its present form, so long as the dogma of sovereignty remains unchanged, just so long must statesmen everywhere give precedence to national interests over general interests, just so long must States pursue power as the supreme good, just so long must international anarchy persist and international violence remain a normal incident in the pursuit of power by national sovereign States.

If the problem be brought down once more to the analysis of French foreign policy and of the forces controlling its course, it may be said that post-war France exhibits the paradox of a State armed to the teeth, linked by alliances to other military Powers, and almost convinced of the inevitability of war, and yet more anxious for permanent peace and more willing to go further in achieving it than most other States. The paradox can be resolved only in terms of the politics of power. France as the dominant Power on the continent in post-Versailles Europe has everything to lose and nothing to gain by war. Her people have not yet forgotten the agony of Verdun, the Aisne, Chemin des Dames, and the Marne. Power considerations are reinforced by a popular will to peace in pushing the Government into a policy of favoring all that seems to promise an end of war. At the same time promises afford little security in the present uneasy equilibrium of forces, little assurance that the patriots in Germany, Italy, Austria, and other States, who resent French hegemony and resist the French preponderance of power, may not push their Governments into policies menacing to the *status quo*. French patriots must insist upon the continuation of French hegemony through the retention of this *status quo* as the only means of assuring peace with power. Hence alliances and preparedness seem essential. But all, save the most fanatic nationalists, perceive that this reliance upon force assures peace only as the Dual Alliance assured peace—as an interlude between wars. Therefore these guarantees must be supplemented by international cooperation, conciliation, and organization. In the traditional formula, foreign policy must progress from Security through Arbitration to Disarmament. Briand's peculiar influence and prestige are due to the fact that while he is everywhere assailed by ultra-patriots for jeopardizing French national interests, he is recognized to be almost the only statesman who can steer a middle course between the exclusive pursuit of those interests, with war as the final outcome, and the subordination of those interests to general interests in the cause of peace. Here lies his strength. But he cannot place peace and the interests of the international community above the power and prestige of France, for he endangers his own domestic position to the degree to which he appears to do this. He cannot, as yet, permit the League of Nations or any other institution or procedure of international cooperation to be utilized as a pacific means of bringing about actual readjustments of power relationships through the revision of existing treaties or the modification of the existing equilibrium. For patriotism and the will to power among patriots forbid this. And yet it may well be that permanent peace can be attained only through what is thus forbidden. Herein lies his weakness. The eventual outcome, mercifully perhaps, is shrouded from view by the mists of the future.

It is this tragic choice which confronts all the members of the Western State System in the crucial transition period through which that System is now passing. National patriotism, the doctrine of sovereignty, the will to power, and the pursuit of political and economic profits through exclusive devotion to national interests dictate foreign policies committed to the old values followed in the old ways. Such policies can lead only to war and to incalculable disaster. War between Great Powers under modern conditions means financial bankruptcy, economic collapse, and social revolution. If it recurs on a grand scale, the final consequence may well be general ruin—and out of ruin the triumph of communism, *i.e.*, of the will to power of the Fourth Estate striving to demolish nationalism, capitalism, and the whole Western State System at a blow. Security and peace demand a subordination of national interests to general interests and the building of new attitudes and institutions which will transform international anarchy into international government and permit national States to pursue power through discussion and compromise on the basis of a common consensus of higher and more permanent values transcending lesser and more immediate goods. The latter course involves a revolutionary modification of national attitudes, habits, and traditions, and a radical transformation of the whole State System. Such a transformation, if it is at all possible, is perhaps the work of decades or generations, and catastrophe may intervene before it is completed. Pessimistic pacifists as well as belligerent patriots may regard it as impossible of achievement. And yet, the strides which have been taken toward the goal since the creation of the League of Nations have been long and steady—so much so as to render plausible the hopes of those who insist that international education and international organization can achieve peace even in a civilization as disorderly, anarchic, and resistant to new values as that which now stands at the crossroads. Another decade should reveal whether the new or the old is to triumph.

THE CONSTITUTION OF THE THIRD FRENCH REPUBLIC

(F. R. and P. Darest, *Les Constitutions Modernes*, Recueil Sirey, Paris, 1928.)

Loi Constitutionnelle du 24 Février 1875, Relative à l'organisation du Sénat

Arts. 1er à 7. (Composition du Sénat. Abrogés et remplacés par la loi du 9 décembre 1884.)

8. Le Sénat a, concurremment avec la Chambre des députés, l'iniative et la confection des lois. Toutefois les lois de finances doivent être, en premier lieu, présentées à la Chambre des députés et votées par elle.

9. Le Sénat peut être constitué en Cour de justice pour juger, soit le président de la République, soit les ministres, et pour connaître des attentats commis contre la sûreté de l'État.

10. Il sera procédé à l'élection du Sénat un mois avant l'époque fixée par l'Assemblée nationale pour sa séparation.

Le Sénat entrera en fonctions et se constituera le jour même où l'Assemblée nationale se séparera.

11. La présente loi ne pourra être promulguée qu'après le vote définitif de la loi sur les pouvoirs publics.

Loi Constitutionnelle du 25 Février 1875, Relative à l'organisation des Pouvoirs Publics

Art. 1er. Le pouvoir législatif s'exerce par deux assemblées: la Chambre des députés et le Sénat.—La Chambre des députés est nommée par le suffrage universel, dans les conditions déterminées par la loi électorale.—La composition, le mode de nomination et les attributions du Sénat seront réglés par une loi spéciale.

2. Le président de la République est élu à la majorité absolue des suffrages par le Sénat et par la Chambre des députés réunis en Assemblée nationale.—Il est nommé pour sept ans. Il est rééligible.

3. Le président de la République a l'initiative des lois, concurremment avec les membres des deux Chambres. Il promulgue les lois lorsqu'elles ont été votées par les duex Chambres; il en surveille et en assure l'exécution.—Il a le droit de faire grâce; les amnisties ne peuvent être accordées que par une loi.—Il dispose de la force armée.—Il nomme à tous les emplois civils et militaires.—Il préside aux solennités nationales; les envoyés et les ambassadeurs des puissances étrangères sont accrédités auprès de lui.—Chacun des actes du président de la République doit être contresigné par un ministre.

4. Au fur et à mesure des vacances qui se produiront à partir de la promulgation de la présente loi, le président de la République nomme, en conseil des ministres, les conseillers d'État en service ordinaire.—Les conseillers d'État ainsi nommés ne pourront être révoqués que par décret rendu en conseil des ministres . . .

5. Le président de la République peut, sur l'avis conforme du Sénat, dissoudre la Chambre des députés avant l'expiration de son mandat.—En ce cas, les collèges électoraux sont réunis pour de nouvelles élections dans le delai de deux mois et la Chambres dans les dix jours qui suivront la clôture des opérations électorales.

6. Les ministres sont solidairement responsables devant les Chambres de la politique générale du gouvernement, et individuellement de leurs actes personnels.—Le président de la République n'est responsable que dans le cas de haute trahison.

7. En cas de vacance par décès ou pour toute autre cause, les deux Chambres réunies procèdent immédiatement à l'élection d'un nouveau président.—Dans l'intervalle, le Conseil des ministres est investi du pouvoir exécutif.

8. Les Chambres auront le droit, par délibérations séparées, prises dans chacune à la majorité absolue des voix, soit spontanément, soit sur la demande du président de la République, de déclarer qu'il y a lieu de réviser les lois constitutionelles.—Après que chacune des deux Chambres aura pris cette résolution, elles se réuniront en Assemblée nationale pour procéder à la révision.— Les délibérations portant révision des lois constitutionelles, en tout ou en partie, devront être prises à la majorité absolue des membres composant l'Assemblée nationale.

(La forme républicaine du gouvernement ne peut faire l'objet d'une proposition de révision. —Les membres des familles ayant régné sur la France sont inéligibiles à la présidence de la République.) (L. 14 août 1884, art. 2)

Loi Constitutionnelle du 16 Juillet 1875, sur les Rapports des Pouvoirs Publics

Art. 1er. Le Sénat et la Chambre des députés se réunissent chaque année le second mardi de janvier, à moins d'une convocation antérieure faite par le président de la République.—Les deux Chambres doivent être réunies en session cinq mois au moins chaque année. La session de l'une commence et finit en même temps que celle de l'autre . . .

2. Le président de la République prononce la clôture de la session. Il a le droit de convoquer extraordinairement les Chambres. Il devra les convoquer si la demande en est faite, dans l'intervalle des sessions, par la majorité absolue des membres composant chaque Chambre.—Le président peut ajourner les Chambres. Toutefois l'ajournement ne peut excéder le terme d'un mois, ni avoir lieu plus de deux fois dans la même session.

3. Un mois au moins avant le terme légal des pouvoirs du président de la République, les Chambres devront être réunies en Assemblée nationale pour procéder à l'élection du nouveau président.—À defaut de convocation, cette réunion aura lieu de plein droit le quinzième jour avant l'expiration de ces pouvoirs.—En cas de décès ou de démission du président de la République, les deux Chambres se réunissent immédiatement et de plein droit.—Dans le cas, ou, par application de l'article 5 de la loi de 25 février 1875, la Chambre des députés se trouverait dissoute au moment où la présidence de la République deviendrait vacante, les collèges électoraux seraient aussitôt convoqués, et le Sénat se réunirait de plein droit.

4. Toute assemblée de l'une des deux Chambres qui serait tenue hors du temps de la session commune est illicite et nulle de plein droit sauf le cas prévu par l'article précédent et celui où le Sénat est réuni comme cour de justice; et, dans ce dernier cas, il ne peut exercer que des fonctions judiciaires.

5. Les séances du Sénat et celles de la Chambre des députés sont publiques.—Néanmoins chaque Chambre peut se former en comité secret, sur la demande d'un certain nombre de ses membres fixés par le règlement.—Elle décide ensuite, à la majorité absolue si la séance doit être reprise en public sur le même sujet.

6. Le président de la République communique avec les Chambres par des messages qui sont lus à la tribune par un ministre.—Les ministres ont leur entrée dans les deux Chambres et doivent être entendus quand ils le demandent. Ils peuvent se faire assister par des commissaires désignés, pour la discussion d'un projet de loi déterminé, par décret du président de la République.

7. Le président de la République promulgue les lois dans le mois qui suit la transmission au gouvernement de la loi définitement adoptée. Il doit promulguer dans les trois jours les lois dont la promulgation, par un vote exprès dans l'une et l'autre Chambre, aura été déclarée urgente.— Dans le délai fixé pour la promulgation, le président de la République peut, par un message motivé, demander aux deux Chambres une nouvelle délibération qui ne peut être refusée.

8. Le président de la République négocie et ratifie les traités. Il en donne connaissance aux Chambres aussitôt que l'intérêt et la sûreté de l'État le permettent.—Les traités de paix, de commerce, les traités qui engagent les finances de l'État, ceux qui sont relatifs à l'état des personnes et au droit de propriété des Français à l'étranger, ne sont définitifs qu'après avoir été votés par les deux Chambres. Nulle cession, nul échange, nulle adjonction de territoire ne peut avoir lieu qu'en vertu d'une loi.

9. Le président de la République ne peut déclarer la guerre sans l'assentiment préalable des deux Chambres.

10. Chacune des deux Chambres est juge de l'éligibilité de ses membres et de la régularité de leur élection; elle peut seule recevoir leur démission.

11. Le bureau de chacune des deux Chambres est élu chaque année pour la durée de la session et pour toute session extraordinaire qui aurait lieu avant la session ordinaire de l'année suivante.—Lorsque les deux Chambres se réunissent en Assemblée nationale, leur bureau se compose des président, vice-présidents et secretaires du Sénat.

12. Le président de la République ne peut être mis en accusation que par la Chambres des députés et ne peut être jugé que par le Sénat.—Les ministres peuvent être mis en accusation par la Chambre des députés pour crimes commis dans l'exercice de leurs fonctions. En ce cas, ils sont jugés par le Sénat. Le Sénat peut être constitué en cour de justice par un décret du président de la République, rendu en Conseil des ministres, pour juger toute personne prévenue d'attentat commis contre la sûreté de l'État.—Si l'instruction est commencée par la justice ordinaire, le décret de convocation du Sénat peut être rendu jusqu'à l'arrêt de renvoi.—Une loi déterminera le mode de procéder pour l'accusation, l'instruction et le jugement.

13. Aucun membre de l'une ou de l'autre Chambre ne peut, pendant la durée de la session, être poursuivi ou recherché à l'occasion des opinions ou votes émis par lui dans l'exercice de ses fonctions.

14. Aucun membre de l'une ou de l'autre Chambre ne peut, pendant la durée dela session, être poursuivi ou arrêté en matière criminelle ou correctionnelle qu'avec l'autorisation de la Chambres dont il fait partie, sauf le cas de flagrant délit.—La détention ou la poursuite d'un membre de l'une ou de l'autre Chambre est suspendue pendant la session, et pour toute sa durée, si la Chambre le requiert.

Loi du 22 *juillet* 1879, relative au siège du pouvoir exécutif et des Chambres. (Transfers seat of executive power and of two chambers to Paris, except when meeting as National Assembly. Also deals with regulation of the chambers. Nine articles.)

Loi du 9 *décembre* 1884, portant modification aux lois organiques sur l'organisation du Sénat et l'élection des sénateurs. (340 members elected triennielly for nine years. Seven articles.)

FOREIGN MINISTERS, PREMIERS, AND PRESIDENTS 1871 to 1931

N.B. The following chronology is intended to indicate only the dates of actual changes of personnel in the three executive offices indicated. It is not, therefore, a list of Cabinets, since new Cabinets are often appointed with the same individual holding the Premiership. The entire Cabinet resigns, moreover, and is usually reappointed *in toto* at each Presidential election. The total number of Cabinets is thus considerably larger than the total number of Premiers. Between September, 1870, and June, 1931, there have been eighty-nine distinct Cabinets, but only sixty-eight successive Premiers.[1]

Minister of Foreign Affairs	*Premier*	*President*
Jules Favre (September 4, 1870–August 2, 1871)	Léon Gambetta (September 4, 1870–February 19, 1871)	Adolphe Thiers (August 31, 1871–May 24, 1873)
Charles de Rémusat (August 2, 1871–May 25, 1873)	Jules Dufaure (February 19, 1871–May 25, 1873)	Marie MacMahon (May 24, 1873–January 30, 1879)
Albert de Broglie (May 25, 1873–November 26, 1873)	Albert de Broglie (May 25, 1873–May 22, 1874)	
Louis Décazes (November 26, 1873–November 23, 1877)	General de Cissey (May 22, 1874–March 10, 1875)	
	Louis Buffet (March 10, 1875–March 9, 1876)	
	Jules Dufaure (March 9, 1876–December 12, 1876)	
	Jules Simon (December 12, 1876–May 17, 1877)	
	Albert de Broglie (May 17, 1877–November 23, 1877)	
Marquis de Banneville (November 23, 1877–December 13, 1877)	General de Grimaudet de Rochebouèt (November 23, 1877–December 13, 1877)	
W. H. Waddington (December 13, 1877–December 28, 1879)	Jules Dufaure (December 13, 1877–February 4, 1879)	Jules Grévy (January 30, 1879–December 3, 1887)

[1] On the problems of computing the number of Cabinets *cf.* Lindsay Rogers, "Ministerial Instability in France," *Political Science Quarterly*, XLVI, pp. 1–24, March, 1931.

Minister of Foreign Affairs	*Premier*	*President*
	W. H. Waddington (February 4, 1879–December 28, 1879)	
Charles de Freycinet (December 28, 1879–September 23, 1880)	Charles de Freycinet (December 28, 1879–September 23, 1880)	
J. Barthélemy-Saint-Hilaire (September 23, 1880–November 14, 1881)	Jules Ferry (September 23, 1880–November 14, 1881)	
Léon Gambetta (November 14, 1881–January 30, 1882)	Léon Gambetta (November 14, 1881–January 30, 1882)	
Charles de Freycinet (January 30, 1882–August 7, 1882)	Charles de Freycinet (January 30, 1882–August 7, 1882)	
Eugène Duclerc (August 7, 1882–January 29, 1883)	Eugène Duclerc (August 7, 1882–January 29, 1883)	
A. Fallières (January 29, 1883–February 21, 1883)	A. Fallières (January 29, 1883–February 21, 1883)	
P. A. Challemel-Lacour (February 21, 1883–November 20, 1883)	Jules Ferry (February 21, 1883–April 6, 1885)	
ules Ferry (November 20, 1883–April 6, 1885)		
Charles de Freycinet (April 6, 1885–December 11, 1886)	Henri Brisson (April 6, 1885–January 7, 1886)	
	Charles de Freycinet (January 7, 1886–December 11, 1886)	
E. Flourens (December 11, 1886–April 3, 1888)	René Goblet (December 11, 1886–May 30, 1887)	
	Maurice Rouvier (May 30, 1887–December 12, 1887)	Marie Sadi-Carnot (December 3, 1887–June 25, 1894)
	Pierre Tirard (December 12, 1887–April 3, 1888)	
René Goblet (April 3, 1888–February 22, 1889)	Charles Floquet (April 3, 1888–February 22, 1889)	
E. Spuller (February 22, 1889–March 17, 1890)	Pierre Tirard (February 22, 1889–March 17, 1890)	
Alexandre Ribot (March 17, 1890–January 11, 1893)	Charles de Freycinet (March 17, 1890–February 27, 1892)	

Minister of Foreign Affairs	Premier	President
	Émile Loubet (February 27, 1892–December 6, 1892)	
Jules Develle (January 11, 1893–December 3, 1893)	Alexandre Ribot (December 6, 1892–April 4, 1893)	
	Charles Dupuy (April 4, 1893–December 3, 1893)	
Jean Casimir-Périer (December 3, 1893–May 30, 1894)	Jean Casimir-Périer (December 3, 1893–May 30, 1894)	
Gabriel Hanotaux (May 30, 1894–November 1, 1895)	Charles Dupuy (May 30, 1894–January 26, 1895)	Jean Casimir-Périer (June 27, 1894–January 17, 1895)
	Alexandre Ribot (January 26, 1895–November 1, 1895)	Félix Faure (January 17, 1895–February 18, 1899)
Pierre Berthelot (November 1, 1895–March 28, 1896)	Léon Bourgeois (November 1, 1895–April 29, 1896)	
Léon Bourgeois (March 28, 1896–April 29, 1896)		
Gabriel Hanotaux (April 29, 1896–June 28, 1898)	Jules Méline (April 29, 1896–June 28, 1898)	
Théophile Delcassé (June 28, 1898–June 17, 1905)	Henri Brisson (June 28, 1898–November 1, 1898)	
	Charles Dupuy (November 1, 1898–June 22, 1899)	Émile Loubet (February 18, 1899–February 18, 1906)
	Pierre Waldeck-Rousseau (June 22, 1899–June 7, 1902)	
	Émile Combes (June 7, 1902–January 23, 1905)	
Maurice Rouvier (June 17, 1905–March 14, 1906)	Maurice Rouvier (January 23, 1905–March 14, 1906)	A. Fallières (February 18, 1906–February 17, 1913)
Léon Bourgeois (March 14, 1906–October 25, 1906)	Jean Sarrien (March 14, 1906–October 25, 1906)	
Stephen Pichon (October 25, 1906–March 2, 1911)	Georges Clemenceau (October 25, 1906–July 24, 1909)	
	Aristide Briand (July 24, 1909–March 2, 1911)	

Minister of Foreign Affairs	Premier	President
J. Cruppi (March 2, 1911–June 27, 1911)	Ernest Monis (March 2, 1911–June 27, 1911)	
Jì de Selves (June 27, 1911–January 14, 1912)	Joseph Caillaux (June 27, 1911–January 14, 1912)	
Raymond Poincaré (January 14, 1912–January 18, 1913)	Raymond Poincaré (January 14, 1912–January 18, 1913)	
Charles Jonnart (January 18, 1913–March 22, 1913)	Aristide Briand (January 18, 1913–March 22, 1913)	Raymond Poincaré (February 17, 1913–February 18, 1920)
Stephen Pichon (March 22, 1913–December 10, 1913)	Louis Barthou (March 22, 1913–December 10, 1913)	
Gaston Doumergue (December 10, 1913–June 9, 1914)	Gaston Doumergue (December 10, 1913–June 9, 1914)	
Léon Bourgeois (June 9, 1914–June 13, 1914)	Alexandre Ribot (June 9, 1914–June 13, 1914)	
René Viviani (June 13, 1914–August 3, 1914)	René Viviani (June 13, 1914–October 29, 1915)	
Gaston Doumergue (August 3, 1914–August 26, 1914)		
Théophile Delcassé (August 26, 1914–October 29, 1915)		
Aristide Briand (October 29, 1915–November 16, 1917)	Aristide Briand (October 29, 1915–November 16, 1917)	
Stephen Pichon (November 16, 1917–January 20, 1920)	Georges Clemenceau (November 16, 1917–January 20, 1920)	
Alexandre Millerand (January 20, 1920–September 24, 1920)	Alexandre Millerand (January 20, 1920–September 24, 1920)	Paul Deschanel (February 18, 1920–September 24, 1920)
Georges Leygues (September 24, 1920–January 16, 1921)	Georges Leygues (September 24, 1920–January 16, 1921)	Alexandre Millerand (September 24, 1920–June 14, 1924)
Aristide Briand (January 16, 1921–January 15, 1922)	Aristide Briand (January 16, 1921–January 15, 1922)	
Raymond Poincaré (January 15, 1922–June 9, 1924)	Raymond Poincaré (January 15, 1922–June 9, 1924)	
L. du Prey (June 9, 1924–June 14, 1924)	Frédéric François-Marsal (June 9, 1924–June 14, 1924)	
Edouard Herriot (June 15, 1924–April 17, 1925)	Edouard Herriot (June 14, 1924–April 17, 1925)	Gaston Doumergue (June 14, 1924–June 13, 1931)

Minister of Foreign Affairs	*Premier*	*President*
Aristide Briand (April 17, 1925–July 21, 1926)	Paul Painlevé (April 17, 1925–November 28, 1925)	
	Aristide Briand (November 28, 1925–July 21, 1926)	
Edouard Herriot (July 21, 1926–July 22, 1926)	Edouard Herriot (July 21, 1926–July 22, 1926)	
Aristide Briand (July 23, 1926– ———	Raymond Poincaré (July 23, 1926–July 30, 1929)	
	Aristide Briand (July 30, 1929–November 2, 1929)	
	André Tardieu (November 2, 1929–February 21, 1930)	
	Camille Chautemps (February 21, 1930–March 3, 1930)	
	André Tardieu (March 3, 1930–December 13, 1930)	
	Théodore Steeg (December 13, 1930–January 27, 1931)	
	Pierre Laval (January 27, 1931– ———	Paul Doumer (June 13, 1931– ———

BIBLIOGRAPHY

N.B. The following list includes only the principal works consulted in the preparation of the present study. All periodical articles, as well as books referred to only incidentally, are cited in full in the footnotes to the text.

A. Official Publications

Chambre des Députés (*or* Sénat) de la République Française,

Débats parlementaires in *Journal official de la République Française, Chambre* or *Sénat*, Imprimerie du Journal Officiel, Paris (annual).

État des travaux législatifs de la Chambre des Députés (one volume for each session), Imprimerie de la Chambre des Députés, Paris.

Rapports fait au nom de la Commission des Finances chargée d'examiner le projet de loi portant fixation du Budget Général de l'Exercise 18— or 19— (Ministère des Affaires Étrangères), Imprimerie de la Chambre des Députés *or* du Sénat, Paris.

Rapports fait au nom de la Commission des Affaires Étrangères . . . in *Impressions projets de loi, propositions, rapports,* etc., Imprimerie de la Chambre des Députés *or* du Sénat, Paris.

Commission de Publication des Documents Relatifs aux Origines de la Guerre de 1914, *Documents diplomatiques français, 1871–1914,* Imprimerie Nationale, Paris, 1929–.

Ministère des Affaires Étrangères,

Documents diplomatiques, affaires de Tunisie, 1870–1881, Imprimerie Nationale, Paris, 1881.

Documents diplomatiques, affaires de Tunisie, supplement, avril–mai, 1881, Imprimerie Nationale, Paris, 1881.

Documents diplomatiques, affaires de Tonkin—Convention de Tien-Tsin du 11 mai 1884; Incident de Long-Son, Imprimerie Nationale, Paris, 1884.

Documents diplomatiques, affaires de Chine et du Tonkin, 1884–1885, Imprimerie Nationale, Paris, 1885.

Documents diplomatiques, affaires de Siam, 1893–1902, Imprimerie Nationale, Paris, 1902.

Documents diplomatiques, affaires du Haut-Mekong, Imprimerie Nationale, Paris, 1893.

Documents diplomatiques, affaires du Siam et du Haut-Mekong, Imprimerie Nationale, Paris, 1896.

Documents diplomatiques, affaires de Madagascar, 1881–1883, Imprimerie Nationale, Paris, 1883.

Documents diplomatiques, affaires de Madagascar, 1882–1883, Imprimerie Nationale, Paris, 1884.

Documents diplomatiques, affaires de Madagascar, 1884–1886, Imprimerie Nationale, Paris, 1886.

Documents diplomatiques, affaires de Madagascar, 1885–1895, Imprimerie Nationale, Paris, 1895.

Documents diplomatiques, affaires de Madagascar, Imprimerie Nationale, Paris, 1896.

Documents diplomatiques, affaires de Maroc, 1901–1905, Imprimerie Nationale, Paris, 1905.

Documents diplomatiques, La Guerre Européenne, 1914, Imprimerie Nationale, Paris, 1914 (French Yellow Book of 1914).

Documents diplomatiques, L'Alliance Franco-Russe, Imprimerie Nationale, Paris, 1918.

Documents diplomatiques, demande de moratorium du Gouvernment Allemand à la Commission des Réparations (14 novembre 1922); Conférence de Londres (9–11 décembre 1922); Conférence de Paris (2–4 janvier 1923), Imprimerie Nationale, Paris, 1923.

Documents diplomatiques, documents relatifs aux notes allemandes des 2 mai et 5 juin sur les réparations, Imprimerie Nationale, Paris, 1923.

Diplomatic Correspondence, Reply of the French Government to the Note of the British Government of August 11, 1923, relating to Reparations (August 20, 1923), Imprimerie Nationale, Paris, 1923.

Documents diplomatiques, documents relatifs aux négociations concernant les garanties de sécurité

contre une agression de l'Allemagne (10 janvier 1919-7 décembre 1923), Imprimerie Nationale, Paris, 1924.

Ministère de la Guerre, État-Major de L'Armée, Service Historique, *Les armées françaises dans la Grande Guerre*, Imprimerie Nationale, Paris, 1923.

B. Unofficial Publications

ALBIN, PIERRE: *L'Allemagne et la France en Europe*, Felix Alcan, Paris, 1913.

ALLEN, GENERAL HENRY T.: *The Rhineland Occupation*, Bobbs-Merrill Company, Indianapolis, Ind., 1927.

ANDERSON, EUGENE N.: *The First Moroccan Crisis, 1904–1906*, The University of Chicago Press, Chicago, Ill., 1930.

ANGAS, LAWRENCE L. B.: *Reparations, Trade, and Foreign Exchange*, P. S. King and Son, London, 1922.

AUGIER, CHARLES: *La France et les traités de commerce*, Chavalier et Rivière, Paris, 1906.

AUGIER, CHARLES, et MARVAUD ANGEL.: *La politique douanière de la France*, Felix Alcan, Paris, 1911.

AULNEAU, J.: *Le Rhin et la France, histoire politique et économique*, Plon-Nourrit, Paris, 1921.

BARCLAY, SIR THOMAS: *Thirty Years (Anglo-French Reminiscences, 1876–1906)*, Constable and Co., London, 1914.

BARDOUX, JACQUES: *De Paris à Spa, La bataille diplomatique pour la paix française*, Alcan, Paris, 1921; *Lloyd George et la France*, Alcan, Paris, 1923.

BARISIEN, PIERRE: *Le parlement et les traités*, A. Rousseau, Paris, 1913.

BARRÈS, MAURICE: *La politique rhénane*, Bloud et Gay, Paris, 1922.

BARTHÉLEMY, JOSEPH: *Démocratie et politique étrangère*, Felix Alcan, Paris, 1917; *Le gouvernement de la France*, Payot, Paris, 1919.

BARUCH, BERNARD M.: *The Making of the Reparation and Economic Sections of the Treaty*, Harper & Brothers, New York, 1920.

BERGMANN, CARL: *The History of Reparations*, Ernest Benn, London, 1927.

BERTHÉLEMY, HENRI: *Traité élementaire de droit administratif*, A. Rousseau, Paris, 1905.

BOUINAIS, A., et PAULUS, A.: *La France en Indo-Chine*, Challamel Ainé, Paris, 1886; *L'Indo-Chine française contemporaine*, 2 vols, Challamel Ainé, Paris, 1885.

BOURGEOIS, ÉMILE: *History of Modern France, 1815–1913*, The University Press, Cambridge, 1919.

BOURGEOIS, É., et G. PAGÈS: *Les origines et les responsibilités de la Grande Guerre, preuves et aveux*, Hachette, Paris, 1921.

BROADLEY, A. M.: *Tunis, Past and Present (The Last Punic War)*, 2 vols., Blackwood and Sons, Edinburgh and London, 1882.

BRUNET, L.: *La France à Madagascar (1815–1895)*, Hachette, Paris, 1895; *l'Oeuvre de la France à Madagascar*, Challamel, Paris, 1913.

BUELL, RAYMOND L.: *Contemporary French Politics*, D. Appleton & Company, New York, 1920.

CAILLAUX, JOSEPH: *Agadir—Ma politique extérieure*, Albin Michel, Paris, 1919.

CARRÈRE, J., G. BOURGIN, et A. GUÉRIN: *Manuel des partis politiques en France*, F. Riederet Cie., Paris, 1924.

CARTER, J. D.: *The Attitude of France in the Austro-Serbian Conflict, 1914*, Ed.Privat, Toulouse, 1927.

CHARDON, HENRI: *L'Administration de la France*, Perrin et Cie., Paris, 1908.

CHARPENTIER, ARMAND: *Le parti radical et radical-socialiste à travers ses congrés (1901–1911)*, Giard et Brière, Paris, 1913.

CHOW, S. R.: *Le contrôle parlementaire de la politique étrangère en Angleterre, en France, et aux États Unis*, Ernest Sagot et Cie., Paris, 1920.

CLARETIE, JULES: *Paul Déroulède*, A. Quantin, Paris, 1883.

COMITÉ D ÉTUDES: *L'Alsace-Lorraine et la frontière du nord-est*, Imprimerie Nationale, Paris, 1918.

CONSTANT, ESTOURNELLES DE (P.H.X.): *La politique française en Tunisie (1854–1891)*, Plon, Paris, 1891.

COUPAYE, L.: *La Ruhr et L'Allemagne*, Dunod, Paris, 1922.

CYON, ÉLIE DE: *Histoire de l'Entente Franco-Russe, 1886–1894*, A. Charles, Paris, 1895.

DAVIE, MAURICE R.: *The Evolution of War*, Yale University Press, New Haven, Conn., 1929.

DAWES, RUFUS C.: *The Dawes Plan in the Making*, Bobbs-Merrill Company, Indianapolis, Ind., 1925.

DEBIDOUR, A.: *Histoire diplomatique de l'Europe*, Felix Alcan, Paris, 1917.

DEMARTIAL, GEORGES: *La guerre de 1914, l'évangile du Quai d'Orsay*, A. Delpeuch, Paris, 1926.

DEPASSE, HECTOR: *De Freycinet*, A. Quantin, Paris, 1883.

DESPAGNET, FRANTZ: *La diplomatie de la troisième République et le droit de gens*, L. Larose, Paris, 1904.

DICKENSON, G. LOWES: *The International Anarchy, 1904–1914*, Allen and Unwin, London, 1926.

DUGUIT, LÉON: *Traité de droit constitutionnel*, 5 vols., E. de Boccard, Paris, 1924.

DUGUIT, LÉON, et HENRI MONNIER: *Les constitutions et les principales lois politiques de la France depuis 1789*, Pichon et Durand-Auzias, Paris, 1915.

DUPUIS, JEAN: *Les origines de la question du Tong-Kin*, A. Challamel, Paris, 1896.

DUPUY, E.: *Comment nous avons conquis le Maroc (1845–1912)*, Pierre Roger et Cie., Paris, 1913.

ESMEIN, ADHEMAR: *Droit constitutionnel français*, 7 vols., Paris, 1921.

FABRE-LUCE, ALFRED: *La crise des alliances, essai sur les relations franco-britanniques depuis la signature de la paix (1919–1922)*, Bernard Grasset, Paris, 1922; *La Victoire*, editions de la *Nouvelle revue française*, Paris, 1924.

FAY, SIDNEY B.: *The Origins of the World War*, 2 vols., The Macmillan Company, New York, 1929.

FEIS, HERBERT: *Europe—The World's Banker 1870–1914*, Yale University Press, New Haven, Conn., 1930.

FLEMING, DENNA F.: *The Treaty Veto of the American Senate*, G. P. Putnam's Sons, New York, 1930.

FLOURNOY, FRANCIS ROSEBRO: *Parliament and War—The Relation of the British Parliament to the Administration of Foreign Policy in Connection with the Initiation of War*, P. S. King and Son., London, 1927.

FOUCHER, LOUIS: *De l'évolution du protectorat de la France sur la Tunisie*, Larose, Paris, 1897.

FULLERTON, MORTON: *Problems of Power*, Constable and Co., London, 1914.

FREYCINET, CHARLES DE: *Souvenirs, 1878–1893*, Ch. Delagrave, Paris, 1913.

GAFFAREL, PAUL: *Notre expansion coloniale en Afrique de 1870 à nos jours*, Félix Alcan, Paris, 1918.

GAUTHEROT, GUSTAV: *Le monde communiste*, "editions Spes," Paris, 1927.

GAUTIER, HIPPOLYTE: *Les Français au Tonkin, 1787–1883*, Challemel Ainé, Paris, 1885.

GIFFEN, MORRISON B.: *Fashoda, The Incident and Its Diplomatic Setting*, The University of Chicago Press, Chicago, Ill., 1930.

GOOCH, G. P.: *History of Modern Europe, 1878–1919*, Henry Holt & Company, New York, 1923; *Franco-German Relations, 1871–1914*, Longmans, Green and Co., London, 1923.

GOUTTENOIRE DE TOURY, FERNAND: *Poincaré a-t-il voulu la guerre?* Clarté, Paris, 1920.

GRANDCHAMP, PIERRE: *La France en Tunisie au debut du XVIIe siècle (1601–1610)*, Tunis, 1921.

GRANDIDIER, G.: *Le Myre de Vilers—Duchesne—Gallieni*, Societé d'Études Geographiques, Maritimes et Coloniales, Paris, 1923.

GREER, GUY: *The Ruhr-Lorraine Industrial Problem*, Allen and Unwin, London, 1925.

GUY-GRAND, GEORGES: *La démocratic et l'après-guerre*, Garnier-Frères, Paris, 1922.

HANOTAUX, GABRIEL: *L'Affaire de Madagascar*, Calmann Levy, Paris, 1896; *Études diplomatiques, 1907–1911*, Plon-Nourrit et Cie., Paris, 1912.

HANSEN, JULES: *L'Alliance Franco-Russe*, Flammarion, Paris, 1897; *Ambassade à Paris du Baron de Mohrenheim, 1884–1898*, Flammarion, Paris, 1907.

HAWTREY, R. G.: *Economic Aspects of Sovereignty*, Longmans, Green and Co., London, 1930.

HAYES, CARLTON, J. H.: *France—A Nation of Patriots*, Columbia University Press, New York, 1929; *The Historical Evolution of Modern Nationalism*, R. R. Smith, New York, 1931.

HELLOT, F.: *La pacification de Madagascar (opérations d'octobre 1896 à mars 1899)*, Chapelot, Paris, 1900.

HIPPEAU, EDMOND: *Histoire diplomatique de la troisième République (1870–1889)*, Dentu, Paris, 1889.

HUDDLESTON, SISLEY: *Poincaré, A Biographical Portrait*, T. Fisher Unwin, London, 1924.

JÈZE, GASTON, et HENRI TRUCHY: *The War Finance of France*, Yale University Press, New Haven, Conn., 1927.

JUDET, ERNEST: *Georges Louis*, F. Rieder et Cie., Paris, 1925.

KAYSER, JASQUES: *Ruhr ou Plan Dawes?*, A. Delpeuch, Paris, 1924.

LACHAPELLE, G.: *Élections législatives, 1910, 1914, 1919 et 1924*, G. Roustan, Paris, 1924.

LANESSAN, J. L. DE: *Histoire de l'Entente Cordiale Franco-Anglaise*, Félix Alcan, Paris, 1916.

LANGER, W. L.: *The Franco-Russian Alliance, 1890–1894*, Harvard University Press, Cambridge, Mass., 1929.

LASSWELL, H. D.: *Psychopathology and Politics*, The University of Chicago Press, Chicago, 1930.

LEBON, ANDRÉ: *La pacification de Madagascar, 1896–1898*, Plon-Nourrit, Paris, 1928; *La politique de la France en Afrique, 1896–1898*, Plon-Nourrit et Cie., Paris, 1901.

LEFEBVRE, HENRI: *Du Rôle respectif du chef de l'état et des chambres dans les traités de commerce*, A. Rousseau, Paris, 1910.

LEWINSOHN, RICHARD: *Das Geld in der Politik*, S. Fischer Verlag, Berlin, 1931.

LEYRET, HENRI: *Le gouvernement et le parlement*, Félix Alcan, Paris, 1919; *Le Président de la République*, A. Colin, Paris, 1913; *Waldeck-Rousseau et la troisième République (1869–1889)*, E. Fasquelle, Paris, 1908.

LICHTENBERGER, HENRI: *Relations between France and Germany*, Carnegie Endowment for International Peace, Washington, D. C., 1923; *The Ruhr Conflict*, Carnegie Endowment for International Peace, Washington, D. C., 1923.

Livre Noir, Un, 2 vols., Librarie du Travail, Paris, 1922.

LOUIS, PAUL: *Histoire du socialism en France*, M. Rivière, Paris, 1925.

LUBERSAC, GUY DE: *Les pouvoirs constitutionnelles de la Président de la République*, E. Paul, Paris, 1913.

MATHEWS, JOHN MABRY: *American Foreign Relations, Conduct and Policies*, The Century Company, New York, 1928.

MICHON, GEORGES: *L'Alliance Franco-Russe, 1891–1917*, A. Delpeuch, Paris, 1927.

MICHON, LOUIS: *Les traités internationaux devant les chambres*, A. Chevalier-Maresq et Cie., Paris, 1901.

MILLET, RENÉ: *Notre politique extérieure de 1898 à 1905*, Felix Javan, Paris, 1905.

MONTEILHET, J.: *Les institutions militaires de la France (1814–1924)*, Felix Alcan, Paris, 1926.

MOON, PARKER T.: *The Labour Problem and the Social Catholic Movement in France*, The Macmillan Company, New York, 1921.

MORHARDT, MATHIAS: *Les preuves*, Librarie du Travail, Paris, 1922.

MORTIER, R., et G. ROUSSEL, Directeurs: "Documents politiques et sociaux" *La politique française en 1923*, Dunod, Paris, 1924.

MOULTON, H. G., and C. E. McGUIRE: *Germany's Capacity to Pay*, McGraw-Hill Book Company, Inc., New York, 1923.

NICOLSON, HAROLD: *Portrait of a Diplomatist*, Houghton Mifflin Company, New York, 1930.

NORTON, HENRY K.: *Foreign Office Organization*, Supplement to Vol. CXLIII of the *Annals of the American Academy of Political and Social Science*, Philadelphia, 1929.

PAIX-SEAILLES, CHARLES: *La diplomatie secrète sous la troisième République, 1910–1911; Homs-Bagdad, Du Quai d'Orsay à la correctionnelle, recueil documentaire*, Editions du *Courrier européen*, Paris, 1911.

PALÉOLOGUE, MAURICE: *La Russie des Tsars pendant la grande guerre*, July 20, 1914–May 17, 1917, 3 vols., Plon, Paris, 1922.

PANGE, JEAN: *France et Allemagne*, Bloud et Gay, Paris, 1925.

PARTI REPUBLICAN RADICAL ET RADICAL-SOCIALISTE: *Compte rendu des les congrés annuelle*, Comité Executif, Paris (Annual).

PAVIE, AUGUSTE: *Mission Pavie, Indo-Chine, 1879–1895*, 7 vols., Ernest Leroux, Paris, 1901-1911; *Le Myre de Vilers, 1833–1919*. Ernest Leroux, Paris, 1919.

PEASE, MARGARET: *Jean Jaurès*, B. W. Huebsch, New York, 1917.

PEVET, ALFRED: *Les responsibles de la guerre*, Librairie de L'Humanite, Paris, 1921.

PINON, RENÉ: *La bataille de la Ruhr*, H. Turgis, Verneuil-sur-Avre, 1924.

PIPKIN, CHARLES W.: *Social Politics and Modern Democracies*, 2 vols., The Macmillan Company, New York, 1931.

PLAYNE, CAROLINE E.: *The Neuroses of the Nations*, Thomas Seltzer, New York, 1925.

POINCARÉ, RAYMOND: *Au service de la France*, 5 vols., Plon-Nourrit et Cie., Paris, 1926–1928.

POUPARD, E.: *L'Occupation de la Ruhr et le droit des gens*, Les Presses Universitaires de France, Paris, 1925.

POUVOURVILLE, ALBERT DE: *L'Affaire de Siam, 1886–1896*, Chameul, Paris, 1897.

RAMBAUD, ALFRED: *Jules Ferry*, Plon-Nourrit et Cie., Paris, 1903.

RECOULY, RAYMOND: *La Barrière du Rhin*, Hachette, Paris, 1923; *La Ruhr*, Flammarion, Paris, 1923.

Reichsministerium für die Besetzten Gebiete, *Die politischen Ordonnanzen der interallilerten Rheinlandkommission, 1920–1924*, Carl Heymanns Verlag, Berlin, 1925.

RENOUVIN, PIERRE: *The Forms of War Government in France*, Yale University Press, New Haven, 1927; *Les origines immédiates de la guerre (28 juin-4 aout 1914)*, St. Amand, Paris.

REYNALD, GEORGES: *La diplomatie française: l'oeuvre de M. Delcassé*, Paris, 1915.

ROBERT, A. E.: *Traités et conventions entre la France et la Russie depuis 1814*, Rousseau et Cie., Paris, 1915.

ROBERTS, STEPHEN H.: *History of French Colonial Policy (1870–1925)*, P. S. King and Son, London, 1929.

ROBIQUET, PAUL (Ed.): *Discours et opinions de Jules Ferry*, 7 vols., Armand Colin et Cie., Paris, 1898.

SAINT-MART, PIERRE DE: *Étude historique et critique sur les interpellations en France*, L. Larose et L.Tenin, Paris, 1912.

SAPIRA, JEAN: *Le rôle des chambres au point de vue diplomatique dans un régime parlementaire (Constitution de 1875)*, L. Tenin, Paris, 1920.

SCHOEN, FREIHERR VON: *The Memoirs of an Ambassador*, Brentano's, Inc., New York, 1923.

SCHMITT, BERNADOTTE E.: *The Coming of the War, 1914*, 2 vols., Charles Scribner's Sons, New York, 1930.

SCOTT, JONATHAN F.: *Five Weeks. The Surge of Public Opinion on the Eve of the Great War*, The John Day Company, Inc., publishers, New York, 1927.

SEAUVE, LE CAPITAINE: *Les relations de la France et du Siam, 1680–1907*, Henri Charles-Lavauzelle, Paris, 1908.

SHARP, WALTER R.: *The French Civil Service—Bureaucracy in Transition*, The Macmillan Company, New York, 1931.

SIMOND, ÉMILE: *Histoire de la troisième République de 1894 à 1896*, Henri Charles-Lavauzelle, Paris, 1921.

STEED, HENRY W.: *Through Thirty Years, 1892–1922*, 2 vols., William Heinemann, London, 1924.

STEPHENS, WINIFRED: *Madame Adam*, E. P. Dutton & Company, Inc., New York, 1917.

STREET, CECIL J. C.: *The Treachery of France*, Philip Allan & Co., London, 1924.

STUART, GRAHAM H.: *French Foreign Policy from Fashoda to Sarajevo, 1898–1914*, The Century Company, New York, 1921.

TARDIEU, ANDRÉ: *La France et les alliances*, Félix Alcan, Paris, 1909; *Le mystère d'Agadir*, Calman-Levy, Paris, 1912.

THOMAZI, A.: *La marine française dans la grande guerre (1914–1918)—La guerre naval dans la zone des armées du nord*, Payot, Paris, 1925.

VALET, RENÉ: *L'Afrique du Nord devant la parlement au XIXme siècle (1828–1838, 1880–1881)*, E. Champion, Paris, 1924.

VIVIANI, RENÉ: *As We See It (Réponse à Kaiser)*, Harper & Brothers, New York, 1923.

VOGELS, DR. WERNER: *Die Verträge über Besetzung und Räumung des Rheinlandes und die Ordonnanzen der Interalliierten Rheinlandoberkommission in Coblenz*, Carl Heymans Verlag, Berlin, 1925.

VIOLLETTE, MAURICE: *A la veille d'Agadir—La N'Goko-Sangha*, Émile Larose, Paris, 1914.

WELSCHINGER, HENRI: *L'Alliance Franco-Russe, Les origines et les résultats*, Félix Alcan, Paris, 1919.

WILLSON, BECKLES: *The Paris Embassy, A Narrative of Franco-British Diplomatic Relations, 1814–1920*, Frederick A. Stokes Co., New York, 1927.

WRIGHT, QUINCY: *The Control of American Foreign Relations*, The Macmillan Company, New York, 1922; *Mandates under the League of Nations*, The University of Chicago Press, Chicago, Ill., 1930.

XYDIAS, JEAN: *L'Intervention française en Russie, 1918–1919*, Les Éditions de France, Paris, 1927.

ZAÏONTCHKOVSKY, A., S. LOUKIRSKY, V. NAITSKY, etc.: *Les Alliés contre la Russie*, A. Delpeuch, Paris, 1927.

ZÉVAÈS, ALEXANDRE B.: *Le parti socialiste de 1904 à 1923*, M. Rivière, Paris, 1923.

INDEX